DICTIONARY OF
COMPUTING

THIRD EDITION

Titles in the series

English Dictionary for Students	1-901659-06-2
Dictionary of Accounting	0-948549-27-0
Dictionary of Agrigulture, 2nd ed	0-948549-78-5
Dictionary of American Business	0-948549-11-4
Dictionary of Automobile Engineering	0-948549-66-1
Dictionary of Banking & Finance, 2nd ed	1-901659-30-5
Dictionary of Business, 2nd ed	0-948549-51-3
Dictionary of Computing, 3rd ed	1-901659-04-6
Dictionary of Ecology & Environment, 3rd ed	0-948549-74-2
Dictionary of Government & Politics, 2nd ed	0-948549-89-0
Dictionary of Hotels, Tourism, Catering Management	0-948549-40-8
Dictionary of Human Resources & Personnel, 2nd ed	0-948549-79-3
Dictionary of Information Technology, 2nd ed	0-948549-88-2
Dictionary of Law, 2nd ed	0-948549-33-5
Dictionary of Library & Information Management	0-948549-68-8
Dictionary of Marketing, 2nd ed	0-948549-73-4
Dictionary of Medicine, 2nd ed	0-948549-36-X
Dictionary of Printing & Publishing, 2nd ed	0-948549-99-8
Dictionary of Science & Technology	0-948549-67-X

Also Available

Professional Series

Dictionary of Astronomy	0-948549-43-2
Dictionary of Multimedia, 2nd ed	1-901659-01-1
Dictionary of PC & the Internet, 2nd ed	1-901659-12-7
Bradford's Crossword Solver's Dictionary, 3rd ed	1-901659-03-8

Workbooks

Check your:

Vocabulary for Banking & Finance	0-948549-96-3
Vocabulary for Business, 2nd ed	1-901659-27-5
Vocabulary for Colloquial English	0-948549-97-1
Vocabulary for Computing	0-948549-72-6
Vocabulary for Hotels, Tourism	0-948549-75-0
Vocabulary for Law, 2nd ed	1-901659-21-6
Vocabulary for Medicine	0-948549-59-9

Visit our web site for full details of all our books

http://www.pcp.co.uk

DICTIONARY OF
COMPUTING

THIRD EDITION

S.M.H. Collin

PETER COLLIN PUBLISHING

OEPE

First published in Great Britain 1988
Second edition published 1994
Third edition published 1998

Reprinted 1999

Published by Peter Collin Publishing Ltd
1 Cambridge Road, Teddington, Middlesex, TW11 8DT
© Copyright S.M.H. Collin, 1988, 1994, 1998

British Library Cataloguing-in-Publication Data

A catalogue record for this book is available from the British Library

ISBN 1-901659-04-6

Text computer typeset by PCP
Printed and bound in Finland by WSOY
Cover artwork by Gary Weston

Preface to the first edition

This dictionary provides the user with a comprehensive vocabulary used in the field of computing. It covers all aspects of computing, including hardware, software, peripherals, networks, programming, as well as many applications in which computers are used, such as desktop publishing

The 5,000 main words are each explained in simple English, using a limited vocabulary of about 500 words, over and above those words which appear in the dictionary as main words. Many examples are given to show how the words and phrases can be used in context. Words which pose particular problems of grammar have short grammatical notes attached.

General comments about particular items of interest, complex ideas or hardware or software applications are given in separate boxes. Quotations from a wide range of magazines and journals are given to show how the words are used in real text. The supplement at the back of the book describes the architecture of single and multi-user computer systems, and a central processing unit; the ASCII and EBCDIC codes are listed and the RS232 interface is described along with examples of different programming languages.

Preface to the second edition

The field of computing has developed considerably since the first edition of this dictionary; the second edition includes an additional 1,000 headwords to provide a completely revised and up-to-date guide to the words used to describe hardware, software, networks and peripherals of modern computer systems. We have covered the whole range of ocmputer platforms from the latest PDAs to PCs, minis and mainframe systems.

Preface to the third edition

This third edition of the dictionary includes an expanded number of headwords, with over 10,000 terms clearly defined. The increase is due in part to the importance of new fields in computing, in particular to the internet which has produced several new programming languages and is very important for business and personal users around the world. We have also updated and expanded the terms that cover hardware as new technology developments are announced. Software development has moved towards applications that run under a GUI user environment, such as Microsoft Windows, and these changes have been reflected in the new terms included in the dictionary.

In this edition of the dictionary we have also included a number of product names and company names. The trademarked names that are included are those that we have judged to be de-facto, important to users or important in the development of computer technology.

Aa

A = AMPERE base SI unit of electrical current; defined as the current flowing through an impedance of one ohm which has a voltage of one volt across it

A hexadecimal equivalent to decimal number 10

Å *see* ANGSTROM

A: (used in some operating systems) denotes the first disk drive on the system; *to see what is stored on your floppy disk, use the DOS command DIR A:*

A/UX version of the Unix operating system for the Apple Macintosh range of computers; *see also* UNIX

A-bus *noun* main internal bus in a microprocessor

A programming language (APL)

noun high-level programming language used for scientific and mathematical work

A to D *or* **A/D** = ANALOG TO DIGITAL changing a signal from an analog form to a digitally coded form; **A to D converter** = (analog to digital converter) device used to convert an analog input to a digital output form which can be understood by a computer; *the speech signal was first passed through an A to D converter before being analysed opposite is* DIGITAL TO ANALOG

abandon *verb* to clear a document or file or work from the computer's memory without saving it to disk or tape; *once you have abandoned your spreadsheet, you cannot retrieve it again*

abbreviated address *noun* (in a network) user name that has fewer characters than the full name, making it easier to remember or type in; *my full network address is over 60 characters long, so you will find it easier to use my abbreviated address;* **abbreviated addressing** *or* **abb. add.** = use of a smaller computer address word than normal which provides faster address decoding operations; **abbreviated installation** = (during installation) to install new hardware *or* software without restoring the previous backup settings of the operating system

◊ **abbreviation** *noun* short form of a word *or* command *or* instruction; *within the text, the abbreviation proc is used instead of processor*

abend *noun* = ABNORMAL END unexpected stoppage of a program being run, due to a fault *or* error *or* power failure; *an interrupt from a faulty printer caused an abend;* **abend code** = special number (generated by the operating system) that identifies the type of error that has caused the problem; **abend recovery program** = software that will reload a program (or system software) and restart it at the point where the abend occurred; *if a fault occurs, data loss will be minimized due to the improved abend recovery program*

ABIOS = ADVANCED BASIC INPUT/OUTPUT SYSTEM set of routines stored on a ROM chip in the IBM PS/2 range of personal computers

COMMENT: the ABIOS is used in addition to the normal BIOS routines; ABIOS routines are used to control the MCA bus in an IBM PS/2 computer

ablation *noun* method of writing data to an optical storage device

COMMENT: a laser burns a hole or pit (that represents digital bits of data) into the thin metal surface of the storage device

abnormal *adjective* not normal; *it's abnormal for two consecutive disk drives to break down; abnormal error;* **abnormal** end *or* **abend** *or* **abnormal termination** = unexpected stoppage of a program being run, caused by a fault *or* error *or* power failure

◊ **abnormally** *adverb* not as normal *or* not as usual; *the signal is abnormally weak; the error rate with this disk is abnormally high*

abort *verb* to end a process (when a malfunction occurs), by switching the computer off manually *or* by an internal feature; *the program was aborted by pressing the red button; abort the program before it erases any more files;* **aborted connection** = connection to a network or online service that has not been shut down correctly; **abort sequence** = unique sequence of bits that indicates that the transmission will be abnormally terminated; *see also* RESET

About... (in the SAA CUA front-end) menu selection that tells you who developed the program and gives copyright information

AB roll *noun* (in a multimedia application) two video or music segments that are synchronised so that one fades as the second starts

ABR *see* AVAILABLE BIT RATE

ABS = ABSOLUTE FUNCTION programming instruction that returns the magnitude of a number without the number's sign; *the command ABS(-13) will return the answer 13*

absolute address *or* **actual address** *or* **machine address** *noun* **(a)** computer storage address that directly, without any modification, accesses a location *or* device *compare* INDEXED ADDRESS; *program execution is slightly faster if you code only with absolute addresses* **(b)** computer storage address that can only

access one location; **absolute addressing** = locating a data word in memory by the use of its absolute address; **absolute assembler** = type of assembly language program designed to produce code which uses only absolute addresses and values; **absolute cell reference** = spreadsheet reference that always refers to the same cell, even when copied to another location; **absolute code** = binary code which directly operates the central processing unit, using only absolute addresses and values (this is the final form of a program after a compiler *or* assembler pass) *see also* OBJECT CODE; **absolute coordinates** = coordinates that describe the distance of a point from the intersection of axes *compare* RELATIVE COORDINATES; **absolute device** = input device such as a tablet or mouse that returns the coordinates of a pointer within specified axes; **absolute error** = value *or* magnitude of an error, ignoring its sign; **absolute expression** = (in assembly language) value of an expression that is not affected by program relocation; **absolute instruction** *or* **code** = (i) instruction which completely describes the operation to be performed (no other data is required); (ii) graphics command that uses absolute coordinates; **absolute loader** = program that loads a section of code into main memory; **absolute maximum rating** = maximum values or limits of a system; **absolute positioning** = position of an object in relation to an origin; **absolute priority** = (in the OS/2 operating system) priority of a process that cannot be changed by the operating system; **absolute program** = computer program written in absolute code; **absolute value** = size *or* value of a number, regardless of its sign; *the absolute value of -62.34 is 62.34; an absolute value of the input is generated*

abstract *noun* short summary of a document; *it's quicker to search through the abstracts than the full text*

◊ **abstract data type** *noun* a general data type that can store any kind of information; *the stack is a structure of abstract data types, it can store any type of data*

AC = ALTERNATING CURRENT electric current whose value varies with time in a regular, sinusoidal way, changing the direction of flow each half cycle

> COMMENT: the mains electricity supply uses alternating current to minimize transmission power loss, with a frequency of 50Hz in U.K., 60Hz in the USA

ACC = ACCUMULATOR most important internal CPU storage register, containing the data word that is to be processed

accelerated graphics port (AGP)

noun dedicated bus between a graphics controller and main memory that allows data to be transferred very quickly without using the main processor, is used with the Intel Pentium II processor to provide very high-speed three-dimensional graphics and video processing; this port does not replace a PCI bus but works with it

acceleration time *noun* (a) time taken

for a disk drive to spin a disk at the correct speed, from rest; *allow for acceleration time in the access time* (b) total time between an access instruction being issued (to a peripheral) and the data being transferred

accelerator *see* ACCELERATOR KEY

accelerator board *or* card *noun*

circuit board that carried a faster or more advanced version of the same processor that runs your computer; adding an accelerator card to your computer makes it run faster

accelerator key *noun* combination of

keys that, when pressed together, carry out a function that would otherwise have to be selected from a menu using a mouse; *instead of selecting the File menu then the Save option, use the accelerator keys Alt and S to do the same thing and save the file*

accent *noun* mark above a character to

indicate a different pronunciation

accept *verb* (a) to agree to do something;

he accepted the quoted price for printing; she has accepted our terms; he did not accept the programming job he was offered (b) to take something which is being offered; *the laser printer will accept a card as small*

as a business card; the multi-disk reader will accept 3.5 inch disks as well as 5.25 inch formats; call **accept signal** = signal sent by a device showing that it is willing to accept (caller's) data **(c)** to establish a session or connection with another device

◊ **acceptable** *adjective* which can be accepted; *the error rate was very low, and is acceptable; for the price, the scratched case is acceptable;* **acceptable use policy (AUP)** = set of rules that describe what a user can write or do on the internet without offending other users

◊ **acceptance** *noun* action of accepting something; **acceptance sampling** = testing a small random part of a batch to see if the whole batch is up to standard; **acceptance test** *or* **testing** = method of checking that a piece of equipment will perform as required *or* will reach required standards

access 1 *noun* being allowed to use a

computer and read *or* alter files stored in it (this is usually controlled by a security device such as a password); **to have access to something** = to be able to get *or* examine *or* reach something; *to have access to a file of data; he has access to numerous sensitive files;* **to bar access to a system** = to prevent a person from using a system; *after he was discovered hacking, he was barred access from the system;* **access arm** = mechanical device in a disk drive used to position the read/write head over the correct track on a disk; *the access arm moves to the parking region during transport;* **access authority** = permission to carry out a particular operation on data; **access barred** = to prevent a user accessing particular data; **access category** = one of several possible predefined access levels; the category defines which files or data a user can access, and which he cannot; **access channel control** = (in Token-Ring network) protocols that manage the data transfer between a station and a medium access control (MAC); **access charge** = cost due when logging onto a system *or* viewing special pages on a bulletin board; **access code** = series of characters *or* symbols that must be entered to identify a user before access to a computer is permitted *see also*

PASSWORD; **access hole** = opening in both sides of a floppy disk's casing allowing the read-write head to be positioned over the disk's surface; **access level** = various predefined access categories; the lowest access level might allow the user to only view data, the highest access level allows a user to do anything; **access line** = permanently connected communications line between a terminal and a computer; **access mechanism** = mechanical device that moves an access arm over the surface of a disk; **access method** = (i) means used for the internal transfer of data between memory and display *or* peripheral devices (differences in the methods used is often the cause of compatibility problems); (ii) set of rules that allows a device to send data onto a network, for example token passing and CSMA/CD are two methods commonly used in a local area network; **access method routines** = software routines that move data between main storage and an output device; **access name** = unique name that identifies an object in a database; **access path** = description of the location of a stored file within a directory structure of a disk; **access path journalling** = recording changes to an access path in case of malfunction; **access period** = period of time during which a user can access data; **access permission** = description of all the access rights for a particular user; **access point** = test point on a circuit board *or* in software, allowing an engineer to check signals *or* data; **access privilege** = status granted to a user that allows them to see or read or alter files; **access rights** = permission for a particular user to access a particular file or data object; **access time** = time taken to find and retrieve a particular piece of data from memory or a hard disk; **access unit** = (in Token-Ring networks) wiring concentrator; **direct access storage device (DASD)** = storage medium whose memory locations can be directly read *or* written to; **direct memory access (DMA)** = direct, rapid link between a peripheral and a computer's main memory which avoids the use of accessing routines for each item of data required; **disk access** = operations required to read from or write to a magnetic disk, including device selection, sector and track address, movement of read/write head

to the correct location and access the location on disk; **disk access management** = regulating the users who can access stored data; **instantaneous access** = storage that has virtually no access time delay, such as access to RAM; *the instantaneous access of the RAM disk was welcome;* **parallel access** = data transfer between two devices with a number of bits (usually one byte wide) being sent simultaneously; **public access terminal** = terminal which can be used by anyone to access a computer; **random access** = ability to access immediately memory locations in any order; **sequential access** = method of retrieving data from a storage device by starting at the beginning of the medium (such as tape) and reading each record until the required data is found; **serial access** = one item of data accessed by reading through all the data in a list until the correct one is found **2** *verb* to call up (data) which is stored in a computer; to obtain data from a storage device; *she accessed the employee's file stored on the computer*

◊ **access control** *noun* security device (such as a password) that only allows selected users to use a computer system *or* read files; **access control byte** = (in Token-Ring network) byte following start marker in the token that indicates if the station can access the network

COMMENT: a good access control system should allow valid users to gain access and operate the computer easily with the minimum of checks, whilst barring entry to hackers or unauthorized users

◊ **accessible** *adjective* which can be reached *or* accessed; *details of customers are easily accessible from the main computer files*

◊ **access time** *noun* **(a)** total time which a storage device takes between the moment the data is requested and the data being returned; *the access time of this dynamic RAM chip is around 200nS - we have faster versions if your system clock is running faster* **(b)** length of time required to find a file *or* program, either in main memory *or* a secondary memory source

accession number *noun* number in a record that shows in which order each record was entered

accessor *noun* person who accesses data

accessory *noun* extra, add-on device (such as a mouse or printer) which is attached to *or* used with a computer; *the printer comes with several accessories, such as a soundproof hood; the special offer includes a range of accessories including a mouse and modem*

accidental *adjective* which happens by accident; *always keep backup copies in case of accidental damage to the master file*

accordion fold *or* **fanfold**   *noun* method of folding continuous paper, one sheet in one direction, the next sheet in the opposite direction, allowing the paper to be fed into a printer continuously with no action on the part of the user

account 1 *noun* (in a network or online system) record of a user's name, password and rights to access a network or online system; *if you are a new user, you will have to ask the supervisor to create an account for you;* **account name** = unique name of a user on a network or online system; *John Smith's account name is JSMITH* **2** *verb* to keep track of how much time and resources each user of a network or online system uses

accounting *or* **accounts package** *noun* software that automates a business's accounting functions; *we now type in each transaction into the new accounting package rather than write it into a ledger*

acoustic coupler *noun* type of modem that has rubber cups that fit around the mouth and ear-piece of a normal telephone handset

accumulate *verb* to gather several things together over a period of time; *we have gradually accumulated a large databank of names and addresses*

◊ **accumulator** *or* **ACC** *or* **accumulator register** *noun* most important internal CPU storage register, containing the result of an operation or the data word that is to be

processed; *store the two bytes of data in registers A and B and execute the add instruction - the answer will be in the accumulator;* **accumulator address** = address accessed by an instruction held in the accumulator; **accumulator shift instruction** = command to shift the contents of an accumulator left *or* right by one bit

accuracy *noun* total number of bits used to define a number in a computer, the more bits allocated the more accurate the definition; **accuracy control character** = code that indicates whether data is accurate or whether the data should be disregarded by a particular device

accurate *adjective* correct; without any errors; *the printed bar code has to be accurate to within a thousandth of a micron*

◊ **accurately** *adverb* correctly *or* with no errors; *the OCR had difficulty in reading the new font accurately; the error was caused because the data had not been accurately keyed*

> COMMENT: most high level languages allow numbers to be represented in a more accurate form by using two or more words to store the number

ACD = AUTOMATIC CALL DISTRIBUTION specialised telephone system that can handle lots of incoming calls and direct them to a particular operator according to programmed instructions in a database

ACDI = ASYNCHRONOUS COMMUNICATIONS DEVICE INTERFACE

ACF = ADVANCED COMMUNICATIONS FUNCTION

achieve *verb* to succeed in doing something; *the hardware designers are trying to achieve compatibility between all the components of the system*

achromatic colour *noun* (grey) colour within the range between black and white displayed by a graphics adapter

ACIA = ASYNCHRONOUS COMMUNICATIONS INTERFACE ADAPTER circuit that allows a computer to transmit and receive serial data using asynchronous access

ACK = ACKNOWLEDGE signal that is sent from a receiver to indicate that a transmitted message has been received and that it is ready for the next one; *the printer generates an ACK signal when it has received data*

Ackerman's function *noun* recursive function used to test the ability of a compiler to cope with recursion

acknowledge 1 *noun* signal that is sent from a receiver to indicate that a transmitted message has been received and that it is ready for the next one **2** *verb* (i) to tell a sender that a message *or* letter has been received; (ii) to send a signal from a receiver to show that a transmitted message has been received; **acknowledge character** = special code sent by a receiver to indicate to the transmitter that the message has been correctly received

◊ **acknowledged mail** *noun* function that signals to the sender when an electronic mail message has been read by the recipient

ACM = ASSOCIATION OF COMPUTING MACHINERY

acoustic *adjective* referring to sound; **acoustic delay line** = original data storage method that delays data (in the form of sound pulses) as it travels across a medium; **acoustic hood** = soundproof hood placed over a printer to reduce the noise; *the acoustic hood allows us to speak and print in the same room;* **acoustic panel** = sound-proofed panel placed behind a device to reduce noise; **acoustic store** *or* **acoustic memory** = (old) regenerative memory that uses an acoustic delay line

◊ **acoustic coupler** *noun* device that connects to a telephone handset, converting binary computer data into sound signals to allow data to be transmitted down a telephone line; *I use an acoustic coupler with my laptop computer*

COMMENT: the acoustic coupler also converts back from sound signals to digital signals when receiving messages; it is basically the same as a modem but uses a handset on which a loudspeaker is placed to send the signals rather than direct connection to the phone line. It is portable, and clips over both ends of a normal telephone handset; it can be used even in a public phone booth

ACPI = ADVANCED CONFIGURATION AND POWER INTERFACE software system (that is part of Microsoft Windows 98) that allows the operating system to automatically configure compatible hardware

acquisition *noun* accepting *or* capturing *or* collecting information; **data acquisition** = gathering data about a subject

ACR = AUDIO CASSETTE RECORDER; **ACR interface** = interface which allows a cassette recorder to be linked to a computer

Acrobat™ *noun* software and proprietary file format (developed by Adobe Systems) that allows formatted text and graphic images to be displayed on different hardware

acronym *noun* abbreviation, formed from various letters, which makes up a word which can be pronounced; *the acronym FORTRAN means Formula Translator; the acronym RAM means Random Access Memory*

ACS *see* ASYNCHRONOUS COMMUNICATION SERVER.

action *noun* **(a)** something which has been done; **to take action** = to do something; *action has been taken to repair the fault* **(b)** (in SAA CUA front-end) user event, such as pressing a special key, that moves the cursor to the action bar at the top of the screen; **action bar** = (in SAA CUA front-end) top line of the screen that displays the menu names; **action bar pull-down** = (in SAA CUA front-end) when a user moves the cursor to a particular menu name on the action bar, the full menu is displayed below the menu name; **action code** = (in SAA CUA front-end) single letter associated with a particular menu option to speed up selection; when the letter action code is pressed, the menu option is selected; **action cycle** = complete set of actions involved in one operation (including reading data, processing, storing results, etc.); **action list** = (in SAA CUA front-end) list of choices; **action message** = message displayed to inform the user that an action *or* input is required; **action-object** = (in SAA CUA front-end) object to which a user specifies an action should be applied

activate *verb* to start a process *or* to make a device start working; *pressing CR activates the printer*

active *adjective* busy *or* working *or* being used; **active application** = (in a multitasking operating system) application currently being used by a user; **active area** = (i) (in a spreadsheet program) the area that contains data bounded by the top left hand corner and the bottom right hand cell; (ii) (in a graphical window) an area that will start or select a function if the user moves the pointer into it with a mouse; **active cell** = spreadsheet cell which is currently selected with a cursor or pointer; **active code page** = code page currently in use by the system; **active database** = database file currently being accessed by a database management program; **active device** = electronic component that requires electrical power to operate and provides gain *or* a logical function *compare* PASSIVE DEVICE; **active file** = file which is being worked on; **active gateway** = (in a network) gateway that exchanges routing information, unlike a passive gateway; **active high** = electronic signal that is valid when it is high *or* logical one *or* at five volts; **active hub** = hub that selectively directs packets of data according to their address *or* content; **active line** = line in a communications link *or* port that is being used to transfer data or carry control signals; **active link** = link currently being used to transfer information; **active low** = electronic signal that is valid when it is low *or* logical zero *or* at zero volts; **active matrix display** = type of colour display used in laptop

computers normally called TFT display; **active menu** = menu selection currently displayed below a menu bar; **active node** = node on a network connected to *or* available to connect to another node; **active pixel region** = area of a computer screen that can display graphic image information; **active printer** = printer that is currently connected to the computer's printer port; **active program** = (in a multitasking system) program that is currently in control of the processor; **active record** = record that is being updated or accessed; **active region** = area on a screen that will start an action or has been defined as a hotspot; **active star** = network consisting of a central point with nodes branching out, in which a central processor controls and routes all messages between devices; **active state** = electronic state in which an action occurs; **active storage** = main storage, fast access RAM whose locations can be directly and immediately addressed by the CPU; **active streaming format (ASF)** = multimedia delivery format developed by Microsoft for delivery over the internet and used in its NetShow product; **active window** = (i) area of display screen in which you are currently working; (ii) (in a GUI *or* SAA CUA front-end), the window that is currently the focus of cursor movements and screen displays; *see also* WINDOW

◊ **ActiveX**™ system, developed by Microsoft, used to create and distribute small programs (called applets) that can be used to enhance the functionality of a Web page or an application; *see also* JAVA

◊ **activity** *noun* **(a)** being active *or* busy; **activity level** = maximum number of jobs that can run in a multitasking system; **activity light** = small light or LED on the front of a disk drive or computer that indicates when the disk drive is reading or writing data to disk; **activity loading** = method of organizing disk contents so that the most often accessed files *or* programs can be loaded quickly; **activity ratio** = number of files currently in use compared to the total stored; **activity trail** = record of activities carried out **(b)**; **activities** = jobs *or* tasks which are being performed on a computer

actual address or absolute

address *noun* computer storage address that directly, without any modification, accesses a location *or* device *compare* INDEXED ADDRESS; **actual code** = binary code which directly operates the central processing unit, using only absolute addresses and values (this is the final form of a program after a compiler *or* assembler pass); **actual data transfer rate** = average number of data bits transferred in a period of time; **actual instruction** = the resulting instruction executed after the modification of an original instruction

actuator *noun* mechanical device that can be controlled by an external signal (such as the read/write head in a disk drive)

ACU = AUTOMATIC CALLING UNIT device which allows a computer to call stations *or* dial telephone numbers automatically

A/D *or* **A to D** = ANALOG TO DIGITAL; *see* ANALOG, A to D

ADA *noun* high-level programming language that is used mainly in military, industrial and scientific fields of computing

adapt *verb* to change *or* to adjust *or* to modify something so that it fits; *can this computer be adapted to take 5.25 inch disks?*

◊ **adaptation** *noun* ability of a device to adjust its sensitivity range according to various situations; *the adaptation of the eye to respond to different levels of brightness*

◊ **adapter** *or* **adaptor** *noun* device that allows two *or* more incompatible devices to be connected together; *the cable adapter allows attachment of the scanner to the SCSI interface; the cable to connect the scanner to the adapter is included in the package;* **adapter card** = add-on interface board that allows incompatible devices to communicate; **adapter plug** = plug which allows devices with different plugs (two-pin, three-pin, etc.) to be fitted into the same socket; **data adapter unit** = device that interfaces a CPU to one or more communications channels; **graphics adapter** = electronic device (normally on an

expansion card) in a computer that provides converts software commands into electrical signals that display graphics on a connected monitor; *the new graphics adapter is capable of displaying higher resolution graphics; see also* CGA, EGA, VGA; **network adapter** = add-in board that connects a computer to a network; the board converts the computer's data into electrical signals that are then transmitted along the network cable

◊ **adaptive channel allocation** *noun* providing communications channels according to demand rather than a fixed allocation; **adaptive differential pulse code modulation (ADPCM)** = CCITT standard that defines a method of converting a voice or analog signal into a compressed digital signal; **adaptive packet assembly** = method used by the MNP error correcting protocol to adjust the size of data packets according to the quality of the telephone line (the better the line, the bigger the packet size); **adaptive routing** = ability of a system to change its communications routes according to various events *or* situations such as line failure; the messages are normally sent along the most cost-effective path unless there is a problem with that route, in which case they are automatically re-routed; **adaptive systems** = ability of a system to alter its responses and processes according to inputs *or* events *or* situations

adaptor *see* ADAPTER

ABD = APPLE DESKTOP BUS

Acorn Computers™ developers of the BBC micro and the Archimedes computer

ADC *noun* = ANALOG TO DIGITAL CONVERTER device used to convert analog input to a digital output form, that can be understood by a computer

add *verb* **(a)** to put figures together to make a total; *in the spreadsheet each column should be added to make a subtotal;* **add register** = register which is an adder; **add time** = period of time taken to perform one addition operation (either of a CPU *or* adder) **(b)** to put things together to form a larger group; *the software house has added a new management package to its range of products; adding or deleting material from the text is easy using function keys;* **add file** = special file in which new records are stored prior to updating the main database

addend *noun* number added to the augend in an addition

adder *noun* device *or* routine that provides the sum of two *or* more (digital *or* analog) inputs; **adder-subtractor** = device that can either add or subtract; **full adder** *or* **three input adder** = binary addition circuit which can produce the sum of two inputs, and can also accept a carry input, producing a carry output if necessary; **half adder** *or* **two input adder** binary addition circuit which can produce the sum of two inputs and a carry output if necessary, but will not accept a carry input; **parallel adder** = a number of full adders arranged in parallel to add two words at once; **serial adder** = one bit full adder used to add two words one bit at a time

COMMENT: a parallel adder takes one clock cycle to add two words, a serial adder takes a time equal to the number of bits in a word to add

◊ **add-in** *noun & adjective* (something) which is added; *the first method is to use a page description language, the second is to use an add-in processor card; can you explain the add-in card method? processing is much faster with add-in cards*

◊ **addition** *adjective* arithmetic operation that produces the sum of an addend and augend; **addition record** = record with changes used to update a master record *or* file; **addition time** = time an adder takes to carry out an add operation; **addition without carry** = addition operation without any carry bits *or* words *same as* EXOR FUNCTION; **destructive addition** = addition operation in which the result is stored in the location of one of the operands used in the sum, so overwriting it

◊ **additional** *adjective* which is added *or* which is extra; *can we link three additional workstations to the network?*

◊ **add-on** *noun & adjective* piece of software *or* hardware that is added to a computer system to improve its performance; *the add-on hard disk will boost the computer's storage capabilities; the new add-on board allows colour graphics to be displayed* (NOTE: the opposite is **built-in**)

address 1 *noun* (i) number allowing a central processing unit to reference a physical location in a storage medium in a computer system; (ii) unique number that identifies a device on a network; *this is the address at which the data starts;* **absolute address** *or* **actual address** *or* **direct address** = (i) computer storage address (within a CPU's address range) that directly, without any modification, accesses a location *or* device; (ii) computer storage address that can only access one location; **address access time** = total time which a storage device takes between the moment the data is requested and the data being returned; **address base** = part of an address that defines the origin to which the logical address is added; **address book** = (i) (in a network) list of node addresses; (ii) (in electronic mail) list of the network addresses of other users to which electronic mail can be sent; **address bus** = physical connection that carries the address data in parallel form from the central processing unit to external devices; **address code** = special code that identifies the part of a document that is an address; **address computation** = operation on address data (in an instruction); **address decoder** = logical circuit that will produce a signal when a certain address *or* range is placed on the address bus; **address field** *or* **operand field** = (i) (in networks) part of a packet that contains the address of the destination node; (ii) (in programming) part of a computer instruction that contains the location of the operand; **address format** = rules defining the way the operands, data and addresses are arranged in an instruction; **address mapping** = virtual address translated to an absolute real address; **address mark** = special code on a disk that indicates the start of sector location data; **address modification** = changing the address field, so that it can refer to a different location; **address register** = register in a computer that is able to store all the bits that make up an address which can then be processed as a single unit (in small micros, the address register is usually made up of two data bytes); *see also* MAR; **address resolution protocol (ARP)** = protocol used within the TCP/IP standard that is used to determine whether the source and destination address in a packet are in the data-link control (DLC) or internet protocol (IP) format; once the format of the address is known, the packet can be correctly routed over a network; *see also* TCP/IP; **address space** = total number of possible locations that can be directly addressed by the program *or* CPU; **address strobe** = signal (pulse) that indicates that a valid address is on the address bus; **address track** = track on a magnetic disk containing the addresses of files, etc., stored on other tracks; **address translation** = an address produced by calculating an expression; **address word** = computer word, usually made up, in a small micro, of two data words that contain the address data; **base address** = initial address in a program used as a reference for others; **destination address** = address of the node to which data is being transferred *or* sent; **initial address** = address at which the first location of a program is stored; **machine address** = storage address that directly, without any modification, accesses a location *or* device; **network address** = unique number that identifies each device on a network; **relative address** = location specified in relation to a reference (address) **2** *verb* to put the location data onto an address bus to identify which word in memory *or* storage device is to be accessed; *a larger address word increases the amount of memory a computer can address*

The world's largest open data network, the Internet, links more than 10,000 local networks and 3 million workstations in 50 countries. It has grown so fast that its address space is 'bust' and is being redesigned to allow further expansion.

Computing

addressability *noun* the control available over pixels on screen

addressable *adjective* which can be addressed; *with the new operating system, all of the 5MB of installed RAM is addressable;* **addressable cursor** = cursor which can be programmed to be placed in a certain position; **addressable point** = any point *or* pixel in a graphics system that can be directly addressed; **addressable terminal** = terminal that will only accept data if it has the correct address and identification number in the message header

addressing *noun* process of accessing a location in memory; **addressing capacity** = largest location that a certain program *or* CPU can directly address, without special features (such as virtual memory *or* memory banks); **addressing level** = zero-level: operand is the address part of the instruction; first-level: operand stored at the address of the instruction; second-level: operand stored at the address given in the instruction; **addressing method** = manner in which a section of memory is located; **addressing mode** = way in which a location is addressed, either sequential, indexed, direct, etc.; **abbreviated addressing** = use of a smaller address word than normal, which provides faster address decoding operations; **absolute addressing** = locating a data word stored in memory, by the use of its absolute address; **bit addressing** = selecting a register and examining one bit within it; **deferred addressing** = (indirect addressing) the location accessed contains the address of the operand to be processed; **direct addressing** = method of addressing where the storage location address given in the instruction is the location to be used; **immediate addressing** = accessing data immediately because it is held in the address field itself; **indexed addressing** = addressing mode, in which the storage location to be accessed is made up of a start (base) address and an offset (index) word, which is then added to it to give the address to be used; **indirect addressing** = way of addressing data, where the first instruction refers to an address which contains a second address

adjacent *adjective* which is near *or* next to something; *the address is stored adjacent to* *the customer name field;* **adjacent domains** = two domains linked by two adjacent nodes; **adjacent nodes** = two nodes connected by a path that does not connect any other node

adjunct register *noun* 32-bit register in which the top 16 bits are used for control information and only the bottom 16 bits are available for use by a program

adjust *verb* to change something to fit new conditions *or* so that it works better; *you can adjust the brightness and contrast by turning a knob*

adjustment *noun* slight change made to something so that it works better; *the brightness needs adjustment; I think the joystick needs adjustment as it sometimes gets stuck*

AdLib type of sound card for the PC with basic sound playback and MIDI functions

administrator *noun* **(a)** individual who is responsible for looking after a network; responsibilities include installing, configuring and maintaining the network **(b)** control *or* supervisor *or* executive software *or* person; **data administrator** = control section of a database management system; **database administrator (DBA)** = person in charge of running and maintaining a database system

Adobe™ software company that developed products including Acrobat, ATM, and PostScript

◊ **Adobe Type Manager** *or* **ATM** standard for describing scalable fonts - used with Apple System 7 and Microsoft Windows to provide fonts that can be scaled to almost any point size, and printed on almost any printer; *see also* OUTLINE FONTS

ADP = AUTOMATIC DATA PROCESSING data processing done by a computer

ADPCM = ADAPTIVE DIFFERENTIAL PULSE CODE MODULATION CCITT standard that defines a method of converting a voice or analog signal into a compressed digital signal

ADSL *see* ASYMMETRIC DIGITAL SUBSCRIBER LINE

advance *verb* to move forward; to make something move forward; *the paper is advanced by turning this knob; advance the cursor two spaces along the line*

advanced *adjective* more complicated *or* more difficult to learn; **advanced configuration and power interface (ACPI)** = software system (that is part of Microsoft Windows 98) that allows the operating system to automatically configure compatible hardware; **advanced program to program communications (APPC)** = set of protocols developed by IBM that allows peer-to-peer communication between workstations connected to an SNA network; also known as LU 6.2 protocols; **advanced peer-to-peer networking (APPN)** = extension to the IBM SNA protocol that allows workstations to share information on a peer-to-peer basis without the need for a central mainframe; often used to route information around a network and dynamically adjusts the route if part of the network is damaged; **advanced run-length limited (ARLL)** = method of storing data onto a hard disk that is faster and more efficient than RLL; **advanced technology attachment packet interface (ATAPI)** = a type of standard interface that is used for CD-ROMs; **advanced version** = program with more complex features for use by an experienced user

adventure game *noun* game played on a computer, where the user pretends to be a hero in an imaginary land and has to get through various dangerous situations, fight monsters, etc.

advisory lock *noun* (in a multitasking system) lock placed on a region of a file by one process to prevent any other process accessing the same data

◊ **advisory system** *noun* expert system that provides advice to a user

affect *verb* to touch *or* to influence *or* to change something; *changes in voltage will affect the way the computer functions*

affirmative *adjective* meaning 'yes'; **the answer was in the affirmative** = the answer was 'yes'; **affirmative acknowledgement** = acknowledge signal from the receiver that it has accepted the message and is ready for the next one

AFIPS = AMERICAN FEDERATION OF INFORMATION PROCESSING SOCIETIES

AFP = APPLETALK FILING PROTOCOL protocol used to communicate between workstations and servers in a network of Apple Macintosh computers

afterglow *see* PERSISTENCE

after-image *noun* copy of a block of data that has been modified

agenda *noun* list of tasks *or* appointments *or* activities that have to be carried out on a particular day; **electronic agenda** = software that allows a user to record appointments for each day

agent *noun* (a) program or software that runs on a workstation in a network; the software sends performance and statistical information about the workstation to a central network management console (b) series of commands or actions that are carried out automatically on a particular file or data

aggregate *noun & adjective* collection of data objects; **data aggregate** = collection of items of data that are related; **aggregate bandwidth** = total bandwidth of a channel carrying a multiplexed data stream; **aggregate function** = mathematical database function performed on a selected field in every record in a selected database; **aggregate line speed** = maximum speed at which data can be transmitted through a particular channel; **aggregate operator** = command in a database management program that starts an aggregate function

AGP = ACCELERATED GRAPHICS PORT dedicated bus between a graphics controller and main memory that allows data to be transferred very quickly without using the main processor, is used with the Intel Pentium II processor to provide very high-speed three-dimensional graphics and video processing; this port does not replace a PCI bus but works with it

AI = ARTIFICIAL INTELLIGENCE the design and development of computer programs that attempt to imitate human intelligence and decision-making functions, providing basic reasoning and other human characteristics; *see also* EXPERT SYSTEM, IKBS

aid 1 *noun* help; *the computer is a great aid to rapid processing of large amounts of information;* **diagnostic aid** = hardware *or* software device that helps find faults **2** *verb* to help; *industrial design is aided by computers see also* COMPUTER-AIDED

aiming symbol *or* **field** *noun* symbol displayed on screen which defines the area in which a light-pen can be detected

airbrush *noun* (in graphics software) a painting tool that creates a diffuse pattern of dots, like an mechanical airbrush; *we used the airbrush tool to create the cloud effects in this image*

air gap *noun* narrow gap between a recording *or* playback head and the magnetic medium

AIX = ADVANCED INTERACTIVE EXECUTIVE version of UNIX produced by IBM to run on its range of PCs, minicomputers and mainframes

alarm *noun* ringing or other sound which warns of a danger; *all staff must leave the building if the alarm sounds; an alarm rings when the printer has run out of paper*

alert *noun* warning message sent from software to warn a person or application that an error or problem has occurred; **alert box** = warning panel displayed on screen to warn a user about something; *the alert box warned me that I was about to delete all my files;* **alert condition** = status of a particular object *or* device that triggers an alarm; **network alert** = message sent from the network operating system to the user warning that the network hardware is not working properly

algebra *noun* use of letters in certain mathematical operations to represent unknown numbers *or* a range of possible numbers; **Boolean algebra** = rules set down to define, simplify and manipulate logical functions, based on statements that are true or false

◊ **algebraic language** *noun* context free language

ALGOL = ALGORITHMIC LANGUAGE high level programming language using algorithmic methods for mathematical and technical applications

algorithm *noun* rules used to define *or* perform a specific task *or* to solve a specific problem

◊ **algorithmic** *adjective* expressed using algorithms; **algorithmic language** = computer language designed to process and express algorithms, such as ALGOL

```
the steps are: acquiring a
digitized image, developing an
algorithm to process it,
processing the image,
modifying the algorithm until
you are satisfied with the
result
```
Byte

```
the complex algorithms needed
for geometrical calculations
make heavy demands on the
processor
```
PC Business World

alias *noun* representative name given to a file, port, device or spreadsheet cell or range of cells; *the operating system uses the alias COM1 to represent the serial port address 3FCh;* **alias name** = (on a network) another name that is used instead of the user name

◊ **aliasing** *noun* jagged edges that appear along diagonal or curved lines displayed on a computer screen caused by the size of each pixel; **anti-aliasing** = (i) (in graphics) method of reducing the effects of jagged edges in graphics by using shades of grey to blend in along edges; (ii) (in sound) to add

sound signals between the sound samples to create a smoother sound

alien *adjective* different *or* not fitting the usual system; **alien disk** = disk formatted on another system *or* containing data in a format which is in a form that cannot be read *or* understood; **alien disk reader** = add-on device which allows a computer to access data on disks from other computers *or* systems; *when you have an alien disk select the multi-disk option to allow you to turn the disk drive into an alien disk reader*

align *verb* **(a)** (i) to make sure that the characters to be printed are spaced and levelled correctly, either vertically or horizontally; (ii) to arrange numbers into a column with all figured lines up against the right hand side (right-aligned) or the left-hand side (left-aligned) **(b)** to ensure that a read/write head is correctly positioned over the recording medium; **align text** = (in a word-processor) to add spaces between words in a line to make sure that the line of text fills the whole line; *see also* JUSTIFY

◊ **aligner** *noun* device used to make sure that the paper is straight in a printer

◊ **aligning edge** *noun* edge of an optical character recognition system used to position a document

◊ **alignment** *noun* correct spacing and levelling of printed characters; **in alignment** = correctly aligned; **out of alignment** = not aligned correctly; **alignment pin** = peg that fits in a hole to ensure that two devices are correctly aligned

allocate *verb* to divide (a period of time *or* a piece of work) in various ways and share it out between users; *the operating system allocated most of main memory to the spreadsheet program*

◊ **allocation** *noun* dividing memory *or* disk space *or* printer use *or* program *or* operating system time *or* device in various ways; *allocation of time or capital to a project;* **allocation unit** = one or more sectors on a hard disk that are used to store a file or part of a file; **allocation routine** = short program that divides the memory resources of a system between the software and peripherals that use it; **dynamic allocation** = system where resources are allocated during a program run, rather than being determined in advance; **memory allocation** = process in which an operating system provides an application with the memory it requires in order to run

> IBM has issued a fix to correct bugs in the latest version of its OS/2 PC operating system which could cause screen crashes. The fix is meant to correct seven problems with OS/2 2.0. They include problems with swapper files and DOS memory allocation.
>
> *Computing*

all points addressable (APA) mode

noun graphics mode in which each pixel can be individually addressed and its colour and attributes defined

ALPHA™   *noun* processor chip developed by Digital Equipment Corporation; the ALPHA chip is a 64-bit RISC processor

alpha *or* **alpha test** *noun* first working attempt of a computer product; *the new software is still in an alpha product stage; see also* BETA TEST

◊ **alpha beta technique**   *noun* (free structure) technique used in artificial intelligence for solving game and strategy problems

◊ **alpha channel** *noun* (in 32-bit graphics systems) the top eight bits that define the properties of a pixel; the lower 24 bits define the pixel's colour

◊ **alpha-particle** *noun* emitted alpha radiation particle; **alpha-particle sensitivity** = problem experienced by certain (MOS) memory devices exposed to alpha radiation, causing loss of stored charge (data)

◊ **alpha radiation**   *noun*   naturally occurring radiation

◊ **alpha test** *see* ALPHA

alphabet *noun* the 26 letters used to make words

◊ **alphabetic character (set)**   *noun* characters (capitals and small letters) that

make up the alphabet; **alphabetic string** = string that only contains alphabetic characters

◊ **alphabetical order** *noun* arrangement of records (such as files, index cards) in the order of the letters of the alphabet (A,B,C,D, etc.)

◊ **alphabetically** *adverb* in alphabetical order; *the files are arranged alphabetically under the customer's name*

◊ **alphabetize** *verb* to put into alphabetical order; *enter the bibliographical information and alphabetize it*

alphageometric *adjective* (set of codes) that instruct a teletext terminal to display various graphics patterns *or* characters

alphameric *US* = ALPHANUMERIC

alphamosaic *adjective* (character set) used in teletext to provide alphanumeric and graphics characters

alphanumeric *adjective;* **alphanumeric characters** *or* **alphanumerics** = roman letters and arabic numerals (and other signs such as punctuation marks); **alphanumeric data** = data that represents the letters of the alphabet and the arabic numerals; **alphanumeric display** = display device able to show characters as well as numbers; **alphanumeric keyboard** = keyboard containing character keys as well as numerical keys; **alphanumeric operand** = operand which can contain alphanumeric characters, such as a string; **alphanumeric string** = series of alphanumeric characters that are manipulated and treated as a single unit

> geometrical data takes up more storage space than alphanumeric data
>
> *PC Business World*

alphaphotographic *adjective* which represents pictures using predefined graphics characters, for teletext services

◊ **alphasort** *verb* to sort data into alphabetical order

Alt key *noun* special key on a PC's keyboard used to activate special functions in an application; *press Alt and P at the same time to print your document*

COMMENT: the Alt key has become the standard method of activating a menu bar in any software running on a PC; for example, Alt-F normally displays the File menu of a program, Alt-X normally exits the program

alter *verb* to change; *to alter the terms of a contract; the program specifications have just been altered*

◊ **alterable** *adjective* which can be altered; *see* EAPROM, EAROM

◊ **alteration** *noun* change which has been made; *the agreement was signed without any alterations; the new version of the software has many alterations and improvements*

alternate 1 *verb* to change from one state to another and back, over and over again **2** *adjective* which change from one to another; **alternate character set** = second set of special characters that can be accessed from a keyboard; *we can print Greek characters by selecting the alternate character set;* **alternate key** = key in a database file that is not the primary key; **alternate mode** = application for multi-user use, where two operators can access and share a single file at the same time; **alternate route** = backup path in a communications system, used in case of a fault *or* breakdown

◊ **alternately** *adverb* switching from one to the other

◊ **alternation** *noun* logical function that produces a true output if any input is true

◊ **alternating current** *or* **AC** *noun* electric current whose value varies with time in a regular, sinusoidal way (changing direction of flow each half cycle)

alternative 1 *noun* something which can be done instead of something else; *what is the alternative to re-keying all the data?;* we **have no alternative** = there is nothing else we can do **2** *adjective* other *or* which can take the place of something; **alternative denial** = logical function whose output is false if all inputs are true and true if any input is false

ALU = ARITHMETIC LOGIC UNIT section of the CPU that performs all arithmetic and logical functions; *see also* CPU

AM = AMPLITUDE MODULATION

ambient *adjective* normal background (conditions); **ambient temperature** = normal average temperature of the air around a device

ambiguity *noun* something which is not clearly defined; **ambiguity error** = error due to incorrect selection of ambiguous data

◊ **ambiguous** *adjective* which has two possible meanings; **ambiguous filename** = filename which is not unique to a single file, making it difficult to locate the file

amendment record *noun* record containing new information used to update a master record *or* file

American National Standards Institute (ANSI)
organization which specifies computer and software standards including those that define network standards and high-level programming languages

American Standard Code for Information Interchange (ASCII)
code which represents alphanumeric characters as binary codes

America Online™ (AOL)
largest internet service provider in the world; *see also* ISP, OSP

Amiga™ range of personal computers developed by Commodore

COMMENT: Amiga computers are based on the Motorola 68000 range of CPUs and are not IBM PC compatible

amount 1 *noun* quantity of data *or* paper, etc.; *what is the largest amount of data which can be processed in one hour?* **2** *verb;* **to amount to** = to make a total of; *the total number of characters amount to ten million*

amp *or* **ampere (A)** *noun* base SI unit of electrical current; defined as the current flowing through an impedance of one ohm which has a voltage of one volt across it; (NOTE: used with figures: **a 13-amp fuse**)

ampersand *noun* printing sign (&) which means 'and'

amplification *noun* the output-to-input signal strength ratio; *increase the amplification of the input signal; the amplification is so high, the signal is distorting*

◊ **amplifier** *noun* electronic circuit that magnifies the power of a signal

◊ **amplify** *verb* to magnify a signal power *or* amplitude; *the received signal needs to be amplified before it can be processed*

amplitude *noun* strength *or* size of a signal; **amplitude modulation** = method of carrying data by varying the size of a carrier signal (of fixed frequency) according to the data; **amplitude quantization** = conversion of an analog signal to a numerical representation

analog *or* **analogue** *noun* representation and measurement of numerical data by continuously variable physical quantities, such as the size of electrical voltages *compare* DIGITAL; **analog channel** = communications line that carries analog signals such as speech; **analog computer** = computer which processes data in analog form (that is, data which is represented by a continuously varying signal - as opposed to digital data); **analog data** = data that is represented as a continuously variable signal; speech is a form of analog data; **analog display** = display or monitor that can display an infinite range of colours or shades of grey (unlike digital displays that can only display a finite range of colours); VGA monitors are a form of analog display; **analog gate** = logic gate whose output is proportional to an input signal; **analog input card** = all circuitry on one PCB required for amplifying and converting analog input signals to a digital form; **analog line** = communications line that carries analog signals, such as a telephone line; **analog loopback** = test mode on a modem used to test the serial port of the local computer or terminal; **analog loopback with selftest** = test mode on a modem used to test

the serial port of the modem; **analog monitor** = display screen that uses a continuously variable input signal to control the colours display so it can display a near infinite range of colours; **analog output card** = all circuitry on one PCB required to convert digital output data from a computer to an analog form; **analog recording** = storing signals in their natural form without conversion to digital form; **analog representation** = value *or* variable in analog form; **analog signal** = continuously varying signal; **analog to digital (A to D** *or* **A/D)** = (changing a signal) from an analog form to a digitally coded form; **analog to digital converter (ADC** *or* **A to D converter)** = device used to convert an analog input signal to a digital output form, that can be understood by a computer; **analog transmission** = data transmission in which the data is sent as a series of changes in a continuously varying signal; **digital to analog converter (DAC** *or* **D to A converter)** = circuit that outputs an analog signal that is proportional to the input digital number, and so converts a digital input to an analog form

COMMENT: a DAC allows the computer to work outside the computer's environment, controlling machines, producing sound or speech, etc. An ADC allows real-world signals to be processed by a computer

analyse *or* **analyze** *verb* to examine in detail; *to analyse a computer printout; to analyse the market potential for a new computer*

analysis *noun* detailed examination and report; *market analysis; sales analysis; to carry out an analysis of the market potential; to write an analysis of the sales position;* **cost analysis** = examination in advance of the costs of a new product; **data analysis** = to extract information and results from data; **systems analysis** = analysing a process *or* system to see if it could be more efficiently carried out by computer; (NOTE: plural is **analyses**)

analyst *noun* person who carries out an analysis of a problem; **systems analyst** = person who specializes in systems analysis

analyzer *noun* electronic test equipment that displays various features of a signal

analytical engine *noun* mechanical calculating machine developed by Charles Babbage in 1833 that is generally considered the first general-purpose digital computer

ancestral file *noun* system of backing up files (son to father to grandfather file), where the son is the current working file

anchor cell *noun* cell in a spreadsheet program that defines the start of a range of cells

ancillary equipment *noun* equipment which is used to make a task easier, but which is not absolutely necessary

AND *or* **coincidence function** *noun* logical function whose output is true if both its inputs are true; **AND** *or* **coincidence gate** *or* **circuit** *or* **element** = electronic gate that performs a logical AND function on electrical signals; **AND** *or* **coincidence operation** = processing two or more input signals, outputting their AND function

COMMENT: if both inputs are 1 the results of the AND function will be 1; if one of the input digits is 0, then AND will produce a 0

angle *noun* measure of the change in direction, usually as the distance turned from a reference line

angstrom (Å) *noun* unit of measurement equal to one thousand millionth of a metre

ANI = AUTOMATIC NUMBER IDENTIFICATION telephone system which displays the telephone number of the caller

animation *or* **computer animation** *noun* creating the illusion of movement by displaying a series of slightly different images on screen; the images are displayed very rapidly to give the effect of smooth movement

annotation *noun* comment *or* note in a program which explains how the program is to be used; **annotation symbol** = symbol used when making flowcharts, to allow comments to be added

annunciator *noun* & *adjective* (signal) which can be heard *or* seen in order to attract attention

anode *noun* positive electrical terminal of a device; (NOTE: the opposite is **cathode**)

ANSI *US* = AMERICAN NATIONAL STANDARDS INSTITUTE organization which specifies computer and software standards, including those of high-level programming languages; **ANSI C** = standard version of the C programming language; **ANSI driver** = (in a PC) small resident software program that interprets ANSI screen control codes and controls the screen appropriately; **ANSI escape sequence** = sequence of ANSI screen control characters that controls the colours and attributes of text on screen; the sequence must begin with the ASCII character Esc (ASCII 27) and the character [(ASCII 91); **ANSI screen control** = standard codes developed by ANSI that control how colours and simple graphics are displayed on a computer screen

answer 1 *noun* reply *or* solution to a question **2** *verb* **(a)** to reply *or* provide the solution to a question **(b)** to reply to a signal and set up a communications link; *the first modem originates the call and the second answers it;* **answer back** = signal sent by a receiving computer to identify itself; **answer mode** = modem that is waiting to receive a telephone call and establish a connection; *see also* MODEM; **answer modem** = mode of a modem that emits an answertone used to establish a connection with an originate modem; **answer time** = time taken for a receiving device to respond to a signal; **answertone** = tone an answering modem emits before the carrier is exchanged

◊ **answering machine** = application software that runs on a PC and controls a modem that has voice-mail functionality

◊ **answer/originate (device)** *noun* communications device, such as a modem, that can receive or send data

anthropomorphic software *noun* (in artificial intelligence) software that appears to react to what a user says

anti- *prefix* meaning against; **anticoincidence circuit** *or* **function** = logical function whose output is true if either (of 2) inputs is true, and false if both inputs are the same; **anti-aliasing** = method of reducing the effects of jagged edges in graphics by using shades of grey to blend in along edges; **anti-static mat** = special rubberised mat which dissipates static electricity charge through an electrical earth connection; an operator touches the mat before handling sensitive electronic components that could be damaged by static electricity; **anti-tinkle suppression** = *(in a modem)* switch which prevents other telephones on a line ringing when a modem dials out; **anti-virus program** = software program that looks for virus software on a computer and destroys it before it can damage data or files

AOL = AMERICA ONLINE

APA = ALL POINTS ADDRESSABLE

Apache HTTPD popular Web server software products, available as freeware, that allow you to set up a Web server

aperture card *noun* method of storing microfilmed information with a card surround, that can contain punched information

◊ **aperture mask** *noun* mask used in colour monitors, used to keep separate the red, green and blue beams

API = APPLICATION PROGRAMMING INTERFACE set of standard program functions and commands that allow any programmer to interface a program with another application; *if I follow the published API for this system, my program will work properly*

APL = A PROGRAMMING LANGUAGE high-level programming language used in scientific and mathematical work

APPC = ADVANCED PROGRAM TO PROGRAM COMMUNICATION set of protocols developed by IBM that allows peer-to-peer communication between workstations connected to an SNA network; also known as LU 6.2 protocols

append *verb* (i) to add data to an existing file *or* record; (ii) to add a file or data to the end of an existing file; *if you enter the DOS command COPY A+B, the file B will be appended to the end of file A*

◊ **appendix** *noun* section at the back of a book, containing additional information; *for further details see the appendices; a complete list is printed in the appendix* (NOTE: plural is **appendices**)

Apple Computer Corporation™

company (formed in 1975) which has developed a range of personal computers including the Apple II, Apple Lisa and, more recently, the Apple Macintosh

◊ **Apple Desktop Bus** *noun* serial bus built into Apple Macintosh computers that allows low-speed devices, such as the keyboard and mouse, to communicate with the processor

◊ **Apple file exchange** *noun* software program that runs on an Apple Macintosh computer allowing it to read disks from a PC

◊ **Apple filing protocol (AFP)** *noun* method of storing files on a network server so that they can be accessed from an Apple Macintosh computer

◊ **Apple Key** *noun* special key on the keyboard of an Apple Macintosh that, when pressed with another key, provides a short-cut to a menu selection

◊ **Apple Mac** *or* **Apple Macintosh™ computer** *noun* range of personal computers developed by Apple Inc. that has a graphical user interface and uses the 68000 family of processors

◊ **Appleshare™** *noun* software that allows Apple Macintosh computers to share files and printers using a file server

◊ **AppleTalk™** *noun* proprietary communications protocol developed by Apple Computer that carries data over network hardware between two or more Apple Macintosh computers and peripherals; similar to the seven-layer OSI protocol model; AppleTalk can link up to 32 devices, uses a CSMA/CA design and transmits data at 230Kbps; **AppleTalk Filing Protocol** (AFP) = protocol used to communicate between workstations and servers in a network of Apple Macintosh computers

---

Apple Computer has fleshed out details of a migration path to the PowerPC RISC architecture for its 7 million Apple Macintosh users. Developments in the pipeline include PowerPC versions of the AppleTalk Remote Access networking protocol.

Computing

---

applet *noun* (i) small utility applications; (ii) small program that is used to enhance the functionality of a web page or application, normally supplied as an ActiveX or Java program; (iii) (in Microsoft Windows) application started from the Control Panel; *there are applets to help format your disk and configure your keyboard; see also* ActiveX, Java, Windows

appliance *noun* machine, especially one used in the home; *all electrical appliances should be properly earthed*

◊ **appliance computer** *noun* ready to run computer system that can be bought in a shop, taken home and used immediately for a particular purpose *see also* TURNKEY

application *noun* **(a)** asking for something, usually in writing; *application for an account on the system;* **application form** = form to be filled in when applying; *to fill in an application (form) for an account on the system* **(b)** task which a computer performs *or* problem which a computer solves (as opposed to an operating system which is the way in which a computer works); **application developer** = programmer who designs the look of an application and defines its functions; **application file** = binary file stored on disk that contains the machine code instructions of a program; **application generator** = special software that allows a programmer to define the main functions and look of an application; the generator then automatically creates the instructions to carry

out the defined application; **application icon** = small image *or* graphical symbol that represents an application program in a graphical user interface; **application layer** = seventh and top layer in an ISO/OSI network, which allows a user to requests functions, such as transfer files, send mail and use resources; the other layers are not normally accessed by users; **application orientated language** = programming language that provides functions which allow the user to solve certain application problems; **application package** = set of computer programs and manuals that cover all aspects of a particular task (such as payroll, stock control, tax, etc.); **application programming interface (API)** = set of standard program functions and commands that allow any programmer to interface a program with another application; *if I follow the published API for this system, my program will work properly;* **application service element** = part of a program in the application layer of an OSI environment that interacts with the layers beneath it; **application software** *or* **application program** = program which is used by a user to make the computer do what is required, designed to allow a particular task to be performed; *the multi-window editor is used to create and edit applications programs;* **application specific integrated circuits (ASIC)** = specially designed ICs for one particular function *or* to special specifications; **application terminal** = terminal (such as at a sales desk) which is specially configured to carry out certain tasks; **application window** = application program running in a window displayed in a graphical user interface such as Microsoft's Windows; *see also* GUI

How do users interact with a computer system? Via a terminal or PC. So what application layer OSI protocol do we need first? The Virtual Terminal. And what do we get? File Transfer Access and Maintenance.

Computing

apply *verb* **(a)** to ask for something, usually in writing **(b)** to affect *or* to touch; *this formula applies only to data received after the interrupt signal*

APPN = ADVANCED PEER-TO-PEER NETWORKING extension to the IBM SNA protocol that allows workstations to share information on a peer-to-peer basis without the need for a central mainframe; often used to route information around a network and dynamically adjusts the route if part of the network is damaged

approval *noun* **(a)** agreement that something can be used; *a BABT approval is needed for modems;* **certificate of approval** = document showing that an item has been approved officially **(b); on approval** = sale where the buyer only pays for goods if they are satisfactory

approve *verb* **(a) to approve of** = to think something is good; *the new graphics monitor was approved by the safety council before being sold; I approve of the new editor - much easier to use* **(b)** to agree to something; *to approve the terms of a contract; the software has to be approved by the board; an approved modem should carry a label with a green circle and the words 'Approved by ....'*

approximate *adjective* not exact, but almost correct; *we have made an approximate calculation of the time needed for keyboarding*

◊ **approximately** *adverb* almost correctly; *processing time is approximately 10% lower than during the previous quarter*

◊ **approximating** *adjective* which is nearly correct

◊ **approximation** *noun* rough calculation; *approximation of keyboarding time; the final figure is only an approximation;* **approximation error** = error caused by rounding off a real number

APT = AUTOMATICALLY PROGRAMMED TOOLS programming language used to control numerically controlled machines

Arabic *adjective;* **Arabic numbers** *or* **figures** = figures such as 1, 2, 3, 4, etc. (as opposed to the Roman numerals I, II, III. IV, etc.); *the page numbers are written in Arabic figures*

arbitration *noun;* **bus arbitration** = protocol and control of transmission over a bus that ensures fair usage by several users

arcade game *noun* adventure game played on a machine in a public place

Archie system of servers on the internet that catalogue the public files available on the internet

Archimedes™ *noun* personal computer developed by Acorn Computers; the Archimedes is based around a RISC central processor and is not compatible with either the IBM PC or Apple Macintosh

architecture *noun* layout and interconnection of a computer's internal hardware and the logical relationships between CPU, memory and I/O devices; **onion skin architecture** = design of a computer system in layers, according to function *or* priority; *the onion skin architecture of this computer is made up of a kernel at the centre, an operating system, a low-level language and then the user's programs*

archive **1** *noun* storage of data over a long period; **archive file** = file containing data which is out of date, but which is kept for future reference; **archive attribute** *or* **bit** *or* **flag** = special attribute attached to a file in DOS and OS/2 that indicates if the file has been archived since it was last changed; *see also* ATTRIBUTE **2** *verb* to put data in storage; **archived copy** = copy kept in storage

◊ **archival quality** *noun* length of time that a copy can be stored before it becomes illegible

ARCNET *or* **ARCnet** = ATTACHED RESOURCE COMPUTER NETWORK network hardware and cable standard; developed by Datapoint Corporation, it is a token bus network that transmits data at between 2.5 and 4Mbps; new versions of ARCnet transfer data at 20 and 100Mbps over fibre optic cable

> ARCNET uses a single token that moves from one workstation to the next carrying data and uses a star-wired cable topology

area *noun* **(a)** measurement of the space taken up by something (calculated by multiplying the length by the width); *the area of this office is 3,400 square feet; we are looking for a shop with a sales area of about 100 square metres;* **area fill** = (in graphics) instruction to fill an area of the screen *or* an enclosed pattern with a colour *or* pattern; **area graph** = line graph in which the area below the line is filled with a pattern or colour **(b)** section of memory *or* code that is reserved for a certain purpose; **area search** = search for specific data within a certain section of memory *or* files; **image area** = region of a display screen in which characters can be displayed; **input area** = section of main memory that holds data transferred from backing store until it is processed

arg *see* ARGUMENT

argue *verb* to discuss something about which you do not agree; *they argued over or about the design of the cover; we spent hours arguing with the managing director about the layout of the new factory* (NOTE: you argue **with** someone **about** *or* **over** something)

argument *or* **arg** *noun* **(a)** discussing something without agreeing; *they got into an argument with the customs officials over the documents; he was sacked after an argument with the managing director* **(b)** variable acted upon by an operator *or* function; *if you enter the words 'MULTIPLY A, B', the processor will recognise the operator, MULTIPLY, and use it with the two arguments, A and B see also* OPERAND; **argument separator** = punctuation mark or symbol that separates several arguments on one line; *the command 'MULTIPLY A, B' uses a comma as the argument separator*

arithmetic *noun* concerned with mathematical functions such as addition, subtraction, division and multiplication; **arithmetic capability** = ability of a device to perform mathematical functions; **arithmetic check** = further arithmetic operation carried out to ensure that a result is correct; **arithmetic functions** = calculations carried out on numbers, such as addition, subtraction, multiplication, division; **arithmetic instruction** = program instruction in which the operator defines the arithmetic operation to be carried out *compare* LOGICAL INSTRUCTION; **arithmetic logic unit** (ALU) *or* **arithmetic unit** = hardware section of a CPU that performs all the mathematical and logical functions; **arithmetic operation** = mathematical function carried out on data; **arithmetic operators** = symbol which indicates an arithmetic function (such as + for addition, x for multiplication); **arithmetic register** = memory location which stores operands; **arithmetic shift** = word *or* data moved one bit to the left *or* right inside a register, losing the bit shifted off the end *compare* LOGICAL SHIFT; **external arithmetic** = arithmetic performed by a coprocessor; **internal arithmetic** = arithmetic performed by the ALU

arm **1** *noun;* **access arm** = mechanical device in a disk drive used to position the read/write head over the correct track on a disk **2** *verb* (i) to prepare a device *or* machine *or* routine for action *or* inputs; (ii) to define which interrupt lines are active; **armed interrupt** = interrupt line which has been made active (using an interrupt mask)

ARP = ADDRESS RESOLUTION PROTOCOL *see also* ADDRESS, TCP/IP

ARQ = AUTOMATIC REPEAT REQUEST error correction system, used in some modems, which asks for data to be re-transmitted if it contains errors

array *noun* ordered structure containing individually accessible elements referenced by numbers, used to store tables *or* sets of related data; **alphanumeric array** = array whose elements are letters and numbers; **array bounds** = limits to the number of elements which can be given in an array; **array dimension** = number of elements in an array, given as rows and columns; **array element** = one individual piece of data within an array; **array processor** = computer that can act upon several arrays of data simultaneously, for very fast mathematical applications; *the array processor allows the array that contains the screen image to be rotated with one simple command;* **string array** = array whose elements can be strings (of alphanumeric characters); **three-dimensional array** = array made up of a number of two dimensional arrays, arranged in parallel, giving rows, columns and depth; **two-dimensional array** = ordered structure whose elements are arranged as a table (of rows and columns)

arrow keys *noun* set of four keys on a keyboard that move the cursor or pointer around the screen; the four keys control movement up, down, left and right

arrow pointer *noun* small arrow on-screen that you can move using the mouse

arsenide *see* GALLIUM ARSENIDE

article *noun* one message in a newsgroup

artificial intelligence (AI) *noun* the design and device of computer programs that attempt to imitate human intelligence and decision making functions, providing basic reasoning and other human characteristics

artwork *noun* graphical work *or* images

ascend *verb* to increase; **ascending order** = to arrange data with the smallest value or date first in the list

◊ **ascender** *noun* part of a character that rises above the main line of printed characters (as the 'tail' of a 'b', 'd', etc.)

ASCII = AMERICAN STANDARD CODE FOR INFORMATION INTERCHANGE code which represents alphanumeric characters in binary code; **ASCII character** = character which is in the ASCII list of codes; **ASCII file** = stored file containing only ASCII coded character data; *use a word processor or other program that generates a standard ASCII file;* **ASCII keyboard** = keyboard which gives all the ASCII characters; **ASCII text** = letter and number characters with an ASCII code between 0 and 127; **ASCIIZ string** = (in programming) a sequence of ASCII characters followed by the ASCII code zero that indicates the end of the sequence *for full listing of ASCII codes see also* APPENDIX (NOTE: when speaking say 'as-key')

ASF = ACTIVE STREAMING FORMAT multimedia delivery format developed by Microsoft for delivery over the internet and used in its NetShow product

ASIC = APPLICATION SPECIFIC INTEGRATED CIRCUITS specially designed ICs for one particular function *or* to special specifications

aspect *noun* way in which something appears; **aspect card** = card containing information on documents in an information retrieval system; **aspect ratio** = ratio of the width to the height of pixel shapes; **aspect system** = method of storing and indexing documents in a retrieval system

ASR = AUTOMATIC SEND/RECEIVE device *or* terminal that can transmit and receive information *compare* KSR

> COMMENT: an ASR terminal can input information via a keyboard or via a tape cassette or paper tape. It can receive information and store it in internal memory or on tape

assemble *verb* **(a)** to put a hardware *or* software product together from various smaller parts; *the parts for the disk drive are made in Japan and assembled in France* **(b)** to translate assembly code into machine code; *there is a short wait during which time the program is assembled into object code; syntax errors spotted whilst the source program is being assembled* **(c)** to insert specific library routines *or* macros *or* parameters into a program

◊ **assembler (program)** *noun* assembly program *or* program which converts a program written in assembly language into machine code; **absolute assembler** = type of assembly language program designed to produce code which uses only absolute addresses and values; **assembler error messages** = messages produced by an assembler program that indicate that errors have been found in the source code; **cross-assembler** = assembler that produces machine-code code for one computer while running on another; **single-pass assembler** = object code produced in one run through the assembler of the source program; **two-pass assembler** = assembler that converts an assembly language program into machine code in two passes, the first pass stores symbolic addresses, the second converts them to absolute addresses

◊ **assembly** *noun* (a) putting an item together from various parts; *there are no assembly instructions to show you how to put the computer together;* **assembly plant** = factory where units are put together from parts made in other factories (b) converting a program into machine code; **assembly code** = mnemonics which are used to represent machine code instructions in an assembler program; **assembly language** *or* **assembler language** = programming language used to code information which will then be converted to machine code; **assembly listing** = display of an assembly program ordered according to memory location; **assembly (language) program** = number of assembly code instructions which perform a task; **assembly routine** *or* **system** *see* ASSEMBLER; **assembly time** = (i) time taken by an assembler program to translate a program; (ii) period during which an assembler is converting a program from assembly language into machine code

assertion *noun* (i) program statement of a fact *or* rule; (ii) fact that is true *or* defined as being true

assets *plural noun* separate data elements (such as video, audio, image) that are used in a multimedia application

assign *verb* (a) to give a computer *or* someone a job of work; *he was assigned the job of checking the sales figures; two PCs have been assigned to outputting the labels* (b) (i) to set a variable equal to a string of

characters *or* numbers; (ii) to keep part of a computer system for use while a program is running

◊ **assignment** *noun* (a) particular job of work (b) setting a variable equal to a value *or* string *or* character; **assignment compatible** = (in the Pascal programming language) check to see if a value is allowed according to its type; **assignment conversion** = (in the C and Fortran programming languages) operation to change the type of a value; **assignment statement** = basic programming command that sets a variable equal to a value *or* string *or* character

associated document *or* **file** *noun* document or file that is linked to its originating application; when you select the file, the operating system automatically starts the originating application

associative addressing *or* **content-addressable addressing** *noun* location addressed by its contents rather than its address; **associative processor** = processor that uses associative storage; **associative memory** *or* **storage** *or* **content-addressable storage** = method of data retrieval that uses part of the data rather than an address to locate the data; **associative storage register** = register that is located by its contents rather than a name *or* address

asterisk *noun* (i) graphical symbol (•) used in programming as a sign for multiplication; (ii) graphical symbol used as a wildcard in many operating systems (including DOS) to mean any characters; *to view all the files beginning with the letter 'L', use the DOS command DIR L•.•;* **asterisk fill** = to fill unused decimal places with the asterisk symbol; *we have used asterisk fill to produce the answer of '***122.33'*

Asymmetric Digital Subscriber Line (ADSL)
high-speed method of carrying data over existing copper twisted-pair wires; provides three channels: one high-speed data channel to the customer (with transfer rates of 1.5-6.1Mbps) a full-duplex data channel (with transfer rates of 576Kbps) and a telephone service

asymmetric transmission   *noun*
method of data transmission used in
high-speed modems

> COMMENT: asymmetric transmission
> splits a communications channel into
> two, one that can support fast data
> transmission at 9,600bps or higher and
> a slower channel that can support
> transmission of around 300bps. The
> slower channel is used to carry control
> and error-correcting data, the
> high-speed channel used to transfer the
> bulk of the data

◊ **asymmetric video compression**
noun using a powerful computer to compress
video, allowing it to be played back on a less
powerful computer

async *(informal)* = ASYNCHRONOUS

asynchronous *adjective* serial data *or*
equipment which does not depend on being
synchronized with another piece of
equipment; **asynchronous access** =
communications using handshaking to
synchronize data transmission;
asynchronous communications = data
transmission between devices that is not
synchronized to a clock, but is transmitted
when ready; **asynchronous communication
server (ACS)** = computer linked to a network
that controls several dial-up modems and
allows remote users to connect to the server
using a modem link and gain access to the
network; **asynchronous communications
interface adapter (ACIA)** = circuit that
allows a computer to transmit and receive
serial data using asynchronous access;
asynchronous computer = (i) computer that
changes from one operation to the next
according to signals received when the
process is finished; (ii) computer in which a
process starts on the arrival of signals *or* data,
rather than on a clock pulse; **asynchronous
data transfer** = transfer of data between two
devices that takes place without any regular
or predictable timing signal; **asynchronous
mode** = linking a terminal linked to another
piece of equipment in a way where the two
need not be synchronized; **asynchronous
port** = connection to a computer allowing
asynchronous data access; *since*

*asynchronous ports are used no special
hardware is required;* **asynchronous
procedure call (APC)** = (in a program)
function that runs separately from the main
program and will execute when a particular
set of conditions exist; **asynchronous
transfer mode (ATM)** = (i) method of
transferring data very rapidly (at up to
155Mbps) across a network using fixed
length data cells (53 octets long); (ii) CCITT
and ANSI standard defining cell relay
transmission; *see also* CELL RELAY
TRANSMISSION;   **asynchronous
transmission** = data transmission that uses
handshaking signals rather than clock signals
to synchronize data pulses

> each channel handles two forms
> of communication: asynchronous
> communication is mainly for
> transferring data between
> computers and peripheral
> devices, while character
> communication is for data
> transfer between computers
> *Electronics & Power*

AT *noun* standard of PC originally developed
by IBM that uses a 16-bit 80286 processor;
AT-bus = expansion bus standard developed
by IBM that uses an edge connector to carry
16-bits of data and address information;
AT-keyboard = standard keyboard layout for
IBM AT personal computers; the keyboard
has 102 keys with a row of 12 function keys
along the top

> COMMENT: AT originally meant IBM's
> Advanced Technology personal
> computer, but is now used to describe
> any IBM PC compatible that uses a
> 16-bit processor

AT = ATTACHMENT (ATA) *or*
ADVANCED   TECHNOLOGY
ATTACHMENT standard interface used to
connect a hard disk or CD-ROM to a
computer; a common alternative to the SCSI
interface that is also known as IDE; **ATA
Fast** = proprietary standard interface
developed by Seagate and based on ATA that
improves the transfer rate and has three
modes of operation that provide either
11.1MBps, 13.3MBps or 16.6MBps transfer

rates; **ATA Packet Interface (ATAPI)** = standard interface that allows a CD-ROM or tape drive to connect to an ATA port; **ATA Ultra** = proprietary extension to ATA-2, developed by Quantum Corp., that provides a high-speed standard interface that provides data transfer at up to 33MBps

AT command set *noun* standard set of commands to control a modem, developed by Hayes Corporation; **AT mode** = mode of a modem that is ready to accept commands using the Hayes AT command set

ATAPI = ADVANCED TECHNOLOGY ATTACHMENT PACKET INTERFACE

Atari ST range of personal computers developed by Atari Corp; Atari ST computers use the 68000 range of processor and are not compatible with IBM PC

ATC = AUTHORIZATION TO COPY permission granted by the software publisher to the user to make a certain number of copies of a program

ATD = ATTENTION, DIAL standard command for compatible modems used to dial a telephone number; defined by Hayes

ATE = AUTOMATIC TEST EQUIPMENT computer controlled testing facilities, that can check a complex circuit *or* PCB for faults *or* problems

ATM = AUTOMATED TELLER MACHINE electronic machine in a bank that dispenses cash when you insert a magnetic card

◊ **ATM** *see* ADOBE TYPE MANAGER

◊ **ATM** = ASYNCHRONOUS TRANSFER MODE (i) method of transferring data very rapidly (at up to 155Mbps) across a network using fixed length data cells (53 octets long); (ii) CCITT and ANSI standard defining cell relay transmission; *see also* CELL RELAY TRANSMISSION; **ATM adaptation layer (AAL)** = part of the ATM system that translates user's data to the standard ATM cell format; **ATM cell format** = data sent over an ATM network in a 53-octet packet that includes a header and address information;

ATM layers = method of dividing the functions of an ATM network system into hierarchical layers; **ATM payload** = section of an ATM cell that contains the data; this section contains 48 octets of data within the 53-octet cell

atom *noun* **(a)** smallest particle of an element that has the same properties as the element **(b)** value *or* string that cannot be reduced to a simpler form

◊ **atomic** *adjective* (i) referring to atoms; (ii) an operation that returns data to its original state if it is stopped during processing; **atomic clock** = very accurate clock which uses changes in energy of atoms as a reference

attach *verb* (i) to fasten *or* to link; (ii) to connect a node *or* login to a server on a network; *I issued the command to attach to the local server*

◊ **attached processor** *noun* separate microprocessor in a system that performs certain functions under the control of a central processor

◊ **attached resource computer network (ARCNET)** *see* ARCNET

◊ **attachment** *noun* **(a)** device which is attached to a machine for a special purpose; *there is a special single sheet feed attachment* **(b)** named file which is transferred together with an electronic mail message; *there is an attachment with my last mail message - it contains the sales report*

attend *verb* to be present at

◊ **attend to** *verb* to give careful thought to (something) and deal with it; *attend to this fault first - it's the worst*

◊ **attended operation** *noun* process which has an operator standing by in case of problems

◊ **attention** *noun* giving careful thought, especially to processing a particular section of a program; *this routine requires the attention of the processor every minute;* **attention interruption** = interrupt signal that requests the attention of the processor; **attention key** = key on a terminal that sends an interrupt signal to the processor

◊ **attention code** *noun* the characters AT used within the Hayes AT command set to tell a modem that a command follows

attenuation *noun* reduction or loss of signal strength; the difference between transmitted and received power measured in decibels; *if the cable is too long, the signal attenuation will start to cause data errors* (NOTE: opposite of **gain**)

attribute *noun* **(a)** (i) field entry in a file; (ii) information concerning the display *or* presentation of information; *this attribute controls the colour of the screen;* screen **attributes** = variables defining the shape, size and colour of text *or* graphics displayed; *pressing Ctrl and B keys at the same time will set the bold attribute for this paragraph of text* **(b)** in some operating systems (such as DOS and OS/2) each file is stored with a set of control data which control particular functions or aspects of the file; **archive attribute** = special attribute attached to a file in DOS and OS/2 that indicates if the file has been archived since it was last changed; **read-only attribute** = special attribute attached to a file which, when switched on, only allows the contents of the file to be viewed, the contents cannot be changed; **system attribute** = special attribute attached to a file used by the operating system; the file is hidden from normal users

auctioneering device *noun* device that will select the maximum *or* minimum signal from a number of input signals

audible *adjective* which can be heard; *the printer makes an audible signal when it runs out of paper*

audio *adjective & noun* referring to sound *or* to things which can be heard; **audio cassette** = reel of magnetic recording tape in a small protective casing inserted into a cassette recorder (for data storage), usually in home computers; **audio cassette recorder (ACR)** = machine to transfer audio signals onto magnetic tape; **audio file** = digital sound sample stored on disk; **audio response unit** = speech synthesizer that allows a computer to speak responses to requests; **audiotex** =

interactive voice response over the telephone in which a computer asks the caller questions and the caller responds by pressing numbers on his telephone; **audio/video interleaved (AVI)** = Windows multimedia video format developed by Microsoft

audit 1 *noun* noting tasks carried out by a computer; **audit trail** = recording details of use of a system by noting transactions carried out (used for checking on illegal use *or* to trace a malfunction) **2** *verb* to examine the state of a system and check that it is still secure or working properly

augend *noun (in an addition)* the number to which another number, the addend, is added to produce the sum

augment *verb* to increase; **augmented addressing** = producing a usable address word from two shorter words
◊ **augmenter** *noun* value added to another

AUI connector *noun* D-connector used to connect thick Ethernet cable to a network adapter

AUP = ACCEPTABLE USE POLICY

authentic *adjective* which is true
◊ **authenticate** *verb* to say that something is true *or* genuine
◊ **authentication** *noun* making sure that something is authentic; **authentication of messages** = using special codes to identify the sender of messages, so that the messages can be recognized as being genuine

author *noun* person who wrote a program
◊ **authoring** *noun* creating a multimedia application by combining sound, video and images; **authoring language** = programming language used to write CAL and training programs; **authoring system** = set of tools normally used to develop multimedia applications; an authoring system provides special commands to control CD-ROM players, play sound files and video clips and display a user-friendly front-end

```
The  authoring  system  is  a
software    product    that
integrates text and fractally
```

```
compressed images, using any
wordprocessor line editor, to
create an electronic book with
hypertext links between
different pages.
```
Computing

authority *noun* power to do something; *he has no authority to delete your account;* **authority file** *or* **list** = list of special terms used by people compiling a database and also by the users of the database

authorization *noun* **(a)** permission *or* power to do something **(b)** giving a user permission to access a system; **authorization code** = code used to restrict access to a computer system to authorized users only

◊ **authorization to copy (ATC)** *noun* permission granted by the software publisher to the user to make a certain number of copies of a program

◊ **authorize** *verb* **(a)** to give permission for something to be done; *to authorize the purchase of a new computer system* **(b)** to give someone the authority to do something

◊ **authorized** *adjective* permitted; **authorized user** = person who is allowed to access a system

auto *adjective & prefix* automatic *or* which works without the user needing to act; **auto advance** = system by which the paper in a printer is automatically moved forward to the next line at the end of a line; **auto-answer** = feature of a modem that will automatically answer a telephone when called; **auto-baud scanning** = ability of a circuit to automatically sense and select the correct baud rate for a line; **auto-boot** = computer system that will initiate a boot-up procedure when it is switched on; **auto-dial** = feature of a modem that dials a number automatically using stored data; **autoflow** = (in DTP or wordprocessor) text that automatically flows around a graphic image or from one page to the next; **auto-login** *or* **auto-logon** = phone number, password and user's number transmitted when requested by a remote system to automate logon; *see also* LOGIN, LOGON; **auto-redial** = feature of a modem that dials a telephone number again if engaged, until it replies; **auto repeat** =

facility where a character is automatically repeated if the key is kept pressed down; **auto restart** = feature of a computer that can initialize and reload its operating system if there is a fault *or* power failure *or* at switch on; **auto save** = feature of some application programs, such as word-processor or database software, that automatically saves the file being used every few minutes in case of a power failure or system crash; **autosizing** = ability of a monitor to maintain the same rectangular image size when changing from one resolution to another; **auto start** = facility to load a program automatically when the computer is switched on; **auto stop** = feature of a tape player which stops when it has reached the end of a tape; **auto trace** = feature of some graphics programs that will transform a bit-mapped image into a vector image by automatically locating the edges of the shapes in the image and drawing lines around them; **auto verify** = verification procedure carried out automatically, as soon as the data has been saved

```
expansion accessories include
auto-dial and auto-answer
```
Electronic & Wireless World

AUTOEXEC.BAT (in an IBM PC running the MS-DOS operating system) batch file that contains commands that are executed when the computer is first switched on or reset; *see also* CONFIG.SYS, BATCH FILE

automate *verb* to install machines to do work previously done by people

automatic *adjective* which works by itself, without being worked by an operator; **automatic backup** = feature of some application programs, such as word-processor or database software, that automatically saves the file being used every few minutes in case of a power failure or system crash; **automatic call distribution (ACD)** = specialised telephone system that can handle lots of incoming calls and direct them to a particular operator according to programmed instructions in a database; **automatic calling unit (ACU)** = device which allows a computer to call telephone numbers automatically; **automatic carriage**

return = system where the cursor automatically returns to the beginning of a new line when it reaches the end of the previous one; **automatic checking** = error detection and validation check carried out automatically on received data; **automatic data capture** = system where data is automatically recorded in a computer system, as it is input; **automatic data processing (ADP)** = data processing done by a computer; **automatic decimal adjustment** = process of lining up all the decimal points in a column of figures; **automatic error correction** = correction of received data, using error detection and correction codes; **automatic error detection** = use of an (alphanumeric) code, such as a grey code, that will allow any errors to be detected; **automatic font downloading** = process in which special font information is sent to a printer by the application; **automatic hyphenation** = feature of a software program that looks up in an electronic dictionary how to correctly split and hyphenate words; **automatic letter writing** = writing form letters (using a word-processor); **automatic loader** = short program (usually in ROM) that will boot up a system and load a program; **automatic mode** *or* **frequency switching** = monitor that can adjust its internal circuits to the different frequencies used by different video standards; **automatic number identification (ANI)** = telephone system which displays the telephone number of the caller; often known as caller-ID; **automatic programming** = process of producing an optimum (operating) system for a particular process; **automatic recalculation** = spreadsheet mode in which the answers to new formula are calculated every time any value or cell changes; **automatic repeat** = facility where a character is automatically repeated if the key is kept pressed down; **automatic repeat request (ARQ)** = error correction system used in some modems that asks for data to be re-transmitted if it contains errors; **automatic sequencing** = ability of a computer to execute a number of programs *or* tasks without extra commands; **automatic speed matching** = ability of a modem to adjust its data rate to the speed of the remote modem;

automatic test equipment (ATE) = computer controlled testing facilities, that can check a complex circuit *or* PCB for faults *or* problems

◊ **automatically** *adverb* (machine) working without a person giving instructions; *the compiler automatically corrected the syntax errors; a SBC automatically limits the movement of the machine; the program is run automatically when the computer is switched on; see also* APT

automation *noun* use of machines to do work with very little supervision by people

autosync *noun* feature of a modem that allows it to transfer sychronous data signals to and from a computer that can only transfer asynchronous signals

AUX = AUXILIARY abbreviation for a serial communications port under the DOS operating system; *see also* COM1 *or* SERIAL PORT

A/UX version of the Unix operating system for the Apple Macintosh range of computers

auxiliary *adjective* which helps; *the computer room has an auxiliary power supply in case there is a mains failure;* **auxiliary equipment** = backup *or* secondary equipment in case of a breakdown; **auxiliary processor** = extra, specialized processor, such as an array *or* numerical processor that can work with a main CPU to increase execution speed; **auxiliary storage** *or* **memory** *or* **store** = any data storage medium (such a magnetic tape *or* floppy disk) that is not the main high speed computer storage (RAM); *disk drives and magnetic tape are auxiliary storage on this machine*

available *adjective* which can be obtained *or* bought; *available in all branches; item no longer available; items available to order only;* **available bit rate (ABR)** = service provided by an ATM network that tries to provide the bandwidth requested by a customer (but cannot guarantee to do so); **available list** = list of unallocated memory and resources in a system; **available point** = smallest single unit *or* point of a display whose colour and brightness can be controlled; **available power** = maximum electrical *or* processing power that a system can deliver; **available time** = time during which a system may be used

◊ **availability** *noun* being easily obtained; *the availability of the latest software package is very good*

avalanche *noun* one action starting a number of other actions; *there was an avalanche of errors after I pressed the wrong key*

average 1 *noun* number calculated by adding together several figures and dividing by the number of figures added; *the average for the last three months or the last three months' average; sales average or average of sales;* **weighted average** = average which is calculated taking several factors into account, giving some more value than others; **on an average** = in general; *we sell, on an average, five computers a day* 2 *adjective* middle (figure); *average cost per unit; average price; average sales per representative;* **average access time** = the average time taken between a request being sent and data being returned from a memory device; **average delay** = average time that a user must wait when trying to access a communication network; *see also* MEAN; *the average delay*

increases at nine-thirty when everyone tries to log-in 3 *verb* to produce as an average figure

◊ **average out** *verb* to come to a figure as an average; *it averages out at 120 dpi*

AVI = AUDIO/VIDEO INTERLEAVED Windows multimedia video format developed by Microsoft

axis *noun* (i) line around which something turns; (ii) reference line which is the basis for coordinates on a graph; *the CAD package allows an axis to be placed anywhere;* **horizontal axis** = reference line used for horizontal coordinates on a graph; **vertical axis** = reference line used for vertical coordinates on a graph; (NOTE: plural is **axes**)

azerty keyboard *noun* method of arranging the keys on a keyboard where the first line begins AZERTY (used mainly in Europe) *compare* QWERTY

azimuth *noun* angle of a tape head to a reference (such as a tape plane); **azimuth alignment** = correct horizontal angle of a tape head to the magnetic tape; *azimuth alignment is adjusted with this small screw; azimuth alignment might not be correct for tape recorded on a different machine*

Bb

b *abbreviation* one bit; **bps (bits per second)** = number of bits transmitted or received per second *compare* B

B *abbreviation* one byte; **KB (kilobyte)** = meaning equal to 1024 bytes

B hexadecimal equivalent to decimal number 11

B: (in personal computers) indicates the second disk drive, normally a floppy disk drive; *copy the files from the hard drive, C:, to the floppy drive, B:*

Babbage Charles Babbage (1792-1871) English inventor of the first automatic calculator and inventor of the forerunner of today's digital computers

babble *noun* crosstalk *or* noise from other sources which interferes with a signal

BABT = BRITISH APPROVALS BOARD FOR TELECOMMUNICATIONS independent organisation that tests and certifies telecommunications equipment; *if you design a new modem, you must have BABT approval before you can sell it*

back 1 *noun* opposite side to the front; *there is a wide range of connectors at the back of the main unit;* **back panel** = panel at the rear of a computer which normally holds the connectors to peripherals such as keyboard, printer, video display unit, and mouse; **back pointer** = (in a tree structure) a pointer that holds the position of the parent node relative to the current node; used in programming to search backwards through a file **2** *verb* to help; **battery-backed** = (volatile storage device) that has a battery backup; *the RAM disk card has the option to be*

battery-backed; battery-backed CMOS memory replaces a disk drive in this portable

> The V3500 has on-board Ethernet and SCSI interfaces, up to 32Mb local DRAM, two programmable timers, a battery-backed real-time clock with 32Kb RAM and four serial ports.
>
> *Computing*

back-end network *noun* a connection between a mainframe computer and a high-speed mass storage device or file server

◊ **back-end processor** *noun* special purpose auxiliary processor

◊ **back-end server** *noun* computer connected to a network that carries out tasks requested by client workstations

backbone *noun* high-speed, high-capacity connection path that links smaller sub-networks; a backbone is normally used to connect servers on a network, smaller workgroups or networks are connected to the backbone as segments or ribs; *we have linked the servers in each office using a high-speed backbone;* **backbone ring** = high-speed ring network that connects a number of smaller ring networks

backdoor *see* TRAP DOOR

background *noun* **(a)** past work *or* experience; *his background is in the computer industry; the company is looking for someone with a background of success in the electronics industry; what is his background or do you know anything about his background?* **(b)** part of a picture which is behind the main object of interest; *the new graphics processor chip can handle background, foreground and sprite movement independently;* **background**

colour = colour of a computer screen display (characters and graphics are normally displayed in a different foreground colour); *white background colour with black characters is less stressful for the eyes;* **background image** = image displayed as a backdrop behind a program or windows of a GUI; the background image does not move and does not interfere with any programs; **background reflectance** = light reflected from a sheet of paper that is being scanned or read by an optical character reader **(c)**; **background noise** = noise which is present along with the required signal; *the other machines around this device will produce a lot of background noise; the modem is sensitive to background noise* **(d)** system in a computer where low-priority work can be done in the intervals when very important work is not being done; **background communication** = data communication activity (such as downloading a file) carried out as a low-priority task in the background; **background job** = low priority task; **background operation** = low priority process that works as and when resources become available from high-priority foreground tasks; **background printing** = printing from a computer while it is processing another task; *background printing can be carried out whilst you are editing another document;* **background program** = computer program with a very low priority; **background recalculation** = (in a spreadsheet program) facility that allows a user to enter new numbers or equations while the program recalculates the solutions in the background; **background task** = process executed at any time by the computer system, not normally noticed by the user

◊ **background processing** *noun* **(a)** low priority job which is executed when there are no higher priority activities for the computer to attend to **(b)** process which does not use the on-line capabilities of a system; (NOTE: opposite is **foreground**)

backing *noun* **backing store** *or* **storage** *or* **memory** = permanent storage medium onto which data can be recorded before being processed by the computer *or* after processing

for later retrieval; *by adding another disk drive, I will increase the backing store capabilities; paper tape is one of the slowest access backing stores; compare* MAIN MEMORY

back-level *noun* earlier release of a product which may not support a current function

backlight *noun* light behind a liquid crystal display (LCD) unit that improves the contrast of characters on the screen and allows it to be read in dim light

◊ **backlit display** *noun* a liquid crystal display (LCD) unit that has a backlight fitted to improve the contrast of the display

backlog *noun* work *or* tasks that have yet to be processed; *the programmers can't deal with the backlog of programming work; the queue was to short for the backlog of tasks waiting to be processed*

backout *verb* to restore a file to its original condition before any changes were made

backplane *noun* part of the body of a computer which holds the circuit boards, buses and expansion connectors (the backplane does not provide any processing functions); *see* MOTHERBOARD, RACK

backslash *noun* ASCII character 92, the sign \ which is used in MS-DOS to represent the root directory of a disk, such as C:\, or to separate subdirectories in a path, such as C:\APPS\DATA

backspace *noun* movement of a cursor *or* printhead left or back by one character; **backspace character (BS)** = code that causes a backspace action in a display device; **backspace key** = key which moves the cursor left on the screen or back by one character; *if you make a mistake entering data, use the backspace key to correct it*

backtab *verb* (in SAA CUA front-end) to move the cursor back to the previous field

backtrack *verb* to carry out list processing in reverse, starting with the goal and working towards the proofs

back up *verb* **(a)** to make a copy of a file *or* data *or* disk; *the company accounts were backed up on disk as a protection against fire damage; the program enables users to back up hard disk files with a single command* **(b)** to support *or* to help; *he brought along a file of documents to back up his claim; the printout backed up his argument for a new system*

◊ **BACKUP** *noun* (in MS-DOS) command to backup data from a hard disk onto floppy disks or a tape drive

◊ **backup** *adjective & noun* **(a)** helping; *we offer a free backup service to customers;* **battery backup** = use of a battery to provide power to a volatile device (RAM chip) to retain data after a computer has been switched off **(b)**; **backup** *or* **backup file** *or* **backup copy** = copy of a file *or* set of data kept for security against errors in the original *or* master copy; **backup copy** = copy of a computer disk to be kept in case the original disk is damaged; *the most recent backup copy is kept in the safe;* **backup domain controller** = server in a network that keeps a copy of database of user accounts to validate login requests in case of a fault with the main server; **backup path** = (in a Token-Ring network) alternative path for a signal around a network avoiding a malfunctioning device; **backup plan** = set of rules that take effect when normal operation has gone wrong; *the normal UPS has gone wrong, so we will have to use our backup plan to try and restore power;* **backup procedure** = method of making backup copies of files; **backup server** = second computer on a network that contains duplicate files and up-to-date data in case of a problem with the main server; **backup utility** = software that simplifies the process of backing up data; backup utilities often allow a user to backup files automatically at a particular time; **backup version** = copy of a file made during a backup; **memory backup capacitor** = (small) very high capacitance device that can provide power for volatile RAM chips for up to two weeks (used instead of a battery)

---

the system backs up at the rate of 2.5Mb per minute
Microcomputer News

the previous version is retained, but its extension is changed to .BAK indicating that it's a back-up
Personal Computer World

Backus-Naur-Form (BNF)   *noun* system of writing and expressing the syntax of a programming language

backward *or* **backwards** *adjective & adverb* towards the back *or* in the opposite direction; **backward chaining** = method used in artificial intelligence systems to calculate a goal from a set of results; **backward channel** = channel from the receiver to transmitter allowing the receiver to send control and handshaking signals; **backward error correction** = correction of errors which are detected by the receiver and a signal is sent to the transmitter to request a re-transmission of the data; **backward LAN channel** = (in a broadband network) channel from receiver to sender used to carry control signals; **backward mode** = negative displacement from an origin; **backward recovery** = data retrieval from a system that has crashed; **backwards compatible** = (i) (new computer) that will work with all the old adapter cards designed for earlier versions of the computer; (ii) (new piece of software) that provides the same functions as the previous version and can read the files created in the previous version; **backwards search** = (in a word-processor or database) search for data that begins at the position of the cursor or end of the file and searches to the beginning of the file; **backwards supervision** = data transmission controlled by the receiver

> COMMENT: backward recovery is carried out by passing the semi-processed data from the crashed computer through a routine that reverses the effects of the main program to return the original data

BACS = BANKERS AUTOMATED CLEARANCE SYSTEM system to transfer money between banks using computer linked via a secure network

bacterium *see* VIRUS

bad break *noun* hyphen inserted in the wrong place within a word; a problem sometimes caused by the automatic hyphenation feature of word-processing software

bad sector *noun* sector which has been wrongly formatted *or* which contains an error or fault and is unable to be correctly written to or read from; *you will probably receive error messages when you copy files that are stored on bad sectors on a disk*

badge reader *noun* machine that reads data from an identification badge; *a badge reader makes sure that only authorized personnel can gain access to a computer room*

bag *noun* number of elements in no particular order

BAK file extension *noun* standard three-letter file extension used in MS-DOS systems to signify a backup or copy of another file

balance 1 *noun* placing of text and graphics on a page in an attractive way; *the dtp package allows the user to see if the overall page balance is correct* **2** *verb* to plan something so that two parts are equal; **balanced circuit** = electronic circuit that presents a correct load to a communications line (the correct load is usually equal to the impedance of a line element); **balanced error** = the probability of any error occurring (from a number of errors) is the same for all errors; **balanced line** = communications line that is terminated at each end with a balanced circuit, preventing signal reflections; **balanced routing** = method of using all possible routes through a network equally; **column balance** = (in a word-processor *or* DTP system) method of making sure that the ends of two columns of text are level

ball printer *noun* impact printer that uses a small metal ball on the surface of which are formed the characters; *see also* GOLF-BALL PRINTER

balun *noun* transformer that matches two circuits which have different impedances; *we have used a balun to connect the coaxial cable to the twisted-pair circuit*

band *noun* **(a)** range of frequencies between two limits; **base band** = frequency range of a signal before it is processed *or* transmitted; *voice base band ranges from 20Hz to 15KHz;* **base band modem** = communications circuit that transmits an unmodulated (base band) signal over a short distance; *do not use a base band modem with a normal phone line;* **base band local area network** = LAN using unmodulated signals transmitted over coaxial cable, often using a CSMA/CD protocol **(b)** group of tracks on a magnetic disk

◊ **band printer** *noun* printer in which the characters are located along a movable steel belt

◊ **banding** *noun;* **elastic banding** = method of defining the limits of an image on the computer screen by stretching a boundary round it; *elastic banding is much easier to control with a mouse*

◊ **bandpass filter** *noun* electronic filter that allows a range of frequencies to pass, but attenuates all frequencies outside the specified range

bandwidth *noun* **(a)** range of frequencies **(b)** measure of the amount of data that can be transmitted along a cable *or* channel *or* other medium; *this fibre-optic cable has a greater bandwidth than the old copper cable and so it can carry data at higher speeds;* **bandwidth on demand** = system used with a switching service (such as ISDN) in a wide area network that allows a user to send as much information as they want, and the network will adjust to transmit this amount of information **(c)** measure of the range of frequencies that a monitor or CRT will accept and display; high resolution monitors display more pixels per area so need high speed data input and so a higher bandwidth

bank *noun* collection of similar devices; *a bank of minicomputers process all the raw data;* **bank switching** = selection of a particular memory bank from a group; **memory bank** = collection of electronic memory devices connected together to form one large area of memory; *an add-on card has a 128Kb memory bank made up of 16 chips; see also* DATABANK

COMMENT: memory banks are used to expand the main memory of a CPU (often above the addressing range of the CPU) by having a number of memory chips arranged into banks. Each bank operates over the same address range but is selected independently by a special code

bankers automated clearance system (BACS) *noun* system to transfer money between banks using computer linked via a secure network

banner *noun* message or advertisement or image that is displayed on a Web page

banner page *noun* page that is printed out first with the time, date, name of the document and the name of the person who has printed it

bar 1 *noun* thick line *or* block of colour **2** *verb* to stop someone from doing something; **to bar entry to a file** = to stop someone accessing a file

◊ **bar chart** *or* **bar graph** *noun* graph on which values are represented as vertical *or* horizontal bars

◊ **bar code** *or* US **bar graphics** *noun* data represented as a series of printed stripes of varying widths; **bar-code reader** *or* **optical scanner** = optical device that reads data from a bar code

COMMENT: bar codes are found on most goods and their packages; the width and position of the stripes is sensed by a light pen or optical wand and provides information about the goods, such as price, stock quantities, etc.

◊ **bar printer** *noun* printer in which the characters are on arms which strike the paper to print characters; *see also* DAISY WHEEL

bare board *noun* circuit board with no components on it; usually refers to a memory expansion board that does not yet have any memory chips mounted on it

barrel *noun* conducting post in a terminal

◊ **barrel printer** *noun* type of printer where characters are located around a rotating barrel

base 1 *noun* **(a)** lowest *or* first position **(b)** collection of files used as a reference; *see* DATABASE **(c)** place where a company has its main office or factory *or* place where a businessman has his office; *the company has its base in London and branches in all European countries* **(d)** initial *or* original position; **base address** = initial address in a program used as a reference for others; **base address register** = register (in a CPU) used to store the base address; **base addressing** = relative addressing; **base font** = default font and point size used by a word-processing program; **base hardware** = minimum hardware requirements that a particular software package needs in order to run; **base language** = assembly language; **base line** = horizontal line along which characters are printed or displayed; the descenders of a character drop below the baseline; **base memory** *or* **conventional memory** *or* **base RAM** = (in an IBM-compatible PC) first 640Kb of random access memory fitted to the PC; *compare* HIGH MEMORY *or* EXPANDED MEMORY; **base register** = register in a CPU (not usually in small computers) that contains the address of the start of a program; **base station** = fixed radio transmitter/receiver that relays radio signals to and from data terminals or radios **(e)** (notation) referring to a number system; **base 2** = binary number system (using the two digits 0 and 1); **base 8** = octal number system (using the eight digits 0 - 7); **base 10** = decimal number system (using the ten digits 0 - 9); **base 16** = hexadecimal number system (using the ten digits 0 - 9 and six letters A - F) **(f)** (in C++ programming language) class from which other classes can be derived by inheritance **2** *verb* **(a)** to start to calculate from a position; *we based our calculations on the basic keyboarding rate;* **based on** = calculating from; *based on last year's figures; the price is based on estimates of keyboarding costs* **(b)** to set up a company *or* a person in a place; *the European manager is based in our London office; a*

London-based system serves the whole country

◊ **baseband** *or* **base band**   *noun*   (i) frequency range of a signal before it is processed *or* transmitted; (ii) digital signals transmitted without modulation; (iii) information modulated with a single carrier frequency; **baseband modem** = communications circuit that transmits an unmodulated (base band) signal over a short range; **baseband local area network** = transmission method in which the whole bandwidth of the cable is used and the data signal is not modulated; Ethernet is a baseband network; *base band local area networks can support a maximum cable length of around 300m;* **baseband signalling** = transmitting data as varying voltage levels across a link

BASIC = BEGINNER'S ALL-PURPOSE SYMBOLIC INSTRUCTION CODE high-level programming language for developing programs in a conversational way, providing an easy introduction to computer programming

basic *adjective* normal *or* from which everything starts; *the basic architecture is the same for all models in this range;* **basic code** = binary code which directly operates the CPU, using only absolute addresses and values (this is the final form of a program after a compiler *or* assembler pass); **basic control system satellite (BCS)** = system that runs dedicated programs *or* tasks for a central computer; it is controlled by using interrupt signals; **basic controller** = part of a communications controller that carries out arithmetic and logic functions; **basic direct access method (BDAM)** = method of directly updating *or* retrieving a particular block of data stored on a direct access device; **basic exchange format** = standard method of storing data on a disk so that it may be accessed by another type of computer; **basic input/output operating system (BIOS)** = system routines that interface between high-level program instructions and the system peripherals to control the input and output to various standard devices, this often includes controlling the screen, keyboard and

disk drives; **basic instruction** = unmodified program instruction which is processed to obtain the instruction to be executed; **basic mode link control** = standardized control of transmission links using special codes; **basic operating system (BOS)** = software that controls the basic, low-level running of the hardware and file management; **basic rate interface (BRI)** = one part of the ISDN service that provides two data transfer channels (also called bearer channels) that can transmit data at 64Kbit/second and one control channel that can transfer extra control information at 16Kbit/second; **basic sequential access method (BSAM)** = method of storing or retrieving blocks of data in a continuous sequence; **basic telecommunications access method (BTAM)** = method to provide access (read *or* write operations) to a remote device

◊ **basically** *adverb* seen from the point from which everything starts; *the acoustic coupler is basically the same as a modem*

◊ **basis** *noun* point *or* number from which calculations are made; *we calculated keyboarding costs on the basis of 5,500 keystrokes per hour*

BAT file extension   *noun*   standard three-letter file extension used in MS-DOS systems to signify a batch file; a text file containing system commands

batch 1 *noun* **(a)** group of items which are made at one time; *the last batch of disk drives are faulty* **(b)** (i) group of documents which are processed at the same time; (ii) group of tasks *or* amount of data to be processed as a single unit; *today's batch of orders; we deal with the orders in batches of fifty;* **batch file** = file stored on disk that contains a sequence of system commands; when the batch file is run, the commands are executed, saving a user typing them in; *this batch file is used to save time and effort when carrying out a routine task;* **(processing data in) batch mode** = (processing the data) in related groups in one machine run; **batch region** = memory area where the operating system executes batch programs; **batch system** = system that executes batch files; **batch total** = sum of a number of batches of data, used for error checking, validation or to provide useful information **2** *verb* **(a)** to put data *or* tasks together in groups; **batched communication** = high-speed transmission of large blocks of data without requiring an acknowledgement from the receiver for each data item **(b)** to put items together in groups

◊ **batch number** *noun* reference number attached to a batch

◊ **batch processing** *noun* **(a)** computer system able to process groups of tasks **(b)** system of data processing where information is collected into batches before being processed by the computer in one machine run

> COMMENT: batch processing is the opposite to interactive processing (where the user gives instructions and receives an immediate response)

battery *noun* chemical device that produces electrical current; **battery backup** = use of a battery to provide power to volatile storage devices (RAM chips) to retain data after a computer has been switched off; **battery-backed** = (volatile storage device) that has a battery backup

baud *or* **baud rate** *noun* measure of the number of signal changes transmitted per second; *the baud rate of the binary signal was 300 bits per second; a modem with auto-baud scanner can automatically sense at which baud rate it should operate;* **baud rate generator** = device that produces various timing signals to synchronize data at different baud rates; **split baud rate** = feature of a modem which receives data at one baud rate but transmits at another; *the viewdata modem uses a 1200/75 split baud rate; see also* (AUTO-BAUD) SCANNER

> COMMENT: baud rate is often considered the same as bits per second, but in fact it depends on the protocol used and the error checking (300 baud is roughly equivalent to 30 characters per second using standard error checking)

Baudot code *noun* five-bit character transmission code, used mainly in teletypewriters

bay *or* **drive bay** *noun* space within a computer's casing where a disk drive is fitted

B box *noun* register in a CPU (not usually in small computers) that contains the address of the start of a program

BBS = BULLETIN BOARD SYSTEM information and message database accessible by modem and computer link

BCC (a) = BLOCK CHARACTER CHECK error detection method for blocks of transmitted data **(b)** = BLIND CARBON COPY feature of many electronic mail programs that allows a user to send one message to several users at a time (carbon copy) but does not display this list to the recipients

BCD = BINARY CODED DECIMAL representation of single decimal digits as a pattern of four binary digits; *the BCD representation of decimal 8 is 1000;* **BCD adder** = full adder able to add two four-bit BCD words

BCH code = BOSE-CHANDHURI-HOCQUENGHEM CODE

BCNF = BOYCE-CODD NORMAL FORM *see* NORMAL FORM

BCPL *noun* high level programming language

BCS (a) = BRITISH COMPUTER SOCIETY **(b)** = BASIC CONTROL SYSTEM (SATELLITE)

beacon *verb* signal transmitted repeatedly by a device that is malfunctioning on a network

◊ **beacon frame** *noun* special frame within the FDDI protocol that is sent after a network break has occurred; *see also* FDDI

bead *noun* small section of a program that is used for a single task

beam *noun* narrow set of light *or* electron rays; *a beam of laser light is used in this printer to produce high-resolution graphics;* **beam deflection** = (in a CRT) to move the electron beam with the CRT across the screen

BEC = BUS EXTENSION CARD

beep 1 *noun* audible warning noise; *the printer will make a beep when it runs out of paper* **2** *verb* to make a beep; *the computer beeped when the wrong key was hit; see also* BLEEP

beginning *noun* first part; **beginning of file (bof)** = character *or* symbol that shows the start of a valid section of data; **beginning of information mark (bim)** = symbol indicating the start of a data stream stored on a disk drive *or* tape; **beginning of tape (bot) marker** = section of material that marks the start of the recording area of a reel of magnetic tape

Beginner's All-Purpose Symbolic Instruction Code (BASIC) *noun*
high-level programming language for developing programs in a conversational way, providing an easy introduction to computer programming

BEL *noun* bell character (equivalent to ASCII code 7)

bell character *noun* control code which causes a machine to produce an audible signal (equivalent to ASCII code 7)

◊ **Bell-compatible modem** *noun* modem that operates according to standards set down by AT&T

bells and whistles *plural noun* advanced features or added extras to an application or peripheral; *this word-processor has all the bells and whistles you would expect - including page preview*

benchmark *noun* **(a)** point in an index which is important, and can be used to compare with other figures **(b)** program used to test the performance of software *or* hardware *or* a system; *the magazine gave the new program's benchmark test results*

◊ **benchmarking** *noun* testing a system *or* program with a benchmark

◊ **benchmark problem** *noun* task *or* problem used to test and evaluate the performance of hardware *or* software

> COMMENT: the same task or program is given to different systems and their results and speeds of working are compared

Berkeley UNIX (BSD) *noun* version of UNIX operating system developed by the University of California, Berkeley

Bernoulli drive *or* **box** *noun* high capacity storage system using exchangeable 20MB cartridges

bespoke software *noun* software that has been written especially for a customer's particular requirements

best fit *noun* (i) (something) which is the nearest match to a requirement; (ii) function that selects the smallest free space in main memory for a requested virtual page

beta site *noun* company or person that tests new software (before it is released) in a real environment to make sure it works correctly

◊ **beta software** *noun* software that has not finished all its testing before release and so may still contain bugs

◊ **beta test** *noun* second stage of tests performed on new software just before it is due to be released; *the application has passed the alpha tests and is just entering the beta test phase*

◊ **beta version** *noun* version of a software application that is almost ready to be released; *we'll try out the beta test software on as many different PCs as possible to try and find all the bugs*

> The client was so eager to get his hands on the product that the managing director bypassed internal testing and decided to let it go straight out to beta test.
>
> *Computing*

bezel *noun* front cover of a computer's casing or disk drive unit

Bézier curve *noun* geometric curve; the overall shape is defined by two midpoints, called control handles

> COMMENT: Bézier curves are a feature of many high-end design software packages; they allow a designer to create smooth curves by defining a number of points. The PostScript page description language uses Bézier curves to define the shapes of characters during printing.

bias *noun* **(a)** electrical reference level **(b)** deviation of statistical results from a reference level

◊ **biased** *adjective* which has a bias; **biased data** = data *or* records which point to one conclusion; **biased exponent** = value of the exponent in a floating point number

bid *verb (of a computer)* to gain control of a network in order to transmit data; *the terminal had to bid three times before there was a gap in transmissions on the network*

bi-directional *adjective* (operation *or* process) that can occur in forward and reverse directions; *bi-directional file transfer;* **bi-directional bus** = data *or* control lines that can carry signals travelling in two directions; **bi-directional printer** = printer which is able to print characters from left to right and from right to left as the head is moving forward *or* backward across the paper (speeding up the printing operation); **bi-directional transmission** = data transfer that can occur to and from a device along a particular channel; *compare* OMNIDIRECTIONAL

bifurcation *noun* system where there are only two possible results; *the result of a binary multiplication is a bifurcation: the result is either 1 or 0*

Big Blue *informal name for* IBM

bilinear filtering *noun* method of removing unwanted image defects (particularly on a texture-mapped object) by looking at the four adjacent pixels that surround each pixel to check that there is no sudden change in colour

billion number equal to one thousand million *or* one million million; (NOTE: in the US it has always meant one thousand million, but in GB it formerly meant one million million, and it is still sometimes used with this meaning. With figures it is usually written **bn: $5bn** say 'five billion dollars')

BIM = BEGINNING OF INFORMATION MARK symbol indicating the start of a data stream stored on a disk drive *or* tape

bin *noun* tray used to hold a supply of paper ready to be fed into a printer

binary *adjective & noun* base 2 *or* number notation system which uses only the digits 0 and 1; **binary adder** = device that provides the sum of two or more binary digits; **binary arithmetic** = rules and functions governing arithmetic operations in base 2; **binary bit** = smallest single unit in (base 2) binary notation, either a 0 or a 1; **binary cell** = storage element for one bit; **binary chop;** *see* BINARY SEARCH; **binary code** = using different patterns of binary digits to represent various symbols, elements, etc.; **binary coded characters** = alphanumeric characters represented as patterns of binary digits; **binary coded decimal (BCD)** = representation of single decimal digits as a pattern of four binary digits; *see also* BCD; **binary counter** = circuit that will divide a binary input signal by two (producing one output pulse for two input pulses); **binary digit** *or* **bit** = smallest single unit in (base 2) binary notation, either a 0 or a 1; **binary dump** = display of a section of memory in binary form; **binary encoding** = representing a character *or* element with a unique combination *or* pattern of bits in a word; **binary exponent** = one word that contains the sign and exponent of a binary number (expressed in exponent and mantissa form); **binary file** = file that contains data rather than alphanumeric characters; a binary file can include any character code and cannot always be displayed or edited; *the program instructions are stored in the binary file;*

your letter is a text file, not a binary file; **binary fraction** = representation of a decimal fraction in binary form; *the binary fraction 0.011 is equal to one quarter plus one eighth (i.e. three eighths);* **binary half adder** = binary adder that can produce the sum of two inputs, producing a carry output if necessary, but cannot accept a carry input; **binary large object (blob)** = field in a database record that can contain a large quantity of binary data, normally a bitmap image; **binary loader** = short section of program code that allows programs in binary form (such as object code from a linker *or* assembler) to be loaded into memory; **binary mantissa** = fractional part of a number (in binary form); **binary notation** *or* **representation** = base 2 numerical system using only the digits 0 and 1; **binary number** = quantity represented in base 2; **binary operation** = (i) operation on two operands; (ii) operation on an operand in binary form; **binary point** = dot which indicates the division between the whole unit bits and the fractional part of a binary number; **binary scale** = power of two associated with each bit position in a word; *in a four bit word, the binary scale is 1,2,4,8;* **binary search** *or* **chop** = fast search method for use on ordered lists of data (the search key is compared with the data in the middle of the list and one half is discarded, this is repeated with the remaining half until only the required data item is left); **binary sequence** = series of binary digits; **binary signalling** = transmission using positive and zero voltage levels to represent binary data; **binary split** = method of iteration in which the existing number is compared to a new value calculated as the mid-point between the high and low limits; **binary synchronous communications (BSC)** = (old) standard for medium/high speed data communication links; **binary system** = use of binary numbers or operates with binary numbers; **binary-to-decimal conversion** = process to convert a binary number into its equivalent decimal value; **binary tree** = tree structure used to define a search method or database, where each item of data can have only two branches; **binary variable** = variable that can contain either a one or zero

with this type of compression you can only retrieve words by scanning the list sequentially, rather than by faster means such as a binary search

Practical Computing

bind *verb* **(a)** to link and convert one or more object code programs into a form that can be executed; **binding time** = time taken to produce actual addresses from an object code program **(b)** to glue or attach sheets of paper along their spine to form a book; **binding offset** = extra wide margin on the inside of a printed page (left margin on a right hand page, right margin on a left hand page) to prevent text being hidden during binding

◊ **binder** *noun* program that converts object code into a form that can be executed

Bindery *noun* special database used in a Novell NetWare network operating system to store user account, access and security details

BIOS = BASIC INPUT/OUTPUT SYSTEM system routines that interface between high-level program instructions and the system peripherals to control the input and output to various standard devices, this often includes controlling the screen, keyboard and disk drives

bipolar *adjective* with two levels; **bipolar coding** = transmission method which uses alternate positive and negative voltage levels to represent a binary one, with binary zero represented by zero level; **bipolar signal** = use of positive and negative voltage levels to represent the binary digits; **bipolar transistor** = transistor constructed of three layers of alternating types of doped semiconductor (p-n-p or n-p-n)

COMMENT: each layer has a terminal labelled emitter, base and collector, usually the base signal controls the current flow between the emitter and collector

biquinary code *noun* decimal digits represented as two digits added together (for decimal digits less than 5, represented as 0 +

the digit, for decimal digits greater than 4, represented as 5 + the digit minus 5)

B-ISDN = BROADBAND ISDN

bistable *adjective* (device *or* circuit) that has two possible states, on and off; **bistable circuit** *or* **multivibrator** = circuit which can be switched between two states

bit *noun* **(a)** = BINARY DIGIT smallest unit in binary number notation, which can have the value 0 or 1 **(b)** smallest unit of data that a system can handle; **bit addressing** = selecting a register *or* word and examining one bit of it; **bit blit** *or* **bitblt** = (in computer graphics) to move a block of bits from one memory location to another; **bit block** = (in computer graphics) group of bits treated as one unit; **bit block transfer** = (in computer graphics) to move a block of bits from one memory location to another; **bit bucket** = area of memory into which data can be discarded; **bit density** = number of bits that can be recorded per unit of storage medium; **bit error rate (BER)** = (normally referring to fibre optics) ratio of the number of bits received compared to the number of errors in a transmission; **bit flipping** = to invert the state of bits from 0 to 1 and 1 to 0; **bit handling** = CPU commands and processes that allow bit manipulation, changing, etc.; **bit image** = collection of bits that represent the pixels that make up an image on screen or on a printer; **bit interleaving** = form of time domain multiplexing used in some synchronous transmission protocols such as HDLC and X.25; **bit manipulation** = various instructions that provide functions such as examine a bit, change *or* set *or* move a bit within a word; **bit parallel** = transmission of a collection of bits simultaneously over a number of lines; the parallel printer port uses bit parallel transmission to transfer eight bits at a time to a printer; **bit pattern** = certain arrangement of bits within a word, that represents a certain character *or* action; **bit plane** = (in computer graphics) one layer of a multiple-layer image; each layer defines one colour of each pixel; **bit position** = place of a bit of data in a computer word; **bit rate** = measure of the number of bits transmitted per second; **bit significant** = using the bits within a byte to describe something; *testing bit six of a byte containing an ASCII character is bit significant and determines if the character is upper or lower case;* **bit slice design** = construction of a large word size CPU by joining a number of smaller word size blocks; *the bit slice design uses four four-bit word processors to construct a sixteen-bit processor;* **most significant bit (MSB)** = bit in a computer word that represents the greatest power of two (in an eight-bit word the MSB is in bit position eight and represents a decimal number of two to the power eight, or 128); **bit stream** = binary data sequence that does not consist of separate, distinct character codes *or* groups; **bit stuffing** = addition of extra bits to a group of data to make up a certain length required for transmission; **bit track** = track on a magnetic disk along which bits can be recorded *or* read back *compare* LOGICAL TRACK; **bits per inch (bpi)** = number of bits that can be recorded per inch of recording medium; **bits per pixel (BPP)** = number of bits assigned to store the colour of each pixel; one bit provides black or white, four bits gives 16 colour combinations, eight bits gives 256 colour combinations; **bits per second (bps)** = measure of the number of binary digits transmitted every second; *see also* BPS; **bit wise** = action or operation carried out on each bit in a byte, one bit at a time; **check bit** = one bit of a binary word that is used to provide a parity check; **mask bit** = one bit (in a mask) used to select the required bit from a word *or* string; **sign bit** = single bit that indicates if a binary number is positive or negative (usually 0 = positive, 1 = negative); *see also* BYTE, WORD

◊ **bitblt** *see* BIT, BLIT

◊ **bit-map** *or* **bitmap** *verb* to define events *or* data using an array of single bits; (this can be an image *or* graphics *or* a table of devices in use, etc.); **bit-mapped font** = font whose characters are made up of patterns of pixels *compare* VECTOR FONT; **bit-mapped graphics** = image whose individual pixels can be controlled by changing the value of its stored bit (one is on, zero is off); in colour displays, more than one bit is used to provide control for the colours red, green, blue the expansion cards fit into the PC's expansion slot and convert bit-mapped screen images to video signals

Publish

it is easy to turn any page into a bit-mapped graphic

PC Business World

microcomputers invariably use raster-scan cathode ray tube displays, and frequently use a bit-map to store graphic images

Soft

BIX online system founded by Byte magazine

biz *noun* type of newsgroup that contains business discussions and oportunities

black 1 *adjective* with no colour; **black and white** = (i) use of shades of grey to represent colours on a monitor *or* display; (ii) an image in which each pixel is either black or white with no shades of grey; **black box** = device that performs a function without the user knowing how

◊ **blackout** *or* **black-out** *noun* complete loss of electrical power *compare* BROWNOUT, BROWN-OUT

◊ **black matrix** *noun* CRT monitor tube in which the color phosphor dots are surrounded by black for increased contrast

◊ **black writer** *noun* printer where toner sticks to the points hit by the laser beam when the image drum is scanned *compare* WHITE WRITER

COMMENT: a black writer produces sharp edges and graphics, but large areas of black are muddy

blank 1 *adjective* empty *or* with nothing written on it; **blank cell** = empty cell in a spreadsheet; **blank character** = character code that prints a space; **blank instruction** = program instruction which does nothing; **blank tape** *or* **blank disk** = magnetic tape *or* disk that does not have data stored on it; **blank string** *or* **empty string** = (i) empty string; (ii) string containing spaces **2** *noun* space on a form which has to be completed;

fill in the blanks and insert the form into the OCR

blast *verb* **(a)** to write data into a programmable ROM device **(b)** to free sections of previously allocated memory *or* resources

◊ **blast-through alphanumerics** *noun* characters that can be displayed on a videotext terminal when it is in graphics mode

bleed *noun* (i) line of printing that runs off the edge of the paper; (ii) badly adjusted colour monitor in which colours of adjoining pixels blend

bleep 1 *noun* audible warning noise; *the printer will make a bleep when it runs out of paper* **2** *verb* to make a bleep; *see also* BEEP

blessed folder *noun* (in an Apple Macintosh system) the System Folder that contains files loaded automatically when the Macintosh is switched on

blind *adjective* which will not respond to certain codes

◊ **blind copy receipt** *or* **blind carbon copy (BCC)** *noun* (in electronic mail) method of sending a message to several users, whose identities are not known to the other recipients *compare* CARBON COPY

◊ **blind dialling** *noun* ability of a modem to dial out even if the line appears dead, used on certain private lines

◊ **blind keyboard** *noun* keyboard whose output is not displayed but is stored directly on magnetic tape *or* disk

B-line counter *noun* address register that is added to a reference address to provide the location to be accessed

blinking *noun* flashing effect caused by varying the intensity of a displayed character

blip *noun* small mark on a tape or film counted to determine the position

blit *or* **bitblt** *verb* (in computer graphics) to move a block of bits from one memory location to another

◊ **blitter** *noun* electronic component designed to process or move a bit-mapped image from one area of memory to another; *the new blitter chip speeds up the graphics display*

blob = BINARY LARGE OBJECT field in a database record that can contain a large quantity of binary data - normally a bitmap image

block 1 *noun* (i) series of items grouped together; (ii) number of stored records treated as a single unit; **block character check (BCC)** = error detection method for blocks of transmitted data; **block code** = error detection and correction code for block data transmission; **block compaction** =; *see* COMPRESS, COMPACT; **block copy** = (i) to duplicate a block of data to another section of memory; (ii) (in a word-processor) to copy a selected area of text from one part of a document to another; **block delete** = (in a word-processor) to delete a selected area of text; **block device** = device that manipulates many bytes of data at once; *the disk drive is a block device that can transfer 256bytes of data at a time;* **block diagram** = illustration of the way the main components in a system are connected, but without detail; *the first step to designing a new computer is to draw out a block diagram of its main components;* **block error rate** = number of blocks of data that contain errors compared with the total number transmitted; **block header** = information at the start of a file describing content organization or characteristics; **block ignore character** = symbol at the start of a block indicating that it contains corrupt data; **block input processing** = input system that requires a whole error-free block to be received before it is processed; **block length** = number of bytes of data in a block; **block list** = list of the blocks and records as they are organized in a file; **block mark** = code that indicates the end of a block; **block move** = (i) (in a word-processor) to move selected text from one area of a document to another; (ii) (in memory) to move the contents of an area of memory to another area of memory; **block operation** = process carried out on a block of data; **block parity** = parity error check on a

block of data; **block protection** = (in a word-processor) to prevent a selected block of text being split by an automatic page break; **block retrieval** = accessing blocks of data stored in memory; **block synchronization** = correct timing of start, stop and message bits according to a predefined protocol; **block transfer** = moving large numbers of records around in memory; **building block** = self-contained unit that can be joined to others to form a system; **data block** = all the data required for *or* from a process; **end of block (EOB)** = code which indicates that the last byte of a block of data has been sent; **interblock gap (IBG)** = space between two blocks of stored data **(b)** wide printed bar; **block cursor** = cursor the shape of a solid rectangle that fills a character position; **block diagram** = graphical representation of a system *or* program operation **(c)**; **block capitals** *or* **block letters** = capital letters (such as A,B,C); *write your name and address in block letters* **2** *verb* to stop something taking place; *the system manager blocked his request for more CPU time*

◊ **blocking factor** *noun* number of records in a block

bloop *verb* to pass a magnet over a tape to erase signals which are not needed

blow *or* **burn** *verb* to program a PROM device with data

blueprint *noun* copy of an original set of specifications *or* design in graphical form

blue-ribbon program *noun* perfect program that runs first time, with no errors *or* bugs

blur 1 *noun* image where the edges *or* colours are not clear **2** *verb* to make the edges *or* colours of an image fuzzy; *the image becomes blurred when you turn the focus knob*

BMP *noun* (in graphics) three-letter extension to a filename that indicates that the file contains a bit-mapped graphics image; *this paint package lets you import BMP files*

bn = BILLION

BNC connector *noun* cylindrical metal connector with a copper core that is at the end of coaxial cable and is used to connect cables together; it attaches by pushing and twisting the outer cylinder onto two locking pins

◊ **BNC T-piece connector** *noun* T-shaped metal connector used to connect an adapter card to the ends of two sections of RG-58 'thin' coaxial cable used in many Ethernet network installations

BNF = BACKUS-NAUR-FORM system of writing and expressing the syntax of a programming language

board *noun* flat insulation material on which electronic components are mounted and connected; **bus board** = PCB containing conducting paths for all the computer signals (for the address, data and control buses); **daughter board** = add-on board that connects to a system motherboard; **expansion board** *or* **add on board** = printed circuit board that is connected to a system to increase its functions *or* performance; **motherboard** = main printed circuit board of a system, containing most of the components and connectors for expansion boards, etc.; **printed circuit board (PCB)** = flat insulating material that has conducting tracks of metal printed *or* etched onto its surface, which complete a circuit when components are mounted on it

> both models can be expanded to the current maximum of the terminals by adding further serial interface boards
>
> *Micro Decision*

body *noun* (i) main section of text in a document; (ii) main part of a program; **body type** = default font and point size that is used for the main section of text in a document *compare* HEADER and FOOTER

bof *or* **BOF** = BEGINNING OF FILE character *or* symbol that shows the start of a valid section of data

boilerplate *noun* final document that has been put together using standard sections of text held in a word processor

◊ **boilerplating** *noun* putting together a final document out of various standard sections of text

bold face *adjective & noun* thicker and darker form of a typeface

bomb 1 *noun* routine in a program designed to crash the system or destroy data at a particular time; **logic bomb** = section of code that performs various unpleasant functions such as fraud *or* system crash when a number of conditions are true (the logic bomb is installed by unpleasant hackers *or* very annoyed programmers); *the system programmer installed a logic bomb when they made him redundant; see also* VIRUS **2** *verb (of software) (informal)* to fail; *the program bombed, and we lost all the data; the system can bomb if you set up several desk accessories or memory-resident programs at the same time*

bookmark *noun* code inserted at a particular point in a document that allows the user to move straight to that point at a later date

Boolean algebra *or* **logic** *noun* rules set down to define, simplify and manipulate logical functions, based on statements which are true or false; *see* AND, NOT, OR

◊ **Boolean connective** *noun* symbol *or* character in a Boolean operation that describes the action to be performed on the operands

◊ **Boolean operation** *noun* logical operation on a number of operands, conforming to Boolean algebra rules; **Boolean operation table** = table showing two binary words (operands), the operation and the result; **Boolean operator** = logical operator such as AND, OR etc.; **dyadic Boolean operation** = logical operation producing a result from two words, such as AND; **monadic Boolean operation** = logical operation on only one word, such as NOT; **Boolean value** = one of two values, either true or false; **Boolean variable** *or* **data type** = binary word in which each bit represents true or false, using the digits 1 or 0

boost 1 *noun* help received; *the prize was a real boost; the new model gave a boost to the sales figures* **2** *verb* to make something increase; *the extra hard disk will boost our storage capacity by 25MB*

boot *verb* to execute a set of instructions automatically in order to reach a required state; **boot block** *or* **record** = first track (track 0) on a boot disk of an IBM-compatible floppy disk; **boot disk** = special disk which contains a bootstrap program and the operating system software; *after you switch on the computer, insert the boot disk;* **boot partition** = on a hard disk with more than one partition, the partition that contains the bootstrap and operating system

◊ **boot up** *or* **booting** *noun* automatic execution of a set of instructions usually held in ROM when a computer is switched on

◊ **bootleg** *noun* illegal copy of recorded material

◊ **bootstrap (loader)** *noun* set of instructions that are executed by the computer before a program is loaded, usually to load the operating system once the computer is switched on *compare* LOADER

```
the  digital  signal  processor
includes    special    on-chip
bootstrap  hardware  to  allow
easy loading of user programs
into the program RAM
```
Electronics & Wireless World

---

border *noun* area around printed *or* displayed text

Borland™ software company which has developed a wide range of programming languages, database management systems and spreadsheet applications (including Turbo C++, Paradox, and QuatroPro)

borrow *verb* operation in certain arithmetic processes, such as subtraction from a smaller number

BOS = BASIC OPERATING SYSTEM software that controls the basic, low-level running of the hardware and file management; *see also* BIOS

Bose-Chandhuri-Hocquenghem code (BCH) *noun* error correcting code

bot *or* **BOT** = BEGINNING OF TAPE; **BOT marker** = section of material that marks the start of the recording area of magnetic tape

bottom up method *or* **programming** *noun* combining low-level instructions to form a high-level instruction (which can then be further combined)

bounce *noun* (error) multiple key contact caused by a faulty switch; **de-bounce** = preventing a single touch on a key producing multiple key contact

boundary *noun* limits of something; **boundary protection** = to prevent any program writing into a reserved area of memory; **boundary punctuation** = punctuation which marks the beginning *or* end of a file; **boundary register** = register in a multi-user system that contains the addresses for the limits of one user's memory allocation

bounding box *noun* rectangle that determines the shape and position of an image that has been placed in a document or on screen

bounds *noun* limits *or* area in which one can operate; **array bounds** = limits to the number of elements which can be given in an array

box *noun* cardboard *or* wood *or* plastic container; *the goods were sent in thin cardboard boxes; the keyboard is packed in plastic foam before being put into the box;* **black box** = device that performs a function without the user knowing how; *see also* B BOX

◊ **boxed** *adjective* put in a box *or* sold in a box; **boxed set** = set of items sold together in a box

Boyce-Codd normal form (BCNF)
see NORMAL FORM

bozo bit *noun* (in an Apple Macintosh system) attribute bit that prevents a file being copied or moved

BPI *or* **bpi** = BITS PER INCH number of bits that can be recorded per inch of recording medium

BPP = BITS PER PIXEL number of bits assigned to store the colour of each pixel; one bit provides black or white, four bits gives 16 colour combinations, eight bits gives 256 colour combinations

bps = BITS PER SECOND number of bits that can be transmitted per second; *their transmission rate is 60,000 bits per second (bps) through a parallel connection;* **bps rate** = rate at which information is sent equal to the number of bits transmitted or received per second; **bps rate adjust** = ability of a modem to automatically adjust the speed of its serial port to match the communications speed

Bps = BYTES PER SECOND

BRA = BASIC RATE ACCESS basic ISDN service that provides two data channels capable of carrying data at a rate of 64Kbps together with a signalling channel used to carry control signals at 16Kbps

braces *noun* curly bracket characters ({ }) used in some programming languages to enclose a routine

bracket 1 *noun* printing sign to show that an instruction *or* operation is to be processed separately; **curly brackets** *or* **braces** = curly bracket characters ({ }) used in some programming languages to enclose a routine; **round brackets** = common form of bracket (( )); **square brackets** = type of bracket with straight sides ([ ]) **2** *verb;* **to bracket together** = to print brackets round several items to show that they are treated in the same way and separated from the rest of the text

branch 1 *noun* **(a)** possible path *or* jump from one instruction to another; **branch instruction** = conditional program instruction that provides the location of the next instruction in the program (if a condition

is met); **branch table** = table that defines where to jump to in a program depending on the result of a test; **program branch** = one or more paths that can be followed after a conditional statement **(b)** line linking one or more devices to the main network; *the faulty station is on this branch;* **branch cable** = cable that runs from a main cable to a node **2** *verb* to jump from one section of a program to another

◊ **branchpoint** *noun* point in a program where a branch can take place

COMMENT: in BASIC, the instruction GOTO makes the system jump to the line indicated; this is an unconditional branch. The instruction IF...THEN is a conditional branch, because the jump will only take place if the condition is met

brand *noun* make of product, which can be recognized by a name *or* by a design; *the number one brand of magnetic tape; the company is developing a new brand of screen cleaner;* **brand name** = name of a brand

breach *noun* failure to carry out the terms of an agreement; **breach of warranty** = supplying goods which do not meet the standards of the warranty applied to them

breadboard *noun* device that allows prototype electronic circuits to be constructed easily without permanent connections or soldering

break 1 *noun* action *or* key pressed to stop a program execution; **Break key** = special key on an IBM-compatible keyboard that halts execution of a program when pressed with the Control key; *I stopped the problem by pressing Ctrl-Break* **2** *verb* **(a)** to fail to carry out the duties of an agreement; *the company has broken the agreement* **(b)** to decipher a difficult code; *he finally broke the cipher system*

◊ **break down** *verb* to stop working because of mechanical failure; *the modem has broken down; what do you do when your line printer breaks down?*

◊ **breakdown** *noun* **(a)** stopping work because of mechanical failure; *we cannot* *communicate with our New York office because of the breakdown of the telex lines*

◊ **breaker** *noun;* **circuit breaker** = device which protects equipment by cutting off the electrical supply

◊ **breakout box** *noun* device that displays the status of lines within an interface, cable or connector; *the serial interface doesn't seem to be working - use the breakout box to see which signals are present*

◊ **breakpoint** *noun* symbol inserted into a program which stops its execution at that point to allow registers, variables and memory locations to be examined (used when debugging a program); **breakpoint instruction** *or* **halt** = halt command inserted in a program to stop execution temporarily, allowing the programmer to examine data and registers while debugging a program; **breakpoint symbol** = special character used to provide a breakpoint in a program (the debugging program allows breakpoint symbols to be inserted, it then executes the program until it reaches one, then halts)

◊ **breakup** *noun* (normally in video) loss *or* distortion of a signal

B register *noun* (i) address register that is added to a reference address to provide the location to be accessed; (ii) register used to extend the accumulator in multiplication and division operations

BRI *see* BASIC RATE INTERFACE

bridge 1 *verb* to use bridgeware to help transfer programs, data files, etc., to another system **2** *noun;* **bridge** *or* **bridging product** = **(a)** device that connects two networks together and allow information to flow between the two networks; bridges function at the data link layer of the OSI network model; *see also* ROUTER; BROUTER **(b)** matching communications equipment that makes sure that power losses are kept to a minimum **(c)** hardware *or* software that allows parts of an old system to be used on a new system; *a bridging product is available for companies with both generations of machines*

Lotus Development and IMRS are jointly developing a bridge linking their respective spreadsheet and client server reporting tools. It will allow users of IMRS' Hyperion reporting tool to manipulate live data from Lotus Improv.

Computing

◊ **bridgeware** *noun* hardware *or* software used to make the transfer from one computer system to another easier (by changing file format, translation etc.)

◊ **bridging** *noun* using bridgeware to help transfer programs, data files, etc., to another system

COMMENT: A bridge connects two similar networks, a gateway connects two different networks. To connect two Ethernet networks, use a bridge.

Briefcase utility *noun* (in Windows 95) a special utility that allows you to keep files stored on a laptop and a desktop PC up to date

brightness *noun* luminance of an object which can be seen; *a control knob allows you to adjust brightness and contrast; the brightness of the monitor can hurt the eyes;* **brightness range** = variation of reflected light intensity

there is a brightness control on the front panel

Micro Decision

brilliant *adjective* very bright and shining (light *or* colour)

bring-up *verb* to start a computer system

British Standards Institute (BSI)

UK organization that monitors design and safety standards in the UK

broadband *or* **wideband** *noun* (in local area networks or communications) transmission method that combines several channels of data onto a carrier signal and can carry the data over long distances; *compare* BASEBAND

◊ **broadband ISDN (B-ISDN)** high speed data transfer service that allows data and voice to be transmitted over a wide area network; currently the Multimegabit Data

Services and Asynchronous Transfer Mode systems are two types of B-ISDN service; *see* MULTIMEGABIT DATA SERVICES, ASYNCHRONOUS TRANSFER MODE

broadcast 1 *noun* (i) (radio communications) data transmission to many receivers; (ii) (in a network) message or data sent to a group of users; **broadcast message** = message sent to everyone on a network; *five minutes before we shut down the LAN, we send a broadcast message to all users;* **broadcast network** = network for sending data to a number of receivers; **broadcast quality** = video image *or* signal that is the same as that used by professional television stations; *we can use your multimedia presentation as the advert on TV if it's of broadcast quality* 2 *verb* to distribute information over a wide area *or* audience; *he broadcast the latest news over the WAN*

brouter *noun* device that combines the functions of a router and bridge to connect networks together; *the brouter provides dynamic routing and can bridge two local area networks; see also* BRIDGE; ROUTER

brown-out *noun* power failure (low voltage level rather than no voltage level); *see also* BLACK-OUT

browse *verb* (a) to view data in a database or online system (b) to search through and access database material without permission

◊ **browser** *noun* software program that is used to display and navigate through WWW pages stored in HTML format on the internet or on a private intranet

COMMENT: a browser program asks the web server (called the HTTP server) to send it a page of information; this page is stored in the HTML layout language that is decoded by the browser and displayed on screen. The browser displays images, text formatting and any hotspots and will jump to another page if the user clicks on a hyperlink

brush *noun* tool in paint package software that draws pixels on screen; *the paint package lets you vary the width of the brush (in pixels) and the colour it produces;* **brush style** = width and shape of the brush tool in a paint package; *to fill in a big area, I select a wide, square brush style*

brute force method *noun* problem-solving method which depends on computer power rather than elegant programming techniques

BS = BACKSPACE

BSAM = BASIC SEQUENTIAL ACCESS METHOD

BSC = BINARY SYNCHRONOUS COMMUNICATIONS (old) standard for medium/high speed data communication links

BSI = BRITISH STANDARDS INSTITUTE organization that monitors design and safety standards in the UK

BTAM = BASIC TELECOMMUNICATIONS ACCESS METHOD method to provide access (read *or* write operations) to a remote device

btree = BINARY TREE

bubble-help *noun* single line that appears on screen to describe what you are pointing at

bubble jet printer *see* INK-JET PRINTER

bubble memory *noun* method of storing binary data using the magnetic properties of certain materials, allowing very large amounts of data to be stored in primary memory; **bubble memory cassette** = bubble memory device on a removable cartridge that can be inserted into a controller card (like an audio cassette) to provide high capacity, high speed, removable memory

◊ **bubble sort** *noun* sorting method which repeatedly exchanges various pairs of data items until they are in order

bucket *noun* storage area containing data for an application; **bit bucket** = area of memory into which data can discarded

buffer 1 *noun* **(a)** (circuit) that isolates and protects a system from damaging inputs from driven circuits *or* peripherals *see also* DRIVER **(b)** temporary storage area for data waiting to be processed; **buffer register** = temporary storage for data read from *or* being written to main memory; **buffer size** = total number of characters that can be held in a buffer; **data buffer** = temporary storage location for data received by a device that is not yet ready to process it; **dynamic** *or* **elastic buffer** = buffer whose size varies with demand; **I/O buffer** = temporary storage area for data waiting to be input *or* output **2** *verb* to use a temporary storage area to hold data until the processor *or* device is ready to deal with it; **buffered input/output** = use of a temporary storage area on input *or* output ports to allow slow peripherals to operate with a fast CPU; **buffered memory** = device that allows instructions *or* data to be entered before it has completed its present ones

◊ **buffering** *noun* using buffers to provide a link between slow and fast devices; **double buffering** = two buffers working together so that one can be read while the other is accepting data

COMMENT: buffers allow two parts of a computer system to work at different speeds (i.e. a high-speed central processing unit and a slower line printer)

```
the    software    allocates    a
portion  of  cache  as  a  print
buffer   to   restore   program
control  faster  after  sending
data to the printer
```
Which PC?

bug *noun* (*informal*) error in a computer program which makes it run incorrectly; **bug patches** = (temporary) correction made to a program; small correction made to software by a user on the instructions of the software publisher; *see also* DEBUG

buggy *noun* small computer-controlled vehicle

build *noun* particular version of a program; *this is the latest build of the new software*

building block *noun* self-contained unit that can be joined to others to form a system

built-in *adjective* (special feature) that is already included in a system; *the built-in adapter card makes it fully IBM compatible; the computer has a built-in hard disk;* **built-in check** = error detection and validation check carried out automatically on received data; **built-in font** = font stored permanently within a peripheral, normally a printer; **built-in function** = special function already implemented in a program; (NOTE: opposite is **add-on**)

◊ **built into** *adjective* (feature) that is already a physical part of a system; *there are communications ports built into all modems*

bulk *noun* large quantity of something; **in bulk** = in large quantities; **bulk erase** = to erase a complete magnetic disk *or* tape in one action; **bulk storage medium** = medium that is able to store large amounts of data in a convenient size and form; *magnetic tape is a reliable bulk storage medium;* **bulk update terminal** = device used by an information provider to prepare videotext pages off-line, then transmit them rapidly to the main computer

bullet *noun* symbol (often a filled circle or square) in front of a line of text, used to draw attention to a particular line in a list

```
For a bullet chart use four to
six bullet points and no more
than six to eight words each
```
Computing

bulletin board system (BBS) *noun* information and message database accessible by modem and computer link

```
The   Council   of   European
Professional      Informatics
Societies  has  instituted  an
experimental   Bulletin   Board
System based at the University
of Wageningen.
```
Computing

bundle 1 *noun* **(a)** number of optic fibres gathered together **(b)** package containing a computer together with software or accessories offered at a special price; *the* *bundle now includes a PC with spreadsheet and database applications for just £999* **2** *verb* to market at a special price a package that contains a computer together with a range of software or accessories

◊ **bundled software** *noun* software included in the price of a computer system

bureau *noun* office which specializes in keyboarding data *or* processing batches of data for other small companies; *the company offers a number of bureau services, such as printing and data collection; our data manipulation is handled by a bureau;* **information bureau** = office which gives information; **output bureau** = office that converts data from a DTP program or a drawing stored on disk into typeset artwork; **word-processing bureau** = office which specializes in word-processing; *we farm out the office typing to a local bureau* (NOTE: the plural is **bureaux**)

IMC has a colour output bureau that puts images onto the uncommon CD-ROM XA format.
Computing

---

burner *noun* device which burns in programs onto PROM chips

◊ **burn-in** *noun* heat test for electronic components

◊ **burn in** *verb* **(a)** to mark a (television *or* monitor) screen after displaying a high brightness image for too long **(b)** to write data into a PROM chip

◊ **burn out** *noun* excess heat *or* incorrect use that causes an electronic circuit *or* device to fail

burst *noun* short isolated sequence of transmitted signals; **burst mode** = transfer of a batch of data across a bus with no interruptions; **error burst** = group of several consecutive errors (in a transmission)

burster *noun* machine used to separate the sheets of continuous fanfold paper

bus *noun* **(a)** communication link consisting of a set of leads *or* wires which connects different parts of a computer hardware system, and over which data is transmitted and received by various circuits in the system; **bus address lines** = wires, each of which carries one bit of an address word; **bus arbitration** = protocol and control of transmission over a bus that ensures fair usage by several users; **bus board** = PCB containing conducting paths for all the computer signals; **bus clock speed** = frequency of the clock that governs the main bus in a computer; **bus control lines** = wires, each of which carries one bit of a control word; **bus data lines** = wires, each of which carries one bit of a data word; **bus driver** = high power transistors *or* amplifier that can provide enough power to transmit signals to a number of devices; **bus extender** *or* **bus extension card (BEC)** = (i) device that extends an 8-bit bus to accommodate 16-bit add-in cards; (ii) special board (used by repair engineers) that moves an add-in board up to a position that is easier to work on; **bus master** = device that controls the bus whilst transmitting (bus master status can move between sending stations); **bus master adapter** = adapter card that fits in a EISA or MCA expansion slot in a PC; the adapter can take control of the main bus and transfer data to the computer's main memory independently of the main processor; *the bus master network adapter provides much faster data throughput than the old adapter;* **bus mouse** = mouse that plugs into the main data bus of a computer (using an interface card) rather than using a serial port; **bus network** = network of computers where the machines are connected to a central bus unit which transmits the messages it receives; **bus slave** = data sink which receives data from a bus master; **bus structure** = way in which buses are organized, whether serial, parallel, bidirectional, etc.; **bus topology** = network topology in which all devices are connected to a single cable which has terminators at each end; *Ethernet is a network that uses the bus topology; token ring uses a ring topology;* **address bus** = bus carrying address data between a CPU and a memory device; **bi-directional bus** = data and control lines that can carry signals travelling in two directions; **control bus** = bus carrying control signals between a CPU and other circuits; **daisy chain bus** = one communications bus that joins one device to the next, each device being able to receive *or* transmit *or* modify data as it passes through to the next device in line; **data bus** = bus carrying data between a CPU and memory and peripheral devices; **dual bus system** = way for linking different parts of a system which keeps the memory bus separate from the input/output bus; **expansion bus** = data and address lines leading to a connector and allowing expansion cards to control and access the data in main memory; **input/output bus (I/O bus)** = links allowing data and control transfer between a CPU and external peripherals; **memory bus** = bus carrying address data between a CPU and memory devices **(b)** central source of information which supplies several devices

---

The slot controller detects when a new board is inserted, it activates power up and assigns a bus arbitration and card slot ID to the board.
Computing

---

mice can either be attached to the PC bus *or* a serial port
PC Business World

---

both buses can be software controlled to operate as either a 16- or 32-bit interface
Electronics & Power

---

business *noun* **(a)** work in buying *or* selling; *business is expanding; business is slow; he does a good business in repairing computers; what's your line of business?;* **business computer** = powerful small computer which is programmed for special business tasks; **business efficiency exhibition** = exhibition which shows products (computers, word-processors) which help a business to be efficient; **business system** *or* **business package** = set of programs adapted for business use (such as payroll, invoicing, customers file, etc.) **(b)** commercial company; *he owns a small computer repair business; she runs a business from her home; he set up in business as an computer consultant;* **business equipment** = machines used in an office

busy *adjective* **(i)** occupied in doing something *or* in working; **(ii)** electrical signal indicating that a device is not ready to receive data; *when the busy line goes low, the printer will accept more data;* **the line is busy** = the telephone line is being used

button *noun* **(a)** (on a mouse or joystick) switch that carries out an action; *use the mouse to move the cursor to the icon and start the application by pressing the mouse button* **(b)** square shape displayed that will carry out a particular action if selected with a pointer or keyboard; *there are two buttons at the bottom of the status window, select the left button to cancel the operation or the right to continue*

buzz 1 *noun* sound like a loud hum **2** *verb* to make a loud hum

◊ **buzzer** *noun* electrical device which makes a loud hum

◊ **buzzword** *noun* (*informal*) word which is popular among a certain group of people

bypass *noun* alternative route around a component *or* device, so that it is not used; *there is an automatic bypass around any faulty equipment*

byte *noun* group of bits *or* binary digits (usually eight) which a computer operates on as a single unit; **byte addresses** = location of data bytes in memory; **byte machine** = variable word length computer; **byte manipulation** = moving, editing and changing the contents of a byte; **byte-orientated protocol** = communications protocol which transmits data as characters rather than as a bit-stream; **byte serial transmission** *or* **mode** = transmission of bytes of data sequentially, the individual bits of which can be sent in a serial *or* parallel way; **bytes-per-inch** = measure of data storage capacity of magnetic tape

---

if you can find a way of packing two eight-bit values into a single byte, you save substantial amounts of RAM or disk space
Practical Computing

Cc

C hexadecimal number equivalent to decimal 12

C high level programming language developed mainly for writing structured systems programs (the C language was originally developed for and with the UNIX operating system)

C++ high level programming language based on its predecessor, C, but providing object oriented programming functions

> these days a lot of commercial software is written in C
>
> *PC Business World*

cable *noun* flexible conducting electrical *or* optical link; *the cable has the wrong connector for this printer;* **cable connector** = connector at either end of a cable; **cable matcher** = impedance matching device that allows non-standard cable to be used with a particular device; **cable plant** = all the cables, connectors and patch panels within a building or office; **cable tester** = test equipment used to find breaks *or* faults *or* cracks in cabling

cabling *noun* cable (as a material); *using high-quality cabling will allow the user to achieve very high data transfer rates; cabling costs up to £2 a foot;* **cabling diagram** = drawing showing where the cable runs throughout an office, including connection points

> It has won a £500,000 contract to supply a structured voice and data cabling system to the bank and its stockbrocking subsidiary.
>
> *Computing*

cache *or* **cache memory** 1 *noun* section of high-speed memory which stores data that the computer can access quickly; **cache controller** = logic circuits that determine when to store data in the high-speed cache memory, when to access data in the cache and when to access data stored in the slower storage device; *file access time is much quicker if the most frequently used data is stored in cache memory;* **instruction cache** = section of high-speed memory which stores the next few instructions to be executed by a processor (to speed up operation) 2 *verb* to file *or* store in a cache; *this CPU caches instructions so improves performance by 15 percent*

> The Alpha AXP PC runs at 150MHz and comes equipped with 256Kb of Cache RAM, 16Mb of RAM (upgradeable to 128Mb) and Microsoft Windows NT.
>
> *Computing*

CAD = COMPUTER-AIDED DESIGN *or* COMPUTER-ASSISTED DESIGN the use of a computer and graphics terminal to help a designer in his work; *all our engineers design on CAD workstations;* **CAD/CAM** = CAD/COMPUTER-AIDED MANUFACTURE; interaction between computers used for designing and those for manufacturing a product

> John Smith of CAD supplier CAD/CAM Limited has moved into sales with responsibilites for the North of England. He was previously a technical support specialist.
>
> *Computing*

CAD software is memory
intensive
PC Business World

caddy *see* CD CADDY

CAI = COMPUTER-AIDED INSTRUCTION *or* COMPUTER-ASSISTED INSTRUCTION use of a computer to assist in teaching a subject

CAL = COMPUTER-AIDED LEARNING *or* COMPUTER-ASSISTED LEARNING use of a computer to assist pupils in learning a subject

calculate *verb* (a) to find the answer to a problem using numbers; *the DP manager calculated the rate for keyboarding; you need to calculate the remaining disk space;* **calculated field** = field within a database record that contains the results of calculations performed on other fields (b) to estimate; *I calculate that we have six months' stock left*

calculation *noun* answer to a problem in mathematics; **rough calculation** = approximate answer; *I made some rough calculations on the back of an envelope; according to my calculations, we have six months' stock left*

calculator *noun* electronic machine which works out the answers to numerical problems; *my pocket calculator needs a new battery; he worked out the discount on his calculator*

calendar program *noun* software diary utility that allows a user to enter and keep track of appointments; **multi-user** *or* **network calendar program** = software diary utility that allows many users to enter appointments and schedule meetings with other users

calibrate *verb* to adjust a monitor or joystick so that is is responding correctly and accurately to the signals or movements

◊ **calibration** *noun* comparing the signal from an input with a known scale to provide a standardized reading

call 1 *noun* conversation (between people or machines) on the telephone; **to log calls** = to note all details of telephone calls made **2** *verb* (a) to transfer control to a separate program *or* routine from a main program; *after an input is received, the first function is called up; the subroutine call instruction should be at this point;* **call instruction** = programming instruction that directs control to a routine (control is passed back once the routine has finished; before the call, the program counter contents are saved to show the return instruction where to return to in the main program) (b); **call accepted signal** = signal sent by a device showing that is is willing to accept (caller's) data; **call back modem** = modem that, on answering a call, immediately hangs up and calls the user back to establish a connection (used to provide better security than a normal dial-up modem); **call control signal** = signal necessary to establish and end a call; **call discrimination** = feature of a modem that allows it to check if an incoming telephone call is from a fax machine, another computer with a modem or from a person; **call duration** = length of time spent between starting and ending a call; *call duration depends on the complexity of the transaction; charges are related to call duration;* **call scheduling** = (in a fax server) arranging calls so that long-distance calls are made at off-peak times; **called party** = person *or* station to which a call is made

caller *noun* person who telephones *or* requests a call; **caller ID** = feature of a digital telephone system that displays the telephone number of the person who is calling you; in a computer, the caller ID number can be accessed by some modems

COMMENT: caller ID is often used to display the name and address of a telephone caller before the telephone has been answered by linking the caller ID to a database

calling *noun* signal to request attention, sent from a terminal *or* device to the main computer; **calling sequence** = series of program commands required to direct execution to or back from a subroutine

call up *verb* to ask for information from a backing store to be displayed; *all the customers addresses were called up; call up the previous file*

calloc (in C programming) instruction to allocate memory to a program

CAM (a) = COMPUTER-AIDED MANUFACTURE *or* COMPUTER-ASSISTED MANUFACTURING use of a computer to control machinery *or* assist in a manufacturing process **(b)** = CONTENT ADDRESSABLE MEMORY memory that is addressed and accessed by its contents rather than a location

Cambridge ring *noun* local area networking standard used for connecting several devices and computers together in a ring with simple cable links

campus environment *noun* large area or location that has lots of users connected by several networks, such as a university or hospital

◊ **campus network** *noun* network that connects together the smaller local area networks in each department within a building or university site

cancel *verb* to stop a process *or* instruction before it has been fully executed; **cancel character** = control code used to indicate that the last data transmitted was incorrect; *the software automatically sends a cancel character after any error*

◊ **cancellation** *noun* action of stopping a process which has been started

canonical schema *noun* model of a database that is independent of hardware *or* software available

capability *noun* being able to do something; *resolution capabilities; electronic mail capabilities;* **capability list** = list of operations that can be carried out

◊ **capable** *adjective* able to do something; *that is the highest speed that this printer is capable of; the software is capable of far more complex functions* (NOTE: a device is capable of something)

capacitance *noun* ability of a component to store electrical charge

◊ **capacitative** *or* **capacititive** *adjective* something which has capacitance

◊ **capacitor** *noun* electronic component that can store charge; **capacitor storage** = device using capacititive properties of a material to store data; **memory backup capacitor** = very high-capacitance, small device that can provide power for volatile RAM chips for up to two weeks (used instead of a battery); *see also* BATTERY BACKUP

capacity *noun* **(a)** amount which can be produced *or* amount of work which can be done; *industrial or manufacturing or production capacity;* **channel capacity** = maximum rate for data transmission over a channel; **to work at full capacity** = to do as much work as possible; **to use up spare** *or* **excess capacity** = to make use of time *or* space which is not fully used **(b)** amount of storage space available in a system *or* on a disk; **storage capacity** = space available for storage; *total storage capacity is now 300Mb*

capitals *or (informal)* **caps** *noun* large form of letters (A,B,C,D, etc.) as opposed to lower case (a,b,c,d, etc.); *the word BASIC is always written in caps;* **caps lock** = key on a keyboard *or* typewriter that allows all characters to be entered as capitals; *the LED lights up when caps lock is pressed*

◊ **capitalization** *noun* function of a word-processor to convert a line or block of text into capitals

capstan *noun* spindle of a tape player *or* tape backup unit that keeps the tape pressed against the magnetic read/write head *or* pinch roller

caption *noun* descriptive text that appears at the top of a window, in white text on a blue background; **caption generator** = computer or electronic device that allows a user to add titles or captions to a video sequence

capture 1 *noun;* **data capture** = action of obtaining data (either by keyboarding *or* by scanning or often automatically from a recording device *or* peripheral); *data capture starts when an interrupt is received* **2** *verb*

(a) to take data into a computer system; *the software allows captured images to be edited; scanners usually capture images at a resolution of 300 dots per inch (dpi)* **(b)** (in a Token-Ring network) to remove a token from the network in order to transmit data across the network *see also* TOKEN-RING

In July it signed a two-year outsourcing and disaster recovery deal for the operation and management of its new data-capture facility.

Computing

---

images can then be captured, stored, manipulated and displayed

Electronics & Wireless World

---

carbon ribbon *noun* thin plastic ribbon, coated with black ink, used in printers *compare* FIBRE RIBBON

card *noun* **(a)** small piece of stiff paper *or* plastic; **card reader** = device which reads data from the magnetic strip on the back of a identity or credit card; **punched card** = card with holes punched in it that represent data; **smart card** = plastic card with a memory and microprocessor device embedded in it, so that it can be used for electronic funds transfer *or* for identification of the user; *smart cards reduce fraud; future smart cards could contain an image of the users fingerprint for identification* **(b)** a punched card; **card code** = combination of punched holes that represent characters on a punched card; **card column** = line of punched information about one character, parallel to the shorter side of the card; **card feed** = device which draws punched cards into a reader automatically; **card field** = part of a card column reserved for one type of data; **card format** = way in which columns and rows are arranged to represent data fields *or* characters in a punched card; **card image** = section of memory that contains an exact representation of the information on a card; **card loader** = short program that transfers data from a punched card into main memory; **card punch (CP)** = machine that punches the holes in punched cards; **card reader** *or* **punched card reader** = device that

transforms data on a punched card to a form that can be recognized by the computer; **card row** = punch positions parallel to the longer edge of a card **(c)** sheet of insulating material on which electronic components can be mounted; **card cage** = metal supporting frame for circuit boards; **card edge connector** = series of metal tracks ending at the edge and on the surface of a card, allowing it to be plugged into an edge connector to provide electrical contact (for data transmission, etc.); **card extender** = card containing only conducting tracks, inserted between a motherboard connector and an expansion card, allowing the expansion card to be worked on and examined easily, outside the card cage; **expansion card** *or* **expansion board** = printed circuit board that is connected to a system (expansion connector) to increase its functions *or* performance; **hard card** = board containing a hard disk drive and the required interfacing electronics, which can be slotted into a system (expansion connector); **card frame** *or* **card chassis** = frame containing a motherboard into which printed circuit boards can be plugged to provide a flexible system

---

A smart card carries an encryption chip, which codifies your ID and password prior to their being transmitted across a network.

Computing

---

this card does not occupy system memory space and provides fifty functions including programmable character sets

Computing Today

---

cardinal *noun & adjective* positive integer; *13, 19 and 27 are cardinal numbers, -2.3 and 7.45 are not*

caret *noun* symbol ' ^ ' that is often used to mean the Control key

carpal tunnel syndrome *see* RSI

carriage *noun* mechanical section of a typewriter *or* printer that correctly feeds *or* moves the paper that is being printed;

carriage control = codes that control the movements of a printer carriage; *carriage control codes can be used to move the paper forward two lines between each line of text*

◊ **carriage return (CR)** *noun* signal *or* key to move to the beginning of the next line of print *or* display; *the carriage return key is badly placed for touch-typists*

carrier *noun* **(a)** device that holds a section of microfilm **(b)** continuous high frequency waveform that can be modulated by a signal; *he's not using a modem - there's no carrier signal on the line;* **carrier detect (CD)** = signal generated by a modem to inform the local computer that it has detected a carrier from a remote modem; **carrier frequency** = frequency of the carrier signal before it is modulated; **carrier sense multiple access - collision detection (CSMA-CD)** = network communications protocol that prevents two sources transmitting at the same time by waiting for a quiet moment, then attempting to transmit; used to control data transmission over an Ethernet network; **carrier signal** = continuous high frequency waveform that can be modulated by a signal; **carrier signalling** = simple data transmission (by switching on and off a carrier signal according to binary data); **carrier system** = method of transmitting several different signals on one channel by using different carrier frequencies; **carrier wave** = waveform used as a carrier; **data carrier** = (i) any device *or* medium capable of storing data; (ii) a waveform used as a carrier for data signals; **data carrier detect (DCD)** = RS232C signal from a modem to a computer, indicating that a carrier wave is being received; *the call is stopped if the software does not receive a DCD signal from the modem*

carry 1 *noun* (extra) digit due to an addition result being greater than the number base used; *when 5 and 7 are added, there is an answer of 2 and a carry which is put in the next column, giving 12;* **carry bit** *or* **flag** = indicator that a carry has occurred; **carry complete signal** = signal from an adder circuit indicating that all carry operations have been completed; **carry look ahead** = high speed adder that can predict if a carry

will be generated by a sum and add it in, removing the delay found in an adder with ripple-through carry; **carry time** = period of time taken to transfer a carry digit to the next higher digit position; **cascade carry** = carry generated in an adder from an input carry signal; **end-around carry** = most significant digit (the carry) is added into the least significant place (used in BCD arithmetic); **high speed carry** = operation when a carry into an adder results in a carry, all produced in one operation; **partial carry** = temporary storage of all carries generated in parallel adders, rather than a direct transfer; **ripple-through carry** = carry generated by a carry in to an adder **2** *verb* to move (something) from one place to another; *the fibre optic link carried all the data; the information-carrying abilities of this link are very good*

cartesian coordinates *noun* positional system that uses two axes at right angles to represent a point which is located with two numbers, giving a position on each

◊ **cartesian structure** *noun* data structure whose size is fixed and the elements are in (a linear) order; *compare* AXIS, POLAR COORDINATES

cartridge *noun* removable cassette, containing a disk *or* tape *or* program *or* data (usually stored in ROM); **data cartridge** = cartridge that contains stored data; **disk cartridge** = removable hard disk; **ink cartridge** = (for use in bubble-jet or ink-jet printers) plastic module that contains ink; **ROM cartridge** = sealed module (with electrical connections) which can be plugged into a computer and contains data *or* extra programs stored in a ROM chip; *the portable computer has no disk drives, but has a slot for ROM cartridges;* **tape cartridge** = cassette box containing magnetic tape; **cartridge drive** = drive which uses a disk *or* tape in a cartridge; **cartridge fonts** = ROM cartridge which can be plugged into a printer, providing a choice of new typefaces, but still limited to the typefaces and styles included in the cartridge *compare* RESIDENT FONTS; **cartridge ribbon** = printer ribbon in a closed cartridge

cascade carry *noun* carry generated in an adder from an input carry signal

◊ **cascade connection** *noun* number of devices *or* circuits arranged in series, the output of one driving the input of the next

◊ **cascade control** *noun* multiple control units, each controlling the next

◊ **cascaded star** *noun* method of the nodes in a star topology network to more than one hub to provide a backup in case of a problem

◊ **cascading style sheet (CSS)** (in DHTML) method of assigning typeface, style, colour and alignment attributes to an identifier (a style sheet) that can then be used to format text in a web page

◊ **cascading windows** *plural noun* (in a GUI) multiple windows that are displayed overlapping so that only the title bar at the top of each window is showing

case 1 *noun* **(a)** protective container for a device *or* circuit **(b); upper case** *or* **lower case** = capital letters *or* ordinary letters; *he corrected the word 'coMputer', replacing the upper case M with a lower case letter;* **case change** = key used to change from upper to lower case on a keyboard; **case sensitive** = command *or* operation that will only work when the characters are entered in a particular case; *the password is case sensitive;* **case sensitive search** = search function that succeeds only if both the search word and the case of the characters in the search word match **(c)** programming command that jumps to various points in a program depending on the result of a test; **case branch** = branch to a part of a program that is dependant upon the result of a test

casing *noun* solid protective box in which a computer *or* delicate equipment is housed

cassette *noun* hard container used to store and protect magnetic tape; *you must back up the information from the computer onto a cassette;* **data cassette** = special high-quality tape for storing data; **cassette recorder** = machine to transfer audio signals onto magnetic tape; **cassette tape** = narrow reel of magnetic tape housed in a solid case for protection

COMMENT: using cassette tape allows data to be stored for future retrieval; it is used as a slow, serial access, high-capacity back-up medium for systems

cast *noun* (in a programming language) instruction that converts data from one type to another; *to convert the variable from an integer to a character type, use the cast command*

CAT (a) = COMPUTER-AIDED *or* COMPUTER-ASSISTED TRAINING use of a computer to demonstrate to and assist pupils in learning a skill **(b)** = COMPUTER-AIDED *or* COMPUTER-ASSISTED TESTING use of a computer to test equipment *or* programs to find any faults

catalogue 1 *noun* list of contents *or* items in order; *all the terminals were catalogued, with their location, call sign and attribute table;* disk catalogue *or* directory = list of files stored on a magnetic disk; *the entry in the disk catalogue is removed when the file is deleted* **2** *verb* to make a catalogue of items stored

catastrophe *noun* serious fault, error *or* breakdown of equipment, usually leading to serious damage and shutdown of a system

◊ **catastrophic error** *noun* error that causes a program to crash *or* files to be accidentally erased; **catastrophic failure** = complete system failure *or* crash

category wiring one of five levels of standards defined by the Electronics Industry Association/Telecommunications Industry Association (EIA/TIA) that defines the type of cable or wire used in a network

◊ **Category 1** standard that defines an older-style unshielded twisted-pair cable that is formed by loosely twisting two insulated wires together to reduce noise and interference; this type of cable is not suitable for data transmission; *see also* unshielded twisted pair

◊ **Category 2** (part of the EIA/TIA 568 specification) standard that defines a type of unshielded twisted-pair cable that can be used to transmit data at rates up to 4MHz

◊ **Category 3** (part of the EIA/TIA 568 specification) standard that defines a type of unshielded twisted-pair cable that can be used to transmit data at rates up to 10MHz; this type of cable is the minimum standard of cable required for a 10BaseT network (NOTE: the standard suggests that the cable should have three twists per foot of cable)

◊ **Category 4** (part of the EIA/TIA 568 specification) standard that defines a type of unshielded twisted-pair cable that is the minimum standard of cable required for data transmission rates up to 16Mbit/second on a Token Ring network

◊ **Category 5** (part of the EIA/TIA 568 specification) standard that defines a type of cable that can carry data transmitted at up to 100MHz and is suitable for FDDI over copper wire, 100BaseT or other high-speed networks; *see also* FDDI, 100BaseT

catena *noun* (i) number of items in a chained list; (ii) series of characters in a word

◊ **catenate** *verb* to join together two or more sets of data

cathode *noun* negative electrical terminal of a device *or* battery; (NOTE: opposite is **anode)**

◊ **cathode ray tube (CRT)** *noun* device used for displaying characters *or* figures *or* graphical information, similar to a TV set; **cathode ray tube storage** = a cathode ray tube with a long persistence phosphor screen coating that retains an image for a long time; (NOTE: CRT is now often used to mean 'monitor')

COMMENT: cathode ray tubes are used in television sets, computer monitors and VDUs; a CRT consists of a vacuum tube, one end of which is flat and coated with phosphor, the other end containing an electron beam source. Characters or graphics are visible when the controllable electron beam strikes the phosphor causing it to glow

CAV *see* CONSTANT ANGULAR VELOCITY

CBL = COMPUTER-BASED LEARNING education or learning using special programs running on a computer

CBMS = COMPUTER-BASED MESSAGE SYSTEM use of a computer system to allow users to send and receive messages from other users (usually in-house); *see also* BBS

CBT = COMPUTER-BASED TRAINING use of a computer system to train students

CCD = CHARGE-COUPLED DEVICE; **CCD memory** = capacitors used (with MOS transistors) to store data, allowing either serial or random access

CCITT = Comité Consultatif International Téléphonique et Télégraphique international committee that defines out communications protocols and standards

CCP = COMMAND CONSOLE PROCESSOR software which interfaces between a user's terminal and system BIOS

CD (a) = COMPACT DISC; **CD caddy** = flat plastic container that is used to hold a compact disc; **CD-ROM** = COMPACT DISC-READ ONLY MEMORY small plastic disc that is used as a high capacity ROM storage device that can store 650Mb of data; data is stored in binary form as holes etched on the surface which are then read by a laser; **CD-ROM drive** = mechanical device that spins a compact disc and reads data stored on the surface of the disc using a tiny laser beam; **CD-ROM player** = disc drive that allows a computer to read data stored on a CD-ROM; the player uses a laser beam to read etched patterns on the surface of the CD-ROM that represent data bits

◊ **CD32** unit with a processor and CD-ROM drive developed by Commodore that uses its Amiga computer

◊ **CD-audio** *or* **CD-DA** = COMPACT DISC-DIGITAL AUDIO standard that defines how music can be stored as a series of numbers (digital form) on a compact disc

◊ **CD-E** = COMPACT DISC ERASABLE format that allows data to be saved to and erased from a compact disc

◊ **CD-I** = COMPACT DISC-INTERACTIVE hardware and software standards that combine sound, data, video and text onto a compact disc and allow a user to interact with the software stored on a CD-ROM; the standard defines encoding, compression and display functions

◊ **CD quality** (something) that can provide recording quality similar to a compact disc; normally refers to equipment that can store 16-bit samples at a sample rate of over 44,000 samples per second; *a sound card in a computer might have several modes of operation: low-quality for general use that does not use up too much memory and CD quality recording mode for final recordings*

◊ **CD-R** = RECORDABLE COMPACT DISC technology that allows a user to write data to and read from a CD-R disc; *a CD-R disc can be played in any standard CD-ROM drive but needs a special CD-R drive to write data to the disc*

◊ **CD-ROM Extended Architecture** *or* **CD-ROM/XA** *noun* extended CD-ROM format that defines how audio, images and data are stored on a CD-ROM disc **(b)** = CHDIR *or* CHANGE DIRECTORY system instruction in MS-DOS and UNIX that moves you around a directory structure; *type in CD DOCS to move into the DOCS subdirectory*

◊ **CD-ROM Extensions** *noun* software required to allow an operating system (typically DOS) to access a CD-ROM drive

◊ **CDRTOS** = CD REAL TIME OPERATING SYSTEM operating system used to run a CD-i hardware platform

CD-WO = COMPACT DISC WRITE ONCE CD-ROM disc and drive technology that allows a user to write data to the disc once only; useful for storing archived documents or for testing a CD-ROM before it is duplicated

---

```
Customers'  images  will   be
captured,    digitised,    and
stored   on   optical   disk   or
CD-ROM, and produced if queries
arise about responsibility for
ATM transactions.
```
Computing

---

cel *noun* single frame in an animation sequence

cell *noun* **(a)** single function *or* number in a spreadsheet program; **cell address** = (in a spreadsheet) code that identifies the position of a cell by row and column; the rows are normally numbered and the columns use the letters of the alphabet; **cell definition** = (in a spreadsheet) formula that is contained in a cell; **cell format** = (in a spreadsheet) way in which the result or data in a cell is displayed; *the cell format is right-aligned and emboldened;* **cell protection** = to prevent the contents of a particular cell or range of cells from being changed; **cell reference variable** = register that contains the reference locating a certain cell that is being operated on; **current** *or* **active cell** = thicker line surrounding the border of the cell being edited **(b)** single memory location, capable of storing a data word, accessed by an individual address **(c)** (in a transmission system such as ATM) fixed-length packet of data; for example, a cell in the ATM system contains 53-octets of data

◊ **cell relay** way of transmitting packets of information over a broadband network, such as Broadband ISDN; for example, the ATM system transfers data by moving cells of data between nodes in a wide area network *see also* ATM

cellar *noun* temporary storage for data *or* registers *or* tasks, in which items are added and retrieved from the same end of the list in a LIFO order

central *adjective* in the middle; **central computer** = HOST COMPUTER; **central memory (CM)** = area of memory whose locations can be directly and immediately addressed by the CPU; **central processing element (CPE)** = short (2, 4 or 8 bit) word length module that can be used to produce large word CPU's using bit slice techniques; **central processing unit (CPU)** *or* **central processor** = group of circuits which perform the basic functions of a computer, made up of three parts: the control unit, the arithmetic and logic unit and the input/output unit; **central terminal** = terminal which controls the communications between a central *or* host computer and remote terminals

centralized *adjective* which is located in a central position; **centralized data processing** = data processing facilities located in a centralized place that can be accessed by other users; **centralized computer network** = network with processing power provided by a central computer

centre *or US* **center 1** *noun* point in the middle of something; **centre holes** = location holes punched along the centre of paper tape; **centre operator** = person who looks after central computer operations; **centre sprocket feed** = centre (sprocket) holes that line up with coding hole positions on punched tape **2** *verb* **(a)** to align the read/write head correctly on a magnetic disk *or* tape **(b)** to place a piece of text in the centre of the paper *or* display screen; *which key do you press to centre the heading?*

◊ **centering** *noun* action of putting text in the centre of the screen; *centering of headings is easily done, using this function key*

Centronics interface *noun* parallel printer interface devised by Centronics Inc

CERN research laboratory in Switzerland where the world wide web was originally invented

certificate authority *noun* independent server or company (on the internet) that is supply or validate a special digital certificate to prove that another company is genuine; a certificate authority issues a special encrypted number that complies with the X.509 standard and is encrypted with a public-key encryption system; *see also* ENCRYPTION, PUBLIC KEY ENCRYPTION, SECURE WEB SITE

COMMENT: if you want to buy goods on the internet, you should use a secure web site, the user's web browser is sent a certificate by the web site and the browser then asks an independent certificate authority to prove that this certificate is genuine. This entire process is invisible to the user and ensures that a web site is run by the company advertised. If you want to set up a web site that allows users to buy goods, you should apply for a certificate of authentication from a certificate authority

CGA = COLOUR GRAPHICS ADAPTER popular microcomputer medium-resolution colour display system; *see also* EGA

CGI = COMMON GATEWAY INTERFACE standard that defines how a WWW page can call special scripts stored on an internet server to carry out functions that enhance a Web page; the web page uses the CGI protocol to run a script or program that might allow a user to search a web site, a script is normally written in Perl

CGM = COMPUTER GRAPHICS METAFILE device-independent file format that provides one method of storing an image as objects

chad *noun* waste material produced from holes punched in tape *or* card; **chadless tape** = punched tape that retains chad by not punching holes through fully

chain 1 *noun* (i) series of files *or* data items linked sequentially; (ii) series of instructions to be executed sequentially; **chain code** = series of words, each word being derived (usually shifted by one bit) from the previous word; **chain list** = list of data with each piece of information providing an address for the next consecutive item in the list; **chain printer** = printer whose characters are located on a continuous belt; **command chain** = list of commands (in a file) executed sequentially by a batch mode system; **daisy chain** = method of connecting equipment with a single cable passing from one machine *or* device to the next (rather than separate cables to each device); **daisy chain bus** = one communications bus that joins one device to the next, each device being able to receive *or* transmit *or* modify data as it passes through to the next device in line **2** *verb* to link files *or* data items in series by storing a pointer to the next file *or* item at each entry; *more than 1,000 articles or chapters can be chained together when printing; see also* CATENA;

chained _or_ **threaded file** = file in which an entry will contain data and an address to the next entry that has the same data content (allowing rapid retrieval of all identical data records); **chained list** = list in which each element contains data and an address to the next element in the list; **chained record** = data record in a chained file

chaining _noun_ execution of a very large program by executing small segments of it at a time, this allows programs larger than memory capacity to be run; **chaining search** = search of a file of elements arranged in a chained list; **daisy-chaining** = connecting equipment using the daisy chain method; _daisy-chaining saves a lot of cable;_ **data chaining** = storing one record that holds the address of the next in the list

---

This comprises separate boxes that can be stacked one on top of the other, linked not by a backplane but by thick cables that daisy-chain from one unit to another.

Computing

---

change _verb_ to make something different; to use one thing instead of another; **change dump** = printout of locations where data has been changed; **change file** = file containing records that are to be used to update a master file; **change record** = record containing new data which is to be used to update a master record; **change tape** = (magnetic) tape containing recent changes _or_ transactions to records which is used to update a master file

◊ **change-over** _verb_ to switch from one (computer system) to another

◊ **changer** _noun_ device which changes one thing for another; **gender changer** = two connectors, used to change a female connector to a male one (or vice-versa); _you can interconnect all these peripherals with just two cables and a gender changer_

channel 1 _noun_ physical connection between two points that allows data to be transmitted (such as a link between a CPU and a peripheral); **channel adapter** = interfacing device allowing different channels to be inter-connected; **channel**

bank = collection of a number of channels, and circuits to switch between them; **channel capacity** = maximum rate of data transmission over a channel; **channel command** = instruction to a channel _or_ control unit, providing control information such as data selection _or_ routes; **channel isolation** = separation of channels measured as the amount of crosstalk between two channels (low crosstalk is due to good channel isolation); **channel overload** = transmission of data at a rate greater than the channel capacity; **channel synchronizer** = interface between a central computer and peripherals, providing a channel, channel command interpretation and status signals from the peripherals; **channel queue** = (i) queue of requests to use a channel; (ii) queue of data that has yet to be sent over a channel; **channel-to-channel connection** = direct link between the main I/O channels of two computers, allowing high speed data transfer; **data channel** = communications link able to carry data signals; **dedicated channel** = communications channel reserved for a special purpose; **I/O channel** = link between a processor and peripheral allowing data transfer 2 _verb_ to send signals _or_ data via a particular path

◊ **channelling** _noun_ protective pipe containing cables _or_ wires

chapter _noun_ section of a main program that can be executed in its own right, without the rest of the main program being required

char _noun_ (in programming) a data type which defines a variable as containing data that represents a character using the ASCII code

character _noun_ graphical symbol which appears as a printed _or_ displayed mark, such as one of the letters of the alphabet, a number or a punctuation mark; **alphanumeric characters** = roman letters and arabic numerals (and other signs such as punctuation marks); **cancel character** = control code used to indicate that the last data transmitted was incorrect; **character assembly** = method of designing characters with pixels on a computer screen; **character-based** = screen design that is drawn using ASCII characters rather than graphical windows; **character blink** = character whose intensity is switched on and off (as an indicator); **character block** = the pattern of dots that will make up a character on a screen *or* printer; **character byte** = byte of data containing the character code and any error check bits; **character check** = check to ensure that a character code protocol and format are correct; **character code** = system where each character is represented by a unique number; *the ASCII code is the most frequently used character coding system;* **character density** = number of characters that can be stored *or* displayed per unit area; **character display** = device that displays data in alphanumeric form; **character fill** = writing one character to every location within an area of memory (for clearing and resetting the memory); **character generator** = ROM that provides the display circuits with a pattern of dots which represent the character (block); *the ROM used as a character generator can be changed to provide different fonts;* **character interleaving** = form of time division multiplexing for asynchronous protocols; **character key** = word processor control used to process text one character at a time; **character machine** = computer in which the number of bits which make up a word is variable, and varies according to the type of data; **Character Map** = utility that is provided with Windows to allow you access the full range of 256 characters that make up every font rather than the limited range that you can access from the keyboard; **character mode** = (of a display adapter) mode that can only display the characters defined in the built-in character set; **character orientated** = computer that addresses character locations rather than words; **character printer** = device that prints characters one at a time; *a daisy wheel printer is a character printer;* **character recognition** = system that optically reads written *or* printed characters into a computer, using various algorithms to ensure that characters are correctly recognized *see also* OCR; **character repertoire** = list of all the characters that can be displayed *or* printed; **character representation** = combination of bits used for each character code; **character rounding** = making a displayed character more pleasant to look at (within the limits of pixel size) by making sharp corners and edges smooth; **character set** = list of all the characters that can be displayed *or* printed; **character string** = storage allocated for a series of alphanumeric characters *compare* NUMERIC STRING; **characters per inch (cpi)** = number of printed characters which fit within the space of one inch; *you can select 10 or 12 cpi with the green button;* **characters per second (cps)** = number of characters which are transmitted *or* printed per second; **character stuffing** = addition of blank characters to a file to increase its length to a preset size; **check character** = additional character inserted into transmitted data to serve as an error detection check, its value is dependent on the text; **device control character** = special code sent in a transmission to a device to instruct it to perform a special function

characteristic 1 *noun* **(a)** value of exponent in a floating point number; *the floating point number 1.345 x 10³, has a characteristic of 3;* **characteristic overflow** = exponent value of a floating point number that is greater than the maximum allowable **(b)** measurements *or* properties of a component 2 *adjective* which is typical *or* special; *this fault is characteristic of this make and model of personal computer*

> This explains a multitude of the database's problems - three-letter months are treated like character strings instead of as dates.
>
> *Computing*

> the screen displays very sharp and stable characters, each cell occupying an 8 by 11 dot matrix
>
> *Computing Today*

charge *noun* (i) a quantity of electricity; (ii) the number of *or* excess of *or* lack of electrons in a material *or* component; **charge-coupled device (CCD)** = electronic device operated by charge; **charge-coupled device memory** = capacitors used (with MOS transistors) to store data, allowing serial and random access; **electric charge** = a number of atoms that are charged (due to an excess *or* deficiency of electrons) **2** *verb* to supply a device with an electric charge; **battery charging** = to replenish the charge stored in a re-chargeable battery

chargeable *adjective* which can be charged; **re-chargeable battery** = battery that can be used to supply power, and then have its charge replenished; *a re-chargeable battery is used for RAM back-up when the system is switched off*

> Compaq Computer and Duracell are developing a new type of standard-size re-chargeable battery for portable computers that lasts 40% longer than those now available.
> *Computing*

chart *noun* diagram showing information as a series of lines *or* blocks, etc.; **bar chart** = graph on which values are represented as vertical *or* horizontal bars of different heights *or* lengths; **flowchart** *or* **flow diagram** = diagram showing the arrangement of various work processes as a series of stages; *see also* FLOWCHART; **logical chart** = graphical representation of logic elements, steps, decisions and interconnections in a system; **pie chart** = diagram where ratios are shown as slices of a circle; *the memory allocation is shown on this pie chart*

chassis *noun* metal frame that houses the circuit boards together with the wiring and sockets required in a computer system *or* other equipment *see also* RACK

chat *verb* to send and receive messages, in real time, with other users on the internet

CHCP (in MS-DOS and OS/2 operating systems) system command that selects which code page to use

CHDIR = CHANGE DIRECTORY; *see* CD

cheapernet *(informal)* THIN-WIRE ETHERNET

check 1 *noun* **(a)** act of making sure that something is correct; **character check** = check to ensure that a character code protocol and format are correct; **check bit** = one bit of a binary word that is used to provide a parity check; **check box** = (in a GUI or front-end) small box displayed with a cross inside it if the option has been selected, or empty if the option is not selected; *select the option by moving the cursor to the check box and pressing the mouse button;* **check character** = additional character inserted into transmitted text to serve as an (error detection) check for the text, its value is dependent on the text; **check digit** *or* **number** = additional digit inserted into transmitted text to monitor and correct errors; **check indicator** = hardware *or* software device that shows that received text is not correct and a check has failed; **check key** = series of characters derived from a text used to check for and correct errors; **check mark** = indicator in a check box that shows if the check box has been selected; often a cross or tick; **check point** = point in a program where data and program status can be recorded *or* displayed; **check point dump** = printout of data and program status at a check point; **check register** = temporary storage for received data before it is checked against the same data received via another path *or* method; **check total** = CHECKSUM; **desk check** = dry run of a program **(b)** short fault *or* pause in a process (that does not stop the process); **data check** = error in reading data due to a fault with the magnetic medium **2** *verb* to examine *or* to make sure that something is in good working order; *the separate parts of the system were all checked for faults before being packaged;* **he checked the computer printout against the invoices** = he examined the printout and the invoices to see if the figures were the same

> Four bits control three multiplexers within the function unit. The last bit is a check bit to read the block's output.
> *Computing*

checkerboarding *noun* (virtual page) memory organization that has resulted in odd pages *or* spread-out pages *or* segments of memory being filled, wasting memory by leaving unusable gaps in between

checking *noun* examination; *the maintenance engineer found some defects whilst checking the equipment;* **checking program** = software that finds errors in program *or* data syntax, format and coding; **self-checking code** = error detection code

checksum *or* **check total** *noun* program which checks that data (retrieved from memory) is correct, summing it and comparing the sum with a stored value; *the data must be corrupted if the checksum is different*

child process *or* **program** *noun* routine or program called by another program which remains active while the second program runs

child window *noun* window within a main window; the smaller window cannot be moved outside the boundary of the main window and is closed when the main window is closed

chip *noun* device consisting of a small piece of a crystal of a semiconductor onto which are etched *or* manufactured (by doping) a number of components such as transistors, resistors and capacitors, which together perform a function; **chip architecture** = design and layout of components on a chip; **chip card** = plastic card with a memory and microprocessor device embedded in it, so that it can be used for electronic funds transfer *or* identification of a user; **chip count** = number of chips on a PCB *or* in a device; *it's no good, the chip count is still too high;* **chip select line** = connection to a chip that will enable it to function when a signal is present; *the data strobe line is connected to the latch chip select line;* **chip set** = chips which together will carry out a function; **diagnostic chip** = chip that contains circuits to carry out tests on circuits *or* other chips; *they are carrying out research on diagnostic chips to test computers that contain processors;* **single chip computer** = complete simple computer including CPU, memory and input/output

ports on one chip; **sound chip** = device that will generate a sound *or* tune

CHKDSK (in MS-DOS) system command that runs a check on the status of a disk drive and installed RAM

choke *see* INDUCTOR

Chooser operating system utility supplied with the Apple Macintosh that allows a user to select the type of printer, network and other peripherals that are connected

chop *see* BINARY

chord keying *noun* action of pressing two *or* more keys at the same time to perform a function

COMMENT: as an example, to access a second window, you may need to press control and F2; pressing shift and character delete keys at the same time will delete a line of text

chroma *noun* measure of colour hue and saturation

◊ **chromatic** *adjective* referring to colours

◊ **chrominance signal** *noun* section of a colour monitor signal containing colour hue and saturation information

chronological order *noun* arrangement of records *or* files according to their dates

CIF COMMON INTERMEDIATE FORMAT

CIM (a) = COMPUTER INPUT FROM MICROFILM coordinated use of microfilm for computer data storage and the method of reading the data **(b)** = COMPUTER-INTEGRATED MANUFACTURING coordinated use of computers in every aspect of design and manufacturing

cipher *noun* system of transforming a message into an unreadable form with a secret key (the message can be read normally after it has passed through the cipher a second time to decrypt it); *always use a secure cipher when sending data over a telephone line;* **cipher key** = secret sequence of characters used with a cipher system to provide a unique ciphertext; **cipher system =** formula used to transform text into a secret form; **public key cipher =** cipher that uses a public key to encrypt messages and a secret key to decrypt them (conventional ciphers use one secret key to encrypt and decrypt messages); *see also* ENCRYPTION, PGP, SSL

◊ **ciphertext** *noun* data output from a cipher; (NOTE: opposite is **plaintext**)

CIR = CURRENT INSTRUCTION REGISTER CPU register that stores the instruction that is currently being executed

circuit *noun* connection between electronic components that perform a function; **circuit analyzer =** device that measures voltage *or* current *or* impedance *or* signal in a circuit; **circuit board** *or* **card =** insulating board used to hold components which are then connected together (electrically) to form a circuit; **circuit breaker =** device which protects equipment by cutting off the electrical supply when conditions are abnormal; **circuit capacity =** information carrying capacity of a particular circuit; **circuit diagram =** graphical description of a circuit; *the CAD program will plot the circuit diagram rapidly;* **circuit switching =** method in which the link or path between two nodes is established at the time of calling for the exclusive use of this call rather than being a fixed, permanent link; **data circuit =** circuit which allows bi-directional data communications; **decision circuit =** logical circuit that operates on binary inputs, producing an output according to the function set in hardware; **digital circuit =** electronic circuit that operates on digital information providing logical functions *or* switching; **logic circuit =** electronic circuit made up of various logical gates, such as AND, OR and EXOR; **printed circuit board (PCB) =** flat insulating material that has conducting tracks of metal printed *or* etched onto its surface, which complete a circuit when components are mounted on it

the motherboard was smothered in patch wires (usually a sign that a design fault in the printed circuit board was rectified at the last minute).
Computing

◊ **circuitry** *noun* collection of circuits; *the circuitry is still too complex*

circular 1 *adjective* which goes round in a circle; **circular buffer =** computer-based queue that uses two markers, for top and bottom of the line of stored items (the markers move as items are read from *or* written to the stack); **circular file =** a data file that has no visible beginning *or* end, each item points to the location of the next item with the last pointing back to the first; **circular list =** list in which each element contains data and an address to the next element in the list with the last item pointing back to the first; **circular reference =** (in a spreadsheet) error condition that occurs when two equations in two cells reference each other; **circular shift =** rotation of bits in a word with the previous last bit inserted in the first bit position

circulate *verb* to go round in a circle, and return to the first point

circulating *adjective* which is moving about freely; **circulating register =** shift register whose output is fed back to its input to form a closed loop; **circulating storage =** storage device that maintains stored data as a series of pulses, that move along the length of the medium, being regenerated and re-input when they reach the end

COMMENT: circulating storage devices are not often used now, being slow (serial access) and bulky: typical devices are acoustic or mercury delay lines

circulation *noun* movement; *the company is trying to improve the circulation of information between departments*

CISC COMPLEX INSTRUCTION SET COMPUTER CPU design whose instruction set contains a number of long, complex instructions, that makes program writing easier, but reduces execution speed; *compare* RISC

cladding *noun* protective material surrounding a conducting core; *if the cladding is chipped, the fibre-optic cable will not function well*

claim frame *noun* (in an FDDI protocol network) special frame which is used to determine which station will initialise the network

clamper *noun* circuit which limits the level of a signal from a scanning head or other input device to a maximum before this is converted to a digital value; used to cut out noise and spikes

clapper *noun* mechanical part of a dot matrix printer that drives the printing needles onto the ribbon to print a character on the paper

class *noun* (in programming language) definition of what a particular software routine will do or what sort of data a variable can hold; **class interval** = range of values that can be contained in a class

classify *verb* to put into classes *or* under various headings; *the diagnostic printouts have been classified under T for test results* ◊ **classification** *noun* way of putting into classes

clean 1 *adjective* not dirty *or* with no errors *or* with no programs; *I'll have to start again - I just erased the only clean copy;* **clean copy** = copy which is ready for keyboarding, and does not have many changes on it; **clean machine** = computer that contains only the minimum of ROM based code to boot its system from disk, any languages required must be loaded in; **clean page** = page (of memory) that has not been changed since it was read; **clean room** = area where hard disks, wafers and chips are manufactured; the air inside has been filtered to ensure no dust or particles are present which could damage a chip **2** *verb* to make something clean; **data cleaning** = to remove errors from data; **head cleaning disk** = special disk which will clean dirt from the read/write head; *use a head cleaning disk every week; write errors occur if you do not use a head cleaning kit*

regularly; **screen cleaning kit** = liquids and cloth which remove any static and dirt from a VDU screen

clear 1 *adjective* easily understood; *the program manual is not clear on how to copy files; the booklet gives clear instructions how to connect the different parts of the system; he made it clear that the system will only work on IBM-compatible hardware* **2** *verb* **(a)** to wipe out *or* erase *or* set to zero a computer file *or* variable *or* section of memory; *type CLS to clear the screen; all arrays are cleared each time the program is run; to clear an area of memory; to clear the data register* **(b)** to release a communications link when transmissions have finished; **clear to send (CTS)** = RS232C signal that a line *or* device is ready for data transmission

clearance *noun* authority to access a file; *you do not have the required clearance for this processor*

click 1 *noun* **(a)** short duration sound, often used to indicate that a key has been pressed **(b)** pressing a key *or* button on a keyboard; *you move through text and graphics with a click of the button* **2** *verb* to press and release a key *or* a button on a keyboard *or* the mouse; *use the mouse to enlarge a frame by clicking inside its border;* **double-click** = two rapid press-release actions on a mouse button; normally to start a program or select an option; **drag-and-click** = to hold down a mouse button while moving the mouse, so moving the object selected

client *noun* (in a network) a workstation *or* PC *or* terminal connected to a network that can send instructions to a server and display results

client-server architecture *noun* distribution of processing power in which a central server computer carries out the main tasks in response to instructions from terminals or workstations; the results are sent back across the network to be displayed on the terminal, the client (the terminal or workstation) does not need to be able to directly access the data stored on the server nor does it need to carry out a lot of processing

client-server network *noun* method of organising a network in which one central dedicated computer, the server, looks after tasks such as security, user accounts, printing and file sharing, while clients (the terminals or workstations connected to the server) run standard applications *compare* PEER-TO-PEER NETWORK

client side data or program that runs on the client's computer rather than on the server, for example a JavaScript program runs on the user's web browser and is a client side application, a cookie is data stored on the user's hard disk; *see also* COOKIE, JAVASCRIPT, SERVER SIDE

clip *verb* to select an area of an image that is smaller than the original

clip-art *noun* set of pre-drawn images or drawings that a user can incorporate into a presentation or graphic; *we have used some clip-art to enhance our presentation*

clipboard *noun* (i) temporary storage area for data; (ii) (in Microsoft Windows and Macintosh Finder) utility that temporarily stores any type of data, such as a word or image; *copy the text to the clipboard, then paste it back into a new document*

clock *noun* (a) machine which shows the time; *the micro has a built-in clock; the time is shown by the clock in the corner of the screen;* **digital clock** = clock which shows the time using numbers (as 12:05) (b) circuit that generates pulses used to synchronize equipment; **clock cycle** = time period between two consecutive clock pulses; **clock doubler** = component that doubles the speed of the main system clock; *the new CPU from Intel has an optional clock doubler that will double performance;* **clock pulse** = regular pulse used for timing *or* synchronizing purposes; **clock rate** *or* **speed** = number of pulses that a clock generates every second; **clock track** = line of marks on a disk *or* tape which provides data about the read head location; **main clock** = clock signal that synchronizes all the components in a system;

programmable clock = circuit whose frequency can be set by the user **2** *verb* to synchronize signals *or* circuits with a clock pulse; **clocked signals** = signals that are synchronized with a clock pulse

clone *noun* computer *or* circuit that behaves in the same way as the original it was copied from; *they have copied our new personal computer and brought out a cheaper clone; higher performance clones are available for all the models in our range*

> On the desktop, the IBM/Motorola/Apple triumvirate is planning to energise a worldwide clone industry based on the PowerPC chip.
> *Computing*

close *verb* to shut down access to a file *or* disk drive; **close file** = to execute a computer instruction to shut down access to a stored file; **closed loop** = number of computer instructions that are repeated; **closed subroutine** = number of computer instructions in a program that can be called at any time, with control being returned on completion to the next instruction in the main program; **closed user group (CUG)** = to restrict the entry to a database *or* bulletin board *or* system (about or on a certain topic *or* subject) to certain known and registered users, usually by means of a password *see also* USER GROUP; **closed bus system** = computer with no expansion bus that makes it very difficult for a user to upgrade

◊ **CLOSE** (in a programming language) command that means the program has finished accessing a particular file *or* device

CLS (in MS-DOS) system command to clear the screen, leaving the system prompt and cursor at the top, left-hand corner of the screen

cluster *noun* (a) one or more sectors on a hard disk that are used to store a file or part of a file (b) number of terminals *or* stations *or* devices *or* memory locations grouped together in one place, controlled by a cluster controller; **cluster controller** = central computer that controls communications to a cluster of devices *or* memory locations

◊ **clustering** *noun* series of elements, occurring in a sequential line within a hash table

CLUT = COLOUR LOOK-UP TABLE table of numbers used in Windows and graphics programs to store the range of colours used in an image; *see also* PALETTE

CLV *see* CONSTANT LINEAR VELOCITY

CM = CENTRAL MEMORY area of memory whose locations can be directly and immediately addressed by the CPU

CMI = COMPUTER MANAGED INSTRUCTION

CMIP = COMMON MANAGEMENT INFORMATION PROTOCOL protocol officially adopted by the ISO used to carry network management information across a network

CMIS = COMMON MANAGEMENT INFORMATION SPECIFICATION powerful network management system

CMOT = CMIP/CMIS OVER TCP use of CMIP and CMIS network management protocols to manage gateways in a TCP/IP network

CML = COMPUTER-MANAGED LEARNING

CMOS = COMPLEMENTARY METAL OXIDE SEMICONDUCTOR integrated circuit design and construction method (using a pair of complementary p- and n-type transistors)

> COMMENT: the final package uses very low power but is relatively slow and sensitive to static electricity as compared to TTL integrated circuits; their main use is in portable computers where battery power is being used

Similarly, customers who do not rush to acquire CMOS companion processors for their mainframes will be rewarded with lower prices when they finally do migrate.

Computergram

CMYK = CYAN-MAGENTA-YELLOW-BLACK (in graphics *or* DTP) method of describing a colour by its four component colours

CNC = COMPUTER NUMERIC CONTROL machine operated automatically by computer; *see also* NUMERICAL CONTROL

coalesce *verb* to merge two or more files

co-axial cable *or* **coax** *noun* cable made up of a central core, surrounded by an insulating layer then a second shielding conductor *compare* TWISTED-PAIR CABLE, UNSHIELDED TWISTED-PAIR CABLE

> COMMENT: co-axial cable is used for high frequency, low loss applications including thin Ethernet network cabling and Arcnet network cabling

COBOL = COMMON ORDINARY BUSINESS-ORIENTED LANGUAGE programming language mainly used in business applications

code 1 *noun* **(a)** rules used to convert instructions *or* data from one form to another; **code conversion** = rules used to change characters coded in one form, to another; **code page** = (in MS-DOS) table that defines the characters that are produced from each key; *in order to enter Swedish characters from an English keyboard, you have to change the system code page* **(b)** sequence of computer instructions; **chain code** = series of words, each word being derived (usually shifted by one bit) from the previous word; **code area** = section of main memory in which program instructions are stored; **code line** = one written *or* displayed computer program instruction; **code segment** = (in an IBM-compatible PC) an area of memory assigned to hold the instructions that form a program; **computer** *or* **machine code** = programming language that consists of commands in binary code which can be directly understood by the central processing unit, without the need for translation; **direct** *or* **one-level** *or* **specific code** = binary code which directly operates the central processing unit, using only absolute addresses and values (this is the final form of a program after a compiler *or* assembler pass); **macro code** = one word that is used to represent a number of instructions, simplifying program writing; **object code** = binary code which directly operates a CPU; program code after it has been translated, compiled or assembled (into machine code); **optimum code** = coding system that provides the fastest access and retrieval time for stored data items; **source code** = set of codes (as a program) written by the programmer which cannot be directly executed by the computer, but have to be translated into an object code program by a compiler *or* assembler *or* interpreter; **symbolic code** = instruction that is in mnemonic form rather than a binary number **(c)** system of signs *or* numbers *or* letters which mean something; **bar code** = data represented as a series of printed stripes of varying widths; **bar-code reader** = optical device that reads data from a bar code; **code bit** = smallest signalling element used by the physical layer (of an OSI model network) for transmission; **code element** = voltage *or* signal used to represent binary digits; **code group** = special sequence of five code bits that represent an FDDI symbol; **cyclic code** = coding system in which the binary representation of decimal numbers changes by only one bit at a time from one number to the next; **device code** = unique identification and selection code for a peripheral; **error code** = code that indicates that a particular type of error has occurred; **error correcting code** = coding system that allows bit errors occurring during transmission to be rapidly corrected by logical deduction methods; **error detecting code** = coding system that allows bit errors occurring during transmission to be detected, but is not complex enough to correct them; **escape codes** = transmitted code sequence which informs the receiver that all following characters represent control actions; **machine-readable codes** = sets of signs *or* letters (such as bar codes *or* post codes) which

can be read by computers; **punched code** = combination of holes that represent characters in a punched card; **self-checking code** = error detecting code **2** *verb* **(a)** to convert instructions *or* data into another form **(b)** to write a program in a programming language

coder *noun* device which encodes a signal

coding *noun* act of putting a code on something; **coding sheet** *or* **coding form** = special printed sheet used by programmers to write instructions for coding a certain type of program

CODEC = CODER/DECODER device which encodes a signal being sent *or* decodes a signal received (used in many advanced PABX systems)

codepages definition of the character produced by each key on the keyboard

coincidence circuit *or* **element** *noun* electronic circuit that produces an output signal when two inputs occur simultaneously *or* two binary words are equal *see also* **AND**

cold *adjective* **(a)** not hot; *the machines work badly in cold weather* **(b)** without being prepared; **cold boot** = switching on a computer; **cold fault** = computer fault *or* error that occurs as soon as it is switched on; **cold standby** = backup system that will allow the equipment to continue running, but with the loss of any volatile data; *compare* HOT STANDBY, WARM STANDBY; **cold start** = switching on a computer *or* to run a program from its original start point; *compare* WARM START; WARM BOOT

collate *verb* to compare and put items in order; **collating sequence** = characters ordered according to their codes

collator *noun* (i) software that collates data; (ii) device that collates punched cards

collect *verb* to receive *or* capture data

collect transfer *verb* to load a register with bits from a number of different locations

collection *noun* (i) gathering together; (ii) series of items put together; **data collection** = act of receiving data from various sources (either directly from a data capture device *or* from a cartridge) and inserting correctly in order into a database; **data collection platform** = station that transmits collected data to a central point (usually via satellite)

collision detection *noun* the detecting and reporting of the coincidence of two actions *or* events; **carrier sense multiple access-collision detection (CSMA-CD)** = network communications protocol that prevents two sources transmitting at the same time by waiting for a quiet moment on the channel, then attempting to transmit

colon *noun* printing sign (:) which shows a break in a string of words; **semi-colon** = printed sign (;) which marks the end of a program line *or* statement in some languages (such as C and Pascal)

colour *noun* sensation sensed by the eye, due to its response to various frequencies of light; **colour bits** = number of data bits assigned to a pixel to describe its colour; one bit provides two colours, two bits give four colours and eight bits allow 256 colour combinations; **colour cell** = smallest area on a CRT screen that can display colour information; **colour depth** = number of different colours that can be displayed by any single pixel in a display; determined by the number of colour bits in each pixel; **colour display** = display device able to represent characters *or* graphics in colour; **colour graphics adapter (CGA)** = popular microcomputer colour display system; *see also* EGA; **colour look-up table (CLUT)** = table of numbers used in Windows and graphics programs to store the range of colours used in an image; **colour monitor** = screen that has a demodulator which shows information in colour; *the colour monitor is great for games;* **colour palette** = selection of colours that are currently being used in an image; **colour printer** = printer that can produce hard copy in colour; includes colour ink-jet, colour dot-matrix and thermal-transfer printers; **colour saturation** = purity of a colour signal; **colour tool** =

utility or icon in a graphics or DTP application that allows the user to create custom colours by specifying the CMYK or RGB values and then draw or fill an area with this colour

column *noun* series of characters, printed one under the other; *to add up a column of figures; put the total at the bottom of the column;* **card column** = line of punched information about one character, parallel to the shorter side of the card; **column guide** = (in a DTP application) vertical line that indicates the position and width of a column; **column indicator** = (in word-processing software) status bar at the bottom of the screen that displays in which column the cursor is positioned; **column parity** = parity check on every punched card *or* tape column; **80-column printer** = printer which has a maximum line width of 80 characters; *an 80-column printer is included in the price*

◊ **columnar** *adjective* in columns; **columnar graph** = graph on which values are shown as vertical *or* horizontal bars; **columnar working** = showing information in columns

COM = COMPONENT OBJECT MODEL D/ standard defined by Microsoft to standardise the way an application can access an object (this is a rival standard to CORBA)

◊ **COM** = COMPUTER OUTPUT ON MICROFILM recording the output from a computer directly onto microfilm

◊ **COM file** *noun* (in operating systems for the PC) three-letter extension to a file name which indicates that the file contains a machine code in binary format and so can be executed by the operating system; *to start the program, type the name of the COM file at the MS-DOS prompt*

◊ **COM1** (in an IBM-compatible PC) name for the first serial port; *see also* AUX

com *suffix* means that the internet domain name is a company and (usually) based in the USA

combi player *noun* hardware drive that can read two or more different CD-ROM formats

combo box *noun* box that displays a number of different input and output objects

comma *noun* symbol (,) that is often used to separate data *or* variables *or* arguments; **comma-delimited file** = data file in which each data item is separated by a comma; *all databases can import and export to a comma-delimited file format*

COMAL = COMMON ALGORITHMIC LANGUAGE structured programming language similar to BASIC

combine *verb* to join together; **combined head** = transducer that can read and write data from the surface of a magnetic storage medium, such as a floppy disk; **combined station** = high-level data link control station that processes commands and responses; **combined symbol matching (CSM)** = efficient optical character recognition system

◊ **combination** *noun* several things which are joined together; series of numbers which open a lock

◊ **combinational** *adjective* which combines a number of separate elements; **combinational circuit** = electronic circuit consisting of a number of connected components; **combinational logic** = logic function made up from a number of separate logic gates

command *noun* (a) electrical pulse *or* signal that will start *or* stop a process (b) word *or* phrase which is recognized by a computer system and starts *or* terminates an action; *interrupt command; the command to execute the program is RUN;* **channel command** = instruction to a channel *or* control unit, providing control actions such as data filtering *or* routes; **command code** = binary code that starts *or* stops an instruction *or* action in a CPU; **command console processor (CCP)** = software which interfaces between a user's terminal and system BIOS; **command control language** = programming language that allows equipment to be easily controlled;

command-driven program = program which requires the user to enter instructions at every stage; **command file** = sequence of frequently used commands stored in a file; **command file processor** = execution of a user's command file, allowing the user to create a customized simple operating environment *or* to carry out a series of frequently used commands; **command interface** = cue and prompts used by a program to inform and accept from a user required inputs (this can be user-friendly such as a WIMP environment, or not so friendly, such as a question mark); **command interpreter** = program within an operating system that recognises a set of system commands and controls the processor, screen and storage devices accordingly; *when you type in the command 'DIR', the command interpreter asks the disk drive for a list of files and instructs the monitor to display the list;* **command key** = (on an Apple Macintosh) special key that gives access to various special functions, similar in effect to the Control key on an IBM PC; **command language** = programming language made up of procedures for various tasks, that can be called up by a series of commands; **command line** = (i) program line that contains a command instruction; (ii) command prompt and system command; **command line argument** = additional items entered following a command; *use the command 'DIR' to view the files on disk, add the command line argument 'A:' to view the files on drive A:;* **command line operating system** = computer system software which is controlled by a user typing in commands (as in MS-DOS), now being replaced by GUI front-ends, such as Microsoft Windows, which allow a user to control the system through images; **command prompt** = symbol displayed by the operating system to indicate a command is expected; **command register** = register that stores the instruction to be carried out *or* that is being processed; **command state** = state of a modem in which it is ready to accept commands; **command window** = area of a screen where commands are entered; **command window history** = list of previous commands entered in the command window;

the user can define the size of the command window; **dot command** = method of writing instructions, with a full stop followed by the command, used mainly for embedded commands in a word-processing system; **embedded command** = printer control command, such as indicating that text should be in italics, inserted into test and used by a word-processor when text formatting

```
This gives Unix a friendly face
instead of the terrifyingly
complex command-line prompts
that make most users reach for
their manuals.
```
Computing

COMMAND.COM (in MS-DOS) program file that contains the command interpreter for the operating system; this program is always resident in memory and recognises and translates system commands into actions; *MS-DOS will not work because you deleted the COMMAND.COM file by mistake*

comment *noun* helpful notes in a program to guide the user; *the lack of comments is annoying; BASIC allows comments to be written after a REM instruction;* **comment field** = section of a command line in an assembly language program that is not executed but provides notes and comments; **comment out** = temporarily disabling a command by enclosing it in a comment field

common *adjective* **(a)** which happens very often; *this is a common fault with this printer model* **(b)** belonging to several different people *or* programs *or* to everyone; **common carrier** = private company that supplies data and voice communications services for a fee to anybody; **common channel signalling** = one channel used as a communications link to a number of devices *or* circuits; **common business orientated language (COBOL)** = programming language mainly used in business applications; **common gateway interface (CGI)** = standard that defines how a WWW page can call special scripts stored on an internet server to carry out functions that enhance a Web page; the web page uses the CGI protocol to run a script or program that

might allow a user to search a web site, a script is normally written in Perl; **common hardware** = hardware items that can be used for a variety of tasks; **common intermediate format (CIF)** = standard for video images that displays an image 352 pixels wide and 288 pixels high; **common language** = data *or* program instructions in a standardized form that can be understood by other processors *or* compilers/interpreters; **common management information protocol (CMIP)** = protocol officially adopted by the ISO used to carry network management information across a network; **common object request broker architecture (CORBA)** = standard defined by the Object Management Group to standardise the way an application can access an object; **common object model (COM)** = standard defined by Microsoft to standardise the way an application can access an object (this is a rival standard to CORBA, above); **common software** = useful (routines) that can be used by any program; **common storage area** = memory *or* storage area used by more than one program; *the file server memory is mainly common storage area, with a section reserved for the operating system*

◊ **common management information protocol (CMIP)** *noun* protocol officially adopted by the ISO used to carry network management information across a network

comms *(informal)* = COMMUNICATIONS

communicate *verb* to pass information to someone; *he finds it impossible to communicate with his staff; communicating with head office has been quicker since we installed the fax*

◊ **communicating word processor** *noun* word processor workstation which is able to transmit and receive data

communication *noun* **(a)** passing of information; *communication with the head office has been made easier by the telex* **(b)**; **communications** = process by which data is transmitted and received, by means of telephones, satellites, radio or any medium capable of carrying signals;

communications buffer = terminal *or* modem that is able to store transmitted data; **communications channel** = physical link over which data can be transmitted; **communications computer** = computer used to control data transmission in a network; **communications control unit** = electronic device that controls data transmission and routes in a network; **communications executive** = main set of programs which ensure that protocol, format and device and line handlers are correct for the type of device *or* line in use; **communications interface adapter** = electronic circuit that allows a computer to communicate with a modem; **communications link** = physical path that joins a transmitter to a receiver; **communications link control** = processor that provides various handshaking and error detection functions for a number of links between devices; **communications network** = group of devices such as terminals and printers that are interconnected with a central computer, allowing the rapid and simple transfer of data; **communications network processor** = processor that provides various interfacing and management (buffering *or* code conversion) between a computer and communications link control; **communications package** = software that allows a user to control a modem and use an online service; **communications port** = socket or physical connection allowing a device to communicate; **communications protocol** = parameters that define how the transfer of information will be controlled; *the communications protocol for most dial-up online services is eight-bit words, no stop bit and even parity;* **communications scanner** = line monitoring equipment to check for data request signals; **communications server** = computer with a modem or fax card attached that allows users on a network to share the use of the modem; **communications software** = software that allows a user to control a modem and use an online service; **data communications** = transmission and reception of data rather than speech *or* images; **data communications buffer** = buffer on a receiver that allows a slow peripheral to accept data from a fast peripheral, without slowing either down; **data communications equipment (DCE)** = equipment (such as a modem) which receives *or* transmits data

---

it requires no additional hardware, other than a communications board in the PC

Electronics & Power

---

comp *noun* type of newsgroup that provides discussion about computers and computer programming

compact 1 *adjective* (thing) which does not take up much space; **compact cassette** = magnetic recording tape contained inside a standard plastic box, used in home personal computers for data storage; **compact code** = minimum number of program instructions required for a task; **compact disc (CD)** = small plastic disc that contains audio signals in digital form etched onto the surface; **compact disc-digital audio (CD-audio** *or* **CD-DA)** = standard that defines how music can be stored as a series of numbers (digital form) on a compact disc; **compact disc erasable (CD-E)** = format that allows data to be saved to and erased from a compact disc; **compact disc-interactive (CD-I)** = set of enhancements to the normal CD-ROM standard, developed by Philips, and aimed for home use; **compact disc player** = machine that reads the digital data from a CD and converts it back to its original form; **compact disc ROM** *or* **CD-ROM** = small plastic disc that is used as a high capacity ROM device: data is stored in binary form as holes etched on the surface which are then read by a laser; *the compact disc ROM can store as much data as a dozen hard disks;* **compact disc write once (CD-WO)** = CD-ROM disc and drive technology that allows a user to write data to the disc once only; **compact model** = memory model in the Intel 80x86 family of CPUs that allows only 64Kb of space for the code of a program, but 1Mb of space for the program's data; **compacting algorithm** = formula for reducing the amount of space required by text **2** *verb* to reduce the space taken by something; **data compacting** = reducing the storage space taken by data by coding it in a more efficient way

companding = COMPRESSING AND EXPANDING two processes which reduce *or* compact data before transmission *or* storage then restore packed data to its original form

COMPAQ™ personal computer company (founded in 1983) that was the first manufacturer to produce a clone of the IBM PC

compare *verb* to check the differences between two pieces of information

◊ **compare with** *verb* to put two things together to see how they differ

comparable *adjective* which can be compared; *the two sets of figures are not comparable*

comparator *noun* logical device whose output is true if there is a difference between two inputs

comparison *noun* way of comparing; **there is no comparison between speeds of the two processors** = one of the two is much faster than the other

compatible 1 *adjective* (two hardware *or* software devices) that function correctly together; **is the hardware IBM-compatible?** = will it work if used with an IBM computer? **2** *noun* hardware *or* software device that functions correctly with other equipment (i.e. is a clone and can run the same software as the other); *buy an IBM PC or a compatible; this computer is much cheaper than the other compatibles*

the compatibles bring computing to the masses
PC Business World

low-cost compatibles have begun to find homes as terminals on LANS
Minicomputer News

this was the only piece of software I found that wouldn't work, but it does show that there is no such thing as a totally compatible PC clone
Personal Computer World

compatibility *noun* ability (of two hardware *or* software devices) to function together; **compatibility box** = window *or* session in an operating system that can execute programs written for a different, but related, operating system; *OS/2 has a compatibility box to allow it to run DOS applications*

COMMENT: by conforming to the standards of another manufacturer or organization, compatibility of hardware and software allows programs and hardware to be interchanged without modification

The manufacturer claims that this card does not require special drivers on the host machine, as a flash-memory card does, and therefore has fewer compatibility problems.
Computing

check for software compatibility before choosing a display or graphics adapter
PC Business World

compile *verb* to convert a high level language program into a machine code program that can be executed by itself; *compiling takes a long time with this old version; debug your program, then compile it; compiled BASIC programs run much faster than the interpretor version;* **compile and go** = computer program not requiring operator interaction that will load, compile and execute a high level language program; **compile phase** = the time during a program run, when the instructions are compiled

◊ **compilation** *noun* translation of an encoded source program into machine readable code; **compilation error** = syntax error found during compilation; *compilation errors result in the job being aborted;* **compilation time** = length of time it takes for a computer to compile a program *compare* DECOMPILATION

This utility divides the compilation of software into pieces and performs the compile in parallel across available machines on the network.

Computergram

◊ **compiler (program)** *noun* piece of software that converts an encoded program into a machine code program; *the new compiler has an in-built editor; this compiler produces a more efficient program;* **compiler diagnostics** = features in a compiler that help the programmer to find any faults; **compiler language** = high level language (such as C, pascal) which will convert a source program that follows the language syntax into a machine code version, then run it; **cross-compiler** = assembler *or* compiler that compiles programs for one computer whilst running on another; *compare* INTERPRETER; *we can use the cross-compiler to develop the software before the new system arrives;* **language compiler** = software that converts an encoded source program into another (machine code) form

complement 1 *noun* (i) inversion of a binary digit; (ii) result after subtracting a number from one less than the radix; *the complement is found by changing the 1s to 0s and 0s to 1s;* **one's complement** = inversion of a binary digit; **nine's complement** = decimal complement (equivalent to binary one's complement) formed by subtracting each digit in the number from nine; **ten's complement** = formed by adding one to the nine's complement of the number; **two's complement** = formed by adding one to the one's complement of a number **2** *verb* to invert a binary digit; **complemented** = (binary digit) that has had a complement performed; **complementary operation** = logical operation that results in the logical NOT of a function

◊ **complementary metal oxide semiconductor (CMOS)** *noun* integrated circuit design and construction method (using a pair of complementary p- and n-type transistors)

◊ **complementation** *noun* number system used to represent positive and negative numbers

complete 1 *adjective* **(a)** finished *or* all ready; *the spelling check is complete; when this job is complete, the next in the queue is processed* **(b)** requiring nothing else (in order to function); **complete operation** = operation that retrieves the necessary operands from memory, performs the operation, returns the results and operands to memory and reads the next instruction to be processed **2** *verb* to finish a task; *when you have completed the keyboarding, pass the text through the spelling checker*

◊ **completion** *noun* point when something is complete; *completion date for the new software package is November 15th*

complex *adjective* very complicated *or* difficult to understand; *the complex mathematical formula was difficult to solve; the controller must work hard to operate this complex network;* **complex instruction set computer (CISC)** = CPU design whose instruction set contains a number of long, complicated instructions, that makes programming easier, but reduces execution speed; *compare* REDUCED INSTRUCTION SET COMPUTER

◊ **complexity** *noun* being complicated; **complexity measure** = measure of the system resources used in an operation *or* job

compliant *adjective* (device) that conforms to a particular set of standards; *if you want to read PhotoCD compact discs in your computer you must be sure that the CD-ROM drive is PhotoCD or CD-ROM XA compliant*

complicated *adjective* with many different parts *or* difficult to understand; *this program is very complicated; the computer design is more complicated than necessary*

component *noun* (i) piece of machinery *or* section which will be put into a final product; (ii) electronic device that produces an electrical signal; **component density** = number of electronic components per unit area on a PCB; *component density increases with production expertise; component density is so high on this motherboard, that no expansion connectors could be fitted;* **component error** = error introduced by a malfunctioning device *or* component rather than incorrect programming

composite circuit *noun* electronic circuit made up of a number of smaller circuits and components

◊ **composite video** *noun* video signal which combines the colour signals and the monochrome signal into one single signal; *most TV set and video players expect a composite video feed;* **composite display** = video display unit that accepts a single composite video signal and can display an infinite number of colours *or* shade of grey

compound *adjective;* **compound device** = Windows MCI multimedia device that requires a data file; **compound document** = document that contains information created by several other applications; **compound file** = individual files grouped together in one file; **compound logical element** = logical circuit *or* function that produces an output from a number of inputs; **compound statement** = a number of program instructions in one line of program; *the debugger cannot handle compound statements*

compress *verb* to squeeze something to fit into a smaller space; *use the archiving program to compress the file*

◊ **compression** *noun;* **data compression** = means of reducing the size of blocks of data by removing spaces, empty sections and unused material; **disk compression software** = resident software that compresses data as it is written to disk and de-compresses it as it is read back

◊ **compressor** *noun* (program *or* device) that provides data compression

CompuServe™ one of the largest US-based online information services

compute *verb* to calculate *or* to do calculations (especially when using a computer); *connect charges were computed on an hourly rate*

◊ **computable** *adjective* which can be calculated

◊ **computation** *noun* calculation

◊ **computational** *adjective* referring to computation; **computational error** = mistake made in calculating

computer *noun* **(a)** machine that receives *or* stores *or* processes data very quickly according to a stored program; **analog computer** = computer which processes data in analog form (that is data which is represented by a continuously variable signal - as opposed to digital data); **business computer** = powerful small computer which is programmed for special business uses; **digital computer** = computer which processes data in digital form (that is data represented in discrete form); **mainframe computer** = large scale powerful computer system that can handle high capacity memory and backing storage devices as well as a number of operators simultaneously; **microcomputer** *or* **micro** = complete small-scale, cheap, low-power computer system based around a microprocessor chip and having limited memory capacity;

minicomputer *or* **mini** = small computer with a greater range of instructions and processing power than a microcomputer, but not able to compete with the speed or data handling capacity of a mainframe computer; **personal computer (PC)** *or* **home computer** = small computer which can be used in the home, in which the various sections (screen, keyboard, disk drives, processing unit, memory etc.) are in one or two small compact cases; **single board computer (sbc)** = micro *or* mini computer whose components are all located on a single printed circuit board; **single chip computer** = complete simple computer, including CPU, memory and I/O ports on one chip; **supercomputer** = very powerful mainframe computer used for high speed mathematical tasks **(b)**; **computer animation** = making a series of computer-generated images displayed in sequence to emulate motion; **computer applications** = the tasks and uses that a computer can carry out in a particular field *or* job; **computer architecture** = (i) layout and interconnection of a computer's internal hardware and the logical relationships between CPU, memory and I/O devices; (ii) way in which the CPU, terminals, printers and network connections are arranged; **computer bureau** = office which offers to do work on its computers for companies which do not have their own; **computer code** = programming language that consists of commands in binary code that can be directly understood by the central processing unit, without the need for translation; **computer conferencing** = connecting a number of computers *or* terminals together to allow a group of users to communicate; **computer crime** = theft, fraud or other crimes involving computers; **computer dating** = use of a computer to match single people who may want to get married; **computer department** = department in a company which manages the company's computers; **computer engineer** = person who maintains *or* programs *or* designs computer equipment; **computer error** = mistake made by a computer; **computer file** = section of information on a computer (such as the payroll, list of addresses, customer accounts); **computer graphics** = information

represented graphically on a computer display; **computer graphics metafile (CGM)** = device-independent file format that provides one method of storing an image as objects; **computer image processing** = analysis of information in an image, usually by electronic means *or* using a computer, also used for recognition of objects in an image; **computer independent language** = programming language that will operate on any computer that has a correct compiler *or* interpreter; **computer input microfilm (CIM)** = use of microfilm for computer data storage, and the method of reading the data; **computer language** = language (formed of figures *or* characters) used to communicate with a computer; **computer listing** = printout of a list of items taken from data stored in a computer; **computer literacy** = understanding the basic principles of computers, related expressions and concepts, and being able to use computers for programming *or* applications; **computer-literate** = (person) able to understand how to use a computer, the expressions and concepts used; *the managing director is simply not computer-literate;* **computer logic** = way in

which the various sections of the CPU, memory and I/O are arranged (in hardware); **computer mail** *or* **electronic mail** = messages sent between users of a bulletin board *or* network; **computer manager** = person in charge of a computer department; **computer network** = number of computers, terminals and peripherals connected together to allow communications between each; **computer numeric control (CNC)** = control of a machine by computer; **computer office system** = computer and related peripherals used for office tasks (filing, word processing, etc.); **computer operator** = person who operates a computer; **computer organization** *see* COMPUTER ARCHITECTURE; **computer output** = data *or* information produced after processing by a computer; **computer output on microfilm (COM)** = information output from a computer, stored directly onto microfilm; **computer power** = measure of speed and capacity of a computer (several tests exist, such as FLOPS *or* benchmark

timings); **computer program** = series of instructions to a computer, telling it to do a particular piece of work; *the user cannot write a computer program with this system;* **computer programmer** = person who writes computer programs; **computer run** = action of processing instructions in a program by a computer; **computer science** = scientific study of computers, the organization of hardware and development of software; **computer services** = work using a computer, done by a computer bureau; **computer system** = a central processor with storage and associated peripherals that make up a working computer; **computer-telephony integration (CTI)** = system that allows normal audio telephone conversations to be transmitted over a computer data network and controlled by a computer; **computer time** = time when a computer is being used (paid for at an hourly rate); *running all those sales reports costs a lot in computer time;* **computer virus** = program which adds itself to an executable file and copies (or spreads) itself to other executable files each time an infected file is run; a virus can corrupt data, display a message or do nothing; **computer word** = number of bits that make up a standard word within a CPU (usually 8, 16 *or* 32 bits long)

◊ **computer generations** *noun* way of defining the advances in the field of computing

> COMMENT: the development of computers has been divided into a series of 'generations': **first generation:** constructed using valves having limited storage; **second generation:** here transistors were used in construction; **third generation:** gated circuits in construction; **fourth generation:** used at present, using low cost memory and IC packages; **fifth generation:** computers using very fast processors, large memory and allowing human input/output

computer- *prefix* referring to a computer; **computer-based learning (CBL)** = learning mainly using a computer; **computer-based message system (CBMS)** = use of a computer system to allow users to send messages to and receive messages from other users (usually in-house); **computer-based training (CBT)** = use of a computer system to train students; **computer-generated** = which has been generated by a computer; *computer-generated graphics;* **computer-integrated manufacturing (CIM)** = coordinated use of computers in every aspect of design and manufacturing; **computer-integrated systems** = coordinated use of computers and other related equipment in a process; *this firm is a very well-known supplier of computer-integrated systems which allow both batch pagination of very long documents with alteration of individual pages;* **computer-managed instruction (CMI)** = using a computer to assist students in learning a subject; **computer-managed learning (CML)** = using a computer to teach students and assess their progress

◊ **computer-aided** *or* **computer-assisted** *adjective* which uses a computer to make the work easier; **computer-aided** *or* **assisted design (CAD)** = the use of computer and graphics terminal to help a designer in his work; **computer-aided** *or* **assisted engineering (CAE)** = use of a computer to

help an engineer solve problems *or* calculate design *or* product specifications; **computer-aided** *or* **assisted instruction (CAI)** = use of a computer to assist in teaching a subject; **computer-aided** *or* **assisted learning (CAL)** = use of a computer to assist pupils to learn a subject; **computer-aided** *or* **assisted manufacture (CAM)** = use of a computer to control machinery *or* to assist in a manufacturing process; **computer-aided** *or* **assisted testing (CAT)** = use of a computer to test equipment *or* programs to find any faults; **computer-aided** *or* **assisted training (CAT)** = use of a computer to demonstrate to and assist pupils in learning a skill

◊ **computer-readable** *adjective* which can be read and understood by a computer; *computer-readable codes*

computerize *verb* to change from a manual system to one using computers; *our stock control has been completely computerized; they operate a computerized invoicing system*

◊ **computerization** *noun* action of introducing a computer system *or* of changing from a manual to a computer system; *computerization of the financial sector is proceeding very fast*

computing *adjective & noun* referring to computers *or* work done on computers; **computing power** = measure of speed and ability of a computer to perform calculations; **computing speed** = speed at which a computer calculates

CON (in IBM-PC compatible systems) name used to identify the console: the keyboard and monitor

concatenate *verb* to join together two or more sets of data; **concatenated data set** = more than one file *or* set of data joined together to produce one set; **concatenation operator** = instruction that joins two pieces of data or variables together

conceal *verb* to hide *or* not display information *or* graphics from a user; *the hidden lines are concealed from view with this algorithm*

concentrate *verb* to combine a number of lines *or* circuits *or* data to take up less space; *the concentrated data was transmitted cheaply*

◊ **concentrator** *noun* **(a)** (in a Token-Ring network) device at the centre of a Token-Ring network which provides a logical star topology in which nodes are connected to the concentrator, but connects each arm of the star as a physical ring within the device **(b)** (in an FDDI network) node which provides access for one or more stations to the network **(c)** (in an 10Base-T Ethernet network) the device at the centre of a star-topology 10Base-T Ethernet network that receives signals from one port and regenerates them before sending them out to the other ports **(d)** (in general networking) device where all the cables from nodes are interconnected

conceptual model *noun* description of a database or program in terms of the data it contains and its relationships

concertina fold *noun* accordion fold *or* method of folding continuous paper, one sheet in one direction, the next sheet in the opposite direction, allowing the paper to be fed into a printer continuously with no action on the part of the user

concurrent *adjective* almost simultaneous (actions *or* sets); *each concurrent process has its own window; three transputers provide concurrent processing capabilities for the entire department;* **concurrent operating system** = operating system software that allows several programs *or* activities to be processed at the same time; **concurrent programming** = running several programs apparently simultaneously, achieved by executing small sections from each program in turn; **concurrent processing** = *see* MULTITASKING

The system uses parallel-processing technology to allow support for large numbers of concurrent users. *Computing*

◊ **concurrently** *adverb* running at almost the same time; *see also the four categories for processors* SISD, SIMD, MISD, MIMD

condition 1 *noun* (i) state of a circuit *or* device *or* register; (ii) series of requirements that have to be met before an action can occur; **condition code register** = register that contains the state of the CPU after the execution of the last instruction; *see also* FLAG; **error condition** = state that is entered if an attempt is made to operate on data containing errors **2** *verb* to modify data that is to be transmitted so as to meet set parameters; *condition the raw data to a standard format*

◊ **conditional** *adjective* **(a)** provided that certain things take place **(b)** (process) which is dependent on the result of another; **conditional breakpoint** = breakpoint inserted, after which the programmer can jump to one of a number of sections, depending on data *or* program status; **conditional jump** *or* **branch** *or* **transfer** = programming instruction that provides a jump to a section of a program if a certain condition is met; *the conditional branch will select routine one if the response is yes and routine two if no;* **conditional statement** = program instruction that will redirect program control according to the outcome of an event

conduct *verb* to allow an electrical current to flow through a material; *to conduct electricity; copper conducts well*

◊ **conduction** *noun* ability of a material to conduct; *the conduction of electricity by gold contacts*

◊ **conductive** *adjective* referring to the ability of a material to conduct

◊ **conductor** *noun* substance (such as a metal) which conducts electricity; *copper is a good conductor of electricity; see also* SEMICONDUCTOR

conduit *noun* protective pipe *or* channel for wires *or* cables; *the cables from each terminal are channelled to the computer centre by metal conduit*

conference *noun* meeting of people to discuss problems

◊ **conferencing** *or* **teleconferencing** *noun* discussion between remote users using computers linked by modem or a network;

computer conferencing = connecting a number of computers *or* terminals together to allow a group of users to communicate; *the multi-user BBS has a computer conferencing facility*

> Small organisations and individuals find it convenient to use online services, offering email, conferencing and information services.
>
> *Computing*

confidence level *noun* likelihood that a number will lie to within a range of values

CONFIG.SYS (in MS-DOS) configuration text file that contains commands to set parameters and load driver software; this file is read automatically once the PC is switched on and the operating system has loaded; *if you add a new adapter card to your PC you will have to add a new command to the CONFIG.SYS file*

configure *verb* to select hardware, software and interconnections to make up a special system; *this terminal has been configured to display graphics; you only have to configure the PC once - when you first buy it*

◊ **configuration** *noun* way in which the hardware and software of a computer system are planned and set up; **configuration state** = state of a computer that allows it *or* the system *or* a program to be configured

◊ **configured-in** *adjective* (device) whose configuration state indicates it is ready and available for use

◊ **configured-off** *or* **configured-out**

adjective (device) whose configuration state indicates it is not available for use

> He said only Banyan Vines had the network configuration and administration capabilities required for implementing an international business plan based on client-server computing.
>
> *Computing*

> the machine uses RAM to store system configuration information
>
> *PC Business World*

> several configuration files are provided to assign memory to the program, depending on the available RAM on your system
>
> *PC Business World*

> users can configure four of the eight ports to handle links at speeds of 64K bit/sec
>
> *Computer News*

> if you modify a program with the editor, or with a word-processor specified in the configuration file, it will know that the program has changed and will execute the new one accordingly
>
> *PC Business World*

confirm *verb* action to indicate that you agree with a particular action; *click on the OK button to confirm that you want to delete all your files*

conform *verb* to work according to set rules; *the software will not run if it does not conform to the operating system standards*

congestion *noun* state that occurs when communication *or* processing demands are greater than the capacity of a system

conjunct *noun* one of the variables in an logical AND function

◊ **conjunction** *noun* logical function whose output is true if all inputs are true

connect *verb* to link together two points in a circuit *or* communications network; **connect charge** = (in a commercial on-line system) the cost per minute of time when you are connected to the remote system; **connect state** = state of a modem in which it is transferring data across a communications line; **connect time** = length of time a user is logged onto an interactive system

◊ **connection** *noun* link *or* something which joins; **connectionless network protocol (CLNP)** = OSI transport protocol that provides an efficient way of routing information around a local area network using a datagram to carry the information; **connection-oriented network services (CONS)** = OSI transport protocol that provides an efficient way of routing information around a wide area network; **parallel connection** = connector on a computer allowing parallel data to be transferred; *their transmission rate is 60,000 bps through parallel connection*

◊ **connector** *noun* physical device with a number of metal contacts that allow devices to be easily linked together; *the connector at the end of the cable will fit any standard serial port;* **card edge connector** = series of metal tracks ending at the edge and on the surface of a circuit board, allowing it to be plugged into an edge connector to provide electrical path (for data transmission, etc.); **connector plug** = (in an FDDI network) device at the end of a fibre-optic or copper cable that connects to a receptacle; **connector receptacle** = (in an FDDI network) device mounted on a panel that connects to a plug; *see also* FEMALE, MALE

connective *noun* symbol between two operands that describes the operation to be performed

connectivity *noun* ability of a device to connect with other devices and transfer information

conscious error *noun* operator error that is immediately spotted, but cannot be prevented in time

consecutive *adjective* following one after another; *the computer ran three consecutive files*

◊ **consecutively** *adverb* one after the other; *the sections of the program run consecutively*

consistency check *noun* check to make sure that objects, data or items conform to their expected formats

console *noun* unit (keyboard and VDU, and usually a printer) which allows an operator to communicate with a computer system; *the console consists of input device such as a keyboard, and an output device such as a printer or CRT see also* CON

constant 1 *noun* item of data, whose value does not change (as opposed to a variable) **2** *adjective* which does not change; *the disk drive motor spins at a constant velocity;* **constant angular velocity (CAV)** = CD-ROM that spins at a constant speed; the size of each data frame on the disc varies so as to maintain a regular data throughput of one frame per second; **constant bit rate (CBR)** = data transfer service that is part of ATM and is used to guarantee a certain data transmission rate over a network even if there is a lot traffic; **constant length field** = data field that always contains the same number of characters; **constant linear velocity (CLV)** = disk technology in which the disk spins at different speeds according to the track that is being accessed; **constant ratio code** = character representation code that has a constant number of binary ones per word length

construct *verb* to build *or* to make (a device *or* a system)

◊ **construction** *noun* building *or* making of a system; *construction of the prototype is advancing rapidly; construction techniques have changed over the past few years*

consult *verb* to ask an expert for advice; *he consulted the maintenance manager about the disk fault*

◊ **consultant** *noun* specialist who gives advice; *they called in a computer consultant to advise them on the system design*

◊ **consulting** *adjective* (person) who gives specialist or professional advice; *a consulting engineer*

consumables *plural noun* small cheap extra items required in the day-to-day running of a computer system (such as paper and printer ribbons); *put all the printer leads and paper with the other consumables*

contact 1 *noun* section of a switch *or* connector that provides an electrical path when it touches another conductor; *the* *circuit is not working because the contact is dirty;* **contact bounce** = (fault on a keyboard) faulty key switch that causes multiple characters to be entered when the key is pressed once; *see* BOUNCE, DE-BOUNCE **2** *verb* to try to call a user *or* device in a network

contain *verb* to hold something inside; *each carton contains two computers and their peripherals; we have lost a file containing important documents*

content *noun* the ideas inside a letter *or* other document

◊ **contents** *plural noun* **(a)** things contained *or* what is inside something; *the contents of the bottle poured out onto the computer keyboard; the customs officials inspected the contents of the box;* **the contents of the letter** = the words written in the letter **(b)** list of items in a file

◊ **content-addressable** *adjective;* **content-addressable file** *or* **location** = method of storing data in which each item may be individually accessed; **content-addressable memory (CAM)** *or* **associative storage** = method of data retrieval which uses part of the data rather than an address to locate the data

contention *noun* situation that occurs when two or more devices are trying to communicate with the same piece of equipment; **contention bus** = communication control system in which a device must wait for a free moment before transmitting data; **contention delay** = length of time spent waiting for equipment to become free for use

context-sensitive *adjective* (information) which relates to the particular context; **context-sensitive help** = help message that gives useful information about the particular function or part of the program you are in rather than general information about the whole program

◊ **context-switching** *noun* process in which several programs are loaded in memory, but only one at a time can be executed

> COMMENT: unlike a true multitasking system which can load several programs into memory and run several programs at once, context-switching only allows one program to be run at a time

contiguous *adjective* which touches; **contiguous file** = file stored in a series of adjacent disk sectors; **contiguous graphics** = graphic cells *or* characters which touch each other; *most display units do not provide contiguous graphics: their characters have a small space on each side to improve legibility*

> If you later edit the file again, some of the new data clusters will not be contiguous with the original clusters but spread around the disk.
>
> *Computing*

contingency plan *noun* secondary plan *or* equipment that will be used if the first fails to work

continue *verb* to go on doing something *or* to do something which you were doing earlier

◊ **continual** *adjective* which happens again and again; *the continual system breakdowns have slowed down the processing*

◊ **continually** *adverb* again and again

◊ **continuation** *noun* act of continuing; **continuation page** = page *or* screen of text that follows on from a main page

◊ **continuity** *noun* clear conduction path between two points

◊ **continuous** *adjective* with no end *or* with no breaks; which goes on without stopping; **continuous data stream** = high speed serial data transmission, in which data words are not synchronized, but follow on immediately one after the other; **continuous feed** = device which feeds continuous stationery into a printer; **continuous loop** = endless piece of recording *or* projection tape; **continuous signal** = analog (continuously variable) signal; **continuous stationery** = paper made as one long sheet, used in computer printers

◊ **continuously** *adverb* without stopping; *the printer overheated after working continuously for five hours*

contrast 1 *noun* **(a)** difference between black and white or between colours; *the control allows you to adjust brightness and contrast;* **contrast enhancement filter** = special filter put over a monitor to increase contrast and prevent eye-strain **(b)** control knob on a display that alters the difference between black and white tones or between colours **2** *verb* to examine the differences between two sets of information; *the old data was contrasted with the latest information*

control 1 *verb* to be in charge of something *or* to make sure that something is kept in check; **controlled vocabulary** = set of terms *or* words used in an indexing language **2** *noun* **(a)** restricting *or* checking something *or* making sure that something is kept in check; **control computer** = dedicated computer used to control a process *or* piece of equipment; **control total** = result of summing certain fields in a computer file to provide error detection; **out of control** = not kept in check **(b)** (i) section of a computer *or* device that carries out instructions and processes signals, etc.; (ii) conditional program statements; **control statement** = program instruction that redirects a program (to another branch, etc.); **control unit (CU)** = section of central processor that selects and executes instructions; **control word** = word which defines the actions (in a particular process) that are to be followed; **device control character** = special code sent in a transmission to a device to instruct it to perform a special function; **line control** = special code used to control a communications link **(c)** (i) key on a computer keyboard which sends a control character; (ii) data *or* a key which controls something; **control block** = reserved area of computer memory that contains control data; **control bus** = set of connections to a microcomputer that carry the control signals between CPU, memory and input/output devices; **control cards** = in a punched card system, the first cards which contain the processor control instructions; **control**

character = special character that provides a control sequence rather than a alphanumeric character; **control cycle** = events required to retrieve, decode and execute an instruction stored in memory; **control data** = data that controls the actions of a device; **control driven** = computer architecture where instructions are executed once a control sequence has been received; **control field** = storage area for control instructions; **control key** *or* **Ctrl** = (on IBM-PC compatible systems) special key (in the lower left corner) that provides a secondary function when pressed with another key; *to halt a program, press Ctrl-C - the control key and letter C - at the same time; to reset your PC, press Ctrl-Alt-Del;* **control instruction** = program instruction that controls the actions of a device; *the next control instruction will switch to italics;* **control language** = commands that describe the identification of and resources required by a job that a computer has to process; **control memory** *or* **ROM** = memory which decodes control instructions into microinstructions which operate the computer *or* microcontroller; **control menu** = (in Microsoft Windows) menu that allows you to move, resize or close the current window; the menu is accessed by pressing Alt-Space; **control mode** = state of a device in which control signals can be received to select options *or* functions; **control panel** = (i) main computer system control switches and status indicators; (ii) (in Windows, Macintosh and OS/2) utility that displays the user-definable options such as keyboard, country-code and type of mouse; **control program/monitor** *or* **control program for microcomputers (CP/M)** = old-fashioned but still popular operating system for microcomputers; **control register** = storage location only used for control data; **control sequence** = (series of) codes containing a control character and various arguments, used to carry out a process *or* change mode in a device; **control signals** = electrical signals transmitted to control the actions of a circuit; **control statement** = program instruction that directs a CPU to provide controlling actions *or* controls the operation of the CPU; **control token** = special sequence of bits transmitted over a

LAN to provide control actions; **control transfer** = redirection of the CPU when a jump *or* call instruction is encountered **(d)**; **control group** = small group which is used to check a sample group; **control systems** = systems used to check that a computer system is working correctly

controllable *adjective* which can be controlled

controller *noun* hardware *or* software device that controls a peripheral (such as a printer) *or* monitors and directs the data transmission over a local area network; **display controller** = device that accepts character *or* graphical codes and instructions, and converts them into dot-matrix patterns that are displayed on a screen; **printer's controller** = main device in a printer that translates output from the computer into printing instructions *see also* DEVICE DRIVER

> a printer's controller is the brains of the machine. It translates the signals coming from your computer into printing instructions that result in a hard copy of your electronic document
>
> *Publish*

> there are seven print control characters which can be placed in a document
>
> *Personal Computer World*

convention *noun* well-known standards *or* rules which have to be followed, so producing hardware *or* software compatibility

◊ **conventional memory** *or* **RAM** *noun* (in an IBM-PC compatible system) the random access memory region installed in a PC from 0 up to 640Kb; this area of memory can be directly controlled by MS-DOS and it is where most programs are loaded when they are executed; *compare* HIGH MEMORY; EXPANDED MEMORY

conversational mode *noun* computer system that provides immediate responses to a user's input; *see also* INTERACTIVE MODE; *compare* BATCH MODE

conversion *noun* change from one system to another; **conversion equipment** = device that will convert data from one format to another (suitable for another system) without changing the content; **conversion tables** *or* **translation tables** = list of source codes *or* statements and their equivalent in another language *or* form; *conversion tables may be created and used in conjunction with the customer's data to convert it to our system codes;* **conversion program** = (i) program that converts programs written for one computer into a suitable form for another; (ii) program that converts data format, coding, etc. for use in another program

convert *verb* to change one thing into another

converter *or* **convertor** *noun* device *or* program that translates data from one form to another; *the convertor allowed the old data to be used on the new system;* **analog to digital converter (ADC)** = device used to convert an analog signal to a digital output form that can be understood by a computer; **digital to analog converter (DAC)** = circuit which outputs an analog signal that is proportional to the input digital number

convertibility *noun* ability to be changed

convertible *adjective* which can be converted

cookie *noun* tiny file that is stored on your computer when you connect to a remote internet site using a browser; the cookie is used by the remote site to store information about your options which can then be read when you next visit the site; *see also* client side

cookie file *noun* file that contains the cookie data supplied by the remote internet site

cooperative processing *noun* system in which two or more computers in a distributed network can each execute a part of a program or work on a particular set of data

coordinate 1 *noun;* **coordinates** = values used to locate a point on a graph *or* map;

coordinate graph = means of displaying one point on a graph, using two values referring to axes which are usually at right angles to each other **2** *verb* to organize complex tasks, so that they fit together efficiently; *she has to coordinate the keyboarding of several parts of a file in six different locations*

◊ **coordination** *noun* organizing complex tasks; synchronizing two *or* more processes

coprocessor *noun* extra, specialized processor, such as an array *or* numerical processor that can work with a main CPU to increase execution speed; **graphics coprocessor** = high speed display adapter that is dedicated to graphics operations such as line drawing, plotting, etc.; **maths coprocessor** = dedicated processor that provides results to mathematical operations much faster than the ALU section of a CPU

```
Inmos is hiring designers to
create   highly   integrated
transputers and co-processors
for   diverse   computer   and
telecoms systems.
```
Computing

---

copy 1 *noun* **(a)** document which looks the same as another; duplicate of an original; **file copy** = copy of a document which is filed in an office for reference **(b)** document; **clean copy** = copy which is ready for keyboarding and does not have many changes to it; **fair copy** *or* **final copy** = document which is written *or* typed without any changes or mistakes; **hard copy** = printout of text *or* data which is stored in a computer; **rough copy** = draft of a program which, it is expected, will have changes made to it before it is complete **2** *verb* to make a second document which is like the first; to duplicate original data; *he copied all the personnel files at night and took them home; there is a memory resident utility which copies the latest files onto backing store every 40 minutes*

◊ **copy protect 1** *noun* switch to prevent copies of a disk being made **2** *verb* to move a switch to prevent copies of a disk being made; *the program is not copy protected*

◊ **copy protection** *noun* preventing copies being made; *a hard disk may crash because of copy protection; the new program will come without copy protection*

◊ **COPY** *noun* (operating system command) that copies the contents of one file to another file on a storage device; *make a copy of your data using the COPY command before you edit it*

copyright 1 *noun* legal right (lasting for fifty years after the death of an artist whose work has been published) which a writer *or* programmer has in his own work, allowing him not to have it copied without the payment of royalties; **Copyright Act** = Act of Parliament making copyright legal, and controlling the copying of copyright material; **work which is out of copyright** = work by a writer, etc., who has been dead for fifty years, and which anyone can publish; **work still in copyright** = work by a living writer, or by a writer who has not been dead for fifty years; **copyright owner** = person who owns the copyright in a work **2** *verb* to state the copyright of a written work by printing a copyright notice and publishing the work **3** *adjective* covered by the laws of copyright; *it is illegal to take copies of a copyright work*

◊ **copyrighted** *adjective* in copyright

CORAL = COMMON REAL-TIME APPLICATIONS LANGUAGE computer programming language used in a real-time system

CORBA *see* = COMMON OBJECT REQUEST BROKER ARCHITECTURE

cord *noun* wire used to connect a device to a socket

core *noun* **(a)** central conducting section of a cable **(b)**; **core memory** *or* **store** = (i) central memory of a computer; (ii) non-volatile magnetic storage method used in old computers; **core program** = computer program stored in core memory

coresident *adjective* (two or more programs) stored in main memory at the same time

corona *noun* electric discharge that is used to charge the toner within a laser printer; **corona wire** = thin wire that charges the powdered toner particles in a laser printer as they pass across it; *if your printouts are smudged, you may have to clean the corona wire*

coroutine *noun* section of a program *or* procedure that can pass data and control to another coroutine then halt itself

correct 1 *adjective* accurate *or* right 2 *verb* to remove mistakes from something; **error correcting code** = coding system that allows bit errors occurring during transmission to be rapidly corrected by logical deduction methods rather than retransmission

◊ **correction** *noun* making something correct; change which makes something correct

◊ **corrective maintenance** *noun* actions to trace, find and repair a fault after it has occurred

corrupt 1 *adjective* data *or* program that contains errors 2 *verb* to introduce errors into data *or* a program; *power loss during disk access can corrupt the data*

◊ **corruption** *noun;* **data corruption** = errors introduced into data, due to noise *or* faulty equipment; *acoustic couplers suffer from data corruption more than the direct connect form of modem; data corruption on the disk has made one file unreadable*

count *verb* to make a total of a number of items

counter 1 *noun* (i) device which counts; (ii) register *or* variable whose contents are increased *or* decreased by a set amount every time an action occurs; *the loop will repeat itself until the counter reaches 100; the number of items changed are recorded with the counter;* **instruction** *or* **program counter** = register in a CPU that contains the location of the next instruction to be processed 2 *prefix* turning the opposite way to normal; **counter-rotating ring** = two signal paths transmitted in opposite directions around a ring network

country file *noun* file within an operating system that defines the parameters (such as character set and keyboard layout) for different countries

couple *verb* to join together; *the two systems are coupled together*

◊ **coupler** *noun* mechanical device used to connect three or more conductors; **acoustic coupler** = device that connects to a telephone handset, converting binary computer data into sound signals to allow it to be transmitted down a telephone line

Courier *noun* fixed-space *or* monospace typeface that is similar to the type produced by an office typewriter

CP = CARD PUNCH

◊ **cp** UNIX command to make a copy of a file

cpi = CHARACTERS PER INCH number of printed characters which fit within the space of one inch

CP/M = CONTROL PROGRAM/MONITOR popular operating system for microcomputers

CPM = CRITICAL PATH METHOD

cps = CHARACTERS PER SECOND number of characters printed *or* processed every second

CPU = CENTRAL PROCESSING UNIT group of circuits which perform the basic functions of a computer, made up of three parts: the control unit, the arithmetic and logic unit and the input/output unit; **CPU bound** = performance of a computer which is limited by the number of instructions the CPU can carry out; effectively, the memory and I/O devices can transfer data faster than the CPU can produce it; **CPU clock** = clock inside a processor device that generates a regular signal millions of times every second to control operations and data transfer within the processor; **CPU clock speed** = frequency of the CPU clock that controls the operations within the processor; **CPU cycle** = period of time taken to fetch and execute an instruction (usually a simple ADD instruction) used as a measure of computer speed; **CPU elements** = main sections that make up a CPU, including ALU, control unit, I/O bus, memory and various registers; **CPU handshaking** = interfacing signals between a CPU and a peripheral *or* I/O device; **CPU time** = total period of time that a CPU is used to actually process instructions

COMMENT: in a file handling program CPU time might be minimal, since data retrieval (from disk) would account for a large part of the program run; in a mathematical program, the CPU time could be much higher in proportion to the total run time

CR = CARRIAGE RETURN, CARD READER

crash 1 *noun* failure of a component *or* a bug in a program during a run, which halts and prevents further use of the system; **disk crash** = fault caused by the read/write head touching the surface of the disk **2** *verb (of a computer or program)* to come to an sudden stop; *the disk head has crashed and the data may have been lost*

◊ **crash-protected** *adjective* (disk) which uses a head protection *or* data corruption protection system; *if the disk is crash-protected, you will never lose your data*

COMMENT: it is sometimes possible to recover data from a crashed hard disk before reformatting, if the crash was caused by a bad sector on the disk rather than contact between the r/w head and disk surface

CRC = CYCLIC REDUNDANCY CHECK

create *verb* to make; *a new file was created on disk to store the document; move to the CREATE NEW FILE instruction on the menu*

crippled leapfrog test *noun* standard leapfrog test that uses a single memory location rather than a changing location

criterion *noun* specification that are to be met; (NOTE: plural is **criteria**)

critical error *noun* error that stops processing or crashes the computer

◊ **critical path analysis** *noun* the definition of tasks *or* jobs and the time each requires arranged in order to achieve certain goals (NOTE: also called PERT - Program Evaluation and Review Techniques); **critical path method (CPM)** = use of analysis and projection of each critical step in a large project to help a management team; **critical resource** = resource that can only be used by one process at a time

Surprisingly, critical path analysis and project management, frequently the next career step for engineers, did not seem to warrant a mention.

Computing

CR/LF = CARRIAGE RETURN/LINE FEED

crop *verb* to reduce the size or margins of an image *or* to cut out a rectangular section of an image

◊ **crop mark** *noun* (in DTP software) printed marks that show the edge of a page or image and allow it to be cut accurately

cross- *prefix* running from one side to another

◊ **cross-assembler** *noun* assembler that produces machine-code code for one computer whilst running on another

◊ **cross-compiler** assembler *or* compiler that compiles programs for one computer whilst running on another

COMMENT: cross-compilers and assemblers are used to compile programs for micros, but are run on larger computers to make the operation faster

◊ **crosshair** *noun* (in a drawing or paint program) shape of the cursor which looks like a cross

◊ **cross-linked files** *plural noun* (in MS-DOS) error in which two files claim to be using the same cluster on disk

◊ **cross-reference generator** *noun* section of an assembler *or* compiler *or* interpreter that provides a list of program labels, variables *or* constants with their location within the program

crossover *noun* change from one system to another; *the crossover to computerized file indexing was difficult*

crosstalk *noun* interference between two communication cables or channels

CRT = CATHODE RAY TUBE device used for displaying characters *or* figures *or* graphical information, similar to a TV set

COMMENT: cathode ray tubes are used in television sets, computer monitors and VDUs; a CRT consists of a vacuum tube, one end of which is flat and coated with phosphor, the other end containing an electron beam source. Characters *or* graphics are visible when the controllable electron beam strikes the phosphor causing it to glow

cruncher, crunching *see* NUMBER

cryogenic memory *noun* storage medium operating at very low temperatures (4deg) to use the superconductive properties of a material

cryptanalysis *noun* study and methods of breaking ciphers

cryptography *noun* study of encryption and decryption methods and techniques

◊ **cryptographic** *adjective* referring to cryptography; **cryptographic algorithm** = rules used to encipher and decipher data; **cryptographic key** = number *or* code that is used with a cipher algorithm to personalize the encryption and decryption of data

crystal *noun* small slice of quartz crystal which vibrates at a certain frequency, used as a very accurate clock signal for computer *or* other high precision timing applications; **crystal shutter printer** = page printer that uses a powerful light controlled by a liquid crystal display to produce an image on a photo-sensitive drum; *see also* LASER PRINTER; **liquid crystal display (LCD)** =

liquid crystals, that turn black when a voltage is applied, used in many watch, calculator and digital displays

CSLIP version of the SLIP protocol that compresses data before it is transmitted, resulting in greater data transfer rate

CSM = COMBINED SYMBOL MATCHING efficient optical character recognition system

CSMA-CA = CARRIER SENSE MULTIPLE ACCESS-COLLISION AVOIDANCE method of controlling access to a network not covered by OSI standards, but used in AppleTalk networks

CSMA-CD = CARRIER SENSE MULTIPLE ACCESS-COLLISION DETECTION network communications protocol that prevents two sources transmitting at the same time by waiting for a quiet moment, then attempting to transmit; used to control data transmission over an Ethernet network

CSS *see* CASCADING STYLE SHEET

CTR *or* **CTRL** *or* **Ctrl** = CONTROL control key *or* key on a computer terminal that sends a control character to the computer when pressed; **Ctrl-Alt-Del** = pressing these three keys at once will cause a PC to carry out a soft reset

CTI *see* COMPUTER-TELEPHONY INTEGRATION

CTS = CLEAR TO SEND RS232C indicating that a line *or* device is ready for data transmission

CU = CONTROL UNIT

cue *noun* prompt *or* message displayed on a screen to remind the user that an input is expected

CUG = CLOSED USER GROUP restricted entry to a database *or* bulletin board system (on a certain topic *or* subject) to certain known and registered users usually by means of a password

cull *verb* to remove hidden or distant objects from a three-dimensional scene or storage space and reduce processing time

cumulative trauma disorder *see* RSI

current 1 *adjective* referring to the present time; **current address** = address being used (accessed) at this time; **current address register (CAR)** = CPU register that stores the address that is currently being accessed; **current directory** = directory within the directory tree which is currently being used; **current drive** = disk drive that is currently being used or has been selected; **current instruction register (CIR)** = CPU register that stores the instruction that is currently being executed **2** *noun* movement of charge-carrying particles in a conductor; **direct current (DC)** = constant value electrical current supply that flows in one direction; **alternating current (AC)** = electrical current whose value varies with time in a regular sinusoidal way (changing direction of flow each half cycle)

COMMENT: mains electricity provides a 240v AC supply at 50Hz in the U.K. and 120v at 60Hz in the USA

cursor *noun* marker on a display device which shows where the next character will appear; **cursor control keys** = keys on a keyboard that allow the cursor to be moved in different directions; **cursor home** = movement of the cursor to the top left hand corner of the screen; **cursor pad** = group of cursor control keys; **addressable cursor** = cursor whose position on the screen can be defined by a program

COMMENT: cursors can take several forms, such as a square of bright light, a bright underline or a flashing light

Probably the most exciting technology demonstrated was ScreenCam, which allows users to combine voice, cursor movement and on-screen activities into a movie which can be replayed.

Computing

further quick cursor movements are available for editing by combining one of the arrow keys with the control function

Personal Computer World

customer *noun* person who buys *or* uses a computer system *or* any peripherals; **customer engineering** = maintenance and repair of a customer's equipment; **customer service department** = department which deals with customers and their complaints and orders

◊ **custom-built** *adjective* made specially for one customer

◊ **custom ROM (PROM)** *noun* ROM produced (usually in small numbers) by a manufacturer to suit a customer's requirements

◊ **customize** *verb* to modify a system to the customer's requirements; *we used customized computer terminals*

cut 1 *noun* removing a piece from a file; piece removed from a file **2** *verb* **(a)**; **cut sheet feeder** = mechanism that automatically feeds single sheets of paper into a printer **(b)** to remove sections of text from a file to make it shorter

◊ **cut and paste** *noun* action of taking a section of text *or* data from one point and inserting it at another (often used in word-processors and DTP packages for easy page editing)

CWP = COMMUNICATING WORD PROCESSOR

cybercafe *noun* company that provides a shop with terminals connected to the internet as well as coffee and pastries

cybernetics *noun* study of the mechanics of human *or* electronic machine movements, and the way in which electronic devices can be made to work and imitate human actions

cyberspace *noun* world in which computers and people interact, normally via the internet

cycle 1 *noun* (i) period of time when something leaves its original position and then returns to it; (ii) one completed operation in a repeated process; **action cycle** = all the steps required to carry out a process *or* operation on data, (such as reading, processing, output and storage); **clock cycle** = period of time between two consecutive clock pulses; **cycle availability** = period of time in a cycle, during which data can be accessed *or* transmitted; **cycle count** = number of times a cycle has been repeated; **cycle index** = number of times a series of instructions have been *or* have to be repeated; **cycle shift** = to shift a pattern of bits within a word, with the bit(s) that are shifted off the end being inserted at the beginning of the word; **cycle stealing** = memory access operation by a peripheral that halts a CPU for one *or* more clock cycles whilst data is being transferred from memory to the device; **cycle time** = time between start and stop of an operation, especially between addressing a memory location and receiving the data, and then ending the operation *compare* ADDRESS TIME **2** *verb* to repeat an operation *or* series of instructions until instructed to stop

cyclic *adjective* (operation) that is repeated regularly; **cyclic access** = access to stored information that can only occur at a certain point in a cycle; **cyclic check** = error detection method that uses *or* examines a bit of data every n bits (one bit examined then n bits transmitted, then another bit examined, etc.); **cyclic code;** *see* GRAY CODE; **cyclic decimal code** = cyclic code that refers to decimal digits; **cyclic redundancy check (CRC)** = error detection code for transmitted data; **cyclic shift** = rotation of bits in a word with the previous last bit inserted in the first bit position

cylinder *noun* (i) group of tracks on a disk; (ii) the tracks in a multi-disk device that can be accessed without moving the read/write head

cypher = CIPHER

Dd

D hexadecimal figure equivalent to decimal number 13

D to A converter = DIGITAL TO ANALOG CONVERTER; *see* DAC

3D = THREE-DIMENSIONAL

```
the software can create 3D
images using data from a
scanner or photographs from an
electronic microscope
                    PC Business World
```

DA = DESK ACCESSORY

DAC *or* **d/a converter** = DIGITAL TO ANALOG CONVERTER circuit that outputs an analog value that is proportional to the input digital number, and so converts a digital input to an analog form; *speech is output from the computer via a D/A converter; the D/A converter on the output port controls the analog machine*

daemon *noun* (in a UNIX system) utility program that performs its job automatically without the knowledge of the user

daisy chain *noun* method of connecting equipment with a single cable passing from one machine *or* device to the next (rather than separate cables to each device); **daisy chain bus** = communications bus that joins one device to the next, each device being able to receive *or* transmit *or* modify data as it passes through to the next device in line; **daisy chain interrupt** = line joining all the interrupt outputs of a number of devices to a CPU; **daisy chain recursion** = subroutines in a program that call another in the series, (the first routine calls the second routine which calls the third routine, etc.)

◊ **daisy-chain** *verb* to connect equipment using the daisy chain method

```
you can often daisy-chain cards
or plug them into expansion
boxes
                                  Byte
```

daisy-wheel *noun* wheel-shaped printing head, with characters on the end of spokes, used in a serial printer; **daisy-wheel printer** *or* **daisy-wheel typewriter** = serial character printer *or* typewriter with characters arranged on interchangeable wheels; *a daisy-wheel printer produces much better quality text than a dot-matrix, but is slower*

DAL *see* = DATA ACCESS LANGUAGE

DAMA = DEMAND ASSIGNED MULTIPLE ACCESS

damage 1 *noun* harm done to things, not to people; **to suffer damage** = to be harmed; **to cause damage** = to harm something; *the breakdown of the electricity supply caused damage estimated at £100,000* **2** *verb* to harm; *the faulty read/write head appears to have damaged the disks; the hard disk was damaged when it was dropped*

◊ **damaged** *adjective* which has suffered damage *or* which has been harmed; *is it possible to repair the damaged files?*

dark fibre *or* **fiber** *noun* optical fibre that is not carrying a signal, often used to refer to fibre optic cable that has just been installed but has not yet been used

DAS = DUAL ATTACHMENT STATION *or* DUAL ATTACHED STATION

DASD = DIRECT ACCESS STORAGE DEVICE storage medium whose memory locations can be directly read *or* written to

DAT = DIGITAL AUDIO TAPE system of recording sound as digital information onto magnetic tape that provides very high-quality reproduction; also used as a high-capacity tape backup system; **DAT drive** = mechanical drive that records data onto a DAT tape and retrieves data from a tape; *we use a DAT drive as the backup device for our network*

data *noun* collection of facts made up of numbers, characters and symbols, stored on a computer in such a way that it can be processed by the computer; *programs act upon data files; data is input at one of several workstations; the company stores data on customers in its main computer file; a user needs a password to access data;* **raw data** = (i) pieces of information which have not been input into a computer system; (ii) data (in a databank) which has to be processed to provide information to the user; (iii) unprocessed data; **data access language (DAL)** = language developed by Apple and used to query a database, based on SQL; **data access management** = regulating the users who can access stored data; **data acquisition** = gathering data about a subject; **data adapter unit** = device that interfaces a CPU to one or more communications channels; **data administrator** = control section of a database management system; **data aggregate** = collection of items of data that are related; **data analysis** = extracting information and results from data; **data area** = amount of storage space that contains data (rather than instructions); **data block** = all the data required for *or* from a process; **data break** = memory access operation by a peripheral that halts a CPU for one or more cycles whilst data is being transferred from memory to the device; **data buffer** = temporary storage location for data received by a device that is not yet ready to accept it; **data bus** = bus carrying the data between a CPU and memory and peripheral devices; **data capture** = act of obtaining data (either by keyboarding or by scanning, or often

automatically from a recording device *or* peripheral); **data carrier** = (i) any device *or* medium capable of storing data; (ii) a waveform used as a carrier for data signals; **data carrier detect (DCD)** = RS232C signal from a modem to a computer indicating a carrier wave is being received; *the call is stopped if the software does not receive a DCD signal from the modem;* **data cartridge** = cartridge that contains stored data; **data chaining** = storing one record that holds the address of the next in the list; **data channel** = communication link able to carry data signals; **data check** = error in reading data due to a fault with the magnetic medium; **data circuit** = circuit which allows bi-directional data communications; **data cleaning** = removing errors from data; **data collection** = act of receiving data from various sources (either directly from a data capture device *or* from a cartridge) and inserting correctly in order into a database; **data collection platform** = station that transmits collected data to a central point (usually via satellite); **data communications** = transmission and reception of data rather than speech *or* images; **data communications buffer** = buffer on a receiver that allows a slow peripheral to accept data from a fast computer, without slowing either down; **data communications equipment (DCE)** = equipment (such as a modem) which receives *or* transmits data; **data communications network** = number of computers, terminals, operators and storage units connected together to allow data transmission between devices *or* files *or* users; **data compacting** = reducing the space taken by data by coding it in a more efficient way; *all the files were stored on one disk with this new data compacting routine;* **data compression** = means of reducing size of data by removing spaces, empty sections and unused material from the blocks of data; *scanners use a technique called data compression which manages to reduce, even by a third, the storage required;* **data concentrator** = data which combines intermittent data from various lines and sends it along a single line in one go; **data connection** = link which joins two devices and allows data transmission; **data control** =

data management to and from a database *or* processing system; **data corruption** = errors introduced into data due to noise *or* faulty equipment; *data corruption occurs each time the motor is switched on;* **data delimiter** = special symbol *or* character that marks the end of a file *or* data item; **data description language (DDL)** = part of database system software which describes the structure of the system and data; **data dictionary** = file or software that lists the structure and types of data used in a database; **data division** = part of a (COBOL) program giving full definitions of the data types and structures; **data-driven** = (computer architecture) in which instructions are executed, once the relevant data has been received; **data element** *see* DATA ITEM;

data element chain = more than one data element treated as a single element; **data encryption** = encrypting data using a cipher system; **data encryption standard (DES)** = standard developed by the US Government for a high-security block data cipher system *compare with* PUBLIC KEY; **data entry** = method of entering data into a system (usually using a keyboard but also direct from disks after data preparation); **data error** = error due to incorrect *or* illegal data; **data field** = part of a computer instruction that contains the location of the data; **data file** = file with data in it (as opposed to a program file); *the data file has to be analysed;* **data flow** = movement of data through a system; **data flowchart** = diagram used to describe a computer *or* data processing system; *the data flowchart allowed us to improve throughput, by using a better structure;* **data flow diagram (DFD)** = diagram used to describe the movement of data through a system; **data format** = rules defining the way in which data is stored *or* transmitted; **data glove** = electronic glove that fits over a user's hand and contains sensors that transmit the position of the user's hand and fingers to a computer; used in virtual reality systems; **data hierarchy** = data structure organized hierarchically; **data highway** = bus carrying data signals between a CPU and peripherals *see also* BUS; **data independence** = structure of a database which can be changed without affecting what the user sees; **data**

input = data transferred into a computer (from an I/O port or peripheral); **data input bus (DIB)** = bus used when transferring data from one section of a computer to another, such as between memory and CPU; **data integrity** = state of data which has not been corrupted by damage *or* errors; **data interchange format (DIF)** = de facto standard method of storing spreadsheet formula and data in a file; **data item** = one unit of data such as the quantity of items in stock, a person's name, age or occupation; **data level** = position of a data item within a database structure; **data link** = connection between two devices to allow the transmission of data; **data link control** = protocol and rules used to define the way in which data is transmitted *or* received; **data link layer** = second layer in the ISO/OSI defined network that sends transmits packets of data to the next link and deals with error correction; this layer is normally split into two further sub-layers: medium access control and logical link control; **data logging** = automatic data collection; **data management** = maintenance and upkeep of a database; **data manipulation language (DML)** = database software that allows the user to access, store and change data; **data medium** = medium which allows data to be stored *or* displayed (such as a VDU *or* magnetic disk *or* screen); **data migration** = data transfer (by a user's instruction) from an on-line device to an off-line device; **data name** = group of characters used to identify one item of data; *problems occur if an ambiguous data name is chosen;* **data network** = networking system which transmits data; **data origination** = conversion of data from its original form to one which can be read by a computer; **data path** = bus *or* connections over which data is transmitted; **data pointer** = register containing the location of the next item of data; **data preparation** = conversion of data into a machine-readable form (usually by keyboarding) before data entry; **data processing (DP** *or* **dp)** = selecting and operating on data to produce useful information; sorting *or* organizing data files; **data processing manager** = person who runs a computer department; **data projector** =

device that uses three large coloured lights (red, green and blue) to project a colour image output from a computer onto a large screen; **data protection** = means of making sure that data is private and secure; **Data Protection Act** = legislation passed in 1984 in the UK that means any owner of a database that contains personal details must register; **data rate** = maximum rate at which data is processed *or* transmitted in a synchronous system, usually equal to the system clock rate; **data record** = one record containing data for use with a program; **data reduction** = production of compact, useful data from raw data; **data register** = area within a CPU used to store data temporarily before it is processed; **data reliability** = measure of the number of data words with errors compared to the total number of words; **data retrieval** = process of searching, selecting and reading data from a stored file; **data routing** = defining the path to be taken by a message in a network; **data security** = protection of data against corruption *or* unauthorized users; **data set ready (DSR)** = signal from a device that is ready to accept data, this signal occurs after a DTR signal is received; **data sharing** = one file *or* set of data that can be accessed by several users; **data signals** = electrical *or* optical pulses *or* waveforms that represent binary data; **data signalling rate** = total amount of data that is transmitted through a system per second; **data sink** = device in a data terminal which receives data; **data source** = device in a data terminal which sends data; **data station** = point that contains a data terminal and a data circuit; **data storage** = medium able to store (large quantities) of data *see also* BACKING STORE; **data stream** = data transmitted serially one bit *or* character at a time; **data strobe** = signal (in the control bus) that indicates that valid data is on the data bus; **data structure** = number of related items that are treated as one by the computer (in an address book record, the name, address and telephone number form separate entries which would be processed as one by the computer); **data switching exchange** = device used to direct and switch data between lines; **data tablet** *see* GRAPHICS TABLET; **data terminal** = device that is able to display

and transmit *or* receive data; *a printer is a data terminal for computer output;* **data terminal equipment (DTE)** = device at which a communications path starts *or* finishes; **data terminal ready (DTR)** = signal from a device that indicates that it is ready to send data; **data transaction** = one complete operation on data; **data transfer rate** = rate at which data is moved from one point to another; **data translation** = conversion of data from one system format to another; **data transmission** = process of sending data from one location to another over a data link; **data type** = sort of data which can be stored in a register (such as string, number, etc.); **data validation** = process of checking data for errors and relevance in a situation; **data vetting** = process of checking data as it is input, for errors and validity; **data word** = piece of data stored as a single word; **data word length** = number of bits that make up a word in a computer; **master data** = reference data which is stored in a master file; **optical data link** = connection between two devices to allow the transmission of data using light (either line-of-sight or using fibre optics); **variable data** = data which can be modified, and is not write protected

COMMENT: Data is different from information in that it is facts stored in machine-readable form. When the facts are processed by the computer into a form which can be understood by people, the data becomes information

Zenith's new notebook models use the power-saving Intel 486 SL microprocessor which offers 32-bit internal and data bus operation.

Computing

data compression is the art of squeezing more and more information into fewer and fewer bytes

Practical Computing

databank *noun* (i) large amount of data stored in a structured form; (ii) personal records stored in a computer

database *noun* integrated collection of files of data stored in a structured form in a large memory, which can be accessed by one or more users at different terminals; **database administrator (DBA)** = person in charge of running and maintaining a database system; **database engine** = program that provides an interface between a program written to access the functions of a DBMS and the DBMS; **database language** = series of languages, such as data description language, that make up a database management system; **database machine** = hardware and software combination designed for the rapid processing of database information; **database management system (DBMS)** *or* **database manager** = series of programs that allow the user to create and modify databases easily; **database mapping** = description of the way in which the records and fields in a database are related; **database schema** = way in which a database is organized and structured; **database server** = database management software that runs on a server computer on a network and is used in a client-server system; the user works with client software that formats and displays data that is retrieved by the server software; **database system** = series of programs that allows the user to create, modify, manage and use a database (often includes features such as a report writer *or* graphical output of data); **on-line database** = interactive search, retrieve and update of database records using an on-line terminal

> This information could include hypertext references to information held within a computer database, or spreadsheet formulae.
> *Computing*

> a database is a file of individual records of information which are stored in some kind of sequential order
> *Which PC?*

datagram *noun* packet of information in a packet switching system that contains its destination address and route

◊ **dataplex** *noun* multiplexing of data signals

◊ **dataset** *noun US* modem; **dataset ready (DSR)** = RS232C signal from a modem to a computer indicating it is ready for use

date 1 *noun* **(a)** number of a day, month and year; *I have received your message of yesterday's date; the date of creation for the file was the 10th of June, 1994* **(b)**; **up to date** = current *or* recent *or* modern; *an up-to-date computer system*; **to bring something up to date** = to add the latest information to something; **to keep something up to date** = to keep adding information to something so that it is always up to date; *we spend a lot of time keeping our files up to date* **(c)**; **out of date** = old-fashioned; *their computer system is years out of date; they are still using out-of-date equipment* **2** *verb* to put a date on a document

daughter board *noun* add-on board that connects to a system motherboard

DBA = DATABASE ADMINISTRATOR person in charge of running and maintaining a database system

dBASE™ popular database software that includes a built-in programming language

> COMMENT: dBASE has several versions, II, III and IV; the software development is currently carried out by Borland International. There have been several versions of dBASE, and files created in dBASE can normally be imported into other database programs

DB connector = DATA BUS CONNECTOR D-shape connector normally with two rows of pins used to connect devices that transfer data; *the most common DB connectors are DB-9, DB-25 and DB-50 with 9, 25 and 50 connections respectively*

DBMS = DATABASE MANAGEMENT SYSTEM series of programs that allow the user to create and modify databases easily

DC = DIRECT CURRENT; **DC signalling** = method of communications using pulses of current over a wire circuit, like a telegraph system

DCA = DOCUMENT CONTENT ARCHITECTURE document format defined by IBM that allows documents to be exchanged between computer systems

DCC = DIGITAL COMPACT CASSETTE magnetic tape in a compact cassette box that is used to store computer data or audio signals in a digital format

DCD = DATA CARRIER DETECT RS232C signal from a modem to a computer indicating a carrier is being received

DCE = DATA COMMUNICATIONS EQUIPMENT

DCT = DISCRETE COSINE TRANSFORM

DD = DOUBLE DENSITY

DDC = DIRECT DIGITAL CONTROL machine operated automatically by machine

DD/D = DATA DICTIONARY/DIRECTORY software which gives a list of types and forms of data contained in a database

DDE 1 = DIRECT DATA ENTRY keying in data directly onto magnetic tape or disk **2** see = DYNAMIC DATA EXCHANGE

DDL = DATA DESCRIPTION LANGUAGE part of database system software which describes the structure of the system and data; *many of DDL's advantages come from the fact that it is a second generation language*

DDP = DISTRIBUTED DATA PROCESSING operations to derive information from data which is kept in different places

dead *adjective* not working; (computer or piece of equipment) that does not function; **dead halt** or **drop dead halt** = program instruction from the user or an error, that causes the program to stop without allowing recovery; *the manual does not say what to do if a dead halt occurs;* **dead keys** = keys on a keyboard that cause a function rather than a character to occur, such as the shift key; **dead time** = period of time between two events, in which nothing happens, to ensure that they do not interfere with each other; *efficient job management minimises dead time*

◊ **deaden** *verb* to make a sound or colour less sharp; *acoustic hoods are used to deaden the noise of printers* •

◊ **deadlock** *noun* situation when two users want to access two resources at the same time, one resource is assigned to each user but neither can use the other

◊ **deadly embrace** *noun* = DEADLOCK

deal 1 *noun* business agreement or contract; **package deal** = agreement where several different items are agreed at the same time; *they agreed a package deal, which involves the development of software, customizing hardware and training of staff* **2** *verb* to **deal with** = to organize; *leave it to the DP manager - he'll deal with it*

◊ **dealer** *noun* person who buys and sells; *always buy hardware from a recognized dealer*

deallocate *verb* to free resources previously allocated to a job or process or peripheral; *when a reset button is pressed all resources are deallocated*

debit *noun* bit transmission rate that is twice the baud rate

deblock *verb* to return a stored block of data to its original form (of individual records)

de-bounce *noun* preventing a single touch on a key giving multiple key contact; **de-bounce circuit** = electronic circuit that prevents a key contact producing more than one signal when pressed

debug *verb* to test a program and locate and correct any faults or errors; *they spent weeks debugging the system; debugging takes up more time than construction;* **debugged program** = software that works correctly and in which all the mistakes have been removed or corrected

DEBUG *noun* (in MS-DOS) software utility that allows a user to view the contents of binary files and assemble small assembly-language programs

debugger *noun* software that helps a programmer find faults *or* errors in a program

> Further questions, such as how you debug an application built from multi- sourced software to run on multisourced hardware, must be resolved at this stage.
>
> *Computing*

> the debug monitor makes development and testing very easy
>
> *Electronics & Wireless World*

decade *noun* ten items *or* events

decay *noun* the process of a (sound) signal fading away; *with a short decay, it sounds very sharp*

deceleration time *noun* time taken for an access arm to come to a stop after it has moved to the correct location over the surface of a hard disk

decentralized computer network

noun network where the control is shared between several computers

decentralized data processing

noun data processing and storage carried out at each location rather than in one central location

deci- *prefix* meaning one tenth of a number

decimal (notation) *noun* arithmetic and number representation using the decimal system; **correct to three places of decimals** = correct to three figures after the decimal point (e.g. 3.485); **decimal point** = dot which indicates the division between the whole unit digits and the smaller (fractional) parts of a decimal number (such as 4.75); **decimal system** = number system using the digits 0 - 9; **decimal tabbing** = adjusting a column of numbers so that the decimal points are vertically aligned; **decimal tab key** = key for entering decimal numbers (using a word processor) so that the decimal points are automatically vertically aligned; **decimal-to-binary conversion** = converting

a decimal (base ten) number into a binary (base two) number

decimalization *noun* changing to a decimal system

decimalize *verb* to change to a decimal system

decipher *verb* to convert an encrypted *or* encoded message (ciphertext) into the original message (plaintext)

decision *noun* making up one's mind to do something; *to come to a decision or to reach a decision;* **decision box** = graphical symbol used in a flowchart to indicate that a decision is to be made and a branch *or* path *or* action carried out according to the result; **decision circuit** *or* **element** = logical circuit that operates on binary inputs, providing an output according to the operation; **decision** *or* **discrimination instruction** = conditional program instruction that directs control by providing the location of the next instruction to be executed if a condition is met; **decision support system** = suite of programs that help a manager reach decisions using previous decisions, information and other databases; **decision table** = chart which shows the relationships between certain variables and actions available when various conditions are met; **decision tree** = graphical representation of a decision table showing possible paths and actions if different conditions are met

deck *noun* **(a) tape deck** = drive for magnetic tape **(b)** pile of punched cards

declare *verb* to define a computer program variable *or* to set a variable equal to a number; *he declared at the start of the program that X was equal to nine*

declaration *or* declarative

statement *noun* statement within a program that informs the compiler *or* interpreter of the form, type and size of a particular element, constant or variable; **procedure declaration** = to write and declare the variable types used and (if any) the routine name and location

declarative language   *noun*
programming language (normally in a
database application) in which you enter
what you want to achieve, rather than enter
instructions

decode *verb* to translate encoded data back
to its original form

◊ **decoder** *noun* program *or* device used to
convert data into another form; **instruction
decoder** = hardware that converts a
machine-code code instruction (in binary
form) into actions

◊ **decoding** *noun* converting encoded data
back into its original form

decollate *verb* to separate continuous
stationery into single sheets; to split two-part
or three-part stationery into its separate parts
(and remove the carbon paper)

◊ **decollator** *noun* machine used to
separate continuous stationery into single
sheets *or* to split 2-part or 3-part stationery
into separate parts

decompilation *noun* conversion of a
compiled program in object code into a
source language; *fast incremental
compilation and decompilation*

decompression *noun* expanding a
compressed image or data file so that it can be
viewed

decrease **1** *noun* fall *or* reduction;
*decrease in price; decrease in value;
decrease in sales; sales show a 10%
decrease on last year* **2** *verb* to fall *or* to
become less; *sales are decreasing; the value
of the pound has decreased by 5%*

decrement *verb* to subtract a set number
from a variable; *the register contents were
decremented until they reached zero*

decrypt *verb* to convert encrypted data
back into its original form; *decryption is
done using hardware to increase speed*

◊ **decryption** *noun* converting of
encrypted data back into its original form

> typically a file is encrypted
> using a password key and
> decrypted using the same key.

A design fault of many systems
means the use of the wrong
password for decryption
results in double and often
irretrievable encryption
PC Business World

dedicated   *adjective* (program *or*
procedure *or* system) reserved for a particular
use; *there's only one dedicated graphics
workstation in this network;* **dedicated
channel** = communications line reserved for
a special purpose; **dedicated computer** =
computer which is only used for a single
special purpose; **dedicated logic** = logical
function implemented in hardware design
(usually for only one task *or* circuit); *the
person appointed should have a knowledge
of micro-based hardware and dedicated
logic; the dedicated logic cuts down the chip
count;* **dedicated print server** = computer
on a network connected to a printer with the
sole task of managing print jobs and print
queues of users on the network; **dedicated
word processor** = computer which has been
configured specially for word processing and
which cannot run any other programs

> The PBX is changing from a
> dedicated proprietary hardware
> product into an open
> application software
> development platform.
> *Computing*

> the server should reduce
> networking costs by using
> standard networking cable
> instead of dedicated links
> *PC Business World*

deduct *verb* to remove something from a
total

de facto standard *noun* a design *or*
method *or* system which is so widely used
that it has become a standard but it has not
been officially recognised by any committee

default *noun* predefined course of action *or*
value that is assumed unless the operator
alters it; **default drive** = disk drive that is
accessed first in a multi-disk system (to try
and load the operating system or a program);
the operating system allows the user to select

the default drive; **default option** = preset value *or* option that is to be used if no other value has been specified; **default printer** = (in systems that allow several printers to be defined) printer that is used unless another is specified; **default rate** = baud rate (in a modem) that is used if no other is selected; **default response** = value which is used if the user does not enter new data; **default value** = value which is automatically used by the computer if no other value has been specified; *screen width has a default value of 80*

The default values of columns cannot be set in the database schema, so different applications can trash the database.

Computing

---

defect *noun* something which is wrong *or* which stops a machine from working properly; *a computer defect or a defect in the computer*

defect skipping *noun* means of identifying and labelling defective magnetic tracks during manufacture so that they will not be used, pointing instead to the next good track to be used

defective *adjective* faulty *or* not working properly; *the machine broke down because of a defective cooling system;* **defective sector** = fault with a hard disk in which data cannot be correctly read from a particular sector; it could be caused by a damaged disk surface or faulty head alignment

defensive computing *noun* method of programming that takes into account any problems *or* errors that might occur

deferred addressing *noun* indirect addressing, where the location accessed contains the address of the operand to be processed

deferred printing *noun* delaying printing a document until a later time

define *verb* (i) to assign a value to a variable; (ii) to assign the characteristics of

processes *or* data to something; *all the variables were defined at initialization*

definition *noun* (i) ability of a screen to display fine detail; (ii) value *or* formula assigned to a variable *or* label; **macro definition** = description (in a program *or* to a system) of the structure, function and instructions that make up a macro operation

deflect *verb* to change the direction of an object *or* beam

deflection *noun;* **deflection yokes** = magnetic coils around a cathode ray tube used to control the position of the picture beam on the screen

DEFRAG (in MS-DOS) defragmentation utility supplied with MS-DOS

defragmentation *noun* reorganisation of files scattered across non-contiguous sectors on a hard disk; **defragmentation utility** = software utility that carries out the process of defragmentation on a hard disk

---

COMMENT: when a file is saved to disk, it is not always saved in adjacent sectors; this will increase the retrieval time. Defragmentation moves files back into adjacent sectors so that the read head does not have to move far across the disk, and it increases performance

---

degauss *verb* to remove unwanted magnetic fields and effects from magnetic tape, disks *or* read/write heads; *the r/w heads have to be degaussed each week to ensure optimum performance*

degausser *noun* device used to remove unwanted magnetic fields from a disk *or* tape *or* recording head

degradation *noun* **(a)** loss of picture *or* signal quality; **image degradation** = loss of picture contrast and quality due to signal distortion *or* bad copying of a video signal **(b)** loss of processing capacity because of a malfunction; **graceful degradation** = allowing some parts of a system to continue to function after a part has broken down

dejagging *see* ANTI-ALIASING

DEL = DELETE (in MS-DOS) command to delete a file; *to delete all files with the extension BAK, use the command DEL *.BAK;* **DEL key** = key on a keyboard that moves the cursor back one character space and deletes any character at that position; *to remove a word from the screen, press the DEL key repeatedly*

delay 1 *noun* time when something is later than planned; *there was a delay of thirty seconds before the printer started printing; we are sorry for the delay in supplying your order, but the computer was not working;* **delay line** = device that causes a signal to take a certain time in crossing it; **delay line store** = (old) method of storing serial data as sound *or* pulses in a delay line, the data being constantly read, regenerated and fed back into the input; **delay vector** = time that a message will take to pass from one packet switching network node to another **2** *verb* to cause something to have a delay

delete *verb* **(a)** to cut out words in a document **(b)** to remove text *or* data *or* a file from a storage device; *the word-processor allows us to delete the whole file by pressing this key;* **delete character** = special code used to indicate data *or* text to be removed

◊ **deletion** *noun* (i) making a cut in a document; (ii) text removed from a document; *the editors asked the author to make several deletions in the last chapter;* **deletion record** = record containing new data which is to be used to update *or* delete data in a master record; **deletion tracking** = method of allowing deleted files to be undeleted; when a file is deleted, the sectors on disk are monitored for a period of time in case the file was deleted by mistake; **undelete** = to restore a file *or* text *or* data that was accidentally deleted; *thankfully, we could undelete the files*

COMMENT: when you delete a file, you are not actually erasing it but you are making its space on disk available for another file by instructing the operating system to ignore the file by inserting a special code in the file header and deleting the entry from the directory

delimit *verb* to set up the size of data using delimiters; **delimited-field file** = data file in which each field is separated by a special character (often a tab character or comma) and each record is separated by a carriage return or a second special character; **comma delimited** = file in which each item *or* field of data is separated by a comma

◊ **delimiter** *noun* (i) character *or* symbol used to indicate to a language *or* program the start *or* end of data *or* a record *or* information; (ii) the boundary between an instruction and its argument

delta clock *noun* clock that provides timing pulses to synchronize a system, and will restart a computer *or* circuit (with an interrupt signal) that has had an error *or* entered an endless loop *or* faulty state

demagnetize *verb* to remove stray *or* unwanted magnetic fields from a disk *or* tape *or* recording head

◊ **demagnetizer** *noun* device which demagnetizes something; *he used the demagnetizer to degauss the tape heads*

demand 1 *noun* asking for something to be done; **demand assigned multiple access (DAMA)** = means of switching in circuits as and when they are required; **demand paging** = system software that retrieves pages in a virtual memory system from backing store when it is required; **demand processing** = processing data when it appears, rather than waiting; **demand protocol architecture (DPA)** = technique of loading protocol stacks in memory only if they are required for a particular session; **demand reading/writing** = direct data transfer between a processor and storage; **demand staging** = moving files *or* data from a secondary storage device to a fast access device when required by a database program **2** *verb* to ask for something and expect to get it; *she demanded her money back; the suppliers are demanding immediate payment*

demarcation *noun* showing the difference between two areas

demo = DEMONSTRATION

democratic network *noun*
synchronized network where each station has
equal priority

demodulation *noun* recovery of the
original signal from a received modulated
carrier wave

demonstrate *verb* to show how
something works; *he demonstrated the file
management program*

◊ **demonstration** *or* **demo** *noun* act of
showing how something works;
demonstration model = piece of equipment
in a shop, used to show customers how the
equipment works; **demonstration software**
= software that shows what an application is
like to use and what it can do, without
implementing all the functions; *the company
gave away demonstration software that lets
you do everything except save your data*

denary notation *noun* number system in
base ten, using the digits 0 to 9; *compare with*
BINARY

denial *noun;* **alternative denial** = logical
function whose output is false if all inputs are
true, and true if any input is false; **joint
denial** = logical function whose output is
false if any input is true

dense index *noun* database index
containing an address *or* entry for every item
or entry in the database; **dense list** = list that
has no free space for new records

◊ **density** *noun* amount of data that can be
packed into a space on a disk *or* tape; **double
density** = system to double the storage
capacity of a disk drive by doubling the
number of bits which can be put on the disk
surface; **double density disk (DD)** = disk
that can store two bits of data per unit area
compared to a standard disk, using a
modified write process; **packing** *or*
recording density = number of bits that can
be stored in a unit area on a magnetic disk *or*
tape; **single density disk (SD)** = (older)
standard of low capacity magnetic disk able
to store data (normally 720Kb for a 3.5-inch
disk

COMMENT: scanner software produces
various shades of grey by using different
densities or arrangements of black and
white dots and/or different size dots

```
diode  lasers  with  shorter
wavelengths will make doubling
of the bit and track densities
possible
```
Byte

deny access *verb* to refuse access to a
circuit *or* system for reasons of workload *or*
security

departmental LAN *noun* small local
network used to connect a group of people
that are working in the same department or
office and allows the users to share files,
printers and other resources; *see also* LAN,
PEER-TO-PEER

dependent *adjective* which is variable
because of something; *a process which is
dependent on the result of another process;
the output is dependent on the physical state
of the link;* **machine dependent** = not
standardized *or* which cannot be used on
hardware *or* software from a different
manufacturer without modification

deposit 1 *noun* thin layer of a substance
which is put on a surface **2** *verb* **(a)** printout
of the contents of all *or* a selected area of
memory **(b)** to coat a surface with a thin layer
of a substance **(c)** to write data into a register
or storage location

◊ **deposition** *noun* process by which a
surface (of a semiconductor) is coated with a
thin layer of a substance

deque *noun* = DOUBLE-ENDED
QUEUE queue in which new items can be
added to either end

derive *verb* to come from; *the results are
derived from the raw data*

◊ **derivation graph** *noun* structure within
a global database that provides information
on the rules and paths used to reach any
element *or* item of data

DES = DATA ENCRYPTION STANDARD
standard developed by the US Government

for a high-security block data cipher system *compare with* PUBLIC KEY

descender *noun* part of a printed letter that is below the line

de-scramble *verb* to reassemble an original message *or* signal from its scrambled form

◊ **de-scrambler** *noun* device which changes a scrambled message back to its original, clear form

describe *verb* to say what someone *or* something is like; *the leaflet describes the services the company can offer; the specifications are described in greater detail at the back of the manual*

◊ **description** *noun* words which show what something is like; **description list** = list of data items and their attributes; **data description language (DDL)** = part of a database system which describes the structure of the system and data; **page description programming language** = programming language that accepts commands to define the size, position and type style for text *or* graphics on a page

◊ **descriptor** *noun* code used to identify a filename *or* program name *or* pass code to a file

design 1 *noun* planning *or* drawing of a product before it is built *or* manufactured; **circuit design** = layout of components and interconnections in a circuit; **product design** = design of products; **design parameters** = specifications for the design of a product **2** *verb* to plan *or* to draw something before it is built *or* manufactured; *he designed a new chip factory; she designs typefaces*

◊ **designer** *noun* person who designs; *she is the designer of the new computer*

desk *noun* writing table in an office, usually with drawers for stationery; *desk diary; desk drawer; desk light;* **desk check** = dry run of a program

◊ **desk accessory (DA)** *noun* (in an Apple Macintosh system) add in utility that enhances the system; *we have installed several DAs that help us manage our fonts*

desktop *adjective* **(a)** which sits on top of a desk; which can be done at a desk; **desktop computer (system)** = small microcomputer system that can be placed on a desk; **desktop media** = combination of presentation graphics, desktop publishing and multimedia; this is a phrase that was originally used by Apple; **desktop presentations** = presentation graphics, text and charts produced and designed on a desktop personal computer; **desktop publishing (DTP)** = design, layout and printing of documents using special software, a small computer and a printer; **desktop video** = combination of special software and extra hardware that allows a user to edit video on a PC **(b)** (i) (in a GUI) workspace that is a graphical representation of a real-life desktop, with icons for telephone, diary, calculator, filing cabinet; (ii) (in Windows 95) main screen layout with a taskbar running along the bottom edge and icons that represent disk drives, network, and printers; **Desktop background** = pattern or image that is displayed by Windows as a backdrop; **Desktop file** = (in an Apple Macintosh system) system file used to store information about all the files on a disk *or* volume (such as version, date, size, author); **Desktop icons** = icons that are displayed on the Desktop; **Desktop taskbar** = status bar that is normally displayed along the bottom of the screen in Windows 95

COMMENT: a desktop makes it easier for a new user to operate a computer, they do not have to type in commands, instead they can point at icons on the desktop using a mouse

---

desktop publishing or the ability to produce high-quality publications using a minicomputer, essentially boils down to combining words and images on pages

Byte

---

despool *verb* to print out spooled files

despotic network *noun* network synchronized and controlled by one single clock

destination *noun* place to which something is sent *or* to which something is going; location to which a data is sent; **destination object** = (in a drag and drop operation) the object or icon onto which you drop an object; **destination page** = target page within a hyperlink; *when a user clicks on the active object in a hyperlink, the software displays the destination page*

destructive addition *noun* addition operation in which the result is stored in the location of one of the operands used in the sum, so overwriting it

◊ **destructive cursor** *noun* cursor that erases the text as it moves over it; *reading the screen becomes difficult without a destructive cursor;* **destructive read** = read operation in which the stored data is erased as it is retrieved; **destructive readout** = form of storage medium that loses its data after it has been read

detail 1 *noun* small part of a description; **detail file** = file containing records that are to be used to update a master file; **in detail** = giving many particulars; *the catalogue lists all the products in detail;* **detail paper** = thin transparent paper used for layouts and tracing **2** *verb* to list in detail; *the catalogue details the shipping arrangements for customers; the terms of the licence are detailed in the contract*

◊ **detailed** *adjective* in detail; **detailed account** = account which lists every item

detect *verb* to sense something (usually something very slight); *the equipment can detect faint signals from the transducer;* **detected error** = error noticed during a program run, but not corrected; **error detecting code** = coding system that allows errors occurring during transmission to be detected, but is not complex enough to correct the errors

◊ **detection** *noun* process of detecting something; *the detection of the cause of the fault is proving difficult*

◊ **detector** *noun* device which can detect

deterministic *adjective* (result of a process) that depends on the initial state and inputs

develop *verb* to plan and produce; *to develop a new product*

◊ **developer** *noun;* **software developer** = person *or* company which writes software

◊ **development** *noun* planning the production of a new product; **research and development** = investigating new products and techniques; **development software** = suite of programs that help a programmer write, edit, compile and debug new software; **development time** = amount of time required to develop a new product

device *noun* small useful machine *or* piece of equipment; **device address** = location within the memory area that is used by a particular device; the CPU can control the device by placing instructions at this address; **device character control** = device control using various characters *or* special combinations to instruct the device; **device code** = unique identification and selection code for each peripheral; **device control (character)** = special code sent in a transmission to a device to instruct it to perform a special function; **device driver** = program *or* routine used to interface and manage an I/O device *or* peripheral; **device flag** = one bit in a device status word, used to show the state of one device; **device independent** = programming technique that results in a program that is able to run with any peripheral hardware; **device name** = abbreviation that denotes a port or I/O device, such as COM for serial port, PRN for printer port, CON for keyboard and monitor; **device priority** = the importance of a peripheral device assigned by the user *or* central computer which dictates the order in which the CPU will serve an interrupt signal from it; *the master console has a higher device priority than the printers and other terminals;* **device queue** = list of requests from users *or* programs to use a device; **device status word (DSW)** = data word transmitted from the device that contains information about its current status; *this routine checks the device status word and*

will not transmit data if the busy bit is set;
I/O device = peripheral (such as a terminal)
which can be used for inputting or outputting
data to a processor; **output device** = device
(such as a monitor *or* printer) which allows
information to be displayed

> Users in remote locations can
> share ideas on the Liveboard
> through the use of a wireless
> pen-input device and network
> connections.
>
> *Computing*

devise *verb* to plan *or* build a system; *they
devised a cheap method to avoid the problem*

DFD = DATA FLOW DIAGRAM diagram
used to describe the movement of data
through a system

Dhrystone benchmark *noun*
benchmarking system developed to try and
measure and compare the performance of
computers; *see also* BENCHMARK

DHTML = DYNAMIC HYPERTEXT
MARKUP LANGUAGE extension to the
HTML web page formatting language that
allows a designer to add simple processing
functions within a web page which are then
interpreted by a compatible web browser;
DHTML allows a developer to create web
pages that change, provide user feedback and
allow animation (currently, only the new
versions of web browsers support this form of
HTML); *see also* HTML

DIA/DCA = DOCUMENT
INTERCHANGE ARCHITECTURE/
DOCUMENT CONTENT
ARCHITECTURE standard method for the
transmission and storage of documents, text
and video over networks; part of the IBM
SNA range of standards

diagnose *verb* to find the cause and effect
of a fault in hardware or error in software

◊ **diagnosis** *noun* finding of a fault *or*
discovering the cause of a fault; results of
diagnosing faulty hardware or software

diagnostic 1 *noun;* **diagnostic aid** =
hardware *or* software device that helps to find
faults; **diagnostic chip** = chip that contains

circuits to carry out tests on other circuits *or*
chips; **diagnostic message** = message that
appears to explain the type, location and
probable cause of a software error *or*
hardware failure; **diagnostic program** =
software that helps find faults in a computer
system; **diagnostic routine** = routine in a
program which helps to find faults in a
computer system; **diagnostic test** = means of
locating faults in hardware and software by
testing circuits *or* programs; **self-diagnostic** =
computer that runs a series of diagnostic
programs (usually when the computer is
switched on) to ensure that all circuits,
memory and peripherals are working
correctly

> the implementation of on-line
> diagnostic devices that
> measure key observable
> parameters
>
> *Byte*

> to check for any hardware
> problems, a diagnostic disk is
> provided
>
> *Personal Computer World*

diagnostics *noun* functions *or* tests that
help a user find faults in hardware *or*
software; **compiler diagnostics** = function in
a compiler that helps a programmer find
faults in the program code; *thorough
compiler diagnostics make debugging easy;*
error diagnostics = information and system
messages displayed when an error is detected
to help a user debug and correct it

diagram *noun* drawing which shows
something as a plan *or* a map; **flow diagram**
= diagram showing the arrangement of work
processes in a series

◊ **diagrammatic** *adjective;* **in
diagrammatic form** = in the form of a
diagram; *the chart showed the sales pattern
in diagrammatic form*

◊ **diagrammatically** *adverb* using a
diagram; *the chart shows the sales pattern
diagrammatically*

dial *verb* to call a telephone number on a
telephone; *to dial a number; to dial the
computer centre;* **auto-dial** = feature of a
modem that can automatically dial a number

(under the control of a computer); **to dial into** = to call a telephone number, which has a modem and computer at the other end; *with the right access code it is possible to dial into a customer's computer to extract the files needed for the report* (NOTE: GB English is **dialling - dialled,** but US spelling is **dialing - dialed)**

Customers will be able to choose a wide variety of telephony products, from basic auto-dial programs to call-centre applications.
Computing

◊ **dial-in modem** *noun* auto-answer modem that can be called at any time to access a system

◊ **dialup** *or* **dial-up service** *noun* online information service that is accessed by dialling into the central computer

dialect *noun* slight variation of a standard language; *this manufacturer's dialect of BASIC is a little different to the one I'm used to*

Dialer *or* **Phone Dialer** Windows 95 utility which, if you have a modem connected to your PC, will dial telephone numbers for you

dialogue *or* **dialog** *noun* speech *or* speaking to another person; communication between devices such as computers; **dialog box** = on-screen message from a program to the user

DIB = DATA INPUT BUS bus used when transferring data from one section of a computer to another, such as between memory and CPU

dibit *noun* digit made up of two binary bits

dichotomizing search *noun* fast search method for use on ordered lists of data (the search key is compared with the data in the middle of the list and one half is discarded, this is repeated with the half remaining until only one data item remains)

dictionary *noun* (i) book which lists words and meanings; (ii) data management

structure which allows files to be referenced and sorted; *see also* DATA DICTIONARY; (iii) part of a spelling checker program: the list of correctly spelled words against which the program checks a text; *see also* SPELL-CHECKER

DIF file = DATA INTERCHANGE FORMAT de facto standard that defines the way a spreadsheet, its formula and data are stored in a file

differ *verb* not to be the same as something else; *the two products differ considerably - one has an external hard disk, the other has internal hard disk and external magnetic tape drive*

◊ **difference** *noun* way in which two things are not the same; *what is the difference between these two products? differences in price or price differences;* **symmetric difference** = logical function whose output is true if either of the inputs is true, and false if both inputs are the same

◊ **different** *adjective* not the same; *our product range is quite different in design from the Japanese models; we offer ten models each in six different colours*

◊ **differential** *adjective* which shows a difference

diffuse *verb* to move *or* insert something over an area *or* through a substance; *the smoke from the faulty machine rapidly diffused through the building; the chemical was diffused into the substrate*

◊ **diffusion** *noun* means of transferring doping materials into an integrated circuit substrate

digit *noun* symbol *or* character which represents an integer that is smaller than the radix of the number base used; *a phone number with eight digits or an eight-digit phone number; the decimal digit 8; the decimal number system uses the digits 0123456789;* **check digit** = additional digit inserted into transmitted text to monitor and correct errors; **digit place** *or* **position** = position of a digit within a number; *see also* RADIX

digital *adjective* which represents data *or* physical quantities in numerical form (especially using a binary system in computer related devices); **digital camera** = camera that uses a bank of CCD units to capture an image and store it digitally on to a miniature disk *or* in RAM in the camera's body; **digital cassette** = high quality magnetic tape housed in a standard size cassette with write protect tabs, and a standard format leader; **digital circuit** = electronic circuit that operates on digital information providing logical functions *or* switching; **digital clock** = clock which shows the time as a series of digits (such as 12:22:04); **digital compact cassette** (DCC) = magnetic tape in a compact cassette box that is used to store computer data or audio signals in a digital format; **digital computer** = computer which processes data in digital form (that is data represented in discrete digital form) *compare* ANALOG; **digital data** = data represented in (usually binary) numerical form; **digital display** = video display that can only show a fixed number of colours *or* shades of grey; **digital logic** = applying Boolean algebra to hardware circuits; **digital monitor** = monitor that can only show a fixed number of colours or shades of grey; **digital optical recording** (DOR) = recording signals in binary form as small holes in the surface of an optical *or* compact disk which can then be read by laser; **digital output** = computer output in digital form *compare with* ANALOG OUTPUT; **digital plotter** = plotter whose pen position is controllable in discrete steps, so that drawings in the computer can be output graphically; **digital read-out** = data displayed in numerical form, such as numbers on an LCD in a calculator; **digital representation** = data *or* quantities represented using discrete quantities (digits); **digital resolution** = smallest number that can be represented with one digit, the value assigned to the least significant bit of a word *or* number; **digital signal** = electric signal that has only a number of possible states, as opposed to analog signals which are continuously variable; **digital signal level zero (DS-0)** = one single circuit in a high-speed T-1 data transmission line, capable of transmitting information in 8-bit frames at a rate of 8,000 frames per second (equal to 64Kbits/second); **digital signal level one (DS-1)** = standard that defines the way data is formatted and transmitted over a T-1 line; *see* T-1; **digital signal processing** (DSP) = special integrated circuit used to manipulate digital signals; **digital signalling** = control and dialling codes sent down a (telephone line) in digital form; **digital signature** = unique identification code sent by a terminal *or* device in digital form; **digital speech** *see* SPEECH SYNTHESIS; **digital system** = system that deals with digital signals; **digital switching** = operating communications connections and switches only by use of digital signals; **digital to analog converter** *or* **D to A converter (DAC)** = circuit that converts a digital signal to an analog one (the analog signal is proportional to an input binary number); **digital transmission system** = communications achieved by converting analog signals to a digital form then modulating and transmitting this (the signal is then converted back to analog form at the receiver); **digital video interactive (DV-I)** = system that defines how video and audio signals should be compressed and displayed on a computer

Xerox Parc's LCD breakthrough promises the digital equivalent of paper, by producing thin, low-cost flat displays with a 600dpi resolution.

Computing

digitally *adverb* (quantity represented) in digital form; *the machine takes digitally recorded data and generates an image*

digitize *verb* to change analog movement *or* signals into a digital form which can be processed by computers, etc.; *we can digitize your signature to allow it to be printed with any laser printer;* **digitized photograph** = image *or* photograph that has been scanned to produce an analog signal which is then converted to digital form and stored *or* displayed on a computer; **digitizing pad** = sensitive surface that translates the position of a pen into numerical form, so that drawings can be entered into a computer

digitizer *noun* analog to digital converter *or* device which converts an analog movement *or* signal to a digital one which can be understood by a computer

DIL = DUAL-IN-LINE PACKAGE standard layout for integrated circuit packages using two parallel rows of connecting pins along each side

DIM = DOCUMENT IMAGE MANAGEMENT software that allows a user to capture, store and index printed text in a digital form; normally works in conjunction with a scanner and a high-capacity storage media such as a recordable CD-ROM

dimension *noun* measurement of size; *the dimensions of the computer are small enough for it to fit into a case*
◊ **dimensioning** *noun* definition of the size of something (usually an array *or* matrix); *array dimensioning occurs at this line*

diminished radix complement
noun number representation in which each digit of the number is subtracted from one less than the radix; *see also* ONE'S, NINE'S COMPLEMENT

DIMM = DUAL IN-LINE MEMORY MODULE system of arranging RAM memory chips on two sides of a tiny expansion card that can be inserted into a slot on the computer's motherboard to upgrade the main memory; *DIMM cards are used to expand the memory in high-performance computers*

DIN = DEUTSCHE INDUSTRIENORM German industry standards organization; often refers to specification for plugs and sockets

Dingbat *noun* font that contains stars, bullets, symbols, images and drawings in place of characters; *to insert a copyright symbol, use the Dingbat font*

diode *noun* electronic component that allows an electrical current to pass in one direction and not the other; **light-emitting diode (LED)** = semiconductor diode that emits light when a current is applied (used in clock and calculator displays, and as an indicator)

> Sullivan would not reveal the launch power of the diode, except that it was twice that of existing LEDs because of the higher efficiency of electron injection in the part.
> *Electronic Times*

DIP = DUAL-IN-LINE PACKAGE standard layout for integrated circuit packages using two parallel rows of connecting pins along each side

DIR = DIRECTORY (in MS-DOS) system command that displays a list of files stored on a disk

direct 1 *verb* to manage *or* to organize; **directed scan** = file *or* array search method in which a starting point and a direction of scan is provided, either up *or* down from the starting point (an address *or* record number) **2** *adjective* straight *or* with no processing *or* going in a straight way; **direct access** = storage and retrieval of data without the need to read other data first; **direct (access) address** = ABSOLUTE ADDRESS; **direct access storage device (DASD)** = storage medium whose memory locations can be directly read *or* written to; **direct addressing** = method of addressing where the storage location address given in the instruction is the location to be used; **direct cable connection** = utility supplied with Windows 95 that allows you to link two computers together using a serial cable plugged into each serial port; **direct change-over** = switching from one computer to another in one go; **direct code** = binary code which directly operates the CPU, using only absolute addresses and values; **direct coding** = program instructions written in absolute code; **direct connect** = (modem) which plugs straight into the standard square telephone socket; **direct current (DC)** = constant value electric current that flows in one direction; **direct data entry (DDE)** = keying in data directly onto a magnetic disk *or* tape; **direct digital control (DDC)** = machine operated automatically by computer; **direct information access network for Europe**

(DIANE) = services offered over the Euronet network; **direct-insert routine** *or* **subroutine** = routine which can be directly copied (inserted) into a larger routine *or* program without the need for a call instruction; **direct instruction** = program command that contains an operand and the code for the operation to be carried out; **direct memory access (DMA)** = direct, rapid link between a peripheral and a computer's main memory which avoids the use of accessing routines for each item of data required; *direct memory access transfer between the main memory and the second processor;* **direct memory access channel** = high speed data transfer link; **direct mode** = typing in a command which is executed once return is pressed; **direct page register** = register that provides memory page access data when a CPU is carrying out a direct memory access, to allow access to any part of memory; **direct reference address** = virtual address that can only be altered by indexing; **direct transfer** = bit for bit copy of the contents of one register into another register (including any status bits, etc.) **3** *adverb* straight *or* with no third party involved

direction *noun* **(a)** organizing *or* managing; *he took over the direction of a software distribution group* (NOTE: no plural in this meaning) **(b)**; **directions for use** = instructions showing how to use something

directive *noun* programming instruction used to control the language translator, compiler, etc.

> directives are very useful for selecting parts of the code for particular purposes
> *Personal Computer World*

directly *adverb* **(a)** immediately **(b)** straight *or* with no third party involved; *we deal directly with the manufacturer, without using a wholesaler*

DirectSound™ (within Microsoft Windows 95) standard for a programming interface used to allow games software to control sound hardware

Director™ multimedia authoring software developed by Macromedia that uses a grid to allow a user to control elements over time

directory *noun* method of organising the files stored on a disk; a directory contains a group of files or further sub-directories, in Windows 95 and on the Macintosh a directory is now called a folder; **directory services** = method of listing all the users and resources linked to a network in a simple and easy-to-access way so that a user can locate another user by name rather than by a complex network address; *with directory services installed, it's much easier for our users to find and connect to the shared printers; see also* NOVELL NETWARE DIRECTORY SERVICES, X.500; **directory synchronisation** = way of ensuring that the files stored in similar directories on two computers contain the same, up-to-date information; **change directory (CD)** = (in MS-DOS, OS/2 and UNIX) system command to move to a directory; **disk directory** = list of names and information about files in a backing storage device; *the disk directory shows file name, date and time of creation;* **make directory (MD)** = (in MS-DOS and OS/2) system command to create a new directory on the disk; **remove directory (RD)** = (in MS-DOS and OS/2) system command to remove an empty directory from disk; **root directory** = directory at the top of the directory tree structure; **sub-directory** = directory within a directory; *see also* TREE STRUCTURE

> COMMENT: a directory is best imagined as a folder within a drawer of a filing cabinet; the folder can contain files or other folders

dirty bit *noun* flag bit set by memory-resident programs (a utility *or* the operating system) to indicate that they have already been loaded into main memory

disable *verb* to prevent a device *or* function from operating; *he disabled the keyboard to prevent anyone changing the data;* **disable interrupt** = command to the CPU to ignore any interrupt signals

disarm *verb* to prevent an interrupt having any effect; **disarmed state** = state of an interrupt that has been disabled, and cannot accept a signal

disassemble *verb* to translate machine code instructions back into assembly language mnemonics

◊ **disassembler** *noun* software that translates a machine code program back into an assembly language form

disaster dump *noun* program and data dump just before *or* caused by a fatal error *or* system crash

disc *noun* disc refers only to compact disc, magnetic media uses the spelling 'disk'; *see* COMPACT DISC, DISK

discard *verb* to throw out something which is not needed

disclose *verb* to reveal details of something which were supposed to be secret

◊ **disclosure** *noun* act of telling details about something

disconnect *verb* to unplug *or* break a connection between two devices; *do not forget to disconnect the cable before moving the printer*

discrete *adjective* (values *or* events *or* energy *or* data) which occur in small individual units; *the data word is made up of discrete bits;* **discrete cosine transform (DCT)** = algorithm used to encode and compress images

discretionary *adjective* which can be used if wanted *or* not used if not wanted; **discretionary hyphen** *or* **soft hyphen** = hyphen which is inserted to show that a word is broken (as at the end of a line), but which is not present when the word is written normally

discrimination instruction *noun* conditional program instruction that directs control by providing the location of the next instruction to be executed (if a condition is met); *see also* BRANCH, JUMP, CALL

disjunction *noun* logical function that produces a true output if any input is true

◊ **disjunctive search** *noun* search for data items that match at least one of a number of keys

disk *noun* flat circular plate coated with a substance that is capable of being magnetized (data is stored on this by magnetizing selective sections to represent binary digits); **disk access** = operations required to read from or write to a magnetic disk, including device selection, sector and track address, movement of read/write head to the correct location, access location on disk; **disk-based (operating system)** = (operating system) held on floppy *or* hard disk; **disk cartridge** = protective case containing a removable hard disk; **disk controller** = IC *or* circuits used to translate a request for data by the CPU into control signals for the disk drive (including motor control and access arm movement); **disk-controller card** = add-on card that contains all the electronics and connectors to interface a disk drive to a CPU; **disk crash** = fault caused by the read/write head touching the surface of the disk; **disk doctor** = utility that can sometimes repair corrupted data stored on a disk; **disk drive** = device that spins a magnetic disk and controls the position of the read/write head; **disk file** = number of related records *or* data items stored under one name on disk; **disk formatting** = initial setting up of a blank disk with track and sector markers and other control information; **disk index holes** = holes around the hub of a disk that provide rotational information to a disk controller *or* number of holes providing sector location indicators on a hard-sectored disk; **disk map** = display of the organization of data on a disk; **disk mirroring** *or* **duplexing** = data protection system in which all or part of a hard disk is duplicated onto another, separate, disk drive; any changes made to the data on the original drive are duplicated on the mirrored drive; **disk operating system (DOS)** = section of the operating system software that controls disk and file management; **MS disk operating system** *or* **Microsoft DOS (MS-DOS)** = popular DOS for microcomputers; **disk pack** = number of disks on a single hub, each with its own read/write head; **disk sector** = smallest area on a magnetic disk that can be addressed by a computer; **disk storage** = using disks as a backing store; **disk track** = one of a series of (thin) concentric rings on a magnetic disk, which the read/write head accesses and along which data is stored in separate sectors; **disk unit** = disk drive; **backup disk** = disk which contains a copy of the information from other disks, as a security precaution; **fixed disk** = magnetic disk which cannot be removed from the disk drive; **floppy disk** = small disk for storing information which can be removed from a computer; **hard disk** = solid disk which will store a large amount of computer information in a sealed case, and cannot usually be removed from the computer; **optical disk** = disk which contains binary data in the form of small holes which are read by a laser beam (also called WORM - write one, read many - when used on computers, and compact disks and video disks for sound *or* film); **Winchester disk** = hard disk with a large storage capacity sealed in a computer

COMMENT: the disk surface is divided into tracks which can be accessed individually; magnetic tapes cannot be accessed in this way

◊ **diskette** *noun* light, flexible disk that can store data in a magnetic form, used in most personal computers

◊ **diskless (workstation)** *adjective* (workstation) which does not have any disk drives for data storage; *diskless system; they want to create a diskless workstation*

disorderly close-down *noun* system crash that did not provide enough warning to carry out an orderly close-down

dispatch *or* **despatch** *noun* action of sending material *or* information *or* messages to a location

dispersion *noun* logical function whose output is false if all inputs are true, and true if any input is false

displacement *noun* offset used in an indexed address

display 1 *noun* device on which information *or* images can be presented visually; **composite display** = video display unit that accepts a single composite video signal and can display an infinite number of colours *or* shades of grey; **digital display** = video display unit that can only show a fixed number of colours *or* shades of grey; **display adapter** = device which allows information in a computer to be displayed on a CRT (the adapter interfaces with both the computer and CRT); **display attribute** = variable which defines the shape *or* size *or* colour of text *or* graphics displayed; **display character** = graphical symbol which appears as a printed *or* displayed item, such as one of the letters of the alphabet *or* a number; **display character generator** = ROM that provides the display circuits with a pattern of dots which form the character; **display colour** = colour of characters in a (videotext) display system; **display controller** = device that accepts character *or* graphics codes and instructions, and converts them into dot-matrix patterns that are displayed on a screen; **display element** = (in computer graphics) any component of an image; **display format** = number of characters that can be displayed on a screen, given as row and column lengths; **display highlights** = emphasis of certain words *or* paragraphs by changing character display colour; **display line** = horizontal printing positions for characters in a line of text; **display mode** = way of referring to the character set to be used, usually graphics *or* alphanumerics; **Display PostScript** = an extension of PostScript that allows PostScript commands to be interpreted and displayed on screen so that a user can see exactly what will appear on the printer *see also* TRUTYPE; **display processor** = processor that changes data to a format suitable for a display controller; **display register** = register that contains character *or* control *or* graphical data that is to be displayed; **display resolution** = number of pixels per unit area that a display can clearly show; **display screen** = the physical part of a Visual Display Unit *or* terminal *or* monitor, which allows the user to see characters *or* graphics (usually a Cathode Ray Tube, but sometimes LCD *or* LED displays are used); **display scrolling** =

movement of a screenful of information up or down one line or pixel at a time; **display space** = memory *or* amount of screen available to show graphics *or* text; **display unit** = computer terminal *or* piece of equipment that is capable of showing data *or* information, usually by means of CRT; **gas discharge** *or* **plasma** *or* **electroluminescent display** = flat lightweight display screen that is made up of two flat pieces of glass covered with a grid of conductors, separated by a thin layer of gas which luminesces when a point of the grid is selected by two electrical signals; *see also* VISUAL DISPLAY UNIT **2** *verb* to show information; *the customer's details were displayed on the screen; by keying HELP, the screen will display the options available to the user*

Barco Chromatics is to supply colour display monitors to the IBM/Siemens Plessey consortium, which is installing the New En Route Centre for air-traffic control.

Computing

the review machine also came with a monochrome display card plugged into one of the expansion slots

Personal Computer World

dissolve *verb* special effect that is used in presentation graphics software or multimedia to fade out one image and fade in the next

distance vector protocols *noun* information about the different routes over a wide area network that can be used by a router to find the shortest and fastest route to send information

distant *adjective* which is located some way away; *the distant printers are connected with cables*

distinguish *verb* to tell the difference between two things; *the OCR has difficulty in distinguishing certain characters*

distort *verb* to introduce unwanted differences between a signal input and output from a device

◊ **distortion** *noun* unwanted differences in a signal before and after it has passed through a piece of equipment

distribute *verb* **(a)** to send out data *or* information to users in a network *or* system; **distributed adaptive routing** = directing messages in a packet network switching system by an exchange of information between nodes; **distributed database system** = database system where the data is stored on several different computers but can be searched as if it is one single location; **distributed data processing (DDP)** = operations to derive information from data which is kept in different places; **distributed file system** = system that uses files stored in more than one location *or* backing store but are processed at a central point; **distributed intelligence** = decentralized system in which a number of small micros *or* mini-computers carry out a set of fixed tasks (rather than using one large computer); **distributed network** = network in which each node can operate as a server storing files or working as a print server; **distributed (data) processing** = system of processing in a large organization with many small computers at different workstations instead of one central computer; **distributed system** = computer system which uses more than one processor in different locations, all connected to a central computer

CORBA sets out a standard for how objects in applications, repositories or class libraries should make requests and receive responses across a distributed computing network.

Computing

◊ **distribution** *noun* act of sending information out, especially via a network; **distribution network;** *see* LAN, WAN

dither *verb* to create a curve or line that looks smoother by adding shaded pixels beside the pixels that make up the image; **dithered colour** = colour that is made up of a pattern of different coloured pixels

divide *verb* **(a) to divide a number by four** = to find out how many fours can be contained in the other number; *twenty-one divided by three gives seven* **(b)** to cut *or* to split into parts; *in the hyphenation program, long words are automatically divided at the end of lines*

division *noun* act of dividing

dividend *noun* operand that is divided by a divisor in a division operation

COMMENT: the dividend is divided by the divisor to form the quotient and a remainder

divisor *noun* operand used to divide a dividend in a division operation

DLL = DYNAMIC LINK LIBRARY (in Microsoft Windows and OS/2) library of utility programs that can be called from a main program; *the word-processor calls a spell-check program that is stored as a DLL;* **DLL file** = file containing a library of routines that can be used by another program

DMA = DIRECT MEMORY ACCESS direct rapid link between a peripheral and a computer's main memory, which avoids accessing routines for each item of data read; **DMA controller** = interface IC that controls high-speed data transfer between a high-speed peripheral and main memory, usually the controller will also halt *or* cycle steal from the CPU; **DMA cycle stealing** = CPU allowing the DMA controller to send data over the bus during clock cycles when it performs internal *or* NOP instructions

A 32-bit DMA controller, 16-bit video I/O ports and I/O filters complete the chip.

Computing

DML = DATA MANIPULATION LANGUAGE

DNS = DOMAIN NAME SYSTEM distributed database used in an Internet system to map names to addresses, for example you can use the name 'www.pcp.co.uk' to locate the Peter Collin Publishing web site rather than a numerical network address (called the IP address)

do-nothing (instruction) *noun* programming instruction that does not carry out any action (except increasing the program counter to the next instruction address

document 1 *noun* (i) piece of paper with writing on it; (ii) file containing text created with a word-processor; **document assembly** *or* **document merge** = creating a new file by combining two or more sections *or* complete documents; **document image management (DIM)** = software that allows a user to capture, store and index printed text in a digital form; normally works in conjunction with a scanner and a high-capacity storage media such as a recordable CD-ROM; **document image processing (DIP)** = process of scanning paper documents, performing OCR on the contents and storing this on disk so that it can be searched for; **document interchange architecture/document content architecture (DIA/DCA)** = standard method for the transmission and storage of documents, text and video over networks; part of the IBM SNA range of standards; **document processing** = processing of documents (such as invoices) by a computer; **document reader** = device which converts written *or* typed information to a form that a computer can understand and process; **document recovery** = program which allows a document which has been accidentally deleted to be recovered **2** *verb* to write a description of a process

◊ **documentation** *noun* **(a)** all documents referring to something; *please send all documentation concerning the product* **(b)** information, notes and diagrams that describe the function, use and operation of a piece of hardware *or* software

dollar sign *noun* printed *or* written character ($) used in some languages to identify a variable as a string type

domain *noun* area *or* group of nodes in a network; **domain name system (DNS)** = distributed database used in an Internet system to map names to addresses, for example you can use the name 'www.pcp.co.uk' to locate the Peter Collin

Publishing web site rather than a numerical network address (called the IP address); **in the public domain** = (information *or* program) which belongs to and is available to the public; **program which is in the public domain** = program which is not copyrighted

dongle *noun* coded circuit *or* chip that has to be present in a system before a piece of copyright software will run

dope *verb* to introduce a dopant into a substance

◊ **dopant** *noun* chemical substance that is diffused *or* implanted onto the substrate of a chip during manufacture, to provide it with n- or p-type properties

◊ **doped** *adjective* (chip) which has had a dopant added

◊ **doping** *noun* adding of dopant to a chip

DOR = DIGITAL OPTICAL READING recording signals in binary form as small holes in the surface of an optical *or* compact disk which can then be read by laser

DOS = DISK OPERATING SYSTEM section of the operating system software, that controls the disk and file access; *boot up the DOS after you switch on the PC;* **DOS prompt** = indicator that shows that DOS is ready to accept a command typed in at the keyboard; **MS-DOS** = operating system developed by Microsoft for the IBM PC; **DR-DOS** = operating system developed by Digital Research for the IBM PC

dot *noun* small round spot; **dot addressable** = display adapter that allows software to control each pixel (or dot) on the display; **dot command** = method of writing instructions with a full stop followed by the command, used mainly for embedded commands in word-processor systems; **dots per inch** *or* **d.p.i.** *or* **dpi** = standard method used to describe the resolution capabilities of a page printer *or* scanner; *some laser printers offer high resolution printing: 400 dpi;* **dot pitch** = spacing between two adjacent pixels displayed on a monitor; **dot prompt** = (in dBASE programming language) command prompt displayed as a single dot on screen

◊ **dot matrix** *noun* method of forming characters by use of dots inside a rectangular matrix

◊ **dot-matrix printer** *noun* printer in which the characters are made up by a series of closely spaced dots (it produces a page line by line; a dot-matrix printer can be used either for printing using a ribbon *or* for thermal *or* electrostatic printing)

Star predicts that 500,000 customers will buy a dot matrix printer in the UK in the next 12 months.

Computing

the characters are formed from an array of dots like in a dot-matrix printer, except that much higher resolution is used

Practical Computing

double *adjective* twice; twice as large; twice the size; **double buffering** = use of two buffers, allowing one to be read while the other is being written to; **double-click** = to click twice, rapidly, on a mouse button to start an action; *move the pointer to the icon then start the program with a double-click;* **double density** = system to double the storage capacity of a disk drive by doubling the number of bits which can be put on the disk surface; **double-density disk** = disk that can store two bits of data per unit area, compared to a standard disk; **double ended queue (deque)** = queue in which new items can be added to either end; **double-length** *or* **double precision arithmetic** = use of two data words to store a number, providing greater precision; **double-sided disk** = disk which can store information on both sides; **double-sided disk drive** = disk drive which can access data on double-sided disks; **double-sided printed circuit board** = circuit board with conducting tracks on both sides; **double-speed drive** = refers to a CD-ROM drive that spins the disc at twice the speed of a normal drive; **double word** = two bytes of data handled as one word, often used for address data

◊ **DoubleSpace** software program that is part of MS-DOS 6 and is used to provide disk compression

doublet *or* **dyad** *noun* word made up of two bits

down *adverb (of computers or programs)* not working; *the computer system went down twice during the afternoon;* **down time** = period of time during which a computer system is not working *or* usable; (NOTE: opposite is **up**)

downsize *verb* to move a company from a computer system based around a central mainframe computer to a networked environment (usually using PCs as workstations) in which the workstations are intelligent; *downsizing is more cost effective and gives more processing power to the end-user*

download *verb* (i) to load a program *or* section of data from a remote computer via a telephone line; (ii) to load data from a CPU to a small computer; (iii) to send printer font data stored on a disk to a printer (where it will be stored in temporary memory *or* RAM); *there is no charge for downloading public domain software from the BBS*

```
The cards will also download
the latest version of the
network drivers from the
server.
```
Computing

◊ **downloadable** *adjective* which can be downloaded; **downloadable fonts** = fonts *or* typefaces stored on a disk, which can be downloaded *or* sent to a printer and stored in temporary memory *or* RAM

downward *adjective* towards a lower position; **downward compatibility** = ability of a complex computer system to work with a simple computer; *the mainframe is downward compatible with the micro*

dp *or* **DP** = DATA PROCESSING operating on data to produce useful information *or* to sort and organize data files

DPA = DEMAND PROTOCOL ARCHITECTURE technique of loading protocol stacks in memory only if they are required for a particular session; *see also* PROTOCOL STACK

d.p.i. *or* **dpi** = DOTS PER INCH standard method used to describe the resolution capabilities of a dot-matrix *or* laser printer *or* scanner; *a 300 d.p.i. black and white A4 monitor; a 300 dpi image scanner*

```
COMMENT: 300 d.p.i. is still the normal
industry standard for a laser printer,
however 600 d.p.i resolution laser
```

```
printers are common in offices and new
technology has made 1200 d.p.i printers
affordable
```

DPM = DATA PROCESSING MANAGER

draft 1 *noun* rough copy of a document before errors have been corrected; **draft printing** = low quality, high speed printing **2** *verb* to make a rough copy *or* drawing; *he drafted out the details of the program on a piece of paper*

drag *verb* to move (a mouse) while holding the button down, so moving an image or icon on screen; *you can enlarge a frame by clicking inside its border and dragging to the position wanted;* **drag and drop** = to drag a section of text *or* icon *or* object onto another program icon which starts this program and inserts the data; *drag and drop the document icon onto the word-processor icon and the system will start the program and load the document;* **drag image** = the cursor, icon or outline image that is displayed when you drag an object across the screen

```
press the mouse button and drag
the mouse: this produces a
dotted rectangle on the screen;
you can easily enlarge the
frame by dragging from any of
the eight black rectangles
round the border, showing that
it is selected
```
Desktop Publishing

DRAM = DYNAMIC RANDOM ACCESS MEMORY

```
cheap bulk memory systems are
always built from DRAMs
```
Electronics & Power

draw direct *noun* process of drawing an object directly to the screen rather than to an off-screen memory buffer

drawing program *noun* software that allows the user to draw and design on screen

drawing tools *noun* range of functions in a paint program that allows the user to draw; normally displayed as icons in a toolbar, the drawing tools might include a circle-draw, line-draw and freehand drawing tools

DR-DOS operating system for the IBM PC developed by Digital Research

drive 1 *noun* part of a computer which operates a tape *or* disk; **drive array** = multiple hard disk drives linked together with an intelligent controller that uses the drives to store multiple copies of the data on each drive for reliability or parts of each data on each drive for speed; **disk drive** = device which spins a magnetic disk and controls the position of the read/write head; **drive letter** *or* **designator** = letter that denotes the disk drive currently being used; A and B are normally floppy disks, C is normally the hard disk in a personal computer; **tape drive** = mechanism that carries magnetic tape over the drive heads **2** *verb* to make a tape *or* disk work; *the disk is driven by a motor*

driven *adjective* operated by something; **control driven** = (computer architecture) where instructions are executed once a control sequence has been received; **event-driven** = (computer program *or* process) where each step of the execution relies on external actions

driver *or* **device driver** *or* **device handler** *noun* program *or* routine used to interface and manage an input/output device *or* other peripheral; **printer driver** = dedicated software that controls and formats users' commands ready for a printer

DRO = DESTRUCTIVE READOUT form of storage medium that loses its data after it has been read

drop *noun* **drop dead halt** *or* **dead halt** = program instruction from the user *or* an error

that causes the program to stop without allowing recovery; **drop in** = small piece of dirt that is on a disk *or* tape surface, which does not allow data to be recorded on that section; **drop out** = failure of a small piece of tape *or* disk to be correctly magnetized for the accurate storage of data

drop cable *noun* section of cable that links an adapter fitted in a workstation to the main network cable (sometimes to a transceiver or T-connector in the main network cable)

drop-down list box *noun* list of options for an entry that appears when you move the cursor to the entry field

drop-down menu *noun* menu that appears below a menu title when it is selected

drum *noun* early type of magnetic computer storage; **magnetic drum** = cylindrical magnetic storage device; **drum plotter** = computer output device that consists of a movable pen and a piece of paper around a drum that can be rotated, creating patterns and text when both are moved in various ways

dry cell (battery) *noun* battery that cannot be recharged *compare with* RECHARGEABLE BATTERY

dry contact *noun* faulty electrical connection, often causing an intermittent fault

dry run *noun* running a program with test data to check everything works

DS-0 *see* DIGITAL SIGNAL LEVEL ZERO

DS-1 *see* DIGITAL SIGNAL LEVEL ONE

DSP = DIGITAL SIGNAL PROCESSING special integrated circuit used to manipulate digital signals

DSR = DATA SET READY signal from a device that it is ready to accept data, this signal occurs after a DTR signal is received

D-SUB connector *noun* (video) connector commonly used on PC monitors to carry all the video signals in one cable

DSW = DEVICE STATUS WORD data word transmitted from a device that contains information about its current status

DTE = DATA TERMINAL EQUIPMENT device at which a communications path starts *or* finishes

DTMF = DUAL TONE MULTI-FREQUENCY method of dialling in a telephone system in which each number on the telephone handset generates a tone *compare with* PULSE DIALLING

DTP = DESKTOP PUBLISHING the design, layout and printing of documents using special software, a desktop computer and a printer

DTR = DATA TERMINAL READY signal from a device that indicates that it is ready to send data

D-type connector *noun* connector that is shaped like an elongated letter D, which prevents the connector being plugged in upside down; *the serial port on a PC uses a 9-pin D-type connector; the video D-type connector has 25 pins*

dual *adjective* using two *or* a pair; **dual attachment** *or* **attached station (DAS)** = (in an FDDI system) station that connects to both rings in an FDDI network, normally used to provide fault tolerance; **dual channel** = two separate audio recording paths, as found in stereo equipment; **dual clocking** = multiplexed data, each set of data is available and valid on a different clock pulse *or* edge; **dual column** = two separate parallel lists of information; **dual homing** = (in an FDDI system) method of arranging cables so that there are two separate routes between servers in case of a fault; **dual in-line memory module (DIMM)** = system of arranging RAM memory chips on two sides of a tiny expansion card that can be inserted into a slot on the computer's motherboard to upgrade the main memory; *DIMM cards are used to expand the memory in high-performance*

computers; **dual-in-line package (DIL** *or* **DIP)** = standard layout for integrated circuit packages using two parallel rows of connecting pins along each edge; **dual port memory** = memory with two sets of data and memory lines to allow communications between CPUs; **dual processor** = computer system with two processors for faster program execution; **dual-scan display** = colour LCD screen that updates the image on screen in two passes *compare with* TFT; **dual systems** = two computer systems, working in parallel on the same data, with the same instructions, to ensure high reliability; **dual tone multi-frequency (DTMF)** = method of dialling in a telephone system in which each number on the telephone handset generates two tones; each row and column of the telephone number grid generates a different tone, so each number will send one tone for the corresponding column and another for the row - if you press number '5' it will send the tone for row two and for column two *compare with* PULSE DIALLING

duct *noun* pipe containing cables, providing a tidy and protective surrounding for a group of cables

dumb terminal *noun* peripheral that can only transmit and receive data from a computer, but is not capable of processing data; *compare* INTELLIGENT TERMINAL

dummy *noun* imitation product to test the reaction of potential customers to its design; **dummy instruction** = instruction in a program that is only there to satisfy language syntax *or* to make up a block length; **dummy variable** = variable set up to satisfy the syntax of a language, but which is replaced when the program is executed

dump 1 *noun* (i) data which has been copied from one device to another for storage; (ii) transferring of data to a disk for storage; (iii) *US* printout of the contents of all *or* selected data in memory; **binary dump** = sections of memory dumped onto another medium *or* printed out in binary form; **change dump** = printout of all the locations whose contents have been changed during a program run; **dump and restart** = software that will stop a program execution, dump any relevant data or program status then restart the program; **dump point** = point in a program where the program and its data are saved onto backing store to minimize the effects of any future faults; **screen dump** = outputting the text *or* graphics displayed on a screen to a printer 2 *verb* to move data from one device *or* storage area to another; *the account results were dumped to the backup disk*

duodecimal number system *noun* number system with a radix of twelve

duplex *noun* simultaneous transmission of two signals on one line; **duplex circuit** = electronic circuit used to transmit data in two directions simultaneously; **duplex computer** = two identical computer systems used in an on-line application, with one used as a backup in case of failure of the other; **duplex operation** = transmission of data in two directions simultaneously; *see also* HALF-DUPLEX, FULL DUPLEX, SIMPLEX

durable *adjective* which will not be destroyed easily; *durable cartridge*

duration *noun* length of time for which something lasts

dustcover *noun* protective cover for a machine

duty-rated *adjective* maximum number of operations which a device can perform in a set time to a certain specification

---

the laser printer can provide
letter-quality print on
ordinary cut-sheet paper and is
duty-rated at up to 3,000 pages
per month

Minicomputer News

DVD = DIGITAL VERSATILE DISC *or* DIGITAL VIDEODISC new development that provides a way of storing over 17Gb of data onto a CD-ROM type disc; **DVD-Recordable (DVD-R)** = DVD disc drive that allows a user to write data once on to a DVD disc; **DVD-RAM** = DVD disc drive that allows a user to write, erase and rewrite

data on to a DVD disc; **DVD-ROM** = DVD disc drive that can read a DVD disc and provides data transfer rates equal to a standard nine-times CD-ROM

DV-I = DIGITAL VIDEO INTERACTIVE system that defines how video and audio signals should be compressed and displayed on a computer

DVORAK keyboard *noun* keyboard layout that is more efficient to use than a normal QWERTY keyboard layout

DX suffix after an Intel processor model number that signifies that the processor has a floating-point arithmetic unit, a 32-bit data path and a built-in cache

dyadic operation *noun* binary operation using two binary operands

dye-polymer recording *noun* (in optical disks) recording method which creates minute changes in a thin layer of dye imbedded in the plastic optical disk; dye-polymer recording has one big advantage - that the data stored on the optical disk using this method can be erased

◊ **dye-sublimation printer** *noun* high-quality colour printer that produces images by squirting tiny drops of coloured ink onto paper; *the new dye-sublimation printer can produce colour images at a resolution of 300dpi*

dynamic *adjective* referring to data which can change with time; **dynamic allocation** = system where resources are allocated during a program run, rather than being determined in advance; **dynamic buffer** = buffer whose size varies with demand; **dynamic data structure** = structure of a data management system which can be changed *or* adapted; **dynamic dump** = dump that is carried out periodically during a program run; **dynamic memory** *or* **dynamic RAM** = random access memory that requires its contents to be updated regularly; **dynamic relocation (program)** = program that is moved from one section of memory to another during its run-time without affecting it *or* its data; **dynamic routing** = process of selecting the shortest or most reliable path for data through exchanges at the time of the connection; **dynamic stop** = stop in a process where the system tells the user that some action must be taken before the processing will continue; **dynamic storage allocation** = to allocate memory to a program when it needs it rather than reserving a block before it has run; **dynamically redefinable character set** = computer *or* videotext character set that can be changed when required; **dynamic subroutine** = subroutine whose function must be defined each time it is called; *compare* STATIC; **dynamic update** = a display (such as a graph) updated in real time as new data arrives

dynamic data exchange (DDE)

noun (in Microsoft Windows and OS/2) method in which two active programs can exchange data; one program asks the operating system to create a link between the two programs

dynamic hypertext markup language *see* DHTML

dynamic link library (DLL) (in Microsoft Windows and OS/2) library of utility programs that can be called from a main program; *the word-processor calls a spell-check program that is stored as a DLL*

dynamic random access memory *see* DRAM

Ee

E hexadecimal number equivalent to decimal number 14

E-1 (in Europe) high-speed telecommunications line that can carry data at 2.048Mbits/second and is normally divided into hundreds of channels that carry information at a lower transmission rate but are more convenient for customers (NOTE: the US equivalent is called T-1)

e-mail = ELECTRONIC MAIL system of sending messages to and receiving messages from other users on a network; *see also* MHS, MIME, POP3, SMTP

EAPROM = ELECTRICALLY ALTERABLE PROGRAMMABLE READ-ONLY MEMORY version of EAROM which can be programmed

early token release *noun* (in a Token-Ring or FDDI network) system that allows two tokens to be present on a ring network, useful when traffic is very busy

EAROM = ELECTRICALLY ALTERABLE READ-ONLY MEMORY

earth 1 *noun* connection in a circuit representing zero potential; *all loose wires should be tied to earth;* **earth wire** = connecting wire between an electrical device and the earth, representing zero potential **2** *verb* to connect an electrical device to the earth; *all appliances must be earthed* (NOTE: US English is **ground**)

easy-to-use *adjective* that is simple to understand and operate

EBCDIC = EXTENDED BINARY CODED DECIMAL INTERCHANGE CODE eight bit binary character coding system

EBNF = EXTENDED BACKUS-NAUR FORM more flexible way of defining the syntax of a language; *see also* BNF

EBR = ELECTRON BEAM RECORDING recording the output from a computer directly onto microfilm using an electron beam

echo 1 *noun* return of a signal back to the source from which it was transmitted; **echo cancellation** = (in high speed modems) technique used to remove echo signals from the line; **echo check** = each character received at a terminal is returned to the transmitter and checked to ensure accurate data transmission **2** *verb* to return a received signal along the same transmission path

ECL = EMITTER COUPLED LOGIC high-speed logic circuit design using the emitters of the transistors as output connections to other stages

ECMA = EUROPEAN COMPUTER MANUFACTURERS ASSOCIATION; **ECMA symbols** = standard set of symbols used to draw flowcharts

ECP = ENHANCED COMMUNICATION PORT system developed by Microsoft to improve the performance and functionality of the parallel printer port

EDAC = ERROR DETECTION AND CORRECTION forward error correction system for data communications

edge *noun* side of a flat object *or* signal *or* clock pulse; **edge board** *or* **card** = printed circuit board that has a series of contact strips along one edge allowing it to be inserted into an edge connector; **edge connector** = long connector with a slot containing metal contacts to allow it to make electrical contact with an edge card; **edge detection** = algorithm and routines used in image recognition to define the edges of an object; **edge notched card** = paper card which has punched holes along an edge to represent data; **edge-triggered** = process *or* circuit which is clocked *or* synchronized by the changing level (edge) of a clock signal rather than the level itself

Connections to the target board are made via IC test clips or the edge connector.

Electronics Today

EDI = ELECTRONIC DATA INTERCHANGE system of sending orders, paying invoices or transferring company information over a network *or* telephone line using an electronic mail system; often used to send instructions to pay money direct from one company to another, or from one bank to a company

edit *verb* to change, correct and modify text *or* programs; **edit commands** = sequence of characters or keys that must be pressed to accomplish a function in an editor; **edit key** = key which starts a function that makes an editor easier to use; *there are several special edit keys - this one will re-format the text;* **edit window** = area of the screen in which the user can display and edit text *or* graphics; **editing run** = processing carried out to check that new data meets certain requirements before actually analysing the data and its information content; **editing terms** = command words and instruction sequences used when editing; **linkage editing** = combining separate programs together, and standardizing the calls and references within them

◊ **editor** *or* **editor program** software that allows the user to select sections of a file and alter, delete or add to them; **line editor** = software in which only one line of a source program can be edited at a time; **text editor** = piece of software used to enter and correct text *or* modify programs under development

The Smartbook authoring system is a software product that integrates text and fractally compressed images, using any wordprocessor line editor.

Computing

while it has many formatting facilities, it does not include an editor with which to create the template for the report

Personal Computer World

EDLIN (in MS-DOS) system utility that allows a user to make changes to a file on a line-by-line basis

EDO memory = EXTENDED DATA OUTPUT MEMORY memory technology that provides better performance by being able to find and read data from a memory location in one operation; it can also store the last piece of data that was saved to memory in a cache ready to be read back from memory

EDP = ELECTRONIC DATA PROCESSING data processing using computers and electronic devices; **EDP capability** = word-processor able to carry out certain data processing functions; (NOTE: **EDP** is more common in US English)

EDS = EXCHANGEABLE DISK STORAGE disk drive using removable disk pack (as opposed to a fixed disk)

edu *suffix* at the end of an internet domain name this indicates that the organisation is an educational institute rather than a commercial company

EEMS = ENHANCED EXPANDED MEMORY SYSTEM (in an IBM PC) development of EMS; standard method of expanding the main memory fitted into a PC; *see also* EMS

EEPROM = ELECTRICALLY ERASABLE PROGRAMMABLE READ-ONLY MEMORY

conventional EEPROM requires two transistors to store each bit of data

Electronics & Power

EEROM = ELECTRICALLY ERASABLE READ-ONLY MEMORY

effective *adjective* which can be used to produce a certain result; **effective address** = address resulting from the modification of an address; **effective instruction** = the resulting instruction executed after the modification of an original instruction; **effective search speed** = rate of finding a particular section of information from a storage device; **effective throughput** = average throughput of a processor

efficiency *noun* working well; *he is doubtful about the efficiency of the new networking system*

efficient *adjective* which works well; *the program is highly efficient at sorting files*

◊ **efficiently** *adverb* in an efficient way; *the word-processing package has produced a series of labelled letters very efficiently*

EFT = ELECTRONIC FUNDS TRANSFER (SYSTEM) system where computers are used to transmit money to and from banks

◊ **EFTPOS** = ELECTRONIC FUNDS TRANSFER POINT-OF-SALE terminal at a POS that is linked to a central computer which automatically transfers money from the customer's account to the shop's

```
Alphameric  has  extended  its
range  specifically  for  the
hospitality  market  and  has
developed  an  eftpos  package
which  allows  most  credit  and
debit  cards  to  be  processed.
```
Computing

EGA = ENHANCED GRAPHICS ADAPTER (in an IBM PC) popular standard for high-resolution colour display adapter; *see also* CGA, VGA

```
although  the  video  BIOS
services  are  enhanced  by  adding
an  EGA  card,  the  DOS  functions
are  not
```
.EXE

EIA = ELECTRONICS INDUSTRY ASSOCIATION; **EIA interface** = standard

defining interface signals, transmission rate and power usually used to connect terminals to modems

EIDE = EXTENDED INTEGRATED DRIVE ELECTRONICS enhanced IDE specification that improves the performance and data transfer rates to and from a hard disk drive

eight-bit (system) *noun* referring to an (old) small, low cost, low power home computer in which the CPU can process eight-bit words; **eight-bit byte** *or* **octet** = byte made up of eight binary digits; *compare* SIXTEEN, THIRTY-TWO BIT

◊ **eight-inch disk** *noun* high-capacity floppy disk which is eight inches in diameter; **eight-inch drive** = disk drive for a eight-inch disk

◊ **eighty-column screen** *noun* screen that can display eighty characters horizontally

◊ **eighty-track disk** *noun* disk formatted to contain eighty tracks

EIS = EXECUTIVE INFORMATION SYSTEM easy-to-use software providing information to a manager or executive about his company; *the EIS software is very easy to use; with this EIS software, we can see how every part of the company performs*

EISA = ELECTRONICS INDUSTRY STANDARDS ASSOCIATION group of PC manufacturers who formed an association to promote a 32-bit expansion bus standard as a rival to the MCA bus standard from IBM

```
COMMENT: the EISA expansion bus
standard is backwards compatible with
the older ISA standard of expansion
cards, but also features 32-bit data path
and allows bus mastering.
```

either-or operation *noun* logical function that produces a true output if any input is true

◊ **either-way operation** *noun* data transmission in one direction at a time over a bi-directional channel

elapsed time *noun* time taken by the user to carry out a task on a computer

elastic banding *noun* method of defining the limits of an image on a computer screen by stretching a boundary around it

◊ **elastic buffer** *noun* buffer size that changes according to demand

electric *adjective* worked by electricity; **electric current** = mass movement of electric charge in a conductor; **electric charge** = a number of atoms that are charged (due to excess *or* deficiency of electrons)

◊ **electrical** *adjective* referring to electricity; *the engineers are trying to repair an electrical fault*

◊ **electrically** *adverb* referring to electricity; *an electrically-powered motor;* **electrically alterable, programmable read-only memory (EAPROM)** = version of EAROM that can be programmed; **electrically alterable read-only memory (EAROM)** = read-only memory chip whose contents can be programmed by applying a certain voltage to a write pin, and can be erased by light *or* a reverse voltage; **electrically erasable programmable read-only memory (EEPROM)** = ROM storage chip which can be programmed and erased using an electrical signal; **electrically erasable read-only memory (EEROM)** EAROM memory chip whose contents can be programmed by applying a certain voltage to a write pin, and can be erased by light *or* a reverse voltage

electricity *noun* electric current used to provide light *or* heat *or* power; *the electricity was cut off, and the computers crashed; electricity prices are an important factor in the production costs*

electrographic printer *noun* *see* ELECTROSTATIC PRINTER

electroluminescence *noun* light emitted from a phosphor dot when it is struck by an electron *or* charged particle

◊ **electroluminescing** *adjective* (object) which is emitting light due to electroluminescence

◊ **electroluminescent** *adjective* capable of emitting light due to electroluminescence; *the screen coating is electroluminescent;* **electroluminescent display** = flat, lightweight display screen made up of two pieces of glass covered with a grid of conductors, separated by a thin layer of gas which luminesces when a point of the grid is selected by two electric signals

electromagnetic *adjective* generating a magnetic field *or* magnetic effect when supplied with electrical power; **electromagnetic interference** = corruption of data due to nearby electrically generated magnetic fields

electron beam *noun* narrow, focussed stream of electrons moving at high speed in the same direction (often in a vacuum); *the electron beam draws the image on the inside of a CRT screen*

◊ **electron beam recording (EBR)** *noun* recording the output from a computer directly onto microfilm using an electron beam

◊ **electron gun** *noun* part of a CRT that produces a beam of electrons

electronic *adjective* referring to something which is controlled by *or* controls electron flow; **electronic blackboard** = means of transmitting handwritten text and diagrams over a telephone line; **electronic book** = term that describes a multimedia title; **electronic data interchange (EDI)** = system of sending orders, paying invoices or transferring company information over a network *or* telephone line using an electronic mail system; often used to send instructions to pay money direct from one company to another, or from one bank to a company; **electronic data processing (EDP)** = data processing using computers and electronic devices; **electronic data processing capability** = ability of a word processor to carry out certain data processing functions; **electronic digital computer** = digital computer constructed with electronic components (the basic form uses a CPU, main memory, backing storage and input/output devices; these are all implemented with electronic components and integrated circuits); **electronic engineer** = person who specializes in work on electronic devices; **electronic filing** = system of storage of documents which can be easily retrieved; **electronic funds transfer (EFT)** = using a computer to transfer money to and from banks; **electronic funds transfer point of sale (EFTPOS)** = terminal at a POS linked to a central computer which automatically transfers money from the customer's account to the shop's account; **electronic keyboard** = keyboard that generates characters electronically in response to a switch making contact when pressed, rather than by mechanical means; **electronic mail** *or* **email** = system of sending messages to and receiving messages from other users on a network; **electronic mailbox** = system for storing messages sent by electronic mail until the person to whom they were sent is ready to read them; *when I log onto the network, I always check my electronic mailbox for new messages;* **electronic pen** *or* **stylus** *or* **wand** = light pen *or* wand; stylus used to draw on a graphics tablet; **electronic point-of-sale (EPOS)** = system that uses a computer terminal at a point-of-sale site for electronic funds transfer *or* stock control as well as product identification, etc.; **electronic publishing** = (i) use of desktop publishing packages and laser printers to produce printed matter; (ii) using computers to write and display information, such as viewdata; **electronic pulse** = short voltage pulse; **electronic shopping** = system of shopping from the home, using computerized catalogues and paying by credit card, all by means of a home computer terminal; **electronic smog** = excessive stray electromagnetic fields and static electricity generated by large numbers of electronic equipment (this can damage equipment *or* a person's health); **electronic traffic** = data transmitted in the form of electronic pulses

---

electronic mail is a system
which allows computer users to
send information to each other
via a central computer
Which PC?

---

electronic publishing will be
used for printing on paper, but
it can be applied equally to
data storage on a database,
transmission via
telecommunications or for use
with visual presentation media
such as AV slides or television
Electronic Publishing & Print Show

◊ **electronically** *adverb* referring to operations using electronic methods; *the text is electronically transmitted to an outside typesetter*

◊ **electronics** *noun* science of applying the study of electrons and their properties to manufactured products, such as components, computers, calculators or telephones; *the electronics industry; an electronics specialist;* **electronics industry association interface (EIA)** = standard defining interface signals, transmission rate and power usually used to connect terminals to modems; (NOTE: takes a singular verb)

electrosensitive *adjective;*
electrosensitive paper = metal-coated printing paper which can display characters using localized heating with a special dot-matrix print head; **electrosensitive printing** = printing using electrosensitive paper

◊ **electrostatic** *adjective* referring to devices using the properties of static electrical charge; **electrostatic printer** = type of printer which forms an image on the paper by charging certain regions to provide character shapes, etc., and using ink with an opposite charge which sticks to the paper where required; **electrostatic screen** = metal cage surrounding sensitive equipment (and connected to ground) to protect it from interference; **electrostatic storage** = storage of data in the form of small electric charged regions on a dielectric material

◊ **electrothermal printer** *noun* printer that uses a printing head with a dot-matrix of heating elements to form characters on electrosensitive paper

elegant programming *noun* writing a well-structured program using the minimum number of instructions

element *noun* **(a)** small part of an object which is made up of many similar parts; **logic element** = gate *or* combination of gates; **picture element** *or* **pixel** = smallest single unit *or* point on a display whose colour *or* brightness can be controlled; **signal element** = smallest basic unit used when transmitting digital data **(b)** one number *or* cell of a matrix *or* array; **array element** = one individual piece of data within an array

◊ **elementary** *adjective* made of many similar small sections *or* objects

elevator *noun* small, square indicator displayed within a scroll bar that indicates where you are within a long document or image; *the user can scroll through the image or text by dragging the elevator up or down the scroll bar*

eliminate *verb* to remove something completely; *using a computer should eliminate all possibility of error in the address system; the spelling checker does not eliminate all spelling mistakes*

◊ **elimination** *noun* removing of something completely; **elimination factor** = during a search, the section of data that is not used

> pointing with the cursor and pressing the joystick button eliminates use of the keyboard almost entirely
>
> *Soft*

else rule *noun* program logical rule used with an IF-THEN instruction to provide an alternative if the IF-THEN condition is not met; *IF X= 20 THEN PRINT 'X is 20' ELSE PRINT 'X not 20'*

EM = END OF MEDIUM

◊ **em** *noun* measure equal to the width of the letter 'm' in a particular font

e-mail *or* **email** = ELECTRONIC MAIL system of sending messages to and receiving messages from other users on a network

> The main uses for a link are to deliver work, to exchange email or take part in a conference.
>
> *Computing*

> to collect telex messages from an e-mail system, you have to remember to dial the system and check whether there are any telex messages in your mailbox
>
> *Which PC?*

embedded code *noun* sections *or* routines written in machine code, inserted into a high-level program to speed up *or* perform a special function; **embedded command** = printer command (such as indicating that text should be in italic) inserted into the text and used by a word-processing system when producing formatted printed text; **embedded computer** *or* **system** = dedicated computer controlling a machine; dedicated computer within a larger system performing one fixed function; **embedded object** = (in Windows) feature of OLE that allows a file or object, such as an image, that is included within another document or file

◊ **embedding** *noun* (in Windows) dragging an object and dropping it into a document or file so that is is embedded within the document

embrace *see* DEADLY

EMI = ELECTROMAGNETIC INTERFERENCE corruption of data due to nearby electrically generated magnetic fields

emitter-coupled logic (ECL) *noun* high-speed logic circuit design using the emitters of the transistors as output connections to other stages

EMM = EXPANDED MEMORY MANAGER utility that manages the extra expanded memory fitted in an IBM PC and makes it available for programs to use

EMS = EXPANDED MEMORY SYSTEM system in a PC that defines the section of memory that lies above the 640Kb mark

empty *adjective* with nothing inside; **empty** *or* **null list** = list with no elements; **empty medium** = blank but formatted storage medium ready to receive data; **empty** *or* **null** *or* **void set** = reserved area for related data items, containing no data; **empty slot** =

(i) packet of data in a packet-switching LAN that is carrying no information; (ii) unused expansion edge connector on a motherboard; **empty** *or* **null string** = variable containing no characters

EMS *or* **LIM EMS** = EXPANDED MEMORY SYSTEM *or* LOTUS-INTEL-MICROSOFT EXPANDED MEMORY SYSTEM (in an IBM PC) standard that defines extra memory added above the 640Kb limit of conventional memory; this memory can only be used by specially-written programs; *see also* LIM

emulate *verb* to copy *or* behave like something else; *some laser printers are able to emulate the more popular office printers*

◊ **emulation** *noun* behaviour by one computer *or* printer which is exactly the same as another, and which allows the same programs to be run and the same data to be processed; **emulation facility** = feature of hardware *or* software which emulates another system

◊ **emulator** *noun* software *or* hardware that allows a machine to behave like another

---

The London Borough of Hackney has standardised on terminal emulator software from Omniplex to allow its networked desktop users to select Unix or DOS applications from a single menu.

Computing

---

full communications error checking built into the software ensures reliable file transfers and a terminal emulation facility enables a user's terminal to be used as if it were a terminal to the remote computer

Byte

---

some application programs do not have the right drivers for a laser printer, so look out for laser printers which are able to emulate the more popular office printers

Publish

---

emulsion laser storage *noun* digital storage technique using a laser to expose light sensitive material

en *noun* unit of measure equal to half the width of an em

enable *verb* **(a)** to allow something to happen; *a spooling program enables editing work to be carried out while printing is going on* **(b)** to use an electronic signal to start a process *or* access a function (on a chip *or* circuit); **enabling signal** = signal that starts a process *or* allows one to take place

encapsulated *adjective* (something) contained within something else; **encapsulated PostScript** = PostScript commands that describe an image *or* page contained within a file that can be placed within a graphics *or* DTP program; **encapsulated PostScript file (EPSF)** = file that contains encapsulated PostScript instructions

◊ **encapsulation** *noun* (in a network) system of sending a frame of data in one format within a frame of another format

encipher *verb* to convert plaintext into a secure coded form by means of a cipher system; *our competitors cannot understand our files - they have all been enciphered* (NOTE: opposite is **decipher**)

enclose *verb* to surround with something; to put something inside something else; **enclosed object** = graphic object that is closed on all sides and so can be filled with a colour or pattern

◊ **enclosure** *noun* protective casing for equipment

encode *verb* to apply the rules of a code to a program *or* data

◊ **encoder** *noun* device that can translate data from one format to another

◊ **encoding** *noun* translation of a message *or* text according to a coding system; **binary encoding** = representing a character *or* element with a unique combination *or* pattern of bits in a word; **encoding format** = method of coding data stored on a magnetic disk (to avoid a series of similar bits); **magnetic**

encoding = storage of binary data signals on a magnetic medium

encrypt *verb* to convert plaintext to a secure coded form, using a cipher system; *the encrypted text can be sent along ordinary telephone lines, and no one will be able to understand it*

◊ **encryption** *noun* conversion of plaintext to a secure coded form by means of a cipher system; **data encryption standard (DES)** = standard for a block data cipher system

end 1 *noun* **(a)** final point *or* last part; *at the end of the data transmission;* in the end = at last *or* after a lot of problems; *in the end the company had to pull out of the US market; in the end the company had to call in a consultant engineer* **(b)**; **end key** = (on an IBM PC keyboard) key that moves the cursor to the end of the current line **(c)** statement *or* character to indicate the last word of a source file; **end about carry** = most significant digit added into the least significant place (used in BCD arithmetic); **end about shift** = data movement to the left *or* right in a word, the bits falling outside the word boundary are discarded and replaced with zeros; **end of address (EOA)** = transmitted code which indicates that address data has been sent; **end of block (EOB)** = code which shows that the last byte of a block of data has been sent through a communications link; **end of data (EOD)** = code which shows that the end of a stored data file has been reached; **end of document** *or* **end of file (EOF)** = marker after the last record in a file; **end of job (EOJ)** = code used in batch processing to show that a job has been finished; **end of line (EOL)** = code to indicate the end of a line (normally either a CR or LF character); **end of medium (EM)** = code that indicates the end of usable physical medium; **end of message (EOM)** = code used to separate the last character of one message from the first of another message; **end of page indicator** = indicator on a typewriter to show that a page is nearly finished; **end of record (EOR)** = code used to show the end of a record; **end of run routines** = routines carried out before a program run finishes to perform certain system housekeeping functions; **end of tape**

= code used to indicate the end of a magnetic tape; **end of text (EOT** *or* **ETX)** = code sent after last character of text; **end of transmission (EOT)** = sequence of characters indicating that all the data from a terminal *or* peripheral has been transmitted **2** *verb* to finish *or* to stop something

◊ **ending** *noun* **(a)** action of coming to an end *or* of stopping something **(b)** end part of something

◊ **endless** *adjective* with no end; **endless loop** = continuous piece of recording tape *or* number of computer instructions that are continuously repeated

◊ **end system** *noun* (on the internet) server or host computer connected to the internet; **end system to intermediate system (ES-IS)** = OSI protocol standard that allows host computers (the end system) to locate a router (the intermediate system)

◊ **end user** *noun* person who will use the device *or* program *or* product; *the company is creating a computer with a specific end user in mind*

Energy Star standard and logo on a monitor, computer or other electrical device; the standard means that the product has been specially designed to save electricity

engine *noun* part of a software package that carries out a particular function; *a search engine is the part of a multimedia title that lets a user search for text in a multimedia book*

enhance *verb* to make better *or* clearer; **enhanced communication port (ECP)** = system developed by Microsoft to improve the performance and functionality of the parallel printer port; **enhanced dot matrix** = clearer character *or* graphics printout (using smaller dots and more dots per inch); **enhanced expanded memory specification (EEMS)** = (in an IBM PC) a development of EMS, standard method of expanding the main memory fitted into a PC; **enhanced graphics adapter (EGA)** = (in an IBM PC) popular standard for high-resolution colour display adapter; **enhanced graphics adapter screen** = high-resolution colour monitor that can display EGA system signals and graphics; **enhanced keyboard** = (in an IBM PC) keyboard with 101 or 102 keys and a row of 12 function keys arranged along the top of the keyboard, with a separate numeric keypad on the right; **enhanced parallel port (EPP)** = standard that defines the way data can be transferred at high speed through a parallel port connector; **enhanced small device interface (ESDI)** = interface standard between a CPU and peripherals such as disk drives; *see also* SCSI; **enhanced mode** = (in an IBM PC with an Intel 80386 CPU) operation of software which uses the CPU's protected mode to allow several MS-DOS programs to run in a multitasking environment

◊ **enhancement** *noun* add-on facility which improves the output *or* performance of equipment

◊ **enhancer** *noun* device *or* software which enhances a process *or* product

ENQ = ENQUIRY

enquiry *noun* request for data *or* information from a device *or* database; accessing data in a computer memory without changing the data; **enquiry character** = special control code that is a request for identification *or* status *or* data from a device

ensure *verb* to make sure; *pushing the write-protect tab will ensure that the data on the disk cannot be erased*

enter *verb* to type in information on a terminal *or* keyboard; *to enter a name on a list; the data has been entered on data capture forms;* **enter key** = key pressed to indicate the end of an input *or* line of text *see also* CARRIAGE RETURN KEY

◊ **entering** *noun* act of typing in data *or* writing items in a record

enterprise network *noun* network which connects all the workstations *or* terminals *or* computers in a company; it can be within one building or linking several buildings in different countries

entity *noun* subject to which the data stored in a file *or* database refers

entry *noun* **(a)** single record *or* data about one action *or* object in a database *or* library **(b)** place where you can enter; **entry condition** = condition that must be satisfied before a routine can be entered; **entry instruction** = first instruction executed in a called subroutine; **entry point** = address from which a program *or* subroutine is to be executed; **entry time** = point in time when a program *or* job *or* batch will be executed by the operating system scheduler

enumerated type *noun* data storage *or* classification using numbers to represent chosen convenient labels

COMMENT: if 'man', 'horse', 'dog', 'cat' are the items of data, stored by the machine as enumerated data types with values of 0, 1, 2, 3, they can still be referred to in the program as man, horse, etc., to make it easier for the user to recognize them

envelope *noun* **(a)** transmitted packet of data containing error-detection and control information **(b)** (in multimedia) shape of the decay curve of a sound **(c)** (in electronic mail) name for the data which contains a mail message with the destination address information **(d)** paper packet that contains a letter; **envelope feeder** = special add-on to a printer used to print on an envelope instead of a sheet of paper; **envelope printer** = special printer used to print the address on an envelope

environment *noun* **(a)** condition in a computer system of all the registers and memory locations; **environment space** = the amount of memory free to be used by a program; **environment variable** = variable set by the system *or* by a user at the system command line which can be used by any program **(b)** surroundings *or* physical conditions

one of the advantages of working in a PC-based environment is the enormous range of software which can run on the same computer

ESL Newsletter

EOA = END OF ADDRESS

EOB = END OF BLOCK

EOD = END OF DATA

EOF = END OF FILE

EOJ = END OF JOB

EOL = END OF LINE

EOM = END OF MESSAGE

EOR = END OF RECORD

EOT = END OF TEXT or TRANSMISSION

EPOS = ELECTRONIC POINT-OF-SALE system that uses a computer terminal at a point-of-sale site for electronic funds transfer or stock control as well as product identification

EPP = ENHANCED PARALLEL PORT standard that defines the way data can be transferred at high speed through a parallel port connector

EPROM = ERASABLE PROGRAMMABLE READ-ONLY MEMORY

EPS = ENCAPSULATED POSTSCRIPT
◊ **EPSF** = ENCAPSULATED POSTSCRIPT FILE

equal 1 *adjective* exactly the same **2** *verb* to be the same as; *production this month has equalled our best month ever*
◊ **equality** *noun* logical function whose output is true if either of two inputs is true, and false if both inputs are the same
◊ **equalize** *verb* to make equal (to preset values); *the received signal was equalized to an optimum shape*
◊ **equally** *adverb* in the same way; *they were both equally responsible for the successful launch of the new system*

equate *verb* to be the same as or to make the same as; *the variable was equated to the input data*
◊ **equation** *noun* formula; **machine equation** = formula which an analog computer has been programmed to solve

equip *verb* to provide with machinery or equipment
◊ **equipment** *noun* machinery and furniture required to make a factory or office work; *office equipment or business equipment; computer equipment supplier; office equipment catalogue;* **equipment failure** = hardware fault, rather than a software fault

equivalent *adjective;* **to be equivalent to** = to have the same value as or to be the same as; *the total characters keyboarded so far is equivalent to one day's printing time*
◊ **equivalence** *noun* **(a)** being equivalent **(b)** logical operation that is true if all the inputs are the same; **equivalence function** or **operation** = (i) AND function; (ii) logical function whose output is true if both inputs are the same; **equivalence gate** = gate which performs an equivalence function; **non-equivalence function (NEQ)** = logical function where the output is true if the inputs are not the same, otherwise the output is false

COMMENT: output is 1 if both inputs are 1 or if both are 0; if the two inputs are different, the output is 0

erase *verb* **(a)** to set all the digits in a storage area to zero **(b)** to remove any signal from a magnetic medium; **erase head** = small magnet that clears a magnetic tape or disk of recorded signals
◊ **erase character** *noun* character which means 'do nothing'
◊ **erasable** *adjective* which can be erased; **erasable storage** or **erasable memory** = (i) storage medium which can be re-used; (ii) temporary storage; **erasable programmable read-only memory (EPROM)** = read-only memory chip which can be programmed by a voltage applied to a write pin and data applied to its output pins, usually erasable with ultraviolet light
◊ **eraser** *noun* device that erases the contents of something (such as using UV light to erase an EPROM); **eraser tool** = (in a graphics program) function that allows areas of an image to be erased, or set to the background colour

ergonomics *noun* science of designing software *or* hardware so that it is comfortable and safe to use

EROM = ERASABLE READ-ONLY MEMORY *same as* EAROM

error *noun* mistake due to an operator; mistake caused by a hardware *or* software fault; mistake in a program that prevents a program *or* system running correctly; *he made an error in calculating the total; the secretary must have made a typing error;* in **error** *or* **by error** = by mistake; **error ambiguity** = error due to an incorrect selection from ambiguous data; **error box** = dialog box displayed with a message alerting the user that an error has occurred; **error burst** = group of several consecutive errors (in a transmission); **error checking code** = general term used to describe all error correcting and error detecting codes; **error code** = code which indicates that a particular type of error has occurred; **error condition** = state that is entered if an attempt is made to operate on data containing errors; **error control** = routines which ensure that errors are minimised and any errors that occur are detected and dealt with rapidly; **error correcting code** = coding system that allows bit errors occurring during transmission to be rapidly corrected by logical deduction methods rather than re-transmission; *see also* GRAY CODE; **error correction** = hardware *or* software that can detect and correct an error in a transmission; **error detecting codes** = coding system that allows errors occurring during transmission to be detected but is not complex enough to correct the errors; **error detection** = using special hardware *or* software to detect errors in a data entry *or* transmission, then usually ask for re-transmission; **error detection and correction (EDAC)** = forward error correction system for data communications; **error diagnosis** = finding the cause of an error; **error diagnostics** = information and system messages displayed when an error is detected to help a user diagnose and correct an error; **error handling** *or* **management** = routines and procedures which can diagnose and correct errors *or* minimise the effects of

errors, so that a system will run when an error is detected; **error interrupts** = interrupt signals sent due to an error in hardware *or* software; **error logging** = recording errors that have occurred; *features of the program include error logging;* **error message** = report displayed to the user saying that an error has occurred; **error propagation** = one error causing another; **error rate** = (i) number of mistakes per thousand entries *or* per page; (ii) number of corrupt bits of data in relation to the total transmission length; *the error rate is less than 1%;* **error recovery** = software *or* hardware which can continue to run after an error has occurred; **error routine** = short routine within a main program that handles any errors when they occur; **error trapping** = detecting and correcting errors before they cause any problems; **compilation error** = error occurring during program compilation time; **diagnostic error message** = explanatory line of text displayed when an error has been found; **execution error** = error occurring during program execution, due to bad inputs *or* a faulty program; **logical error** = fault in a program design causing incorrect branching *or* operation; **margin of error** = number of mistakes which are acceptable in a document *or* in a calculation; **permanent error** = error in a system which cannot be repaired; **quantization error** = error in converting an analog signal into a numerical form due to limited accuracy *or* a rapidly changing signal; **recoverable error** = error that does not cause complete system shut-down, and allows the user to restart the program; **syntax error** = error resulting from incorrect use of programming language syntax; **transient read error** = error from which a program can recover (caused by bad data recording); **undetected error** = error which is not detected by a coding system

syntax errors, like omitting a bracket, will produce an error message from the compiler
Personal Computer World

ES-IS = END SYSTEM TO INTERMEDIATE SYSTEM OSI protocol standard that allows host computers (the end system) to locate a router (the intermediate system)

ESC escape character code *or* key on a computer

escape character *noun* character used to represent an escape code; **escape codes** = transmitted code sequence which informs the receiver that all following characters represent control actions; **escape key** = key on a keyboard which allows the user to enter escape codes to control the computer's basic modes *or* actions

◊ **escapement** *noun* preset vertical movement of a sheet of paper in a printer

ESDI = ENHANCED SMALL DEVICE INTERFACE interface standard between a CPU and peripherals such as disk drives; *see also* SCSI

establish *verb* (i) to discover and prove something; (ii) to define the use *or* value of something; *they established which component was faulty*

Ethernet (refers to IEEE 802.3 standard) standard defining the protocol and signalling method of a local area network; **Blue Book Ethernet** = version of Ethernet developed by DEC, Intel and Xerox; **fibre** *or* **fiber Ethernet** = high-speed network that uses optical fibre to link one node to another in a point-to-point topology; **thick-Ethernet** = network implemented using thick coaxial cable and transceivers to connect branch cables; can stretch long distances; **thin-Ethernet** = (the most popular type of Ethernet) network implemented using thin coaxial cable and BNC connectors; it is limited to distances of around 1000m *compare* ARCNET, TOKEN-RING; **twisted-pair Ethernet** = star-topology network that uses twisted-pair cable and transmits data at 10Mbps; normally called 10BaseT

COMMENT: Ethernet has several implementations: 10Base5 (the most common) is a bus-based topology running over coaxial cable; 10BaseT uses unshielded-twisted-pair cable in a star-based topology; Ethernet normally has a data transmission rate of 10Mbps

◊ **EtherTalk** (in Apple Macintosh systems) variation of the standard Ethernet network developed to connect Macintoshes together as an alternative to the slower AppleTalk

ETX = END OF TEXT (NOTE: same as **EOT**)

Eudora common commercial software program used to send, receive and manage electronic mail messages sent via the internet

evaluate *verb* to calculate a value *or* a quantity

◊ **evaluation** *noun* action of calculating a value *or* a quantity

even *adjective* (quantity *or* number) that is a multiple of two; *the first three even numbers are 2, 4, 6;* **even parity (check)** = error checking method that only transmits an even number of binary ones in each word *compare* ODD PARITY

event *noun* an action *or* activity

◊ **event-driven** *adjective* (computer program *or* process) where each step of the execution relies on external actions

◊ **event focus** *noun* object that is currently receiving messages from an action or event

◊ **event handler** *noun* routine that responds to an event or message within an object-oriented programming environment; *if a user clicks the mouse button this generates a message which can be acted upon by the event handler*

Forthcoming language extensions will include object-oriented features, including classes with full inheritance, as well as event-driven programming.
Computing

except *preposition & conjunction* not including; *all the text has been keyboarded, except the last ten pages;* **except gate** = logical function whose output is true if either (of two) inputs is true, and false if both inputs are the same

◊ **exception** *noun* something which is different from all others in the same category; **exception dictionary** = store of words and their special word-break requirements, for word-processing and photocomposition; **exception handling** *or* **error handling** = routines and procedures that diagnose and correct errors *or* minimise the effects of errors, so that a system will run when an error is detected

exceptional *adjective* not usual *or* different

excess *noun* too much of something; **excess-3 code** = code in which decimal digits are represented by the binary equivalent of three greater than the number; *the excess-3 code representation of 6 is 1001*

◊ **excessive** *adjective* too much *or* too large; *the program used an excessive amount of memory to accomplish the job*

exchange 1 *noun* giving of one thing for another; **part exchange** = giving an old product as part of the payment for a new one **2** *verb* **(a)**; **to exchange one article for another** = to give one thing in place of something else; **exchange selection** = sorting method which repeatedly exchanges various pairs of data items until they are in order **(b)** to swap data between two locations

◊ **exchangeable** *adjective* which can be exchanged; **exchangeable disk storage (EDS)** = disk drive using a removable disk pack (as opposed to a fixed disk)

Exchange application supplied with Windows 95 that provides features that allow you to manage your communications including electronic mail and fax

exclude *verb* to keep out *or* not to include

◊ **excluding** *preposition* not including

◊ **exclusion** *noun* **(a)** act of not including **(b)** restriction of access to a system

◊ **exclusive** *adjective* which excludes; **exclusive NOR (EXNOR)** = logical function whose output is true if all inputs are the same level, and false if any are different; **exclusive NOR gate** = electronic implementation of the EXNOR function

◊ **exclusive OR (EXOR)** = logical function whose output is true if any input is true, and false if all the inputs are the same;

exclusive OR gate = electronic implementation of the EXOR function

EXE file *noun* (in an operating system) three-letter extension to a filename which indicates that the file contains binary data of a program; the file can be executed directly by the operating system; *in DOS, to start a program type in its EXE file name*

executable file *noun* file that contains a program rather than data

◊ **executable form** *noun* program translated *or* compiled into a machine code form that a processor can execute

execute *verb* to run *or* carry out a computer program *or* process; **execute cycle** = events required to fetch, decode and carry out an instruction stored in memory; **execute mode** = state of a computer that is executing a program *compare* DIRECT MODE; **execute phase** = section of the execute cycle when the instruction is carried out; **execute signal** = signal that steps the CPU through the execute cycle; **execute statement** = basic operating system command to start a program run; **fetch-execute cycle** = EXECUTE CYCLE

◊ **execution** *noun* carrying out a computer program *or* process; **execution address** = location in memory at which the first instruction in a program is stored; **execution cycle** = period of time during which the instruction is executed; **execution error** = error detected while a program is being run; **execution phase** = EXECUTE PHASE; **execution time** = (i) time taken to run *or* carry out a program *or* series of instructions; (ii) time taken for one execution cycle

---

```
fast execution speed is the
single most important feature
of a C compiler
```
.EXE

---

executive *adjective* normally refers to the operating system of a computer; **executive program** *or* **supervisor program** = master program in a computer system that controls the execution of other programs; **executive control program** = OPERATING SYSTEM; **executive instruction** = instruction used to control and execute programs under the control of an operating system

executive information system

(EIS) *noun* easy-to-use software providing information to a manager or executive about his company; *the EIS software is very easy to use; with this EIS software, we can see how every part of the company performs*

exerciser *noun* tester for a device

exhaustive search *noun* search through every record in a database

exit *verb* to stop program execution *or* to leave a program and return control to the operating system *or* interpreter; **exit point** = point in a subroutine where control is returned to the main program; *you have to exit to another editing system to add headlines*

◊ **EXIT** (in MS-DOS) system command to stop and leave a child process and return to the parent process

exjunction *noun* logical function whose output is true if either (of two) inputs is true, and false if both inputs are the same

EXNOR = EXCLUSIVE NOR logical function whose output is true if all inputs are the same level, false if any are different; **EXNOR gate** = electronic implementation of the EXNOR function *see also* NOR

EXOR = EXCLUSIVE OR logical function whose output is true if any input is true, and false if all the inputs are the same; **EXOR gate** = electronic implementation of the EXOR function; *see also* OR

expand *verb* to make larger; *if you want to hold so much data, you will have to expand the disk capacity*

◊ **expandable** *adjective* which can be expanded; **expandable system** = computer system that is designed to be able to grow (in power *or* memory) by hardware *or* software additions

◊ **expanded memory system (EMS)** *noun* (in an IBM PC) standard that defines extra memory added above the 640Kb limit of conventional memory; this memory can

only be used by specially-written programs; *see also* LIM; **expanded memory board** = expansion card used to add extra memory to an IBM PC; the memory follows the EMS standard; **expanded memory manager (EMM)** = utility which manages the extra expanded memory fitted in an IBM PC and makes it available for programs to use

◊ **expansion** *noun* increase in computing power *or* storage size; **expansion box** = device that plugs into an expansion bus and provides several more free expansion slots; **expansion bus** = data and address lines leading to a connector and allowing expansion cards to control and access the data in main memory; **expansion card** *or* **expansion board** = printed circuit board connected to a system to increase its functions *or* performance; **expansion slot** = connector inside a computer into which an expansion card can be plugged; *insert the board in the expansion slot;* **macro expansion** = process in which a macro call is replaced with the instructions in the macro

---

it can be attached to most kinds of printer, and, if that is not enough, an expansion box can be fitted to the bus connector

Personal Computer World

---

expert *noun* person who knows a lot about something; *he is a computer expert; she is an expert in programming languages;* **expert system** = software which applies the knowledge, advice and rules defined by experts in a particular field to a user's data to help solve a problem

explicit address *noun* address provided in two parts, one is the reference point, the other a displacement *or* index value

◊ **explicit reference** *noun* (within a program or script) a way of identifying a particular object, such as a field or button, by a unique name

Explorer™ program supplied with Windows 95 that lets you manage all the files stored on a disk

exponent *noun* number indicating the power to which a base number is to be raised; **binary exponent** = one word that contains the sign and exponent of a binary number (expressed in exponent and mantissa form); *see also* MANTISSA

exponentiation *noun* raising a base number to a certain power

export *verb* to save data in a different file format from the default; *to use this data with dBASE, you will have to export it as a DBF file*

express *verb* to state *or* to describe; *express the formula in its simplest form; the computer structure was expressed graphically*

◊ **expression** *noun* (a) mathematical formula *or* relationship (b) definition of a value *or* variable in a program

extend *verb* to make longer; **extended arithmetic element** = section of a CPU that provides hardware implementations of various mathematical functions; **extended binary coded decimal interchange code (EBCDIC)** = 8-bit character coding system; **extended BNF (EBNF)** = more flexible way of defining the syntax of a language; **extended character set** = set of 128 special characters that includes accents, graphics, and symbols; **extended data output memory (EDO memory)** = memory technology that provides better performance by being able to find and read data from a memory location in one operation; it can also store the last piece of data that was saved to memory in a cache ready to be read back from memory; **extended industry standard architecture (EISA)** = group of PC manufacturers who formed an association to promote a 32-bit expansion bus standard as a rival to the MCA bus standard from IBM; **extended integrated drive electronics (EIDE)** = enhanced IDE specification that improves the performance and data transfer rates to and from a hard disk drive; **extended graphics array (XGA)** = high resolution graphics standard developed by IBM; capable of displaying resolutions of up to 1024x768 pixels; **extended memory** = (in an IBM PC) most popular standard method of adding extra memory above 1Mb which can be used directly by many operating systems

or programs; **extended memory manager** = software utility that configures extra memory fitted in a PC to conform to the extended memory standard; **extended memory specification (XMS)** = rules that define how a program should access extended memory fitted in a PC; **extending serial file** = file which can be added to *or* which has no maximum size

◊ **extensible** *adjective* which can be extended; **extensible language** = computer programming language that allows the user to add his own data types and commands

◊ **extension** *noun* making something longer; something added to something else to make it longer; **extension cable** = cable that allows a device located at some distance to be connected; **extension memory** = storage which is located outside the main computer system but which can be accessed by the CPU; **filename extension** = additional information after a filename, indicating the type *or* use of the file; *in MS-DOS, there is a three-character filename extension that indicates the type of file*

external *adjective* outside a program *or* device; **external clock** = clock *or* synchronizing signal supplied from outside a device; **external data file** = file containing data for a program but stored separately from it; **external device** = (i) item of hardware (such as terminals, printers, etc.) which is attached to a main computer; (ii) any device that allows communications between the computer and itself, but which is not directly operated by the main computer; **external disk drive** = device not built into the computer, but which is added to increase its storage capabilities; **external interrupts** = interrupt signal from a peripheral device indicating that attention is required; **external label** = identifying piece of paper stuck to the outside of a device *or* disk; **external memory** = memory which is located outside the main computer system confines but which can be accessed by the CPU; **external modem** = modem which is self-contained with its own power supply unit that connects to a serial port of a computer; **external registers** = a user's registers located in main memory rather than within the CPU; **external schema**

= user's view of the structure of data *or* a program; **external sort** = method of sorting which uses a file stored in secondary memory, such as a disk, as its data source and uses the disk as temporary memory during sorting; **external storage** *or* **external store** = storage device which is located outside the main computer system but which can be accessed by the CPU

extra 1 *adjective* added *or* which is more than usual **2** *noun* item which is additional to the package; *the mouse and cabling are sold as extras*

◊ **extracode** *noun* short routines within the operating system that emulate a hardware function

extract *verb* to remove required data *or* information from a database; *we can extract the files required for typesetting;* **extract instruction** = instruction to select and read required data from a database *or* file

◊ **extractor** *noun see* MASK

eye-strain *noun* pain in the eyes, caused by looking at bright lights *or* at a VDU for too long

```
to minimize eye-strain, it is
vital  to  have  good  lighting
conditions with this LCD system
```
Personal Computer World

Ff

f = FEMTO- *prefix* equal to one thousandth of a million millionth (10^{-15})

F hexadecimal number equivalent to decimal number 15

face *see* TYPEFACE

facet *noun* one surface *or* plane

◊ **faceted code** *noun* code which indicates various details of an item, by assigning each one a value

facility *noun* **(a)** being able to do something easily; *we offer facilities for processing a customer's own disks* **(b)**; **facilities** = equipment *or* buildings which make it easy to do something; *storage facilities* **(c)** US single large building; *we have opened our new data processing facility*

facsimile *noun* exact copy of an original; **facsimile character generator** = means of displaying characters on a computer screen by copying preprogrammed images from memory; **facsimile copy** = exact copy of a document; **facsimile transmission (FAX)** = method of sending and receiving images in digital form over a telephone *or* radio link

factor *noun* **(a)** something which is important *or* which has an influence on something else; **deciding factor** = most important factor which influences someone's decision; *the deciding factor was the superb graphics;* **elimination factor** = (during a search) the section of data that is not used **(b)** any number in a multiplication that is the operand; **by a factor of ten** = ten times

◊ **factorial** *noun* the product of all the numbers below a number; *example: 4 factorial (written 4!) = 1x2x3x4 = 24*

◊ **factorize** *verb* to break down a number into two whole numbers which when multiplied will give the original number; *when factorized, 15 gives the factors 1, 15 or 3, 5*

factory *noun* building where products are manufactured; *computer factory; they have opened a new components factory;* **factory price** *or* **price ex factory** = price not including transport from the maker's factory

fade *verb (of radio or electrical signal)* to become less strong

fail *verb* not to do something which should be done; not to work properly; *the company failed to carry out routine maintenance of its equipment; the prototype disk drive failed its first test; a computer has failed if you turn on the power supply and nothing happens;* **fail safe system** = system which has a predetermined state it will go to if a main program or device fails, so avoiding a total catastrophe that a complete system shutdown would produce; **fail soft system** = system that will still be partly operational even after a part of the system has failed; *see also* GRACEFUL DEGRADATION

The DTI is publishing a new code of best practice which covers hardware reliability and fail-safe software systems.
Computing

if one processor system fails, the other takes recovery action on the database, before taking on the workload of the failed system
Computer News

failure *noun* breaking down *or* stopping; not doing something which should be done;

failure logging = section of the operating system that automatically saves the present system states and relevant data when an error *or* fault is detected; **failure rate** = number of a certain type of failure within a specified period of time; **failure recovery** = resuming a process *or* program after a failure has occurred and has been corrected; **induced failure** = failure of a device due to external effects; **mean time between failures (MTBF)** = average period of time that a piece of equipment will operate for between breakdowns; **power failure** = loss of the electric power supply; *see also* BLACK, BROWN OUT

fall back *noun* special *or* temporary instructions *or* procedures *or* data used in the event of a fault *or* failure; **fall back recovery** = resuming a program after a fault has been fixed, from the point at which fall back routines were called; **fall back routines** = routines that are called *or* procedures which are executed by a user when a machine *or* system has failed

false *adjective* (i) wrong; not true *or* not correct; (ii) a logical term, equal to binary 0, opposite of true; **false code** = code that contains values not within specified limits; **false drop** *or* **retrieval** = unwanted files retrieved from a database through the use of incorrect search codes; **false error** = error warning given when no error has occurred

FAM = FAST ACCESS MEMORY

family *noun* (a) range of different designs of a particular typeface (b) range of machines from one manufacturer that are compatible with other products in the same line from the same manufacturer

fan 1 *noun* (i) mechanism which circulates air for cooling; (ii) a spread of data items *or* devices; *if the fan fails, the system will rapidly overheat* **2** *verb* (i) to cool a device by blowing air over it; (ii) to spread out a series of items *or* devices; **fan-in** = maximum number of inputs that a circuit *or* chip can deal with; **fan-out** = maximum number of outputs that a circuit *or* chip can drive without exceeding its power dissipation limit;

fanning strip = cable supporting insulated strip

> Intel is investigating other options to solve the Pentium system overheating problems, including selling the chip with its own miniature fan.
> *Computing*

> a filtered fan maintains positive air pressure within the cabinet, to keep dust and dirt from entering
> *Personal Computer World*

◊ **fanfold** *or* **accordion fold paper** *noun* method of folding continuous paper, one sheet in one direction, the next sheet in the opposite direction, allowing the paper to be stored conveniently and fed into a printer continuously

FAQ FREQUENTLY ASKED QUESTIONS Web page or help file that contains common questions and their answers related to a particular subject

Faraday cage *noun* wire *or* metal screen, connected to ground, that completely encloses sensitive equipment to prevent any interference from stray electromagnetic radiation

fascia plate *noun* front panel on a device; *the fascia plate on the disk drive of this model is smaller than those on other models*

fast *adjective* which moves quickly; which works quickly; (storage *or* peripheral device) that performs its functions very rapidly; *fast program execution; this hard disk is fast, it has an access time of 8mS;* **fast access memory (FAM)** = storage locations that can be read from *or* written to very rapidly; **fast core** = high speed, low access time working memory for a CPU; *the fast core is used as a scratchpad for all calculations in this system;* **fast line** = special telecommunications line which allows data to be transmitted at 64K *or* 128K baud rates; **fast packet** = asynchronous method of transferring data over a network; **fast page RAM (FPM RAM)** = older type of memory component that seeks and reads data from a memory location in two separate operations; this component has now been replaced by EDO memory; *see* EDO; **fast peripheral** = peripheral that communicates with the computer at very high speeds, limited only by the speed of the electronic circuits, as opposed to a slow peripheral, such as a card reader, where mechanical movement determines speed; **fast time-scale** = operation in which the time-scale factor is less than one

FAT = FILE ALLOCATION TABLE (in a PC operating system) data file stored on disk that contains the names of each file stored on the disk, together with its starting sector position, date and size

fatal error *noun* fault in a program *or* device that causes the system to crash

FatBits MacPaint option which allows a user to edit an image one pixel at a time

father file *noun* backup of the previous version of a file; *see also* GRANDFATHER, SON

fault *noun* situation where something has gone wrong with software *or* hardware, causing it to malfunction; *the technical staff are trying to correct a programming fault; we think there is a basic fault in the product design*; *see also* BUG, ERROR; **fault detection** = (automatic) process which logically *or* mathematically determines that a fault exists in a circuit; **fault diagnosis** = process by which the cause of a fault is located; **fault location program** = routine that is part of a diagnostic program that identifies the cause of faulty data *or* equipment; **fault management** = one of the five categories of network management specified by the ISO that will detect, isolate and correct network faults; **fault time** = period of time during which a computer system is not working or usable due to a fault; **fault tolerance** = ability of a system to continue functioning even when a fault has occurred; *see also* RAID, REDUNDANT; **fault-tolerant** = (system *or* device) that is able to continue functioning even when a fault occurs; *they market a highly successful*

range *of fault-tolerant minis*; **fault trace** = program that checks and records the occurrences of faults in a system

faulty *adjective* which does not work properly; *there must be a faulty piece of equipment in the system; they traced the fault to a faulty cable*; **faulty sector** = sector of a magnetic disk that cannot be written to *or* read from correctly

Hampshire fire brigade is investing £2 million in a command and control system based on the new SeriesFT fault-tolerant Unix machine from Motorola.

Computing

before fault-tolerant systems, users had to rely on cold standby

Computer News

fault tolerance is usually associated with a system's reliability

Computer News

fax *or* **FAX** *noun & verb* (*informal*) = FACSIMILE COPY, FACSIMILE TRANSMISSION method of sending and receiving images in digital form over a telephone *or* radio link; *we will send a fax of the design plan; I've faxed the documents to our New York office; the fax machine is next to the telephone switchboard*; **fax card** *or* **board** = adapter card which plugs into an expansion slot and allows a computer to send or receive fax data; **fax modem** = modem that can be used to send and receive faxes to and from a standard fax machine as well as being used as a modem to connect to other computers; **fax server** = computer connected to a network and fitted with a fax card that is shared by all users on the network

investment in a good modem and communications system could reduce your costs considerably on both courier and fax services

Which PC?

FCB = FILE CONTROL BLOCK area of memory (used by the operating system) that contains information about the files in use *or* those stored on a disk drive

fd *or* **FD** **(a)** = FULL DUPLEX data transmission down a channel in two directions simultaneously **(b)** = FLOPPY DISK

fdc = FLOPPY DISK CONTROLLER

FDD = FLOPPY DISK DRIVE

FDDI = FIBRE DISTRIBUTED DATA INTERFACE ANSI standard for high-speed networks which use fibre optic cable in a dual ring topology; data is transmitted at 100Mbps; **FDDI II** = enhanced ANSI standard for high-speed networks that uses fibre optic cable and transmits data at 100Mbps but can also allocate part of the bandwidth to a 64Kbits/second analog channel for audio or video data

FDISK (in MS-DOS) system utility that configures the partitions on a hard disk

FDM = FREQUENCY DIVISION MULTIPLEXING to assign a number of different signals to different frequencies (or bands) to allow many signals to be sent along one channel; *using FDM we can transmit 100 telephone calls along one main cable*

fdx *or* **FDX** = FULL DUPLEX

feasibility *noun* ability to be done; *he has been asked to report on the feasibility of a project;* **feasibility study** = examination and report into the usefulness and cost of a new product that is being considered for purchase; **to carry out a feasibility study on a project** = to carry out an examination of costs and profits to see if the project should be started

feature *noun* special function *or* ability *or* design of hardware *or* software; **key feature** = most important feature; *the key features of this system are: 20Mb of formatted storage with an access time of 60ms*

FED = FIELD EMISSION DISPLAY

FEDS = FIXED AND EXCHANGEABLE DISK STORAGE magnetic disk storage system that contains some removable disks, such as floppy disks and some fixed *or* hard disk drives

feed 1 *noun* device which puts paper *or* tape into and through a machine, such as a printer *or* photocopier; **continuous feed** = device which feeds in continuous computer stationery into a printer; **front feed** *or* **sheet feed attachment** = device which can be attached to a line printer to allow individual sheets of paper to be fed in automatically; **feed holes** = punched sprocket holes along the edge of continuous paper; **feed reel** = reel of tape which is being fed into a machine; **paper feed** = mechanism which pulls paper through a printer; **sheet feed** = device which puts in one sheet at a time into a printer; **tractor feed** = method of feeding paper into a printer, sprocket wheels on the printer connect with sprocket holes on each edge of the paper **2** *verb* to put paper into a machine *or* information into a computer; *this paper should be manually fed into the printer; data is fed into the computer*

feedback *noun* information from one source which can be used to modify something *or* provide a constructive criticism of something; *we are getting customer feedback on the new system; they asked the sales teams for feedback on the reception of the new model; have you any feedback from the sales force about the customers' reaction to the new model?;* **feedback control** = information about the effects of a controlling signal on a machine *or* device, returned to the controlling computer

feeder *noun* **(a)** channel that carries signals from one point to another **(b)** mechanism that automatically inserts the paper into a printer

female *adjective;* **female connector** = connector with connecting sockets into which the pins *or* plugs of a male connector can be inserted; **female socket** = hole into which a pin *or* plug can be inserted to make a connection

femto- (f) *prefix* equal to ten exponent minus fifteen (10^{-15}); **femtosecond** = thousandth of a picosecond

FEP = FRONT END PROCESSOR processor placed between an input source and the central computer, whose function is to preprocess received data to relieve the workload of the main computer

ferric oxide or **ferrite** noun substance (iron oxide) used as tape or disk coating that can be magnetized to store data or signals

◊ **ferrite core** noun small bead of magnetic material that can hold an electromagnetic charge, used in (old) core memory

◊ **ferromagnetic material** noun any ferrite material that can be magnetized

FET = FIELD EFFECT TRANSISTOR electronic device that can act as a variable current flow control: an external signal varies the resistance of the device and current flow by changing the width of a conducting channel

fetch noun command that retrieves the next instruction from memory; **demand fetching** = virtual page management system in which the pages are selected as required; **fetch cycle** = events that retrieve the next instruction to be executed from memory (by placing the program counter contents on the address bus); **fetch-execute cycle** = events required to retrieve, decode and carry out an instruction stored in memory; **fetch instruction** = computer instruction to select and read the next instruction or data to be processed; **fetch phase** = section of the fetch-execute cycle that retrieves and decodes the instructions from memory; **fetch protect** = to restrict access to a section of memory; **fetch signal** = signal that steps the CPU through the fetch cycle

FF (a) = FORM FEED **(b)** = FLIP-FLOP

fibre or **fiber** noun very thin glass or plastic strand that can carry data in the form of light signals; **fibre connectors** = type of connector that can be used to connect two fibre optic cables together; **multimode fibre** = commonly used type of optic fibre that uses a glass fibre with a diameter of between 50 to 125 microns and can carry several different frequencies of light with a maximum

bandwidth of 2.5Gbps; the disadvantage is that because the fibre is wide, the light disperses quickly and so repeaters need to be installed to boost the signal; **single mode fibre** = optic fibre that has a very narrow diameter (of 10 microns or less) and is designed to transmit a single light signal over a long distance; this type of fibre has a bandwidth of 5Gbits/second and is normally used for long distance telephone networks

fibre channel noun ANSI standard that defines a high-speed serial interface that can transfer data at up to 1.06Gbps and is often used as a backbone technology to link servers or high-speed devices; the technology is normally used over optic fibre, but will work over twisted-pair cable or coax cable

fibre distributed data interface

(FDDI) noun ANSI standard for high-speed networks that uses fibre optic cable in a dual ring topology; data is transmitted at 100Mbps

fibre distributed data interface II

(FDDI-2) noun enhanced ANSI standard for high-speed networks that uses fibre optic cable and transmits data at 100Mbps but can also allocate part of the bandwidth to a 64Kbits/second analog channel for audio or video data

fibre optics noun thin strands of glass or plastic that can transmit light signals at the speed of light; the light or laser signal is pulsed or modulated to represent data being transmitted; **fibre optic cable** or **connection** = fine strands of glass or plastic protected by a surrounding material, used for transmission of light signals that carry data at very high speeds; *fibre optic connections enabling nodes up to one kilometre apart to be used*

Honeywell has won a contract worth £380,000 to cable Abbey National's Milton Keynes-based administration offices. The installation will be based on copper wire and fibre optics and will be carried out by Honeywell's PDS Group.

Computing

fibre over Etherenet *noun* enhanced version of the 802.3 Ethernet network protocol standard that allows data to be transferred at 10Mbits/second (10BaseFX) or 100Mbits/second (100BaseFX)

fibre ribbon *noun* fabric-based ribbon used in dot-matrix and golf ball printers

fiche *see* MICROFICHE

field *noun* **(a)** area of force and energy distribution, caused by magnetic *or* electric energy sources; **field effect transistor (FET)** = electronic device that can act as a variable current flow control: an external signal varies the resistance of the device and current flow by changing the width of a conducting channel; **field emission display (FED)** = method of producing thin, flat displays for laptop computers in which a miniature colour CRT is located at each pixel point; **field programmable device;** *see* PLA; **field programming** = writing data into a PROM; *see also* BLOW **(b)** sections containing individual data items in a record; *the employee record has a field for age;* **address** *or* **operand field** = part of a computer instruction containing the location of the operand; **card field** = part of a card column reserved for one type of data *or* record; **data field** = part of a computer instruction that contains the location of the data; **field label** *or* **name** = series of characters used to identify a field or its location; **field length** = number of characters that a field can contain; **field marker** *or* **separator** = code used to indicate the end of one field and the start of the next; **protected field** = storage *or* display area that cannot be altered by the user **(c)**; **in the field** = outside an office *or* factory; **field engineer** = engineer who does not work at one single company, but travels between customers carrying out maintenance on their computers; **field tested** = product tested outside a company *or* research laboratory, in a real situation

◊ **fielding** *noun* arrangement of field allocations inside a record and file

FIF = FRACTAL IMAGE FORMAT file format used to store graphics images which have been highly compressed using fractals

FIFO = FIRST IN FIRST OUT storage read/write method in which the first item stored is the first read; **FIFO memory** = memory using a FIFO access scheme; *the two computers operate at different rates, but can transmit data using a FIFO memory;* **FIFO queue** = temporary (queue) storage, in which the first item written to the queue is the first to be read; *compare* LIFO

fifth generation computers *noun* next stage of computer system design using fast VLSI circuits and powerful programming languages to allow human interaction

figure *noun* printed number; **figures shift** = (i) transmitted code which indicates to the receiver that all following characters should be read as upper case; (ii) mechanical switch which allows a typewriter to print *or* keyboard to produce special characters and symbols located on the same keys as the numbers; **in round figures** = not totally accurate, but correct to the nearest 10 or 100; *they have a workforce of 2,500 in round figures*

file 1 *noun* **(a)** documents kept for reference; **to place something on file** = to keep a record of something **(b)** section of data on a computer (such as payroll, address list, customer accounts), in the form of individual records which may contain data, characters, digits *or* graphics; **file activity ratio** = ratio of the number of different records accessed within a file compared to the total number in store; **file allocation table (FAT)** = (in a PC operating system) data file stored on disk containing the names of each file stored on the disk, together with its starting sector position, date and size; **file attributes** = control bits of data stored with each file which control particular functions or aspects of the file such as read-only, archived or system file; **file cleanup** = tidying and removing out of date *or* unnecessary data from a file; **file collating** = putting the contents of a file into order; **file control block (FCB)** = area of memory (used by the operating system) that contains information about the files in use *or* those stored on a disk drive; **file conversion** = change of format *or* structure of a file system, usually when using a new program *or* file handling routine; **file**

creation = writing file header information onto a disk and writing an entry into the directory; **file deletion** = erasing a file from storage *see also* DELETE; **file descriptor** = code *or* series of characters used to identify a file; **file defragmentation** *see* DEFRAGMENTATION; **file directory** = list of names and information about files in a backing storage device; **file extent** = actual area *or* number of tracks required to store a file; **file format** = way in which data is stored in a file; **file fragmentation** = file that is stored in non contiguous sectors on a disk; **file gap** = section of blank tape *or* disk that indicates the end of a file; **file handle** = number by which an open file is identified within a program; *the new data is written to the file identified by file handle 1;* **file handling routine** = short computer program that manages the reading/writing and organization of stored files; **file header** = information about the file stored at the beginning of the file; *the file header in the database file shows the total number of records and lists the index fields;* **file identification** = unique label *or* name used to identify and locate a file stored on backing store; **file index** = sorted table of the main entries in a file, with their address, allowing the rapid location of entries; **file label** = character(s) used to identify a file; **file layout** = set of rules defining internal file structure; **file locking** = software mechanism that prevents data in a file being updated by two different users at the same time; only one user can change the particular information at any one time; **file maintenance** = process of updating a file by changing, adding *or* deleting entries; **file management (system)** = section of a DOS that allocates disk space to files, keeping track of the sections and their sector addresses; **file manager** = routines used to create, locate and maintain files on backing store; **file merger** = (i) to combine two data files, but still retaining an overall structure; (ii) one file created from more than one file written one after the other (no order preserved); **file name** = word used to identify a particular stored file; *in MS-DOS a file name has eight characters, together with a three character extension to identify the type of file;* **file organization** = *see* FILE

LAYOUT; **file processing** = applying a set of rules *or* search limits to a file, in order to update *or* find information; **file protection** = (i) software *or* physical device used to prevent any accidental deletion *or* modification of a file *or* its records; (ii) *see* FILE SECURITY; **file protect tab** = plastic tab on a disk which prevents accidental erasure of a file; **file purge** = erasing the contents of a file; **file-recovery utility** = software which allows files that have been accidentally deleted *or* damaged to be read again; *a lost file cannot be found without a file-recovery utility;* **file security** = hardware *or* software organization of a computer system to protect users' files from unauthorized access; **file server** = computer connected to a network that runs a network operating system software to manage user accounts, file sharing and printer sharing; **file set** = number of related files treated as one unit; **file sharing** = one file that can be used by two or more users *or* programs in a network (often using file locking); **file size** = the number of bytes a file occupies on disk; **file sort** = to put the contents of a file into order; **file storage** = physical means of preserving data in a file, such as a disk drive *or* tape machine; **file store** = files that are available in main memory at any time; **file structure** = way in which a (data) file is organized; **file transfer** = moving a file from one area of memory to another *or* to another storage device *or* between computers; **file transfer access and management (FTAM)** = OSI standard method of transferring files between different computer systems; **file transfer protocol (FTP)** = TCP/IP standard for transferring files between computers; it is a file sharing protocol that operates at layers 5, 6 and 7 of an OSI model network; **file transfer utility** = software utility that links two computers together (normally via a physical serial cable) and allows files to be transferred between the computers; **file type** = method of classifying what a file contains; (in an MS-DOS system this is often by the filename extension); *files with the extension EXE are file types that contain program code;* **file update** = (i) recent changes *or* transactions to a file; (ii) new version of software which is sent to users of an existing version; **file validation** =

checking that a file is correct; **data file** = file containing data (as opposed to a program file); **disk file** = number of related records *or* data items stored under one name on disk; **distributed file system** = system that uses files stored in more than one location *or* backing store, but which are processed at a central point; **hidden file** = important system file which is not displayed in a directory and cannot normally be read by a user; **indexed file** = sequential file with an index of all the entries and their addresses; **inverted file** = file with an index entry for every data item; **output file** = set of records that have been completely processed according to various parameters; **program file** = file containing a program rather than data; **text file** = file that contains text rather than digits *or* data; **threaded file** = file in which an entry contains data and an address to the next entry that contains the same data (allowing rapid retrieval of all identical entries); **transaction** *or* **change** *or* **detail** *or* **movement file** = file containing recent changes to records *or* transactions used to update a master file **2** *verb* **to file documents** = to put documents in order so that they can be found easily; *the correspondence is filed under 'complaints'; he filed the new papers in chronological order*

The first problem was solved by configuring a Windows swap file, which I hadn't done before because my 4Mb 486 had never been overloaded.

Computing

it allows users to back up or restore read-only security files and hidden system files independently

Minicomputer News

the lost file, while inaccessible without a file-recovery utility, remains on disk until new information writes over it

Publish

filename *noun* unique identification code allocated to a program, on a PC running MS-DOS filename can be up to eight characters long together with a three

character filename extension, under Windows 95, a filename can be up to 254 characters long; **filename extension** = (in MS-DOS) additional three-character name that is used together with a filename, indicating the type *or* use of the file; *the filename extension SYS indicates that this is a system file;* **long filename** = feature of Windows 95 that allows a filename to be up to 254 characters long

when the filename is entered at the prompt, the operating system looks in the file and executes any instructions stored there

PC User

filing *noun* (i) putting documents in order; (ii) documents which have to be put in order

◊ **filing system** *noun* **(a)** way of putting documents in order for reference **(b)** software which organizes files

fill 1 *verb* **(a)** to make something full; *the screen was filled with flickering images* **(b)** to put characters into gaps in a field so that there are no spaces left; **fill character** = character added to a string of characters to make up a required length **(c)** to draw an enclosed area in one colour *or* shading

◊ **fill up** *verb* to make something completely full; *the disk was quickly filled up*

filter 1 *noun* **(a)** electronic circuit that allows certain frequencies to pass while stopping others **(b)** pattern of binary digits used to select various bits from a binary word (a one in the filter retains that bit in the source word) **2** *verb* **(a)** to remove unwanted elements from a signal *or* file **(b)** to select various bits word; *filter the top three bits of the video attribute word* **(c)** to select various records from a database file; *we filtered the data to select those customers based in New York*

final *adjective* last *or* coming at the end of a period; *to keyboard the final data files; to make the final changes to a document*

find 1 *verb* to get something back which has been lost; *it took a lot of time to find the* *faulty chip; the debugger found the error very quickly* **2** *noun* command to locate a piece of information; **find and replace** = feature on a word-processor that allows certain words *or* sections of text to be located and replaced with others

Find utility program supplied with Windows 95 that will search through any disk for a particular file, folder or computer; *to use the Find function, select the Start/Find menu option*

Finder *noun* (in an Apple Macintosh system) graphical user interface to the Macintosh; allowing a user to view files and folders and start applications using a mouse

fine *adjective* excellent *or* of very high quality

◊ **fine tune** *verb* to adjust by small amounts the features *or* parameters of hardware *or* software to improve performance; *fine-tuning improved the speed by ten per cent*

finger *noun* (on the internet) software program that will retrieve information about a user based on their electronic mail address

finish 1 *noun* **(a)** final appearance; *the product has an attractive finish* **(b)** end of a process *or* function **2** *verb* **(a)** to do something *or* to make something completely; *the order was finished in time; she finished all the keyboarding before lunch* **(b)** to come to an end; *the contract is due to finish next month*

◊ **finished** *adjective* which has been completed; **finished document** = document which is typed, and is ready to be printed; **finished goods** = manufactured goods which are ready to be sold

finite-precision numbers *noun* use of a fixed number of bits to represent numbers

firewall *noun* hardware or software security system between a server or intranet and the public internet; the system allows information to pass out to the internet but checks any incoming data before passing it on to the private server; *we have installed a firewall in our intranet to prevent hackers accessing company data via the internet link*

firmware *noun* computer program *or* data that is permanently stored in a hardware memory chip, such as a ROM *or* EPROM *compare* HARDWARE, SOFTWARE

first fit *noun* routine *or* algorithm that selects the first, largest section of free memory in which to store a (virtual) page

◊ **first generation computer** *noun* original computer made with valve based electronic technology, started around 1951; **first generation image** = master copy of an original image, text *or* document

◊ **first in first out (FIFO)** *noun* temporary queue where the first item stored is the first read; *see also* FIFO

◊ **first-level address** *noun* computer storage address that directly, without any modification, accesses a location *or* device

fit *verb* to plot or calculate a curve that most closely approximates a number of points *or* data

fix *verb* **(a)** to make something permanent *or* to attach something permanently; *the computer is fixed to the workstation;* **fixed and exchangeable disk storage (FEDS)** = magnetic disk storage system that contains some removable disks, such as floppy disks and some fixed *or* hard disk drives; **fixed cycle operation** = (i) process in which each operation is allocated a certain, fixed time limit; (ii) actions within a process that are synchronized to a clock; **fixed data** = data written to a file *or* screen for information *or* identification purposes and which cannot be altered by the user; **fixed disk storage** = hard disk *or* magnetic disk which cannot be removed from the disk drive; **fixed field** = area in a stored record that can only contain a certain amount of data; **fixed head disk (drive)** = use of a separate immovable read/write head over each disk track making access time very short; **fixed-length field** = field whose size cannot be changed; **fixed-length record** = record whose size cannot be changed; **fixed-length word** = preset number of bits that make up a computer word; **fixed program computer** =

(hardwired) computer program that cannot be altered and is run automatically; **fixed routing** = communications direction routing that does not consider traffic *or* efficient paths; **fixed word length** = (computer) whose word size (in bits) cannot be changed **(b)** to mend; *the technicians are trying to fix the switchboard; can you fix the photocopier?*

◊ **fixed-point notation** = *noun* number representation that retains the position of the digits and decimal points in the computer, so limiting the maximum manageable numbers; *storage of fixed point numbers has two bytes allocated for the whole number and one byte for the fraction part;* **fixed-point arithmetic** = arithmetic rules and methods using fixed-point numbers *compare* FLOATING POINT

flag 1 *noun* (i) way of showing the end of field *or* of indicating something special in a database; (ii) method of reporting the status of a register after a mathematical *or* logical operation; *if the result is zero, the zero flag is set;* **flag bit** = single bit of a word used as a flag for certain operations; **flag code** = code sequence which informs the receiver that following characters represent control actions; **flag event** = process *or* state *or* condition that sets a flag; **flag register** = register that contains the status and flag bits of a CPU; **flag sequence** = sequence of codes sent on a packet switching network as identification of the start and finish of a frame of data; **carry flag** = indicator that a carry has occurred after a subtraction *or* addition; **device flag** = one bit in a device status word, used to show the state of a device; **overflow bit** *or* **flag** = single bit in a word that is set to one (1) if a mathematical overflow has occurred; **zero flag** = indicator that the contents of a register *or* result is zero **2** *verb* to attract the attention of a program while it is running to provide a result *or* to report an action *or* to indicate something special

◊ **flagging** *noun* putting an indicator against an item so that it can be found later

flame *verb* (on the internet) to send a rude or angry message to a user

flash *verb* to switch a light on and off; to increase and lower the brightness of a cursor to provide an indicator; **flash A/D** = parallel high speed A/D converter; **flash memory** = nonvolatile memory similar to an EEPROM device but that operates with blocks of data rather than single bytes; most often used as an alternative to a disk drive; **flash ROM** = electronic memory component that contains data that can normally only be read, but does allow new data to be stored in the memory using a special electrical signal; **flashing character** = character intensity that is switched on and off (as an indicator)

flat *adjective* **(a)** smooth (surface); **flat address space** = area of memory in which each location has a unique address (OS/2, Macintosh use a flat address space, MS-DOS does not) *compare* SEGMENTED ADDRESS SPACE; **flat file** = two-dimensional file of data items; **flat file database** = database program that does not allow relational data; it can only access data stored in one file at a time; **flat pack** = integrated circuit package whose leads extend horizontally, allowing the device to be mounted directly onto a PCB without the need for holes; **flat screen** = display monitor that has been manufactured with a flat, square-edged front to the monitor **(b)** fixed *or* not changing; **flat rate** = set pricing rate that covers all the uses of a facility

◊ **flatbed** *noun* printing *or* scanning machine that holds the paper *or* image on a flat surface while processing; *scanners are either flatbed models or platen type, paper-fed models; paper cannot be rolled through flatbed scanners;* **flatbed plotter** = movable pen that draws diagrams under the control of a computer onto a flat piece of paper; **flatbed scanner** = device with a flat sheet of glass on which the artwork is placed; the scan head moves below the glass and converts the image into a graphics file

flex *noun* wire *or* cable used to connect an appliance to the mains electricity supply; (NOTE: no plural: for one item, say **a piece of flex**)

flexible *adjective* which can be altered *or* changed; **flexible array** = array whose size and limits can be altered; **flexible disk** = FLOPPY DISK; **flexible disk cartridge** = FLOPPY DISK; **flexible machining system (FMS)** = computer numeric control (CNC) *or* control of a machine by a computer; **flexible manufacturing system (FMS)** = use of CNC machines, robots and other automated devices in manufacturing

◊ **flexibility** *noun* ability of hardware *or* software to adapt to various conditions *or* tasks

flicker 1 *noun* computer graphic image whose brightness alternates due to a low image refresh rate *or* signal corruption **2** *verb* to move very slightly; *the image flickers when the printer is switched on*

◊ **flicker-free** *adjective* (display) that does not flicker

---

the new 640 by 480 pixel standard, coupled with the flicker-free displays on the four new monitors and a maximum of 256 colours from a palette of more than quarter of a million

PC User

---

flip-flop (FF) *noun* electronic circuit *or* chip whose output can be one of two states, which is determined by one or two inputs, can be used to store one bit of digital data

flippy *noun* disk that is double-sided but used in a single-sided drive, so it has to be turned over to read the other side

float *noun* addition of the origin address to all indexed *or* relative addresses to check the amount of memory a program will require; **float factor** = location in memory at which the first instruction of a program is stored; **float relocate** = to convert floating addresses to absolute addresses

◊ **floating** *adjective* not fixed; character which is separate from the character it should be attached to; **floating address** = location specified in relation to a reference address; **floating head** = FLYING HEAD; **floating point arithmetic** = arithmetic operations on floating point numbers; **floating point (notation)** = numerical notation in which a fractional number is represented with a point

after the first digit and a power, so that any number can be stored in a standard form; *the fixed number 56.47 in floating-point arithmetic would be 0.5647 and a power of 2;* **floating point number** = number represented using floating point notation; **floating point operation (FLOP)** = mathematical operation carried out on a floating point number; **floating point unit** *or* **processor (FPU)** = specialized CPU that can process floating point numbers very rapidly; *the floating point processor speeds up the processing of the graphics software; this model includes a built-in floating point processor;* **floating symbolic address** = symbol *or* label that identifies a particular instruction *or* word, regardless of its location; **floating window** = window that can be moved anywhere on screen

FLOP = FLOATING POINT OPERATION; **FLOPs per second** = measure of computing power as the number of floating point operations that a computer can execute every second

floppy disk *or* **floppy** *or* **FD** *noun* secondary storage device, in the form of a flat, circular flexible disk onto which data can be stored in a magnetic form (a floppy disk cannot store as much data as a hard disk, but is easily removed, and is protected by a flexible paper *or* plastic sleeve); **floppy disk controller (FDC)** = combination of hardware and software devices that control and manage the read/write operations of a disk drive from a computer; **floppy disk drive (FDD)** *or* **unit** = disk drive for floppy disks and ancillary electronics as a separate assembly; **floppy disk sector** = smallest area on a magnetic (floppy) disk that can be individually addressed by a computer; **floppy tape** *or* **tape streamer** = continuous loop of tape, used for backing storage; *see also* MICROFLOPPY

COMMENT: floppy disks are usually available in 3.5 inch format, but the older sizes of 5.25 inch and 8 inch are still available. The size refers to the diameter of the disk inside the sleeve

flow 1 *noun* regular movement; *automatic text flow across pages; the device controls the copy flow; current flow is regulated by a resistor;* **flow control** = management of the flow of data into queues and buffers, to prevent heavy traffic; **data flow** = movement of data through a system 2 *verb* to move smoothly; *work is flowing normally again after the breakdown of the printer;* **flow text** = to insert text into a page format in a DTP system; the text fills all the space around pictures, and between set margins

◊ **flowchart** *or* **flow diagram** 1 *noun* chart which shows the arrangement of the steps in a process *or* program; **data flowchart** = diagram used to describe a computer *or* data processing system structure; **flowchart symbols** = special symbols used to represent devices, decisions and operations in a flowchart; **flowchart template** = plastic sheet with template symbols cut out, to allow symbols to be drawn quickly and clearly; **logical flowchart** = diagram showing where the logical decisions occur in a structure and their effects on program execution 2 *verb* to describe a process, its control and routes graphically; **flow diagram** = FLOWCHART; **flow direction** = order in which events occurring a flowchart

◊ **flowline** *noun* lines connecting flowchart symbols, showing the direction of flow within a flowchart

fluctuate *verb* to move up and down; *the electric current fluctuates between 1 Amp and 1.3 Amp*

◊ **fluctuating** *adjective* moving up and down; *fluctuating signal strength*

◊ **fluctuation** *noun* up and down movement; *voltage fluctuations can affect the functioning of the computer system*

flush 1 *verb* to clear *or* erase all the contents of a queue, buffer, file or section of memory; **flush buffers** = to erase any data remaining in a buffer, ready for a new job *or* after a job has been aborted 2 *adjective* level *or* in line with; **flush left** *or* **flush right** *see* JUSTIFY LEFT, JUSTIFY RIGHT

flutter *noun* fluctuations of tape speed due to mechanical *or* circuit problems, causing

signal distortion; *wow and flutter and common faults on cheap tape recorders*

flyback *or* **line flyback** *noun* electron picture beam return from the end of a scan to the beginning of the next

flying head *noun* hard disk read/write head that is wing-shaped to fly just above the surface of the spinning disk

FMS (a) = FLEXIBLE MACHINING SYSTEM computer numeric control (CNC) *or* control of a machine by a computer **(b)** = FLEXIBLE MANUFACTURING SYSTEM use of CNC machines, robots and other automated devices in manufacturing

focus 1 *noun* a particular window or field that is currently ready to accept a user's command; *in Windows, the object that currently has the user's focus has a dotted line around it;* **focus window** = window in a GUI that is currently active and accepting user input or is being controlled by a program and accepting commands from the program 2 *verb* to adjust a monitor so that the image that is displayed on the screen is sharp and clear

fogging *or* **haze** *noun* graphic effect that is used to simulate atmospheric fog or haze, used to make a three-dimensional scene more realistic

fold *noun* **accordion fold** *or* **fanfold** = method of folding continuous stationery, one sheet in one direction, the next sheet in the opposite direction, allowing the paper to stored conveniently and fed into a printer continuously

-fold *suffix* times; **four-fold** = four times

folding *noun* hashing method (that generates an address by splitting the key into parts and adding them together)

folder *noun* (in Windows 95 and the Apple Macintosh) group of files stored together under a name, similar to a directory under MS-DOS; *see also* DIRECTORY

font *or* **fount** *noun* set of characters all of the same style, size and typeface; **font card** = ROM device that fits into a socket on a printer and adds another resident font; **font change =** function on a computer to change the style of characters used on a display screen; **Font/DA Mover =** (in an Apple Macintosh system) system utility that allows a user to add fonts and DA files to the system environment; **font disk =** magnetic disk that contains the data to drive a character generator to make up the various fonts on a computer display; **Fonts Folder =** (in Windows 95) location for all the fonts that are currently installed on your PC; **downloadable fonts** or **resident fonts =** fonts or typefaces which are stored on a disk and can be downloaded to a printer and stored in temporary memory

---

Word Assistant is designed to help wordprocessing users produce better- looking documents. It has style templates and forms providing 25 TrueType fonts, 100 clip-art images and two font utility programs.

Computing

---

laser printers store fonts in several ways: as resident, cartridge and downloadable fonts

Desktop Publishing Today

---

foot *noun* bottom part; *he signed his name at the foot of the letter*

◊ **footer** or **footing** *noun* message at the bottom of all the pages in a printed document (such as the page number)

◊ **footnote** *noun* note at the bottom of a page, which refers to the text above it, usually using a superior number as a reference

◊ **footprint** *noun* **(a)** area covered by a transmitting device such as a satellite or antenna **(b)** area that a computer takes up on a desk

---

Acer has overhauled its desktop PC range with the launch of 16 new models ranging from s m a l l - f o o t p r i n t , single-processing systems to large multiprocessing boxes.

Computing

---

for-next loop *noun* loop or routine that is repeated until a condition no longer occurs;

for X= 1 to 5: print X: next X - this will print out 1 2 3 4 5

forbid *verb* to say that something must not be done; *the contract forbids sale of the goods to the USA;* **forbidden character** or **combination =** bit combination in a computer word that is not allowed according to the rules defined by the programmer or system designer

force 1 *noun* strength; **to come into force =** to start to operate or to work; *the new regulations will come into force on January 1st* **2** *verb* to make someone do something; *competition has forced the company to lower its prices;* **forced page break =** embedded code which indicates a new page start

foreground *noun* **(a)** front part of an illustration (as opposed to the background); **foreground colour =** colour of characters and text displayed on a screen **(b)** high priority task done by a computer; **foreground/background modes =** computer system in which two modes for program execution are possible: foreground mode for interactive user programs, background mode for housekeeping and other necessary system programs; **foreground processing memory =** region of a multitasking operating system in which high priority jobs or programs are executed; **foreground program =** high priority program in a multitasking system, whose results are usually visible to the user *compare* BACKGROUND

This brighter - but still anti-glare - type of screen is especially useful for people using colourful graphic applications, where both the background and foreground are visually important.

Computing

◊ **foregrounding** *noun* execution of high priority jobs or programs in a multitasking operating system

forest *noun* number of interconnected data structure trees

fork *noun* (in an Apple Machintosh) special folder that contains system files and information about a file or application

form 1 *noun* **(a)** (i) preprinted document with blank spaces where information can be entered; (ii) graphical display that looks like an existing printed form and is used to enter data into a database; *it's been easy to train the operators to use the new software since its display looks like the existing printed forms;* **form type** = four-character code that identifies the type of data chunk within a RIFF file **(b)** page of computer stationery; **form feed (FF)** = command to a printer to move to the next sheet of paper; **form flash** = text heading held in store and printed out at the same time as the text; **form handling equipment** = peripherals (such as decollator) which deal with output from a printer; **form letter** = standard letter into which personal details of each addressee are inserted, such as name, address and job; **form mode** = display method on a data entry terminal, the form is displayed on the screen and the operator enters relevant details; **form overlay** = heading *or* other matter held in store and printed out at the same time as the text; **form stop** = sensor on a printer which indicates when the paper has run out **2** *verb* to create a shape; to construct; *the system is formed of five separate modules*

format 1 *noun* **(a)** specific method of arranging text *or* data; way of arranging data on disk; **address format** = way in which address data is stored including which bits select pages, memory protect, etc.; **card format** = way in which columns and rows are arranged to represent data *or* characters in a punched card; **data format** = rules defining the way in which data is stored *or* transmitted; **display format** = number of characters that can be displayed on a screen, given as row and column lengths; **format mode** = use of protected display fields on a screen to show a blank form *or* page which cannot be altered, but into which a user can enter information; **instruction format** = rules defining the way the operands, data and address are arranged in an instruction; **local format storage** = format of an empty form *or* repeated page

stored in a terminal rather than being repeatedly transmitted; **variable format** = changing method of arranging data *or* text within an area **(b)** precise syntax of instructions and arguments; **symbolic-coding format** = assembly language instruction syntax, using a label, operation and operand fields **2** *verb* **(a)** to arrange text as it will appear in printed form on paper; *style sheets are used to format documents;* **formatted dump** = text *or* data printed in a certain format **(b)**; **to format a disk** = (i) to set up a blank disk so that it is ready for data, by writing control and track location information on it; (ii) to define the areas of a disk reserved for data and control; **disk formatting** = setting up a blank disk by writing control and track location information on it; *disk formatting has to be done before you can use a new floppy disk;* **low-level format** = process that defines the physical pattern and arrangement of tracks and sectors on a disk

◊ **formatter** *noun* hardware *or* software that arranges text *or* data according to certain rules; **print formatter** = software that converts embedded codes and print commands to printer control signals; **text formatter** = program that converts text to a new form or layout according to parameters or embedded codes (such as line width, page size, justification, etc.)

there are three models, offering 53, 80 and 160 Mb of formatted capacity
Minicomputer News

As an increasing amount of information within businesses is generated in wordprocessed format, text retrieval tools are becoming a highly attractive pragmatic solution.
Computing

formula *noun* set of mathematical rules applied to solve a problem; **formula portability** = feature in a spreadsheet program to find a value in a single cell from data in others, with the possibility of using the same formula in other cells; **formula translator** = FORTRAN (NOTE: plural is **formulae**)

FORTH computer programming language mainly used in control applications

---

the main attraction of FORTH over other computer languages is that it is not simply a language, rather it is a programming tool in which it is possible to write other application specific languages
Electronics & Power

FORTRAN = FORMULA TRANSLATOR programming language developed in the first place for scientific use

forty-track disk *noun* floppy disk formatted to contain forty tracks of data

forward 1 *adjective* moving in advance *or* in front; **forward error correction** = error detection and correction method that is applied to received data to correct errors rather than requesting another transmission; **forward pointer** = (in a linked list) pointer that contains the address of the next item in the list **2** *verb* **(a)** (in e-mail) to send an electronic mail message that you have received on to another user; *I did not know the answer to the question, so I have forwarded your message to my colleague* **(b)** (in a network) action by a bridge to copy a packet of data from one segment to another; *see also* BRIDGE

◊ **forward mode** *noun* to add a number *or* index *or* displacement to an origin

FOSDIC = FILM OPTICAL SCANNING DEVICE FOR INPUT INTO COMPUTERS storage device for computer data using microfilm

fount = FONT set of characters all of the same style, size and typeface

four-address instruction *noun* program instruction which contains four addresses within its address field, usually the location of the two operands, the result and the location of the next instruction; **four-plus-one address** = instruction that contains the locations of four registers and the location of the next instruction

fourth generation computers *noun* computer technology using LSI circuits, developed around 1970 and still in current use; **fourth generation languages (4GL)** = languages that are user-friendly and have been designed with the non-expert in mind

FPU = FLOATING POINT UNIT

fractal *noun* geometric shape that repeats itself within itself and always appears the same, however much you magnify the image; **fractal compression** = technique used to compress images; **fractal image format (FIF)** = file format used to store graphics images which have been highly compressed using fractals

fraction *noun* (i) part of a whole unit, expressed as one figure above another (such as 1/4, 1/3, 1/2, etc.); (ii) mantissa of a floating point number

◊ **fractional** *adjective* made of fractions; referring to fractions; *the root is the fractional power of a number;* **fractional part** = mantissa of a floating point number; **fractional services** = allocation of parts of a bandwidth to different signals or customers; *the commercial carrier will sell you fractional services that provide 64Kbps data transmission*

◊ **fractional T-1** *noun* method of dividing the capacity of a 1.544Mbits/second T-1 communications line into smaller 64Kbits/second channels that are more convenient and cheaper for a customer to use

fragmentation *noun* **(a)** (in main memory) memory allocation to a number of files, which has resulted in many small, free sections *or* fragments that are too small to be of any use, but waste a lot of space **(b)** (on a disk drive) files stored scattered across non-contiguous sectors on a hard disk; **defragmentation utility** = software utility that carries out the process of defragmentation on a hard disk

---

COMMENT: when a file is saved to disk, it is not always saved in adjacent sectors; this will increase the retrieval time. Defragmentation moves files back into adjacent sectors so that the read

> head does not have to move far across
> the disk, so it increases performance.

frame *noun* (i) space on magnetic tape for one character code; (ii) packet of transmitted data including control and route information; **frame buffer** = section of memory used to store an image before it is displayed on screen; **frame error** = error due to a faulty bit within a frame on magnetic tape; **frame relay** = communications protocol (similar but more efficient to X.25) that operates at OSI level 2; the system is used in wide area networks and is a subset of the HDLC (high level data-link control) called LAP-D (link access procedure-D) that allows data to be sent in packets over a shared high-speed channel such as a T-1 line; **frame window** = controls (including the minimise and maximise buttons, scroll bar and window title) and border that surround a window area

◊ **framework** *noun* basic structure of a database *or* process *or* program; *the program framework was designed first*

fraud *noun* making money by tricking people *or* by making them believe something which is not true; **computer fraud** = theft of data *or* dishonest use *or* other crimes involving computers

> the offences led to the arrest
> of nine teenagers who were all
> charged with computer fraud
> *Computer News*

free 1 *adjective* available for use *or* not currently being used; (spare bytes) available on disk *or* in memory; **free form database** = database that can store any type of data and does not have a fixed record structure; **free running mode** = interactive computer mode that allows more than one user to have simultaneous use of a program; **free wheeling** = transmission protocol where the computer transmitting receives no status signals from the receiver **2** *verb* to erase *or* remove *or* backup programs *or* files to provide space in memory

◊ **freedom** *noun* being free to do something without restriction; **freedom of information** = being able to examine computer records (referring both to

government activities and to records kept about individuals)

◊ **freely** *adverb* with no restrictions

◊ **freeware** *noun* software that is in the public domain and can be used by anyone without having to pay

free WAIS non-commercial version of the WAIS search index server; *see also* WAIS

freeze *see* HANG, CRASH

frequency *noun* number of cycles *or* periods of a regular waveform that are repeated per second; **clock frequency** = frequency of the main clock that synchronizes a computer system; *the main clock frequency is 10MHz;* **frequency division multiplexing (FDM)** = to assign a number of different signals to different frequencies (or bands) to allow many signals to be sent along one channel; *using FDM we can transmit 100 telephone calls along one main cable;* **line frequency** = (in a CRT) the number of times that the picture beam scans a horizontal row of pixels in a monitor

◊ **frequent** *adjective* which comes *or* goes *or* takes place often

◊ **frequently** *adverb* often; **frequently asked questions (FAQ)** = Web page or help file that contains common questions and their answers related to a particular subject

friction feed *noun* printer mechanism where the paper is advanced by holding it between two rollers (as opposed to tractor feed)

friendly front-end *noun* design of the display of a program that is easy to use and understand

FROM = FUSIBLE READ ONLY MEMORY

front *noun* part of something which faces away from the back; *the disks are inserted in slots in the front of the terminal;* **front panel** = main computer system control switches and status indicators

◊ **front-end** *adjective* **(a)** located at the start *or* most important point of a circuit *or* network; **front-end processor (FEP)** =

processor placed between an input source and the central computer whose function is to preprocess received data to relieve the workload of the main computer **(b)** visible part of an application that is seen by a user and is used to view and work with information; *the program is very easy to use thanks to the uncomplicated front-end*

FTAM = FILE TRANSFER, ACCESS, AND MANAGEMENT OSI standard method of transferring files between different computer systems

FTP = FILE TRANSFER PROTOCOL TCP/IP standard for transferring files between computers; it is a file sharing protocol that operates at layers 5, 6 and 7 of an OSI model network

full *adjective* **(a)** with as much inside as possible; *the disk is full, so the material will have to be stored on another disk* **(b)** complete *or* including everything; **full adder** = binary addition circuit that can produce the sum of two inputs and can also accept a carry input, producing a carry output if necessary; **full duplex** = data transmission down a channel in two directions simultaneously; *see also* DUPLEX, HALF-DUPLEX, SIMPLEX; **full motion video adapter** = computer fitted with a digitising card that is fast enough to capture and display moving video images (at a rate of 25 or 30 frames per second); **full path** = description of the position of a directory (in relation to the root directory) in which a file is stored; **full-screen** = (program display) that uses all the available screen; it is not displayed within a window; **full-size display** = large screen VDU which can display a whole page of text; **full subtractor** = binary subtractor circuit that can produce the difference of two inputs and can also accept a carry input, producing a carry output if necessary; **full-text search** = to carry out a search for something through all the text in a file or database rather than limiting the search to an area or block

```
transmitter and receiver can be
operated independently, making
full  duplex  communication
possible
```

◊ **fully** *adverb* completely; **fully formed characters** = characters produced by a printer in a single action; *a daisy wheel printer produces fully formed characters;* **fully populated board** = circuit board which has all components in place, including any optional or extra components

function 1 *noun* **(a)** mathematical formula, where a result is dependent upon several other numbers **(b)** sequence of computer program instructions in a main program that perform a certain task; **function call** = program instruction that moves execution to a predefined function *or* named sequence of instructions; **function digit** = code used to instruct a computer as to which function *or* branch in a program to follow; **function library** = collection of functions that can be used by a program; **function overloading** = programming system in which several different functions can have the same name, but are differentiated because they operate on different data types; **function table** = list that gives the relationship between two sets of instructions *or* data **(c)** special feature available on a computer *or* word-processor; *the word-processor had a spelling-checker function but no built-in text-editing function;* **function code** = printing codes that control an action rather than representing a character **2** *verb* to operate *or* perform correctly; *the new system has not functioned properly since it was installed*

◊ **functional** *adjective* which refers to the way something works; **functional diagram** = drawing of the internal workings and processes of a machine *or* piece of software; **functional specification** = specification which defines the results which a program is expected to produce; **functional unit** = hardware *or* software that works as it should

◊ **function key** *or* **programmable function key** *noun* key *or* switch that has been assigned a particular task *or* sequence of instructions; *tags can be allocated to function keys*

COMMENT: function keys often form a separate group of keys on the keyboard, and have specific functions attached to them. They may be labelled F1, F2, etc.

they made it clear that the PC was to take its place as part of a much larger computing function that comprised of local area networks, wide area networks, small systems, distributed systems and mainframes

Minicomputer News

the final set of keys are to be found above the main keyboard and comprise 5 function keys, which together with shift, give 10 user-defined keys

Computing Today

fuse 1 *noun* electrical protection device consisting of a small piece of metal, which will melt when too much power passes through it; **to blow a fuse** = to melt a fuse by passing too much current through it **2** *verb* to draw too much current, causing a fuse to melt; *when the air-conditioning was switched on, it fused the whole system*

◊ **fusible link** *noun* small link in a PLA that can be blown to program the device permanently

◊ **fusible read only memory (FROM)** *noun* PROM that is made up of a matrix of fusible links which are selectively blown to program it

fuzzy logic *or* **fuzzy theory** *noun* type of logic applied to computer programming, which tries to replicate the reasoning methods of the human brain

Gg

G = GIGA *prefix* meaning one thousand million

> COMMENT: in computing G refers to 2^{30}, equal to 1,073,741,824

G.711 standard used in multimedia and telephony to define an audio signal with a 3.4KHz bandwidth transferred over a 64Kbits/second data channel

GaAs = GALLIUM ARSENIDE

gain 1 *noun* increase *or* becoming larger; amount by which a signal amplitude is changed as it passes through a circuit, usually given as a ratio of output to input amplitude **2** *verb* to get; **to gain access to a file** = to be able to access a file; *the user cannot gain access to the confidential information in the file without a password*

gallium arsenide (GaAs) *noun* semiconductor compound, a new material for chip construction, that allows faster operation than silicon chips

game *noun* something which is played for enjoyment *or* relaxation; **computer game** = game played on a computer, using special software; **game cartridge** = ROM device that contains the program code for a computer game, and which is plugged into a game console; **game console** = dedicated computer, joystick and display adapter that is designed to be only used to play games; **game paddle** = device held in the hand to move a cursor *or* graphics in a computer game; **game port** = connection that allows a joystick to be plugged into a computer

ganged *adjective* mechanically linked devices that are operated by a single action; **ganged switch** = series of switches that operate on different parts of a circuit, but which are all switched by a single action; *a ganged switch is used to select which data bus a printer will respond to*

gap *noun* (a) space between recorded data; **block gap** *or* **interblock gap (IBG)** = blank magnetic tape between the end of one block of data and the start of the next in backing store; **gap character** = an extra character added to a group of characters (for parity or another purpose, but not data *or* instructions); **gap digit** = an extra digit added to a group of data (for parity or another purpose, but not data *or* instructions); **record gap** = blank section of magnetic tape between two consecutive records (b) space between a read head and the magnetic medium; **gap loss** = signal attenuation due to incorrect alignment of the read/write head with the storage medium; **air** *or* **head gap** = narrow gap between a recording *or* playback head and the magnetic medium

garbage *noun* (a) radio interference from adjacent channels (b) data *or* information that is no longer required because it is out of date *or* contains errors; **garbage collection** = reorganization and removal of unwanted *or* out of date files and records; clearing a section of memory of a program *or* its data that is not in use; **garbage in garbage out (GIGO)** = expression meaning that the accuracy and quality of information that is output depends on the quality of the input

> COMMENT: GIGO is sometimes taken to mean 'garbage in gospel out': i.e. that whatever wrong information is put into a computer, people will always believe that the output results are true

gas discharge display *or* **gas plasma display** *noun* flat, lightweight display screen that is made of two flat pieces of glass covered with a grid of conductors, separated by a thin layer of a gas which luminesces when one point of the grid is selected by two electric signals

COMMENT: mainly used in modern portable computer displays, but the definition is not as good as in cathode ray tube displays

gate *noun* **(a)** logical electronic switch whose output depends on the states of the inputs and the type of logical function implemented; **AND gate** = gate that performs a logical AND function; **coincidence gate** = gate that produces a logical output depending on various input coincidences (an AND gate requires the coincidence in time of all logically true inputs); **EXNOR gate** = electronic implementation of the EXNOR function; **EXOR gate** = electronic implementation of the EXOR function; **NAND gate** = electronic circuit that provides a NAND function; **negation** *or* **NOT gate** = single input gate whose output is equal to the logical inverse of the input; **NOR gate** = electronic circuit which performs a NOR function; **OR gate** = electronic circuit that provides the OR function; **gate array** = number of interconnected logic gates built into an integrated circuit to perform a complex function; **gate delay** *or* **propagation time** = time taken for a gate to produce an output after it has received inputs; **gate circuit** = electronic components that implement a logical function **(b)** connection pin of a FET device

gateway *noun* **(a)** (i) device that links two dissimilar networks; (ii) software protocol translation device that allows users working in one network to access another; *we use a gateway to link the LAN to WAN* **(b)** (in electronic mail) software that allows mail messages to be sent via a different route *or* to another network; *to send messages by fax instead of across the network, you'll need to install a fax gateway;* **fax gateway** = computer or software that allows users to

send information as a fax transmission instead of as a file stored on a disk

gather *verb* to receive data from various sources (either directly from a data capture device or from a cartridge) and sort and insert it in correct order into a database; **gather write** = to write a group of separate records as one block of data

gender changer *noun (informal)* device for changing a female connection to a male or vice versa

general *adjective* **(a)** ordinary *or* not special; **general office** = main administrative office **(b)** dealing with everything; **general purpose computer** = computer whose processing power may be applied to many different sorts of applications, depending on its hardware *or* software instructions; **general purpose interface bus (GPIB)** = standard for an interface bus between a computer and laboratory equipment; **general purpose program** = program *or* device able to perform many different jobs *or* applications; **general register** *or* **general purpose register (gpr)** = data register in a computer processing unit that can store items of data for many different mathematical *or* logical operations

generate *verb* to use software *or* a device to produce codes *or* a program automatically; *to generate an image from digitally recorded data; the graphics tablet generates a pair of co-ordinates each time the pen is moved;* **computer-generated** = produced using a computer; *they analyzed the computer-generated image;* **generated address** = location used by a program that has been produced by instructions within the program; **generated error** = error occurring due to inaccuracies in data used (such as a sum total error due to a series of numbers which are rounded up)

generation *noun* **(a)** producing data *or* software *or* programs using a computer; *the computer is used in the generation of graphic images; code generation is automatic; program generation; see* GENERATOR **(b)** state *or* age of the technology used in the design of a system;

first generation = earliest type of technology; **first generation computers** = original computers made with valve-based electronic technology, started around 1951; **first generation image** = master copy of an original image, text *or* document; **second generation computers** = computers which used transistors instead of valves; **third generation computers** = computers which used integrated circuits instead of transistors; **fourth generation computers** = computer technology using LSI circuits, developed around 1970 and still in current use; **fourth generation languages** = languages that are user-friendly and have been designed with the non-expert in mind; **fifth generation computers** = next stage of computer system design using fast VLSI circuits and powerful programming languages to allow human interaction **(c)** distance between a file and the original version, used when making backups; *the father file is a first generation backup*

◊ **generator** *noun* **(a)** (program) that generates new programs according to rules *or* specifications set out by the user **(b)** device which generates electricity; *the computer centre has its own independent generator, in case of mains power failure*

> vector and character
> generation are executed in
> hardware by a graphics display
> processor
> *Computing Today*

generic *adjective* (something) that is compatible with a whole family of hardware *or* software devices from one manufacturer

genuine *adjective* real *or* correct; *authentication allows the system to recognize that a sender's message is genuine*

geometry and rendering *noun* the two stages used to create and display a three-dimensional object

geometry processing *noun* process required to calculate the x, y and z coordinates of a three-dimensional object that is to be displayed on screen; *geometry processing is usually carried out by the CPU or by a specialized graphics processor*

get *noun* instruction to obtain a record from a file *or* database

ghost *noun;* **ghost cursor** = second cursor which can be used in some programs

GHz = GIGAHERTZ

gibberish *noun* useless and meaningless information

GIF file *noun* graphics file format of a file containing a bit-mapped image

giga- *or* **G** *prefix* meaning one thousand million
◊ **gigabyte** *noun* 10^9 bytes
◊ **gigaflop** *noun* one thousand million floating-point operations per second
◊ **gigahertz (GHz)** *noun* frequency of one thousand million cycles per second

> COMMENT: in computing giga refers to 2^{30}, which is equal to 1,073,741,824

GIGO = GARBAGE IN GARBAGE OUT expression meaning that the accuracy and quality of information that is output depends on the quality of the input

> COMMENT: GIGO is sometimes taken to mean 'garbage in gospel out': i.e. that whatever wrong information is put into a computer, people will always believe that the output results are true

GINO = GRAPHICAL INPUT OUTPUT graphical control routine written in FORTRAN

GKS = GRAPHICS KERNEL SYSTEM standard for software command and functions describing graphical input/output to provide the same functions, etc. on any type of hardware

glare *noun* very bright light reflections, especially on a VDU screen; *the glare from the screen makes my eyes hurt;* **glare filter** = coated glass or plastic sheet placed in front of a screen to cut out bright light reflections

glitch *noun (informal)* anything which causes the sudden unexpected failure of a computer *or* equipment

> The programmer was upgrading a
> verification system at Visa's
> UK data centre when his work
> triggered a software glitch
> causing hundreds of valid cards
> to be rejected for several
> hours.
>
> *Computing*

global *adjective* covering everything; **global backup** = (i) backup of all data stored on all nodes *or* workstations connected to a network; (ii) backup of all files on a hard disk *or* file server; **global exchange** = replace function which replaces one piece of text (such as a word) with another throughout a whole text; **global knowledge** = all the knowledge about one problem *or* task; **global memory** = (in Microsoft Windows) memory available to all Windows applications; **global search and replace** = word-processor search and replace function covering a complete file *or* document; **global variable** = variable *or* number that can be accessed by any routine *or* structure in a program *compare* LOCAL VARIABLE

> In an attempt to bring order to
> an electronic Tower of Babel,
> pharmaceutical   giant
> Rhone-Poulenc has assembled an
> X.400-based global messaging
> network   and   a   patchwork
> directory system that will be
> used   until   a   single   email
> system is deployed worldwide.
>
> *Computing*

GND = GROUND electrical circuit connection to earth *or* to a point with a zero voltage level

goal *noun* (i) aim *or* what you are trying to do; (ii) final state reached when a task has been finished *or* has produced satisfactory results

gold contacts *noun* electrical contacts, (usually for low-level signals) that are coated with gold to reduce the electrical resistance

golf-ball *noun* metal ball with characters on its surface, which produces printed characters by striking a ribbon onto paper;

golf-ball printer = computer printer using a golf-ball as a printing head

Gopher *noun* (on the internet) system that allows a user to find information and files stored on the internet using a series of commands; *see also* SEARCH ENGINE, VERONICA, WAIS

GOSIP = GOVERNMENT OPEN SYSTEMS INTERCONNECT PROFILE standards defined by the US Government to ensure that computers and communications systems can interact

gospel *see note at* GARBAGE

Government Open Systems Interconnect Profile *see* GOSIP

GOSUB programming command which executes a routine then returns to the following instruction

GOTO programming command which instructs a jump to another point *or* routine in the program; *GOTO 105 instructs a jump to line 105*

> COMMENT: GOTO statements are frowned upon by software experts since their use discourages set, structured programming techniques

GPIB = GENERAL PURPOSE INTERFACE BUS standard for an interface bus between a computer and laboratory equipment

gpr = GENERAL PURPOSE REGISTER data register in a computer processing unit that can store items of data for many different mathematical *or* logical operations

grab *verb* to take something and hold it

> sometimes a program can grab
> all the available memory, even
> if it is not going to use it
>
> *Byte*

grabber *or* **frame grabber** *noun* high speed digital sampling circuit that stores a TV picture in memory so that it can then be processed by a computer

```
the    frame    grabber    is
distinguished by its ability to
acquire a TV image in a single
frame interval
```
Electronics & Wireless World

graceful degradation *noun* allowing some parts of a system to continue to function after a part has broken down

grade *noun* level *or* rank; *a top-grade computer expert*

grammar *noun* rules for the correct use of language; **grammar checker** = software utility used to check a document or letter to make sure it is grammatically correct

◊ **grammatical error** *noun* incorrect use of a computer programming language syntax

grandfather file *noun* third most recent version of a backed up file, after father and son files; **grandfather cycle** = period in which the grandfather file is retrieved and updated to produce a new father file, the old father file becoming the new grandfather file

granularity *noun* size of memory segments in a virtual memory system

graph *noun* diagram showing the relationship between two *or* more variables as a line *or* series of points; **graph plotter** = printing device with a pen which takes data from a computer and plots it in graphic form

◊ **graphic** *adjective* (representation of information) in the form of pictures *or* plots instead of by text; **graphic data** = stored data that represents graphical information (when displayed on a screen); **graphic display** = computer screen able to present graphical information; **graphic display resolution** = number of pixels that a computer is able to display on the screen; **graphic language** = computer programming language with inbuilt commands that are useful when displaying graphics; *this graphic language can plot lines, circles and graphs with a single command*

◊ **graphical** *adjective* referring to something represented by graphics

◊ **graphical user interface (GUI)** *noun* interface between an operating system *or*

program and the user; it uses graphics *or* icons to represent functions or files and allow the software to be controlled more easily; system commands do not have to be typed in *compare* COMMAND LINE INTERFACE

COMMENT: GUIs normally use a combination of windows, icons and a mouse to control the operating system. In many GUIs, such as Microsoft Windows, Apple Macintosh System 7 and DR-GEM, you can control all the functions of the operating system just using the mouse. Icons represent programs and files; instead of entering the file name, you select it by moving a pointer with a mouse.

◊ **graphically** *adverb* by using pictures; *the sales figures are graphically represented as a pie chart*

◊ **graphics** *noun* pictures *or* lines which can be drawn on paper *or* on a screen to represent information; *graphics output such as bar charts, pie charts, line drawings, etc.;* **graphics accelerator** = special card that fits inside a computer and uses a dedicated processer chip to speed up the action of drawing lines and images on the screen; **graphics adapter** = electronic device (normally on an expansion card) in a computer that converts software commands into electrical signals that display graphics on a connected monitor; *the new graphics adapter is capable of displaying higher resolution graphics;* **graphics character** = preprogrammed shape that can be displayed on a non-graphical screen instead of a character, used extensively in videotext systems to display simple pictures; **graphics coprocessor** *see* GRAPHICS PROCESSOR; **graphics file** = (binary) file which contains data describing an image; *there are many standards for graphics files including TIFF, IMG and EPS;* **graphics file format** = method in which data describing an image is stored; **graphics kernel system (GKS)** = standard for software command and functions describing graphical input/output to provide the same functions etc. on any type of hardware; **graphics library** = number of routines stored in a library file that can be added to any user program to simplify the task of writing graphics programs; **graphics light pen =** high-accuracy light pen used for drawing onto a graphics display screen; **graphics mode =** videotext terminal whose displayed characters are taken from a range of graphics characters instead of text; **graphics overlay card =** expansion card for a PC or Macintosh that combines generated text or images with an external video source; **graphics pad** *or* **tablet =** flat device that allows a user to input graphical information into a computer by drawing on its surface; **graphics primitive =** basic shape (such as an arc, line or filled square) that is used to create other shapes or objects; **graphics printer =** printer capable of printing bit-mapped images; **graphics processor** *or* **graphics coprocessor =** secondary processor used to speed up the display of graphics: it calculates the position of pixels that form a line *or* shape and display graphic lines *or* shapes; *this graphics adapter has a graphics coprocessor fitted and is much faster;* **graphics software =** prewritten routines which perform standard graphics commands such as line drawing, plotting, etc., that can be called from within a program to simplify program writing; **graphics terminal =** special terminal with a high-resolution graphic display and graphics pad *or* other input device; **graphics VDU =** special VDU which can display high-resolution *or* colour graphics as well as text

---

one interesting feature of this model is graphics amplification, which permits graphic or text enlargement of up to 800 per cent

Byte

---

the custom graphics chips can display an image that has 640 columns by 400 rows of 4-bit pixel

Byte

---

several tools exist for manipulating image and graphical data: some were designed for graphics manipulation

Byte

Gray code *noun* coding system in which the binary representation of decimal numbers changes by only one bit at a time from one number to the next; **gray scale =** *see* GREY SCALE

COMMENT: used in communications systems to provide error detection facilities

---

greeked *adjective* (in a DTP program) font with a point size too small to display accurately, shown as a line rather than individual characters

Green Book formal specification for CD-i standard published by Philips; *see also* CD-I

green phosphor *noun* most commonly used phosphor for monochrome screen coating, which displays green characters on a black background

---

COMMENT: a new popular screen type is paper-white, using a white phosphor to display black characters on a white background

---

gremlin *noun (informal)* unexplained fault in a system; **line gremlin =** unexplained fault when data is lost during transmission

grey scale *noun* **(a)** shades of grey used to measure the correct exposure when filming **(b)** shades which are produced from displaying what should be colour information on a monochrome monitor

grid *noun* system of numbered squares used to help when drawing; matrix of lines at right angles allowing points to be easily plotted *or* located; **grid snap =** (in a graphics program) patterns *or* lines drawn on screen limited to the points of a grid; *if you want to draw accurate lines, you'll find it easier with grid snap turned on*

grip *verb* to hold something tightly; *in friction feed, the paper is gripped by the rollers*

ground *noun* electrical circuit connection to earth *or* to a point with a zero voltage level;

(NOTE: **ground** is more common in US English; the British English is **earth**)

group 1 *noun* **(a)** set of computer records containing related information; **group mark** *or* **marker** = code used to identify the start and end of a group of related records *or* items of data; **group poll** = polling a number of devices at once **(b)** six-character word used in telegraphic communications **(c)** (in a GUI) collection of icons of files *or* programs displayed together in a window; *all the icons in this group are to do with painting;* **group icon** = (in a GUI) icon that represents a window which contains a collection of icons of files *or* programs **(d)** (in a network) collection of users conveniently identified by one name; *the group ACCOUNTS contains all the users who work in the accounts department* **2** *verb* to bring several things together

◊ **groupware** *noun* (on a network) software specially written to be used by a group of people connected to a network and help them carry out a particular task; it provides useful functions such as a diary or electronic mail that can be accessed by all users

guarantee *noun* legal document promising that a machine will work properly *or* that an item is of good quality; *the system is still under guarantee and will be repaired free of charge*

guard band *noun* section of magnetic tape between two channels recorded on the same tape

◊ **guard bit** *noun* one bit within a stored word that indicates to the computer whether it can be altered or if it is protected

GUI = GRAPHICAL USER INTERFACE interface between an operating system *or* program and the user; it uses graphics *or* icons to represent functions or files and allow the software to be controlled more easily; system commands do not have to be typed in; *compare* COMMAND LINE INTERFACE (NOTE: pronounced 'gooey')

COMMENT: GUIs normally use a combination of windows, icons and a mouse to control the operating system. In many GUIs, such as Microsoft Windows, and Apple Macintosh System 8, you can control all the functions of the operating system just using the mouse. Icons represent programs and files; instead of entering the file name, you select it by moving a pointer with a mouse.

guide bars *noun* special lines in a bar code that show the start and finish of the code; *the standard guide bars are two thin lines that are a little longer than the coding lines*

gulp *noun* a group of words, usually two bytes; *see also* BYTE, NIBBLE

gun *or* **electron gun** *noun* source of an electron beam located inside a cathode ray tube

COMMENT: black and white monitors have a single beam gun, while colour monitors contain three, one for each primary colour (Red, Green and Blue) used

gutter *noun* (in a DTP system) blank space or inner margin between two facing pages

Hh

H & J = HYPHENATION AND JUSTIFICATION

hack *verb* **(a)** to experiment and explore computer software and hardware **(b)** to break into a computer system for criminal purposes

◊ **hacker** *noun* person who hacks

> The two were also charged with offences under the Computer Misuse Act and found guilty of the very actions upon which every hacker is intent.
>
> *Computing*

> software manufacturers try more and more sophisticated methods to protect their programs and the hackers use equally clever methods to break into them
>
> *Electronics & Wireless World*

> the hackers used their own software to break into the credit card centre
>
> *Computer News*

> any computer linked to the system will be alerted if a hacker uses its code number
>
> *Practical Computing*

hairline rule *noun* (in a DTP system) very thin line

half *noun* one of two equal parts; *half the data was lost in transmission; the second half of the program contains some errors;* **half adder** = binary adder that can produce the sum of two inputs, producing a carry output if necessary, but cannot accept a carry input; **half card** = expansion card that is half full length; **half duplex** = data transmission in one direction at a time over a bidirectional channel; **half-duplex modem** = modem which works in one mode at a time (either transmitting *or* receiving); *some modems can operate in half-duplex mode if required; see also* DUPLEX; **half-height drive** = disk drive whose front is half the height of a standard drive (half height drives, usually 5.25 inches are now the norm on PCs); **half-intensity** = character *or* graphics display at half the usual display brightness; **half word** = sequence of bits occupying half a standard computer word, but which can be accessed as a single unit

◊ **halftone** *adjective* photograph *or* image that originally had continuous tones, displayed *or* printed by a computer using groups of dots to represent the tones

hall effect *noun* description of the effect of a magnetic field on electron flow; **hall effect switch** = solid state electronic switch operated by a magnetic field

halt 1 *noun* computer instruction to stop a CPU carrying out any further instructions until restarted, or until the program is restarted, usually by external means (such as a reset button); **halt condition** = operating state reached when a CPU comes across a fault or faulty instruction or halt instruction in the program that is being run; **halt instruction** = program instruction that causes a CPU to halt, suspending operations, usually until it is reset; **dead halt** *or* **drop-dead halt** = program instruction from the user *or* an error that causes the program to stop without allowing recovery; **programmed halt** = instruction within a program which when executed, halts the processor (to restart the program, a reset is usually required) **2** *verb* to stop; *hitting CTRL S will halt the program*

Hamming code *noun* coding system that uses check bits and checksums to detect and correct errors in transmitted data, mainly used in teletext systems; **Hamming distance** = the number of digits that are different in two equal length words

hand *noun;* **hands off** = working system where: (i) the operator does not control the operation which is automatic; (ii) the operator does not need to touch the device in use; **hands on** = working system where the operator controls the operations by keying instructions on the keyboard; *the sales representatives have received hands-on experience of the new computer; the computer firm gives a two day hands-on training course*

◊ **hand-held** *adjective* which can be held in the hand; **hand-held computer** *or* **programmable** = very small computer which can be held in the hand, useful for basic information input, when a terminal is not available; **hand-held scanner** = small hand-held device used to scan small photographs and line drawings and convert these into graphic images that can be used on a computer *compare* FLATBED SCANNER

> A year ago the hand-held computer business resembled that of PCs a decade ago, with a large number of incompatible models, often software incompatible and using proprietary displays, operating systems and storage media.
>
> *Computing*

◊ **handler** *or* **driver** *noun* section of the operating system *or* program which controls a peripheral

handle *noun* **(a)** (in programming) number used to identify an active file within the program that is accessing the file **(b)** (in a GUI) small square displayed that can be dragged to change the shape of a window or graphical object; *to stretch the box in the DTP program, select it once to display the handles then drag one handle to change its shape*

◊ **handler** *noun* special software routine that controls a device or function; *the disk drive handler code is supplied in the library* *see also* DEVICE DRIVER; **error handler** = software routine that controls and reports on an error when it occurs

handshake *or* **handshaking**   *noun* standardized signals between two devices to make sure that the system is working correctly, the equipment is compatible and data transfer is correct (signals would include ready to receive, ready to transmit, data OK); **handshake I/O control** = use of handshake signals meaning ready-to-send and ready-to-receive, that allow a computer to communicate with a slower peripheral; **full handshaking** = signals transmitted between two communicating devices indicating ready to transmit, ready to receive, received, transmitted, etc.

handwriting recognition   *noun* software that is capable of recognising handwritten text and converting it into ASCII characters; *the new PDA has excellent handwriting recognition*

hang *verb* to enter an endless loop and not respond to further instruction

◊ **hangover** *noun* sudden tone change on a document that is transmitted over a fax machine as a gradual change, caused by equipment faults

◊ **hangup** *noun* sudden stop of a working program (often due to the CPU executing an illegal instruction *or* entering an endless loop)

hard *adjective* solid, as opposed to soft; (parts of a computer system) that cannot be programmed *or* altered; **hard card** = board containing a hard disk drive and the required interfacing electronics, which can be slotted into a system's expansion connector; **hard copy** = printed document *or* copy of information contained in a computer *or* system, in a form that is readable (as opposed to soft copy); **hard copy interface** = serial *or* parallel interface used to transmit data between a computer and a printer; **hard disk** = rigid magnetic disk that is able to store many times more data than a floppy disk, and usually cannot be removed from the disk drive; **hard disk drive (HDD)** *or* **hard drive** = unit used to store and retrieve data from a spinning hard disk (on the commands of a computer); **hard disk model** = model of computer with a hard disk; **hard error** = error which is permanent in a system; **hard failure** = fault (in hardware) that must be mended before a device will function correctly; *the hard failure was due to a burnt-out chip;* **hard reset** = switch that generates an electrical signal to reset the CPU and all devices, equivalent to turning a computer off and back on again; **hard return** = code in a word-processing document that (normally) indicates the end of a paragraph

◊ **hard-sectoring** *noun* method of permanently formatting a disk, where each track is split into sectors, sometimes preformatted by a series of punched holes around the central hub, where each hole marks the start of sector

hardware *noun* physical units, components, integrated circuits, disks and mechanisms that make up a computer *or* its peripherals; **hardware compatibility** = architecture of two different computers that allows one to run the programs of the other without changing any device drivers *or* memory locations, or the ability of one to use the add-on boards of the other; **hardware configuration** = way in which the hardware of a computer system is connected together; **hardware dependent** = something which will only work with a particular model *or* brand of hardware; *the communications software is hardware dependent and will only work with Hayes-compatible modems;* **hardware failure** = fault with a hardware device *or* hardware that has stopped working properly; **hardware graphics cursor** = electronic component that is used to calculate the position on screen of a pointer (according to the movement of a mouse) and display the pointer; **hardware interrupt** = interrupt signal generated by a piece of hardware rather than by software; **hardware platform** = standard of a particular computer (such as IBM PC, Apple Macintosh); **hardware reliability** = ability of a piece of hardware to function normally over a period of time; **hardware reset** = switch that generates an

electrical signal to reset the CPU and all devices, equivalent to turning a computer off and back on again; **hardware security** = making a system secure by means of hardware (such as keys, cards, etc.); *compare* SOFTWARE

> COMMENT: computer hardware can include the computer itself, the disks and disk drive, printer, VDU, etc.

Seuqent's Platform division will focus on hardware and software manufacture, procurement and marketing, with the Enterprise division concentrating on services and client-server implementation.
Computing

hardwired connection *noun* permanent phone line connection, instead of a plug and socket

hardwired logic *noun* logical function *or* program, which is built into the hardware, using electronic devices such as gates, rather than in software

hardwired program *noun* computer program built into the hardware, and which cannot be changed

hartley *noun* unit of information, equal to 3.32 bits, or the probability of one state out of ten equally probable states

hash 1 *verb* to produce a unique number derived from the entry itself, for each entry in a database; **hashing function** = algorithm used to produce a hash code for an entry and ensure that it is different from every other entry **2** *noun* **(a)** *see* HASHMARK **(b)**; **hash code** = coding system derived from the ASCII codes, where the code numbers for the first three letters are added up, giving a new number used as hash code; **hash-code system** = coding system using hash codes; **hash index** = list of entries according to their hashed numbers; **hash table** = list of all entries in a file with their hashed key address; **hash total** = total of a number of hashed entries used for error detection; **hash value** = number arrived at after a key is hashed

hashmark or **hash mark** noun printed sign (#) used as a hard copy marker or as an indicator

COMMENT: in US usage # 32 means number; # = number 32 (apartment number in a postal address, paragraph number in a text, etc.).

Hayes Corporation™ modem manufacturer who developed standard control language for modems; **Hayes AT command set** = set of commands to control a modem prefixed with the letters AT; *to dial the number 1234, use the Hayes AT command ATD1234;* **Hayes compatible** = modem that is compatible with the Hayes AT command set

hazard noun fault in hardware due to incorrect signal timing; **hazard-free implementation** = logical function design that has taken into account any hazards that could occur, and solved them

HD = HALF DUPLEX data transmission in one direction only, over a bidirectional channel

HDD = HARD DISK DRIVE

HDLC = HIGH LEVEL DATA LINK CONTROL

HDX = HALF DUPLEX

head 1 noun **(a)**; **combined head** or **read/write head** = transducer that can read or write data from the surface of a magnetic storage medium, such as a floppy disk; **head alignment** = (i) correct position of a tape or disk head in relation to the magnetic surface, to give the best performance and correct track location; (ii) location of the read head in the same position as the write head was (in relation to the magnetic medium); **head cleaning disk** = special disk which is used to clean the disk read/write heads; **head crash** = component failure in a disk drive, where the head is allowed to hit the surface of the spinning disk, causing disk surface damage and data corruption; **head demagnetizer** = device used to remove any stray magnetic effects that might have built up on the tape

head; **head park** = moving the read/write head in a (hard) disk drive to a safe position, not over the disk, so that if the unit is knocked or jarred the head will not damage the disk surface; **head positioning** = moving the read/write head to the correct track on a disk; **head wheel** = wheel that keeps video tape in contact with the head; **disk head** = head which reads or writes on a floppy disk; **flying head** = hard disk read/write head that uses a 'wing' to fly just over the surface of the spinning disk; **playback head** = transducer that reads signals recorded on a storage medium and usually converts them to an electrical signal; **read head** = transducer that can read data from a magnetic storage medium such as a floppy disk; **tape head** = head which reads or writes signals on a magnetic tape; **write head** = transducer that can write data onto a magnetic medium **(b)** data that indicates the start address of a list of items stored in memory **(c)** top edge of a book or of a page; **head of form** = first line on a form or sheet of paper that can be printed on **(d)** start of a reel of recording tape **(e)** top part of a device, network or body; **head end** = interconnection equipment between an antenna and a cable television network **2** verb to be the first item of data in a list; *the queue was headed by my file*

header noun **(a)** (in a local area network) a packet of data that is sent before a transmission to provide information on destination and routing **(b)** information at the beginning of a list of data relating to the rest of the data; **header block** = block of data at the beginning of a file containing data about file characteristics; **header card** = punched card containing information about the rest of the cards in the set; **header label** = section of data at the beginning of a magnetic tape, that contains identification, format and control information; **tape header** = identification information at the beginning of a tape **(c)** words at the top of a page of a document (such as title, author's name, page number, etc.); *see also* FOOTER

heading noun **(a)** title or name of a document or file **(b)** header or words at the top of each page of a document (such as the title, the page numbers, etc.)

headlife *noun* length of time that a video *or* tape head can work before being serviced *or* replaced

headline *noun* = HEADING

heap *noun* **(a)** temporary data storage area that allows random access *compare* STACK **(b)** binary tree

heat-sensitive paper *noun* *see* ELECTROSTATIC PRINTING

heat-sink *noun* metal device used to conduct heat away from an electronic component to prevent damage

help *noun* **(a)** anything which makes it easier to do something; *he finds his word-processor a great help in the office; they need some help with their programming* **(b)** function in a program *or* system that provides useful information about the program in use; *hit the HELP key if you want information about what to do next;* **context sensitive help** = help message that gives useful information about the particular function or part of the program you are in, rather than general information about the whole program; **help key** = (i) (on an Apple Macintosh) special key that displays help information; (ii) (on an IBM PC) F1 function key used to display help information; **help screen** = display of information about a program or function

COMMENT: most software applications for IBM PCs have standardized the use of the F1 function key to display help text explaining how something can be done

Hercules graphics adapter (HGA)

noun (old) standard for mono graphics adapter developed by Hercules Corporation

Hertz *noun* SI unit of frequency, defined as the number of cycles per second of time

COMMENT: Hertz rate is the frequency at which mains electricity is supplied to the consumer. The Hertz rate in the USA and Canada is 60; in Europe it is 50

heterogeneous network *noun* computer network joining computers of many different types and makes; **heterogeneous multiplexing** = communications multiplexing system that can deal with channels with different transmission rates and protocols

heuristic *adjective* which learns from past experiences; *a heuristic program learns from its previous actions and decisions*

Hewlett Packard™ manufacturer of computers, test equipment, and printers; **Hewlett Packard Graphics Language (HPGL)** = standard set of commands used to describe graphics; **Hewlett Packard Interface Bus (HPIB)** = standard method of interfacing peripheral devices *or* test equipment and computers; **Hewlett Packard LaserJet** *or* **HP LaserJet**= laser printer manufactured by Hewlett Packard that uses its PCL language to describe a page; **Hewlett Packard Printer Control Language (HP-PCL)** = standard set of commands developed by Hewlett Packard to allow a software application to control a laser printer's functions

hex *or* **hexadecimal notation** *noun* number system using base 16 and digits 0-9 and A-F; **hex dump** = display of a section of memory in hexadecimal form; **hex pad** = keypad with keys for each hexadecimal digit

HFS = HIERARCHICAL FILE SYSTEM (in an Apple Macintosh system) method used to store and organise files on a disk

HGA = HERCULES GRAPHICS ADAPTER

hidden *adjective* which cannot be seen; **hidden defect in a program** = defect which was not seen when the program was tested; **hidden files** = important system files which are not displayed in a directory listing and cannot normally be read by a user; *it allows users to backup or restore hidden system files independently;* **hidden lines** = lines which make up a three-dimensional object, but are obscured when displayed as a two-dimensional image; **hidden line algorithm** = mathematical formula that removes hidden lines from a two-dimensional computer image of a 3-D object; **hidden line removal** = erasure of lines which should not be visible when looking at a two-dimensional image of a three-dimensional object

hierarchy *noun* way in which objects *or* data *or* structures are organized, usually with the most important *or* highest priority *or* most general item at the top, then working down a tree structure; **data hierarchy** = data structure organized hierarchically

◊ **hierarchical communications system** *noun* network in which each branch has a number of separate minor branches dividing from it; **hierarchical computer network** = method of allocating control and processing functions in a network to the computers which are most suited to the task; **hierarchical database** = database in which records can be related to each other in a defined structure; **hierarchical directory** = directory listing of files on a disk, showing the main directory and its files, branches and any sub-directories; **hierarchical filing system (HFS)** = (in an Apple Macintosh system) method used to store and organise files on a disk

high *adjective* **(a)** large *or* very great; **high density storage** = very large number of bits stored per area of storage medium; *a hard disk is a high density storage medium compared to paper tape;* **high-end** = expensive or high-performance device; **high memory** = (on an IBM PC) memory area between 640Kb and 1Mb; **high memory area (HMA)** = (in an IBM PC) first 64Kb of extended memory above 1Mb that can be used by programs; **high order** = digit with the greatest weighting within a number; **high-order language** = HIGH-LEVEL LANGUAGE; **high performance equipment** = very good quality *or* high specification equipment; **high performance filing system (HPFS)** = (in OS/2 operating system) method of storing file information that is faster and more flexible than MS-DOS FAT; **high priority program** = program that is important *or* urgent and is processed before others; **high specification** *or* **high spec** =

giving a high degree of accuracy *or* having a large number of features; *high spec cabling needs to be very carefully handled;* **high speed carry** = single operation in which a carry into an adder results in a carry out **(b)**; **logical high** = equal to logic TRUE state or 1; *compare* LOGICAL LOW, FALSE

◊ **high-level** *adjective;* **high-level data link control (HLDLC)** = ISO standard that provides a link-layer protocol and defines how data is formatted before being transmitted over a synchronous network; **high-level data link control station** = equipment and programs which correctly receive and transmit standard HLDLC data frames; **high-level (programming) language (HLL)** = computer programming language which is easy to learn and allows the user to write programs using words and commands that are easy to understand and look like English words, the program is then translated into machine code, with one HLL command often representing a number of machine code instructions; *programmers should have a knowledge of high-level languages, particularly PASCAL; compare* LOW-LEVEL LANGUAGE

```
they      have      proposed      a
standardized            high-level
language  for  importing  image
data  into  desktop  publishing
and      other      applications
programs
```
Byte

highlight 1 *noun;* **highlights** = characters *or* symbols treated to make them stand out from the rest of the text, often by using bold type 2 *verb* to make part of the text stand out from the rest; *the headings are highlighted in bold*

highlight bar *noun* bar that a user can move up and down a list of options to choose an option

high-resolution *or* **hi-res** *noun* ability to display *or* detect a very large number of pixels per unit area; *high-resolution graphics; this high-resolution monitor can display 1280x1024 pixels; the new hi-res optical scanner can detect 2400 dots per inch* the computer is uniquely suited to image processing because of its high-resolution graphics

Byte

◊ **high Sierra specification**   *noun* industry standard method of storing data on a CD-ROM disc

◊ **high-speed** *adjective* which operates faster than normal data transmission *or* processing; **high-speed serial interface (HSSI)** = serial link that can transfer data at data rates up to 52Mbits/second; used in some wide area network systems; *see also* USB; **high-speed skip** = rapid movement in a printer to miss the perforations in continuous stationery

◊ **high-tech** *or* **high technology** *adjective* technologically advanced

◊ **highway** *or* **bus** *noun* communications link consisting of a set of leads *or* wires which connect different parts of a computer hardware system and over which data is transmitted and received by various circuits inside the system; **address highway** = physical connections that carry the address data in a parallel form between the central processing unit and memory *or* external devices; **data highway** = bus carrying the data signals in parallel form between the central processing unit and memory *or* external devices

hill climbing *noun* method of achieving a goal in an expert system

hi-res = HIGH RESOLUTION; *hi-res graphics; this hi-res monitor can display 1280x1024 pixels; the new hi-res optical scanner can detect 2400 dots per inch*

histogram *noun* graph on which values are represented as vertical *or* horizontal bars

history *noun* feature of some applications that keeps a log of the actions a user has carried out, the places within a hypertext document they have visited, or the sites on the internet they have explored

hit 1 *noun* successful match *or* search of a database; *there was a hit after just a few seconds; there are three hits for this search key;* **cache hit** = data retrieved from cache

memory rather than from the storage device; indicates that time was saved and the cache was useful; **hit on the line** = short period of noise on a communications line, causing data corruption **2** *verb* to press a key; *to save the text, hit ESCAPE S*

the cause of the data disaster is usually due to your finger hitting the wrong key

PC Business World

HLDLC = HIGH-LEVEL DATA LINK CONTROL

HLL = HIGH-LEVEL LANGUAGE

HMA = HIGH MEMORY AREA (in an IBM PC) first 64Kb of extended memory above 1Mb that can be used by programs

HMI = HUMAN MACHINE INTERFACE facilities provided to improve the interaction between a user and a computer system

HOF = HEAD OF FORM

hold 1 *noun* synchronization timing pulse for a television time base signal **2** *verb* to retain *or* keep a value *or* communications line *or* section of memory; **holding loop** = section of program that loops until it is broken by some action, most often used when waiting for a response from the keyboard *or* a device; **holding time** = time spent by a communications circuit on call

COMMENT: the hold feature keeps the picture steady and central on the screen; some televisions have horizontal and vertical hold controls to allow the picture to be moved and set up according to various conditions

◊ **holdup** *noun* (i) time period over which power will be supplied by a UPS; (ii) pause in a program *or* device due to a malfunction

hole *noun* punched gap in a punched paper tape *or* card, representing data; **index hole** = hole in the edge of a hard-sectored disk

Hollerith code *noun* coding system that uses punched holes in a card to represent characters and symbols: the system uses two sets of twelve rows to provide possible positions for each code

hologram *noun* imaginary three-dimensional image produced by the interference pattern when a part of a coherent light source, such as a laser, is reflected from an object and mixed with the main beam

◊ **holographic image** *noun* hologram of a three-dimensional object; **holographic storage** = storage of data as a holographic image which is then read by a bank of photocells and a laser (a new storage medium with massive storage potential)

home *noun* (a) place where a person lives; **home banking** = method of examining and carrying out bank transactions in the user's home via a terminal and modem; **home computer** = microcomputer designed for home use, whose applications might include teaching, games, personal finance and word-processing (b) starting point for printing on a screen, usually taken as the top left hand corner; **home key** = (on an IBM PC keyboard) key that moves the cursor to the beginning of a line of text; **home record** = first *or* initial data record in a file

◊ **home page** *noun* opening page of a Web site (normally stored in a file called index.html)

homogeneous computer network

noun network made up of similar machines, that are compatible *or* from the same manufacturer; **homogeneous multiplexing** = switching multiplexer system where all the channels contain data using the same protocol and transmission rate

hood *noun* cover which protects something; **acoustic hood** = soundproof cover put over a line printer to cut down its noise

hook *noun* point in a program at which a programmer can insert test code or debugging code

hop *noun* path taken by a packet of data as it moves from one server or router to another

hopper *noun* device which holds punched cards and feeds them into the reader

horizontal *adjective* lying flat *or* going from side to side, not up and down; **horizontal blanking period** = time taken for the picture beam in a monitor to return to the start of the next line from the end of the previous line; **horizontal check** = error detection method for transmitted data; *see also* CYCLIC CHECK; **horizontal scan frequency** = the number of lines on a video display that are refreshed each second; **horizontal scrollbar** = (in a GUI) bar along the bottom of a window that indicates that the page is wider than the window; a user can move horizontally across the page by dragging the indicator bar on the scrollbar; **horizontal scrolling** = to move across a page, horizontally; **horizontal wraparound** = movement of a cursor on a computer display from the end of one line to the beginning of the next

host *noun & adjective;* **host adapter** = adapter which connects to a host computer; *the cable to connect the scanner to the host adapter is included;* **host name** = name given to a web site on the internet

◊ **host computer** *noun* (a) main controlling computer in a multi-user *or* distributed system (b) computer used to write and debug software for another computer, often using a cross compiler (c) computer in a network that provides special services *or* programming languages to all users

```
you select fonts manually or
through commands sent from the
host computer along with the
text
```
Byte

hot *adjective;* **hot chassis** = metal framework *or* case around a computer that is connected to a voltage supply rather than being earthed; **hot fix** = to detect and repair a fault (normally a corrupt sector on a hard disk) without affecting normal operations; **hot key** = special key or key combination which starts a process or activates a program; **hot link** = command within a hypertext program that links a hotspot or hotword on one page with a second destination page which is displayed if the user selects the hotspot; **hot standby** = piece of hardware that is kept operational at all times and is used as backup in case of system failure; **hot zone** = text area to the left of the right margin in a word-processed document (if a word does not fit in completely, a hyphen is automatically inserted); **hotword** = word within displayed text that does something when the cursor is moved onto it or it is selected

◊ **hotspot** *noun* special area on an image or display that does something when the cursor is moved onto it; *the image of the trumpet is a hotspot and will play a sound when you move the pointer over it*

house 1 *noun* company (especially a publishing company); *one of the biggest software houses in the US;* **house style** = (i) style of spelling and layout, used by a publishing company in all its books; (ii) design of a company's products, used to identify them from the products of competitors **2** *verb* to put a device in a case; *the magnetic tape is housed in a solid plastic case*

◊ **housekeeping** *noun* tasks that have to be regularly carried out to maintain a computer system (checking backups, deleting unwanted files, etc.); **housekeeping routine** = set of instructions executed once, at the start of a new program to carry out system actions such as clear memory, configure function keys or change screen display mode; *see also* IN-HOUSE

◊ **housing** *noun* solid case; *the computer housing was damaged when it fell on the floor*

howler *noun* **(a)** buzzer which indicates to a telephone exchange operator that a user's telephone handset is not on the receiver **(b)** very bad and obvious mistake; *what a howler, no wonder your program won't work*

HP = HEWLETT PACKARD

HPFS = HIGH PERFORMANCE FILING SYSTEM (in OS/2 operating system) method of storing file information that is faster and more flexible than MS-DOS FAT

HPGL = HEWLETT PACKARD GRAPHICS LANGUAGE

◊ **HPIB** = HEWLETT PACKARD INTERFACE BUS

◊ **HP-PCL** = HEWLETT PACKARD PRINTER CONTROL LANGUAGE

HRG = HIGH RESOLUTION GRAPHICS ability to display a large number of pixels per unit area; *the HRG board can control up to 300 pixels per inch*

HSSI HIGH-SPEED SERIAL INTERFACE serial link that can transfer data at data rates up to 52Mbits/second; used in some wide area network systems; *see also* USB

HTML = HYPERTEXT MARKUP LANGUAGE series of special codes that define the typeface and style that should be used when displaying the text and also allow hypertext links to other parts of the document or to other documents; *HTML is normally used to create documents for the World Wide Web; see also* DHTML, HYPERTEXT, WWW

HTTP = HYPERTEXT TRANSFER PROTOCOL commands used by a browser to ask an internet Web server for information about a Web page

HTTPD = HYPERTEXT TRANSFER PROTOCOL DAEMON Web server that carries out the functions required to process forms, image maps, authentication and searching

hub *noun* **(a)** (in a floppy disk) central part of a disk, usually with a hole and ring which the disk drive grips to spin the disk **(b)** (in a star-topology network) central ring *or* wiring cabinet where all circuits meet (and form an electrical path for signals); **stackable hub** = hub device that has an external connector to allow several devices to be connected together to allow network information to pass from one network ring to another

Huffman code *noun* data compression code, where frequent characters occupy less bit space than less frequent ones

huge model *noun* (in programming) memory model of an Intel processor that allows data and program code to exceed 64Kb (but the total of both must be less than 1Mb)

human-computer *or* human-machine interface (HMI) *noun*
facilities provided to improve the interaction between a user and a computer system

hung *see* CRASH

hunting *noun* process of searching out a data record in a file

hybrid circuit *noun* connection of a number of different electronic components such as integrated circuits, transistors, resistors and capacitors in a small package, which since the components are not contained in their own protective packages, requires far less space than the individual discrete components; **hybrid computer** = combination of analog and digital circuits in a computer system to achieve a particular goal; **hybrid interface** = one-off interface between a computer and a piece of analog equipment; **hybrid system** = combination of analog and digital computers and equipment to provide an optimal system for a particular task

HyperCard™ *noun* database system controlled by HyperTalk programming language used to produce hypertext documents

hyperlink *noun* word or image or button in a Web page or multimedia title that moves the user to another page when clicked

hypermedia *noun* hypertext document that is also capable of displaying images and sound

HyperTalk *noun* programming language used to control a HyperCard database

HyperTerminal *noun* communications program that is included with Windows 95

and allows a user to call a remote computer via a modem and transfer files

hypertext *adjective & noun* **(a)** (multimedia) system of organising information; certain words in a document link to other documents and display the text when the word is selected; *in this hypertext page, click once on the word 'computer' and it will tell you what a computer is* **(b)** (internet) a way of linking one word or image to another page; when the user selects the word or image, they jump directly to the new page; **dynamic hypertext markup language** = *see* DHTML; **hypertext markup language** = *see* HTML; **hypertext transfer protocol** = *see* HTTP; **hypertext transfer protocol daemon** = *see* HTTPD

hyphen *noun* printing sign (-) to show that a word has been split; **soft** *or* **discretionary hyphen** = hyphen which is inserted when a word is split at the end of a line in word-processed text, but is not present when the word is written normally

hyphenated *adjective* written with a hyphen; *the word 'high-level' is usually hyphenated*

hyphenation *noun* splitting of a word (as at the end of a line, when the word is too long to fit); **hyphenation and justification** *or* **H & J** = justifying lines to a set width, splitting the long words correctly at the end of each line; *an American hyphenation and justification program will not work with British English spellings*

> the hyphenation program is useful for giving a professional appearance to documents and for getting as many words onto the page as possible
>
> *Micro Decision*

Hz = HERTZ

Ii

IAM = INTERMEDIATE ACCESS MEMORY memory storage that has an access time between that of main memory and a disk based system

IAB = INTERNET ACTIVITIES BOARD independent committee that is responsible for the design, engineering and management of the internet

IAR = INSTRUCTION ADDRESS REGISTER register in a CPU that contains the location of the next instruction to be processed

IAS = IMMEDIATE ACCESS STORE high-speed main memory area in a computer system

I-beam *noun* cursor shaped like the letter 'I' used (in a GUI) to edit text *or* indicate text operations

IBG = INTERBLOCK GAP

IBM = INTERNATIONAL BUSINESS MACHINES largest computer company in the world; developed the first PC based on the Intel processor; **IBM AT** = personal computer based on the Intel 80286 16-bit processor and featured an ISA expansion bus; **IBM AT keyboard** = keyboard layout that features 12 function keys in a row along the top of the keyboard, with a separate numeric keypad; **IBM compatible** = generic term for a personal computer that is hardware and software compatible with the IBM PC regardless of which Intel processor it uses; it features an ISA, EISA or MCA expansion bus; **IBM PC** = personal computer based on the Intel 8088 8-bit processor; **IBM PC keyboard** = keyboard layout that features 10 function keys arranged to the left of the main

keys, with no separate numeric keypad; **IBM PS/2** *or* **IBM Personal System/2** = range of personal computers based on the Intel 8086, 80286 and 80386 processors that feature an MCA expansion bus; **IBM XT** = personal computer based on the IBM PC but with an internal hard disk drive and featuring an ISA expansion bus

IC = INTEGRATED CIRCUIT (NOTE: plural is **ICs**)

icand *noun* = MULTIPLICAND

icon *or* **ikon** *noun* graphic symbol *or* small picture displayed on screen, used in an interactive computer system to provide an easy way of identifying a function; *the icon for the graphics program is a small picture of a palette; click twice over the word-processor icon - the picture of the typewriter*

> Despite (or because of?) the swap file, loading was slow and the hourglass icon of the mouse pointer frequently returned to the arrow symbol well before loading was complete.
>
> *Computing*

> the system has on-screen icons and pop-up menus and is easy to control using the mouse
>
> *Electronics & Power*

> an icon-based system allows easy use of a computer without the need to memorize the complicated command structure of the native operating system
>
> *Micro Decision*

ID = IDENTIFICATION; **ID card** = card which identifies a person; **ID code** =

password *or* word that identifies a user so that he can access a system; *after you wake up the system, you have to input your ID code then your password*

IDE = INTEGRATED DRIVE ELECTRONICS *or* INTELLIGENT DEVICE ELECTRONICS popular standard for a hard disk drive controller unit that allows data transfer rates up to 4.1MBps and can support two hard disk drives on each conroller; enhanced versions of the IDE standard provide more flexibility and speed (also known as AT Attachment - ATA - interface); *IDE drives are the standard fitted to most PCs; see also* ATA, SCSI

identical *adjective* exactly the same; *the two systems use identical software; the performance of the two clones is identical*

identify *verb* to establish who someone is *or* what something is; *the user has to identify himself to the system by using a password before access is allowed; the maintenance engineers have identified the cause of the system failure*

◊ **identification** *noun* procedure used by a host computer to establish the identity and nature of the calling computer *or* user (this could be for security and access restriction purposes *or* to provide transmission protocol information); **identification character** = single character sent to a host computer to establish the identity and location of a remote computer *or* terminal; **identification division** = section of a COBOL program source code, in which the identifiers and formats for data and variables to be used within the program are declared

◊ **identifier** *noun* set of characters used to distinguish between different blocks of data *or* files; **identifier word** = word that is used as a block *or* file identifier

◊ **identity** *noun* who someone *or* what something is; **identity burst** = pattern of bits before the first block of data on a magnetic tape that identifies the tape format used; **identity gate** *or* **element** = logical gate that provides a single output that is true if the inputs are both the same; **identity number** = unique number, used usually with a password

to identify a user when logging into a system; *don't forget to log in your identity number;* **identity operation** = logical function whose output is true only if all the operands are of the same value; **identity palette** = 256-colour palette in which the first and last 10 colours are the system colours

idle *adjective* (machine *or* telephone line *or* device) which is not being used, but is ready and waiting to be used; **idle character** = symbol *or* code that means 'do nothing' *or* a code which is transmitted when there is no data available for transmission at that time; **idle time** = period of time when a device is switched on but not doing anything

IDP = INTEGRATED DATA PROCESSING

IE = INTERNET EXPLORER web browser developed by Microsoft, currently available free, that allows a user to view Web pages

IEC connector *noun* standard for a three-pin connector used on sockets that carry mains electricity to the computer; *all PCs use a male IEC connector and a mains lead with a female IEC connector*

IEE *UK* = INSTITUTION OF ELECTRICAL ENGINEERS

IEEE *US* = INSTITUTE OF ELECTRICAL AND ELECTRONIC ENGINEERS; **IEEE bus** = interface that conforms to IEEE standards; **IEEE-488** = interfacing standard as laid down by the IEEE, where only data and handshaking signals are used, mainly used in laboratories to connect computers to measuring equipment; **IEEE-802.2** = standard defining data links used with 802.3, 802.4 and 802.5; **IEEE-802.3** = standard defining Ethernet network system (CSMA/CD access using a bus-topology); **IEEE-802.4** = standard defining Token Bus; **IEEE-802.5** = standard defining IBM Token-Ring network system (access using a token passed around a ring network)

ier *noun* = MULTIPLIER

IETF = INTERNET ENGINEERING TASK FORCE committee that is part of the IAB (see above) and determines internet standards

IFF (a) = INTERNATIONAL FILE FORMAT standard for compressed files stored on a CD-i **(b)** = INTERCHANGE FILE FORMAT standard that defines how palette data is stored in an Amiga and some graphics programs

IF statement *noun* computer programming statement, meaning do an action IF a condition is true (usually followed by THEN); **IF-THEN-ELSE** = high-level programming language statement, meaning IF something cannot be done, THEN do this, or ELSE do that

ignore *verb* not to recognize *or* not to do what someone says; *this command instructs the computer to ignore all punctuation;* **ignore character** = null *or* fill character

IH = INTERRUPT HANDLER

IIL = INTEGRATED INJECTION LOGIC

IIS = INTERNET INFORMATION SERVER internet Web server software developed by Microsoft

IKBS = INTELLIGENT KNOWLEDGE-BASED SYSTEM

ikon *or* **icon** *noun* graphic symbol *or* picture displayed on screen, used in an interactive computer system to provide an easy way of identifying a function *see also* ICON

illegal *adjective* which is not legal *or* which is against the law *or* against rules of syntax; **illegal character** = invalid combination of bits in a computer word, according to preset rules; **illegal instruction** = instruction code not within the repertoire of a language; **illegal operation** = instruction *or* process that does not follow the computer system's protocol *or* language syntax

◊ **illegally** *adverb* against the law *or* against rules; *the company has been illegally copying copyright software*

illiterate *adjective* (person) who cannot read; **computer illiterate** = (person) who does not understand computer-related expressions *or* operations; *see also* LITERATE

> three years ago the number of people who were computer illiterate was much higher than today
>
> *Minicomputer News*

IMA = INTERACTIVE MULTIMEDIA ASSOCIATION professional organisation that covers subjects including authoring languages, formats, and intellectual property

image *noun* **(a)** exact duplicate of an area of memory **(b)** copy of an original picture *or* design; **image area** = region of microfilm *or* display screen on which characters *or* designs can be displayed; **image buffer** = area of memory that is used to build up an image before it is transferred to screen; **image compression** = compressing the data that forms an image; **image editing** = altering or adjusting an image using a paint package or special image editing program; **image enhancement** = adjusting parts of an image using special image editing program, normally to change the contrast, brightness or sharpness of an image; **image processing** = analysis of information contained in an image, usually by electronic means *or* using a computer which provides the analysis *or* recognition of objects in the image, etc.; **image processor** = electronic *or* computer system used for image processing, and to extract information from the image; **image scanner** = input device which converts documents *or* drawings *or* photographs into a digitized, machine-readable form; **image sensor** = photoelectric device that produces a signal related to the amount of light falling on it (this scans horizontally over an image, reading in one line at a time); **image setter** = typesetting device that can process a PostScript page and produce a high-resolution output; *see also* TYPESETTER; **image stability** = ability of a display screen to provide a flicker-free picture; **image storage space** = region of memory in which a digitized image is stored;

image table = two bit-mapped tables used to control input and output devices *or* processes

> The Max FX also acts as a server to a growing number of printers, including a Varityper 5300 with emerald raster image processor and a Canon CLC 500 colour photocopier.
>
> *Computing*

◊ **imaging** *noun* technique for creating pictures on a screen (in medicine used to provide pictures of sections of the body, using scanners attached to computers)

IMAP4 = INTERNET MESSAGE ACCESS PROTOCOL protocol used to retrieve electronic mail messages from a mail server; used in advanced mail software to provide extra features such as the ability to edit messages stored on the server (rather than download the message to the client); *see also* POP3, SMTP

immediate *adjective* which happens at once; **immediate access store (IAS)** = high-speed main memory area in a computer system; **immediate addressing** = accessing data immediately because it is held in the address field of an instruction; **immediate instruction** = computer instruction in which the operand is included within the instruction, rather than an address of the operand location; **immediate mode** = mode in which a computer executes an instruction as soon as it is entered; **immediate operand** = operand which is fetched at the same time as the instruction (within an immediate addressing operation); **immediate processing** = processing data when it appears, rather than waiting for a synchronizing clock pulse *or* time; *compare* BATCH

impact *noun* hitting *or* striking something; **impact printer** = printer that prints text and symbols by striking an ink ribbon onto paper with a metal character, such as a daisy-wheel printer (as opposed to a non-impact printer like a laser printer); *see also* DAISY-WHEEL PRINTER, DOT MATRIX PRINTER

impedance *noun* measurement of the effect an electrical circuit has on signal current magnitude and phase when a steady voltage is applied; *see also* OHM

> COMMENT: for network cables need to have the correct impedence for the type of network card installed; 10BaseT unshielded twisted-pair cable normally has an impedence between 100-105 Ohms, while 10Base2 coaxial cable has an impedence of 50 Ohms

implement *verb* to carry out *or* to put something into action

◊ **implementation** *noun* version of something that works; *the latest implementation of the software runs much faster*

implication *noun* logical operation that uses an IF-THEN structure, if A is true and if B is true this implies that the AND function of A and B will be true

implicit reference *noun* (in a multimedia programming language) a reference to an object that does not give its exact page location, but assumes that the object is on the current page or is currently visible

implied addressing *noun* assembler instruction that operates on only one register (this is preset at manufacture and the user does not have to specify an address; *implied addressing for the accumulator is used in the instruction LDA,16*

import *verb* (a) to bring goods into a country to resell (b) (i) to bring something in from outside a system; (ii) to convert a file stored in one format to the default format used by a program; *you can import images from the CAD package into the DTP program; select import if you want to read a TIFF file*

◊ **importation** *noun* the act of importing something into a system from outside

impulse *noun* (voltage) pulse which lasts a very short time

impulsive *adjective* lasting a very short time

inaccurate *adjective* not correct *or* wrong; *he entered an inaccurate password*

◊ **inaccuracy** *noun* mistake *or* error; *the bibliography is full of inaccuracies*

inactive *adjective* not working *or* not running; **inactive window** = (in a GUI) window still displayed, but not currently being used

in-band signalling *noun* data transmission in which the signal carrying the data is within the bandwidth of the cable *or* transmission media

InBox (in Windows 95) feature of the Windows messaging system (Exchange) that can gather together a user's electronic messages including mail sent over the network, fax messages and mail sent over the internet

inbuilt *adjective* (feature *or* device) included in a system; *this software has inbuilt error correction*

inches-per-second (ips) way of showing the speed of tape past the read/write heads

in-circuit emulator *noun* (circuit) that emulates a device *or* integrated circuit and is inserted into a new *or* faulty circuit to test if it is working correctly; *this in-circuit emulator is used to test the floppy disk controller by emulating a disk drive*

inclusion *noun* logical operation that uses an IF-THEN structure, if A is true and if B is true this implies that the AND function of A and B will be true

◊ **inclusive** *adjective* which counts something in with other things; *prices are inclusive of VAT;* **inclusive OR** = *see* OR

incoming *adjective* which is coming in from outside; **incoming message** = message received in a computer; **incoming traffic** = amount of data *or* messages received

incompatible *adjective* not compatible *or* which cannot work together; *they tried to link the two systems, but found they were incompatible*

incorrect *adjective* not correct *or* with mistakes; *the input data was incorrect, so the output was also incorrect*

◊ **incorrectly** *adverb* not correctly *or* with mistakes; *the data was incorrectly keyboarded*

increment 1 *noun* **(a)** addition of a set number, usually one, to a register, often for counting purposes; *an increment is added to the counter each time a pulse is detected* **(b)** value of the number added to a register; *increase the increment to three* **2** *verb* **(a)** to add something *or* to increase a number; *the counter is incremented each time an instruction is executed* **(b)** to move forward to the next location **(c)** to move a document *or* card forward to its next preset location for printing *or* reading

◊ **incremental backup** *noun* backup procedure that only backs up the files which have changed since the last full *or* incremental backup

◊ **incremental computer** *noun* computer that stores variables as the difference between their actual value and an absolute initial value; **incremental data** = data which represents the difference of a value from an original value; **incremental plotter** = graphical output device that can only move in small steps, with input data representing the difference between present position and the position required, so drawing lines and curves as a series of short straight lines

indent 1 *noun* space *or* series of spaces from the left margin, when starting a line of text **2** *verb* to start a line of text with a space in from the left margin; *the first line of the paragraph is indented two spaces*

◊ **indentation** *noun* leaving a space at the beginning of a line of text

Indeo (video) software technology developed by Intel that allows a computer to store and play back compressed video sequences using software compression techniques

independent *adjective* free *or* not controlled by anyone

◊ **independently** *adverb* freely *or* without being controlled *or* without being connected; *in spooling, the printer is acting independently of the keyboard*

indeterminate system *noun* system whose logical (output) state cannot be predicted

index 1 *noun* **(a)** list of items in a computer memory, usually arranged alphabetically; **index build** = creation of an ordered list from the results of a database *or* file search; **index page** = (i) page of a multimedia book that lists all the other pages within the book and allows a user to locate other pages or areas of interest; (ii) initial opening web page of a site on the internet or on a company's intranet **(b)** alphabetical list printed, usually at the back of a book, giving references to items in the main part of the book **(c)** list of terms classified into groups *or* put in alphabetical order; **index letter** *or* **index number** = letter *or* number which identifies an item in an index **(d)** address to be used that is the result of an offset value added to a start location; *see* INDEXED ADDRESSING; **index register (IR)** = computer address register that is added to a reference address to provide the location to be accessed; **index value word** = offset value added to an address to produce a usable address **(e)** guide marks along the edge of a piece of film *or* strip of microfilm; **index hole** = hole in the edge of a hand-sectored disk **2** *verb* to put marks against items, so that they will be selected and sorted to form an index; **indexed address** = address of the location to be accessed, which is found in an index register; **indexed addressing** = method of addressing where the storage location is addressed with a start address and an offset word which is added to give the destination address; **indexed file** = sequential file with an index of all entries and their addresses; **indexed instruction** = instruction which contains an origin and offset that are added to provide the location to be accessed; **indexed sequential access**

method (ISAM) = data retrieval method using a list containing the address of each stored record, where the list is searched, then the record is retrieved from the address in the list; **indexed sequential storage** = method of storing records in a consecutive order, but in such a way that they can be accessed rapidly

indexing *noun* **(a)** use of indexed addressing methods in a computer **(b)** process of building and sorting a list of records; **indexing language** = language used in building library *or* book indexes **(c)** writing an index for a book; **computer indexing** = using a computer to compile an index for a book by selecting relevant words *or* items from the text

```
in           microcomputer
implementations   of   COBOL,
indexed files are usually based
on  some  type  of  B-tree
structure which allows rapid
data retrieval based on the
value of the key being used
                        PC-User
```

indicate *verb* to show

indication *noun* sign *or* something which shows

indicator *noun* something which shows the state of a process, usually a light *or* buzzer; **indicator chart** = graphical representation of the location and use of indicator flags within a program; **indicator flag** = register *or* single bit that indicates the state of the processor and its registers, such as a carry or overflow; **indicator light** = light used to warn *or* to indicate the condition of equipment

indirect *adjective* not direct; **indirect addressing** = way of addressing data, where the first instruction refers to an address which contains a second address

individual 1 *noun* single person; *each individual has his own password to access the system* **2** *adjective* single *or* belonging to a single person; *the individual workstations are all linked to the mainframe*

induce *verb* **(i)** to generate an electrical current in a coil of wire by electromagnetic effects; (ii) to prove (something) mathematically; **induced failure** = failure of a device due to external effects; **induced interference** = electrical noise on a signal due to induced signals from nearby electromagnetic sources

inductance *noun* measurement of the amount of energy a device can store in its magnetic field

induction *noun* (i) generation of an electrical current due to electromagnetic effects from a nearby source; (ii) mathematically proving a formula *or* fact

inductive coordination *noun* agreement between electrical power suppliers and communication providers on methods of reducing induced interference

inductor *noun* electrical component consisting of a coil of wire used to introduce inductance effects into a circuit (by storing energy in its magnetic field)

Industry Standard Architecture (ISA) *noun* standard used for the 16-bit expansion bus in an IBM PC or compatible *compare* EISA, MCA

inequality operator *noun* symbol used to indicate that two variables *or* quantities are not equal; *the C programming language uses the symbol '!= ' as its inequality operator*

inequivalence *noun* logical function whose output is true if the inputs are not the same, otherwise the output is false

inert *adjective* (chemical substance *or* gas) that does not react with other chemicals

infected computer *noun* computer that carries a virus program

inference *noun* (a) deduction of results from data according to certain rules; **inference engine** *or* **machine** = set of rules used in an expert system to deduce goals *or* results from data (b) method of deducing a result about confidential information concerning an individual by using various data related to groups of people; **inference**

control = determining which information may be released without disclosing personal information about a single individual

inferior figures *noun* smaller numbers *or* characters that are printed slightly below normal characters, used in mathematical and chemical formulae *see also* SUBSCRIPT, SUPERSCRIPT, SUPERIOR; (NOTE: used with figures and letters: CO_2)

infinite *adjective* with no end; **infinite loop** = loop which has no exit (except by ending the running of the program by switching off the machine *or* resetting)

◊ **infinity** *noun* **(a)** very large incomprehensible quantity even bigger than the biggest you can think of **(b)** distance of an object from a viewer where beams of light from the object would be seen to be parallel (i.e. very far away)

infix notation *noun* method of computer programming syntax where operators are embedded inside operands (such as C - D or X + Y) *compare* PREFIX, POSTFIX NOTATION

informatics *noun* science and study of ways and means of information processing and transmission

information *noun* **(a)** knowledge presented to a person in a form which can be understood **(b)** data that has been processed *or* arranged to provide facts which have a meaning; **information bearer channel** = communications channel that is able to carry control and message data, usually at a higher rate than a data only channel; **information content** = measurement of the amount of information conveyed by the transmission of a symbol *or* character, often measured in shannons; **information flow control** = regulation of access to certain information; **information input** = information received from an input device; **information line** = line running across the screen which gives the user information about the program running *or* the file being edited, etc.; **information management system** = computer program that allows information to be easily stored, retrieved, searched and updated;

information networks = number of databases linked together, usually by telephone lines and modems, allowing a large amount of data to be accessed by a wider group of users; **information output** = display of information on an output device; **information processing** = organizing, processing and extracting information from data; **information processor** = machine that processes a received signal, according to a program, using stored information, and provides an output (this is an example of a computer that is not dealing with mathematical functions); **information provider (IP)** = company *or* user who provides an information source for use in a videotext system (such as the company providing weather information *or* stock market reports); **information rate** = amount of information content per character multiplied by the number of characters transmitted per second; **information retrieval (IR)** = locating quantities of data stored in a database and producing useful information from the data; **information storage** = storing data in a form which allows it to be processed at a later date; **information storage and retrieval (ISR)** = techniques involved in storing information and retrieving data from a store; **information structure** = *see* DATA STRUCTURE; **information system** = computer system which provides information according to a user's requests; **information technology (IT)** = technology involved in acquiring, storing, processing and distributing information by electronic means (including radio, television, telephone, computers); **information theory** = formulae and mathematics concerned with data transmission equipment and signals; **information transfer channel** = connection between a data transmitter and a receiver; *see also* DATA TERMINAL EQUIPMENT

Racal-Datacom has picked up a £1.5 million order for its ISDN digital access multiplexers from financial information provider Telerate, its second from the company this year.

Computing

---

infra-red link *noun* system that allows two computers or a computer and a printer to exchange information using an infra-red light beam to carry the data; **Infrared Data Association (IrDA)** = standard method used to transfer information via an infrared light beam; often used to transfer information from a laptop or PDA to a printer or desktop computer; to use this feature, your computer or printer needs to have an IrDA port

infrastructure *noun* basic structure *or* basic services

infringement *noun* breaking the law *or* a rule; **copyright infringement** = illegally making a copy of a book which is in copyright

inherent addressing *noun* instruction that contains all the data required for the address to be accessed with no further operation *compare* EXTENDED, INDEXED

inherit *verb* (in object-oriented programming) one class *or* data type that acquires the characteristics of another

◊ **inheritance** *noun* (in object-oriented programming) to pass the characteristics of one class *or* data type to another (called its descendant)

◊ **inherited error** *noun* error that is the result of a fault in a previous process *or* action

inhibit *verb* to stop a process taking place *or* to prevent an integrated circuit *or* gate from operating, (by means of a signal *or* command); **inhibiting input** = one input of a gate which blocks the output signal

in-house *adverb* & *adjective* (working) inside a company's building; *all the data processing is done in-house; the in-house maintenance staff deal with all our equipment*

initial 1 *adjective* first *or* at the beginning; **initial address** = address at which the first instruction of a program is stored; **initial condition** = condition that must be satisfied before a routine can be entered; **initial error** = error in data that is the difference between the value of the data at the start of processing and its present actual value; **initial**

instructions = routine that acts as an initial program loader; **initial program header** = small machine-code program usually stored in a read-only memory device that directs the CPU to load a larger program *or* operating system from store into main memory (such as a boot up routine which loads the operating system when a computer is switched on); **initial program loader (IPL)** = short routine that loads a program (the operating system) from backing store into main memory; **initial value** = starting point (usually zero) set when initializing variables at the beginning of a program **2** *noun* first letter of a word, especially of a name; *what do the initials IBM stand for?*

◊ **initialization** *noun* process of initializing; *initialization is often carried out without the user knowing;* **initialization string** = series of AT commands sent to a modem to configure it before it is used

◊ **initialize** *verb* to set values *or* parameters *or* control lines to their initial values, to allow a program *or* process to be re-started

ink 1 *noun* dark liquid used to mark *or* write with; **ink-jet printer** = computer printer that produces characters by sending a stream of tiny drops of electrically charged ink onto the paper (the movement of the ink drops is controlled by an electric field; this is a non-impact printer with few moving parts); *colour ink-jet technology and thermal transfer technology compete with each other* **2** *verb* to draw lines on paper by the use of a plotter device

ink-jet   printers   work   by
squirting a fine stream of ink
onto the paper
Personal Computer World

inlay card *noun* identification card inside a tape *or* disk box

in-line 1 *noun* connection pins on a chip arranged in one or two rows **2** *adverb* way in which unsorted *or* unedited data is processed; **in-line program** = program that contains no loops; **in-line processing** = processing data when it appears rather than waiting for a synchronizing *or* clock pulse

inner loop *noun* loop contained inside another loop; *see also* NESTED LOOP

input (i/p *or* **I/P) 1** *verb* to transfer data *or* information from outside a computer to its main memory; *the data was input via a modem* **2** *noun* **(a)** action of inputting information **(b)** data *or* information that is transferred into a computer; **input area** = section of main memory that holds data transferred from backing store until it is processed *or* distributed to other sections; **input block** = block of data transferred to an input area; **input bound** = computer *or* device in which the slowest part is data transfer; **input buffer register** = temporary store for data from an input device before it is transferred to main *or* backing store; **input device** = device such as a keyboard *or* bar code reader, which converts actions *or* information into a form which a computer can understand and transfers the data to the processor; **input lead** = lead which connects an input device to a computer; **input limited (program)** = (program) which is not running as fast as it could, due to limiting input rate from a slower peripheral; **input mode** = computer which is receiving data; **input port** = circuit *or* connector that allows a computer to receive data from other external devices; **input register** = temporary store for data received at slow speeds from an I/O device, the data is then transferred at high speed to main memory; **input routine** = set of instructions which control an I/O device and direct data received from it to the correct storage location; **input section** = (i) input routine; (ii) input area; **input statement** = computer programming command that waits for data entry from a port *or* keyboard; **input storage** = *see* INPUT AREA; **input unit** = an input device; **input work queue** = list of commands to be carried out in the order they were entered (or in order of priority) **(c)** electrical signals which are applied to relevant circuits to perform the operation

In fact, the non-Qwerty format
of the Maltron keyboard did
cause a few gasps when it was
first shown to the staff, but
within a month all the Maltron

users had regained normal input speeds.

Computing

input-bound *or* **input-limited** *adjective* (program) which is not running as fast as it could, due to limiting input rate from a slower peripheral

input/output (I/O) *noun* receiving *or* transmitting data between a computer and its peripherals, and other points outside the system; **input/output buffer** = temporary storage area for data waiting to be output or input; **input/output bus** = links allowing data and control signal transfer between a CPU *or* peripheral devices; **input/output channel** = link between a processor and peripheral allowing data transfer; **input/output control program** = monitoring and control of I/O operations and data flow by a section of the operating system *or* supervisory program; **input/output controller** = intelligent device that monitors, directs and controls data flow between a CPU and I/O devices; **input/output device** *or* **unit** = peripheral (such as a terminal in a workstation) which can be used both for inputting and outputting data to a processor; **input/output executive** = master program that controls all the I/O activities of a computer; **input/output instruction** = computer programming instruction that allows data to be input *or* output from a processor; **input/output interface** = circuit allowing controlled data input and output from a CPU, consisting usually of: input/output channel, parallel input/output port and a DMA interface; **input/output interrupt** = interrupt signal from a peripheral device *or* to indicate that an input or output operation is required; **input/output instruction** = programming instruction that transfers data from memory to an input/output port; **input/output library** = set of routines that can be used by the programmer to help simplify input/output tasks (such as printer drivers *or* port control routines); **input/output port** = circuit *or* connector that provides an input/output channel to another device; *the joystick can be connected to the input/output port;* **input/output processor (IOP)** = processor

that carries out input/output transfers for a CPU, including DMA and error correction facilities; **input/output referencing** = use of labels to refer to specific input/output devices, the actual address of the device being inserted at run-time; **input/output register** = temporary store for data received from main memory before being transferred to an I/O device, or for data from an I/O device to be processed or stored in main memory; **input/output request (IORQ)** = request signal from the CPU for data input or output; **input/output status word** = word whose bits describe the state of peripheral devices (busy, free, etc.); **parallel input/output (PIO)** = data input *or* output from a computer in a parallel form

inquiry *noun* (i) asking a question; (ii) accessing data held in a computer system; **inquiry character (ENQ)** = code transmitted by a computer to a remote terminal, asking for a response; **inquiry station** = terminal that is used to access and interrogate files stored on a remote computer; **inquiry/response** = interactive computer mode, in which a user's commands and enquiries are responded to very quickly

Ins *or* **insert key** *noun* key (on a keyboard) that switches a word-processor or editor program into insert mode rather than overwrite mode

insert *verb* **(a)** to put something into something; *first insert the system disk in the left slot* **(b)** to add new text inside a word *or* sentence; **insert key** *or* **Ins key** = key that switches a word-processor or editor program into insert mode rather than overwrite mode; **inserted subroutine** = series of instructions that are copied directly into the main program where a call instruction appears *or* where a user requires

insert mode *noun* (in a wordprocessor) mode of operation in which any characters typed in at the keyboard are inserted into the existing text

insertion loss *noun* attenuation to a signal caused by adding **a** device into an existing channel *or* circuit

insertion point *noun* cursor positioned to show where any text typed in will be entered within a document

> COMMENT: this is a standard feature on most word-processing packages where the cursor is placed at the required point in the document and any characters typed will be added, with the existing text moving on as necessary

install *verb* to put a machine into an office *or* factory; to set up a new computer system to the user's requirements *or* to configure a new program to the existing system capabilities; *the system is easy to install and simple to use;* **install program** = software utility that transfers program code from the distribution disks onto a computer's hard disk and configures the program

◊ **installable device driver** *noun* device driver that is loaded into memory and remains resident, replacing a similar function built-into the operating system

◊ **installation** *noun* **(a)** computer and equipment used for one type of work and processing; *the engineers are still testing the new installation* **(b)** setting up a new computer system; *the installation of the equipment took only a few hours*

instance *noun* (in object-oriented programming) an object *or* duplicate object that has been created

instantaneous access *noun* extremely short access time to a random access device

instruct *verb* to tell someone *or* a computer what to do

instruction *noun* word used in a programming language that is understood by the computer to represent an action; *the instruction PRINT is used in this BASIC dialect as an operand to display the following data;* **instruction address** = location of an instruction; **instruction address register (IAR)** register in a CPU that contains the location of the next instruction to be processed; **instruction area** = section of memory that is used to store

instructions; **instruction cache** = area of high-speed memory which stores the next few instructions to be executed by a processor; **instruction character** = special character that provides a control sequence rather than an alphanumeric character; **instruction codes** = set of symbols *or* codes that a CPU can directly understand and execute; **instruction counter** *or* **instruction address register (IAR)** *or* **program counter** = register in a CPU that contains the location of the next instruction to be processed; **instruction cycle** = sequence of events and their timing that is involved when fetching and executing an instruction stored in memory; **instruction cycle time** = amount of time taken for one instruction cycle; **instruction decoder** = program which decodes instructions in machine code; **instruction execution time** = time taken to carry out an instruction; **instruction format** = rules defining the way the operands, data and addresses are arranged in an instruction; **instruction modification** = altering a part of an instruction (data *or* operator) so that it carries out a different function when next executed; **instruction pipelining** = beginning processing a second instruction while still processing the present one (this increases program speed of execution); **instruction pointer** = register in a CPU that contains the location of the next instruction to be processed; **instruction processor** = section of the central processing unit that decodes the instruction and performs the necessary arithmetic and logical functions; **instruction register (IR)** = register in a central processing unit that stores an instruction during decoding and execution operations; **instruction repertoire** *or* **set** = total number of instructions that a processor can recognize and execute; **instruction storage** = *see* INSTRUCTION AREA; **instruction time** = amount of time taken for a central processing unit to carry out a complete instruction; **instruction word** = fixed set of characters used to initiate an instruction; *the manufacturers of this CPU have decided that JMP will be the instruction word to call the jump function;* **absolute instruction** = instruction which completely describes the operation to be performed (i.e. no other data is required); **arithmetic instruction** = instruction to perform an arithmetic operation on data rather than a logical function; **blank** *or* **null** *or* **dummy instruction** = instruction in a program that is only there to satisfy language syntax *or* to make up a block length; **breakpoint instruction** = halt command inserted in a program to temporarily stop execution, allowing the programmer to examine data and registers whilst debugging a program; **decision** *or* **discrimination instruction** = conditional program instruction that directs control by providing the location of the next instruction to be executed (if a condition is met); **dummy instruction** = instruction in a program that is only there to satisfy language syntax *or* to make up a block length; **executive instruction** = instruction used to control and execute programs under the control of an operating system; **four-address instruction** = program instruction which contains four addresses within its address field, usually the location of the two operands, the result and the location of the next instruction; **indexed instruction** = instruction that contains an origin and location of an offset that are added together to provide the address to be accessed; **input/output instruction** = computer programming instruction that allows data to be input *or* output from a processor; **jump instruction** = program command to end one set of instructions and direct the processor to another section of the program; **macro instruction** = one programming instruction that refers to a number of instructions within a routine *or* macro; **no-op instruction** = instruction that does not carry out any functions, but increments the program counter; **n-plus-one instruction** = instruction made up of a number (n) of addresses and one other address that is the location of the next instruction to be executed; **supervisory instruction** = instruction used to control and execute programs under the control of an operating system; **three-address-instruction** = instruction format which contains the addresses of two operands and the location where the result is to be stored; **two-address-instruction** =

instruction format containing the locations of two operands, the result being stored in one of the operand locations; **two-plus-one-address instruction** = instruction containing locations of two operands and an address for the storage of the result

COMMENT: in a high level language the instructions are translated by the compiler *or* interpreter to a form that is understood by the central processing unit

A Taos kernel, typically 15Kb in size, resides at each processing node to 'translate', non-native instructions - on the fly when needed. This kernel contains the only code which has to be written in the processor's native instruction set.

Computing

insulate *verb* to prevent energy from a conductor reaching another point by separating the two points with an insulation material

◊ **insulator** *noun* material that does not conduct electricity; *plastic is a good insulator*

integer *noun* mathematical term to describe a whole number (it may be positive *or* negative *or* zero); **integer BASIC** = faster version of BASIC that uses only integer mathematics and cannot support fractions; **double-precision integer** = two computer words used to store an integer

integral *noun* add-on device *or* special feature that is already built into a system; *the integral disk drives and modem reduced desk space*

an integral 7 inch amber display screen, two half-height disk drives and terminal emulation for easy interfacing with mainframes
Computing Today

integrated *adjective* (system) that contains many peripherals grouped together in order to provide a neat, complete system;

integrated database = database that is able to provide information for varied requirements without any redundant data; **integrated data processing (IDP)** = organizational method for the entry and retrieval of data to provide maximum efficiency; **integrated device electronics (IDE)** = popular standard for a hard disk drive controller unit that allows data transfer rates up to 4.1MBps and can support two hard disk drives on each conroller; enhanced versions of the IDE standard provide more flexibility and speed (also known as AT Attachment - ATA - interface); **integrated emulator** = emulator program run within a multitasking operating system; **integrated injection logic (IIL)** = type of circuit design able to produce very small, low-power components; **integrated modem** = modem that is an internal part of the system; **integrated office** = office environment in which all operations are carried out using a central computer (to store information, to print, etc.); **integrated services digital network** = *see* ISDN; **integrated software** = software such as an operating system *or* word-processor that is stored in the computer system and has been tailored to the requirements of the system

integrated circuit (IC)   *noun*   circuit where all the active and passive components are formed on one small piece of semiconductor, by means of etching and chemical processes

integration   *noun*   bringing several operations together; *small scale integration (SSI); medium scale integration (MSI); large scale integration (LSI); very large scale integration (VLSI)*

> COMMENT: integrated circuits can be classified as follows: **Small Scale Integration (SSI)**: 1 to 10 components per IC; **Medium Scale Integration (MSI)**: 10 to 100 components per IC; **Large Scale Integration (LSI)**: 100 to 5000 components per IC; **Very Large Scale Integration (VLSI)**: 5,000 to 50,000 components per IC; **Ultra Large Scale Integration (ULSI)**: over 100,000 components per IC.

integrity   *noun*   reliability of data (when being processed *or* stored on disk); **integrity of a file** = the fact that a file that has been stored on disk is not corrupted *or* distorted in any way; **the data in this file has integrity** = the data has not been corrupted

> it is intended for use in applications demanding high data integrity, such as archival storage or permanent databases
>
> *Minicomputer News*

Intel™   company which developed the first commercially available microprocessor (the 4004); they also developed the range of processors that is used in IBM PCs and compatible computers; **Intel 8086** = microprocessor that uses a 16-bit data bus and can address up to 1Mb of RAM; **Intel 8088** = microprocessor that uses a 16-bit data bus internally, but uses an 8-bit data bus externally; used in the first IBM PC computers; **Intel 80286** = microprocessor that uses a 16-bit data bus and can address up to 16Mb of RAM; **Intel 80386** = microprocessor that uses a 32-bit data bus and can address up to 4Gb of RAM; **Intel 80486** = microprocessor that uses a 32-bit data bus and can address up to 64Gb of RAM; **Intel Indeo** = (video) software technology developed by Intel that allows a computer to store and play back compressed video sequences using software compression techniques; **Intel MMX** = range of processors developed by Intel that include components that are used to improve the performance when dealing with multimedia and communications; **Intel Pentium** = advanced microprocessor that has replaced the 80486 and uses a 32-bit data bus; **Intel Pentium Pro** = currently the most powerful 32-bit processor developed by Intel

intelligence   *noun*   (i) ability to reason; (ii) ability of a device to carry out processing *or* run a program; **artificial intelligence (AI)** = the design of computer programs and systems that attempt to imitate human intelligence and decision-making functions, providing basic reasoning and human characteristics

intelligent *noun (of a machine)* (program *or* device) that is capable of limited reasoning facilities, giving it human-like responses; **intelligent device** = peripheral device that contains a central processing unit allowing it to process data; **intelligent knowledge-based system (IKBS)** *or* **expert system** = software that applies the knowledge, advice and rules defined by an expert in a particular field to a user's data to help solve a problem; **intelligent spacer** = facility on a word-processing system used to prevent words from being hyphenated *or* separated at the wrong point; **intelligent terminal** = computer terminal which contains a CPU and memory, usually with a facility to allow the user to program it independently of the main CPU; (NOTE: the opposite is **dumb terminal**); **intelligent tutoring system** = computer-aided learning system that provides responsive and interactive teaching facilities for users; **intelligent wiring hub** = wiring hub that can be controlled from a workstation to direct which circuits to connect to each other

intensity *noun* measure of the strength of a signal *or* the brightness of a light source

inter- *prefix* meaning between; **interblock** = between blocks

interact *verb (of two things)* to act on each other

◊ **interaction** *noun* action of two things on each other

◊ **interactive** *adjective* (system *or* piece of software) that allows communication between the user and the computer (in conversational mode); **interactive debugging system** = software development tool that allows the user to run a program under test, set breakpoints, examine source and object code, examine registers and memory contents and trace the instruction execution; **interactive graphics** = display system that is able to react to different inputs from the user; *the space invaders machine has great interactive graphics, the player controls the position of his spaceship on the screen with the joystick;* **interactive media** = communication between a group of people

using different transmission means; **interactive mode** *or* **processing** = computer mode that allows the user to enter commands *or* programs *or* data and receive immediate responses; *see also* INQUIRY/RESPONSE; **interactive multimedia** = multimedia system in which a user can issue a command and the program responds *or* the user can control actions and control the way a program works; *this interactive multimedia title allows a user to make music with a synthesizer program;* **Interactive Multimedia Association (IMA)** = professional organisation that covers subjects including authoring languages, formats, and intellectual property; **interactive routine** = computer program able to accept data from an operator, process it and provide a real-time reaction to it; **interactive system** = system which provides an immediate response to the user's commands *or* programs *or* data; **interactive terminal** = terminal in an interactive system which sends and receives information; **interactive videotext** = viewdata service that allows the operator to select pages, display them, ask questions, or use a service such as teleshopping

◊ **interactive video** *noun* system that uses a computer linked to a video disk player to provide processing power and real images *or* moving pictures

COMMENT: this system is often used in teaching to ask a student questions, which if answered correctly will provide him with a filmed sequence from the videodisk

Oracle today details its interactive information superhighway aims, endorsed by 17 industry partners. The lynchpin to the announcement will be software based on the Oracle Media Server, a multimedia database designed to run on massively parallel computers.

Computing

interactivity is a buzzword you've been hearing a lot lately. Resign yourself to it

because you're going to be
hearing a lot more of it
Music Technology

interblock gap (IBG) *noun* blank
magnetic tape between the end of one block
of data and the start of the next in backing
store

interchange 1 *noun* exchange of one
thing for another; *the machine allows
document interchange between it and other
machines without reformatting* **2** *verb* to
exchange one thing for another

◊ **interchangeable** *adjective* which can
be exchanged

◊ **interchange file format (IFF)** *noun*
standard that defines how palette data is
stored in an Amiga and some graphics
programs

intercharacter spacing *noun*
word-processor feature that provides variable
spacing between words to create a justified
line

interconnect *verb (of several things)* to
connect together; *a series of interconnected
terminals*

◊ **interconnection** *noun* section of
connecting material between two devices

interface 1 *noun* (i) point at which one
computer system ends and another begins;
(ii) circuit *or* device *or* port that allows two or
more incompatible units to be linked together
in a standard communication system,
allowing data to be transferred between them;
(iii) section of a program which allows
transmission of data to another program;
interface card = add-on board that allows a
computer to interface to certain equipment *or*
conform to a certain standard; **interface
message processor** = computer in a packet
switching network that deals with the flow of
data, acting as an interface processor;
interface processor = computer that controls
data transfer between a processor and a
terminal *or* network; **interface routines** =
software that allows programs *or* data for one
system to run on another; **EIA interface** =
standard defining interface signals,
transmission rate and power usually used to

connect terminals to modems; **general
purpose interface adapter (GPIA)** =
usually used to interface a processing unit to
a IEEE-488 bus; **general purpose interface
bus (GPIB)** = standard for an interface bus
between a computer and laboratory
equipment; **input/output interface** = circuit
allowing controlled data input and output
from a CPU, consisting usually of:
input/output channel, parallel input/output
port and a DMA interface; **parallel interface**
= computer circuit *or* connector that allows
parallel data to be transmitted *or* received;
(NOTE: parallel interfaces are usually used to drive
printers); **serial interface** = circuit that
converts parallel data in a computer to and
from a serial form, allowing serial data to be
transmitted to *or* received from other
equipment; (NOTE: the most common serial
interface is RS232C but USB is gaining popularity)
2 *verb* (i) to modify a device by adding a
circuit *or* connector to allow it to conform to a
standard communications system; (ii) to
connect two or more incompatible devices
together with a circuit, to allow them to
communicate

◊ **interfacing** *noun* hardware *or* software
used to interface two computers *or* programs
or devices

The original release of ODBC
only included a driver for
Microsoft's own SQL Server
database. Microsoft has
subsequently published the
ODBC application program
interface enabling third-party
vendors to create drivers for
other databases and tools.
Computing

interfere *verb* to stop something working
properly; to get in the way; *to interfere with
something*

◊ **interference** *noun* noise on a signal;
electromagnetic interference = corruption
of data due to nearby electrically generated
magnetic fields; **induced interference** =
electrical noise on a signal due to induced
signals from nearby electromagnetic sources

interior label *noun* identification label
stored on a storage medium (magnetic tape *or*

disk) rather than an exterior *or* physical label stuck to the case

interlace *verb* method of building up an image on a television screen using two passes, each displaying alternate lines

> COMMENT: this system uses two picture fields made up of alternate lines to reduce picture flicker effects

interleave factor *noun* ratio of sectors skipped between access operations on a hard disk

> COMMENT: in a hard disk with an interleave of 3, the first sector is read, then three sectors are skipped and the next sector is read. This is used to allow hard disks with slow access time to store more data on the disk.

◊ **interleaved** *adjective* sections of two programs executed alternately to give the impression that they are running simultaneously; **interleaved memory** = two separate banks of memory used together in sequence

◊ **interleaving** *noun* **(a)** processor dealing with slices *or* sections of processes alternately, so that they appear to be executed simultaneously **(b)** dividing data storage into sections so that each can be accessed separately

> there are two separate 40-bit arrays on each card to allow interleaved operation, achieving data access every 170ns machine cycle
> *Minicomputer News*

interlock *noun* security device which is part of the logon prompt and requires a password **2** *verb* to prevent a device from performing another task until the present one has been completed

interlude *noun* small initial routine at the start of a program that carries out housekeeping tasks

intermediate *adjective* which is at a stage between two others; **intermediate access memory (IAM)** = memory storage that has an access time between that of main memory and disk based systems; **intermediate code** = code used by a computer *or* assembler during the translation of a high-level code to machine code; **intermediate file** = series of records which contain partially processed data, that will be used at a later date to complete that task; **intermediate system (IS)** = (on the internet) router or other device that links a network or user to the internet; **intermediate system to intermediate system (IS-IS)** = OSI protocol that allows data to be transferred between routers; **intermediate storage** = temporary area of memory for items that are currently being processed

intermittent error *noun* error which apparently occurs randomly in a computer *or* communications system due to a program fault *or* noise

> COMMENT: these errors are very difficult to trace and correct due to their apparent random appearance

internal *adjective* which is inside; **internal arithmetic** = arithmetic operations performed by the ALU; **internal character code** = representation of characters in a particular operating system; **internal command** = command that is part of the operating system, rather than a separate utility program; *in MS-DOS, the internal command DIR is used frequently;* **internal** *or* **resident font** = font that is stored on a ROM in a printer; **internal format** = way in which data and instructions are represented within a CPU *or* backing store; **internal hard disk** = hard disk drive mounted inside the main case of a computer; **internal language** = language used in a computer system that is not under the direct control of the operator

> COMMENT: many compiled languages are translated to an internal language

◊ **internal memory** *or* **store**   *noun* section of RAM and ROM to which the central processing unit is directly connected without the use of an interface (as in external memory devices such as disk drives)

◊ **internal modem** *noun* modem on an expansion card that fits into an expansion connector and transfers information to the processor through the bus rather than connecting to a serial port

◊ **internal sort** *noun* sorting program using only the main memory of a system

◊ **internally stored program** *noun* computer program code that is stored in a ROM device in a computer system (and does not have to be loaded from backing store)

international *adjective* referring to different countries

◊ **international file format (IFF)** *noun* standard for compressed files stored on a CD-i

◊ **International Standards Organization (ISO)** *noun* organization which creates and regulates standards for many types of computer and networking products; **International Standards Organization Open System Interconnection (ISO/OSI)** = standardized ISO network design which is constructed in layered form, with each layer having a specific task, allowing different systems to communicate if they conform to the standard

internet *noun* international wide area network that provides file and data transfer, together with electronic mail functions for millions of users around the world; anyone can use the Internet; *see also* HTTP, POP3, SMTP, WWW; **internet activities board (IAB)** = independent committee that is responsible for the design, engineering and management of the internet; **internet engineering task force (IETF)** = committee that is part of the IAB (see above) and determines internet standards; **internet research task force (IRTF)** = committee that is part of the IAB (see above) and researches new internet standards before referring them to the IETF for approval; **Internet Explorer** (IE) = web browser developed by Microsoft, currently available free, that allows a user to view Web pages; **Internet Information Server** (IIS) = web server software developed by Microsoft; **internet protocol (IP)** = one part of the TCP/IP standard that defines how data is transferred over a network; **internet protocol address (IP Address)** = unique, 32-bit number which identifies computers that want to connect to a TCP/IP network; **internet relay chat (IRC)** = system that allows many users to participate in a chat session in which each user can send messages and sees the text of any other user; **internet service provider (ISP)** = company that provides one of the permanent links that make up the internet and sells connections to private users and companies to allow them to access the internet

internetwork *noun* number of networks connected together using bridges or routers to allow users on one network to access any resource on any other of the connected networks

◊ **Internetwork Packet Exchange (IPX)** network protocol developed by Novell that is used to transfer packets of information over a network

InterNIC organisation that manages the way domain names and unique network addresses are assigned to companies

interoperability *noun* the ability of two devices *or* computers to exchange information

interpolation *noun* calculation of intermediate values between two points

interpret *verb* to translate what is said in one language into another; **interpreted language** = programming language that is executed by an interpreter

◊ **interpreter** *noun* software used to translate (at the time of execution) a user's high-level program into machine code; *compare* COMPILER

> COMMENT: a compiler translates the high-level language into machine code and then executes it, rather than the real-time translation by an interpreter

◊ **interpretative** *adjective;* **interpretative code** = code used with an interpretative program; **interpretative program** = software that translates (at run-time) high level interpretative code into machine code instructions

interrecord gap = INTERBLOCK GAP

interrogation *noun* asking questions; **file interrogation** = questions asked to select various records *or* data items from a file

interrupt 1 *verb* to stop something happening while it is happening 2 *noun* **(a)** stopping of a transmission due to an action at the receiving end of a system **(b)** signal which diverts a central processing unit from one task to another which has higher priority, allowing the CPU to return to the first task later; *this printer port design uses an interrupt line to let the CPU know it is ready to receive data;* **armed interrupt** = interrupt line which has been made active (using an interrupt mask); **interrupt enable** = to arm an interrupt (by setting a bit in the interrupt mask); **interrupt disable** = to disable an interrupt (by resetting a bit in the interrupt mask to zero); **interrupt-driven** = (program) that works in response to an interrupt; **interrupt handler (IH)** = software that accepts interrupt signals and acts on them (such as running a special routine *or* sending data to a peripheral); **interrupt level** = priority assigned to the interrupt from a peripheral; **interrupt line** = connection to a central processing unit from outside the system that allows external devices to use the CPU's interrupt facility; **interrupt mask** = term in computer programming that selects which interrupt lines are to be activated *see also* NON-MASKABLE INTERRUPT; **interrupt priorities** = deciding which interrupt is given highest priority; **interrupt request (IRQ)** = signal from a device that indicates to the CPU that it requires attention; **interrupt servicing** = carrying out some action when an interrupt is detected (such as running a routine); **interrupt signal;** *see* INTERRUPT; **interrupt stacking** = storing interrupts in a queue and processing according to priority; **maskable interrupt** = interrupt line that can be disabled and ignored using an interrupt mask; **non-maskable interrupt (NMI)** = high priority interrupt signal that cannot be blocked and overrides all other commands; **polled interrupt** =

interrupt signal determined by polling; **priority interrupt table** = list of peripherals and their priorities when they send an interrupt signal (used instead of a hardware priority scheduler); **transparent interrupt** = mode in which if an interrupt occurs, all machine and program states are saved, the interrupt is serviced then the system restores all previous states and continues normally; **vectored interrupt** = interrupt which directs the CPU to transfer to a particular location

intersection *noun* logical function whose output is only true if both its inputs are true

interval *noun* short pause between two actions; *there was an interval between pressing the key and the starting of the printout*

intervention *noun* acting to make a change in a system

interword spacing *noun* variable spacing between words in a text, used to justify lines

intimate *adjective* (software) that operates and interacts closely with hardware in a system

intranet *noun* private network of computers within a company that provide similar functions to the internet (electronic mail, newsgroups and the WWW), without the associated security risks of making the information public or linking the company to a public network; *see also* FIREWALL, INTERNET, WEB SERVER

introduce *verb* to put something into something; *errors were introduced into the text at keyboarding*

intruder *noun* person who is not authorized to use a computer or connect to a network

invalid *adjective* not valid; *he tried to use an invalid password; the message was that the instruction was invalid*

inverse *noun* changing the logical state of a signal *or* device to its logical opposite; *the inverse of true is false; the inverse of 1 is 0;* **inverse video** = television effect created by swapping the background and foreground text display colours

◊ **inversion** *noun* changing over the numbers in a binary word (one to zero, zero to one); *the inversion of a binary digit takes place in one's complement*

◊ **invert** *verb* to change all binary ones to zeros and zeros to ones; **inverted backbone** = network architecture in which the hub is the centre of the network and all sub networks connect to the hub; in a traditional backbone network the sub networks connect to the cable that is the main backbone; **inverted commas** = printing sign (") which is usually used to indicate a quotation; **inverted file** = file with an index entry for all the data items

◊ **inverter** *noun* **(a)** logical gate that provides inversion facilities **(b)** circuit used to provide alternating current supply from a DC battery source; **inverter (AC/DC)** = device which changes alternating current to direct current, or direct current to alternating current

invisible *adjective* (guide or object) visible on a DTP page or graphics layout during the design phase, but not printed

invitation *noun* action by a processor to contact another device and allow it to send a message; **invitation to send (ITS)** = special character transmitted to indicate to a device that the host computer is willing to receive messages

◊ **invite** *verb* to ask someone to do something

invoke *verb* to start *or* to run a program (often a memory resident utility)

> when an error is detected, the editor may be invoked and positioned at the statement in error
>
> *Personal Computer World*

involve *verb* to have to do with; to include (something) in a process; *backing up involves copying current working files onto a separate storage disk*

I/O = INPUT/OUTPUT referring to the receiving *or* transmitting of data; **I/O address** = the memory location that is used by an I/O

port to transfer data with the CPU; **I/O bound** = processor that is doing very little processing since its time is taken up reading *or* writing data from a I/O port; **I/O buffer** = temporary storage area for data waiting to be input *or* output; **I/O bus** = links allowing data and control signal transfer between a CPU and memory *or* peripheral devices; **I/O channel** = link between a processor and peripheral, allowing data transfer; **I/O device** = peripheral (such as a terminal in a workstation) which can be used for both inputting and outputting data to a processor; **I/O file** = file whose contents have been *or* will be transferred from storage to a peripheral; **I/O instruction** = computer programming instruction that allows data to be input *or* output from a processor; **I/O mapping** = method of assigning a special address to each I/O port that does not use any memory locations; *compare* MEMORY MAPPING; **I/O port** = circuit *or* connector that provides an input/output channel to another device; *see also* SERIAL PORT, PARALLEL PORT; **I/O redirection** = transferring data to an I/O port rather than to its normal destination; *using I/O redirection, we send all the data from the keyboard to the printer port instead of the monitor*

ion deposition *noun* printing technology that uses a printhead that deposits ions to create a charged image which attracts the toner

IOP = INPUT/OUTPUT PROCESSOR

IORQ = INPUT/OUTPUT REQUEST

i/p *or* **I/P** = INPUT

ip = INFORMATION PROVIDER company *or* user who provides an information source for use in a videotext system; **ip terminal** = special visual display unit that allows users to create and edit videotext pages before sending them to the main videotext page database

◊ **IP** = INTERNET PROTOCOL one part of the TCP/IP standard that defines how data is transferred over a network; **IP Address** = unique, 32-bit number which identifies computers that want to connect to a TCP/IP network; **IP Datagram** = packet of data transferred across a TCP/IP network

IPL = INITIAL PROGRAM LOADER

ips = INCHES PER SECOND

IPSE = INTEGRATED PROJECT SUPPORT ENVIRONMENT

IPX = INTERNETWORK PACKET EXCHANGE network protocol developed by Novell that is used to transfer packets of information over a network

IR (a) = INFORMATION RETRIEVAL **(b)** = INDEX REGISTER **(c)** = INSTRUCTION REGISTER

IRC = INTERNET RELAY CHAT

IrDA = INFRARED DATA ASSOCIATION standard method used to transfer information via an infrared light beam; often used to transfer information from a laptop or PDA to a printer or desktop computer; to use this feature, your computer or printer needs to have an IrDA port

IRQ = INTERRUPT REQUEST a signal sent to the CPU to temporarily suspend normal processing and transfer control to an interrupt handling routine

irregular polygon *noun* enclosed graphic object that has a number of sides of unequal length

irretrievable *adjective* which cannot be retrieved; *the files are irretrievable since the computer crashed*

irreversible process *noun* process which, once carried out, cannot be reversed

IRTF = INTERNET RESEARCH TASK FORCE committee that is part of the IAB (see above) and researches new internet standards before referring them to the IETF for approval

IS-IS *see* INTERMEDIATE SYSTEM TO INTERMEDIATE SYSTEM

ISA = INDUSTRY STANDARD ARCHITECTURE standard used for the

16-bit expansion bus in an IBM PC or compatible *compare* EISA, MCA

ISAM = INDEXED SEQUENTIAL ACCESS METHOD

ISDN = INTEGRATED SERVICES DIGITAL NETWORK

ISO = INTERNATIONAL STANDARDS ORGANIZATION

◊ **ISO/OSI model** = INTERNATIONAL STANDARDS ORGANIZATION/OPEN SYSTEM INTERCONNECTION layered architecture that defines how computers and networks should interact

isochronous network *noun* network in which all the components on the network run from a common clock so that their timing is uniform

◊ **isochronous transmission** *noun* transfer of asynchronous data over a synchronous link

isolate *verb* (i) to separate something from a system; (ii) to insulate (something) electrically; **isolated location** = (hardware) storage location which cannot be directly accessed by a user's program, protecting it against accidental erasure

◊ **isolation** *noun* being isolated; **isolation transformer** = transformer used to isolate equipment from direct connection with the mains electricity supply, in case of voltage spikes, etc.

◊ **isolator** *noun* device *or* material which isolates

isometric view *noun* (in graphics) a drawing that shows all three dimensions of an object in equal proportion; *an isometric view does not show any perspective*

ISP = INTERNET SERVICE PROVIDER company that provides one of the permanent links that make up the internet and sells connections to private users and companies to allow them to access the internet

ISR = INFORMATION STORAGE AND RETRIEVAL

IT = INFORMATION TECHNOLOGY

italic *adjective & noun* type of character font in which the characters slope to the right; *the headline is printed in italic and underlined;* italics = italic characters; *all the footnotes are printed in italics; hit CTRL I to print the text in italics*

item *noun* single thing among many; *a data item can be a word or a series of figures or a record in a file;* item size = number of characters *or* digits in an item of data

iterate *or* **iterative routine** *noun* loop *or* series of instructions in a program which repeat over and over again until the program is completed

◊ **iteration** *noun* repeated application of a program to solve a problem

◊ **iterative process** *noun* process that is continuously repeated until a condition is met

ITS = INVITATION TO SEND

Jj

jabber *noun* continuous random signal transmitted by a faulty adapter card *or* node on a network

jack *noun* plug which consists of a single pin; **data jack** = plug that allows a modem to be connected directly to the telephone system

jaggies *plural noun* jagged edges which appear along diagonal or curved lines displayed on a computer screen, caused by the size of each pixel; *see also* ALIASING, ANTI-ALIASING

Jaguar™ *noun* multimedia console hardware developed by Atari; uses a 64-bit RISC processor and includes a high-speed graphics adapter and sound

jam 1 *noun* stoppage of a process *or* mechanism due to a fault; *a jam in the paper feed* **2** *verb (of a device)* to stop working because something is blocking the functioning; *the recorder's not working because the tape is jammed in the motor; lightweight copier paper will feed without jamming*

jar *verb* to give a sharp shock to a device; *you can cause trouble by turning off or jarring the PC while the disk read heads are moving; hard disks are very sensitive to jarring*

Java™ programming language and program definition developed by Sun Microsystems used to create small applications designed to enhance the functionality of a Web page; the language is similar to object-oriented languages such as C++ and can run on any compatible platform *compare with* ACTIVEX; **Java Database Connectivity (JDBC)** = set of standard functions that allow a programmer to access a database from within a Java application

◊ **JavaScript**™ set of programming commands that can be included within a normal Web page (that is written using HTML commands); when the web browser loads the web page, it runs the JavaScript commands, normally used to create special effects to a web page *compare with* PERL, VBSRIPT

JCL = JOB CONTROL LANGUAGE commands which describe the identification of and resources required by a job that a computer has to process

jet *see* INK-JET

jitter *noun* **(a)** fault where there is rapid small up-and-down movement of characters *or* pixels on a screen of image bits in a facsimile transmission; *looking at this screen jitter is giving me a headache* **(b)** fault in a transmission line that causes some of the data bits being transmitted to be corrupted

JK-flip-flop *noun* flip-flop device with two inputs (J and K) and two complementary outputs that are dependent on the inputs

job *noun* task *or* number of tasks *or* work to be processed as a single unit; *the next job to be processed is to sort all the records;* **job control file** = file which contains instructions in a JCL; **job control language (JCL)** = commands which describe the identification of and resources required by a job that a computer has to process; **job control program** = short program of job control instructions loaded before a particular application is run, setting up the system as required by the application; **job file** = file containing jobs *or* job names waiting to be processed; **job mix** = the jobs being executed at any one time in a system; **job number** = number which is given to a job in a queue, waiting to be processed; **job orientated language** = computer programming language that provides specialized instructions relating to job control tasks and processing; **job orientated terminal** = computer terminal designed for and used for a particular task; **job priority** = importance of a job compared to others; **job processing** = to read in job control instructions from an input source and execute them; **job queue** *or* **job stream** = number of tasks arranged in an order waiting to be processed in a multitasking *or* batch system; **job scheduling** = arranging the order in which jobs are processed; **job statement control** = use of instructions and statements to control the actions of the operating system of a computer; **job step** *or* **stream** = one unit of processing involved in a task; **remote job entry (RJE)** = use of an interactive user terminal to enter job control instructions; **stacked job control** = queue of job control instructions that are processed in the order in which they were received

join *verb* **(a)** to link *or* to put several things together **(b)** to combine two or more pieces of information to produce a single unit of information; **join files** = instruction to produce a new file consisting of one file added to the end of another **(c)** logical function that produces a true output if any input is true

joint denial *noun* logical function whose output is false if any input is true

Joint Photographic Experts Group *see* JPEG

journal *noun* **(a)** record of all communications to and from a terminal; **journal file** = stored record of every communication between a user and the central computer, used to help retrieve files after a system crash *or* fault **(b)** list of any changes *or* updates to a file; *the modified records were added to the master file and noted in the journal*

joystick *noun* device that allows a user to move a cursor around the screen by moving an upright rod connected to an I/O port on the computer; **joystick port** = circuit and connector used to interface a joystick with a computer; *a joystick port is provided with the home computer*

COMMENT: mostly used for computer games or CAD or desktop publishing packages

JPEG = JOINT PHOTOGRAPHIC EXPERTS GROUP standard that defines a way of storing graphic images in a compressed format in a file on disk

◊ **JPEG++** *noun* an extension to JPEG that allows different parts of an image to be compressed at different levels of compression

jukebox *noun* CD-ROM drive that can hold several CD-ROM discs and select the correct disc when required

jumbo chip *noun* integrated circuit made using the whole of a semiconductor wafer; *see also* WAFER SCALE INTEGRATION

jump (instruction) 1 *noun* programming command to end one set of instructions and direct the processor to another section of the program; **conditional jump** = situation where the processor is directed to another section of the program only if a condition is met; **jump operation** = situation where the CPU is sent from the instruction it is currently executing to another point in the program; **unconditional jump** = instruction which transfers control from one point in the program to another, without requiring any condition to be met 2 *verb* to direct a CPU to another section of a program; **jump on zero** = conditional jump executed if a flag *or* register is zero

jumper *noun* temporary wire connection on a circuit board; **jumper-selectable** = circuit *or* device whose options can be selected by positioning various wire connections; *the printer's typeface was jumper-selectable*

junction *noun* connection between wires *or* cables; **junction box** = small box where a number of wires can be interconnected

junk 1 *noun* information *or* hardware which is useless *or* out-of-date *or* non-functional **2** *verb* to get rid of a file; to make a file *or* piece of hardware redundant; **to junk a file** = to erase *or* delete from storage a file that is no longer used

justify *verb* **(a)** to change the spacing between words *or* characters in a document so that the left and right margins will be straight; **justify inhibit** = instruction to prevent a word processor justifying a document; **justify margin** = *see* LEFT *or* RIGHT JUSTIFY; **hyphenate and justify** = to break long words correctly where they split at the ends of lines, so as to give a straight right margin; **left justify** = to print with a straight left-hand margin; **right justify** = to print with a straight right-hand margin **(b)** to shift the contents of a computer register by a set amount

◊ **justification** *noun* moving data bits *or* characters to the left *or* right so that the lines have straight margins; **hyphenation and justification** *or* **H & J** = justifying lines to a set width, splitting the long words correctly at the end of each line; *an American hyphenation and justification program will not work with British English spellings*

juxtaposition *noun* arranging *or* placing items next to or adjacent to each other

Kk

K *prefix* **(a)** = KILO symbol used to represent one thousand **(b)** symbol used to represent 1,024, equal to 2^{10}

◊ **Kbit** = KILOBIT measure of 1,024 bits

◊ **Kb** *or* **Kbyte** = KILOBYTE unit of measure for high capacity storage devices meaning 1,024 bytes; *the new disk drive has a 100Kb capacity; the original PC cannot access more than 640K bytes of RAM*

> COMMENT: 1,024 is the strict definition in computer or electronics applications, being equal to a convenient power of two; these abbreviations can also be taken to equal approximately one thousand, even in computing applications. 1Kb is roughly equal to 1,000 output characters in a PC

◊ **Kbps** = KILO BITS PER SECOND measure of the amount of data that a device can transfer each second; *a fast modem can transfer data at a rate of 33.6Kbps, whereas an ISDN adapter can transfer data at a rate of 64Kbps*

K6 64-bit processor developed by AMD Corporation as a rival to the Intel Pentium series of processors

Kaleida Labs company formed as a joint venture between Apple and IBM to produce cross-platform multimedia authoring tools

Karnaugh map *noun* graphical representation of states and conditions in a logic circuit; *the prototype was checked for hazards with a Karnaugh map*

Kermit *noun* file transfer protocol usually used when downloading data with a modem

kern *verb* to adjust the space between pairs of letters so that they are printed closer together; *we have kerned 'T' and 'o' so they are closer together*

kernel *noun* basic essential instruction routines required as a basis for any operations in a computer system; **graphics kernel system (gks)** = number of basic commands required to illuminate in various shades and colours the pixels on a screen (these are then used to provide more complex functions such as line *or* shape plotting)

> COMMENT: kernel routines are usually hidden from the user; they are used by the operating system for tasks such as loading a program or displaying text on a screen

key 1 *noun* **(a)** button on a keyboard that operates a switch; *there are 64 keys on the keyboard;* **hot key** = special key or key combination which starts a process or activates a program; **key combination** *or* **shortcut** = combination of two or more keys that carry out a function when pressed at the same time; **key click** = sound produced by a computer to allow the operator to know that the key he pressed has been registered; **key number** = numeric code used to identify which key has been pressed; **key overlay** = paper placed over the keys on a keyboard describing their functions for a particular application; *without the key overlay, I would never remember which function key does what;* **key punch** = machine used for punching data into punched cards by means of a keyboard; **key rollover** = use of a buffer between the keyboard and computer to provide rapid key stroke storage for fast typists who hit several keys in rapid succession; **key strip** = piece of paper above certain keys used to remind the operator of their special functions **(b)** *(names of keys);*

alphanumeric key *or* **character key** = key which produces a character (letter *or* symbol *or* figure); **carriage return key** = key which moves a cursor *or* printhead to the beginning of the next line on screen *or* on a typewriter *or* in printing; **function key** = key which has a specific task *or* sequence of instructions; *tags can be allocated to function keys;* **shift key** = key which provides a second function for a key (usually by moving the output into upper case) **(c)** important object *or* group of characters in a computer system, used to represent an instruction *or* set of data; **key terminal** = most important terminal in a computer system *or* one with the highest priority **(d)** special combination of numbers *or* characters that are used with a cipher to encrypt *or* decrypt a message; *type this key into the machine, it will decode the last message* **(e)** identification code *or* word used for a stored record *or* data item; *we selected all the records with the word disk in their keys;* **index key** = one field which is used to index a record; **key field** = field which identifies entries in a record **2** *verb* **(a)**; **to key in** = to enter text *or* commands via a keyboard; *they keyed in the latest data* **(b)**; **keyed sequential access method (KSAM)** = file structure that allows data to be accessed using key fields or key field content

◊ **keyboard 1** *noun* number of keys fixed together in some order, used to enter information into a computer *or* to produce characters on a typewriter; **keyboard to disk entry** = system where information entered on a keyboard is stored directly onto disk with no processing; **ANSI keyboard** = standard for a keyboard that provides either upper case or upper and lower case characters on a typewriter style keyboard; **ASCII keyboard** = keyboard that provides a key for every ASCII code; **ASR keyboard** = communications console keyboard that has all the characters and punctuation keys and special control, send and receive keys; **AZERTY keyboard** = non-English language key layout (the first six letters on the top left row of the keyboard being AZERTY); **interactive keyboard** = keyboard that helps to direct the user *or* prompts for an input by lighting up certain keys on the keyboard (under program control); **keyboard contact**

bounce = multiple signals from a key pressed just once, due to a faulty switch and key bounce; **keyboard encoder** = way in which each key generates a unique word when pressed; **keyboard layout** = way in which various function and character keys are arranged; **keyboard overlay** = paper placed over the keys on a keyboard describing their special functions for a particular application; **keyboard send/receive (KSR)** = terminal which has a keyboard and monitor, and is linked to a CPU; **keyboard to disk entry** = system where information entered on a keyboard is stored directly onto disk without any processing; **QWERTY keyboard** = standard English language key layout (the first six letters on the top left row of keys are QWERTY); **touch sensitive keyboard** = thin, flat membrane type keyboard whose keys are activated by touching a particular key, with no movement involved (often used for heavy duty or dirty environments where normal keys would not function correctly) **2** *verb* to enter information by using a keyboard; *it was cheaper to have the manuscript keyboarded by another company*

---

the new keyboard is almost unchanged, and has sixteen programmable function keys
Micro Decision

---

the main QWERTY typing area is in the centre of the keyboard with the 10 function keys on the left
Personal Computer World

keyboarder *noun* person who enters data via a keyboard

keyboarding *noun* action of entering data using a keyboard; *the cost of keyboarding is calculated in keystrokes per hour*

keypad *noun* group of special keys used for certain applications; *you can use the numeric keypad to enter the figures;* **hex keypad** = keypad with 16 keys (0-9 and A-F) for all the hexadecimal digits; **numeric keypad** = set of ten keys with figures (0-9), included in most computer keyboards as a separate group, used for entering large amounts of data in numeric form

it uses a six button keypad to select the devices and functions

Byte

keystone *or* trapezoidal distortion
noun image distortion in which the vertical lines slant out towards the horizontal edges of the monitor

keystroke *noun* action of pressing a key; *he keyboards at a rate of 3500 keystrokes per hour;* **keystroke count** = counting of each keystroke made, often used to calculate keyboarding costs; **keystroke verification** = check made on each key pressed to make sure it is valid for a particular application

key-to-disk *noun* system where data is keyed in and stored directly on disk without any processing

keyword *noun* (i) command word used in a programming language to provide a function; (ii) important *or* informative word in a title *or* document that describes its contents; (iii) word which is relevant *or* important to a text; *the BASIC keyword PRINT will display text on the screen; computer is a keyword in IT*

KHz = KILOHERTZ

kill *verb* to erase a file *or* stop a program during execution; **kill file** = command to erase a stored file completely; **kill job** = command to halt a computer job while it is running

kilo *prefix* **(a)** meaning one thousand; **kilobaud** = = 1,000 bits per second; **kilohertz (KHz)** = frequency of one thousand cycles per second; **kilo instructions per second (KIPS)** = one thousand computer instructions processed every second, used as a measure of computer power **(b)** meaning 1,024 units, equal to 2^{10} (used only in computer and electronics applications); **kilobit** *or* **Kbit** = 1,024 bits of data; **kilo bits per second (Kbps)** = measure of the amount of data that a device can transfer each second; **kilobyte** *or* **Kb** *or* **Kbyte** = unit of measurement for high capacity storage devices meaning 1,024 bytes of data; **Kilostream** = leased line connection

supplied by British Telecom that provides data transfer rates of 64Kbit per second; **kiloword** *or* **KW** = unit of measurement of 1,024 computer words

kiosk *noun* small booth with a screen, means of user input and a computer, used to provide information for the general public

KIPS = KILO INSTRUCTIONS PER SECOND one thousand computer instructions processed every second, used as a measure of computer power

Klamath code name for the low-cost version of the Intel Pentium Pro processor

kludge *or* **kluge** *noun* *(informal)* (i) temporary correction made to a badly written *or* constructed piece of software *or* to a keyboarding error; (ii) hardware which should only be used for demonstration

◊ **kluged** *adjective* temporarily repaired

knob *noun* round button (such as on a monitor), which can be turned to control some process; *turn the on/off knob; the brightness can be regulated by turning a knob at the back of the monitor*

knowledge *noun* what is known; **intelligent-knowledge based system (IKBS)** = software that applies the knowledge, advice and rules defined by experts in a particular subject, to a user's data to help solve a problem; **knowledge-based system** = computer system that applies the stored reactions, instructions and knowledge of experts in a particular field to a problem; *see also* EXPERT SYSTEM; **knowledge engineering** = designing and writing expert computer systems

KSAM = KEYED SEQUENTIAL ACCESS METHOD file structure that allows data to be accessed using key fields or key field content

KSR = KEYBOARD SEND/RECEIVE terminal which has a keyboard and monitor, and is linked to a CPU *compare* ASR

KW = KILOWORD

LI

L1 cache = LEVEL ONE CACHE small area of high-speed static RAM fitted to a processor chip that stores frequently used data to improve processing speed; *the Intel Pentium processor contains 16Kb of L1 cache; see also* CACHE

◊ **L2 cache** = LEVEL TWO CACHE high-speed cache memory that is fitted to the computer's motherboard and supplies data to the processor faster than the main memory to improve performance; *see also* BURST CACHE, PIPELINE

label 1 (a) *noun* (i) word *or* other symbol used in a computer program to identify a routine *or* statement; (ii) character(s) used to identify a variable *or* piece of data *or* a file; *BASIC uses many program labels such as line numbers;* **label field** = an item of data in a record that contains a label; **label record** = record containing identification for a stored file **(b)** piece of paper *or* card attached to something to show instructions for use *or* an address; **continuous labels** = removable adhesive labels attached to a backing sheet that can be fed into a printer; **external label** = identifying piece of paper stuck to the outside of a device *or* disk; **label printer** = special printer used to print addresses onto continuous labels **2** *verb* to print an address on a label

◊ **labelling** *noun* (i) putting a label on something; (ii) printing labels; *the word-processor has a special utility allowing simple and rapid labelling*

lag *noun* time taken for an image to be no longer visible after it has been displayed on a CRT screen (this is caused by long persistence phosphor)

LAN *or* **lan** = LOCAL AREA NETWORK network where various terminals and equipment are all within a short distance of one another (at a maximum distance of about 500m, for example in the same building), and can be interconnected by cables; **LAN segment** = part of a network separated from the rest by a bridge; **LAN server** = computer which runs a network operating system and controls the basic network operations; all the workstations in a LAN are connected to the central network server and users log onto the network server; *see also* PEER-TO-PEER *compare* WAN

◊ **LAN Manager** *noun* network operating system developed for the PC by Microsoft

◊ **LAN Server** *noun* network operating system for the PC developed by IBM

> The opportunities to delete and destroy data are far greater on our LAN than in the days when we had a mainframe. PC people are culturally different from mainframe people. You really don't think about security problems when you can physically lock your system up in a closet.
>
> *Computing*

landing zone *noun* area of a hard disk which does not carry data, the head can come into contact with the disk in this area without damaging the disk or data; *see also* PARKING

landline *noun* communications link that uses cable to physically and electrically link two devices

landscape *noun* orientation of a page *or* piece of paper where the longest edge is horizontal *compare* PORTRAIT

language *noun* system of words *or* symbols which allows communication with computers (such as one that allows computer instructions to be entered as words which are easy to understand, and then translates them into machine code); **language assembler** = program used to translate and assemble a source code program into a machine executable binary form; **language compiler** = software that converts an encoded source program into another (machine code) form, and then executes it; **language interpreter** = any program that takes each consecutive line of source program and translates it into another (machine code) language at run-time; **language processor** = language translator from one language to machine code (there are three types of language processor: assembler, compiler and interpreter); **language rules** = syntax and format for instructions and data items used in a particular language; **language support environment** = hardware and software tools supplied to help the programmer write programs in a particular language; **language translation** = using a computer to translate text from one language to another; **language translator** = program that converts code written in one language into equivalent instructions in another language; **assembly language** *or* **assembler language** = programming language using mnemonics to code instructions which will then be converted to machine code; **command language** = programming language made up of procedures for various tasks, that can be called up by a series of commands; **control language** = commands that identify and describe the resources required by a job that a computer has to perform; **graphic language** = computer programming language with inbuilt commands that are useful when displaying graphics; **high-level language (HLL)** = computer programming language which is easy to learn and allows the user to write programs using words and commands that are easy to understand and look like English words, the program is then translated into machine code, with one HLL instruction often representing more than one machine code instruction; **low-level language (LLL)** = language which is long and complex to program in, where each instruction represents a single machine code instruction; **machine language** = programming language that consists of commands in binary code form that can be directly understood by the CPU; **programming language** = software that allows a user to enter a program in a certain language and then to execute it; **query language** = language in a database management system that allows a database to be easily searched and queried; **source language** = original language in which a program is written prior to processing by a computer

COMMENT: There are three main types of computer languages: machine code, assembler and high-level language. The higher the level the language is, the easier it is to program and understand, but the slower it is to execute. The following are common high-level languages: ADA, ALGOL, APL, BASIC, C, C++, COBOL, COMAL, CORAL, FORTH, FORTRAN, LISP, LOGO, PASCAL, PL/1, POP-2, PROLOG, Visual Basic. Assembly language uses mnemonics to represent machine code instructions; machine code is the lowest level of programming language and consists of binary patterns that instruct the processor to perform various tasks

lap *noun* **(a)** a person's knees, when he is sitting down; *he placed the computer on his lap and keyboarded some orders while sitting in his car* **(b)** overlap of printed colours which prevents any gaps showing

◊ **laptop (computer)** *noun* computer that is light enough to carry but not so small as to fit in a pocket, usually containing a screen, keyboard and disk drive; *compare with* PDA

COMMENT: a laptop is usually designed in two parts joined with a hinge; the processor and disk drives are located beneath the keyboard and the display is in the upper hinged section that folds down over the keyboard for safety

in our summary of seven laptops we found features to admire in every machine
PC Business World

LAP = LINK ACCESS PROTOCOL CCITT standard protocol used to start and maintain links over an X.25 network; **LAP-B** = CCITT standard setup routine to establish a link between a DCE and DTE (such as a computer and modem); **LAP-M** = LINK ACCESS PROTOCOL FOR MODEMS variation of LAP-B protocol used in V.42 error correcting modems

large model *noun* (in an Intel processor) memory model in which both code and data can exceed 64Kb in size, but combined size should be less than 1Mb

large-scale computer *noun* high-powered (large word size) computer system that can access high capacity memory and backing storage devices as well as multiple users

◊ **large-scale integration (LSI)** *noun* integrated circuit with 500 to 10,000 components

laser *noun* = LIGHT AMPLIFICATION BY STIMULATED EMISSION OF RADIATION; device that produces coherent light of a single wavelength in a narrow beam, by exciting a material so that it emits photons of light; **laser disc** = COMPACT DISC; **laser emulsion storage** = digital storage technique using a laser to expose light-sensitive material; **laser printer** = high-resolution computer printer that uses a laser source to print high-quality dot matrix character patterns on paper (these have a much higher resolution than normal printers, usually 300 dpi)

LaserJet™ *or* **Hewlett Packard™ LaserJet** *or* **HP LaserJet** *noun* laser printer manufactured by Hewlett Packard that uses its PCL language to describe a page

LaserWriter *noun* laser printer manufactured by Apple that uses the PostScript page description language

last in first out (LIFO) *noun* queue system that reads the last item stored, first; *this computer stack uses a last in first out data retrieval method;* compare FIRST IN FIRST OUT

latch *verb* to set an output state; *the output latched high until we reset the computer*

latency *noun* time delay between the moment when an instruction is given to a computer and the execution of the instruction *or* return of a result (such as the delay between a request for data and the data being transferred from memory)

launch 1 *noun* putting a new product on the market; *the launch of the new PC has been put back six months; the launch date for the network will be September 2* verb (a) to put a new product on the market; *the new PC was launched at the Computer Show; launching costs for the computer range were calculated at $250,000* (b) to start *or* run a program; *you launch the word-processor by double-clicking on this icon*

layer *noun* (a) ISO/OSI standards defining the stages a message has to pass through when being transmitted from one computer to another over a local area network; **application layer** = the program that requests a transmission; **data link layer** = layer that sends packets of data to the next link, and deals with error correction; **network layer** = layer that decides on the routes to be used, the costs, etc.; **physical layer** = the ISO/OSI standard network layer that defines rules for bit rate, power and medium for signal transmission; **presentation layer** = section that agrees on format, codes and request for start/end of a connection; **session layer** = layer that makes the connection/disconnection between a transmitter and receiver; **transport layer** = layer that checks and controls the quality of the connection

◊ **layered** *adjective* which consists of layers; *the kernel has a layered structure according to user priority*

◊ **layout** *noun* (i) rules governing the data input and output from a computer (ii) way of using a sheet of paper; *see also* LANDSCAPE, PORTRAIT

LCD = LIQUID CRYSTAL DISPLAY liquid crystal that turns black when a voltage is applied, used in many watches, calculators and other small digital displays; **LCD shutter printer** = page printer that uses an LCD panel in front of a bright light to describe images onto the photosensitive drum; the LCD panel stops the light passing through, except at pixels that describe the image

---

LCD screens can run for long periods on ordinary or rechargeable batteries

Micro Decision

LCP = LINK CONTROL PROCEDURE rules defining the transmission of data over a channel

LDAP = LIGHTWEIGHT DIRECTORY ACCESS PROTOCOL method of locating and accessing folders, files and resources via a wide area network or the internet; new internet software uses LDAP to allow a remote user to easily find and access resources such as a folder on a company intranet linked to the internet; *see also* DIRECTORY SERVICES, GLOBAL NAMING

lead *noun* **(a)** electrical conducting wire

◊ **lead in page** *noun* videotext page that directs the user to other pages of interest

◊ **leader** *noun* section of magnetic tape that contains no signal, used at the beginning of the reel for identification and to aid the tape machine to pick up the tape; **leader record** = initial record containing information (such as titles, format, etc.) about following records in a file

◊ **leading** *noun* space between lines of text printed or displayed

◊ **leading edge** *noun* first edge of a punched card that enters the card reader

◊ **leading zero** *noun* zero digit used to pad out the beginning of a stored number

leaf *noun* final node in a tree structure

leap-frog test *noun* memory location test, in which a program skips from one location to another random location, writing data then reading and comparing for faults, until all locations have been tested; **crippled leap-frog test** = standard leap-frog test that uses a single memory location rather than a changing location

learning curve *noun* graphical description of how someone can acquire knowledge (about a product) over time; **steep learning curve** = (a product) that is very difficult to use

lease 1 *noun* written contract for letting *or* renting a piece of equipment for a period against payment of a fee **2** *verb* **(a)** to let *or* rent equipment for a period; *the company has a policy of only using leased equipment;* **leased line** = communications channel, such as a telephone line, which is rented for the exclusive use of the subscriber **(b)** to use equipment for a time and pay a fee; *the company leases all its computers*

least cost design *noun* best money-saving use of space *or* components; *the budget is only £1000, we need the least cost design for the new circuit*

◊ **least recently used algorithm (LRU)** *noun* algorithm which finds the page of memory that was last accessed before any other, and erases it to make room for another page

◊ **least significant bit (LSB)** *noun* binary digit occupying the right hand position of a word and carrying the least power of two in the word (usually equal to two raised to zero = 1)

◊ **least significant digit (LSD)** *noun* digit which occupies the right hand position in a number and so carries the least power (equal to the number radix raised to zero = 1)

leaving files open *phrase* meaning that a file has not been closed *or* does not contain an end of text marker (this will result in the loss of data since the text will not have been saved)

LED = LIGHT EMITTING DIODE semiconductor diode that emits light when a current is applied; **LED printer** = page printer (similar to a laser printer) that uses an LED light source instead of a laser

> COMMENT: LED displays are used to display small amounts of information, as in pocket calculators, watches, indicators, etc.

left-handed mouse *noun* configuration of a mouse so that the function of the two buttons are reversed

left justification *noun* **(a)** shifting a binary number to the left hand end of the word containing it **(b)** making the left hand margin of the text even

◊ **left justify** *verb* printing command that makes the left hand margin of the text even

◊ **left shift** *noun* left arithmetic shift by one bit of data in a word; a binary number is doubled for each left shift

leg *noun* one possible path through a routine

legal *adjective* statement or instruction that is acceptable within language syntax rules

leightweight directory access protocol *see* LDAP

length *noun* how long something is; the number of data items in a variable *or* list; **block length** = number of records *or* fields *or* characters in a block of data; **buffer length** = number of data item that can be stored in a buffer while waiting for the processor to attend to them; **field length** = number of characters stored in a field; **file length** = number of characters *or* bytes in a stored file; **length of filename** = number of characters allowed for identification of a file; **line length** = number of characters which can be displayed horizontally on one line of a display (CRT displays often use an 80 character line length); **record length** = total number of characters contained in the various fields within a stored record; **register length** = number of bits that make up a register

letter *noun* piece of writing sent from one person to another *or* from a company to another, to give information, to send an instructions, etc.; **form letter** *or* **standard**

letter = letter sent to several addressees by name without any change to the text

◊ **letter-quality (LQ) printing** *noun* feature of some dot-matrix printers to provide characters of the same quality as a typewriter by using dots which are very close together; **near-letter-quality (NLQ) printing** = printing by a dot-matrix printer that provides higher quality type, which is almost as good as a typewriter, by decreasing the space between the dots

> the printer offers reasonable speeds of printing in both draft and letter-quality modes
> *Which PC?*

level *noun* quantity of bits that make up a digital transmitted signal; **quaternary level quantization** = use of four bits of data in an A/D conversion process

◊ **level two cache** *or* **L2 cache** high-speed cache memory that is fitted to the computer's motherboard, except on a computer using the Pentium Pro processor where the memory is part of the processor chip design

lexical analysis *noun* stage in program translation when the compiling *or* translating software replaces program keywords with machine code instructions

LF = LINE FEED

library *noun* **(a)** collection of files *or* documents *or* books *or* records, etc., which can be consulted *or* borrowed by the public, usually kept in a public place **(b)**; **program library** *or* **software library** = collection of programs *or* books belonging to a person; *he has a large library of computer games* **(c)**; **library function** = software routine that a user can insert into his program to provide the function with no effort; **library program** = (i) number of specially written *or* relevant software routines, which a user can insert into his own program, saving time and effort; (ii) group of functions which a computer needs to refer to often, but which are not stored in main memory; *the square root function is already in the library program;* **macro library** = number of useful, independent routines that can be incorporated into any program to ease program writing; **library routine** = prewritten routine that can be inserted into a main program and called up when required; **library subroutine** = tried and tested subroutine stored in a library, and which can be inserted into a user's program when required; **library track** = one track on a magnetic disk *or* tape used to store information about the contents (such as titles, format and index data)

---

a library of popular shapes and images is supplied

Practical Computing

---

licence *noun* permission given by one manufacturer to another manufacturer to make copies of his products against payment of a fee; *the software is manufactured in this country under licence*

lifetime *noun* period of time during which a device is useful *or* not outdated; *this new computer has a four-year lifetime*

LIFO = LAST IN FIRST OUT queue system that reads the last item stored, first; *this computer stack uses a LIFO data retrieval method; see also* FIFO

lifter *noun* mechanical device that lifts magnetic tape away from the heads when rewinding the tape

light *noun* perception of brightness due to electromagnetic effects in the frequency range 400 - 750 nm, which allows a person to see; *the VDU should not be placed under a bright light;* **light emitting diode (LED)** = semiconductor diode that emits light when a current is applied (used in calculators and clock displays and as indicators); **light pen** = computer accessory in the shape of a pen that contains a light-sensitive device that can detect pixels on a video screen (often used with suitable software to draw graphics on a screen *or* position a cursor)

◊ **lightweight** *adjective* which is not heavy; *a lightweight computer which can easily fit into a suitcase*

LIM EMS = LOTUS, INTEL, MICROSOFT EXPANDED MEMORY SYSTEM (in an IBM PC) standard that

defines extra memory added above the 640Kb limit of conventional memory; this memory can only be used by specially-written programs

limits *noun* predefined maximum ranges for numbers in a computer

◊ **limited distance modem** *noun* data transmission device with a very short range that sends pure digital data rather than data sent on a modulated carrier

line *noun* **(a)** physical connection for data transmission (such as a cable between parts of a system *or* a telephone wire); **telephone line** = cable used to connect a telephone handset with a central exchange; **line busy tone** = signal generated to indicate that a connection *or* telephone line is already in use; **access line** = permanently connected communications line between a terminal and a DSE; **fast line** = special communications link that allows data to be transmitted at 48K *or* 96K baud; **line adapter** = electronic circuit that matches the correct signal voltage and impedance for a particular line; **line analyzer** = test equipment that displays the characteristics of a line *or* the signals carried on the line; **line communications** = signal transmission using a cable link *or* telegraph wire; **line conditioning** = (techniques) used to keep the quality of data transmissions *or* signals on a line to a certain standard; **line control** = special codes used to control a communications channel; **line driver** = high power circuit and amplifier used to send signals over a long distance line without too much loss of signal; **line level** = amplitude of a signal transmitted over a cable; **line speed** = rate at which data is sent along a line; **line switching** = communications line and circuit established on demand and held until no longer required **(b)** single long thin mark drawn by a pen *or* printed on a surface; *the printer has difficulty in reproducing very fine lines* **(c)** one trace by the electron picture beam on a screen *or* monitor; **line flyback** = electron beam returning from the end of one line to the beginning of the next; **line frequency** = number of picture lines that are scanned per second **(d)** row of characters (printed on a page *or* displayed on a computer screen *or* printer); *each page has 52 lines of text; several lines of manuscript seem to have been missed by the keyboarder; can we insert an extra line of spacing between the paragraphs?;* **command line** = program line that contains a command; **information line** = line running across the screen which gives the user information about the program being executed *or* the file being edited; **line editor** = piece of software that allows the operator to modify one line of text from a file at a time; **line ending** = character which shows that a line has ended (instructed by pressing the carriage return key); **line feed (LF)** = control on a printer *or* computer terminal that moves the cursor down by one line; **line length** = number of characters contained in a displayed line (on a computer screen this is normally 80 characters, on a printer often 132 characters); **line spacing** = distance between two rows of characters; **lines per minute (LPM)** = number of lines printed by a line printer per minute; **line style** = appearance of a line displayed on screen or printed **(e)** series of characters received as a single input by a computer; **line input** = command to receive all characters including punctuation entered up to a carriage return code **(f)** one row of commands *or* arguments in a computer program; **line number** = number that refers to a line of program code in a computer program

COMMENT: the programming language will sort out the program into order according to line number

straight lines are drawn by clicking the points on the screen where you would like the line to start and finish
Personal Computer World

while pixel editing is handy for line art, most desktop scanners have trouble producing the shades of grey or half-tones found in black and white photography
Publish

◊ **line printer** *noun* device for printing draft quality information at high speeds, typical output is 200 to 3000 lines per minute

COMMENT: line printers print a whole line at a time, running from right to left and left to right, and are usually dot matrix printers with not very high quality print. Compare page printers, which print a whole page at a time

linear *adjective;* **linear list** = list that has no free space for new records within its structure; **linear program** = computer program that contains no loops *or* branches; **linear programming** = method of mathematically breaking down a problem so that it can be solved by computer; **linear search** = search method which compares each item in a list with the search key until the correct entry is found (starting with the first item and working sequentially towards the end)

link 1 *noun* **(a)** communications path *or* channel between two components *or* devices; *to transmit faster, you can use the direct link with the mainframe;* **data link layer** = ISO/OSI layer that sends packets of data to the next link, and deals with error correction; **link control procedure (LCP)** = rules defining the transmission of data over a channel **(b)** software routine that allows data transfer between incompatible programs; **link trials** = testing computer programs so as to see if each module works in conjunction with the others **2** *verb* to join *or* interface two pieces of software *or* hardware; *the two computers are linked;* **link files** = command to merge together a list of separate files; **linked list** = list of data where each entry carries the address of the next consecutive entry; **linked object** = one piece of data that is referred to in another file or application; **linked subroutine** = number of computer instructions in a program that can be called at any time, with control being returned on completion to the next instruction in the main program

◊ **linkage** *noun* act of linking two things; **linkage editing** = combining separate programs together, and standardizing the calls *or* references within them; **linkage software** = special software which links sections of program code with any library routines *or* other code; *graphics and text are joined without linkage software*

◊ **linking** *noun* merging of a number of small programs together to enable them to run as one unit; **linking information** = (in Windows) feature that allows you to insert data from one application into a another application using its OLE function; **linking loader** = short software routine that merges sections of programs to allow them to be run as one

LIPS = LOGICAL INFERENCES PER SECOND standard for the measurement of processing power of an inference engine

> COMMENT: one inference often requires thousands of computer instructions

liquid crystal display (LCD) *noun*
liquid crystals that turn black when a voltage is applied, used in many watch, calculator and digital displays; **liquid crystal display shutter printer;** *see* LCD SHUTTER PRINTER

> COMMENT: LCDs do not generate light and so cannot be seen in the dark without an external light source (as opposed to LEDs)

LISP = LIST PROCESSING high-level language used mainly in processing lists of instructions *or* data and in artificial intelligence work

list 1 *noun* series of ordered items of data; **chained list** = list in which each element contains data and an address to the next element in the list; **linear list** = list that has no free space for new records within its structure; **linked list** = list of data where each entry carries the address of the next consecutive entry; **pushdown list** = temporary storage, in a LIFO format, for a list of items of data; **reference list** = list of routines *or* instructions and their location within a program; **stop list** = list of words that are not to be used *or* are not significant for a file search; **list box** = number of items or options displayed in a list; **list processing** = (i) computation of a series of items of data such as adding *or* deleting *or* sorting *or*

updating entries; (ii) LISP *or* a high-level language used mainly in processing lists of instructions *or* data, and in artificial intelligence work; **listserv** *or* **listserver** = server on the internet that sends a newsletter or articles to a list of registered users **2** *verb* to print *or* display certain items of information; **to list a program** = to display a program line by line in correct order

◊ **listing** *noun* program lines printed *or* displayed in an ordered way; **computer listing** = printout of a list of items, taken from data stored in a computer; **a program listing** = a printed copy of the lines of a program; **listing paper** = continuous stationery used in computer printers

LIST chunk (in a RIFF file) four-character code LIST that contains a series of subchunks

literal *noun* **(a)** (operand) computer instruction that contains the actual number *or* address to be used, rather than a label *or* its location **(b)** printing error when one character is replaced by another *or* when two characters are transposed

literate *adjective* (person) who can read; **computer-literate** = able to understand expressions relating to computers and how to use a computer

◊ **literacy** *noun* being able to read; **computer literacy** = understanding the basic principles of computers, related expressions and being able to use computers for programming *or* applications

liveware *noun* the operators and users of a computer system (as opposed to the hardware and software)

LLC = LOGICAL LINK CONTROL IEEE 802.2 standard defining the protocol for data-link-level transmissions

LLL = LOW-LEVEL LANGUAGE

load 1 *noun* job *or* piece of work to be done; **load sharing** = use of more than one computer in a network to even out the work load on each processor; **work load** = number of tasks that a machine has to complete **2** *verb* **(a)** to transfer a file *or* program from disk *or* tape to main memory; **load and run** *or* **load**

and go = computer program that is loaded into main memory and then starts to execute itself automatically; **load high** = (using MS-DOS on a PC) to transfer a program into high *or* expanded memory; **scatter load** = to load sequential data into various non-continuous locations in memory **(b)** to put a disk *or* tape into a computer, so that it can be run

◊ **loader** *noun* program which loads another file *or* program into computer memory; **absolute loader** = program that loads a section of code into main memory *compare* BOOTSTRAP; **binary loader** = short section of program code that allows programs in binary form (such as object code from a linker *or* assembler) to be loaded into memory; **card loader** = short program that transfers data from a punched card into main memory; **initial program loader (IPL)** = short routine that loads the first section of a program, after which it continues the loading process itself

◊ **loading** *noun* action of transferring a file *or* program from disk to memory; *loading can be a long process*

◊ **load point** *noun* start of a recording section in a reel of magnetic tape

local *adjective* **(a)** device that is physically attached and close to the controlling computer; **local bridge** = bridge that links two local networks; *we use a local bridge to link the two LANs in the office;* **local bus** = direct link *or* bus between a device and the processor; with no logic circuits *or* buffers *or* decoders in between; *the fastest expansion cards fit into this local bus connector;* **local drive** = disk drive that is physically attached to a computer rather than a resource being accessed across a network; **local memory** = high speed RAM that is used instead of a hardware device to store bit streams *or* patterns; **local printer** = printer physically attached to a computer rather than a shared resource available on a network **(b)** (variable *or* argument) that is only used in a certain section of a computer program *or* structure; **local declaration** = assignment of a variable that is only valid in a section of a computer program *or* structure; **local variable** = variable which can only be accessed by

certain routines in a certain section of a computer program *compare* GLOBAL VARIABLE **(c)** referring to a system with limited access *(of a terminal);* **on local** = not working with a CPU, but being used as a stand-alone terminal; **local mode** = operating state of a computer terminal that does not receive messages

◊ **local area network (LAN** *or* **lan)** *noun* network where various terminals and equipment are all a short distance from one another (at a maximum distance of about 500m, for example in the same building) and can be interconnected by cables *compare* WAN; **local area network server** = computer which runs a network operating system and controls the basic network operations; all the workstations in a LAN are connected to the central network server and users log onto the network server

> COMMENT: LANs use cables or optical fibre links; WANs use modems, radio and other long distance transmission methods

◊ **LocalTalk** *noun* network standard developed by Apple that defines the physical layer such as the cabling system and connectors used in Apple's AppleTalk network; the network transfers data at 230Kbits/second over unshielded twisted-pair cable

locate *verb* (i) to place *or* to set; (ii) to find; *the computer is located in the main office building; have you managed to locate the programming fault?*

◊ **location** *noun* number *or* absolute address which specifies the point in memory where a data word can be found and accessed

lock *verb* to prevent access to a system *or* file; **locking a file** = the action of preventing any further writing to a file; **to lock onto** = to synchronize an internal clock with a received signal

◊ **lockout** *noun* preventing a user sending messages over a network by continuously transmitting data

◊ **lock up** *noun* faulty operating state of computer that cannot be recovered from without switching off the power

> COMMENT: this can be caused by an
> infinite program loop or a deadly
> embrace

log 1 *noun* record of computer processing operations **2** *verb* **(a)** to record a series of actions; **to log calls** = to keep a record of telephone calls **(b)** to make a connection and start using a remote device such as a network server; **log on script** = series of batch instructions that are automatically executed when you connect *or* log on to network a server; **log on server** = computer that checks user identification and password data against a user database to authorize connection to a network *or* server; **to log in** *or* **log on** = to enter various identification data, such as a password, usually by means of a terminal, to the central computer before accessing a program *or* data (used as a means of making sure that only authorized users can access the computer system); **automatic log on** = telephone number, password and user number transmitted when requested by a remote system to automate logon; **to log off** *or* **log out** = to enter a symbol *or* instruction at the end of a computing session to close all files and break the channel between the user's terminal and the main computer (NOTE: the verbs can be spelled **log on, log-on,** or **logon; log off, log-off** or **logoff**)

◊ **logger** *noun* device which keeps a record of a series of actions; **call logger** = device which keeps a record of telephone calls

◊ **logging** *noun* input of data into a system; **logging in** *or* **logging on** = process of opening operations with a system; **logging off** *or* **logging out** = process of ending operations with a system; **error logging** = recording errors met; *features of the program include error logging*

logging on and off from terminals is simple, requiring only a user name and password
Micro Decision

facilities for protection against hardware failure and software malfunction include log files
Computer News

logic *noun* **(a)** science which deals with thought and reasoning; **formal logic** = treatment of form and structure, ignoring content **(b)** mathematical treatment of formal logic operations such as AND, OR, etc., and their transformation into various circuits; *see also* BOOLEAN ALGEBRA; **logic map** = graphical representation of states and conditions in a logic circuit; **logic state** = one out of two possible levels in a digital circuit, the levels being 1 and 0 or TRUE and FALSE; **logic state analyzer** = test equipment that displays the logic states of a number of components *or* circuits; **logic symbol** = graphical symbol used to represent a type of logic function **(c)** system for deducing results from binary data; **logic bomb** = section of code that performs various unpleasant functions such as system crash when a number of conditions are true (the logic bomb is installed by unpleasant hackers *or* very annoyed programmers); **logic level** = voltage used to represent a particular logic state (this is often five volts for a one and zero volts for a zero); **logic operation** = computer operation *or* procedure in which a decision is made **(d)** components of a computer *or* digital system; **sequential logic** = logic circuit whose output depends on the logic state of the previous inputs; **logic card** *or* **logic board** = printed circuit board containing binary logic gates rather than analog components; **logic circuit** = electronic circuit made up of various logical gates such as AND, OR and EXOR; **logic element** = gate *or* combination of logic gates; **logic flowchart** = graphical representation of logic elements, steps and decisions and the interconnections; **logic gate** = electronic circuit that applies a logical operator to an input signal and produces an output; *see also* GATE

the removal of complex but infrequently used logic makes the core of the processor simpler and faster, so simple operations execute faster
Electronics & Power

◊ **logical** *adjective* that uses logic in its operation; *logical reasoning can be simulated by an artificial intelligence machine;* **logical channel** = electronic circuit between a terminal and a network node in a packet switching system; **logical chart** = graphical representation of logic elements, steps and decisions and their interconnections; **logical comparison** = function to see if two logic signals are the same; **logical decision** = one of two paths chosen as a result of one of two possible answers to a question; **logical drive** = letter assigned to a disk drive *or* storage area on a disk drive that can be used as if it were a local drive; *the logical drive F: actually stores data on part of the server's disk drive;* **logical error** = fault in a program design causing incorrect branching *or* operations; **logical expression** = function made up from a series of logical operators such as AND and OR; **logical high** = equal to logic true state *or* 1; **logical inferences per second (LIPS)** = standard for the measurement of processing power of an inference engine; **logical link control (LLC)** = IEEE 802.2 standard defining the protocol for data-link-level transmissions; **logical low** = equal to logic false state *or* 0; **logical operator** = character *or* word that describes the logical action it will perform (the most common logical operators are AND, NOT, and OR); **logical palette** = (in Windows) graphics object that includes the colour palette information it requires; **logical record** = unit of information ready for processing that is not necessarily the same as the original data item in storage, which might contain control data, etc.; **logical ring** = (in a Token-Ring or FDDI network) the path a token follows through the layers of each node; in FDDI the physical topology does not effect the logical ring; **logical shift** = data movement to the left *or* right in a word, the bits falling outside the word boundary are discarded, the free positions are filled with zeros *compare* ARITHMETIC SHIFT; **logical unit (LU)** = set of protocols developed by IBM to allow communication over an SNA network; LU1, LU2 and LU3 provide control of the session, LU4 supports communication between the devices and LU6.2 is a peer-to-peer protocol

◊ **logic-seeking** *adjective* printer that can print the required information with the minimum head movement, detecting ends of lines, justification commands, etc.

login = LOGGING IN

LOGO *noun* high-level programming language used mainly for educational purposes, with graphical commands that are easy to use

◊ **logo** *noun* special printed set of characters *or* symbols used to identify a company *or* product

logoff = LOG OFF, LOGGING OFF

◊ **logon** = LOG ON, LOGGING ON

◊ **logout** = LOGGING OUT

long filename *noun* feature of Windows 95 that lets a user give files a long name (up to 254 characters long)

◊ **long haul network** *noun* communications network between distant computers that usually uses the public telephone system

◊ **long integer** *noun* (in programming languages) an integer represented by several bytes of data

look ahead *noun* action by some CPUs to fetch instructions and examine them before they are executed (to speed up operations); **carry look ahead** = high speed adder that can predict if a carry will be generated by a sum and add it in, removing the delay found in a ripple through carry adder

◊ **binary look-up** *noun* fast search method for use on ordered lists of data; the search key is compared with the data in the middle of the list and one half is discarded, this is repeated with the remaining half until only one data item remains

◊ **look-up table** *or* **LUT** *noun* collection of stored results that can be accessed very rapidly by a program without the need to calculate each result whenever needed; *lookup tables are preprogrammed then used in processing so saving calculations for each result required*

a lookup table changes a pixel's value based on the values in a table

Byte

loop 1 *noun* procedure *or* series of instructions in a computer program that are performed again and again until a test shows that a specific condition has been met *or* until the program is completed; **closed loop** = computer control operation in which data is fed back from the output of the controlled device to the controlling loop; **endless loop** *or* **infinite loop** = loop which has no end, except when the program is stopped; **holding loop** = section of program that loops until it is broken by some action, most often used when waiting for a response from the keyboard *or* a device; **modification loop** = instructions within a loop that change other instructions *or* data within a program; **nested loop** = loop contained inside another; **loopback** = diagnostic test that returns the transmitted signal to the sending device after it has passed through a device *or* across a link; **loop body** = main section of instructions within a loop that carry out the primary function rather than being used to enter or leave or set up the loop; **loop check** = check that data has been correctly transmitted down a line by returning the data to the transmitter; **loop counter** = register that contains the number of times a loop has been repeated; **loop program** = sequence of instructions that are repeated until a condition is met **2** *verb* to make a piece of wire *or* tape into a circle; **looping program** = computer program that runs continuously

lose *verb* not to have something any more; *all the current files were lost when the system crashed and we had no backup copies*

lossless compression *noun* image compression techniques that can reduce the number of bits used for each pixel in an image, without losing any information or quality; *see also* HUFFMAN ENCODING

lossy compression *noun* image compression techniques that can reduce the number of bits used for each pixel in an image, but in doing so lose information; *see also* JPEG

lost cluster *noun* number of sectors on a disk whose identification bits have been corrupted; the operating system has marked this area of disk as being used by a file, but

the data they contain can no longer be identified with a particular file

Lotus software company best known for its spreadsheet program, 1-2-3

◊ **Lotus-Intel-Microsoft Expanded Memory System** *see* LIM EMS

loudspeaker *noun* electromagnetic device that converts electrical signals into audible noise

low end *noun* hardware *or* software that is not very powerful or sophisticated and is designed for beginners

low-level language (LLL) *noun* programming language similar to assembler and in which each instruction has a single equivalent machine code instruction (the language is particular to one system *or* computer); *see also* HIGH-LEVEL LANGUAGE

◊ **low-level format** *noun* process that defines the physical pattern and arrangement of tracks and sectors on a disk

◊ **low memory** *noun* (in a PC) memory locations up to 640Kb; *compare* HIGH MEMORY

◊ **low-order digit** *noun* digit in the position within a number that represents the lowest weighting of the number base; *the number 234156 has a low-order digit of 6*

◊ **low-power standby** *noun* energy-saving feature of laptop computers and many monitors connected to a desktop

◊ **low-priority work** *noun* task which is not particularly important

◊ **low-resolution graphics** *or* **low-res graphics** *noun* ability to display character-sized graphic blocks *or* preset shapes on a screen rather than using individual pixels; *compare* HIGH-RESOLUTION

◊ **low-speed communications** *noun* data transmission at less than 2400 bits per second

lower case *noun* small characters (such as a, b, c, as opposed to upper case A, B, C)

LPM = LINES PER MINUTE

LPT1 (in a PC) name given to the first, main parallel printer port in the system

LQ = LETTER QUALITY

LRU = LEAST RECENTLY USED ALGORITHM *noun* algorithm which finds the page of memory that was last accessed before any other, and erases it to make room for another page

LSB = LEAST SIGNIFICANT BIT binary digit occupying the right hand position of a word and carrying the least power of two in the word, usually equal to two raised to zero = 1

LSD = LEAST SIGNIFICANT DIGIT digit which occupies the right hand position in a number and so carries least power (equal to the number radix raised to zero = 1)

LSI = LARGE SCALE INTEGRATION system with between 500 and 10,000 circuits on a single IC

LU = LOGICAL UNIT set of protocols developed by IBM to allow communication over an SNA network; LU1, LU2 and LU3 provide control of the session, LU4 supports communication between the devices and LU6.2 is a peer-to-peer protocol

luggable *noun* personal computer that is just about portable and usually will not run off batteries (it is much heavier and less compact than a laptop or true transportable machine)

LUT LOOK-UP TABLE

an image processing system can have three LUTs that map the image memory to the display device

Byte

Mm

m *prefix* = MILLI one thousandth

M *prefix* = MEGA **(a)** one million; **Mbps** = MEGA BITS PER SECOND number of million bits transmitted every second; **MFLOPS** = MEGA FLOATING POINT OPERATIONS PER SECOND measure of computing power and speed, equal to one million floating point operations per second **(b)** symbol for 1,048,576, used only in computer and electronic related applications, equal to 2^{20}; **Mbyte (MB)** = measurement of mass storage equal to 1,048,576 bytes; *the latest model has a 30Mbyte hard disk*

mA = MILLIAMPERE electrical current measure equal to one thousandth of an ampere

MAC **(a)** = MESSAGE AUTHENTICATION CODE special code transmitted at the same time as a message as proof of its authenticity **(b)** = MEDIA ACCESS CONTROL

◊ **Mac** *see* MACINTOSH

◊ **MacBinary** *noun* file storage and transfer system that allows Macintosh files, together with their icons and long file names, to be stored on other computer systems

machine *noun* **(a)** number of separate moving parts *or* components, acting together to carry out a process **(b)** computer *or* system *or* processor made of various components connected together to provide a function *or* perform a task; **clean machine** = computer that contains only the minimum of ROM based code to boot its system from disk, any languages required must be loaded separately; **machine address** = number *or* absolute address which specifies the point in memory where a data word can be found and accessed; **machine check** = fault caused by equipment failure; **machine code** *or* **machine language** = programming language that consists of commands in binary code that can be directly understood by the central processing unit without the need for translation; **machine code format** = a machine code instruction is usually made up of 1,2 or 3 bytes for operand, data and address; **machine code instruction** = instruction that directly controls the CPU and is recognized without the need for translation; **machine cycle** = minimum period of time taken by the CPU for the execution of an instruction; **machine dependent** = not standardized *or* which cannot be used on hardware *or* software from a different manufacturer without modifications; **machine error** = error caused by a hardware malfunction; **machine equation** = formula which an analog computer has been programmed to solve; **machine independent** = (computer software) that can be run on any computer system; **machine independent language** = programming language that can be translated and executed on any computer that has a suitable compiler; **machine instruction** = an instruction which can be recognized by a machine and is part of its limited set of commands; **machine intelligence** = the design of computer programs and devices that attempt to imitate human intelligence and decision-making functions, providing basic reasoning and other human characteristics; **machine intimate** = software that operates and interacts closely with the hardware in a system; **machine language** = (i) the way in which machine code is written; (ii) MACHINE CODE; **machine language compile** = to generate a machine code program from a HLL program by translating and assembling each HLL instruction; **machine language programming** = slowest and most complex method of programming a CPU, but the fastest in execution, achieved by entering directly into RAM or ROM the binary representation for the machine code instructions to be carried out (rather than using an assembler with assembly language programs *or* a compiler with HLL programs); **machine-readable** = (commands *or* data) stored on a medium that can be directly input to the computer; *the disk stores data in machine-readable form;* **machine run** = action of processing instructions in a program by a computer; **machine translation** = computer system that is used to translate text and commands from one language and syntax to another; **machine word** = number of bits of data operated on simultaneously by a CPU in one machine cycle, often 8, 16 or 32 bits; **source machine** = computer which can compile source code; **virtual machine** = simulated machine and its operations

Macintosh™ *noun* range of personal computers designed by Apple Corporation; the Macintosh uses the Motorola family of processors, the 68000, and offers similar computing power to a PC. The Macintosh is best known for its graphical user interface which allows a user to control the computer using icons and a mouse.; *Macintosh computers are not compatible with an IBM PC unless you use special emulation software*

macro- *prefix* very large *or* applying to the whole system

macro *noun* program routine *or* block of instructions identified by a single word *or* label; **macro assembler** *or* **assembly program** = assembler program that is able to decode macro instructions; **macro call** = use of a label in an assembly language program to indicate to an assembler that the macro routine is to be inserted at that point; **macro code** *or* **macro command** = one word that is used to represent a number of instructions, simplifying program writing; **macro definition** = description (in a program *or* to the operating system) of the structure, function and instructions that make up a

macro operation; **macro expansion** = process in which a macro call is replaced with the instructions in the macro; **macro flowchart** = graphical representation of the logical steps, stages and actions within a routine; **macro language** = programming language that allows the programmer to define and use macro instructions; **macro programming** = writing a program using macro instructions *or* defining macro instructions

Microsoft has released a developer's kit for its Word for Windows wordprocessing package. The 900-page kit explains how to use the WordBasic macro language supplied with the software.

Computing

macroelement *noun* number of data items treated as one element

macroinstruction *noun* one programming instruction that refers to a number of instructions within a routine *or* macro Macromedia Director authoring software for the PC and Macintosh using the Lingo scripting language

magazine *noun* number of pages in a videotext system

magnet *noun* something that produces a magnetic field

magnetic *adjective* which has a magnetic field associated with it; **magnetic bubble memory** = method of storing large amounts of binary data as small magnetized areas in the medium (made of certain pure materials); **magnetic card** = plastic card with a strip of magnetic recording material on its surface, allowing data to be stored (used in automatic cash dispensers); **magnetic card reader** *or* **magnetic strip reader** = machine that can read data stored on a magnetic card; **magnetic cartridge** *or* **cassette** = small box containing a reel of magnetic tape and a pick up reel; **magnetic cell** = small piece of material whose magnetic field can be altered to represent the two states of binary data; **magnetic core** = early main memory system for storing data in the first types of computer, each bit of data was stored in a magnetic cell; **magnetic disk** = flat circular piece of material coated with a substance, allowing signals and data to be stored magnetically; *see also* FLOPPY DISK, HARD DISK; **magnetic disk unit** = computer peripheral made up of a disk drive and necessary control electronics; **magnetic drum** = computer data storage peripheral that uses a coated cylinder to store data magnetically(not often used now); **magnetic encoding** = storage of (binary) data signals on a magnetic medium; **magnetic field** = description of the polarity and strength of magnetic effects at a point; **magnetic flux** = measure of magnetic field strength per unit area; **magnetic head** = electromagnetic component that converts electrical signals into a magnetic field, allowing them to be stored on a magnetic medium; **magnetic ink** = printing ink that contains a magnetic material, used in some character recognition systems; **magnetic ink character recognition (MICR)** = system that identifies characters by sensing the magnetic ink patterns (as used on bank cheques); **magnetic master** = original version of a recorded tape *or* disk; **magnetic material** *or* **medium** = substance that will retain a magnetic flux pattern after a magnetic field is removed; **magnetic media** = magnetic materials used to store signals, such as disk, tape, etc.; **magnetic memory** *or* **store** = storage that uses a medium that can store data bits as magnetic field changes; **magnetic recording** = transferring an electrical signal onto a moving magnetic tape *or* disk by means of an magnetic field generated by a magnetic head; **magnetic storage** = method of storing information as magnetic changes on a sensitive tape or disk, such as a floppy disk or hard disk; **magnetic strip** = layer of magnetic material on the surface of a plastic card, used for recording data; **magnetic transfer** = copy signals stored on one type of magnetic medium to another

◊ **magnetic tape** *noun* narrow length of thin plastic coated with a magnetic material used to store signals magnetically; **magnetic tape cartridge** *or* **cassette** = small box containing a reel of magnetic tape and a pick up reel, used in a cassette player *or* tape drive; **magnetic tape encoder** = device that directly writes data entered at a keyboard onto magnetic tape; **magnetic tape reader** = machine that can read signals stored on magnetic tape and convert them to an electrical form that can be understood by a computer; **magnetic tape recorder** = device with a magnetic head, motor and circuitry to allow electrical signals to be recorded onto *or* played back from a magnetic tape; **magnetic tape transport** = computer-controlled magnetic tape drive mechanism

> COMMENT: magnetic tape is available on spools of between 200 and 800 metres. The tape is magnetized by the read/write head. Tape is a storage medium which only allows serial access, that is, all the tape has to be read until the required location is found (as opposed to disk storage, which can be accessed randomly)

◊ **magnetize** *verb* to convert a material *or* object into a magnet

◊ **magneto-optical disc** *noun* optical disc that is used in a magneto-optical recording device

◊ **magneto-optical recording** *noun* storage media that uses an optical disc

> COMMENT: the optical disk has a thin layer of magnetic film which is heated by a laser, the particles are then polarised by a weak magnetic field. Magneto-optical media has very high capacity (over 600Mb) and is re-writable

mag tape *noun (informal)* = MAGNETIC TAPE

magnitude *noun* level *or* strength of a signal *or* variable

mail 1 *noun* **(a)** system for sending letters and parcels from one place to another **(b)** letters sent *or* received **(c)** electronic messages to and from users of a bulletin board *or* network; **electronic mail** *or* **email** *or* **e-mail** = messages sent between users of a bulletin board *or* interconnecting network; **mail-enabled** = (application) that has access to an electronic mail system without leaving the application; *this word-processor is mail-enabled - you can send messages to other users from within it* **2** *verb* to send something by post; *to mail a letter; we mailed our order last Wednesday*

mail application programming interface (MAPI) *noun* set of standards (developed by Microsoft) that defines how electronic mail is sent and delivered; *compare* MHS, POP3, SMTP

mailbox *or* **mail box** *noun* electronic storage space with an address in which a user's incoming messages are stored

mailing *noun* sending something using the post

mail-merge *noun* word-processing program which allows a standard form letter to be printed out to a series of different names and addresses

mail server *noun* computer that stores incoming mail and sends it to the correct user and stores outgoing mail and transfers it to the correct destination server on the internet

Spreadsheet views for data and graphical forms for data entry have been added to the Q&A database, with the traditional reporting, mailmerge, and labels improved through Windows facilities.

Computing

main *adjective* most important; **main body (of a program)** = set of instructions that form the main part of a program and from which other subroutines are called; **main clock** = clock signal that synchronizes all the components in a system; **main entry** = entry in a catalogue under which is contained the most important information about the document; **main index** = more general index that directs the user gradually to more specific index areas; **main loop (of a program)** = series of instructions performed repeatedly that carry out the main action of a program; this loop is often used to wait for user input before processing the event; **main memory** *or* **main storage** = fast access RAM whose locations can be directly and

immediately addressed by the CPU; *the 16-bit system includes up to 3Mb of main memory;* **main routine** = section of instructions that make up the main part of a program (a program often consists of a main routine and several subroutines, which are called from the main routine)

mainframe (computer) *noun*

large-scale high power computer system that can handle high capacity memory and backing storage devices as well as a number of operators simultaneously; **mainframe access** = using microcomputers to access a mainframe computer

mains electricity *noun* normal domestic electricity supply to consumers

COMMENT: in UK this is 240 volts at 50Hz; in the USA, it is 110 volts at 60Hz

maintain *verb* to ensure a system is in good condition and functioning correctly; **well maintained** = well looked after

◊ **maintainability** *noun* the ability to have repairs carried out quickly and efficiently if a failure occurs

◊ **maintenance** *noun* (i) keeping a machine in good working condition; (ii) tasks carried out in order to keep a system running, such as repairing faults, replacing components, etc.; **file maintenance** = process of updating a file by changing *or* adding *or* deleting entries; **preventive maintenance** = regular inspection and cleaning of a system to prevent faults occurring; **maintenance contract** = arrangement with a repair company that provides regular checks and special repair prices in the event of a fault; **maintenance release** = program revision that corrects a minor problem or bug but does not offer any major new features; *the maintenance release of the database program, version 2.01, corrects the problem with the margins;* **maintenance routine** = software diagnostic tool used by an engineer during preventative maintenance operations

major cycle *noun* minimum access time of a mechanical storage device

male connector *noun* plug with conducting pins that can be inserted into a female connector to provide an electrical connection

malfunction 1 *noun* (*of hardware or software*) not working correctly; *the data was lost due to a software malfunction;* **malfunction routine** = software routine used to find and help diagnose the cause of an error or fault 2 *verb* not to work properly; *some of the keys on the keyboard have started to malfunction*

◊ **malfunctioning** *noun* not working properly

MAN = METROPOLITAN AREA NETWORK network extending over a limited area (normally a city) *compare* LAN, WAN

man machine interface (MMI) *noun* hardware and software designed to make it easier for users to communicate effectively with a machine

manage *verb* to direct *or* to be in charge of

◊ **manageable** *adjective* which can be dealt with easily; *processing problems which are still manageable; the problems are too large to be manageable; data should be split into manageable files*

◊ **management** *noun* directing *or* organizing (work *or* a business); **network management** = organization, planning, running and upkeep of a network

◊ **management information service (MIS)** *noun* department within a company that is responsible for information and data processing; in practice, this department is often responsible for the computer system in a company

◊ **management information system (MIS)** *noun* software that allows managers in a company to access and analyse data

◊ **manager** *noun* (a) user-friendly front end software that allows easy access to operating system commands; **file manager** = section of a disk operating system that allocates disk space to files, keeping track of the file sections (if it has to be split) and their sector addresses; **queue manager** = software

which orders tasks waiting to be processed; **records manager** = program which maintains records and can access and process them; **text manager** = facilities that allow text to be written, stored, retrieved, edited and printed (b) head of a department in a company; *a department manager; data processing manager; production manager;* **system manager** = person responsible for the computers or network in a company

Manchester coding *noun* method of encoding data and timing signals that is used in communications; the first half of the bit period indicates the value of the bit (1 or 0) and the second half is used as a timing signal

Mandlebrot set *noun* mathematical equation that is called recursively to generate a set of values; when plotted these form a fractal image; *see also* FRACTAL

manipulate *verb* to move, edit and change text *or* data; *an image processor that captures, displays and manipulates video images*

◊ **manipulation** *noun* moving *or* editing *or* changing text *or* data; *the high-speed database management program allows the manipulation of very large amounts of data*

mantissa *noun* fractional part of a number; *the mantissa of the number 45.897 is 0.897*

manual 1 *noun* document containing instructions about the operation of a system *or* piece of software; *the manual is included with the system;* **installation manual** = booklet showing how a system should be installed; **instruction manual** = document describing how to use a system *or* software; **user's manual** = booklet showing how a device *or* system should be used 2 *adjective* (work) done by hand; (process) carried out by the operator without the help of a machine; **manual data processing** = sorting and processing information without the help of a computer; **manual entry** *or* **manual input** = act of entering data into a computer, by an operator via a keyboard

map 214 **mask**

◊ **manually** *adverb* done by hand, not automatically; *the paper has to be fed into the printer manually*

map 1 *noun* diagram representing the internal layout of a computer's memory *or* communications regions; **memory map =** diagram indicating the allocation of address ranges to various memory devices, such as RAM, ROM and memory-mapped input/output devices **2** *verb* to retrieve data and display it as a map; **database mapping =** description of the way in which the records and fields in a database are related; **I/O mapping =** method of assigning a special address to each (I/O) port in a microcomputer rather than a memory location; **to map out =** to draw *or* set down the basic way in which something should be done; **memory-mapped =** with addresses allocated to a computer's input *or* output devices to allow them to be accessed as if they were a memory location; *a memory-mapped screen has an address allocated to each pixel, allowing direct access to the screen by the CPU;* **memory-mapped I/O** *or* **memory-mapped input/output =** an I/O port which can be accessed as if it were a memory location within the CPU's normal address range; *see also* BIT-MAP, BIT-MAPPED

MAPI = MAIL APPLICATION PROGRAMMING INTERFACE set of standards (developed by Microsoft) that defines how electronic mail is sent and delivered

MAR = MEMORY ADDRESS REGISTER register within the CPU that contains the next location to be accessed

marching display *noun* display device that contains a buffer to show the last few characters entered

margin *noun* **(a)** blank space around a section of printed text; *when typing the contract leave wide margins; the left margin and right margin are the two sections of blank paper on either side of the page;* **to set the margin =** to define the size of a margin **(b)** extra time *or* space; **margin of error =**

number of mistakes which are accepted in a document *or* in a calculation; **safety margin =** time *or* space allowed for something to be safe

mark 1 *noun* **(a)** sign put on a page to show something **(b)** transmitted signal that represents a logical one *or* true condition; **mark space =** two-state transmission code using a mark and a space (without a mark) as signals **2** *verb* to put a mark on something; **mark block =** to put a block marker at the beginning and end of a block of text; **mark sense =** to write characters with conductive *or* magnetic ink so that they are then machine readable; **mark sense device** *or* **reader =** device that reads data from special cards containing conductive *or* magnetic marks; **mark sensing card =** preprinted card with spaces for mark sense characters

◊ **marker** *noun* code inserted in a file *or* text to indicate a special section; **block markers =** two markers inserted at the start and finish of a section of data *or* text to indicate a special block which can then be moved *or* deleted *or* copied as a single unit; **field marker =** code used to indicate the end of one field and the start of the next; **word marker =** symbol indicating the start of a word in a variable word length machine

marquee *noun* (in a graphics application) area selected by a selection tool

mask 1 *noun* **(a)** integrated circuit layout that is used to define the pattern to be etched *or* doped onto a slice of semiconductor; *a mask or stencil is used to transfer the transistor design onto silicon* **(b)** pattern of binary digits used to select various bits from a binary word (a one in the mask retains that bit in the word); **mask bit =** one bit used to select the required bit from a word *or* string; **mask register =** storage location in a computer that contains the pattern of bits used as a mask; **interrupt mask =** data word in a computer that selects which interrupt lines are to be activated **2** *verb* to cover an area of (something) with (something); **masked ROM =** read-only memory device that is programmed during manufacture, by depositing metal onto selected regions dictated by the shape of a mask

maskable *adjective* which can be masked; **maskable interrupt** = interrupt which can be activated by using an interrupt mask; **non-maskable interrupt (NMI)** = high priority interrupt signal that cannot be deactivated

masking *noun* operation used to select various bits in a word

---

the device features a maskable interrupt feature which reduces CPU overheads

Electronics & Power

---

mass storage *noun* storage and retrieval of large amounts of data; **mass storage device** = computer backing store device that is able to store large amounts of data; *the hard disk is definitely a mass storage device;* **mass storage system** = data storage system that can hold more than one million million bits of data

master 1 *noun* main *or* most important device *or* person in a system; most up-to-date and correct file; *the master computer controls everything else;* **master card** = first punched card in a pack that provides information about the rest of the pack; **master clock** = timing signal to which all components in a system are synchronized; **master computer** = computer in a multiprocessor system that controls the other processors and allocates jobs, etc.; **master control program (MCP)** = software that controls the operations in a system; **master data** = reference data which is stored in a master file; **master disk** = (i) disk containing all the files for a task; (ii) disk containing the code for a computer's operating system that must be loaded before the system will operate; **master file** = set of all the reference data required for an application, which is updated periodically; **master/master computer system** = system in which each processor is a master, dedicated to one task; **master program file** = magnetic medium which contains all the programs required for an application; **master/slave computer system** = system with a master controlling computer and a slave that takes commands from the master; **master tape** = magnetic tape which contains all the vital operating system routines, loaded once when the computer is switched on (by the initial program loader); **master terminal** = one terminal in a network that has priority over any other, used by the system manager to set up the system *or* carry out privileged commands **2** *verb* to learn and understand a language *or* process; *we mastered the new word-processor quite quickly; the user-friendly package is easier to master*

◊ **mastering** *noun* process to convert finished data to a master disc

mat *noun* plain coloured border that is displayed around an image that is smaller than the window in which it is displayed

match *verb* **(a)** to search through a database for a similar piece of information **(b)** to set a register equal to another

material *noun* substance which can be used to make a finished product; *gold is the ideal material for electrical connections*

mathematics *noun* science of the relationship between numbers, their manipulation and organization to (logically) prove facts and theories; *see also* ALGEBRA

◊ **mathematical** *adjective* referring to mathematics; **mathematical model** = representation of a system using mathematical ideas and formulae; **mathematical subroutines** = library routines that carry out standard mathematical functions, such as square root, logarithm, cosine, sine, etc.

◊ **maths** *or US* **math** *(informal)* = MATHEMATICS; **maths chip** *or* **coprocessor** = dedicated IC that can be added to a system to carry out mathematical functions far more rapidly than a standard CPU, speeding up the execution of a program

matrix *noun* **(a)** array of numbers *or* data items arranged in rows and columns; **matrix rotation** = swapping the rows with the columns in an array (equal to rotating by 90 degrees) **(b)** array of connections between logic gates providing a number of possible logical functions; **key matrix** = way in which the keys of a keyboard are arranged as an array of connections **(c)** pattern of the dots that make up a character on a computer screen *or* dot-matrix *or* laser printer; **matrix printer** *or* **dot-matrix printer** = printer in which the characters are made up by a series of dots printed close together, producing a page line by line; a dot-matrix printer can be used either for printing using a ribbon or for thermal *or* electrostatic printing; **character matrix** = pattern of dots that makes up a displayed character

matter *noun* **(a)** question *or* problem to be discussed **(b)** main section of text on a page as opposed to titles *or* headlines

MAU = MULTISTATION ACCESS UNIT

maximise *verb* (in MS-Windows) to expand an application icon back to its original display window; *compare* MINIMISE

> COMMENT: you maximise a window by clicking once on the up arrow in the top right hand corner

maximum *adjective & noun* highest value used *or* which is allowed; **maximum capacity** = greatest amount of data that can be stored; **maximum transmission rate** = greatest amount of data that can be transmitted every second; **maximum users** = greatest number of users that a system can support at any one time

Mb = MEGABIT equal to 1,048,576 bits of storage, equal to 131,072 bytes

MB *or* **MByte** = MEGABYTE equal to 1,048,576 bytes of storage, equal to 2^{20} bytes

> the maximum storage capacity is restricted to 8 Mbytes
> *Micro Decision*

◊ **Mbps** = MEGA BITS PER SECOND

MBR = MEMORY BUFFER REGISTER register in a CPU that temporarily buffers all inputs and outputs

MCA = MICRO CHANNEL ARCHITECTURE design of the expansion bus within IBM's PS/2 range of personal computers that has taken over from the older

ISA/AT bus; MCA is a 32-bit bus that supports bus master devices; **MCA chipset** = number of electronic components required to manage the timing and data signals over an MCA expansion bus

MCGA = MULTICOLOR GRAPHICS ADAPTER colour graphics adapter standard fitted in low-end IBM PS/2 computers

MCI = MEDIA CONTROL INTERFACE commands that allow any program to control multimedia, such as a sound card or video clip

◊ **MCI device** *noun* recognised multimedia device that is installed in a computer with the correct drivers

MCP = MASTER CONTROL PROGRAM

MD *or* **MKDIR** = MAKE DIRECTORY DOS command used to create a new directory on a disk

MDA MONOCHROME DISPLAY ADAPTER video adapter standard used in early PC systems that could display text in 25 lines of 80 columns

MDK *see* MULTIMEDIA DEVELOPER'S KIT

MDR = MEMORY DATA REGISTER register in a CPU that holds data before it is processed *or* moved to a memory location

MDRAM = MULTIBANK DYNAMIC RANDOM ACCESS MEMORY high performance memory normally used in video adapter cards to provide fast graphic display

mean 1 *noun & adjective* average value of a set of numbers *or* values; **mean time between failures (MTBF)** = average period of time that a piece of equipment will operate between failures; **mean time to failure (MTF)** = average period of time for which a device will operate (usually continuously) before failing; **mean time to repair** = average period of time required to repair a faulty piece of equipment **2** *verb* to signify something; *the message DISK FULL means* *that there is no more room on the disk for further data*

measure 1 *noun* (a) way of calculating size *or* quantity; **square measure** = area in square feet or square metres, calculated by multiplying width and length (b) total width of a printed line of text (c) type of action; **to take measures to prevent something happening** = to act to stop something happening; **safety measures** = actions to make sure that something is safe **2** *verb* (i) to find out the size *or* quantity of something; (ii) to be of a certain size *or* quantity

measurement *noun* (a); **measurements** = size; *to write down the measurements of a package* (b) way of judging something; *performance measurement or measurement of performance is carried out by running a benchmark program*

mechanical *adjective* referring to machines

◊ **mechanical mouse** *noun* pointing device that is operated by moving it across a flat surface; as the mouse is moved, a ball inside spins and turns two sensors that feed the horizontal and vertical movement back to the computer *compare* OPTICAL MOUSE

mechanism *noun* piece of machinery; *the printer mechanism is very simple; the drive mechanism appears to be faulty*

media any physical material that can be used to store data; *computers can store data on a variety of media, such as disk, punched card or CD-ROM;* **magnetic media** = magnetic materials used to store signals, such as disk, tape, etc.; **media access control (MAC)** = sublayer within the data-link layer of the OSI network model that provides access to the transmission media; *see also* DATA-LINK LAYER, LOGICAL LINK CONTROL; **media control interface (MCI)** = commands that allow any program to control multimedia, such as a sound card or video clip; **media conversion** = to copy data from one type of storage media to another; *to transfer from magnetic tape to floppy disk, you need a media conversion device;* **media**

error = fault in the storage media that corrupts data

Media Player™ *noun* Windows utility program that allows a user to control installed multimedia hardware including video disc or audio CDs, or play back multimedia files including sound, animation and video files

MediaServer™ *noun* system developed by Netscape to provide audio and video delivery over the internet

```
The Kontron IN Lite notebook,
said to continue working even
when fully immersed in a metre
of liquid, includes an Intel
i386 25MHz processor, between
4Mb and 20Mb of RAM, a 80Mb or
200Mb hard disk and a 40Mb
removable media option.
```
Computing

medium 1 *adjective* middle *or* average; *a medium-sized computer system;* **medium model** = memory model of the Intel 80x86 processor family that allows 64Kb of data and up to 1MB of code **2** *noun;* **storage medium** = any physical material that can be used to store data for a computer application; *data storage mediums such as paper tape, magnetic disk, magnetic tape, optical disk, magneto optical disk, paper, card and microfiche are available;* **data medium** = medium which allows data to be stored *or* displayed such as magnetic disk *or* a VDU; **empty medium** = blank but formatted storage medium that is ready to accept data; **magnetic medium** *or* **material** = substance that will retain a magnetic flux pattern after a magnetic field is removed (NOTE: plural is **mediums** or **media**)

medium scale integration (MSI) *noun* integrated circuit with 10 to 500 components

medium speed *noun* data communication speed between 2400 and 9600 bits per second

COMMENT: medium speed transmission describes the maximum rate of transfer for a normal voice grade channel

meet *noun* logical function whose output is true if both inputs are true

meg *abbreviation* *(informal)* = MEGABYTE; *this computer has a seven-hundred-meg hard disk*

mega- *prefix* **(a)** meaning one million; **megabits per second (Mbps)** = number of million bits transmitted every second; **megaflops (MFLOPS)** = measure of computing power and speed equal to one million floating point instructions per second; **megahertz (MHz)** = measure of frequency equal to one million cycles per second; **Megastream** = data link provided by British Telecom that offers data transfer at rates up to 8Mbits/second **(b)** meaning 1,048,576 (equal to 2^{20}) and used only in computing and electronic related applications; **megabit (Mb)** = equal to 1,048,576 bits; **megabyte (MB)** = equal to 1,048,576 bytes of storage; **megapixel display** = display adapter and monitor that are capable of displaying over one million pixels; this means a resolution of at least 1,024x1,024 pixels

---

The component manufacturers sell flash memory at an average price of $30 a megabyte. By comparison, the hard-disk components sell at $3 a megabyte.

Computing

---

melody *noun* series of musical notes that form the basis for a musical tune

member *noun* (i) one object on a page of a multimedia book; (ii) individual record *or* item in a field

membrane keyboard *noun* keyboard that uses a thin plastic or rubber sheet with key shapes moulded into it; when the user presses on a key, it activates a pressure sensor

---

COMMENT: the keys in a membrane keyboard have less travel than normal mechanical keys, but since they have no moving parts, they are more robust and reliable

---

Memmaker software utility supplied with some versions of Microsoft MS-DOS and used to automatically configure the computer's memory settings to provide optimum performance

memo field *noun* field in a database *or* text window in an application that allows a user to add comments or a memo about the entry

memory *noun* storage space in a computer system *or* medium that is capable of retaining data *or* instructions; **associative memory** = method of data retrieval that uses part of the data rather than an address to locate data; **backing memory** = any data storage medium, such as a magnetic tape *or* floppy disk, that is not the main high speed memory; **bootstrap memory** = permanent memory within a terminal *or* microcomputer, that allows a user to customize the attributes, booting the system and loading programs; **bubble memory** = method of storing large amounts of binary data, as small magnetized areas in the medium (certain pure materials); **cache memory** = section of high-speed memory which stores data that the CPU needs to access quickly; **charge coupled device (CCD) memory** = volatile, low-cost, high-storage capability memory device; **content-addressable memory** = memory that is addressed and accessed by its contents rather than a location; **control memory** = memory which decodes control instructions into microinstructions which operate the computer *or* microcontroller; **core memory** *or* **primary memory** = central fast-access memory which stores the programs and data currently in use; **disk memory** = memory held on magnetic disk, not on tape; **dynamic memory** = random access memory that requires its contents to be updated regularly; **external memory** = memory which is located outside the main computer system confines, but which can be accessed by the CPU; **fast access memory (FAM)** = storage locations that can be read from *or* written to very rapidly; **FIFO memory** *or* **first in first out memory** = memory using a FIFO access scheme; **internal memory** = storage available within and under the direct control of the main computer, such as main memory; **magnetic memory** = storage that uses a medium that can store data bits as magnetic field changes; **main memory** = fast access RAM whose locations can be directly and immediately addressed by a CPU; **memory access time** = time delay between requesting access to a location and being able to do so; **memory address register (MAR)** = register within the CPU that contains the address of the next location to be accessed; **memory bank** = number of smaller storage devices connected together to form one large area of memory; **memory board** = printed circuit board containing memory chips; **memory buffer register (MBR)** = register in a CPU that temporarily buffers all inputs and outputs; **memory capacity** = number of bits *or* bytes that can be stored within a memory device; **memory cell** = smallest location that can be individually accessed; **memory chip** = electronic component that is able to store binary data; **memory cycle** = period of time from when the CPU reads *or* writes to a location and the action being performed; **memory data register (MDR)** = register in a CPU which holds data before it is processed *or* moved to a memory location; **memory diagnostic** = software routine that checks each memory location in main memory for faults; **memory dump** = printout of all the contents of an area of memory; **memory edit** = to change (selectively) the contents of various memory locations; **memory expansion** = adding more electronic memory chips to a computer; **memory hierarchy** = the different types (capacity and access time) of memory available in a system; **memory-intensive software** = software that uses large amounts of RAM or disk storage during run-time, such as programs whose entire code has to be in main memory during execution; **memory management** = software that controls and regulates the flow and position in memory of files and data; **memory management unit (MMU)** = electronic logic circuits that generate the memory refresh signals and manage the mapping of virtual memory addresses to physical memory locations; the MMU is normally integrated into the processor chip; **memory map** = diagram indicating the allocation of address ranges to various devices such as RAM, ROM and memory-mapped input/output devices;

memory-mapped = with addresses allocated to a computer's input *or* output devices to allow them to be accessed as if they were a memory location; *a memory-mapped screen has an address allocated to each pixel, allowing direct access to the screen by the CPU;* **memory-mapped I/O** = an I/O port which can be accessed as if it were a memory location within the CPU's normal address range; **memory model** = method used in a program to address the code and data that is used within that program; the memory model defines how much memory is available for code and data; processors with a segmented address space (like the Intel 80x86 range) can support multiple memory models; **memory page** = one section of main store which is divided into pages, and which contains data *or* programs; **memory protect** = feature on most storage systems to prevent the accidental overwriting of data; **memory-resident** = (program) that is held permanently in memory; *the system can bomb if you set up too many memory-resident programs at the same time;* **memory switching system** = system which communicates information, stores it in memory and then transmits it according to instructions; **memory workspace** = amount of extra memory required by a program to store data used during execution; **nonvolatile memory** = storage medium that retains data even when power has been switched off; **random access memory (RAM)** = memory that allows access to any location in any order without having to access the rest of memory; **read only memory (ROM)** = memory device that has had data written into it at manufacture, which can only be read; **scratchpad memory** = workspace *or* area of high-speed memory that is used for the temporary storage of data currently in use; **serial memory** = storage whose locations can only be accessed in a serial way: locating one item requires a search through every location; *magnetic tape is a high capacity serial memory;* **static memory** = non-volatile memory that does not require refreshing; **virtual memory** = system of providing extra main memory by using a disk drive as if it were RAM *see also* PAGING; **volatile memory** = memory *or* storage medium which loses data stored in it when its power supply is switched off

---

The lower-power design, together with an additional 8Kb of on-board cache memory, will increase the chip's performance to 75 million instructions per second.

Computing

---

when a program is loaded into memory, some is used for the code, some for the permanent data, and some is reserved for the stack which grows and shrinks for function calls and local data

Personal Computer World

◊ **memorize** *verb* to remember *or* to retain in the memory

menu *noun* list of options *or* programs available to the user; **menu-bar** = (in a GUI) list of options available to a user which are displayed on a horizontal line along the top of the screen or window: each menu option activates a pull-down menu; **menu-driven software** = program where commands *or* options are selected from a menu by the operator rather than commands typed in by the user at a prompt; **menu item** = one of the choices in a menu; **menu selection** = choosing commands from a list of options presented to the operator; **menu shortcuts** = key combination of two or more keys that have the same function as selecting a menu option; **main menu** = list of primary options available; **pop-up menu** = set of options that are displayed in the centre of the screen; **pull-down menu** = set of options that are displayed below the relevant entry on a menu-bar; *the pull-down menu is viewed by clicking on the menu bar at the top of the screen*

The London Borough of Hackney has standardised on terminal emulator software from Omniplex to allow its networked desktop users to select Unix or DOS applications from a single menu.

Computing

---

when the operator is required to make a choice a menu is displayed

Micro Decision

---

mercury delay line *noun* (old) method of storing serial data as pulses in a length of mercury, the data was constantly read, regenerated and fed back into the input

merge *verb* to combine two data files, but still retaining an overall order; *the system automatically merges text and illustrations into the document;* **merge sort** = software application in which the sorted files are merged into a new file; *see also* MAIL-MERGE

mesh *noun* any system with two *or* more possible paths at each interconnection; **mesh network** = method of connecting several machines together, where each device is directly connected to every other device in the network

message *noun* (a) information sent from one person to another (b) certain defined amount of information; **message box** = small window that is displayed on screen to warn of an event or condition or error; **message format** = predetermined rules defining the coding, size and speed of transmitted messages; **message handling service (MHS)** = independent, open standard used to transfer electronic mail, uses the store and forward method of transfer and is often used in Novell NetWare networks and as a method of linking mail systems from different manufacturers; **message header** = sequence of data at the beginning of a message that contains routing and destination information; **message routing** = selection of a suitable path between the source and destination of a message in a network; **message slot** = number of bits that can hold a message which circulates around a ring network; **message text** = information that concerns the user at the destination without routing *or* network control data; **message transfer agent (MTA)** = software that temporarily stores a new mail message and then sends it to its correct destination; in some electronic mail software applications, there are several message transfer agents, one for each type of delivery method (internet, fax, LAN)

metabit *noun* extra identifying bit for each data word

metacompilation *noun* compiling a program that will compile other programs when executed; **metacompiler** = compiler that is used to create another compiler

metafile *noun* (i) file that contains other files; (ii) file that defines or contains data about other files; *the operating system uses a metafile to hold data that defines where each file is stored on disk*

metalanguage *noun* language which describes a programming language

metal oxide semiconductor (MOS) *noun* production and design method for a certain family of integrated circuits using patterns of metal conductors and oxide deposited onto a semiconductor; **complementary metal oxide semiconductor (CMOS)** = integrated circuit design and construction method, using a pair of complementary p- and n-type transistors

meter - power supply *noun* utility within Windows 95 that indicates how much power is left in a laptop's battery and whether a laptop is running from a battery or mains electricty power

metropolitan area network (MAN) *noun* network extending over a limited area (normally a city); *compare* LAN, WAN

MFLOPS = MEGA FLOATING POINT INSTRUCTIONS PER SECOND measure of computing speed calculated as the number of floating point instructions that can be processed each second

MFM = MODIFIED FREQUENCY MODULATION method of storing data on magnetic media (such as a magnetic disk) that encodes the data bit according to the state of the previous bit; MFM is more efficient than FM, but less efficient than RLL encoding

MFS = MACINTOSH FILING SYSTEM

MHS = MESSAGE HANDLING SERVICE independent, open standard used to transfer electronic mail, uses the store and forward method of transfer and is often used in Novell NetWare networks and as a method of linking mail systems from different manufacturers

MHTML = MIME HYPERTEXT MARKUP LANGUAGE method of sending documents formatted with HTML commands as a MIME attachment to an electronic mail; *see also* HTML, MIME

MHz = MEGAHERTZ measure of frequency equal to one million cycles per second

MICR = MAGNETIC INK CHARACTER RECOGNITION system that identifies characters by sensing magnetic ink patterns (as used on bank cheques)

micro *noun* = MICROCOMPUTER

micro- *prefix* **(a)** meaning one millionth of a unit; **micrometre** = one millionth of a metre; **microsecond** = one millionth of a second **(b)** meaning very small; **microcassette** = small format audio cassette used mainly in pocket dictating equipment

◊ **microchip** *noun* circuit in which all the active and passive components are formed on one small piece of semiconductor, by means of etching and chemical processes

◊ **microcircuit** *noun* complex integrated circuit

◊ **microcode** *noun* ALU control instructions implemented as hardwired software

◊ **microdevice** *noun* very small device, such as a microprocessor

◊ **microelectronics** *noun* design and manufacture of electronic circuits with integrated circuits and chips

◊ **microfloppy** *noun* small size magnetic floppy disk (usually refers to 3.5 inch disks)

Micro Channel Architecture (MCA) design of the expansion bus within IBM's PS/2 range of personal computers that has taken over from the older ISA/AT bus; MCA is a 32-bit bus that supports bus master devices; **Micro Channel Architecture chipset** = number of electronic components that are required to manage the timing and data signals over an MCA expansion bus

◊ **Micro Channel Bus** *noun* proprietary 32-bit expansion bus defined by IBM in its Micro Channel Architecture

Microcom Networking Protocol™

(MNP) error detection and correction system developed by Microcom Inc. used in modems and some communications software

microcomputer *or* micro *noun*

complete small-scale, cheap, low-power computer system based around a microprocessor chip and having limited memory capacity; **microcomputer architecture** = layout and interconnection of a microcomputer's internal hardware; **microcomputer backplane** = main printed circuit board of a system, containing most of the components and connections for expansion boards, etc.; **microcomputer bus** = main data, address and control buses in a microcomputer; **microcomputer development kit** = basic computer based around a new CPU chip that allows hardware and software designers to experiment with the new device; **single-board microcomputer** = microcomputer whose components are all contained on a single printed circuit board

◊ **microcomputing** *noun* referring to microcomputers and their use; *the microcomputing industry*

COMMENT: micros are particularly used as home computers or as small office computers

microcontroller *noun* small

self-contained microcomputer for use in dedicated control applications; **single-chip microcontroller** = one integrated circuit that contains a CPU, I/O ports, RAM and often a basic programming language

microcycle *noun* unit of time (usually a multiple of the system clock period) used to give the execution time of instructions

microinstruction *noun* one hardwired instruction (part of a microcode) that controls the actions of the ALU in a processor

micron *noun* one millionth of a metre

microphone *noun* device that converts sound waves into electrical signals

microprocessor *noun* central processing unit elements, often contained on a single integrated circuit chip, which when combined with other memory and I/O chips will make up a microcomputer; **bit-slice microprocessor** = large word size CPU constructed by joining a number of smaller word size blocks; *the bit-slice microprocessor uses four 4-bit processors to make a 16-bit word processor;* **microprocessor addressing capabilities** = highest address that a CPU can directly address, without special features (this depends on the address word size - the bigger the word the greater the addressing capacity); **microprocessor architecture** = layout of the basic parts within a CPU (I/O, ALU, etc.); **microprocessor chip** = integrated circuit that contains all the elements of a central processing unit, connected with other memory and I/O chips to make a microcomputer; **microprocessor unit (MPU)** = unit containing the main elements of a microprocessor

microprogram *noun* series of microinstructions; **microprogram assembly language** = each assembly language instruction of a computer is carried out by a microprogram; **microprogram counter** = register that stores the address of the next microinstruction to be carried out (the microprogram counter is the same as the memory address register); **microprogram instruction set** = complete set of basic microinstructions available in a CPU; **microprogram store** = storage device used to hold a microprogram

◊ **microprogramming** *noun* writing microcode using microinstructions

microsecond *noun* one millionth of a second

microsequence *noun* series of microinstructions

Microsoft™ the biggest developer and publisher of software for the PC and Macintosh; Microsoft developed the MS-DOS operating system for the IBM PC and later Windows together with a range of application software; **Microsoft DOS (MS-DOS)** = operating system for IBM PC range of personal computers that manages data storage onto disks, display output and user input; MS-DOS is a single-user, single-tasking operating system that is controlled by a command-line interface; **Microsoft Exchange** = program included with Windows 95 that coordinates the electronic mail, fax and network messages sent and received on a PC; **Microsoft Exchange Server** = program that runs on a server under Microsoft Windows NT and provides sophisticated groupware functions using the Exchange client software supplied with Windows 95; **Microsoft Fax** = series of programs supplied with Windows 3.1 and 95 that let a user send and receive fax transmissions from a PC; **Microsoft internet Explorer** = Web browser developed by Microsoft, currently available free, that allows a user to view Web pages; **Microsoft Word** = popular wordprocessor software that runs on a range of platforms; **Microsoft Word for Windows** = popular wordprocessor software that runs on the Windows platform; **Microsoft Network (MSN)** = online service that was launched by Microsoft to provide information, weather updates, database links to the internet and electronic mail especially for Windows 95 users; **Microsoft Windows** = multi-tasking graphical user interface designed to be easy to use; Windows uses icons to represent files and devices and can be controlled using a mouse, unlike MS-DOS which requires commands to be typed in *see also* WINDOWS

microwriter *noun* portable keyboard and display, used for keyboarding when travelling

mid-user *noun* operator who retrieves relevant information from a database for a customer *or* end user

middleware *noun* system software that has been customized by a dealer for a particular user

MIDI = MUSICAL INSTRUMENT DIGITAL INTERFACE serial interface that connects electronic instruments; the MIDI interface carries signals from a controller or computer that instructs the different instruments to play notes

◊ **MIDI file** *noun* file stored on a PC that contains musical notes and sound information that can be sent via a MIDI interface card to a musical instrument

◊ **MIDI interface card** *noun* adapter card that plugs into an expansion connector in a PC and allows it to send and receive MIDI data

◊ **MIDI Mapper** *noun* program supplied with Windows 3.1x that allows experienced MIDI users to change the way in which musical notes are sent to each instrument that is connected to the PC; *you could use the MIDI Mapper to re-direct all the notes meant for the drum machine to the electronic piano*

◊ **MIDI sequencer** *noun* (i) software that allows a user to record, edit, add special effects and play back MIDI data through a synthesizer; (ii) hardware device that records or plays back stored MIDI data

◊ **MIDI setup map** *noun* (used with MIDI Mapper) file that contains all the data required to define the settings for MIDI Mapper

migration *noun* moving users from one hardware platform to another; **data migration** = moving data between a high priority or on-line device to a low-priority or off-line device

milk disk *noun* disk used to transfer data from a small machine onto a larger computer, which provides greater processing power

◊ **milking machine** *noun* portable machine which can accept data from different machines, then transfer it to another larger computer

milli- *prefix* meaning one thousandth

◊ **milliampere (mA)** *noun* electrical current measure equal to one thousandth of an ampere

◊ **millisecond (mS)** *noun* one thousandth of a second

million instructions per second
(MIPS) measure of processor speed that defines the number of instructions it can carry out per second *compare* MEGAFLOPS

MIMD = MULTIPLE INSTRUCTION STREAM - MULTIPLE DATA STREAM architecture of a parallel processor that uses a number of ALUs and memory devices in parallel to provide high speed processing

MIME = MULTIPURPOSE INTERNET MAIL EXTENSIONS standard that defines a way of sending files using electronic mail software; **secure/MIME** = method of sending encrypted mail messages and file attachments, the encryption is public-key so it also provides authentication of the identity of the sender

COMMENT: MIME allows a user to send files over the internet to another user without having to carry out any other encoding or conversion actions. MIME was developed to get around a problem of many electronic mail systems that could only transmit text which is stored in a 7-bit data format; programs, multimedia, graphics and other files are stored using an 8-bit data format

MIME HYPERTEXT MARKUP
LANGUAGE *see* MHTML

mini- *prefix* meaning small; **minidisk** = magnetic disk smaller than the 5.25 inch standard, usually 3.5 inch; **minifloppy** = magnetic disk (usually refers to the 5.25 inch standard); *(slang)* **miniwinny** = small Winchester hard disk

◊ **miniaturization** *noun* making something very small

minicomputer *or* **mini** *noun* small computer, with a greater range of instructions and processing power than a microcomputer, but not able to compete with the speed *or* data handling capacity of a mainframe computer

minimal latency coding *see* MINIMUM ACCESS CODE

◊ **minimal tree** *noun* tree whose nodes are organized in the optimum way, providing maximum efficiency

minimise *verb* **(a)** to make as small as possible; *we minimised costs by cutting down the number of components* **(b)** (in MS-Windows) to shrink an application window to an icon *compare* MAXIMISE

COMMENT: the application can continue to run in the background; you minimise a window by clicking once on the down arrow in the top right hand corner

minimum *noun* the smallest amount of something; **minimum access code** *or* **minimum delay code** = coding system that provides the fastest access and retrieval time for stored data items

◊ **minimize** *see* MINIMISE

minmax *noun* method used in artificial intelligence to solve problems

minuend *noun* number from which another is subtracted

minus *or* **minus sign** *noun* printed *or* written sign (like a small dash) to indicate subtraction *or* to show a negative value

MIP mapping *noun* method of calculating pixels within texture mapping to take into account the perceived distance of the scene from the viewer

MIPS = MILLION INSTRUCTIONS PER SECOND measure of processor speed *compare* MEGAFLOPS

ICL has staked its claim to the massively parallel market with the launch of the Goldrush MegaServer, providing up to 16,000 Unix MIPS of processing power.

Computing

mirror *verb* **(a)** to create an identical copy **(b)** to duplicate all disk operations onto a second disk drive that can be used if the first breaks down; *there's less chance of losing our data now that we have mirrored the server's disk drive*

---
disks are also mirrored so that
the system can continue to run
in the event of a disk crash
Computer News

MIS = MANAGEMENT INFORMATION SYSTEM

MISD = MULTIPLE INSTRUCTION STREAM - SINGLE DATA STREAM architecture of a parallel computer that has a single ALU and data bus with a number of control units

mission-critical *adjective* (application or hardware) on which your company depends; **mission-critical application** = software program without which your company cannot function

MMI = MAN MACHINE INTERFACE hardware and software designed to make it easier for users to communicate effectively with a machine

MMU = MEMORY MANAGEMENT UNIT electronic logic circuits that generate the memory refresh signals and manage the mapping of virtual memory addresses to physical memory locations; the MMU is normally integrated into the processor chip

MMX = MULTIMEDIA EXTENSIONS enhanced Intel processor chip that includes special features and components that are used to improve the performance when dealing with multimedia and communications

mnemonic *noun* shortened form of a word *or* function that is helpful as a reminder (such as INCA for increment register A); **assembler mnemonics** *or* **mnemonic operation codes** = standard word abbreviations used when writing a program for a particular CPU in assembly language (such as LDA for load register A)

MNP = MICROCOM NETWORKING PROTOCOL error detection and correction system developed by Microcom Inc., used in modems and some communications software

MNP 2-4 error-correcting communications protocol developed by Microcom Inc. and adopted into the CCITT V.42 standard

MNP 5 communications standard that provides data compression, providing up to 2-to-1 compression (though averaging less)

MNP 10 error correcting communications protocol that can transfer data accurately even over poor-quality telephone connections

mock-up *noun* model of a new product for testing *or* to show to possible customers

mode *noun* way of doing something; method of operating a computer; *when you want to type in text, press this function key which will put the terminal in its alphanumeric mode;* Mode 1 = encoding format used on compact discs, that has error-detection and correction codes; **Mode 2** = encoding format with two forms: form 1 is the same as Mode 1, form 2 requires no processing and the data can be sent straight to the output channel; **burst mode** = data transmission using intermittent bursts of data; **byte mode** = way of transmitting data one byte at a time; **control mode** = state of a device in which control signals can be received to select options *or* functions; **deferred mode** = entering a command as a program line, then executing the program; **direct mode** = typing in a command which is executed once carriage return has been pressed; **execute mode** = entering a command in direct mode to start a program run; **form mode** = display method on a data entry terminal, the form is displayed on the screen and the operator enters relevant details; **input mode** = mode in which a computer is receiving data; **insert mode** = interactive computer mode in which new text is entered within the previous text, which adjusts to make room for it; **interactive mode** = mode in which a computer allows the user to enter commands *or* programs *or* data and receive an immediate response; **noisy mode** = floating point arithmetic in which a digit other than a zero is deliberately added in the least significant position during the normalization of a floating point number; **replace mode** = interactive computer mode in which new text entered replaces any previous text; **sequential mode** = mode in which each instruction in a program is stored in consecutive locations

---

The approach being established by the Jedec committee provides for burst mode data transfer clocked at up to 100MHz.

Computing

---

the printer gives print quality in three modes: high speed, data processing and letter-quality

Minicomputer News

modal *adjective* (i) referring to modes; (ii) (in Windows) window that is displayed and does not allow a user to do anything outside it; *dialog boxes are normally modal windows*

model 1 *noun* **(a)** small copy of something to show what it will look like when finished; *he showed us a model of the new computer centre building* **(b)** style *or* type of product; version of a product; *the new model B has taken the place of model A; this is the latest model; the model on display is last year's; they are selling off the old models at half price;* **demonstration model** = piece of equipment used in demonstrations (and then sold cheaply) **2** *adjective* which is a perfect example to be copied; *a model agreement* **3** *verb* to make a computerized model of a new product *or* of the economic system, etc.

◊ **modelling** *noun* creating computer models

modem *or* **MODEM** *noun* = MODULATOR/DEMODULATOR device that allows data to be sent over telephone lines by converting binary signals from a computer into analog sound signals which can be transmitted over a telephone line; **dial-in modem** = auto-answer modem that can be called at any time to access a system; **modem eliminator** = cable *or* device that allows two computers to communicate via their serial ports without using modems; **null modem** = circuit *or* cable that allows two computers to communicate via their serial ports; *this cable is configured as a null modem, which will allow me to connect*

these two computers together easily; see also STANDARD; *compare* ACOUSTIC COUPLER

COMMENT: the process of converting binary signals to analog is called 'modulation'. When the signal is

received, another modem reverses the process (called 'demodulation'). Both modems must be working according to the same standards

---

AST Research has bundled together a notebook PC with a third-party PCMCIA fax modem technology for a limited-period special offer.

Computing

---

moderated list *noun* mailing list in which someone reads all the material that has been submitted before it is distributed to the users on the list

modification *noun* change made to something; *the modifications to the system allow it to be run as part of a LAN;* **modification loop** = instructions within a loop that changes other instructions *or* data within a program

◊ **modifier** *noun* programming instruction that alters the normal action of a command

◊ **modified frequency modulation (MFM)** *noun* method of storing data on magnetic media (such as a magnetic disk) that encodes the data bit according to the state of the previous bit; MFM is more efficient than FM, but less efficient than RLL encoding

◊ **modify** *verb* to change something *or* to make something fit a different use; *the keyboard was modified for European users; we are running a modified version of the mail-merge system; the software will have to be modified to run on a small PC*

Modula-2 *noun* high-level programming language derived from Pascal that supports modular programming techniques and data abstraction

modular *adjective* (method of constructing hardware *or* software products) by connecting several smaller blocks together to produce a customized product; **modular programming** = programming small individually written sections of computer code that can be made to fit into a structured program and can be called up from a main program

◊ **modularity** *noun* being made up from modules; *the modularity of the software or hardware allows the system to be changed*

◊ **modularization** *noun* designing programs from a set of standard modules

modulate *verb* to change a carrier wave so that it can carry data; **modulated signal** = constant frequency and amplitude carrier signal that is used in a modulated form to transmit data; **modulating signal** = signal to be transmitted that is used to modulate a carrier

◊ **modulator** *noun* electronic circuit that varies a carrier signal according to an applied signal; **modulator/demodulator** = MODEM

module *noun* (a) small section of a large program that can, if required, function independently as a program in its own right (b) self-contained piece of hardware that can be connected with other modules to form a new system; *a multifunction analog interface module includes analog to digital and digital to analog converters*

modulo arithmetic *noun* branch of arithmetic that uses the remainder of one number when divided by another; **modulo-N** = modulo arithmetic using base N; **modulo-N check** = error detection test using the remainder from a modulo arithmetic operation on data

modulus *or* **MOD** *noun* the remainder after the division of one number by another; *7 mod 3 = 1*

momentary switch *noun* switch that only conducts while it is being pressed

monadic (Boolean) operator *noun* logical operator with only one operand; *the monadic operator NOT can be used here;* **monadic operation** = operation that uses one operand to produce one result

monitor 1 *noun* (a) visual display unit used to display high quality text *or* graphics, generated by a computer; **multi-scan** *or* **multi-sync monitor** = monitor which has circuitry to lock onto the required scanning frequency for any type of graphics card; **monitor unit** *see* VDU (b) **monitor program** = computer program that allows basic commands to be entered to operate a system (such as load a program, examine the state of devices, etc.) *see also* OPERATING SYSTEM; **firmware monitor** = monitor program that is resident in a ROM device, used to load in the operating system when a machine is switched on (c) system that watches for faults *or* failures in a circuit; **power monitor** = circuit that shuts off the electricity supply if it is faulty *or* likely to damage equipment **2** *verb* (i) to check *or* to examine how something is working; (ii) to look after and supervise a process *or* experiment to make sure it is operating correctly; *he is monitoring the progress of the trainee programmers; the machine monitors each signal as it is sent out*

mono- *prefix* meaning single *or* one

◊ **monochrome** *adjective & noun* (image) in one colour, usually shades of grey and black and white; **monochrome display adapter (MDA)** = video adapter standard used in early PC systems that could display text in 25 lines of 80 columns; **monochrome monitor** = computer monitor that displays text and graphics in black, white and shades of grey instead of colours

◊ **monoprogramming system** *noun* computer batch processing system that executes one program at a time *compare* MULTIPROGRAMMING SYSTEM

◊ **monospaced font** *noun* font in which each character has the same width, making it easy to align tables and columns; *in Windows, the monospaced font is called Courier*

Monte Carlo method *noun* statistical analysis technique

morphing *noun* special effect used in multimedia and games in which one image gradually turns into another

MOS = METAL OXIDE SEMICONDUCTOR production and design method for a certain family of integrated circuits using patterns of metal conductors and oxide deposited onto a semiconductor; *see also* MOSFET; **MOS memory** = solid-state memory using MOSFETs to store binary data; **CMOS** = COMPLEMENTARY METAL OXIDE SEMICONDUCTOR integrated circuit design and construction (using a pair of complementary p- and n-type transistors)

integrated circuits fall into one of two distinct classes, based either on bipolar or metal oxide semiconductor (MOS) transistors

Electronics & Power

mosaic *noun* display character used in videotext systems that is made up of small dots

MOSFET = METAL OXIDE SEMICONDUCTOR FIELD EFFECT TRANSISTOR high power and high speed field effect transistor manufactured using MOS techniques

most significant bit *or* msb *or* MSB

noun bit in a word that represents the greatest value *or* weighting (usually the bit which is furthest to the left); *the most significant bit in an eight bit binary word represents 128 in decimal notation*

◊ **most significant character** *or* **most significant digit (MSD)** *noun* digit at the far left of a number, that represents the greatest power of the base (NOTE: the opposite is **LSD**)

motherboard *noun* main printed circuit board of a system, containing most of the components and connections for expansion boards, etc.

Motorola™ manufacturer of electronic components, including the 68000 range of processors used in Apple Macintosh computers; **Motorola 68000** = processor that can manage 32-bit words internally, but transfers data externally via a 16-bit data bus; used in the Apple Macintosh SE and Macintosh Plus; **Motorola 68020** = processor similar to the 68000 that uses full internal and external 32-bit architecture; **Motorola 68030** = processor similar to the 68020, that can manage 32-bit words internally and externally, but can run at much faster clock rates than the 68020; **Motorola Power PC** = high performance RISC-based processor used in top-end Macintosh and workstation computers

mount *verb* **(a)** to fix a device *or* a circuit onto a base; *the chips are mounted in sockets on the PCB* **(b)** operation to insert a disk in a disk drive or inform an operating system that a disk drive is ready to be used

mouse *noun* small hand-held input device moved on a flat surface to control the position of a cursor on the screen; **mouse acceleration** = feature of some mouse driver software that will move the mouse pointer at different speeds according to the speed (not the distance) at which you move the mouse; **mouse-driven** = (software) which uses a mouse rather than a keyboard for input; **mouse driver** = program which converts positional data sent from a mouse to a standard form of coordinates that can be used by any software; **mouse pointer** = small arrow displayed on screen that moves around as the mouse is moved; **mouse sensitivity** = ratio of how far the pointer moves on screen in relation to the distance you move the mouse; *high mouse sensitivity means that a small movement of the mouse results in a small movement of the pointer;* **mouse tracking** = inverse of mouse sensitivity; *high mouse tracking means that a small movement of the mouse results in a large movement of the pointer;* **bus mouse** = mouse that connects to a special expansion card plugged into the computer's expansion bus; **mechanical mouse** = pointing device that is operated by moving it across a flat surface; as the mouse is moved, a ball inside spins and turns two sensors that feed the horizontal and vertical movement back to the computer; **optical mouse** = pointing device that is operated by moving it across a special flat mat; on the mat is printed a grid of lines, as the mouse is moved, two light sensors count the number of lines that have been passed to produce a measure of the distance and direction of travel; an optical mouse has fewer moving parts than a mechanical mouse and so is more reliable, but requires an accurately printed mat; **serial mouse** = mouse that connects to the serial port of a PC and transfers positional data via the serial port (NOTE: the plural is **mice)**

```
This project has now borne
fruit, with the announcement
last week of Windots, a project
which allows users to 'see'
Windows screens in a Braille
form of Ascii. Other areas of
research include a sound system
which allows a sound to 'move',
mirroring the movement of a
mouse.
```
Computing

M out of N code *noun* coding system providing error detection, each valid character which is N bits long must contain M binary 'one' bits

move *verb* to change the place of something; **move block** = command which changes the place of a block of text identified by block markers

◊ **movable** *adjective* which can be moved; **movable head disk** = magnetic disk head assembly that moves across the disk until the required track is reached

◊ **movement** *noun* changing the place of something; **movement file** = file which continues recent changes *or* transactions to records, which is then used to update a master file

MPS = MICROPROCESSOR SYSTEM

MPU = MICROPROCESSOR UNIT

ms = MILLISECOND one thousandth of a second

msb *or* **MSB** = MOST SIGNIFICANT BIT bit in a word that represents the greatest value *or* weight (usually the bit furthest to the left)

MSD = MOST SIGNIFICANT DIGIT

MS-DOS = MICROSOFT DOS operating system for IBM PC range of personal computers that manages data storage onto disks, display output and user input; MS-DOS is a single-user, single-tasking operating system that is controlled by a command-line interface

MSI = MEDIUM SCALE INTEGRATION

MSN *see* MICROSOFT NETWORK

MS-Windows *see* MICROSOFT WINDOWS

MSX *noun* hardware and software standard for home computers that can use interchangeable software

MTA = MESSAGE TRANSFER AGENT software that temporarily stores a new mail message and then sends it to its correct destination; in some electronic mail software applications, there are several message transfer agents, one for each type of delivery method (internet, fax, LAN)

MTBF = MEAN TIME BETWEEN FAILURES average period of time that a piece of equipment will operate between failures

MTF = MEAN TIME TO FAILURE average period of time for which a device will operate (usually continuously) before failing

multi- *prefix* meaning many *or* more than one; *multimegabyte memory card; a multistandard unit;* **multi-access system** = computer system that allows several users to access one file *or* program at the same time; *see also* MULTI-USER; **multi-address** *or* **multi-address instruction** = instruction that contains more than one address (of data *or* locations *or* input/output)

multibank dynamic random access memory (MDRAM) *noun* high performance memory normally used in video adapter cards to provide fast graphic display

multi-board computer *noun* computer which has several integrated circuit boards connected with a motherboard

multi-bus system   *noun*   computer architecture that uses a high speed bus between CPU and main memory and a slower bus between CPU and other peripherals

multicast packet *noun* data packet that is sent to a selected set of network addresses; a broadcast packet is sent to all stations in a network

multichannel *adjective* with more than one channel

multicolour   *adjective*   with several colours; **multicolour graphics adapter (MCGA)** = colour graphics adapter standard fitted in low-end IBM PS/2 computers

multidimensional   *adjective*   with features in more than one dimension; **multidimensional array** = number of arrays arranged in parallel, providing depth; **multidimensional language** = programming language that can be represented in a number of ways

multi-disk *adjective* referring to several types of disk; **multi-disk option** = system that can have disk drives installed in a number of sizes; **multi-disk reader** = device which can read from various sizes and formats of disk

multidrop circuit   *noun*   network allowing communications between a number of terminals and a central computer, but not directly between terminals

MultiFinder version of Apple Macintosh Finder that supports multitasking

multifrequency monitor   *see* MULTISYNC MONITOR

multifunction   *adjective*   which has several functions; *a multifunction analog interface module includes analog to digital and digital to analog converters;* **multifunction card** = add-on circuit board that provides many features to upgrade a computer; **multifunction workstation** = workstation where several tasks can be carried out

◊ **multifunctional** *adjective* which has several functions; *a multifunctional scanner*

◊ **multilayer** *noun* printed circuit board that has several layers *or* interconnecting conduction tracks

◊ **multilevel** *adjective* (signal) with a number of possible values (quaternary signals have four levels)

◊ **multilink system** *noun* system where there is more than one connection between two points

multimedia *adjective* the combination of sound, graphics, animation, video and text within an application; **multimedia developer's kit (MDK)** = product developed by Microsoft that allows developers to produce multimedia applications more easily using the supplied libraries of routines to control video playback, process images and display text; **multimedia extensions (MMX)** = processor chip that includes components that are used to improve the performance when dealing with multimedia and communications; **multimedia PC** = computer that can run multimedia application; normally equipped with a sound card, CD-ROM drive and high-resolution colour monitor; **multimedia-ready** = PC that has all the extra equipment requirement to run most multimedia software

> The Oracle Media Server is a multimedia database designed to run on massively parallel computers, running hundreds of transactions per second and managing multiple data types, such as video, audio and text.
>
> *Computing*

multimode fibre *or* **fiber**   *noun* commonly used type of optic fibre that uses a glass fibre with a diameter of between 50 to 125 micros and can carry several different frequencies of light with a maximum bandwidth of 2.5Gbps; the disadvantage is that because the fibre is wide, the light disperses quickly and so repeaters need to be installed to boost the signal; *see also* **fibre, single-mode fibre**

multi-part stationery *noun* continuous stationery with two or more sheets together, either with carbons between *or* carbonless

◊ **multipass overlap** *noun* system of producing higher quality print from a dot matrix printer by repeating the line of characters but shifted slightly, so making the dots less noticeable

◊ **multiphase program** *noun* program that requires more than one fetch operation before execution is complete

multi-platform *adjective* (software) that can run on several different hardware platforms

multiple *adjective* having many parts *or* acting in many ways; **multiple access;** *see* MULTI-ACCESS; **multiple address code** = instruction with more than one address for the operands, result and the location of the next instruction to be executed; *see also* THREE-PLUS-ONE; FOUR-PLUS-ONE ADDRESS; **multiple bus architecture** = computer architecture that uses a high speed bus between CPU and main memory and a slower bus between CPU and other peripherals; **multiple instruction stream - multiple data stream (MIMD)** = architecture of a parallel processor that uses a number of ALUs and memories in parallel to provide high speed processing; **multiple instruction stream - single data stream (MISD)** = architecture of a parallel computer that has a single ALU and data bus with a number of control units; **multiple precision** = use of more than one byte of data for number storage to increase possible precision

multiplex *verb* to combine several messages in the same transmission medium; **multiplexed bus** = one bus used to carry address, data and control signals at different times; **dynamic multiplexing** = multiplexing method which allocates time segments to signals according to demand; **homogeneous multiplexing** = switching multiplexor system where all the channels contain data using the same protocol and transmission rate

the displays use BCD input signals and can be multiplexed to provide up to six digits

Electronics & Power

◊ **multiplexor (MUX)** *noun* circuit that combines a number of inputs into a smaller number of outputs; *a 4 to 1 multiplexor combines four inputs into a single output compare* DEMULTIPLEXOR

multiply *verb* to perform the multiplication of a number (the multiplicand) by another number (the multiplier)

◊ **multiplicand** *noun* number which is multiplied by another number (the multiplier)

◊ **multiplication** *noun* mathematical operation that adds one number to itself a number of times; *the multiplication of 5 and 3 = 15;* **multiplication sign** = printed *or* written sign (x) used to show that numbers are multiplied

◊ **multiplier** *noun* number which multiplies a multiplicand

multipoint *adjective* (connection) with several lines, attaching several terminals to a single line to a single computer

multiprecision *noun* use of more than one data word to represent numbers (increasing the range *or* precision possible)

multiprocessing system *noun* system where several processing units work together sharing the same memory

◊ **multiprocessor** *noun* number of processing units acting together *or* separately but sharing the same area of memory; **multiprocessor interleaving** = operation where each processor in a multiprocessor system deals with a section of one or more processes

multi-programming *noun* operating system used to execute more than one program apparently simultaneously (each program being executed a little at a time)

multipurpose internet mail extensions *see* MIME

multi-scan monitor *noun* monitor which contains circuitry to lock onto the required scanning frequency of any type of graphics card

multisession compatible *adjective* (CD-ROM drive) that can read PhotoCD discs or other discs that have been created in several goes

multi statement line *noun* line from a computer program that contains more than one instruction *or* statement

multistation access unit (MAU)

noun central hub used to connect together cables in a Token Ring network

multi-strike printer ribbon   *noun*

inked ribbon in a printer that can be used more than once

multisync monitor *noun* monitor which contains circuitry to lock onto the required scanning frequency of any type of graphics card; *if you want to plug a monitor into PCs with VGA, EGA and MDA adapters, you'll need a multisync monitor*

multitasking *or* **multi-tasking**   *noun* ability of a computer system to run two or more programs at the same time; *the system is multi-user and multi-tasking;* real-time **multitasking** = executing several (real-time) tasks simultaneously without slowing the execution of any of the processors

> COMMENT: few small systems are capable of simultaneous multitasking, since each program would require its own processor; this is overcome by allocating to each program an amount of processing time, executing each a little at a time so that they will appear to run simultaneously due to the speed of the processor and the relatively short gaps between programs

X is the underlying technology which allows Unix applications to run under a multi-user, multitasking GUI. It has been adopted as the standard for the Common   Open   Software

Environment, proposed recently by top Unix vendors
Computing

this is a true multi-tasking system, meaning that several computer applications can be running at the same time
Which PC?

multi-terminal system *noun* system where several terminals are linked to a single CPU

multithread *noun* program design using more than one logical path through it, each path being concurrently executed

multi-user system   *noun*   computer system that can support more than one user at a time; *the program runs on a standalone machine or a multi-user system*

multi-window editor   *noun*   program used for creating and editing a number of applications programs independently, each in a separate window on screen at the same time

Murray code   *noun*   code   used   for teleprinters that uses only 5 bits

music chip   *noun*   integrated   circuit capable of generating musical sounds and tunes

◊ **musical instrument digital interface (MIDI)** *noun* serial interface that connects electronic instruments

> COMMENT: the MIDI interface carries signals from a controller or computer that instructs the different instruments to play notes

MUX = MULTIPLEXOR circuit that combines a number of inputs into a smaller number   of   outputs   *compare* DEMULTIPLEXOR

My Computer icon that is normally in the upper left-hand corner of the screen on a computer running Windows 95; contains an overview of the PC

n *prefix* meaning nano-

N-key rollover *noun* facility on a keyboard where each keystroke (up to a maximum of N) is registered in sequence even if they are struck very fast

NAK = NEGATIVE ACKNOWLEDGEMENT

name *noun* **(a)** word used to call a thing *or* a person; **brand name** = name of a particular make of product; **corporate name** = name of a large corporation; *the company buys computer parts from several suppliers, and packages them together to make their own name product* **(b)** ordinary word used to identify an address in machine language; **name server** = computer on the internet that provides a domain name service to any other computer; **name table** *or* **symbol table** = list of reserved words *or* commands in a language and the addresses in the computer that refer to them; **file name** = word used to identify a particular stored file; **program name** = identification name for a stored program file; **variable name** = word used to identify a variable in a program

◊ **naming services** *noun* method of assigning each user or node or computer on a network a unique name that allows other users to access shared resources even over a wide area network.

NAND function *noun* logical function whose output is false if all inputs are true, and true if any input is false; **NAND gate** = electronic circuit that provides a NAND function

COMMENT: the NAND function is equivalent to an AND function with a NOT function at the output. The output

is 0 only if both inputs are 1; if one input is 1 and the other 0, or if both inputs are 0, then the output is 1

nano- *or* **n** *prefix* meaning one thousand millionth *or* US one billionth; **nanocircuit** *or* **nanosecond circuit** = electronic and logic circuits that can respond to impulses within nanoseconds; **nanosecond** *or* **ns** = one thousand millionth of a second; NOTE: US billion is the same as UK one thousand million (10 to the power of nine); UK billion is one million million (10 to the power of 10)

the cache's internal RAM is accessed in under 70ns from address strobe to ready signal
Electronics & Power

narrative *noun* explanatory notes or comments to help a user operate a program

◊ **narrative statement** *noun* statement which sets variables and allocates storage at the start of a program

narrow band ISDN another name for the common ISDN communications system; *see* ISDN

National Center for Supercomputing Applications (NCSA) organisation that helped define and create the world wide web with its Mosaic Web browser

National Television System Committee *see* NTSC

native *adjective*; **native compiler** = compiler that produces code that will run on the same system on which it is running (a cross-compiler produces code that will run on another hardware platform); **native file format** = (normally proprietary) default file format that is used by an application to store its data on disk; **native format** = first *or* basic format; **native language** = language that can be executed by a processor without the need for any special software (normally this means the processor's native machine code)

natural *adjective* occurring in nature *or* not created artificially; **natural binary coded decimal (NBCD)** = representation of single decimal digits as a pattern of 4 bits; **natural language** = language that is used *or* understood by humans; *the expert system can be programmed in a natural language*

```
there are two main types of
natural-language interface:
those based on menus, and those
where the user has to discover
what questions the computer
will respond to by trial and
error
```
Electronics & Power

navigation *noun* moving around a multimedia title using hotspots, buttons and a user interface

NBCD = NATURAL BINARY CODED DECIMAL

NC 1 = NETWORK COMPUTER **2** = NUMERICAL CONTROL

NCR paper = NO CARBON REQUIRED special type of paper impregnated with chemicals and used in multipart forms; when NCR paper is printed on by an impact printer, the writing also appears on the sheets below

NDIS = NETWORK DRIVER INTERFACE SPECIFICATION standard command interface (defined by Microsoft) between network driver software and network adapter cards

NDR = NON DESTRUCTIVE READOUT display system that continues to display previous characters when new ones are displayed

near-letter-quality (NLQ) *noun* printing by a dot-matrix printer which provides higher quality type, almost as good

as a typewriter, by decreasing the spaces between the dots; *switch the printer to NLQ for these form letters*

needle *noun* tiny metal pin on a dot matrix printer which prints one of the dots

negate *verb* to reverse the sign of a number; *if you negate 23.4 the result is -23.4*

◊ **negation** *noun* reversing the sign of a number (such as from 5 to -5)

◊ **negative** *adjective* meaning 'no'; **negative acknowledgement (NAK)** = signal sent by a receiver to indicate that data has been incorrectly *or* incompletely received; **negative number** = number which represents the number subtracted from zero, indicated by a minus sign in front of the number; **negative-true logic** = use of a lower voltage level to represent binary 1 than for binary 0

neither-nor function *noun* logical function whose output is false if any input is true

NEQ = NON-EQUIVALENCE; **NEQ function** = logical function where the output is true if the inputs are not the same, otherwise the output is false; **NEQ gate** = electronic implementation of an NEQ function

nerd *noun (slang)* person who is obsessed with computers and rarely talks or thinks about anything that is not technologically exciting

nest *verb* (i) to insert a subroutine within a program *or* another routine; (ii) to use a routine that calls itself recursively; **nested loop** = loop inside another loop in the same program; **nested macro call** = a macro called from within another macro; **nested structure** = section of a program in which one control loop or subroutine is used within another; **nesting level** = number of subroutines within a subroutine; **nesting store** = hardware stack (normally stacks are implemented with software)

NetBEUI = NETBIOS EXTENDED USER INTERFACE extended version of the NetBIOS network protocol developed by

Microsoft; NetBEUI cannot be routed in a network, making it unsuitable for very large internetworks

NetBIOS = NETWORK BASIC INPUT OUTPUT SYSTEM commonly used standard set of commands (originally developed by IBM) that allow application programs to carry out basic operations over a network (operations such as file sharing and transferring data between nodes); *this software uses NetBIOS calls to manage file sharing*

Netscape™ company that develops a range of internet applications including web browser and web server applications

◊ **Netscape Navigator**™ one of the most popular WWW browsers that still dominates the marketplace; includes many features including a news reader, and supports Java applets; *compare* MICROSOFT INTERNET EXPLORER

NetShow™ system developed by Microsoft to provide audio and video delivery over the internet without interruption or glitches in the video sequence

NetView™ network management architecture developed by IBM

NetWare™ proprietary network operating system, developed by Novell, that runs on a range of hardware platforms and supports file and print sharing and client-server applications; **NetWare Loadable Module** = application that can run under the NetWare operating system

network 1 *noun* any system made of a number of points *or* circuits that are interconnected; **communications network** = group of devices such as terminals and printers that are interconnected with a central computer allowing the rapid and simple transfer of data; **computer network** = shared use of a series of interconnected computers, peripherals and terminals; **information network** = number of databases linked together, usually using telephone lines and modems, allowing a large amount of data to be accessed by a wider number of users; **local area network (LAN)** = network where the various terminals and equipment are all within a short distance of one another (at a maximum distance of 500m, for example in the same building) and can be interconnected by cables; *see also* LOCAL; **long haul network** = communications network between distant computers that usually uses the public telephone system; **mesh network** = network in which each node is directly connected to every other node in the network; **network adapter** = add-in board that connects a computer to a network; the board converts the computer's data into electrical signals that are then transmitted along the network cable; **network administrator** = individual who is responsible for looking after a network; responsibilities include installing, configuring and maintaining the network; **network analysis** = study of messages, destinations and routes in a network to provide a better operation; **network architecture** = way in which a network is constructed, such as layers in an OSI system; **Network Basic Input Output System;** *see* NetBIOS; **network control program** = software that regulates the flow of and channels for data transmitted in a network; **network controller** = network user responsible for allocating disk space, answering queries and solving problems from other users of the same network; **network database** = database structure in which data items can be linked together; **network device driver** = software which controls and manages a network adapter card to ensure that it functions correctly with other hardware and software in the computer; **network diagram** = graphical representation describing the interconnections between points; **network directory** = directory that is stored on a disk drive on another computer in the network, but it can be accessed by anyone on the network; not on the local disk drive; **network drive** = disk drive that is part of another computer on a network, but it can be used by anyone on the network; **network hardware** = physical links, computers and control equipment that make up a network; **network interface card (NIC)** = add-in board that connects a computer to a network; the board converts the computer's data into electrical signals that are then transmitted along the network cable; **network-intrinsic application** = application that makes use of a network and the shared resources; **network layer** = third ISO/OSI layer that decides on the route to be used to send a packet of data; *see also* LAYER; **network management** = organization, planning, running and upkeep of a network; **Network Neighborhood** = Windows 95 utility that allows you to view and manage connections to your computer; **network news transfer protocol (NNTP)** = set of commands used to interact with and control a news server on the internet or an intranet to allow a newsreader to access news articles; **network operating system (NOS)** = operating system running on a (normally dedicated) server computer that controls access to the network resources, manage network links, printing, and users; **network printer** = printer attached to a server or workstation that can be used by any user connected to the network; **network processor** = signal multiplexer controlled by a microprocessor in a network; **network protocol** = set of handshaking signals that defines how a workstation sends data over a network without clashing with other data transmissions; **network redundancy** = extra links between points allowing continued operation in the event of one failing; **network server** = computer which runs a network operating system and controls the basic network operations; all the workstations in a LAN are connected to the central network server and users log onto a network server; **network software** = software which is used to establish the link between a user's program and the network; **network structure** = data structure that allows each node to be connected to any of the others; **network timing** = signals that correctly synchronize the transmission of data; **network topology** = arrangement of nodes and links within a network; a bus network topology; ring network topology; **neural network** = system running an artificial intelligence program that attempts to simulate the way the brain works, how it learns and remembers *see also* BUS, MESH, PROTOCOL, RING, STAR, TOPOLOGY; **wide area network (WAN)** = network where the various terminals are far apart and linked by radio *or* satellite **2** *verb* to

link points together in a network; *they run a system of networked micros; the workstations have been networked together rather than used as standalone systems*

◊ **network computer (NC)** *noun* new type of computer that is designed to run Java programs and access information using a web browser

COMMENT: the network computer has a small desktop box that does not have a floppy disk drive; instead it downloads any software it requires from a central server. Network computers are simpler and cheaper than current PCs and Macintosh computers, and are designed to be easier to manage in a large company

◊ **networking** *noun* (i) working *or* organization of a network; (ii) interconnecting two *or* more computers either in the same room *or* different buildings, in the same town *or* different towns, allowing them to exchange information; **networking hardware** *or* **network hardware** = physical links, computers and control equipment that make up a network; **networking software** *or* **network software** = software which is used to establish the link between a user's program and the network; **networking specialist** = company *or* person who specializes in designing and setting up networks; *this computer firm is a UK networking specialist*

COMMENT: networking allows a machine with a floppy disk drive to use another PC's hard disk when both machines are linked by a cable and are using networking software

It has expanded its range of Ethernet-to-LocalTalk converters with the release of AsantePrint 8, which connects up to eight LocalTalk printers, or other LocalTalk devices, to a high-speed Ethernet network.
Computing

the traditional way of operating networks involves having a network manager and training network users to

> familiarize themselves with a special set of new commands
>
> *Which PC?*

> workstations are cheaper the more you buy, because they are usually networked and share resources
>
> *PC Business World*

neural network *noun* system running an artificial intelligence program that attempts to simulate the way the brain works, how it learns and remembers

neutral *adjective* with no state *or* bias *or* voltage; **neutral transmission** = (transmission) system in which a voltage pulse and zero volts represent the binary digits 1 and 0

new *adjective* recent *or* not old; *they have installed a new computer system; the new programmer does not seem as efficient as the old one;* **new (command)** = program command that clears main memory of the present program ready to accept a new program to be entered; **new line character** = character that moves a cursor *or* printhead to the beginning of the next line; *see also* CARRIAGE RETURN (CR); LINEFEED (LF); **new technology** = electronic instruments which have recently been invented

news network transfer protocol

see NNTP

newsgroup or usenet *noun* feature of the internet that provides free-for-all discussion forums; a central server stores the articles that are in each group and these can be accessed using the NNTP protocol with a news reader utility; *see also* NNTP

news reader *noun* software that allows a user to view the list of newsgroups and read the articles posted in each group or submit a new article

Newton™ range of handheld computers developed by Apple, operated by writing on a touch-sensitive screen

next instruction register *noun* register in a CPU that contains the location where the next instruction to be executed is stored; *see also* REGISTER

nexus *noun* connection point between units in a network

nibble *or* **nybble** *noun* half the length of a standard byte

> COMMENT: a nibble is normally 4 bits, but can vary according to different computer hardware designs or people

NIC = NETWORK INTERFACE CARD add-in board that connects a computer to a network; the board converts the computer's data into electrical signals that are then transmitted along the network cable

NiCad = NICKEL-CADMIUM type of rechargeable battery used in laptops but now superseded by the NiMH battery

> COMMENT: NiCad batteries unfortunately have one problem called 'memory' which gradually reduces their ability to retain charge; to remove the memory you should condition a battery by running it right down so that it has no charge, before re-charging it

nil pointer *noun* pointer used to indicate the end of a chained list of items

NiMH = NICKEL METAL HYDRIDE type of rechargeable battery now used in laptops; has better charge-carrying ability than a NiCad battery, is quicker to charge and does not suffer from 'memory'

nine's complement *noun* decimal complement (equivalent to the binary one's complement) formed by subtracting each digit in the number from nine; *see also* TEN'S COMPLEMENT

n-key rollover *noun* use of a buffer between the keyboard and computer to provide key stroke storage (up to 'n' keys can be stored) for fast typists who hit several keys in rapid succession

n-level logic *noun* logic gate design in which no more than n gates occur in a series

NLQ = NEAR-LETTER-QUALITY

NMI NON-MASKABLE INTERRUPT

NNTP = NEWS NETWORK TRANSFER PROTOCOL one of the protocols that is part of the TCP/IP suite) allows news articles to be sent to or retrieved from a news server; *see also* HTTP, FTP, NEWSGROUPS, TCP/IP

no-address operation *noun* instruction which does not require an address within it

◊ **no-drop image** *noun* (in a GUI) icon image displayed during a drag and drop operation when the pointer is over an object that cannot be the destination object (the object being dragged cannot be dropped onto it)

◊ **no op** *or* **no operation instruction** = NO OPERATION programming instruction which does nothing

◊ **no parity** *noun* data transmission which does not use a parity bit

node *noun* interconnection point in a structure *or* network; *a tree is made of branches that connect together at nodes; this network has fibre optic connection with nodes up to one kilometre apart*

noise *noun* random signal present in addition to any wanted signal, caused by static, temperature, power supply, magnetic or electric fields and also from stars and the sun; **noise immunity** = ability of a circuit to ignore *or* filter out *or* be protected from noise; **impulsive noise** = interference on a signal caused by short periods of noise

◊ **noisy mode** *noun* floating point arithmetic system, in which a digit other than a zero is deliberately added in the least significant position during the normalization of a floating point number; **noisy digit** = digit, usually not zero, added during the normalization of a floating point number when in noisy mode

nomenclature *noun* predefined system for assigning words and symbols to represent numbers or terms

nomogram *or* **nomograph** *noun* graphical system for solving one value given two others

non- *prefix* meaning not

◊ **nonaligned** *adjective* (two devices) which are not correctly positioned in relation to each other, for optimum performance; **nonaligned read head** = read head that is not in the same position on a magnetic medium as the write head was, producing a loss of signal quality

◊ **non-arithmetic shift** *see* LOGICAL SHIFT

◊ **non-breaking space** *noun* (in word-processing or DTP software) space character that prevents two words being separated by a line break

◊ **noncompatibility** *noun* two or more pieces of hardware *or* software that cannot exchange data *or* use the same peripherals

◊ **non-dedicated server** *noun* computer that runs a network operating system in the background and can also be used to run normal applications at the same time

◊ **non-destructive cursor** *noun* cursor on a display that does not erase characters already displayed as it passes over them; *the screen quickly became unreadable when using a non-destructive cursor;* **non-destructive readout (NDR)** = display device that retains previous characters when displaying new characters; **non-destructive test** = series of tests carried out on a piece of equipment without destroying it; *I will carry out a number of non-destructive tests on your computer, if it passes, you can start using it again*

◊ **non-equivalence function (NEQ)** *noun* logical function where the output is true if the inputs are not the same, otherwise the output is false; **non-equivalence gate** = electronic implementation of an NEQ function

◊ **nonerasable storage** *noun* storage medium that cannot be erased and re-used; *paper tape is a nonerasable storage*

◊ **non-impact printer** *noun* printer (like an ink-jet printer) where the character form does not hit a ribbon onto the paper

◊ **non-interlaced** *adjective* (in a monitor) system in which the picture electron beam scans each line of the display once during each refresh cycle; the beam in an interlaced display scans every alternate line

◊ **nonlinear** *adjective* electronic circuit whose output does not change linearly in proportion to its input

◊ **non-maskable interrupt (NMI)** *noun* high priority interrupt signal that cannot be blocked by software and overrides other commands

◊ **non-operable instruction** *noun* instruction that does not carry out any function, but increments the program counter

◊ **non-printing codes** *noun* codes that represent an action of the printer rather than a printed character; *the line width can be set using one of the non-printing codes, .LW, then a number*

◊ **non-procedural language** *noun* programming language which does not execute statements one after another, nor calls subroutines; instead it defines a set of facts that can be queried

◊ **non return to zero (NRZ)** *noun* signalling system in which a positive voltage represents one binary digit and a negative voltage the other; representation of binary data in which the signal changes when the data changes state, and does not return to zero volts after each bit of data

◊ **non-scrollable** *adjective* (part of the screen display) which is always displayed (in a WP, the text can scroll while instructions, etc., are non-scrollable); *see also* STATUS LINE

◊ **non-volatile** *adjective;* **non-volatile memory** *or* **non-volatile store** *or* **storage** = storage medium *or* memory that retains data even when the power has been switched off; *bubble memory is a non-volatile storage; using magnetic tape provides non-volatile memory;* **non-volatile random access memory (NVRAM)** = memory that can permanently retain information (NOTE: opposite is **volatile**)

COMMENT: disks (both hard and floppy) and tapes are non-volatile memory stores; solid-state memory, such as RAM chips are volatile unless battery backed

100 sets of test results can be stored in non-volatile memory for later hard-copy printout.
Computing

NOR function *noun* logical function whose output is false if either input is true; **NOR gate** = electric circuit *or* chip which performs a NOR function on an electrical input signal

COMMENT: the output is 1 only if both inputs are 0; if the two inputs are different or if both are 1, the output is 0

normal *adjective* usual *or* which happens regularly; *the normal procedure is for backup copies to be made at the end of each day's work;* **normal form** = method of structuring information in a database to avoid redundancy and improve storage efficiency; **normal format** = standardized format for data storage; **normal range** = expected range for a result *or* number, any outside this range are errors

◊ **normalize** *verb* **(a)** to convert data into a form which can be read by a particular computer system **(b)** to convert characters into just capitals or into just a lower case form **(c)** to store and represent numbers in a pre-agreed form, usually to provide maximum precision; *all the new data has been normalized to 10 decimal places;* **normalized form** = floating point number that has been normalized so that its mantissa is within a certain range

◊ **normalization** *noun* process of normalizing data; **normalization routine** = routine that normalizes a floating point number and adds extra (noisy) digits in the least significant position

NOS = NETWORK OPERATING SYSTEM

NOT function *noun* logical inverse function where the output is true if the input is false; **NOT-AND** = equivalent to the NAND function; **NOT gate** = electronic circuit *or* chip which performs a NOT function

> COMMENT: if the input to a NOT function is 1, the output is 0; if the input is 0, the output is 1

notation *noun* method of writing *or* representing numbers; **binary notation** = base two numerical system using only the digits 0 and 1; **decimal notation** = number representation in base 10, using the digits 0-9; **hexadecimal notation** = number system using base 16 and the digits 0-9 and A-F; **infix notation** = mathematical syntax where operators are embedded inside operands (such as C - D or X + Y); **octal notation** = number system using base 8 and the digits 0-7; **postfix notation** = mathematical operations written in a logical way, so that the operator appears after the operands, this removes the need for brackets; *normal notation: (x-y) + z, but using postfix notation: xy - z +;* **prefix notation** = mathematical operations written in a logical way, so that the operator appears before the operands, this removes the need for brackets; *normal notation: (x-y) + z, but using prefix notation: - xy + z*

notched *see* EDGE NOTCHED CARD

notebook computer *noun* very small portable computer (normally smaller than a laptop computer) that can be carried easily but has a small keyboard and display

notepad *noun;* **screen notepad** = part of the screen used to store information even when the terminal is switched off

notice board *noun* (i) board fixed to a wall where notices can be pinned up; (ii) type of bulletin board on which messages to all users can be left

notification message *noun* message within authoring software to notify other objects that a particular task has been completed; *if an object is moved, the application will generate a notification message to tell other processes when it has finished moving the object*

notify handler *noun* series of commands that are executed when a particular notification message is received

Novell™ large company that produces network software; it is best known for its NetWare range of network operating system software that runs on a PC server

n-plus-one address instruction

noun instruction made up of a number (n) of addresses and one other address that is the location of the next instruction

npn transistor *noun* bipolar transistor design using p-type semiconductor for the base and n-type for the collector and emitter; *see also* TRANSISTOR, BIPOLAR

NRZ = NON RETURN TO ZERO

ns *abbreviation* nanosecond

NT *see* WINDOWS NT

NTSC = NATIONAL TELEVISION SYSTEM COMMITTEE US committee that defines standards for television and video

n-type material *or* N-type material *or* n-type semiconductor *noun*
semiconductor doped with a substance which provides extra electrons in the material, giving it an overall negative charge compared to the intrinsic semiconductor; *see also* NPN TRANSISTOR

NuBus™ *noun* high-speed 96-pin expansion bus used within Apple Macintosh II computers

null *noun* nothing; **null** *or* **NUL character** = character which means nothing (usually code 0); **null instruction** = program instruction that does nothing; **null list** = list which contains nothing; **null modem** = circuit *or* cable that allows two computers to communicate via their serial ports; *this cable is configured as a null modem, which will allow me to connect these 2 computers together easily;* **null set** = set that only contains zeros; **null string** = string that contains no characters; **null terminated string** = string of characters that has a null character to indicate the end of the string

---

you have to connect the two RS232 ports together using a crossed cable, or null modem

PC Business World

Num Lock key *noun* (on a keyboard) key that switches the function of a numeric keypad from cursor control to numeric entry

number 1 *noun* **(a)** representation of a quantity; **number cruncher** = dedicated processor used for high-speed calculations; **number crunching** = performing high-speed calculations; *a very powerful processor is needed for graphics applications which require extensive number crunching capabilities;* **number range** = set of allowable values **(b)** written figure; *each piece of hardware has a production number; please note the reference number of your order;* **check number** = number produced from data for parity *or* error detection **2** *verb* **(a)** to put a figure on a document; *the pages of the manual are numbered 1 to 196* **(b)** to assign digits to a list of items in an ordered manner

◊ **numeral** *noun* character *or* symbol which represents a number; **Arabic numerals** = figures written 1, 2, 3, 4, etc.; **Roman numerals** = figures written I, II, III, IV, etc.

◊ **numeric** *adjective* (i) referring to numbers; (ii) (field, etc.) which contains only numbers; **numeric array** = array containing numbers; **numeric character** = letter used in some notations to represent numbers (for example in hex the letters A-F are numeric characters); **numeric keypad** = set of ten keys with figures, included in most computer keyboards as a separate group, used for entering large amounts of data in numeric form; **numeric operand** = operand that only uses numerals; **numeric pad** = numeric keypad; **numeric punch** = punched hole in rows 0-9 of a punched card

◊ **numerical** *adjective* referring to numbers; **numerical analysis** = study of ways of solving mathematical problems; **numerical control (NC)** *or* **computer numerical control (CNC)** = machine operated automatically by computer *or* circuits controlled by stored data

---

Hewlett-Packard's   100LX Palmtop PC weighs 11oz and has a separate numeric keypad.

Computing

NVRAM = NON-VOLATILE RANDOM ACCESS MEMORY memory that can permanently retain information

nybble *or* **nibble** *noun* (*informal*) half the length of a standard byte

---

COMMENT: a nybble is normally 4 bits, but can vary according to different micros

Oo

OA = OFFICE AUTOMATION

object *noun* **(a)** the data that makes up a particular image *or* sound **(b)** variable used in an expert system within a reasoning operation **(c)** data in a statement which is to be operated on by the operator; *see also* ARGUMENT, OPERAND; **object** *or* **object-orientated architecture** = structure where all files, outputs, etc., in a system are represented as objects; **object code** = binary code which directly operates a central processing unit (a program code after it has been translated, compiled or assembled into machine code); **object computer** = computer system for which a program has been written and compiled; **object deck** = punched cards that contain a program; **object file** = file that contains object code for a routine *or* program; **object hierarchy** = order in which messages are passed from one object to another; **object language** = the language of a program after it has been translated *compare* SOURCE LANGUAGE; **object linking and embedding (OLE)** = (in Microsoft Windows) method of including data formatted in one application within another application; for example, an object (such as an image or sound) can be inserted into a document or spreadsheet, OLE2 is currently used in Microsoft Windows and provides more flexibility and allows applications to exchange information; *see also* DDE; **object linking and embedding 2 (OLE-2)** = (in Windows) extends the functions of OLE to include visual editing to allow the embedded object to be edited without leaving the document in which it is embedded; for example, if you insert an image into a document, you can now edit the image without leaving the wordprocessor; **Object Packager** = utility included with Windows

3.x that lets you convert data from an application that does not support OLE so that it can be used as an OLE object in another application; **object program** = computer program in object code form, produced by a compiler *or* assembler; **Object Request Broker (ORB)** = software that links objects together using the CORBA standard; *see* CORBA

◊ **object-oriented** *adjective* (system or language) that uses objects; **object-oriented graphics** = image which uses vector definitions (lines, curves) to describe the shapes of the image rather than pixels in a bit-map image; *this object-oriented graphics program lets you move shapes around very easily;* **object-oriented language** = programming language that is used for object-oriented programming, such as C++; **object-oriented programming (OOP)** = method of programming, such as C++, in which each element of the program is treated as an object that can interact with other objects within the program; *see also* OBJECT

◊ **objective** *noun* something which someone tries to do

> UK PC-maker Elonex has signed a strategic agreement with NeXT Computer designed to create a volume market in Europe for NeXT's pioneering object based operating system.
>
> *Computing*

obtain *verb* to get *or* to receive; *to obtain data from a storage device*

OCCAM computer programming language, used in large multiprocessor *or* multi-user systems

COMMENT: this is the development language for transputer systems

occur *verb* to happen *or* to take place; *data loss can occur because of power supply variations*

OCE = OPEN COLLABORATION ENVIRONMENT set of standards that allow networked Macintosh users to share objects and files

OCP = ORDER CODE PROCESSOR (in a multiprocessor system) a processor which decides and performs the arithmetic and logical operations according to the program code

OCR (a) = OPTICAL CHARACTER READER device which scans printed *or* written characters, recognizes them, and converts them into machine-readable form for processing in a computer **(b)** = OPTICAL CHARACTER RECOGNITION (software) process that allows printed *or* written characters to be recognized optically and converted into machine-readable code that can be input into a computer, using an optical character reader; **OCR font** = character design that can be easily read using an OCR reader

COMMENT: there are two OCR fonts in common use: OCR-A, which is easy for scanners to read, and OCR-B, which is easier for people to read than the OCR-A font

In 1986, Calera Recognition Systems introduced the first neural-network-based OCR system that could read complex pages containing any mixture of non-decorative fonts without manual training.

Computing

octal (notation) *noun* number notation using base 8, with digits 0 to 7; **octal digit** = digit (0 to 7) used in the octal system; **octal scale** = power of eight associated with each digit position in a number

COMMENT: in octal, the digits used are 0 to 7; so decimal 9 is octal 11

octet *noun* a group of eight bits treated as one unit; word made up of eight bits; *see also* BYTE

odd *adjective* (number, such as 5 or 7) which cannot be divided by two; **odd-even check** = method of checking that transmitted binary data has not been corrupted; **odd parity (check)** = error checking system in which any series of bits transmitted must have an odd number of binary ones (NOTE: opposite is **even**)

ODI = OPEN DATALINK INTERFACE standard interface, defined by Novell, for a network interface card that allows users to have just one network driver that will work with all network interface cards; the standard also supports more than one protocol, such as IPX and NetBEUI *compare* NDIS

OEM = ORIGINAL EQUIPMENT MANUFACTURER company which produces equipment using basic parts made by other manufacturers, and customizes the product for a particular application

IBM UK has appointed Steve Wainwright as regional sales manager, northern Europe, for micro-electronics products. He was previously OEM sales manager, north Europe, for Harris Corporation

Computing

office *noun* room *or* building where a company works *or* where business is done; **office automation (OA)** = use of machines and computers to carry out normal office tasks; **office computer** = small computer (sometimes with a hard disk and several terminals) suitable for office use

off-hook *adverb* condition in a modem similar to picking up a telephone receiver; a modem goes off-hook to answer a call and remains off-hook whilst connected

off-line *adverb & adjective* (i) (processor *or* printer *or* terminal) that is not connected to a network *or* central computer (usually temporarily); (ii) (peripheral) connected to a network, but not available for use; *before changing the paper in the printer, switch it off-line;* **off-line printing** = printout operation that is not supervised by a computer; **off-line processing** processing by devices not under the control of a central computer; **off-line storage** = storage that is not currently available for access, such as a magnetic tape that must first be loaded into the tape machine (NOTE: opposite is **on-line**)

off-screen buffer *noun* area of RAM used to hold an off-screen image before it is displayed on screen

◊ **off-screen image** *noun* image that is first drawn in memory and then is transferred to the display memory to give the impression of fast display action

offset *noun* quantity added to a number *or* address to give a final number; **offset value** *or* **offset word** = value to be added to a base address to provide a final indexed address

O.K. used as a prompt in place of 'ready' in some systems; **OK button** = (in a GUI) button with 'OK' label that is used to start or confirm an action

OLE = OBJECT LINKING AND EMBEDDING (in Microsoft Windows) method of including data formatted in one application within another application; for example, an object (such as an image or sound) can be inserted into a document or spreadsheet, OLE2 is currently used in Microsoft Windows and provides more flexibility and allows applications to exchange information; *see also* DDE

◊ **OLE-2** (in MS-Windows) extends the functions of OLE to include visual editing to allow the embedded object to be edited without leaving the document in which it is embedded; for example, if you insert an image into a document, you can now edit the image without leaving the wordprocessor

◊ **OLE container object** object that contains a reference to a linked object or a copy of an embedded object

omission factor *noun* number of relevant documents that were missed in a search

OMR (a) = OPTICAL MARK READER device that can recognize marks *or* lines on a special forms (such as on an order form *or* a reply to a questionnaire) and convert them into a form a computer can process **(b)** = OPTICAL MARK RECOGNITION process that allows certain marks *or* lines on special forms (such as on an order form *or* a reply to a questionnaire) to be recognized by an optical mark reader, and input into a computer

on-board *adjective* (feature *or* circuit) which is contained on a motherboard *or* main PCB

the	electronic	page	is
converted		to	a
printer-readable	video	image
by the	on-board	raster	image
processor			

the key intelligence features
of these	laser	printers	are
emulation	modes	and	on-board
memory			
			Byte

on chip *noun* circuit constructed on a chip

◊ **on-chip** *adjective* (circuit) constructed on a chip; *the processor uses on-chip bootstrap software to allow programs to be loaded rapidly;* **on-chip cache** = cache memory and controller circuitry built into a processor chip

on-hook *adverb* condition similar to replacing a telephone receiver; a modem goes on-hook when it has finished a call

one address computer *noun* computer structure whose machine code only uses one address at a time; **one address instruction** = instruction made up of an operator and one address

◊ **one element** *noun* logical function that produces a true output if any input is true

◊ **one for one** *noun* programming language, usually assembler, that produces one machine code instruction for each instruction *or* command word in the language

> COMMENT: compilers and interpreters are usually used for translating high-level languages which use more than one machine code instruction for each high-level instruction

◊ **one-level address** *noun* storage address that directly, without any modification, accesses a location *or* device; **one-level code** = binary code which directly operates the CPU, using only absolute addresses and values (this is the final form of a program after a compiler *or* assembler pass); **one-level store** = organization of storage in which each different type of storage device is treated as if it were the same; **one-level subroutine** = subroutine which does not call another subroutine during its execution

◊ **one's complement** *noun* inverse of a binary number; *the one's complement of 10011 is 01100; see also* COMPLEMENT; TWO'S COMPLEMENT

◊ **one-pass assembler** *noun* assembler program that translates the source code in one action; *this new one-pass assembler is very quick in operation*

◊ **one-plus-one address** *noun* address format that provides the location of one register and the location of the next instruction

◊ **one-time pad** *noun* coding system that uses a unique cipher key each time it is used

> COMMENT: two identical pieces of paper with an encrypted alphabet printed on each one are used, one by the sender, one by the receiver; this is one of the most secure cipher systems

◊ **one to zero ratio** *noun* ratio between the amplitude of a binary one and zero output

onion skin architecture *noun* design of a computer system in layers, according to function *or* priority; *the onion skin architecture of this computer is made up of a kernel at the centre, an operating system, a low-level language and then the user's program*

◊ **onion skin language** *noun* database manipulation language that can process hierarchical data structures

on-line *adverb & adjective* (terminal *or* device) connected to and under the control of a central processor; *the terminal is on-line to the mainframe;* **on-line database** = interactive search, retrieve and update of database records, with a terminal that is on-line; **on-line help** = text screen displayed from within an application that explains how to use the application; **on-line information retrieval** = system that allows an operator of an on-line terminal to access, search and display data held in a main computer; **on-line processing** = processing by devices connected to and under the control of the central computer (the user remains in contact with the central computer while processing); **on-line storage** = data storage equipment that is directly controlled by a computer; **on-line system** = computer system that allows users who are on-line to transmit and receive information; **on-line transaction processing** = interactive processing in which a user enters commands and data on a terminal which is linked to a central computer, with results being displayed on the screen

on-screen *adjective* (information) that is displayed on a computer screen rather than printed out

◊ **on-site** *adjective* at the place where something is; *the new model has an on-site upgrade facility*

on the fly *adverb* (to examine and modify data) during a program run without stopping the run

OOP = OBJECT ORIENTED PROGRAMMING

O/P *or* **o/p** = OUTPUT

op code = OPERATION CODE part of the machine code instruction that defines the action to be performed

```
the subroutine at 3300 is used
to    find    the    op    code
```

corresponding to the byte whose hex value is in B

Computing Today

open 1 *adjective* **(a)** (command) to prepare a file before reading *or* writing actions can occur; *you cannot access the data unless the file is open;* **open file** = file that can be read from or written to; the application opens the file which locates the file on disk and prepares it for an operation **(b)** not closed; **open access** = system where many workstations are available for anyone to use; **open architecture** = computer with a published expansion interface that has been designed to allow add-on hardware to be plugged in; **open collaboration environment (OCE)** = set of standards that allow networked Macintosh users to share objects and files; **open code** = extra instructions required in a program that mainly uses macroinstructions; **open datalink interface;** *see* ODI; **open-ended program** = program designed to allow future expansion and easy modification; **open reel** = magnetic tape on a reel that is not enclosed in a cartridge *or* cassette; **open routine** = routine which can be inserted into a larger routine *or* program without using a call instruction; **open shortest path first (OSPF)** = protocol used with a TCP/IP network that will send packets of data on a route that has the least amount of traffic; **open subroutine** = code for a subroutine which is copied into memory whenever a call instruction is found, rather than executing a jump to the subroutine's address; **open system** = (i) non-proprietary system that is not under the control of one company; (ii) system which is constructed in such a way that different operating systems can work together; **Open System Interconnection (OSI)** = standardized ISO network which is constructed in layered form, with each layer having a specific task, allowing different systems to communicate if they conform to the standard; the sever layers are Physical, Data Link, Network, Transport, Session, Presentation, and Application; *see also* ISO/OSI MODEL, INTERNATIONAL **2** *verb* **(a)** to take the cover off *or* to make a door open; *open the disk drive door; open the top*

of the computer by lifting here **(b)** to prepare a file before accessing *or* editing *or* carrying out other transactions on stored records; *you cannot access the data unless the file has been opened*

X.400 messaging company Isocor has appointed Steve McDaniel to the position of sales director. Steve previously worked for Retix, where he was European sales manager for the company's OSI products.

Computing

operand *noun* data (in a computer instruction) which is to be operated on by the operator; *in the instruction ADD 74, the operator ADD will add the operand 74 to the accumulator;* **immediate operand** = within an immediate addressing operation, the operand is fetched at the same time as the instruction; **literal operand** = actual number *or* address to be used rather than a label *or* its location; **numeric operand** = operand that only contains numerals; **operand field** = space allocated for an operand in a program instruction; *see also* ARGUMENT, MACHINE-CODE INSTRUCTION

operate *verb* to work *or* to make a machine work; *do you know how to operate the telephone switchboard?;* **disk operating system (DOS)** = section of the operating system software that controls disk and file management; **operating code (op code)** = part of the machine code instruction that defines the action to be performed; **operating console** = terminal in an interactive system which sends and receives information; **operating instructions** = commands and instructions used to operate a computer; **operating system (OS)** = software that controls the basic, low-level hardware operations, and file management, without the user having to operate it (the operating system is usually supplied with the computer as part of the bundled software in ROM); **operating time** = total time required to carry out a task

◊ **operation** *noun* working (of a machine); **arithmetic operation** = mathematical function carried out on data; **binary**

operation = (i) operation on two operands; (ii) operation on an operand in binary form; **block operation** = process carried out on a block of data; **Boolean operation** = logical operation on a number of operands, conforming to Boolean algebra rules; **complete operation** = operation that retrieves the necessary operands from memory, performs the operation and returns the results and operands to memory, then reads the next instruction to be processed; **dyadic Boolean operation** = logical operation that produces an output from two inputs; **no-address operation** = instruction which does not require an address within it; **no-operation instruction (no-op)** = programming instruction which does nothing; **operation code (op code)** = part of a machine-code instruction that defines the action to be performed; **operation cycle** = section of the machine cycle during which the instruction is executed; *see also* FETCH-EXECUTE CYCLE, MACHINE CYCLE; **operation decoder** = hardware that converts a machine-code instruction (in binary form) into actions; **operation field** = part of an assembly language statement that contains the mnemonic or symbol for the op code; **operation priority** = the sequence order in which the operations within a statement are carried out; **operation register** = register that contains the op code during its execution; **operation time** = period of time that an operation requires for its operation cycle; **operation trial** = series of tests to check programs and data preparation; **operations manual;** *see* INSTRUCTION MANUAL

◊ **operational** *adjective* which is working *or* which refers to the way a machine works; **operational information** = information about the normal operations of a system

operator *noun* **(a)** person who makes a machine *or* process work; *the operator was sitting at his console;* **computer operator** = person who operates a computer; **operator's console** = input and output devices used by an operator to control a computer (usually consisting of a keyboard and VDU); **operator procedure** = set of actions that an operator has to carry out to work a machine *or*

process **(b)** character *or* symbol *or* word that defines a function *or* operation; *x is the multiplication operator;* **arithmetic operator** = symbol which indicates an arithmetic function (such as + for addition, x for multiplication); **operator overloading** = assigning more than one function to a particular operator (the function often depends on the type of data being operated on and is used in the C++ and Ada programming languages); **operator precedence** = order in which a number of mathematical operations will be carried out

op register *noun* register that contains the operating code for the instruction that is being executed

optic fibres = OPTICAL FIBRES; *see also* FIBRE OPTICS

optical *adjective* referring to *or* making use of light; *an optical reader uses a light beam to scan characters or patterns or lines;* **optical bar reader** *or* **bar code reader** *or* **optical wand** = optical device that reads data from a bar code; **optical character reader (OCR)** = device which scans printed *or* written characters, recognizes them, and converts them into machine-readable code for processing in a computer; **optical character recognition (OCR)** = process that allows printed *or* written characters to be recognized optically and converted into machine-readable code that can be input into a computer, using an optical character reader; **optical communication system** = communication system using fibre optics; **optical data link** = connection between two devices to allow the transmission of data using light signals (either line-of-sight or optic fibre); **optical disk** = disk that contains binary data in the form of small holes in a metal layer under the surface which are read with a laser beam (NOTE: also called WORM (write once, read many times) which can be programmed once or compact disk (CD) which is programmed at manufacture); **optical fibre** = fine strand of glass *or* plastic protected by a surrounding material, that is used for the convenient transmission of light signals; **optical font** *or* **OCR font** = character design that can be easily read using an OCR reader;

optical mark reader (OMR) = device that can recognize marks *or* lines on a special forms (such as on an order form *or* a reply to a questionnaire) and convert them into a form a computer can process; **optical mark recognition (OMR)** = process that allows certain marks *or* lines on special forms (such as on an order form *or* a reply to a questionnaire) to be recognized by an optical mark reader, and input into a computer; **optical memory** = optical disks; **optical mouse** = pointing device that is operated by moving it across a special flat mat; on the mat is printed a grid of lines, as the mouse is moved, two light sensors count the number of lines that have been passed to produce a measure of the distance and direction of travel; an optical mouse has fewer moving parts than a mechanical mouse and so is more reliable, but requires an accurately printed mat; **optical scanner** = equipment that converts an image into electrical signals which can be stored in and displayed on a computer; **optical storage** = data storage using mediums such as optical disk, etc.; **optical transmission** = use of fibre optic cables, laser beams and other light sources to carry data, in the form of pulses of light; **optical wand** = OPTICAL BAR READER

optimization *noun* making something work as efficiently as possible

◊ **optimize** *verb* to make something work as efficiently as possible; **optimized code** = program that has been passed through an optimizer to remove any inefficient code *or* statements; **optimizing compiler** = compiler that analyses the machine code it produces in order to improve the speed or efficiency of the code

◊ **optimizer** *noun* program which adapts another program to run more efficiently

optimum *noun & adjective* best possible; **optimum code** *or* **minimum access code** *or* **minimum delay code** = coding system that provides the fastest access and retrieval time for stored data items

option *noun* action which can be chosen; *there are usually four options along the top of the screen; the options available are* described in the main menu; **Option key** = (on an Apple Macintosh) key on the keyboard that gives access to other functions of keys; similar to Ctrl or Alt keys on an IBM PC keyboard

◊ **optional** *adjective* which can be chosen; *the system comes with optional 3.5 or 5.25 disk drives*

> with the colour palette option, remarkable colour effects can be achieved on an RGB colour monitor
>
> *Electronics & Wireless World*

optomechanical mouse   *see* MECHANICAL MOUSE

Orange Book *noun* set of standards published by Philips that define the format for a recordable CD-ROM

OR function *noun* logical function that produces a true output if any input is true; **OR gate** = electronic implementation of the OR function

> COMMENT: the result of the OR function will be 1 if either or both inputs are 1; if both inputs are 0, then the result is 0

ORB   *see*   =   OBJECT   REQUEST BROKER

order *noun* **(a)** instruction; **order code** = operation code; **order code processor (OCP)** = (in a multiprocessor system) a processor which decodes and performs the arithmetic and logical operations according to the program code **(b)** sorted according to a key; *in alphabetical order* **2** *verb* **(a)** to direct *or* instruct **(b)** to sort according to a key; **ordered list** = list of data items which has been sorted into an order

organize *verb* to arrange something so that it works efficiently

◊ **organization** *noun* way of arranging something so that it works efficiently

◊ **organizational** *adjective* referring to the way in which something is organized

orientated *adjective* aimed towards; **problem-orientated language (POL)** =

high-level programming language that allows certain problems to be expressed easily

◊ **orientation** *noun* (i) direction *or* position of an object; (ii) (in word-processing or DTP software) direction of a page, either landscape (long edge horizontal) or portrait (long edge vertical)

origin *noun* **(a)** position on a display screen to which all coordinates are referenced, usually the top left hand corner of the screen **(b)** location in memory at which the first instruction of a program is stored; *see also* INDEXED

original 1 *adjective* used first *or* made first **2** *noun* (first used) master data disk, from which a copy can be made

◊ **original equipment manufacturer (OEM)** *noun* company which produces equipment using basic parts made by other manufacturers, and customizes the product for a particular application; *one OEM supplies the disk drive, another the monitor; he started in business as a manufacturer of PCs for the OEM market*

◊ **originate** *verb* to start *or* come from; *the data originated from the new computer;* **originate modem** = modem that (normally) makes a call to another modem that is waiting to answer calls; the originate modem emits a carrier in response to an answertone from the remote modem

◊ **origination** *noun* work involved in creating something

orphan *noun* first line of a paragraph of text printed alone at the bottom of a column, with the rest of the paragraph at the top of the next column; an orphan makes a page look ugly

orthogonal *adjective* (instruction) made up of independent parameters *or* parts

OS = OPERATING SYSTEM software that controls the basic, low-level hardware operations, and file management, without the user having to operate it (the operating system is usually supplied with the computer as part of the bundled software in ROM)

◊ **OS/2** multitasking operating system for PC computers developed by IBM and Microsoft, development is now continued by IBM to make it an alternative to Microsoft Windows

OSI = OPEN SYSTEM INTERCONNECTION; *see also* ISO/OSI

OSPF ; *see* OPEN SHORTEST PATH FIRST

out of range *adjective* (number *or* quantity) that is outside the limits of a system

outage *noun* time during which a system is not operational

outlet *noun* connection *or* point in a circuit *or* network where a signal *or* data can be accessed

outline *noun* the main features of something; **outline flowchart** = flowchart of the main features, steps and decisions in a program *or* system; **outline font** = printer or display font (collection of characters) stored as a set of outlines that mathematically describe the shape of each character (which are then used to draw each character rather than actual patterns of dots); outline fonts can be easily scaled, unlike bit-map fonts; *see also* BIT-MAP FONTS

outliner *noun* (utility program) used to help a user order sections and sub-sections of a list of things to do or parts of a project

output (o/p *or* **O/P) 1** *noun* **(a)** information *or* data that is transferred from a CPU *or* the main memory to another device such as a monitor *or* printer *or* secondary storage device; **computer output** = data *or* information produced after processing by a computer (NOTE opposite is **input) (b)** action of transferring the information *or* data from store to a user; **output area** *or* **block** = section of memory that contains data to be transferred to an output device; **output bound** *or* **limited** = (processor) that cannot function at normal speed because of a slower peripheral; **output buffer register** = temporary store for data that is waiting to be output; **output device** = device (such as a monitor *or* printer) which allows information to be displayed; **output file** = set of records that have been completely processed according to various parameters; **output formatter** = (i) software used to format data *or* programs (and output them) so that they are compatible with another sort of storage medium; (ii) part of a word processor program that formats text according to embedded commands; **output mode** = computer mode in which data is moved from internal storage *or* the CPU to external devices; **output port** = circuit and connector that allow a computer to output *or* transmit data to other devices *or* machines; *connect the printer to the printer output port;* **output register** = register that stores data to be output until the receiver is ready *or* the channel is free; **output stream** = communications channel carrying data output to a peripheral; **input/output (I/O)** = (i) receiving *or* transmitting of data between a computer and its peripherals and other points outside the system; (ii) all data received *or* transmitted by a computer; *see also* INPUT **2** *verb* to transfer data from a computer to a monitor *or* printer; *finished documents can be output to the laser printer*

---

most CAD users output to a
colour plotter
PC Business World

---

outsource *verb* to employ another company to manage and support a network for your company

OV = OVERFLOW

Overdrive processor chip that is used as a more powerful replacement for a conventional Intel 80486 processor

overflow *or* **OV** *noun* **(a)** mathematical result that is greater than the limits of the computer's number storage system; **overflow bit** *or* **flag** *or* **indicator** = single bit in a word that is set to one (1) if a mathematical overflow has occurred; **overflow check** = examining an overflow flag to see if an overflow has occurred **(b)** situation in a network when the number of transmissions is greater than the line capacity and are transferred by another route

overhead *noun* extra code that has to be stored to organize the program; *the line numbers in a BASIC program are an overhead;* **overhead bit** = single bit used for error detection in a transmission; **polling overhead** = amount of time spent by a computer calling and checking each terminal in a network

overheat *verb* to become too hot; *the system may overheat if the room is not air-conditioned*

overlap 1 *noun* where one thing covers part of another *or* two sections of data that are placed on top of each other; **multipass overlap** = system of producing higher quality print from a dot matrix printer by repeating the line of characters but shifted slightly, so making the dots less noticeable (used to produce NLQ print) **2** *verb* to cover part of an item with another

overlay *noun* **(a)**; **keyboard overlay** = strip of paper that is placed above keys on a keyboard to indicate their function **(b)** small section of a program; the entire program is bigger than the main memory capacity of a computer, and so the overlay is loaded into memory when required, so that main memory only contains the sections it requires; **form overlay** = heading *or* other matter held in store and printed out at the same time as the text; **overlay manager** = system software that manages (during run-time) the loading and execution of sections of a program when they are required; **overlay region** = area of main memory that can be used by the overlay manager to store the current section of the program being run; **overlay segments** = short sections of a long program that can be loaded into memory when required, and executed *contrast with* VIRTUAL MEMORY MANAGEMENT

Many packages also boast useful
drawing and overlay facilities
which enable the user to
annotate specific maps.
Computing

---

overload *verb* to demand more than the device is capable of; *the computer is overloaded with that amount of processing;*

channel overload = transmission of data at a rate greater than the channel capacity

overpunching *noun* altering data on a paper tape by punching additional holes

overrun *verb* data that was missed by a receiver because it was not synchronized with the transmitter *or* because it operates at a slower speed than the transmitter and has no buffer

overscan *noun* (i) faulty or badly adjusted monitor in which the displayed image runs off the edge of the screen; (ii) display equipment in which the picture beam scans past the screen boundaries to ensure that the image fills the screen

overwrite *verb* to write data to a location (memory *or* tape *or* disk) and, in doing so, to destroy any data already contained in that location; *the latest data input has overwritten the old information*

over-voltage protection *noun* safety device that prevents a power supply voltage exceeding certain specified limits

oxide *noun* chemical compound of oxygen; **ferric oxide** = iron oxide used as a coating for magnetic disks and tapes; **metal oxide semiconductors (MOS)** = production and design method for a certain family of integrated circuits using patterns of metal conductors and oxide deposited onto a semiconductor; *see also* MOSFET, CMOS

Pp

p = PICO-

◊ **P** = PETA equal to one quadrillion (2$_{50}$)

◊ **PB** = PETABYTE one quadrillion bytes

P-code *noun* intermediate code produced by a compiler that is ready for an interpreter to process, usually for PASCAL programs

pack 1 *noun* number of punched cards or magnetic disks; **disk pack** = number of magnetic disks on a single spindle, either fixed or removable (from the drive) **2** *verb* **(a)** to put things into a container for selling *or* sending; *to pack goods into cartons; the diskettes are packed in plastic wrappers; the computer is packed in expanded polystyrene before being shipped* **(b)** to store a quantity of data in a reduced form, often by representing several characters of data with one stored character; **packed decimal** = decimal digits stored in a small space, by using only four bits for each digit; **packed format** = two binary coded decimal digits stored within one computer word *or* byte (usually achieved by removing the check *or* parity bit)

package *noun* **(a)** group of different items joined together in one deal; **package deal** = agreement where several different items are agreed at the same time; *we are offering a package deal which includes the whole office computer system, staff training and hardware maintenance* **(b)**; **applications package** = set of computer programs and manuals covering all aspects of a particular task (such as payroll, stock control, invoicing, etc.); **software package** = computer programs and manuals designed for a special purpose; *the computer is sold with accounting and word-processing packages*

◊ **packaged software** *see* SOFTWARE PACKAGE

◊ **packaging** *noun* material used to protect goods which are being packed; attractive material used to wrap goods for display; *airtight packaging; packaging material*

packet *noun* group of data bits which can be transmitted as a group from one node to another over a network; **packet assembler/disassembler (PAD)** = dedicated computer which converts serial data from asynchronous terminals to a form that can be transmitted along a packet switched (synchronous) network; *the remote terminal is connected to a PAD device through which it accesses the host computer;* **packet scheduler** = part of a network router that determines when to transmit the packet of data to the final destination based on the route that has been selected; **packet switched data service** *or* **packet switched network (PSN)** = service which transmits data in packets of a set length; **packet switching** = method of sending data across a WAN in small packets, these are then re-assembled in the correct order at the receiving end; **packet switching service (PSS)** = commercial data transmission service that sends data over its WAN using packet switching *compare* STORE-AND-FORWARD

```
The network is based on
Northern Telecom DPN data
switches over which it will
offer X.25 packet switching,
IBM  SNA,  and  frame-relay
transmission.
```
Computing

packing *noun* **(a)** action of putting goods into boxes and wrapping them for shipping; *what is the cost of the packing? packing is* *included in the price* **(b)** putting large amounts of data into a small area of storage; **packing density** = amount of bits of data which can be stored in a unit area of a disk *or* tape; **packing routine** = program which packs data into a small storage area **(c)** material used to protect goods; *packed in airtight packing* (NOTE: opposite is **padding**)

PAD = **PACKET ASSEMBLER/DISASSEMBLER**

pad 1 *noun* number of keys arranged together; **cursor pad** = group of four arrowed cursor control keys, used to move the cursor up and down or to the right or left; **keypad** = group of special keys used for certain applications; **hex keypad** = set of sixteen keys, with all the figures (0-9, A-F) needed to enter hexadecimal numbers; **numerical keypad** = set of ten keys with figures (0-9), included on most computer keyboards as a separate group, used for entering large amounts of data in numeric form **2** *verb* to fill out

◊ **pad character** *noun* extra character added to a string *or* packet *or* file until it is a required size

◊ **padding** *noun* characters or digits added to fill out a string *or* packet until it is the right length (NOTE: opposite is **packing**)

paddle *noun* computer peripheral consisting of a knob *or* device which is turned to move a cursor *or* pointer on the screen; **game paddle** = device held in the hand to move a cursor *or* graphics in a computer game

page *noun* **(a)** sheet of paper **(b)** amount of text, displayed on a computer monitor *or* screen (which if printed out would fill a page of paper *or* which fills the screen); **page break** = (i) point at which a page ends and a new page starts (in continuous text); (ii) marker used when word-processing to show where a new page should start; **page description language (PDL)** = software that controls a printer's actions to print a page of text to a particular format according to a user's instructions; **page display** = showing on the screen a page of text as it will appear when printed out; **page down key** = (on a keyboard) key that moves the cursor position

down by the number of lines on one screen; **page image buffer** = memory in a page printer that holds the image as it is built up before it is printed; **page layout** = arrangement of text and pictures within a page of a document; *we do all our page layout using desktop publishing software;* **page length** = length of a page (in word-processing); **page makeup** = action of pasting images and text into a page ready for printing; **page number** = unique number assigned to each page within a multimedia application, to be used within hyperlinks and when moving between pages; **page orientation** = direction of the long edge of a piece of paper; *see* **PORTRAIT, LANDSCAPE**; **pages per minute (ppm)** = number of pages that a printer can print in one minute; measurement of the speed of a printer shown as the number of pages of text printed every minute; *this laser printer can output eight pages per minute;* **page preview** = (in WP or DTP software) graphical representation of how a page will look when printed, with different type styles, margins, and graphics correctly displayed; **page printer** = printer which composes one page of text within memory and then prints it in one pass (normally refers to laser printers); *this dot-matrix printer is not a page printer, it only prints one line at a time;* **page reader** = device which converts written *or* typed information to a form that a computer can understand and process; **page setup** = (within software) options that allow a user to set up how the page will look when printed - normally setting the margins, size of paper, and scaling of a page; **page up key** = (on a keyboard) key that moves the cursor position up by the number of lines in one screen **(c)** section of main store, which contains data *or* programs; **multiple base page** = multi-user system in which each user and the operating system have one page of main memory, which can then call up other pages within main memory; **page addressing** = main memory which has been split into blocks, with a unique address allocated to each block of memory which can then be called up and accessed individually, when required; **page boundary** = point where one page ends and the next starts; **page frame** = physical address to which a page of virtual (or logical) memory can be mapped; **page-mode RAM =** dynamic RAM designed to access sequential memory locations very quickly; *the video adapter uses page-mode RAM to speed up the display;* **page protection** = software controls used to ensure that pages are not overwritten by accident or copied into a reserved section of memory; **page table =** list of all the pages and their locations within main memory, used by the operating system when accessing a page **(d)** one section of a main program which can be loaded into main memory when required **2** *verb* **(a)** to make up a text into pages **(b)** to divide computer backing store into sections to allow long programs to be executed in a small main memory

◊ **paged address** *noun* (in a paged-memory scheme) actual physical memory address that is calculated from a logical address and its page address; **paged-memory scheme** = way of dividing memory into areas (pages) which are then allocated a page number; memory addresses are relative to a page which is then mapped to the real, physical memory (this system is normally used to implement virtual memory); **paged-memory management unit** = electronic logic circuit that manages the translation between logical addresses that refer to a particular page and the real physical address that is being referenced

◊ **pagination** *noun* process of dividing text into pages; arrangement of pages in a book

◊ **paging** *noun* virtual memory technique of splitting main memory into small blocks (pages) which are allocated an address and which can be called up when required; **paging algorithm** = formula by which the memory management allocates memory to pages, also covering the transfer from backing storage to main memory in the most efficient way

> COMMENT: a virtual memory management system stores data as pages in memory to provide an apparently larger capacity main memory by storing unused pages in backing store, copying them into main memory only when required

> Mannesmann Tally has launched the T9005, a five-page-a-minute page printer designed to handle over 3,000 pages a month.
> *Computing*

paint 1 *noun* (in a graphics program) colour and pattern used to fill an area **2** *verb* (in a graphics program) to fill an enclosed graphics shape with a colour

◊ **Paintbrush/Paint** *noun* application supplied with Microsoft Windows 3.1x and Windows 95 for creating or editing bitmap images

◊ **paint program** *noun* software that allows a user to draw pictures on screen in different colours, with different styles of brush and special effects; *I drew a rough of our new logo with this paint program*

> COMMENT: paint programs normally operate on bitmap images; drafting or design software normally works with vector-based images

paired registers *noun* two basic word size registers used together as one large word size register (often used for storing address words); *the 8-bit CPU uses a paired register to provide a 16-bit address register*

palette *noun* range of colours which can be used (on a printer *or* computer display); **palette shift** = image displayed using the wrong palette with the unwanted effect that the colours appear distorted

> the colour palette option offers sixteen colours from a range of over four thousand
> *Electronics & Wireless World*

palmtop *noun* personal computer that is small enough to be held in one hand and operated with the other; *this palmtop has a tiny keyboard and twenty-line LCD screen*

pan *verb* (i) (in computer graphics) to smoothly move a viewing window horizontally across an image that is too wide to display all at once; (ii) (in MIDI or sound) to adjust the balance of a sound between the two stereo channels

panel *noun* flat section of a casing with control knobs *or* sockets; *the socket is on the back panel;* **back panel** = panel at the rear of a computer which normally holds the connectors to peripherals such as keyboard, printer, video display unit, and mouse; **control panel** = panel with indicators and switches which allows an operator to monitor and control the actions of a computer *or* peripheral; **front panel** = main computer system control switches and status indicators

pan *verb* (in computer graphics) to move a viewing window horizontally across an image that is too wide to display all at once

Pantone Matching System (PMS)

standard method of matching ink colours on screen and on printed output using a book of pre-defined colours

paper *noun* thin material used for making books *or* newspapers *or* stationery items; **paper feed** = mechanism that moves paper through a printer; *the paper feed in this printer is complex, so it often jams US;* **paper slew** = PAPER THROW; **paper tape** = long strip of paper on which data can be recorded, usually in the form of punched holes; **paper tape feed** = method by which paper tape is passed into a machine; **paper tape punch** = device which punches holes in paper tape to carry data; **paper tape reader** = device which accepts punched paper tape and converts the punched information stored on it into signals which a computer can process; **paper throw** = rapid vertical movement of paper in a printer; **paper tray** = container used to hold paper to be fed into a printer

◊ **paper-fed** *adjective* (device) which is activated when paper is introduced into it; *a paper-fed scanner*

◊ **paper-white monitor** *noun* monitor that normally displays black text on a white background, rather than the normal illuminated text on a black background

◊ **paperless** *adjective* without using paper; **paperless office** = electronic office *or* office which uses computers and other electronic devices for office tasks and avoids the use of paper

Indeed, the concept of the paperless office may have been a direct attack on Xerox and its close ties to the paper document. Yet, as we all know, the paperless office has so far been an empty promise.

Computing

paragraph *noun* **(a)** (in a document) section of text between two carriage return characters; **paragraph marker** = (in a document) non-printing character that shows where a carriage return is within a document **(b)** (in a memory map) 16-byte section of memory which starts at a hexadecimal address that can be evenly divided by 16

parallel *adjective* (i) (computer system) in which two or more processors operate simultaneously on one or more items of data; (ii) two or more bits of a word transmitted over separate lines at the same time; **parallel access** = data transfer between two devices with a number of bits (usually one byte wide) being sent simultaneously; **parallel adder** = number of adders joined together, allowing several digits to be added at once; **parallel computer** = computer with one or more logic *or* arithmetic units, allowing parallel processing; **parallel connection** = transmission link that handles parallel data; *their average transmission rate is 60,000 bps through parallel connection;* **parallel data transmission** = transmission of bits of data simultaneously along a number of data lines; **parallel input/output (PIO)** = data input *or* output from a computer in a parallel form; **parallel input/output chip** = dedicated integrated circuit that performs all handshaking, buffering, etc., needed when transferring parallel data to and from a CPU; **parallel input/parallel output (PIPO)** = device that can accept and transmit parallel data; **parallel input/serial output (PISO)** = device that can accept parallel data and transmit serial data; **parallel interface** *or* **port** = circuit and connector that allows parallel data to be received *or* transmitted; **parallel operation** = number of processes carried out simultaneously on a number of inputs; **parallel port** *see* PARALLEL INTERFACE; **parallel priority system** = number of peripherals connected in parallel to one bus, if they require attention, they send their address and an interrupt signal, which is then processed by the computer according to device priority; **parallel printer** = printer that is connected to a computer via a parallel interface and accepts character data in parallel form; **parallel processing** = computer operating on several tasks simultaneously; **parallel running** = running an old and a new computer system together to allow the new system to be checked before it becomes the only system used; **parallel search storage** = data retrieval from storage that uses part of the data other than an address to locate the data; **parallel transfer** = data transfer between two devices with a number of bits (usually one byte wide) being sent simultaneously; **parallel transmission** = data transmitted over a number of data lines carrying all the bits of a data word simultaneously (NOTE: opposite is **serial transmission**)

The Wheelwriter 7000 offers 172Kb of document storage and mail-merge capabilities: it can be connected to a PC using the parallel printer port.

Computing

---

parameter *noun* information which defines the limits *or* actions of something, such as a variable or routine or program; *the X parameter defines the number of characters displayed across a screen; the size of the array is set with this parameter;* **parameter-driven software** = software whose main functions can be modified and tailored to a user's needs by a number of variables; **parameter passing** = (in a program) value passed to a routine or program when it is called; **parameter testing** = using a program to examine the parameters and set up the system *or* program accordingly; **parameter word** = data word that contains information defining the limits *or* actions of a routine or program; **physical parameter** = description of the size, weight, voltage or power of a system

◊ **parametric (subroutine)** *noun* subroutine that uses parameters to define its limits *or* actions; **parametric equalizer** = device that can enhance or reduce the levels of particular frequencies within an audio signal

◊ **paramterization** *noun* action of setting parameters for software

parent directory *noun* (in DOS filing system) the directory above a sub-directory

◊ **parent folder** *noun* (in Macintosh filing system) one folder that contains other folders

◊ **parent object** *noun* page that contains the object that is being referenced

◊ **parent program** *noun* program that starts another program (a child program), whilst it is still running; control passes back to the parent program when the child program has finished

parity *noun* being equal; **block parity** = parity check on a block of data; **column parity** = parity check on every punched card *or* tape column; **even parity (check)** = error checking system in which any series of bits transmitted must have an even number of binary ones; **no parity** = data transmission which does not use a parity bit; **odd parity (check)** = error checking system in which any series of bits transmitted must have an odd number of binary ones; **parity bit** = extra bit added to a data word as a parity checking device; **parity check** = method of checking (odd *or* even parity check) for errors and that transmitted binary data has not been corrupted; **parity flag** = indicator that shows if data has passed a parity check or if data has odd or even parity; **parity interrupt** = interrupt signal from an error checking routine which indicates that received data has failed a parity check and is corrupt; **parity track** = one track on magnetic *or* paper tape that carries the parity bit

---

The difference between them is that RAID level one offers mirroring, whereas level five stripes records in parity across the disks in the system.

Computing

park *verb* to move the read/write head of a hard disk drive over a point on the disk where no data is stored; *when parked, the disk head will not damage any data if it touches the disk surface*

parse *verb* to break down high-level language code into its element parts when translating into machine code

part *noun* (a) section of something; **part page display** = display of only a section of a page, and not the whole page (b); **spare part** = small piece of a machine which is needed to replace a piece which is broken *or* missing; *the printer won't work - we need to get a spare part;* **parts per quarter note (PPQN)** = most common time format used with standard MIDI sequences

partial carry *noun* temporary storage of all carries generated by parallel adders rather than a direct transfer

◊ **partial RAM** *noun* RAM chip in which only a certain area of the chip functions correctly, usually in newly released chips (partial RAM's can be used by employing more than one to make up the capacity of one fully functional chip)

partition 1 *noun* (a) area of a hard disk that is treated as a logical drive and can be accessed as a separate drive; *I defined two partitions on this hard disk - called drive C: and D:* (b) section of computer memory set aside as foreground *or* background memory; **partitioned file** = one file made up of several smaller sequential files, each part can be accessed individually by the control program **2** *verb* (a) to divide a hard disk into two or more logical drives that can be accessed as separate drives (b) to divide a large file *or* block into several smaller units which can be accessed and handled more easily

PASCAL high-level structured programming language used both on micros and for teaching programming

pass 1 *noun* (i) the execution of a loop, once; (ii) single operation; **single-pass assembler** = assembler program that translates the source code in one action;

sorting pass = single run through a list of items to put them into order **2** *verb* action of moving the whole length of a magnetic tape over the read/write heads

password *noun* word *or* series of characters which identifies a user so that he can access a system; *the user has to key in the password before he can access the database;* **password protection** = computer *or* software that requires the user to enter a password before he can gain access

> the system's security features
> let you divide the disk into up
> to 256 password-protected
> sections
>
> *Byte*

paste *verb* to insert text or graphics that has been copied or cut into a file; *now that I have cut this paragraph from the end of the document, I can paste it in here;* **cut-and-paste** = action of taking a section of text *or* data from one point and inserting it at another (often used in word-processors and DTP packages for easy page editing)

◊ **Paste Special** to insert a special object (sound, images, or data from other applications) into a document

patch *noun* (temporary) correction made to a program; small correction made to software by the user, on the instructions of the software publisher; **patch cord** = short cable with a connector at each end, used to make an electrical connection on a patch panel; **patch panel** = electrical terminals that can be interconnected using short patch cords, allowing quick and simple re-configuration of a network

path *noun* (a) possible route or sequence of events *or* instructions within the execution of a program (b) route from one point in a communications network to another (c) (in the DOS operating system) list of subdirectories where the operating system should look for a named file; *you cannot run the program from the root directory until its directory is added to the path;* **pathname** = location of a file with a listing of the subdirectories leading to it; *the pathname for*

the Word letter file is
\FILES\SIMON\DOCS\LETTER.DOC

pattern *noun* series of regular lines *or* shapes which are repeated again and again; **pattern palette** = range of predefined patterns that can be used to fill an area of an image; **pattern recognition** = algorithms *or* program functions that can identify a shape from a video camera, etc.

◊ **patterned** *adjective* with patterns

pause key *noun* (in a keyboard) key that temporarily stops a process, often a scrolling screen display, until the key is pressed a second time

PBX = PRIVATE BRANCH EXCHANGE

PC (a) = PERSONAL COMPUTER (originally referring to a microcomputer specification with an 8086-based low-power computer); now normally used to refer to any computer that uses an Intel 80x86 processor and is based on the IBM PC-style architecture; **PC-compatible** = computer that is compatible with the IBM PC; **PC/AT** = (IBM PC compatible) computer that used an Intel 80286 processor and was fitted with 16-bit ISA expansion connectors; **PC/AT keyboard** = keyboard that features twelve function keys arranged in one row along the top of the keyboard; **PC/XT** = (IBM PC compatible) computer that was fitted with a hard disk drive and used a 8086 Intel processor; **PC/XT keyboard** = keyboard that features ten function keys arranged in two columns along the left hand side of the keyboard **(b)** = PRINTED CIRCUIT (BOARD) **(c)** = PROGRAM COUNTER

in the UK, the company is known not for PCs but for PC printers
Which PC?

PCB = PRINTED CIRCUIT BOARD

PC-DOS version of MS-DOS that is sold by IBM

PCI = PERIPHERAL COMPONENT INTERCONNECT specification produced by Intel defining a type of fast local bus that allows high-speed data transfer between the processor and the PCI-compatible expansion cards

PCL = PRINTER CONTROL LANGUAGE standard set of commands, defined by Hewlett Packard, that allow a computer to control a printer

PCM 1 = PLUG-COMPATIBLE MANUFACTURER company that produces add-on boards which are compatible with another manufacturer's computer **2** = PULSE-CODE MODULATION way of storing sounds in an accurate, compact format that is used by high-end sound cards

PCMCIA = PERSONAL COMPUTER MEMORY CARD INTERNATIONAL ASSOCIATION specification for add-in expansion cards that are the size of a credit card with a connector at one end; *the extra memory is stored on this PCMCIA card and I use it on my laptop;* **PCMCIA card** = memory *or* peripheral which complies with the PCMCIA standard; **PCMCIA connector** = 68-pin connector that is inside a PCMCIA slot and on the end of a PCMCIA card; **PCMCIA slot** = expansion slot (normally on a laptop) that can accept a PCMCIA expansion card

PCS *see* = PERSONAL COMMUNICATIONS SERVICES

PCU = PERIPHERAL CONTROL UNIT device used to convert input and output signals and instructions to a form that a peripheral device will understand

PCX file *noun* method of storing a bitmap graphic image file on disk

PDA = PERSONAL DIGITAL ASSISTANT lightweight palmtop computer that provides the basic functions of a diary, notepad, address-book and to-do list together with fax or modem communications; current PDA designs do not have a keyboard, but use a touch-sensitive screen with a pen and handwriting-recognition to control the software

PDF = PORTABLE DOCUMENT FORMAT file format used by Adobe Acrobat

PDL = PAGE DESCRIPTION LANGUAGE, PROGRAM DESIGN LANGUAGE

PDN = PUBLIC DATA NETWORK

peak 1 *noun* highest point; maximum value of a variable *or* signal; **peak period** = time of the day when most power is being used; **time of peak demand** = time when something is being used most; **peak output** = highest output **2** *verb* to reach the highest point

peek *noun* BASIC computer instruction that allows the user to read the contents of a memory location; *you need the instruction PEEK 1452 here to examine the contents of memory location 1452* compare POKE

peer *noun* any two similar devices operating on the same network protocol level

◊ **peer-to-peer network** *noun* local area network (normally using network adapter cards in each computer) that does not use a central dedicated server, instead each computer in the network shares the jobs; *we have linked the four PCs in our small office using a peer-to-peer network*

pel *see* PIXEL

pen *see* LIGHT PEN; **pen computer** = type of computer that uses a pen instead of a keyboard for input; the computer has a touch-sensitive screen and uses handwriting recognition software to interpret the commands written on the screen using the pen; **pen plotter** = plotter that uses removable pens to draw on paper; **pen recorder** = peripheral which moves a pen over paper according to an input (a value or coordinate)

Pentium™ *noun* processor developed by Intel; it is backwards compatible with the 80x86 family used in IBM PCs; the processor uses a 32-bit address bus and a 64-bit data bus

◊ **Pentium Pro** *noun* currently the most powerful processor developed by Intel; this processor replaced the Pentium for high-performance PCs

per *preposition* **(a)**; **as per** = according to; **as per sample** = as shown in the sample; **as**

per specification = according to the details given in the specification **(b)** at a rate of; **per hour** *or* **per day** *or* **per week** *or* **per year** = for each hour *or* day *or* week *or* year **(c)** out of; *the rate of imperfect items is about twenty-five per thousand; the error rate has fallen to twelve per hundred*

◊ **percentile** *noun* one of a series of ninety-nine figures below which a certain percentage of the total falls

perfect 1 *adjective* completely correct *or* with no mistakes; *we check each batch to make sure it is perfect; she did a perfect typing test* **2** *verb* to make something which is completely correct; *he perfected the process for making high grade steel*

◊ **perfectly** *adverb* with no mistakes *or* correctly; *she typed the letter perfectly*

perforations *noun* line of very small holes in a sheet of paper *or* continuous stationery, to help when tearing

◊ **perforated tape** *noun* paper tape *or* long strip of tape on which data can be recorded in the form of punched holes

◊ **perforator** *noun* machine that punches holes in a paper tape

perform *verb* to do well *or* badly

◊ **performance** *noun* way in which someone *or* something works; **as a measure of the system's performance** = as a way of judging if the system is working well; *in benchmarking, the performances of several systems or devices are tested against a standard benchmark;* **high performance equipment** = high quality *or* high specification equipment

period *noun* **(a)** length of time; *for a period of time or for a period of months or for a six-year period; sales over a period of three months* **(b)** *US* printing sign used at the end of a piece of text (NOTE: GB English is **full stop**)

◊ **periodic** *or* **periodical** *adjective* **(a)** from time to time; *a periodic review of the company's performance* **(b)**; **periodic** = (signal *or* event) that occurs regularly; *the clock signal is periodic*

◊ **periodically** *adverb* from time to time

peripheral 1 *adjective* which is not essential *or* which is attached to something else **2** *noun* (i) item of hardware (such as terminals, printers, monitors, etc.) which is attached to a main computer system; (ii) any device that allows communication between a system and itself, but is not directly operated by the system; *peripherals such as disk drives or printers allow data transfer and are controlled by a system, but contain independent circuits for their operation;* **fast peripheral** = peripheral that communicates with the computer at very high speeds, limited only by the speed of the electronic circuits; **slow peripheral** = peripheral such as a card reader, where mechanical movement determines speed; **peripheral component interconnect (PCI)** = high-speed local bus designed by Intel that runs at 33MHz and is most often used in Pentium-based personal computers for network or graphics adapters; **peripheral control unit (PCU)** = device that converts the input/output signals and instructions from a computer to a form and protocol which the peripheral will understand; **peripheral driver** = program *or* routine used to interface, manage and control an input/output device *or* peripheral; **peripheral equipment** = (i) external devices that are used with a computer, such as a printer *or* scanner; (ii) (communications) equipment external to a central processor that provides extra features; **peripheral interface adapter (PIA)** = circuit that allows a computer to communicate with a peripheral by providing serial and parallel ports and other handshaking signals required to interface the peripheral; **peripheral limited** = CPU that cannot execute instructions at normal speed because of a slow peripheral; **peripheral memory** = storage capacity available in a peripheral; **peripheral processing units (PPU)** = device used for input, output or storage which is controlled by the CPU; **peripheral software driver** = short section of computer program that allows a user to access and control a peripheral easily *same as* DEVICE DRIVER; **peripheral transfer** = movement of data between a CPU and peripheral; **peripheral unit** = (i) item of hardware (such as terminal, printer, monitor,

etc.) which is attached to a main computer system; (ii) any device that allows communication between a system and itself, but is not operated only by the system

Perl = PRACTICAL EXTRACTION AND REPORT LANGUAGE *noun* interpreted programming language (that is usually used under Unix) used to create CGI scripts that can process forms or carry out functions on a Web server to enhance a web site; *if you want to add a search engine to your web site, you will need to write a Perl program*

permanent *adjective* which will last for a very long time *or* for ever; **permanent dynamic memory** = storage medium which retains data even when power is removed; **permanent error** = error in a system which cannot be mended; **permanent file** = data file that is stored in a backing storage device such as a disk drive; **permanent memory** = computer memory that retains data even when power is removed; *see also* NON-VOLATILE MEMORY; **permanent swap file** = file on a hard disk, made up of contiguous disk sectors, which stores a swap file for software that implements virtual memory, such as Microsoft's Windows

◊ **permanently** *adverb* done in a way which will last for a long time; *the production number is permanently engraved on the back of the computer casing*

permission *noun* authorization given to a particular user to access a certain shared resource or area of disk; *this user cannot access the file on the server because he does not have permission; see also* RIGHTS

permutation *noun* number of different ways in which something can be arranged; *the cipher system is very secure since there are so many possible permutations for the key*

persistence *noun* length of time that a CRT will continue to display an image after the picture beam has stopped tracing it on the screen; *slow scan rate monitors need long persistence phosphor to prevent the image flickering*

person *noun* human being

◊ **personal** *adjective* referring to one person; **personal communications services (PCS)** = range of wireless communication systems that allow computers to exchange data with other devices such as a printer or PDA; **personal computer (PC)** = low-cost microcomputer intended mainly for home and light business use; **Personal Computer Memory Card International Association** *see* PCMCIA; **personal digital assistant (PDA)** = lightweight palmtop computer that provides the basic functions of a diary, notepad, address-book and to-do list together with fax or modem communications; current PDA designs do not have a keyboard, but use a touch-sensitive screen with a pen and handwriting-recognition to control the software; **personal identification device (PID)** = device (such as a card) connected *or* inserted into a system to identify *or* provide authorization for a user; **personal identification number (PIN)** = unique sequence of digits that identifies a user to provide authorization to access a system (often used on automatic cash dispensers *or* with a PID or password to enter a system); **personal information manager (PIM)** = software utility that stores and manages a user's everyday data, such as diary, telephone numbers, address book and notes

◊ **personalize** *verb* to customize *or* to adapt a product specially for a certain user

perspective *noun* appearance of depth in an image in which objects that are further away from the viewer appear smaller; **perspective correction** = (in a three-dimensional scene) method that is used to change the size and shape of an object to give the impression of depth and distance

PERT = PROGRAM EVALUATION AND REVIEW TECHNIQUE definition of tasks *or* jobs and the time each requires, arranged in order to achieve a goal

peta (P) equal to one quadrillion (2^{50})

◊ **petabyte (PB)** *noun* one quadrillion bytes

petal printer = DAISY WHEEL PRINTER

PgDn *see* PAGE DOWN KEY

◊ **PgUp** *see* PAGE UP KEY

PGP = PRETTY GOOD PRIVACY encryption system developed to allow anyone to protect the contents of their email messages from unauthorised readers; this system is often used when sending credit card or payment details over the internet

phantom ROM *noun* duplicate area of read-only memory that is accessed by a special code

phase 1 *noun* one part of a larger process; **run phase** = period of time when a program is run; **compile phase** = period of time during which a program is compiled **2** *verb;* **to phase in** *or* **to phase out** = to introduce something gradually *or* to reduce something gradually; **phased change-over** = new device that is gradually introduced as the old one is used less and less

PHIGS = PROGRAMMER'S HIERARCHICAL INTERACTIVE GRAPHICS STANDARD standard application interface between software and a graphics adapter that uses a set of standard commands to draw and manipulate 2D and 3D images

phone 1 *noun* telephone *or* machine used for speaking to someone over a long distance; *we had a new phone system installed last week;* **phone call** = speaking to someone on the phone; **to make a phone call** = to dial a number to try to speak to someone on the telephone; **to answer the phone** *or* **to take a phone call** = to reply to a call on the phone; **phone number** = set of figures for a particular telephone; *he keeps a list of phone numbers in a little black book; the phone number is on the company notepaper; can you give me your phone number?*

◊ **Phone Dialer** *noun* utility supplied with Windows 95 that allows a user to dial telephone numbers from their computer

phoneme *noun* one small sound, several of which may make up a spoken word; used to analyse voice input to recognise words or to produce speech by playing back a sequence of phonemes

phosphor *noun* substance that produces light when excited by some form of energy, usually an electron beam, used for coating the inside of a cathode ray tube; *see* TELEVISION; **phosphor coating** = thin layer of phosphor on the inside of a CRT screen; **phosphor dots** = individual dots of red, green and blue phosphor on a colour CRT screen; **phosphor efficiency** = measure of the amount of light produced in ratio to the energy received from an electron beam; **long persistence phosphor** = television screen coating that retains the displayed image for a period of time longer than the refresh rate, so reducing flicker effects

COMMENT: a thin layer of phosphor is arranged in a pattern of small dots on the inside of a television screen which produces an image when scanned by the picture beam

photo- *prefix* referring to light

◊ **photodigital memory** *noun* computer memory system that uses a LASER to write data onto a piece of film which can then be read many times but not written to again (NOTE: also called WORM (Write Once Read Many times memory)

◊ **photoresist** *noun* chemical *or* material that hardens into an etch resistant material when light is shone on it; *to make the PCB, coat the board with photoresist, place the opaque pattern above, expose, then develop and etch, leaving the conducting tracks;* **positive photoresist** = method of forming photographic images where exposed areas of photoresist are removed; it is used in making PCBs

◊ **phototypesetter** *noun* device that can produce very high-resolution text on photo-sensitive paper or film

PhotoCD™ *noun* standard developed to store 35mm photographic slides or negatives in digital format on a CD-ROM

photorealistic *adjective* (computer image) that has almost the same quality and clarity as a photograph

physical *adjective* real *or* solid *or* which can be touched; **physical address** = memory address that corresponds with a hardware memory location in a memory device; **physical database** = organization and structure of a stored database; **physical layer** = lowest ISO/OSI standard network layer that defines rules for bit rate, power and medium for signal transmission; *see also* LAYER, OSI; **physical memory** = memory fitted in a computer *compare* VIRTUAL MEMORY; **physical topology** = actual arrangement of the cables in a network

◊ **physical record** *noun* (a) maximum unit of data that can be transmitted in a single operation (b) all the information, including control data, for one record stored in a computer system

PIA = PERIPHERAL INTERFACE ADAPTER circuit which allows a computer to communicate with a peripheral by providing serial and parallel ports and other handshaking signals required to interface the peripheral

PIC = PICTURE IMAGE COMPRESSION image compression algorithm used in Intel's DVI video system; *see also* DV-I

pica *noun* typeface used on a printer, giving ten characters to the inch

PICK *noun* multiuser, multitasking operating system that runs on mainframe, mini or PC computers

pickup reel *noun* empty reel used to take the tape as it is played from a full reel

pico- (p) *prefix* representing one million millionth of a unit; **picosecond (pS)** = one million millionth of a second

PICS file format used to import a sequence of PICT files on a Macintosh

PICT = PICTure (Apple Macintosh) graphics file format that stores images in a vector format

PICture method of storing vector graphic images, developed by Lotus for its 1-2-3 spreadsheet charts and graphs

picture 1 *noun* printed *or* drawn image of an object or scene; *this picture shows the new design;* **picture beam** = moving electron beam in a TV, that produces an image on the screen by illuminating the phosphor coating and by varying its intensity according to the received signal; **picture element** *or* **pixel** = smallest single unit *or* point on a display whose colour *or* brightness can be controlled; *see also* PIXEL; **picture image compression (PIC)** = image compression algorithm used in Intel's DVI video system; **picture processing** = analysis of information contained in an image, usually by computer *or* electronic methods, providing analysis *or* recognition of objects in the image; **picture transmission** = transmission of images over a telephone line; *see also* FACSIMILE TRANSMISSION **2** *verb* to visualize an object *or* scene; *try to picture the layout before starting to draw it in*

PID = PERSONAL IDENTIFICATION DEVICE device (such as a bank card) connected with or inserted into a system to identify or provide authorization for a user

PIF *see* PROGRAM INFORMATION FILE

piggyback *verb* to connect two integrated circuits in parallel, one top of the other to save space; *piggyback those two memory chips to boost the memory capacity;* **piggyback entry** = unauthorized access to a computer system gained by using an authorized user's password *or* terminal

◊ **piggybacking** *noun* using transmitted messages to carry acknowledgements from a message which has been received earlier

PILOT *noun* computer programming language that uses a text-based format and is mainly used in computer-aided learning

pilot 1 *adjective* used as a test, which if successful will then be expanded into a full operation; *the company set up a pilot project to see if the proposed manufacturing system was efficient; the pilot factory has been built to test the new production process;* **pilot system** = system constructed to see if it can be manufactured, if it works and if the end-user likes it **2** *verb* to test; *they are piloting the new system*

PIM = PERSONAL INFORMATION MANAGER software utility that stores and manages a user's everyday data, such as diary, telephone numbers, address book and notes

PIN = PERSONAL IDENTIFICATION NUMBER unique sequence of digits that identifies the user

COMMENT: the PIN is commonly used in automatic cash machines in banks, along with a card (PID) which allows the user to be identified

pin *noun* **(a)** one of several short pieces of wire attached to an integrated circuit package that allows the IC to be connected to a circuit board; **pin compatible** = an electronic chip that can directly replace another because the arrangement of the pins is the same and they carry the same signals; *it's easy to upgrade the processor because the new one is pin-compatible* **(b)** short piece of metal, part of a plug which fits into a hole in a socket; *use a three-pin plug to connect the printer to the mains;* **three-pin mains plug** = plug with three pins (one neutral, one live and one earthed); **two-pin mains plug** = plug with two pins (one neutral, one live)

◊ **pincushion distortion** *noun* fault with a monitor that causes the distortion of an image displayed in which the edges curve in towards the centre

◊ **pinfeed** *see* TRACTOR FEED

◊ **pinout** *noun* description of the position of all the pins on an integrated circuit together with their function and signal

pinchwheel *noun* small rubber wheel in a tape machine that holds the tape in place and prevents flutter

PING *noun* software utility that will test all the nodes on a network or internet to ensure that they are working correctly

PIO = PARALLEL INPUT/OUTPUT; *see also* PIPO, PISO

pipe *noun* (in DOS and UNIX) symbol, normally (|), that tells the operating system to send the output of one command to another command, instead of displaying it

◊ **pipeline 1** *noun;* **pipeline (computer)** = CPU or ALU that is constructed in blocks and executes instructions in steps, each block dealing with one part of the instruction, so speeding up program execution; **pipeline burst cache** = secondary synchronous cache that uses very high speed memory chips (with access speeds of around 9ns) **2** *verb* **(a)** to schedule inputs to arrive at the microprocessor when nothing else is happening, so increasing apparent speed **(b)** to begin the processing of a second instruction while still processing the present one to increase speed of execution of a program

PIPO = PARALLEL INPUT/PARALLEL OUTPUT

pirate 1 *noun* person who copies a patented invention *or* a copyright work and sells it; *the company is trying to take the software pirates to court* **2** *adjective;* **pirate copy** = copy of software or other copyright material which has been made illegally; *a pirate copy of a computer program* **3** *verb* to manufacture copies of an original copyrighted work illegally; *a pirated tape or a pirated design; the designs for the new system were pirated in the Far East; he used a cheap pirated disk and found the program had bugs in it*

◊ **piracy** *noun* copying of patented inventions *or* copyright works

COMMENT: the items most frequently pirated are programs on magnetic disks and tapes which are relatively simple to copy

PISO = PARALLEL INPUT/SERIAL OUTPUT

pitch *noun* number of characters which will fit into one inch of line, when the characters are typed in single spacing (used on line printers, the normal pitches available being 10, 12 and 17 characters per inch); **pitch scale factor** = instruction to a waveform audio device to change the pitch of the sound by a factor

pix *noun* picture *or* pictures

pixel *or* **picture element** *noun* smallest single unit *or* point of a display whose colour *or* brightness can be controlled

COMMENT: in high resolution display systems the colour or brightness of a single pixel can be controlled; in low resolution systems a group of pixels are controlled at the same time

an EGA display and driver give a resolution of 640 x 350 pixels and support sixteen colours
PC Business World

adding 40 to each pixel brightens the image and can improve the display's appearance
Byte

PL/1 = PROGRAMMING LANGUAGE/1 high level programming language mainly used in commercial and scientific work on large computers, containing features of ALGOL, COBOL and FORTRAN

PLA = PROGRAMMABLE LOGIC ARRAY IC that can be permanently programmed to perform logic operations on data

COMMENT: a PLA consists of a large matrix of paths between input and output pins, with logic gates and a fusible link at each connection point which can be broken or left to conduct when programming to define a function from input to output

place *noun* position of a digit within a number

plaintext *noun* text *or* information that has not been encrypted *or* coded; *the messages* *were sent as plaintext by telephone; enter the plaintext message into the cipher machine*

PLAN low-level programming language

plan 1 *noun* **(a)** organized way of doing something **(b)** drawing which shows how something is arranged *or* how something will be built **2** *verb* to organize carefully how something should be done

◊ **planner** *noun* software program that allows appointments and important meetings to be recorded and arranged in the most efficient way

◊ **planning** *noun* organizing how something should be done; *long-term planning or short-term planning*

planar *noun* **(a)** method of producing integrated circuits by diffusing chemicals into a slice of silicon to create the different components **(b)** graphical objects or images arranged on the same plane

◊ **plane** *noun* (in a graphics image) one layer of an image that can be manipulated independently within a graphics program

plant *verb* to store a result in memory for later use

plasma display *or* **gas plasma display** *noun* display screen using the electroluminescing properties of certain gases to display text

> COMMENT: this is a thin display usually used in small portable computers

> the disadvantage of using plasma technology is that it really needs mains power to work for any length of time
> *Micro Decision*

plastic bubble keyboard *noun* keyboard whose keys are small bubbles in a plastic sheet over a contact which when pressed completes a circuit

> COMMENT: these are very solid and cheap keyboards but are not ideal for rapid typing

platform *noun* standard type of hardware that makes up a particular range of computers; *this software will only work on the IBM PC platform;* **platform independence** = software or a network that can work with or connect to different types of incompatible hardware

platter *noun* one disk within a hard disk drive

> COMMENT: the disks are made of metal or glass and coated with a magnetic compound; each platter has a read/write head that moves across its surface to access stored data

play back *verb* to read data *or* a signal from a recording medium; *after you have recorded the music, press this button to play back the tape and hear what it sounds like*

◊ **playback head** *noun* transducer that reads signals recorded on a storage medium and usually converts them to an electrical signal; *disk playback head; tape playback head*

◊ **playback rate scale factor** *noun* (i) (in waveform audio) sound played back at a different rate, directed by another application, to create a special effect; (ii) (video displayed on a computer) point at which video playback is no longer smooth and appears jerky due to missed frames

player missile graphics *see* SPRITES

PLD = PROGRAMMABLE LOGIC DEVICE

plex database *noun* database structure in which data items can be linked together

◊ **plex structure** *noun* network structure *or* data structure in which each node is connected to all the others

PL/M = PROGRAMMING LANGUAGE FOR MICROPROCESSORS high level programming language derived from PL/1 for use on microprocessors

plot 1 *noun* graph *or* map **2** *verb* to draw an image (especially a graph) based on information supplied as a series of coordinates; **plotting mode** = ability of some word-processors to produce graphs by printing a number of closely spaced characters rather than individual pixels (this results in a broad low-resolution line)

◊ **plotter** *noun* computer peripheral that draws straight lines between two coordinates; **plotter driver** = dedicated software that converts simple instructions issued by a user into complex control instructions to direct the plotter; **plotter pen** = instrument used in a plotter to mark the paper with ink as it moves over the paper; **digital plotter** = plotter which receives the coordinates to plot to in a digital form; **drum plotter** = computer output device consisting of a movable pen and a piece of paper wrapped around a drum that rotates, creating patterns and text; **incremental plotter** = plotter which receives positional data as increments to its current position rather than separate coordinates; **pen plotter** = plotter that uses removable pens to draw an image on paper; **printer-plotter** = high-resolution printer that is able to mimic a plotter and produce low-resolution plots; **x-y plotter** *or* **graph plotter** = plotter which plots to coordinates supplied, by moving the pen in two planes while the paper remains stationary

COMMENT: plotters are used for graph and diagram plotting and can plot curved lines as a number of short straight lines

plug 1 *noun* connector with protruding pins that is inserted into a socket to provide an electrical connection; *the printer is supplied with a plug;* **adapter plug** = plug which allows devices with different plugs (two-pin, three-pin, etc.) to be fitted into the same socket; **plug-compatible** = equipment manufactured to operate with another system when connected to it by a connector *or* cable; *this new plug-compatible board works much faster than any of its rivals, we can install it by simply plugging it into the expansion port* **2** *verb;* **to plug in** = to make an electrical connection by pushing a plug into a socket; *no wonder the computer does nothing, you have not plugged it in at the mains;* **plug-in unit** = small electronic circuit that can be simply plugged into a system to increase its power (NOTE: opposite is **unplug**)

it allows room for up to 40K of RAM via plug-in memory cartridges

Which PC?

adding memory is simply a matter of plugging a card into an expansion bus connector

Byte

◊ **Plug and Play** (PNP) development in PCs that is part of the Windows 95 system; when a user plugs a new adapter card into their PC they do not have to configure it or set any switches

◊ **plug-compatible** *adjective* (equipment) that can work with several different types of computer, so long as they have the correct type of connector

plus *or* **plus sign** *noun* printed *or* written sign (+) showing that figures are added *or* showing a positive value

PLV = PRODUCTION LEVEL VIDEO highest-quality video compression algorithm used with DVI full-motion video sequences

PMOS = P-channel METAL OXIDE SEMICONDUCTOR metal oxide semiconductor transistor that conducts via a small region of p-type semiconductor

PMS *see* PANTONE MATCHING SYSTEM

PNP *see* PLUG AND PLAY

pnp transistor *noun* layout of a bipolar transistor whose collector and emitter are of p-type semiconductor and whose base is n-type semiconductor

point 1 *noun* (a) place *or* position; **access point** = point on a circuit board *or* in software, allowing an engineer to check signals *or* data; **re-entry point** = point in a program *or* routine where it is re-entered; **starting point** = place where something starts; *see also* BREAKPOINT (b); **binary point** = dot which indicates the division between the bits for the numbers' whole units and the fractional part of the binary number; **decimal point** = dot (in a decimal number) which indicates the division between a whole unit and its fractional parts (such as 4.25); **percentage point** = 1 per cent **2** *verb;* **to point out** = to show

◊ **point-of-sale (POS)** place in a shop where goods are paid for; **electronic point-of-sale (EPOS)** = system that uses a computer terminal at a point-of-sale site for electronic fund transfer *or* stock control as well as product pricing, etc.

◊ **pointer** *noun* **(a)** variable in a computer program that contains the address to a data item *or* instruction; *increment the contents of the pointer to the address of the next instruction;* **pointer file** = file of pointers referring to large amounts of stored data **(b)** graphical symbol used to indicate the position of a cursor on a computer display; *desktop publishing on a PC is greatly helped by the use of a pointer and mouse*

◊ **pointing device** *noun* input device that controls the position of a cursor on screen as it is moved by the user; *see also* MOUSE

---

the arrow keys, the spacebar or the mouse are used for pointing, and the enter key or the left mouse button are to pick

PC User

---

pointing with the cursor and pressing the joystick button eliminates use of the keyboard entirely

Soft

◊ **point of presence (POP)** *noun* telephone access number for a service provider that can be used to connect to the internet via a modem

◊ **point size** *noun* (typography) unit of measure equal to 1/72-inch - used to measure type or text

◊ **point to point** *noun* (i) direct link between two devices; (ii) communications network in which every node is directly connected to every other node; **point to point protocol (PPP)** = protocol that supports a network link over an asynchronous (modem) connection and is normally used to provide data transfer between a user's computer and a remote server on the internet using the TCP/IP network protocol

poke *noun* computer instruction that modifies an entry in a memory by writing a number to an address in memory; *poke 1423,74 will write the data 74 into location 1423 compare* PEEK

POL = PROBLEM-ORIENTATED LANGUAGE

polar *adjective* referring to poles; **polar coordinates** = system of defining positions as an angle and distance from the origin *compare* CARTESIAN COORDINATES

◊ **polarized** *adjective;* **polarized plug** = plug which has a feature (usually a peg or a special shape) which allows it to be inserted into a socket only in one way; **polarized edge connector** = edge connector that has a hole or key to prevent it being plugged in the wrong way round

◊ **polarity** *noun* definition of direction of flow of flux *or* current in an object; **electrical polarity** = definition of whether an electrical signal is positive *or* negative, indicating if a point is a source or collector of electrical current (positive polarity terminals are usually marked red, negative are black); **magnetic polarity** = method of indicating if a point is a source *or* collector of magnetic flux patterns; **polarity test** = check to see which electrical terminal is positive and which negative; **reverse polarity** = situation where positive and negative terminals have been confused, resulting in the equipment not functioning

Polish notation *see* REVERSE

poll *verb* (of computer) to determine the state of a peripheral in a network; **polled interrupt** = interrupt signal determined by polling devices

◊ **polling** *noun* system of communication between a controlling computer and a number of networked terminals (the computer checks each terminal in turn to see if it is ready to receive *or* transmit data, and takes the required action); **polling characters** = special sequence of characters for each terminal to be polled (when a terminal recognises its sequence, it responds); **polling interval** = period of time between two polling operations; **polling list** = order in which terminals are to be polled by a computer; **polling overhead** = amount of time spent by a computer in calling and checking each terminal in a network

> COMMENT: the polling system differs from other communications systems in that the computer asks the terminals to transmit or receive, not the other way round

polygon *noun* graphics shape with three or more sides

polynomial code *noun* error detection system that uses a set of mathematical rules applied to the message before it is transmitted and again when it is received to reproduce the original message

pop *verb* (instruction to a computer) to read and remove the last piece of data from a stack

◊ **pop-down menu** *or* **pop-up menu** *noun* menu that can be displayed on the screen at any time by pressing the appropriate key, usually displayed over material already on the screen

◊ **pop-up window** *noun* window that can be displayed on the screen at any time on top of anything that is already on the screen

> you can use a mouse to access pop-up menus and a keyboard for word processing
>
> *Byte*

POP = POINT OF PRESENCE telephone access number for a service provider that can be used to connect to the internet via a modem

POP 2 high level programming language used for list processing applications

POP 3 system used to transfer electronic mail messages between a user's computer and a server located at an ISP; *compare with* SMTP

populate *verb* to fill the sockets on a printed circuit board with components; **fully-populated** = (i) all the options or memory is fitted into a computer; (ii) printed

circuit board that has components in all free sockets

port *noun* socket *or* physical connection allowing data transfer between a computer's internal communications channel and another external device; **asynchronous port** = connection to a computer allowing asynchronous data communications; **input port** = circuit *or* connector that allows a computer to receive data from other external devices; **joystick port** = socket and interfacing circuit into which a joystick can be plugged; **output port** = circuit *or* connector that allows a computer to output *or* transmit data to another machine *or* device; **parallel port** = circuit and connector that allows parallel data to be received *or* transmitted; **printer port** = output port of a computer with a standard connector to which a printer is connected to receive character data (either serial *or* parallel); **serial port** = circuit that converts parallel data in a computer to and from a serial form, allowing serial data access; **port selector** = switch that allows the user to choose which peripheral a computer (via its o/p port) is connected to; **port sharing** = device that is placed between one I/O port and a number of peripherals, allowing the computer access to all of them

portable 1 *noun* compact self-contained computer that can be carried around and used either with a battery pack *or* mains power supply **2** *adjective* (any hardware *or* software *or* data files) that can used on a range of different computers; **portable document format (PDF)** = file format used by Adobe Acrobat; **portable operating system interface** *see* POSIX; **portable software** *or* **portable programs** = programs that can be run on several different computer systems

◊ **portability** *noun* extent to which software *or* hardware can be used on several systems

> although portability between machines is there in theory, in practice it just isn't that simple
>
> *Personal Computer World*

portrait *adjective* orientation of a page or piece of paper where the longest edge is vertical

POS = POINT-OF-SALE place in a shop where goods are paid for; **EPOS** = ELECTRONIC POINT-OF-SALE system that uses a computer terminal at a point-of-sale site for electronic fund transfer *or* stock control as well as product pricing, etc.

position 1 *noun* place where something is; *this is the position of that chip on the PCB* **2** *verb* to place something in a special place; *the VDU should not be positioned in front of a window; position this photograph at the top right-hand corner of the page;* **positioning time** = amount of time required to access data stored in a disk drive *or* tape machine, including all mechanical movements of the read head and arm

◊ **positional** *adjective* referring to position; in a certain position

positive *adjective* **(a)** meaning 'yes'; **positive response** = communication signal that indicates correct reception of a message; **positive terminal** = connection to a power supply source that is at a higher electrical potential than ground and supplies current to a component **(b)** (image) which shows objects as they are seen; **positive display** = (screen) where the text and graphics are shown as black on a white background to imitate a printed page; **positive presentation** = screen image which is coloured on a white background *compare* NEGATIVE **(c)** electrical voltage greater than zero; **positive logic** = logic system in which a logical one is represented by a positive voltage level, and a logical zero represented by a zero or negative voltage level

POSIX = PORTABLE OPERATING SYSTEM INTERFACE IEEE standard that defines a set of services provided by an operating system; software that works to the POSIX standard can be easily ported between hardware platforms

post *verb* **(a)** to enter data into a record in a file **2** *prefix* action that occurs after another;

post-editing = editing and modifying text after it has been compiled *or* translated by a machine; **post-formatted** = (text) arranged at printing time rather than on screen; **post mortem** = examination of a computer program *or* piece of hardware after it has failed to try to find out why the failure took place

◊ **postbyte** *noun* in a program instruction, the data byte following the op code that defines the register to be used

◊ **postfix** *noun* word *or* letter written after another; **postfix notation** = mathematical operations written in a logical way, so that the operator appears after the operands, this removes the need for brackets; *normal notation: (x-y) + z, but using postfix notation: xy - z + (often referred to as* **reverse Polish notation)**

◊ **postprocessor** *noun* **(a)** microprocessor that handles semi-processed data from another device **(b)** program that processes data from another program, which has already been processed

post office *noun* central store for the messages for users on a local area network

PostScript standard page description language developed by Adobe Systems; PostScript offers flexible font sizing and positioning; it is most often found in laser printers; *if you do a lot of DTP work, you will benefit from a PostScript printer;* **Display PostScript** = graphics language system that allows a user to see on the screen exactly what would appear on the printer

potential *noun* ability of energy to carry out work (by transformation); **potential difference** = voltage difference between two points in a circuit

power *noun* **(a)** unit of energy in electronics equal to the product of voltage and current, measured in Watts; **automatic power off** = equipment that will switch itself off if it has not been used for a certain time; **power down** = to turn off the electricity supply to a computer or other electronic device; **power dump** = to remove all power from a computer; **power failure** = stoppage of the electrical power supply (for a long *or* very short period of time) which will cause electrical equipment to stop working or malfunction, unless they are battery backed; **power loss** = amount of power lost (in transmission *or* due to connection equipment); **power management** = software built into laptop computers and some newer desktop PCs and monitors that, to save energy, will automatically turn off components that are not being used; **'power off'** = switching off *or* disconnecting an electrical device from its power supply; **'power on'** = indication that a voltage is being supplied to a piece of electrical equipment; **power on self test (POST)** = series of hardware tests that a computer carries out when it is first switched on; **power-on reset** = automatic reset of a CPU to a known initial state immediately after power is applied (some CPUs will not automatically start with clear registers, etc., but might contain garbage); **power pack** = self-contained box that will provide a voltage and current supply for a circuit; **power supply** *or* **power supply unit (PSU)** = electrical circuit that provides certain direct current voltage and current levels from an alternating current source for use in other electrical circuits (a PSU will regulate, smooth and reduce the mains voltage level for use in low power electronic circuits); **uninterruptable power supply (UPS)** = power supply that can continue to provide a regulated supply to equipment even after mains power failure **(b)** mathematical term describing the number of times a number is to be multiplied by itself; *5 to the power 2 is equal to 25* (NOTE: written as small figures in superscript: 10^5: say: 'ten to the power five') **(c)** **power user** = user who needs the latest, fastest model of computer because he runs complex or demanding applications **2** *verb* to provide electrical or mechanical energy to a device; *the monitor is powered from a supply in the main PC;* **power down** = to turn off the power to a device; *once you have shut down the software, you can power off the server;* **power up** = to switch on *or* apply a voltage to a electrical device

PowerBook™ *noun* laptop version of the Macintosh, designed by Apple Corp.

PowerPC™ *noun* high-performance RISC-based processor developed by Motorola

ppm = PAGES PER MINUTE number of finished pages that a printer can print each minute, used as a measure of the speed of a printer

PPP = POINT TO POINT PROTOCOL protocol that supports a network link over an asynchronous (modem) connection and is normally used to provide data transfer between a user's computer and a remote server on the internet using the TCP/IP network protocol

PPQN = PARTS PER QUARTER NOTE most common time format used with standard MIDI sequences

practical extraction and report language (PERL) *noun* interpreted programming language (that is usually used under Unix) used to create CGI scripts that can process forms or carry out functions on a Web server to enhance a web site; *if you want to add a search engine to your web site, you will need to write a Perl program*

pre- *prefix* meaning before; **pre-agreed** = which has been agreed in advance; **pre-allocation** = execution of a process which does not begin until all memory and peripheral requirements are free for use; **pre-fetch** = instructions read and stored in a short temporary queue with a CPU that contains the next few instructions to be processed, increasing the speed of execution of the program

precede *verb* to come before; *instruction which cancels the instruction which precedes it*

precedence *noun* computational rules defining the order in which mathematical operations are calculated (usually multiplications are done first, then divisions, additions, and subtractions last); **operator precedence** = order in which a number of mathematical operations will be carried out

precise *adjective* very exact; *the atomic clock will give the precise time of starting the process*

◊ **precision** *noun* being very accurate; **precision of a number** = number of digits in a number; **double precision** = using two data words to store a number, providing greater precision; **multiple precision** = using more than one byte of data for number storage to increase possible precision; **single precision** = number stored in one word

precompiled code *noun* code that is output from a compiler, ready to be executed

precondition *verb* to condition data before it is processed

predefined *adjective* which has been defined in advance

predicate *noun* function *or* statement used in rule-based programs such as expert systems

we should stick to systems which we know are formally sound, such as predicate logic
Personal Computer World

pre-edit *verb* to change text before it is run through a machine to make sure it is compatible

preemptive multitasking *noun* form of multitasking in which the operating system executes a program for a period of time, then passes control to the next program so preventing any one program using all the processor time

pre-fetch CPU instructions stored in a short temporary queue before being processed, increasing the speed of execution

prefix *noun* **(a)** code *or* instruction *or* character at the beginning of a message *or* instruction **(b)** word attached to the beginning of another word to give it a special meaning

◊ **prefix notation** *noun* mathematical operations written in a logical way, so that the operator appears before the operands, this removes the need for brackets; *normal*

notation: $(x\text{-}y) + z$, but using prefix notation: $-xy + z$

preformatted *adjective* which has been formatted already; *a preformatted disk*

pre-imaging *noun* generating one frame of an animation or video in a memory buffer before it is transferred on-screen for display

preparation *noun* getting something ready; **data preparation** = conversion of data into a machine-readable form (usually by keyboarding) before data entry

preprocessor *noun* **(a)** software that partly processes *or* prepares data before it is compiled *or* translated **(b)** small computer that carries out some initial processing of raw data before passing it to the main computer

◊ **preprocess** *verb* to carry out initial organization and simple processing of data

the C preprocessor is in the first stage of converting a written program into machine instructions
Personal Computer World

preprogrammed *adjective* (chip) which has been programmed in the factory to perform one function

prescan feature of many flat-bed scanners that carry out a quick, low-resolution scan to allow you to re-position the original or mark the area that is to be scanned at a higher resolution

presentation graphics *noun* graphics used to represent business information or data; *the sales for last month looked even better thanks to the use of presentation graphics*

◊ **presentation layer** *noun* sixth ISO/OSI standard network layer that agrees on formats, codes and requests for start and end of a connection; *see also* ISO/OSI, LAYER

◊ **Presentation Manager** *noun* graphical user interface supplied with the OS/2 operating system

◊ **presentation software** *noun* software application that allows a user to create a business presentation with graphs, data, text and images

preset *verb* to set something in advance; *the printer was preset with new page parameters*

press *verb* to push with the fingers; *to end the program press ESCAPE*

prestore *verb* to store data in memory before it is processed

presumptive address *noun* initial address in a program, used as a reference for others

◊ **presumptive instruction** *noun* unmodified program instruction which is processed to obtain the instruction to be executed

pretty good privacy (PGP) *noun* encryption system developed to allow anyone to protect the contents of their email messages from unauthorised readers; this system is often used when sending credit card or payment details over the internet

prevent *verb* to stop something happening; *we have changed the passwords to prevent hackers getting into the database*

◊ **preventative** *or* **preventive** *adjective* which tries to stop something happening; **preventive maintenance** = regular checks on equipment to correct and repair any small faults before they cause a major problem; *we have a preventive maintenance contract for the system*

◊ **prevention** *noun* preventing something happening

preview *verb* to display text *or* graphics on a screen as it will appear when it is printed out

◊ **previewer** *noun* feature that allows a user to see on screen what a page will look like when printed; *the built-in previewer allows the user to check for mistakes*

previous *adjective* which happens earlier; *copy data into the present workspace from the previous file*

◊ **previously** *adverb* happening earlier; *the data is copied onto previously formatted disks*

PRI = PRIMARY RATE INTERFACE high-performance ISDN communications link that supports 23 separate B channels that can transfer 64Kbits/second plus one D channel for signalling and control

primary *adjective* first *or* basic *or* most important; **primary channel** = channel that carries the data transmission between two devices *compare* SECONDARY CHANNEL; **primary key** = unique identifying word that selects one entry from a database; **primary memory** *or* **storage** *or* **main memory** = (i) small fast-access internal memory of a computer system (whose main memory is slower secondary storage) which stores the program currently being used; (ii) main internal memory of a computer system *compare* SECONDARY STORAGE; **primary rate interface (PRI)** = high-performance ISDN communications link that supports 23 separate B channels that can transfer 64Kbits/second plus one D channel for signalling and control; **primary station** = the single station in a data network that can select a path and transmit; the primary station status is temporary and is transferred from one station to another

◊ **primarily** *adverb* mainly

prime 1 *adjective* very important; **prime attribute** = most important feature *or* design of a system **2** *noun* number that can only be divided by itself and by one; *the number seven is a prime*

primer *noun* manual *or* simple instruction book with instructions and examples to show how a new program *or* system operates

primitive *noun* (i) (in programming) basic routine that can be used to create more complex routines; (ii) (in graphics) simple shape (such as circle, square, line, curve) used to create more complex shapes in a graphics program

print 1 *noun* **(a)** characters made in ink on paper; *the print from the daisy-wheel printer* is clearer than that from the line printer; **print control character** = special character sent to a printer that directs it to perform an action or function (such as change font), rather than print a character; **print control code** = special character sent to a printer that directs it to perform an action or function (such as change font), rather than print a character; **print format** = way in which text is arranged when printed out, according to embedded codes, etc., used to set the margins, headers, etc.; **print hammer** = moving arm in a daisy-wheel printer that presses the metal character form onto the printer ribbon leaving a mark on the paper; **print job** = file in a print queue that contains all the characters and printer control codes needed to print one document or page; **print life** = number of characters a component can print before needing to be replaced; *the printhead has a print life of over 400 million characters;* **print modifiers** = codes in a document that cause a printer to change mode, i.e. from bold to italic; **printout** = final printed page; **print pause** = temporarily stopping a printer while printing (to change paper, etc.); **print preview** = function of a software product that lets the user see how a page will appear when printed; **print quality** = the quality of the text or graphics printed; normally measured in dots per inch; *a desktop printer with a resolution of 600dpi provides good print quality;* **print queue** = area of memory that stores print jobs ready to send to the printer when it has finished its current work; **Print Screen key** = special key in the top right-hand side of the keyboard that under DOS will send the characters that are displayed on the screen to the printer; **print server** = computer in a network that is dedicated to managing print queues and printers; **print spooling** = automatic printing of a number of different documents in a queue at the normal speed of the printer, while the computer is doing some other task; **print style** = typeface used on a certain printer or for a certain document **2** *verb* to put letters or figures in ink on paper; *printed agreement; printed regulations; the printer prints at 60 characters per second*

◊ **printed circuit** or **printed circuit board (PCB)** noun flat insulating material that has conducting tracks of metal printed or etched onto its surface which complete a circuit when components are mounted on it

◊ **printer** noun **(a)** device that converts input data in an electrical form into a printed readable form; **barrel printer** = type of printer where characters are located around a rotating barrel; **bi-directional printer** = printer which is able to print characters from left to right or from right to left as the head moves backwards and forwards across the paper; **bubble-jet printer** = printer that produces characters by sending a stream of tiny drops of ink onto the paper; **chain printer** = printer whose characters are located on a continuous belt; **computer printer** = machine which prints information from a computer; **daisy-wheel printer** = printer with characters arranged on interchangeable daisy-wheels; **dot-matrix printer** = printer which forms characters from a series of tiny dots printed close together; **impact printer** = printer that prints text and symbols by striking an inked ribbon onto paper with a metal character; **ink-jet printer** = printer that produces characters by sending a stream of tiny drops of electrically charged ink onto the paper (the movement of the ink drops is controlled by an electric field); **laser printer** = high-resolution printer that uses a laser source to print high quality dot-matrix characters; **line printer** = printer which prints draft-quality information at high speed (typical output is 200 - 3000 lines per minute); **page printer** = printer which composes one page of text, then prints it rapidly; **thermal printer** = printer where the character is formed on thermal paper with a printhead containing a matrix of small heating elements; **printer buffer** = temporary store for character data waiting to be printed (used to free the computer before the printing is completed making the operation faster); **printer control characters** = command characters in a text which transmit printing commands to a printer; **printer control language (PCL)** = standard set of commands, defined by Hewlett Packard, that allow a computer to control a printer; **printer driver** = dedicated software that converts and formats users' commands ready for a printer; **printer emulation** = printer that is able to interpret the standard set of commands used to control another brand of printer; *this printer emulation allows my NEC printer to emulate an Epsom;* **printer-plotter** = high resolution printer that is able to operate as a low resolution plotter; **printer port** = output port of a computer to which a printer is connected to receive character data (either parallel or serial); **printer quality** = standard of printed text from a particular printer (high resolution dot-matrix printers produce near letter-quality, daisy-wheel printers produce letter-quality text); **printer ribbon** = roll of inked material which passes between a printhead and the paper

◊ **printhead** *noun* (i) row of needles in a dot-matrix printer that produce characters as a series of dots; (ii) metal form of a character that is pressed onto an inked ribbon to print the character on paper

◊ **printing** *noun* action of printing

◊ **Print Manager** software utility that is part of Microsoft Windows and is used to manage print queues

◊ **print out** *verb* to print information stored in a computer with a printer

◊ **printout** *noun* final printed page; **computer printout** = printed copy of information from a computer; *the sales director asked for a printout of the agents' commissions*

◊ **printwheel** *noun* daisy-wheel *or* the wheel made up of a number of arms, with a character shape at the end of each arm, used in a daisy-wheel printer

prior **1** *adjective* happening before **2** *adverb;* **prior to** = before; *the password has to be keyed in prior to accessing the system*

◊ **priority** *noun* importance of a device *or* software routine in a computer system; *the operating system has priority over the application when disk space is allocated; the disk drive is more important than the printer, so it has a higher priority;* **job priority** = importance of a job compared to others; **priority interrupt** = signal to a computer that takes precedence over any

other task *see* *also* INTERRUPT, NON-MASKABLE INTERRUPT; **priority interrupt table** = list of peripherals and their priority when they send an interrupt signal (used instead of a hardware priority scheduler); **priority sequence** = the order in which various devices that have sent an interrupt signal are processed, according to their importance or urgency (a disk drive will usually come before a printer in a priority sequence); **priority scheduler** = system that organizes tasks into correct processing priority (to improve performance)

privacy *noun* the right of an individual to limit the extent of and control the access to the data that is stored about him; **privacy of data** = rule that data is secret and must not be accessed by users who have not been authorized; **privacy of information** = rule that unauthorized users cannot obtain data about private individuals from databases *or* that each individual has the right to know what information is being held about him *or* her on a database

private *adjective* belonging to an individual *or* to a company, not to the public; **private address space** = memory address range that is reserved for a single user, not for public access; **private branch exchange (PBX)** = small telephone exchange located within a company that allows the people in the company to dial each other or to dial out to an external telephone number

privilege *noun* status of a user referring to the type of program he can run and the resources he can use; *the systems manager has a privileged status so he can access any file on the system;* **privileged account** = computer account that allows special programs *or* access to sensitive system data; *the system manager can access anyone else's account from his privileged account;* **privileged instructions** = computer commands which can only be executed via a privileged account, such as delete another account *or* set up a new user *or* examine passwords; **privileged mode** = mode of an Intel 80286 processor that is in protected mode and allows a program to modify vital parts of the operating environment

PRN = PRINTER acronym used in MS-DOS to represent the standard printer port

problem *noun* **(a)** question to which it is difficult to find an answer; **to solve a problem** = to find an answer to a problem; **problem definition** = the clear explanation, in logical steps, of a problem that is to be solved; **problem-orientated language (POL)** = high-level programming language that allows certain problems to be expressed easily **(b)** malfunction *or* fault with hardware or software; **problem diagnosis** = finding the cause and method of repairing a fault *or* error

procedure *noun* **(a)** small section of computer instruction code that provides a frequently used function and can be called upon from a main program; *this procedure sorts all the files into alphabetical order, you can call it from the main program by the instruction SORT see also* SUBROUTINE **(b)** method *or* route used when solving a problem; *you should use this procedure to retrieve lost files; the procedure is given in the manual;* **procedure-orientated language** = high-level programming language that allows procedures to be programmed easily

◊ **procedural** *adjective* using a procedure (to solve a problem); **procedural language** = high-level programming language in which the programmer enters the actions required to achieve the result wanted

proceed *verb* to move forward; *after spellchecking the text, you can proceed to the printing stage*

process 1 *noun* a number of tasks that must be carried out to achieve a goal; *the process of setting up the computer takes a long time; there are five stages in the process;* **process bound** = program that spends more time executing instructions and using the CPU than in I/O operations; **process chart** = diagram that shows each step of the computer procedures needed in a system; **process control** = automatic control of a process by a computer; **process control computer** = dedicated computer that controls and manages a process; **process control system** = complete input, output modules, a CPU with memory and a program (usually stored in ROM) and control and feedback devices (such as A/D and D/A converters) that completely monitors, manages and regulates a process **2** *verb* to carry out a number of tasks to produce a result (such as sorting data *or* finding the solution to a problem); *we processed the new data; processing all the information will take a long time*

◊ **processing** *noun* sorting of information; using a computer to solve a problem *or* organize data; *page processing time depends on the complexity of a given page; see also* CPU; **batch processing** = computer system, where information is collected into batches before being loaded into the computer; **data processing** *or* **information processing** = selecting and examining data in a computer to produce information in a special form; **image processing** = analysis of information contained in an image (usually by electronic means or by using a computer to provide the analysis or for recognition of objects in the image); **immediate processing** = processing data when it appears, rather than waiting for a certain clock pulse or time; **off-line processing** = processing by devices not under the control of a central computer; **on-line processing** = processing by devices connected to and under the control of the central computer (the user remains in contact with the central computer while processing); **query processing** = processing of queries, either by extracting information from a database *or* translating query commands from a query language; **real-time processing** = processing operations that take a time of the same order of magnitude as the problem to be solved; **serial processing** = executing one instruction at a time *compare* PARALLEL PROCESSING; **word-processing** *or* **text processing** = working with words, using a computer to produce, check and change texts, reports, letters, etc.

COMMENT: the central processing unit is a hardware device that allows a computer to manipulate and modify

> data; a compiler is a software language processor that translates data and instructions in one language into another form

processor *noun* hardware *or* software device that is able to manipulate *or* modify data according to instructions; **array processor** = computer that can act upon several arrays of data simultaneously for very fast mathematical applications; **associative processor** = processor that uses associative storage; **attached processor** = separate microprocessor in a system that performs certain functions under the control of a central processor; **auxiliary processor** = extra, specialized processor, such as an array or numerical processor, that can work with a main processor to improve performance; **back-end processor** = special purpose auxiliary processor; **bit-slice processor** = construction of a large word size CPU by joining a number of smaller word size blocks; **distributed processor** = using many small computers at different workstations instead of one central computer; **front-end processor (FEP)** = processor placed between an input source and the central computer, whose function is to preprocess received data to reduce the main computer's workload; **input/output processor** = processor that handles data communications, including DMA and error correcting functions; **language processor** = program that translates from one language to machine code (there are three type of translator: (i) assembler; (ii) compiler; (iii) interpreter); **network processor** = signal multiplexer controlled by a microprocessor in a network; **order code processor** = (in a multiprocessor system) a processor which decodes and performs the arithmetic and logical operations according to the program code; **processor controlled keying** = data entry by an operator which is prompted and controlled by a computer; **processor interrupt** = to send an interrupt signal to a processor requesting attention, that will usually cause it to stop what it is doing and attend to the calling device; **processor status word (PSW)** = word which contains a number of status bits, such as carry flag, zero flag and overflow flag; **processor-limited** = (operation *or* execution time) that is set by the speed of the processor rather than a peripheral; **dual processor** = computer system with two processors for faster program execution; **image processor** = electronic *or* computer system used for image processing; **word-processor** = small computer which is used for working with words, to produce texts, reports, letters, etc.

> each chip will contain 128 processors and one million transistors
>
> *Computer News*

produce *verb* to make *or* manufacture

◊ **producer** *noun* person *or* company *or* country which manufactures; *country which is a producer of high quality computer equipment; the company is a major magnetic tape producer*

◊ **producing** *adjective* which produces; **producing capacity** = capacity to produce

product *noun* **(a)** item which is made *or* manufactured; **basic product** = main product made from a raw material; **end product** *or* **final product** *or* **finished product** = product made at the end of a production process **(b)** manufactured item for sale; **product engineer** = engineer in charge of the equipment for making a product; **product line** *or* **product range** = series of different products made by the same company, which form a group (such as printers in different models *or* different colours, etc.) **(c)** result after multiplication

◊ **production** *noun* making *or* manufacturing of goods for sale; *production will probably be held up by industrial action; we are hoping to speed up production by installing new machinery;* **batch production** = production in batches; **mass production** = manufacturing of large quantities of goods; *mass production of monitors or of calculators;* **rate of production** *or* **production rate** = speed at which items are made; **production control** = control of the manufacturing of a product (using computers); **production level video (PLV)** = highest-quality video compression algorithm used with DVI full-motion video sequences

◊ **productive** *adjective* during *or* in which something useful is produced; **productive time** = period of time during which a computer can run error-free tasks

profile *noun* feature of Windows 95 that stores the settings for different users on one PC

PROFS electronic mail system developed by IBM that runs on mainframe computers

program 1 *noun* complete set of instructions which direct a computer to carry out a particular task; **assembly program** = number of assembly code instructions which perform a task; **background program** = computer program with a very low priority; **blue-ribbon program** = perfect program that runs first time without errors; **control program/monitor** *or* **control program for microcomputers (CP/M)** = popular operating system for microcomputers; **diagnostic program** = software that helps find faults in a computer system; **executive program** = master program in a computer system that controls the execution of other programs; **foreground program** = high priority program in a multitasking system; **hardwired program** = computer program built into the hardware (and which cannot be changed); **job control program** = short program of job control instructions loaded before a particular application is run, that sets up the system as required by the application; **library program** = (i) number of specially written *or* relevant software routines, which a user can insert into his own program, saving time and effort; (ii) group of functions which a computer needs to refer to often, but which are not stored in main memory; **linear program** = computer program that contains no loops *or* branches; **user program** = program written by a user (often in a high-level language); **program address counter** = register in a CPU that contains the location of the next instruction to be processed; **program branch** = one or more paths that can be followed after a conditional statement; **program cards** = punched cards that contain the instructions that make up a

program; **program coding sheet** = specially preprinted form on which computer instructions can be written, simplifying program writing; **program compatibility** = ability of two pieces of software to function correctly together; **program compilation** = translation of an encoded source program into machine code; **program counter (PC)** *or* **instruction address register (IAR)** = register in a CPU that contains the location of the next instruction to be processed; *see also* INSTRUCTION ADDRESS REGISTER; SEQUENCE CONTROL REGISTER; **program crash** = unexpected failure of a program due to a programming error *or* a hardware fault; *I forgot to insert an important instruction which caused a program to crash, erasing all the files on the disk!;* **program design language (PDL)** = programming language used to design the structure of a program; **program development** = all the operations involved in creating a computer program from first ideas to initial writing, debugging and the final product; **program development system** = all the hardware and software needed for program development on a system; **program documentation** = set of instruction notes, examples and tips on how to use a program *see also* MANUAL; **program editor** = software that allows the user to alter, delete and add instructions to a program file; **program execution** = instructing a processor to execute in sequence the instructions in a program; **program file** = file containing a program rather than data; **program flowchart** = diagram that graphically describes the various steps in a program; **program generator** = software that allows users to write complex programs using a few simple instructions; **program group** = (in Windows 3.1x) window that contains icons relating to a particular subject or program; **program icon** = (in a GUI) icon that represents an executable program file; *to run the program, double-click on the program icon;* **program information file (PIF)** = (in Microsoft Windows) file that contains the environment settings for a particular program; **program instruction** = single word *or* expression that represents one operation (in a high level program each program instruction can consist of a number of low level machine code instructions); **program item** = (in a GUI) an icon that represents a program; **program library** = collection of useful procedures and programs which can be used for various purposes and included into new software; **program line** = one row of commands *or* arguments in a computer program; **program line number** = number that refers to a line of program code in a computer program; **program listing** = list of the set of instructions that make up a program (program listings are displayed in an ordered manner, BASIC listings by line number, assembly listings by memory location; they do not necessarily represent the order in which the program will be executed, since there could be jumps *or* subroutines); **program maintenance** = keeping a program free of errors and up to date; **program name** = identification name for a stored program file; **program origin** = address at which the first instruction of a program is stored; **program overlay** = portion of a big program that is loaded from disk into memory when it is needed; **program register** = register in a CPU that contains an instruction during decoding and execution operations; **program relocation** = moving a stored program from one area of memory to another; **program report generator** = software that allows users to create reports from files, databases and other stored data; **program run** = executing (in correct order) the instructions in a program; **program segment** = section of a main program that can be executed in its own right, without the rest of the main program being required; **program specification** = document that contains details on all the functions and abilities of a computer program; **program stack** = section of memory reserved for storing temporary system *or* program data; **program statement** = high level program instruction that is made up of a number of machine code instructions; **program step** = one operation within a program, usually a single instruction; **program storage** = section of main memory in which programs (rather than operating system or data) can be stored; **program structure** = the way in which sections of program code are interlinked and operate;

program testing = testing a new program with test data to ensure that it functions correctly; **program verification** = a number of tests and checks performed to ensure that a program functions correctly **2** *verb* to write *or* prepare a set of instructions which direct a computer to perform a certain task; **programmed halt** = instruction within a program that when executed, halts the processor (to restart the CPU a reset action is required); **programmed learning** = using educational software which allows a learner to follow a course of instruction

◊ **programmable 1** *adjective* (device) that can accept and store instructions then execute them; **programmable calculator** = small calculator which can hold certain basic mathematical calculating programs; **programmable interrupt controller** = circuit *or* chip which can be programmed to ignore certain interrupts, accept only high priority interrupts and select the priority of interrupts; **programmable key** = special key on a computer terminal keyboard that can be programmed with various functions *or* characters; **programmable logic array (PLA)** *or* **programmable logic device (PLD)** = integrated circuit that can be permanently programmed to perform logic operations on data using a matrix of links between input and output pins; **programmable memory (PROM)** = electronic device in which data can be stored *see also* EAROM; EEPROM; EPROM; ROM; **programmable read only memory (PROM)** = memory integrated circuit that can be programmed with data by a user (some PROMs provide permanent storage, others such as EPROMs are erasable) **2** *noun;* **hand-held programmable** = very small computer, which can be held in the hand, used for inputting information when a larger terminal is not available (as by a salesman on a call)

---

each of the 16 programmable
function keys has two modes -
normal and shift - giving 32
possible functions

Micro Decision

◊ **Program Manager** (in Windows 3.x) main part of Windows that the user sees

programmer *noun* **(a)** person who is capable of designing and writing a working program; *the programmer is still working on the new software;* **applications programmer** = programmer who writes applications software; **systems programmer** = programmer specializes in writing systems software **(b)** device that allows data to be written into a programmable read only memory

programming *noun* **(a)** writing programs for computers; **programming in logic** = PROLOG; **programming language** = software that allows a user to write a series of instructions to define a particular task, which will then be translated to a form that is understood by the computer; **programming standards** = rules to which programs must conform to produce compatible code **(b)** writing data into a PROM device

> COMMENT: programming languages are grouped into different levels: the high-level languages such as BASIC and PASCAL are easy to understand and use, but offer slow execution time since each instruction is made up of a number of machine code instructions; low-level languages such as assembler are more complex to read and program in but offer faster execution time

Programs menu sub-menu that is accessed from the Start button in Windows 95

> we've included some useful program tools to make your job easier. Like the symbolic debugger
>
> *Personal Computer World*

project 1 *noun* planned task; *his latest project is computerizing the sales team; the design project was entirely worked out on computer; CAD is essential for accurate project design* **2** *verb* to forecast future figures from a set of data; *the projected sales of the new PC*

◊ **projection** *noun* forecast of a situation from a set of data; *the projection indicates that sales will increase*

PROLOG = PROGRAMMING IN LOGIC high-level programming language

using logical operations for artificial intelligence and data retrieval applications

PROM **(a)** = PROGRAMMABLE READ-ONLY MEMORY read-only memory which can be programmed by the user (as opposed to ROM, which is programmed by the manufacturer); **PROM blaster** *or* **burner** *or* **programmer** = electronic device used to program a PROM; *see also* EPROM **(b)** = PROGRAMMABLE MEMORY electronic memory in which data can be stored

prompt *noun* message *or* character displayed to remind the user that an input is expected; *the prompt READY indicates that the system is available to receive instructions;* **command prompt** = symbol displayed to indicate a command is expected; *MS-DOS normally displays the command prompt C:\ to indicate that it is ready to process instructions typed in by a user*

propagate *verb* to travel *or* spread; **propagated error** = one error in a process that has affected later operations; **propagating error** = an error that occurs in one place *or* operation and affects another operation *or* process

◊ **propagation delay** *noun* (i) time taken for an output to appear in a logic gate after the input is applied; (ii) time taken for a data bit to travel over a network from the source to the destination

properties *noun* (in Windows 95) attributes of a file or object; *see* ATTRIBUTES

proportion *noun* size of something as compared to others

◊ **proportional spacing** *noun* printing system where each letter takes a space proportional to the character width ('i' taking less space than 'm'); *compare* MONOSPACING

proprietary file format *noun* method of storing data devised by a company for its products and incompatible with other products; *you cannot read this spreadsheet file because my software saves it in a proprietary file format*

protect *verb* to stop something being damaged; **protected location** = memory location that cannot be altered *or* cannot be accessed without authorization; **protected mode** = operating mode of an Intel processor (the 80286 or higher) that supports multitasking, virtual memory, and data security *compare* REAL MODE; **protected storage** = section of memory that cannot be altered; **copy protect** = switch used to prevent copies of a disk being made; *all the disks are copy protected;* **crash protected** = (disk) which uses a head protection *or* data corruption protection system; *if the disk is crash protected, you will never lose your work*

◊ **protection** *noun* action of protecting; **protection key** = signal checked to see if a program can access a section of memory; **protection master** = spare copy of a master film *or* tape; **copy protection** = preventing copies being made; *a hard disk may crash because of faulty copy protection; the new product will come without copy protection;* **data protection** = making sure that data is not copied by an unauthorized user; **Data Protection Act** = act which prevents confidential data about people being copied without their permission (also every organization that keeps information subject to the act on a computer, must protect it adequately)

◊ **protective** *adjective* which protects; *the disks are housed in hard protective cases*

protocol *noun* pre-agreed signals, codes and rules to be used for data exchange between systems; **protocol standards** = standards laid down to allow data exchange between any computer system conforming to the standard

> there is a very simple protocol
> that would exclude hackers from
> computer networks using the
> telephone system
>
> *Practical Computing*

prototype *noun* first working model of a device *or* program, which is then tested and adapted to improve it

◊ **prototyping** *noun* making a prototype

provider *noun;* **information provider (ip)** = company *or* user that provides an information source for use in a videotext system (such as the company providing weather information *or* stock exchange reports)

proxy server *noun* computer that stores copies of files and data normally held on a slow server and so allows users to access files and data quickly; proxy servers are often used as a firewall between an intranet in a company and the public internet

◊ **proxy agent** *noun* software that can translate network management commands to allow management software to control a device that uses a different protocol

PrtSc = PRINT SCREEN (on an IBM PC keyboard) key that sends the contents of the current screen to the printer

pS = PICOSECOND

PS/2 range of IBM PC computers that are software compatible with the original IBM PC, but use a different MCA expansion bus; *see also* MCA

pseudo- *prefix* meaning similar to something, but not genuine

◊ **pseudo-code** *noun* English sentence structures, used to describe program instructions which are translated at a later date into machine code

◊ **pseudo-digital** *adjective* (modulated analog signals) produced by a modem and transmitted over telephone lines

◊ **pseudo-instruction** *noun* label (in an assembly language program) that represents a number of instructions

◊ **pseudo-operation** *noun* command in an assembler program that controls the assembler rather than producing machine code

◊ **pseudo-random** *noun* generated sequence that appears random but is repeated over a long period; **pseudo-random number generator** = hardware *or* software that produces pseudo-random numbers; **pseudo-static** = dynamic RAM memory chips that contain circuitry to refresh the contents and so have the same appearance as a static RAM component

PSN = PACKET SWITCHED NETWORK

PSS = PACKET SWITCHING SYSTEM

PSU = POWER SUPPLY UNIT electrical circuit that provides certain direct current voltage and current levels from an alternating current source to other electrical circuits

COMMENT: a PSU will regulate, smooth and step down a higher voltage supply for use in small electronic equipment

PSW = PROCESSOR STATUS WORD

PTR = PAPER TAPE READER

public *adjective* open to anyone to use; made for the use of everyone; **public data network (PDN)** = data transmission service for the public, such as the main telephone system in a country; **public domain (PD)** = documents *or* text *or* program that has no copyright and can be copied by anyone *compare* SHAREWARE; **public key cipher system** = cipher that uses a public key to encrypt messages and a secret key to decrypt them (conventional cipher systems use one secret key to encrypt and decrypt messages); *see also* CIPHER, KEY; **public key encryption** = method of encrypting data that uses one key to encrypt the data and another different key to decrypt the data

publish *verb* to produce and sell software; **desktop publishing (DTP)** = design, layout and printing of documents using special software, a small computer and a printer; **electronic publishing** = (i) use of desktop publishing packages and laser printers to produce printed matter; (ii) using computers to write and display information (such as viewdata)

pull *verb* to remove data from a stack *compare* PUSH

pull-down menu *noun* set of options that are displayed below the relevant entry on a menu-bar; *the pull-down menu is viewed by*

clicking on the menu bar at the top of the screen compare POP-UP MENU

pull up *verb;* **to pull up a line** = to connect *or* set a line to a voltage level; *pull up the input line to a logic one by connecting it to 5 volts*

the gated inputs lower the standby current and also eliminate the need for input pull-up or pull-down resistors
Electronics & Power

pulse 1 *noun* short period of a voltage level; **pulse-code modulation (PCM)** = way of storing sounds in an accurate, compact format that is used by high-end sound cards; **pulse stream** *or* **train** = continuous series of similar pulses **2** *verb* to apply a short-duration voltage level to a circuit; *we pulsed the input but it still would not work*

COMMENT: electric pulse can be used to transmit information, as the binary digits 0 and 1 correspond to 'no pulse' and 'pulse' (the voltage level used to distinguish the binary digits 0 and 1, is often zero and 5 or 12 volts, with the pulse width depending on transmission rate)

◊ **pulse-dialling** *noun* telephone dialling that dials a telephone number by sending a series of pulses along the line; *pulse-dialling takes longer to dial than the newer tone-dialling system*

punch 1 *noun* device for making holes in punched cards **2** *verb* to make a hole; **punch** *or* **punched card** = small piece of card which contains holes representing various instructions *or* data; **punched card reader** = device which transforms data on a punched card to a form that can be recognized by a computer; **punched tag** = card attached to a product in a shop, with punched holes containing data about the product; **punched (paper) tape** = strip of paper tape that contains holes to represent data

◊ **punch-down block** *noun* device ·used in a local area network to connect UTP cable

punctuation mark *noun* printing symbol, which cannot be spoken, but which helps to understand the text

> COMMENT: the main punctuation marks are the question mark and exclamation mark; inverted commas (which show the type of text being written); the comma, full stop, colon and semicolon (which show how the words are broken up into sequences); the apostrophe (which shows that a letter or word is missing); the dash and hyphen and brackets (which separate or link words)

pure *adjective* clean *or* not mixed with other things; **pure code** = code that does not modify itself during execution

purge *verb* to remove unnecessary *or* out of date data from a file or disk; *each month, I purge the disk of all the old email messages*

push *verb* to press something *or* to move something by pressing on it; **push instruction** *or* **operation** = computer instruction that stores data on a LIFO list *or* stack

◊ **pushbutton** *adjective* which works by pressing on a button

◊ **push-down list** *or* **stack** *noun* temporary storage queue system where the last item added is at the top of the list; *see also* LIFO

◊ **push-up list** *or* **stack** *noun* temporary storage queue system where the last item added is at the bottom of the list; *see also* FIFO

put *verb* to push *or* place data onto a stack

Qq

QAM = QUADRATURE AMPLITUDE MODULATION

QBE = QUERY BY EXAMPLE simple language used to retrieve information from a database management system by, normally, entering a query with known values, which is then matched with the database and used to retrieve the correct data; *in most QBE databases, the query form looks like the record format in the database - retrieving data is as easy as filling in a form*

Q Channel *noun* (in a CD audio disc) one of the eight information channels that holds data indentifying the track and the absolute playing time

QISAM = QUEUED INDEXED SEQUENTIAL ACCESS METHOD indexed sequential file that is read item by item into a buffer

QL = QUERY LANGUAGE

QOS = QUALITY OF SERVICE

QSAM = QUEUED SEQUENTIAL ACCESS METHOD queue of blocks waiting to be processed, which are retrieved using a sequential access method

quad *noun* meaning four times; **quad density** = four bits of data stored in the usual place of one; **quadbit** = four bits that are used by modems to increase transmission rates when using QAM; **quad-speed drive** = CD-ROM drive that spins the disc at four times the speed of a single-speed drive, providing higher data throughput of 600Kbps and shorter seek times

◊ **quadding** *noun* insertion of spaces into text to fill out a line

in this case, interfacing is done by a single quad-wide adapter

Minicomputer News

quadr- *prefix* meaning four

◊ **quadruplex** *noun* four signals combined into a single one

quadrature amplitude modulation (QAM)
noun data encoding method used by high-speed modems (transmitting at rates above 2,400bps); QAM combines amplitude modulation and phase modulation to increase the data transmission rate

◊ **quadrature encoding** *noun* system used to determine the direction in which a mouse is being moved; in a mechanical mouse, two sensors send signals that describe its horizontal and vertical movements - these signals are transmitted using quadrature encoding

quality *noun* what something is like *or* how good or bad something is; *there is a market for good quality secondhand computers;* **high quality** *or* **top quality** = very best quality; *the store specializes in high quality imported items;* **printer quality** = standard of printed text from a particular printer (high-resolution dot-matrix printers produce near-letter quality, daisy-wheel printers produce letter-quality text) *see also* LETTER, NEAR-LETTER, DRAFT; **quality control** = checking that the quality of a product is good; **quality of service** = phrase used to refer to a network that can transfer information without error or fault; if you want to transfer video or multimedia over a network you need to be sure that the data will arrive correctly, in a certain period of time and in the correct order (otherwise the video sequence will be distorted)

the computer line printer operates at 120cps in draft quality mode and 30cps in near letter-quality mode
Minicomputer News

quantify *verb;* **to quantify the effect of something** = to show the effect of something in figures; *it is impossible to quantify the effect of the new computer system on our production*

◊ **quantifiable** *adjective* which can be quantified; *the effect of the change in the pricing structure is not quantifiable*

◊ **quantifier** *noun* sign *or* symbol which indicates the quantity *or* range of a predicate

quantity *noun* (a) amount *or* number of items; *a small quantity of illegal copies of the program have been imported; he bought a large quantity of spare parts* (b) large amount; *the company offers a discount for quantity purchases*

quantize *verb* to convert an analog signal into a numerical representation; *the input signal is quantized by an analog to digital converter;* **quantizing noise** = noise on a signal due to inaccuracies in the quantizing process

◊ **quantizer** *noun* device used to convert an analog input signal to a numerical form, that can be processed by a computer

◊ **quantization** *noun* conversion of an analog signal to a numerical representation; **quantization error** = error in converting an analog signal into a numerical form due to limited accuracy *or* rapidly changing signal; *see also* **A/D**

quantum *noun* (in communications) a packet of data that is the result of a signal being quantized

quartz (crystal) clock *noun* small slice of quartz crystal which vibrates at a certain frequency when an electrical voltage is supplied, used as a very accurate clock signal for computers and other high precision timing applications

quasi- *prefix* almost *or* which seems like; **quasi-instruction** = label (in an assembly program) which represents a number of instructions

quaternary *adjective* referring to four bits *or* levels *or* objects

query 1 *noun* question; **query by example (QBE)** = simple language used to retrieve information from a database management system by, normally, entering a query with known values, which is then matched with the database and used to retrieve the correct data; **query facility** = program (usually a database *or* retrieval system) which allows the user to ask questions and receive answers *or* access certain information according to the query; **query language (QL)** = language in a database management system, which allows a database to be searched and queried easily; *see also* **SQL**; **query message** = message sent to an object to find out the value of one of the object's properties, such as its name, active state or position; **query processing** = processing of queries, either by extracting information from a database *or* by translating query commands from a query language; **query window** = (i) window that appears when an error has occurred, asking the user what action they would like to take; (ii) window that is displayed with fields a user can fill in to search a database **2** *verb* to ask a question about something *or* to suggest that something may be wrong

The Query By Example features now found on some database packages, Foxpro in particular, are easy to use and very powerful.
Computing

question mark *noun* the character (?) which is often used as a wildcard to indicate that any single character in the position will produce a match; *to find all the letters, use the command DIR LETTER?.DOC which will list LETTER1.DOC, LETTER2.DOC and LETTER3.DOC; see also* **ASTERISK**

queue 1 *noun* (a) line of people waiting one behind the other; *to form a queue or to join a queue* (b) list of data *or* tasks that are waiting to be processed; series of documents (such as orders, application forms) which are dealt with in order; **channel queue** = (i) queue of requests to use a channel; (ii) queue of data that has yet to be sent over a channel; **file queue** = number of files temporarily stored in order before being processed; *output devices such as laser printers are connected on-line with an automatic file queue;* **job queue** = number of tasks arranged in order waiting to be processed in a batch system; **his order went to the end of the queue** = his order was dealt with last; **queue discipline** = method used as the queue structure, either LIFO or FIFO; **queue management** *or* **queue manager** = software which orders tasks to be processed; *this is a new software spooler with a built-in queue management* **2** *verb* to add more data *or* tasks to the end of a queue; **queued access method** = programming method which minimises input/output delays by ensuring that data transferred between software and an I/O device is synchronised with the I/O device; **queued indexed sequential access method (QISAM)** = indexed sequential file that is read item by item into a buffer; **queued sequential access method (QSAM)** = queue of blocks waiting to be processed, which are retrieved using a sequential access method; **queuing time** = period of time messages have to wait before they can be processed *or* transmitted

---

Citibank Global Asset Management had two weeks of parallel running, which threw out some problems. For example, you can have 120 elements in a System/36 job queue, but you can only have 30 elements in a Baby/36 environment.

Computing

---

quick *adjective* fast *or* not taking any time; *the company made a quick recovery; he is looking for a quick return on his investment; we are hoping for a quick sale*

◊ **QuickDraw** (in an Apple Macintosh) graphics routines built into the Macintosh's operating system that control displayed text and images

◊ **quick format** *noun* command (in DOS on a PC) that does not delete all the existing data on a floppy disk during a format process; it is faster than a full format and allows data to be recovered

◊ **quickly** *adverb* without taking much time

◊ **quicksort** *noun* very rapid file sorting and ordering method

◊ **QuickTime™** (in an Apple Macintosh and Windows) graphics routines and file format that allow allow animation, video and images to be stored displayed

quiescent *adjective* state of a process *or* circuit *or* device when no input signal is applied

quiet *adjective* not making very much noise; *laser printers are much quieter than dot-matrix*

quintet *noun* byte made up of five bits

quit *verb* to leave a system *or* a program; *do not forget to save your text before you quit the system*

quotation *noun* part of a text borrowed from another text

◊ **quotation marks** *noun* inverted commas, signs printed at the beginning and end of text to show that it has been quoted from another source

quote 1 *verb* to repeat words used by someone else; to repeat a reference number **2** *noun* (a) quotation (b); **quotes** = quotation marks *or* inverted commas; **single quotes** = single inverted commas; **double quotes** = double inverted commas; *the name of the company should be put in double quotes*

quotient *noun* result of one number divided by another

COMMENT: when two numbers are divided, the answer is made up of a quotient and a remainder (the fractional part), 16 divided by 4 is equal to a quotient of 4 and zero remainder, 16 divided by 5 is equal to a quotient of 3 and a remainder of 1

quoting *noun* feature of many electronic mail applications that allows you to reply to a message and include the text of the original message

QWERTY *noun;* **QWERTY keyboard =** English language keyboard for a typewriter *or* computer, where the top line of letters are Q-W-E-R-T-Y; *the computer has a normal QWERTY keyboard; see also* AZERTY

the keyboard does not have a QWERTY layout but is easy to use

Micro Decision

Rr

R & D = RESEARCH AND DEVELOPMENT; **R & D department** = department in a company that investigates new products, discoveries and techniques

race *noun* error condition in a digital circuit, in which the state *or* output of the circuit is very dependent on the exact timing between the input signals (faulty output is due to unequal propagation delays on the separate input signals at a gate)

rack *noun* metal supporting frame for electronic circuit boards and peripheral devices such as disk drives; **rack mounted** = system consisting of removable circuit boards in a supporting frame

radial transfer *noun* data transfer between two peripherals *or* programs that are on different layers of a structured system (such as an ISO/OSI system)

radio button *noun* (in a GUI) circle displayed beside an option that, when selected, has a dark centre; radio buttons are a method of selecting one of a number of options, only one radio button can be selected at one time (select another and the first is deselected)

◊ **radio frequency (RF)** *noun* electromagnetic spectrum that lies between the frequency range 10KHz and 3000GHz

radix *noun* the value of the base of the number system being used; *the hexadecimal number has a radix of 16;* **radix complement** *see* TEN'S, TWO'S COMPLEMENT; **radix notation** = numbers represented to a certain radix; *see also* BASE; **radix point** = dot which indicates the division between a whole unit and its fractional parts

ragged *adjective* not straight *or* with an uneven edge; **ragged left** = printed text with a flush right-hand margin and uneven left-hand margin; **ragged right** = printed text with a flush left-hand margin and uneven right-hand margin; **ragged text** = unjustified text, text with a ragged right margin

RAID = REDUNDANT ARRAY of INEXPENSIVE DISKS fast, fault tolerant disk drive system that uses multiple drives which would, typically, each store one byte of a word of data, so allowing the data to be saved faster; one drive in the array would also store a check byte for error detection

A Japanese investor group led by system distributor Technography has pumped $4.2 million (#2.8 million) into US disk manufacturer Storage Computer to help with the development costs of RAID 7 hard disk technology.

Computing

RAM = RANDOM ACCESS MEMORY memory that allows access to any location in any order, without having to access the rest first *compare* SEQUENTIAL ACCESS MEMORY; **partial RAM** = RAM chip in which only a certain area of the chip functions correctly, usually in newly released chips (partial RAM's can be used by employing more than one to make up the capacity of one fully functional chip); **RAM cache** = section of high-speed RAM that is used to buffer data transfers between the (faster) processor and a (slower) disk drive; *see also* CACHE, L1 CACHE, L2 CACHE; **RAM card** = expansion card which contains RAM chips; it is plugged into a computer *or* device to increase the main memory capacity;

RAM cartridge = plug-in device that contains RAM chips and increases a computer *or* device's memory; *you can increase the printer's memory by plugging in another RAM cartridge;* **RAM chip** = chip which stores data, allowing random access; **RAMDAC** = RANDOM ACCESS DIGITAL TO ANALOG CONVERTER electronic component on a video graphics adapter that converts the digital colour signals into electrical signals that are sent to the monitor; **RAM disk** = section of RAM that is made to look like and behave as a high-speed disk drive (using special software); **RAM loader** = routine that will transfer a program from external backing store into RAM; **RAM refresh** = signals used to update the contents of dynamic RAM chips every few thousandths of a second, involving reading and rewriting the contents; it is needed to retain data; **RAM refresh rate** = number of times every second that the data in a dynamic RAM chip has to be read and rewritten; **RAM resident program** *or* **TSR** = program that loads itself into main memory and carries out a function when activated; *when you hit Ctrl-F5, you will activate the RAM resident program and it will display your day's diary;* **dynamic RAM** = most common RAM ICs, which use capacitative charge to retain data but which must be refreshed (read from and rewritten to) every few thousandths of a second; **self-refreshing RAM** = dynamic RAM chip that has built-in circuitry to generate refresh signals, allowing data to be retained when the power is off by using a battery; **static RAM** = RAM ICs that do not have to be refreshed but cannot store as much data per chip as dynamic RAM; *see also* CHIP, ROM (NOTE: there is no plural for RAM, and it often has no article: **16Mb of RAM; the file is stored in RAM)**

COMMENT: dynamic RAM which uses a capacitor to store a bit of data (as a charge) needs to have each location refreshed from time to time to retain the data, but is very fast and can contain more data per unit area than static RAM which uses a latch to store the state of a bit, and has the advantage of not requiring to be refreshed to retain its

data, and will keep data for as long as power is supplied

The HP Enterprise Desktops have hard-disk capacities of between 260Mb and 1Gb, with RAM ranging from 16Mb up to 128Mb.
Computing

in addition the board features 512K of video RAM, expandable up to a massive 1MB
PC Business World

fast memory is RAM that does not have to share bus access with the chip that manages the video display
Byte

random *adjective* (event) which cannot be anticipated; **random process** *or* **direct access** = system whose output cannot be related to its input *or* internal structure; *see also* PSEUDO-RANDOM

◊ **random access** *noun* ability to access immediately memory locations in any order; *disk drives are random access, magnetic tape is sequential access memory;* **random access device** = device whose access time to retrieve data is not dependent on the location or type of data; **random access digital to analog converter (RAMDAC)** = electronic component on a video graphics adapter that converts the digital colour signals into electrical signals that are sent to the monitor; **random access files** = file in which each item *or* record can be immediately accessed by its address, without searching through the rest of the file, and is not dependent on the previous location; **random access memory (RAM)** = memory that allows access to any location in any order, usually in the form of ICs; **random access storage** = storage medium that allows access to any location in any order

◊ **random number** *noun* number which cannot be predicted; **random number generation** = method of creating a sequence of numbers which appears to be random so that no number appears more often than another; **random number generator** = program which generates random numbers (used in lotteries, games, etc.)

◊ **random processing** *noun* processing of data in the order required rather than the order in which it is stored

range 1 *noun* **(a)** series of items from which the customer can choose; *a wide range of products; the catalogue lists a wide range of computer stationery* **(b)** set of allowed values between a maximum and minimum; **number range** = set of allowable values **(c)** (in a spreadsheet) a cell or group of cells **2** *verb* **(a)** to vary *or* to be different; *the company's products range from a cheap lapheld micro to a multistation mainframe* **(b)** to put text in order to one side; **range left** = move text to align it to the left margin; to move the contents of a word to the left edge

rank *verb* to sort data into an order, usually according to size *or* importance

rapid *adjective* fast; **rapid access** = device *or* memory whose access time is very short; **rapid access memory** *or* **fast access memory (FAM)** = storage locations that can be read from *or* written to very quickly

raster *noun* system of scanning the whole of a CRT screen with a picture beam by sweeping across it horizontally, moving down one pixel *or* line at a time; **raster graphics** = graphics where the picture is built up in lines across the screen *or* page; **raster image processor (RIP)** = raster which translates software instructions into an image *or* complete page which is then printed by the printer; *an electronic page can be converted to a printer-readable video image by an on-board raster image processor;* **raster scan** = one sweep of the picture beam horizontally across the front of a CRT screen

rate 1 *noun* quantity of data *or* tasks that can be processed in a set time; *the processor's instruction execution rate is better than the older version;* **error rate** = number of errors that occur within a certain time; **information rate** = amount of information content per character multiplied by the number of characters transmitted per second **2** *verb* to evaluate how good something is *or* how large something is; **rated throughput** = maximum throughput of a device that will still meet original specifications

ratio *noun* proportion of one number to another; *the ratio of 10 to 5 is 2:1; the ratio of corrupt bits per transmitted message is falling with new technology*

◊ **rational number** *noun* number that can be written as the ratio of two whole numbers; *24 over 7 is a rational number; 0.333 can be written as the rational number 1/3*

raw *adjective* in the original state *or* not processed; **raw data** = (i) pieces of information that have not yet been input into a computer system; (ii) data in a database which has to be processed to provide information to the user; *this small computer collects raw data from the sensors, converts it and transmits it to the mainframe;* **raw mode** = (in DOS and UNIX operating systems) method of accessing a file which, when data is read from the file, does not carry out any data translation or filtering

ray tracing *noun* (in graphics) method of creating life-like computer-generated graphics which correctly show shadows and highlights on an object as if coming from a light source; ray tracing software calculates the direction of each ray of light, its reflection and how it looks on an object; *to generate this picture with ray tracing will take several hours on this powerful PC*

RD = REMOVE DIRECTORY (in DOS) command to remove an empty subdirectory

RDBMS = RELATIONAL DATABASE MANAGEMENT SYSTEM

react *verb;* **to react to something** = to act in response to something; **to react with something** = to change because a substance is present

◊ **reactive mode** *noun* computer operating mode in which each entry by the user causes something to happen but does not provide an immediate response *compare* INTERACTIVE; BATCH

read *verb* **(a)** (i) to look at printed words and understand them; (ii) (of an electronic device) to scan printed text; *conditions of* *sale are printed in such small characters that they are difficult to read; can the OCR read typeset characters?* **(b)** to retrieve data from a storage medium; *this instruction reads the first record of a file; access time can be the time taken to read from a record;* **destructive read** = read operation in which the stored data is erased as it is retrieved; **read back check** = system to ensure that data was correctly received, in which the transmitted data is sent back and checked against the original for any errors; **read cycle** = period of time between address data being sent to a storage device and the data being returned; **read error** = error that occurs during a read operation, often because the stored data has been corrupted; **read head** = transducer that reads signals stored on a magnetic medium and converts them back to their original electrical form; **read only** = device *or* circuit whose stored data cannot be changed; **read only attribute** = attribute bit of a file that, if set, prevents new data being written to the file or its contents edited; **read only memory (ROM)** = memory device that has had data written into it at the time of manufacture, and now its contents can only be read; *the manufacturer provided the monitor program in two ROM chips;* **read rate** = number of bytes *or* bits that a reader can read in a certain time; **read/write channel** = channel that can carry signals travelling in two directions; **read/write cycle** = sequence of events used to retrieve and store data; **read/write head** = transducer that can read *or* write data from the surface of a magnetic storage medium, such as a floppy disk; **read/write memory** = storage medium that can be written to and read from *compare* READ ONLY

readable *adjective* that can be read *or* understood by someone *or* an electronic device; *the electronic page is converted to a printer-readable video image;* **machine readable** = (commands *or* data) stored on a medium that can be directly input to the computer

reader *noun* device which reads data stored on one medium and converts it into another form; **reader level** = (in authoring software)

one of two modes that allows a user to run and interact with a multimedia application, but not modify it in any way; **card reader** = device which transforms data on a punched card to a form that can be recognized by the computer; **tape reader** = machine which reads punched holes in paper tape *or* signals on magnetic tape; *see also* OPTICAL

read-in *or* **read in** *verb* to transfer data from an external source to main memory; *the computer automatically read-in thirty values from the A/D converter*

reading *noun* note taken of figures *or* degrees, especially of degrees on a scale

readme file *noun* file that contains last-minute information about an application

readout *noun* display of data; *the readout displayed the time; the clock has a digital readout;* **destructive readout** = display device that erases previous characters when displaying new ones; **readout device** = device that allows information (numbers *or* characters) to be displayed

---

some OCR programs can be taught to read typefaces that are not in their library

Publish

---

the machine easily reads in text from typewriters and daisy-wheel printers

PC Business World

---

ready *adjective* fit to be used *or* sold; (equipment) that is waiting and able to be used; *the green light indicates the system is ready for another program; the programming will not be ready until next week; the maintenance people hope that the system will be ready for use in 24 hours;* **ready state** = communications line *or* device that is waiting to accept data

real address *noun* absolute address that directly accesses a memory location *compare* PAGED ADDRESS

RealAudio™ system used to transmit sound, usually live, over the internet (to listen to RealAudio sound you need to have a connection to the internet a web browser and a RealAudio plug-in for the web browser)

real memory *noun* actual physical memory that can be addressed by a CPU *compare* VIRTUAL MEMORY

real mode *noun* (in an IBM PC) the default operating mode for an IBM PC and the only mode in which DOS operates; real mode normally means a single-tasking operating system in which software can use any available memory *or* I/O device

real number *noun* (in computing) number that is represented with a fractional part (sometimes refers to numbers represented in a floating-point form)

real time *noun* actions *or* processing time which is of the same order of magnitude as the problem to be solved (i.e. the processing time is within the same time as the problem to be solved, so that the result can influence the source of the data); *a navigation system needs to be able to process the position of a ship in real time and take suitable action before it hits a rock US*; **real-time animation** = animation in which objects appear to move at the same speed as they would in real life; real-time animation requires display hardware capable of displaying a sequence with tens of different images every second; **real-time clock** = clock in a computer that provides the correct time of day *compare* RELATIVE-TIME CLOCK; **real-time input** = data input to a system as it happens *or* is required; **real-time multi-tasking** = executing several real-time tasks simultaneously without slowing the execution of any of the processes; **real-time operating system** = operating system designed to control a real-time system *or* process-control system; **real-time processing** = processing operation that takes a time of the same order of magnitude as the problem to be solved; **real-time simulation** = computer model of a process where each process is executed in a similar time to the real process; **real-time system** = system whose processing time is within that of the problem, so that it can influence the source of the data; *in a real-time system, as you move*

the joystick left, the image on the screen moves left. If there is a pause for processing it is not a true real-time system; **real time transport protocol (RTP)** = data transport protocol developed by the IETF that provides a guaranteed data delivery over a network that does not normally provide this type of quality of service; normally used to transfer video or multimedia data over a packet network, such as the internet; *see also* QUALITY OF SERVICE

> Quotron provides real-time quotes, news and analysis on equity securities through a network of 40,000 terminals to US brokers and investors.
>
> *Computing*

> a real-time process is one which interacts with a real external activity and respects deadlines imposed by that activity
>
> *.EXE*

> define a real-time system as any system which is expected to interact with its environment within certain timing constraints
>
> *British Telecom Technology Journal*

realize *or* **realizing the palette** *verb* to select a particular set of colours for a 256-colour palette and use this palette when displaying an image, normally by mapping the colours in a logical palette into the system palette

reboot *verb* to reload an operating system during a computing session; *we rebooted and the files reappeared; see also* BOOT

recall 1 *noun* bringing back text *or* files from store **2** *verb* to bring back text *or* files from store for editing

> automatic recall provides the facility to recall the last twenty commands and to edit and re-use them
>
> *Practical Computing*

receipt notification *noun* feature of many electronic mail applications that will send an automatic message to confirm that the recipient has received the message

receive *verb* to accept data from a communications link; *the computer received data via the telephone line;* receive only = computer terminal that can only accept and display data (but not transmit)

◊ **receiver** *noun* electronic device that can detect transmitted signals and present them in a suitable form; **receiver register** = temporary storage register for data inputs, before processing

recode *verb* to code a program which has been coded for one system, so that it will work on another

recognition *noun* (i) being able to recognize something; (ii) process that allows something to be recognized, such as letters on a printed text *or* bars on bar codes, etc.; **recognition logic** = logical software used in OCR, AI, etc.; **optical character recognition** = process that allows printed *or* written characters to be recognized optically (using an optical character reader), and converted into a form that can be input into a computer; **optical mark recognition** = process that allows certain marks *or* lines *or* patterns to be recognized optically (using an optical character reader), and converted into a form that can be input into a computer

◊ **recognize** *verb* to see something and remember that it has been seen before; *the scanner will recognize most character fonts*

◊ **recognizable** *adjective* which can be recognized

recompile *verb* to compile a source program again, usually after changes *or* debugging

reconfiguration *noun* altering the structure of data in a system

reconfigure *verb* to alter the structure of data in a system; *I reconfigured the field structure in the file; this program allows us to reconfigure the system to our own requirements; see also* CONFIGURE, SET UP

reconstitute *verb* to return a file to a previous state, usually to restore a file after a crash *or* corruption

record 1 *noun* set of items of related data; *your record contains several fields that have been grouped together under the one heading; this record contains all their personal details;* **chained record** = data record in a chained file; **change** *or* **transaction record** = record containing new data which is to be used to update a master record; **logical record** = number of items of related data which are held in temporary memory ready to be processed; **physical record** = record and control data combination stored on a backing device; **record count** = number of records within a stored file; **record format** *or* **layout** = organization and length of separate fields in a record; **record length** = quantity of data in a record; **record locking** = (in a multiuser system) software method of preventing more than one user writing data to a record at the same time; the first user's software sets a locked flag for the record during write operations, preventing other users from corrupting data by also writing data; **record structure** = list of the fields which make up a record, together with their length and data type; **records manager** = program which maintains records and can access and process them to provide information **2** *verb* to store data *or* signals on tape *or* on disk *or* in a computer; *record the results in this column; this device records signals onto magnetic tape; digitally recorded data are used to generate images;* **record button** = key pressed on a recorder when ready to record signals onto a medium; **record gap** *see* BLOCK GAP; **record head** *or* **write head** = transducer that converts an electrical signal into a magnetic field to write the data onto a magnetic medium

Micro Focus provides Fileshare 2, which it claims substantially reduces network traffic, and provides features such as full record locking, update logging and roll-forward recovery.

Computing

```
records may be sorted before
the report is created, using up
to nine sort fields
```
Byte

```
file    and    record-locking
procedures     have    to    be
implemented to make sure that
files cannot be corrupted when
two users try to read or write
to     the     same     record
simultaneously
```
Micro Decision

◊ **recordable CD (CD-R)** technology that allows a user to write data to and read from a CD-R disc; a CD-R disc can be played in any standard CD-ROM drive, but needs a special CD-R drive to write data to the disc

recorder *noun* equipment able to transfer input signals onto a storage medium; **magnetic tape recorder** = device with a motor, read/write head and circuitry to allow electrical signals to be recorded onto *or* played back from magnetic tape

> COMMENT: the signal recorded is not always in the same form as the input signal: many recorders record a modulated carrier signal for better quality. A recorder is usually combined with a suitable playback circuit since the read and write heads are often the same physical device

recording *noun* action of storing signals *or* data on tape *or* in a computer; **recording density** = number of bits of data that can be stored in a unit area on a magnetic disk *or* tape

recover *verb* to get back something which has been lost; *it is possible to recover the data but it can take a long time*

◊ **recoverable error** *noun* error type that allows program execution to be continued after it has occurred

◊ **recovery** *noun* (a) returning to normal operating after a fault; **recovery procedure** = processes required to return a system to normal operation after an error; **automatic recovery program** = software that is automatically run when a piece of equipment fails, to ensure that the system continues to operate; **failure recovery** = resuming a

process *or* program after a failure has occurred and has been corrected; **fall back recovery** = resuming a program after a fault has been fixed, from a point at which the fall back routines were called; **sense recovery time** = time that a RAM device takes to switch from read to write mode **(b)** getting back something which has been lost; *the recovery of lost files can be carried out using the recovery procedure*

rectify *verb* to correct something *or* to make something right; *they had to rectify the error at the printout stage*

Recycle Bin *noun* icon displayed on the Windows 95 Desktop that looks like a wastepaper bin; *if you want to delete a file or folder, drag it onto the Recycle Bin icon or press the Delete key*

recursion *or* **recursive routine** *noun* subroutine in a program that calls itself during execution; **recursive call** = subroutine that calls itself when it is run

red, green, blue (RGB) *noun* **(a)** high-definition monitor system that uses three separate input signals controlling red, green and blue colour picture beams **(b)** the three colour picture beams used in a colour TV

> COMMENT: there are three colour guns producing red, green and blue beams acting on groups of three phosphor dots at each pixel location

redefine *verb* to change the function *or* value assigned to a variable *or* object; *we redefined the initial parameters;* **to redefine a key** = to change the function of a programmable key; *I have redefined this key to display the figure five when pressed*

◊ **redefinable** *adjective* which can be redefined

```
the idea of the packages is that
they enable you to redefine the
keyboard
```
Practical Computing

> one especially useful command
> lets you redefine the printer's
> character-translation table
>
> *Byte*

redirect *verb* **(a)** to send a message to its destination by another route **(b)** (in DOS and UNIX operating systems) process of treating the output of one program as input for another program; *you can sort the results from a DIR command by redirecting to the SORT command;* **redirect** *or* **redirection operator** = character used by an operating system to indicate that the output of one program is to be sent as input to another; in DOS, the '>' character is used

◊ **redirection** *noun* sending a message to its destination by another route; *call forwarding is automatic redirection of calls*

redliner *noun* feature of workgroup *or* word-processor software that allows a user to highlight text in a different colour

redo *verb* to do something again; **redo from start** = start again from the beginning

redraw *verb* to draw again; *can the computer redraw the graphics showing the product from the top view?*

reduce *verb* **(a)** to make smaller **(b)** to convert raw data into a more compact form which can then be easily processed

◊ **reduced instruction set computer (RISC)** *noun* CPU design whose instruction set contains a small number of simple fast-executing instructions, that makes program writing more complex, but increases speed *compare* WISC

redundant *adjective* **(a)** (data) that can be removed without losing any information; *the parity bits on the received data are redundant and can be removed;* **redundant array of inexpensive disks (RAID)** = fast, fault tolerant disk drive system that uses multiple drives which would, typically, each store one byte of a word of data, so allowing the data to be saved faster; one drive in the array would also store a check byte for error detection; **redundant character** = character added to a block of characters for error detection *or* protocol purposes, and carries no

information; **redundant code** = check bit *or* data added to a block of data for error detection purposes, and carries no information **(b)** extra piece of equipment kept ready for a task in case of faults

◊ **redundancy** *noun* providing extra components in a system in case there is a breakdown; **longitudinal redundancy check** = check on received blocks of data to detect any errors; **network redundancy** = extra links between points allowing continued operation in the event of one failing; **vertical redundancy check** = (odd) parity check on each character of a block received, to detect any errors; **redundancy checking** = checking of received data for correct redundant codes to detect any errors

reel *noun* holder around which a tape is rolled; *he dropped the reel on the floor and the tape unwound itself;* **pick-up reel** = empty reel used to store tape as it is played from a full reel

◊ **reel to reel** *noun* copying one tape of data onto another magnetic tape; **reel to reel recorder** = magnetic tape recording machine that uses tape held on one reel and feeds it to a pick-up reel

re-entrant program *or* **code** *or* **routine** *noun* one program *or* code shared by many users in a multi-user system (it can be interrupted *or* called again by another user before it has finished its previous run, and returns to the point at which it was interrupted when it has finished that run)

◊ **re-entry** *noun* calling a routine from within that routine; running a program from within that program; **re-entry point** = point in a program *or* routine where it is re-entered

refer *verb* to mention *or* to deal with *or* to write about something; *the manual refers to the serial port, but I cannot find it*

◊ **reference 1** *noun* **(a)** value used as a starting point for other values, often zero; **reference address** = initial address in a program used as an origin *or* base for others **(b)** mentioning *or* dealing with something; **reference file** = file of data which is kept so that it can be referred to; **reference instruction** = command that provides access to sorted *or* stored data; **reference list** = list of routines *or* instructions and their location within a program; **reference mark** = printed symbol to indicate the presence of a note *or* reference not in the text; **reference retrieval system** = index which provides a reference to a document; **reference table** = list of ordered items; **reference time** = point in time that is used as an origin for further timings *or* measurements **2** *verb* to access a location in memory; *the access time taken to reference an item in memory is short*

```
a    referencing    function
dynamically    links    all
references    throughout    a
document
```
                                        Byte

---

reflected code *noun* coding system in which the binary representation of decimal numbers changes by only one bit at a time from one number to the next

reformat *verb* to format a disk that already contains data, and erasing the data by doing so; *do not reformat your hard disk unless you can't do anything else*

◊ **reformatting** *noun* act of formatting a disk which already contains data; *reformatting destroys all the data on a disk; see also* FORMAT

refresh *verb* **(a)** to update regularly the contents of dynamic RAM by reading and rewriting stored data to ensure data is retained; *memory refresh signal;* **RAM refresh rate** = number of times every second that the data in a dynamic RAM chip has to be read and rewritten; **refresh cycle** = period of time during which a controller updates the contents of dynamic RAM chips; **self-refreshing RAM** = dynamic RAM chip that has built-in circuitry to generate refresh signals, allowing data to be retained when the power is off, using a battery backup **(b)**; **screen refresh** = to update regularly the images on a CRT screen by scanning each pixel with a picture beam to make sure the image is still visible; **refresh rate** = number of times every second that the image on a CRT is redrawn

```
Philips    autoscan    colour
monitor, the 4CM6099, has SVGA
refresh rates of 72Hz (800 x
600) and EVGA refresh rates of
70Hz (1,024 x 768).
```
                                   Computing

regenerate *verb* (i) to redraw an image on a screen many times a second so that it remains visible; (ii) to receive distorted signals, process and error check them, then retransmit the same data

◊ **regenerative memory** *noun* storage medium whose contents need to be regularly refreshed to retain its contents; *dynamic RAM is regenerative memory - it needs to be refreshed every 250ns; the CRT display can be thought of as regenerative memory, it requires regular refresh picture scans to prevent flicker;* **regenerative reading** = reading operation that automatically regenerates and rewrites the data back into memory

◊ **regenerator** *noun* device used in communications that amplifies or regenerates a received signal and transmits it on; regenerators are often used to extend the range of a network

region *noun* special *or* reserved area of memory or program or screen; **region fill** = to fill an area of a the screen or a graphics shape with a particular colour

◊ **regional breakpoint** *noun* breakpoint that can be inserted anywhere within a program that is being debugged; *see also* BREAKPOINT, DEBUGGING

register 1 *noun* (i) special location within a CPU (usually one or two words wide) that is used to hold data and addresses to be processed in a machine code operation; (ii) reserved memory location used for special storage purposes; **register addressing** = instruction whose address field contains the register in which the operand is stored; **register file** = number of registers used for temporary storage; **register length** = size (in bits) of a register; **register map** = display of the contents of all the registers; **accumulator register** = most important internal storage register in a CPU, containing the data to be processed; **address register** = register in a computer that is able to store all the bits of an address which can then be processed as a single unit; **base register** = register in a CPU (not usually in small computers) that contains the address of the start of a program; **buffer register** = temporary storage for data being written to *or* read from memory; **circulating register** = shift register whose output is fed back into its input (to form a closed loop); **control register** = storage location for control data; **data register** = area within a CPU used to store data temporarily before it is processed; *in this small micro, the data register is eight bits wide, an address register is sixteen bits wide;* **external registers** = a user's registers located in main memory rather than within the CPU; **index register** = computer address register that is added to a reference address to provide the location to be accessed; **input/output register** = temporary storage for data received from memory before being transferred to an I/O device *or* data from an I/O device waiting to be stored in main memory or to be processed; **instruction register** = temporary storage for the instruction that is being executed; **instruction address register (IAR)** = register in a CPU that stores the location where instructions are found; **memory address register (MAR)** = register within the CPU that contains the address of the next location to be accessed; **next instruction register** = register in the CPU that contains the address of the next instruction to be processed; **program status word register (PSW register)** = register which contains a number of status bits, such as carry flag, zero flag, overflow flag; **sequence control register (SCR)** = CPU register that contains the address of the next instruction to be processed; *see also* NEXT INSTRUCTION REGISTER; **shift register** = temporary storage into which data can be shifted **2** *verb* to react to a stimulus

◊ **registry** *noun* database that forms the basis of Windows 95

regulate *verb* to control a process (usually using sensors and a feedback mechanism); **regulated power supply** = constant, controlled voltage *or* current source whose output will not vary with input supply variation

COMMENT: a regulated power supply is required for all computers where components cannot withstand voltage variations

rehyphenation *noun* changing the hyphenation of words in a text after it has been put into a new page format *or* line width

reject *verb* to refuse to accept something; *the computer rejects all incoming data from incompatible sources*

◊ **rejection** *noun* refusing to accept something; **rejection error** = error by a scanner which cannot read a character and so leaves a blank

relational database *or* **relational database management system (RDBMS)** *noun* database in which all the items of data can be interconnected; data is retrieved by using one item of data to search for a related field; *if you search the relational database for the surname, you can pull out his salary from the related accounts database;* **relational operator** *or* **logical operator** = symbol that compares two items; **relational query** = database query that contains relational operators; *the relational query 'find all men under 35 years old' will not work on this system*

◊ **relationship** *noun* way in which two similar things are connected

Data replication is the process of duplicating data on, or distributing it between, databases, usually on different servers. It is not new, having been around for many years: nor is it confined to relational databases.

Computing

relative *adjective* which is compared to something; **relative address** *or* **indirect address** = location specified in relation to a reference or base address; **relative coding** = writing a program using relative address instructions; **relative coordinates** = positional information given in relation to a reference point; **relative data** = data that gives new coordinate information relative to previous coordinates; **relative error** = difference between a number and its correct value (caused by rounding off); **relative pointing device** = input device (such as a mouse) in which the movement of a pointer on screen is relative to the movement of the input device; **relative-time clock** = regular pulses that allow software in a computer to calculate the real time

relay 1 *noun* electromagnetically controlled switch; *there is a relay in the circuit; it is relay-rated at 5 Amps* **2** *verb* to receive data from one source and then retransmit it to another point; *all messages are relayed through this small micro*

release 1 *noun* version of a product; *the latest software is release 5;* **release number** = number of the version of a product; *see also* VERSION **2 (a)** to put a new product on the market **(b)** (of software) to relinquish control of a block of memory *or* file

relevant *adjective* which has an important connection

◊ **relevance** *noun* (i) way in which something has a connection with something else; (ii) importance of something in a situation *or* process

reliability *noun* the ability of a device to function as intended, efficiently and without failure; *it has an excellent reliability record; the product has passed its reliability tests*

◊ **reliable** *adjective* which can be trusted to work properly; *the early version of the software were not completely reliable*

reload *verb* to load again; *we reloaded the program after the crash; see also* LOAD

relocate *verb* to move data from one area of storage to another; *the data is relocated during execution;* **self-relocating program** = program that can be loaded into any part of memory (that will modify its addresses depending on the program origin address)

◊ **relocatable** *adjective* which can be moved to another area of memory without affecting its operation; **relocatable program** = computer program that can be loaded into and executed from any area of memory; *the operating system can load and run a relocatable program from any area of memory*

◊ **relocation** *noun* moving to another area in memory; **dynamic relocation** = moving data *or* coding *or* assigning absolute locations during a program execution; **relocation constant** = quantity added to all addresses to move them to another section of memory, (equal to the new base address); **static relocation** = moving data *or* coding *or* assigning absolute locations before a program is run

REM = REMARK statement in a BASIC program that is ignored by the interpreter, allowing the programmer to write explanatory notes

remainder *noun* number equal to the dividend minus the product of the quotient and divider; *7 divided by 3 is equal to 2 remainder 1; compare* QUOTIENT

remark (REM) statement in a BASIC program that is ignored by the interpreter, allowing the programmer to write explanatory notes

remedial maintenance *noun* maintenance to repair faults which have developed in a system

remote *adjective* (communications) with a computer at a distance from the systems centre; *users can print reports on remote printers;* **remote access** = link that allows a user to access a computer from a distance (normally using a modem); **remote client** = user who is accessing mail without being connected to the mail server's local network; **remote console** *or* **device** = input/output device located away from the computer (and send data to it by line *or* modem); **remote control** = system that allows a remote user to control (run programs, copy files, control resources) a computer from a distance; the remote user has the impression of using the remote computer locally; **remote control software** = software that runs on a local computer and a remote computer allowing a user to control the remote computer; *this remote control software will work with Windows and lets me operate my office PC from home over a modem link;* **remote job entry (RJE)** = batch processing system where instructions are transmitted to the computer from a remote terminal; **remote procedure call (RPC)** = method of communication between two programs running on two separate, but connected, computers; a software routine asks another computer on the network to process a problem and then displays the results; normally used with client-server applications; **remote station** = communications station that can be controlled by a central computer; **remote terminal** = computer terminal connected to a distant computer system

removable *adjective* which can be removed; *a removable hard disk*

◊ **removal** *noun* taking away; *the removal of this instruction could solve the problem*

remove *verb* to take away *or* to move to another place; *the file entry was removed from the floppy disk directory*

REN = RINGER EQUIVALENCE NUMBER number that defines the load a device places on a telephone network

rename *verb* to give a new name to a file; *save the file and rename it CUSTOM*

render *verb* to colour and shade a graphic object so that it looks solid and real; *we rendered the wire-frame model*

renumber *noun* feature of some computer languages which allows the programmer to allocate new values to all *or* some of a program's line numbers; *see also* LINE NUMBER

reorganize *verb* to organize again; *wait while the spelling checker database is being reorganized*

repaginate *verb* to change the lengths of pages of text before they are printed; *the text was repaginated with a new line width*

◊ **repagination** *noun* action of changing pages lengths; *the dtp package allows simple repagination*

repeat *verb* to do an action again; **repeat counter** = register that holds the number of times a routine *or* task has been repeated; **repeat key** = key on a keyboard which repeats the character pressed; **repeat rate** = number of times that a character will be entered on screen if you press and hold down one key on the keyboard

◊ **repeater** *noun* device used in communications that amplifies or regenerates a received signal and transmits it on; regenerators are often used to extend the range of a network; the repeater works at the physical layer of the OSI network model; *see also* BRIDGE, OSI, ROUTER

◊ **repeating group** *noun* pattern of data that is duplicated in a bit stream

reperforator *noun* machine that punches paper tape according to received signals; **reperforator transmitter** = reperforator and a punched tape transmitter connected together

repertoire *noun* the range of functions of a device *or* software; *the manual describes the full repertoire;* **character repertoire** = list of all the characters that can be displayed *or* printed; **instruction repertoire** = all the commands that a system can recognise and execute; *see also* RESERVED WORD

> the only omissions in the editing repertoire are dump, to list variables currently in use, and find
>
> *Computing Today*

repetitive letter *noun* form letter *or* standard letter into which the details of each addressee (such as name and address) are inserted

repetitive strain injury *or* repetitive stress injury (RSI)

noun pain in the arm felt by someone who performs the same movement many times over a certain period, as when operating a computer terminal; *RSI can be avoided by adjusting your chair so that you do not excessively flex your wrists when typing*

replace *verb* **(a)** to put something back where it was before; to put something in the place of something else; *the printer ribbons need replacing after several thousand characters* **(b)** instruction to a computer to find a certain item of data and put another in its place; *see also* SEARCH AND REPLACE

replay 1 *noun* playback *or* reading back data *or* a signal from a recording **2** *verb* to play back (something which has been recorded)

replenish *verb* to charge a battery with electricity again

replicate *verb* to copy; *the routine will replicate your results with very little effort*

◊ **replication** *noun* (i) extra components in a system in case there is a breakdown *or* fault in one; (ii) copying a record *or* data to another location

reply *verb* to answer an electronic mail message

report generator *noun* software that allows data from database files to be merged with a document (in the form of graphs or tables) to provide a complete report

◊ **report program generator (RPG)** *noun* programming language used mainly on personal computers for the preparation of business reports, allowing data in files, databases, etc., to be included

represent *verb* **(a)** to act as a symbol for something; *the hash sign is used to represent a number in a series* **(b)** to act as a salesman for a product

◊ **representation** *noun* action of representing something; **character representation** = combination of bits used for each character code

reproduce *verb* to copy data *or* text from one material *or* medium to another similar one

reprogram *verb* to alter a program so that it can be run on another type of computer

request 1 *noun* something which someone asks for; **request for comment (RFC)** = document that contains information about a proposed new standard and asks users to look at the document and make any comments; **request to send signal (RTS)** = signal sent by a transmitter to a receiver asking if the receiver is ready to accept data (used in the RS232C serial connection) **2** *verb* to ask for something

require *verb* to need something *or* to demand something; *delicate computer systems require careful handling*

◊ **requirements** *noun* things which are needed; *memory requirements depend on the application software in use*

re-route *verb* to send by a different route

rerun *verb* to run a program *or* a printing job again; **rerun point** = place in the program from where to start a running again after a crash *or* halt

res *see* RESOLUTION; **hi-res** = HIGH RESOLUTION; **lo-res** = LOW RESOLUTION

resample *verb* to change the number of pixels used to make up an image

resave *verb* to save again; *it automatically resaves the text*

rescue dump *noun* data automatically saved on disk when a computer fault occurs (it describes the state of the system at that time; it is used to help in debugging)

research *noun* scientific investigation to learn new facts about a field of study; **research and development (R & D)** = investigation of new products, discoveries and techniques; *the company has spent millions of dollars on R & D*

reserved character *noun* special character which is used by the operating system *or* which has a particular function to control an operating system and cannot be used for other uses; *in DOS, the reserved* *character* \ *is used to represent a directory path;* **reserved sector** = area of disk space that is used only for control data storage; **reserved word** = word *or* phrase used as an identifier in a programming language (it performs a particular operation *or* instruction and so cannot be used for other uses by the programmer *or* user)

---

sometimes a process will demand cache space when the only free cache space is reserved for higher priority processes

.EXE

---

reset *verb* **(a)** to return a system to its initial state, to allow a program *or* process to be started again; **reset button** *or* **key** = switch that allows a program to be terminated and reset manually; **hard reset** = electrical signal that usually returns the system to its initial state when it was switched on, requiring a reboot; **soft reset** = instruction that terminates any program execution and returns the user to the monitor *or* BIOS **(b)** to set a register *or* counter to its initial state; *when it reaches 999 this counter resets to zero* **(c)** to set data equal to zero

---

COMMENT: hard reset is similar to soft reset but with a few important differences: it is a switch that directly signals the CPU, while soft reset signals the operating system; hard reset clears all memory contents, a soft reset does not affect memory contents; hard reset should always reset the system, a soft reset does not always work (if, for example, the operating system cannot recover, then a soft reset will not work)

---

reshape handle *noun* (in a GUI) small square displayed on a frame around an object or image that a user can select and drag to change the shape of the frame or graphical object

resident *adjective* (data *or* program) that is always in a computer; **resident engineer** = engineer who works permanently for one company; **resident font** = font data which is always present in a printer *or* device and which does not have to be downloaded; **resident software** *or* **memory-resident software** = program that is held permanently in memory (whilst the machine is on); **terminate and stay resident software (TSR)** = program that is started from the command line, then loads itself into memory, ready to be activated by an action, and passes control back to the command line

residual *adjective* which remains behind; **residual error rate** = ratio between incorrect and undetected received data and total data transmitted

◊ **residue check** *noun* error detection check in which the received data is divided by a set number and the remainder is checked against the required remainder

resist 1 *verb* to fight against something *or* to refuse to do something **2** *noun* substance used to protect a pattern of tracks on a PCB, which is not affected by etching chemicals; *see also* PHOTORESIST

resolution *noun* number of pixels that a screen *or* printer can display per unit area; *the resolution of most personal computer screens is not much more than 70 dpi (dots per inch);* **graphic display resolution** = number of pixels that a computer is able to display on the screen; **high-resolution (hi-res)** = ability to display *or* detect a very large number of pixels per unit area; *the high-resolution screen can display 640 by 450 pixels;* **limiting resolution** = maximum number of lines that make up an image on a CRT screen; **low resolution (low-res)** = ability of a display system to control a number of pixels at a time rather than individual pixels

---

Group IV fax devices can send a grey or colour A4 page in about four seconds, at a maximum resolution of 15.7 lines per millimetre over an Integrated Services Digital Network circuit.

Computing

---

the resolution is 300 dots per inch and the throughput is up to eight pages per minute

Practical Computing

---

resolving power *noun* measurement of the ability of an optical system to detect fine black lines on a white background (given as the number of lines per millimetre)

resonance *noun* situation where a frequency applied to a body being the same as its natural frequency, causes it to oscillate with a very large amplitude

resource *noun* device *or* products *or* program *or* software *or* graphic object which are useful or used by something; **resource allocation** = dividing available resources in a system between jobs; **resource fork** = (in an Apple Macintosh) one of two forks of a file; the resource fork contains the resources that the file needs (fonts, code or icons); **resource interchange file format (RIFF)** = multimedia data format jointly introduced by IBM and Microsoft that uses tags to identify parts of a multimedia file structure and allows the file to be exchanged between platforms; **resource sharing** = the use of one resource in a network *or* system by several users

respond *verb* to reply *or* to react because of something

◊ **response** *noun* reaction caused by something; **response frame** = page in a videotext system that allows a user to enter data; **response position** = area of a form that is to be used for optical mark reading data; **response time** = (i) time which passes between the user starting an action (by pressing a key) and the result appearing on the screen; (ii) speed with which a system responds to a stimulus; *the response time of this flight simulator is very good*

restart *verb* to start again; *first try to restart your system*

restore *verb* to put back into an earlier state

```
first you have to restore the
directory that contains the
list of deleted files
                Personal Computer World
```

restrict *verb* to keep something within a certain limit; to allow only certain people to access information; *the document is restricted, and cannot be placed on open access*

◊ **restriction** *noun* something which restricts (data flow *or* access)

result *noun* answer *or* outcome of an arithmetic *or* logical operation

◊ **result code** *noun* message sent from a modem to the local computer indicating the state of the modem

resume *verb* to restart the program from the point where it was left, without changing any data

retain *verb* to keep

◊ **retention** *noun* keeping; **image retention** = time taken for a TV image to disappear after it has been displayed, caused by long persistence phosphor

retrain *verb* to re-establish a better quality connection when the quality of a line if very bad

retrieval *noun* the process of searching, locating and recovering information from a file *or* storage device; **information retrieval** = locating quantities of data stored in a database and producing information from the data; **information retrieval centre** = research system, providing specific information from a database for a user; **text retrieval** = information retrieval system that allows the user to examine complete documents rather than just a reference to a document

◊ **retrieve** *verb* to extract information from a file *or* storage device; *these are the records retrieved in that search; this command will retrieve all names beginning with S*

retro- *prefix meaning* going back; progress backwards

◊ **retrofit** *noun* device *or* accessory added to a system to upgrade it

retrospective parallel running *noun* running a new computer system with old data to check if it is accurate

retrospective search *noun* search of documents on a certain subject since a certain date

return *noun* **(a)** instruction that causes program execution to return to the main program from a subroutine; *the program is not working because you missed out the return instruction at the end of the subroutine;* **return address** = address to be returned to after a called routine finishes **(b)** key on a keyboard used to indicate that all the required data has been entered; *you type in your name and code number then press return* **(c)** indication of an end of line (in printing); **carriage return (CR)** = code *or* key to indicate the end of an input line and to move the cursor to the start of the next line

◊ **return to zero signal** *noun* recording reference mark taken as the level of unmagnetized tape (NOTE: opposite is **non return to zero)**

> COMMENT: the return address is put on the stack by the call instruction and provides the address of the instruction after the call, which is to be returned to after the called routine has finished

reveal *verb* to display previously hidden information once a condition has been met

reverse 1 *adjective* going in the opposite direction; **reverse channel** = low speed control data channel between a receiver and transmitter; **reverse characters** = characters which are displayed in the opposite way to other characters for emphasis (as black on white *or* white on black, when other characters are the opposite); **reverse engineering** = method of product design in which the finished item is analysed to determine how it should be constructed; **reverse index** = movement of a printer head up half a line to print superscripts; **reverse interrupt** = signal sent by a receiver to request the termination of transmissions; **reverse polarity** = situation where the positive and negative terminals have been confused, resulting in the equipment not functioning; **reverse Polish notation (RPN)** = mathematical operations written in a logical way, so that the operator appears after the numbers to be acted upon, this removes the need for brackets; *three plus four, minus two is written in RPN as 3 4 + 2 - = 5; normal notation: (x-y) + z, but using RPN:*

xy - z + same as POSTFIX NOTATION; **reverse video** = screen display mode where white and black are reversed (colours are complemented) **2** *verb* to go *or* travel in the opposite direction; to send (control) data from a receiver to a transmitter

```
the options are listed on the
left side of the screen, with
active options shown at the top
left in reverse video
```
PC User

revert *verb* to return to a normal state; *after the rush order, we reverted back to our normal speed;* **revert command** = command (in text) that returns a formatted page to its original state

review *verb* to see again *or* replay and check; *the program allows the user to review all wrongly spelled words*

revise *verb* to update *or* correct a version of a document *or* file; *the revised version has no mistakes*

rewind *verb* to return a tape *or* film *or* counter to its starting point; *the tape rewinds onto the spool automatically*

rewrite 1 *verb* to write something again; *see also* REGENERATE **2** *noun* act of writing something again; *the program is in its second rewrite*

RF = RADIO FREQUENCY electromagnetic spectrum that lies between the frequency range 10KHz and 3000GHz; **RF shielding** = thin metal foil wrapped around a cable that prevents the transmission of radio frequency interference signals; *without RF shielding, the transmitted signal would be distorted by the interference*

RFC = REQUEST FOR COMMENT document that contains information about a proposed new standard and asks users to look at the document and make any comments

RGB = RED, GREEN, BLUE method of producing colours by mixing the light made up of three primary colours red, green and blue

RGB display *or* **monitor**   *noun*
high-definition monitor system that uses three separate input signals controlling red, green and blue colour picture beams

> COMMENT: there are three colour guns producing red, green and blue beams acting on groups of three phosphor dots at each pixel location

RJ11 connector *noun* popular standard of four-wire modular connector

RJ45 connector *noun* popular name for an eight-pin modular connector used in 10BaseT networks to connect UTP cables

ribbon *noun* long thin flat piece of material; **printer ribbon** = roll of inked material which passes between a printhead and the paper; **ribbon cable** = number of insulated conductors arranged next to each other forming a flat cable

rich text format (RTF) *noun* way of storing a document that includes all the commands that describe the page, type, font and formatting

RIFF = RESOURCE INTERCHANGE FILE FORMAT multimedia data format jointly introduced by IBM and Microsoft that uses tags to identify parts of a multimedia file structure and allows the file to be exchanged between platforms; **RIFF chunk** = chunk with the ID RIFF; **RIFF file** = file that contains tagged information that complies with the RIFF file format

right *adjective* not left; **right-click menu** = small pop-up menu that appears when you click on the right-hand button of a two-button mouse; **right-hand button** = button on the right-hand side of a two or three-button mouse; **right justify** = to align the right margin so that the text is straight; **right justification** = aligning the text and spacing characters so that the right margin is straight; **right shift** = to move a section of data one bit to the right; *see also* LOGICAL SHIFT, ARITHMETIC SHIFT

rightsizing *noun* process of moving a company's information technology structure to the most cost-effective hardware platform; often used to mean moving from a mainframe-based network to a PC-based network

rigid *adjective* hard *or* which cannot bend; **rigid disk** = rigid magnetic disk that is able to store many times more data than a floppy disk, and usually cannot be removed from the disk drive

ring 1 *noun* **(a)** data list whose last entry points back to the first entry; *see also* CHAINED LIST **(b)** topology of a network in which the wiring sequentially connects one workstation to another; **ring topology network** = type of network where each terminal is connected one after the other in a circle *compare with* BUS, STAR; **Token Ring network** = IEEE 802.5 standard that uses a token passed from one workstation to the next in a ring network; a workstation can only transmit data if it captures the token (Token Ring networks, although logically a ring, are often physically wired in a star topology); *Token Ring networks are very democratic and retain performance against increasing load compare* BUS NETWORK, ETHERNET **2** *verb* to telephone; **ring back system** = remote computer system in which a user attempting to access it phones once, allows it to ring a number of times, disconnects, waits a moment, then redials (usually in a bulletin board system)

ring shift *noun* data movement to the left *or* right in a word, the bits falling outside the word boundary are discarded, the free positions are filled with zeros

ring topology *noun* network architecture in which each node (computer or printer) is connected together in a loop

ringer equivalence number (REN) *noun* number that defines the load a device places on a telephone network

RIP 1 = RASTER IMAGE PROCESSOR **2** = ROUTING INFORMATION PROTOCOL

ripple-through effect *noun* (in a spreadsheet) results *or* changes *or* errors appearing in a spreadsheet as a result of the value in one cell being changed

◊ **ripple-through carry** *noun* one operation producing a carry out from a sum and a carry in

RISC REDUCED INSTRUCTION SET COMPUTER CPU design whose instruction set contains a small number of simple fast-executing instructions, that makes program writing more complex, but increases speed; *see also* WISC

RJ-11 connector with four connections normally used in telephone sockets in the USA

RJ-45 connector used in telephone systems with eight connections; a similar looking connector, often referred to as an RJ-45 connector is used to connect 10BaseT UTP cable in an Ethernet local area network, this type of connector looks the same but has different electrical properties

RJE = REMOTE JOB ENTRY batch processing system where instructions are transmitted to the computer from a remote terminal

RLL encoding = RUN-LENGTH LIMITED ENCODING fast and efficient method of storing data onto a disk in which the changes in a run of data bits is stored

rm (in UNIX) command to remove an empty subdirectory

◊ **RMDIR** *or* **RD** = REMOVE DIRECTORY (in DOS) command to remove an empty subdirectory

RO = RECEIVE ONLY computer terminal which can only accept and display data, not transmit

roam *verb* (in wireless communications) to move around freely and still be in contact with a wireless communications transmitter

robot *noun* device which can be programmed to carry out certain manufacturing tasks which are similar to tasks carried out by people

◊ **robotics** *noun* study of artificial intelligence, programming and building involved with robot construction

robust *adjective* solid *or* (system) which can resume working after a fault

◊ **robustness** *noun* **(a)** strength of a system's casing and its ability to be knocked *or* dropped; *this hard disk is not very robust* **(b)** system's ability to continue functioning even with errors *or* faults during a program execution

rogue indicator *noun* special code used only for control applications such as end of file marker

◊ **rogue value** *or* **terminator** *noun* item in a list of data, which shows that the list is terminated

role indicator *noun* symbol used to show the role of a index entry in its particular context

roll back *verb* function of a database application to stop a transaction and return the database to its previous state; *see also* COMMIT, TRANSACTION

◊ **roll forward** *verb* function of a database application that allows the user to recover from a disaster (such as a power cut) by reading the transaction log and re-executing all the instructions to return the database to the state just before the disaster

◊ **roll-in** *verb* to transfer data from backing store into main memory

◊ **roll-out** *verb* to save the contents of main memory onto backing store

◊ **rollover** *noun* keyboard with a small temporary buffer so that it can still transmit correct data when several keys are pressed at once; **key rollover** = use of a buffer between the keyboard and computer to provide rapid key stroke storage for fast typists who hit several keys in rapid succession

◊ **roll scroll** *verb* displayed text that moves up *or* down the computer screen one line at a time

ROM = READ ONLY MEMORY; **CD-ROM** *or* **compact disc-ROM** = small plastic disc which is used as a high capacity

ROM device; data is stored in binary form as holes etched on the surface which are then read by a laser; **ROM BIOS** = code which makes up the BIOS routines stored in a ROM chip (normally executed automatically when the computer is switched on); **ROM cartridge** = software stored in a ROM mounted in a cartridge which can easily be plugged into a computer (NOTE: there is no plural for ROM, and it is often used without the article: **the file is stored in ROM**)

◊ **romware** *noun* software which is stored in ROM

root *noun* (a) starting node from which all paths branch in a data tree structure; **root directory** = (in a disk filing system) the topmost directory from which all other directories branch; *in DOS, the root directory on drive C: is called C:* (b) fractional power of a number; **square root** = number raised to the power one half; *the square root of 25 is 5*

rot13 simple encoding that is used to scramble offensive messages posted in newsgroups

rotate *verb* to move data within a storage location in a circular manner

◊ **rotation** *noun* amount by which an object has been rotated; **bit rotation** *or* **rotate operation** = shifting a pattern of bits in a word to the left or right, the old last bit moving to the new first bit position; **matrix rotation** = swapping the rows with the columns in an array (equal to rotating by 90 degrees); *see also* SHIFT (CYCLIC)

round 1 *adjective* which goes in a circle; **round robin** = way of organizing the use of a computer by several users, who each use it for a time and then pass it on the next in turn **2** *verb*; **to round down** = to approximate a number to a slightly lower one of lower precision; *we can round down 2.651 to 2.65;* **to round off** = to approximate a number to a slightly larger *or* smaller one of lower precision; *round off 23.456 to 23.46;* **round off errors** = inaccuracies in numbers due to rounding off; **to round up** = to approximate a number to a slightly larger one of lower precision; *we can round up 2.647 to 2.65*

◊ **rounding** *noun* (a) approximation of a number to a slightly larger *or* smaller one of lower precision; **rounding error** = error in a result caused by rounding off the number (b) giving graphics a smoother look; **character rounding** = making a displayed character more pleasant to look at (within the limits of pixel size) by making sharp corners and edges smooth

route *noun* path taken by a message between a transmitter and receiver in a network; *the route taken was not the most direct since a lot of nodes were busy*

router *noun* (i) communications device that receives data packets in a particular protocol and forwards them to their correct location via the most efficient route; (ii) (in a LAN) device that connect two or more LANs that use the same protocol and allows data to be transmitted between each network, the router works at the network-layer level of the OSI model; *see also* BRIDGE, OSI

◊ **routing** *noun* determining a suitable route for a message through a network; *there is a new way of routing data to the central computer;* **routing overheads** = actions that have to be taken when routing messages; *the information transfer rate is very much less once all routing overheads have been accommodated;* **routing page** = videotext page describing the routes to other pages; **routing table** = list of preferred choices for a route for a message stored within a router

routine *noun* a number of instructions that perform a particular task, but are not a complete program; they are included as part of a program; *the routine copies the screen display onto a printer; the RETURN instruction at the end of the routine sends control back to the main program;* **closed routine** *or* **closed subroutine** = one section of code at a location, that is used by all calls to the routine; **fall back routines** = routines that are called *or* processes which are executed by a user when a machine *or* system has failed; **floating-point routines** = set of routines that allow floating-point numbers to be handled and processed; **input routine** = short section of code that accepts data from an external device, such as reading an entry from a keyboard; **open routine** *or* **open subroutine** = set of instructions in a routine, that are copied to whichever part of the program requires them; **packing routine** = program which packs data into a small storage area; *see also* CALL, RETURN

COMMENT: routines are usually called from a main program to perform a task, control is then returned to the part of the main program from which the routine was called once that task is complete and the program continues

row *noun* **(a)** (i) line of printed *or* displayed characters; (ii) horizontal line on a punched card; *the figures are presented in rows, not in columns; each entry is separated by a row of dots* **(b)** horizontal set of data elements in an array *or* matrix

RPC = REMOTE PROCEDURE CALL method of communication between two programs running on two separate, but connected, computers; a software routine asks another computer on the network to process a problem and then displays the results; used with client-server applications

RPG = REPORT PROGRAM GENERATOR

RS-232C EIA approved standard used in serial data transmission, covering voltage and control signals

◊ **RS-422** EIA approved standard that extends the RS-232's 50ft limit

◊ **RS-423** EIA approved standard that extends the RS-232's 50ft limit, introduced at the same time as the RS-422 standard, but less widely used

COMMENT: RS232C has been superseded by the RS423 and RS422 interface standards, similar to the RS232, but allowing higher transmission rates

RSI = REPETITIVE STRAIN INJURY

RTE = REAL TIME EXECUTION

RTF = RICH TEXT FORMAT

RTFM common abbreviation used in messages to mean 'read the manual'

RTP = REAL TIME TRANSPORT PROTOCOL

RTS = REQUEST TO SEND SIGNAL

rubber banding *see* ELASTIC BANDING

rub out *see* ERASE

rule *noun* set of conditions which describe a function; *the rule states that you wait for the clear signal before transmitting;* **rule-based system** = software that applies the rules and knowledge defined by experts in a particular field to a user's data to solve a problem

ruler *noun* bar displayed on screen that indicates a unit of measurement; often used in DTP or word-processor software to help with layout

rules *noun* method of testing incoming messages for certain conditions (such as the name of the sender or the contents) and acting upon them

run 1 *noun* execution by a computer of a set of instructions *or* programs *or* procedures; *the next invoice run will be on Friday;* **program run** = executing (in correct order) the instructions in a program; **Run command** = (in Windows) command that lets the user type in the name of a program that they want to run or a DOS command they want to execute; **run indicator** = indicator bit *or* LED which shows that a computer is currently executing a program **2** *verb* to make a device work; *the computer has been running ten hours a day; do not interrupt the spelling checker while it is running; the new package runs on our PC;* **parallel running** = running old and new computer systems together to allow the new system to be checked before it becomes the only system used; **run in** = to operate a system at a lower capacity for a time in case of any faults

run around *verb* to fit text around an image on a printed page

runaway *noun* uncontrolled operation of a device *or* computer (due to a malfunction *or* error)

run-length limited encoding (RLL) fast and efficient method of storing data onto a disk in which the changes in a run of data bits is stored

running head *noun* title line of each page in a document

run on *verb* to make text continue without a break; *the line can run on to the next without any space*

run-time *or* **run-duration 1** *noun* **(a)** period of a time a program takes to run **(b)** time during which a computer is executing a program **2** *adjective* (operation) carried out only when a program is running; **run-time error** = fault only detected when a program is run *or* error made while a program is running; *see also* EXECUTION ERROR; **run-time library** = library of routines that are only accessed by an application when it is running; *the software is designed with all the graphics routines in this run-time library file;* **run-time licence** = licence granted to a user to run an application; **run-time system** = software that is required in main storage while a program is running (to execute instructions to peripherals, etc.); **run-time version** = (i) program code that has been compiled and is in a form that can be directly executed by the computer; (ii) commercial interpreter program that is sold with an application developed in a high-level language that allows it to run

R/W = READ/WRITE

◊ **R/W cycle** = READ/WRITE CYCLE sequence of events used to retrieve *or* store data

◊ **R/W head** = READ/WRITE HEAD electromagnetic device that allows data to be read from *or* written to a storage medium

RX = RECEIVE, RECEIVER; *the RXed signal needs to be amplified*

Ss

S100 bus *or* **S-100 bus** *noun* IEEE-696 standard bus, old 8- and 16-bit microcomputer bus using 100 lines and a 100-pin connector; *see also* BUS (NOTE: say 'S one hundred bus')

SAA = SYSTEMS APPLICATION ARCHITECTURE standard developed by IBM which defines the look and feel of an application regardless of the hardware platform; SAA defines which keystrokes carry out standard functions (such as F1 to display help), the application's display and how the application interacts with the operating system

safe format *noun* format operation that does not destroy the existing data and allows the data to be recovered in case you formatted the wrong disk

◊ **safe mode** *noun* special operating mode of Windows 95 that is automatically selected if Windows 95 detects that there is a problem when starting

safety net *noun* software *or* hardware device which protects the system *or* files from excessive damage in the event of a system crash; *if there is a power failure, we have a safety net in the form of a UPS*

sag *noun* short drop in the voltage level from a power supply

salami technique *noun* computer fraud involving many separate small transactions that are difficult to detect and trace

SAM = SERIAL ACCESS MEMORY storage where a particular data item can only be accessed by reading through all the previous items in the list (as opposed to random access)

COMMENT: magnetic tape is a form of SAM; you have to go through the whole tape to access one item, while disks provide random access to stored data

sample 1 *noun* measurement of a signal at a point in time; *the sample at three seconds showed an increase;* **sample and hold circuit** = circuit which freezes an analog input signal for long enough for an A/D converter to produce a stable output

◊ **sample size** *noun* size of the word used to measure the level of the signal when it is sampled: normally either 8-bit or 16-bit words are used **2** *verb* to obtain a number of measurements of a signal which can be used to provide information about the signal; **sampling interval** = time period between two consecutive samples; **sampling rate** = number of measurements of a signal recorded every second; *see also* ANALOG/DIGITAL CONVERSION, QUANTIZE

◊ **sampler** *noun* electronic circuit that takes many samples of a signal and stores them for future analysis

SAR = STORE ADDRESS REGISTER register within the CPU that contains the address of the next location to be accessed

SAS = SINGLE ATTACHMENT STATION

satellite *noun* small system that is part of a larger system; **satellite computer** = computer doing various tasks under the control of another computer; **satellite terminal** = computer terminal that is outside the main network

saturated colour *noun* bright colours (such as red and orange) that do not reproduce well on video and can cause distortion or can spread over the screen

saturation *noun* point where a material cannot be further magnetized; **saturation noise** = errors due to saturation of a magnetic storage medium; **saturation testing** = testing a communications network, by transmitting large quantities of data and messages over it

save *verb* to store data *or* a program on an auxiliary storage device; *this WP saves the text every 15 minutes in case of a fault; don't forget to save the file before switching off;* **save area** = temporary storage area of main memory, used for registers and control data; **save as** = option in an application that allows the user to save the current work in a file with a different name

SBC = SINGLE BOARD COMPUTER computer whose main components such as processor, input/output and memory are all contained on one PCB

scalable font *noun* method of describing a font so that it can produce characters of different sizes; *see also* OUTLINE FONT

◊ **scalable software** *noun* groupware application that can easily accommodate more users on a network without having to invest in new software

scalar *noun* variable which has a single value assigned to it; *a scalar has a single magnitude value, a vector has two or more positional values;* **scalar data** = data type containing single values which are predictable and follow a sequence; **scalar processor** = processor designed to operate at high-speed on scalar values; **Scalar Processor Architecture (SPARC)** = RISC processor designed by Sun Microsystems and used in its range of workstations; **scalar variable** = variable which can contain a single value rather than a complex data type (such as an array or record); **scalar value** = single value rather than a matrix or record (scalar values are not normally floating-point numbers)

scale 1 *noun* ratio of two values; **large scale** *or* **small scale** = working with large *or* small amounts of data; **large scale**

integration (LSI) = integrated circuit with 500 - 10,000 components; **medium scale integration (MSI)** = integrated circuit with 10 - 500 components; **small scale integration (SSI)** = integrated circuit with 1 - 10 components; **very large scale integration (VLSI)** = integrated circuit with 10,000 - 100,000 components **2** *verb;* **to scale down** *or* **scale up** = to lower *or* increase in proportion

scan 1 *noun* examination of an image *or* object *or* list of items to obtain data describing it; *the heat scan of the computer quickly showed which component was overheating; the scan revealed which records were now out of date;* **scan area** = section of an image read by a scanner; **scan code** = number transmitted from the keyboard to an IBM PC compatible computer to indicate that a key has been pressed and to identify the key; **scan conversion** = process of converting an interlaced video signal to a non-interlaced signal or a composite to a separated RGB signal; **scan head** = device used in scanners, photocopiers and fax machines, which uses photo-electric cells to turn an image into a pattern of pixels; *this model uses a scan head that can distinguish 256 different colours;* **scan length** = number of items in a file *or* list that are examined in a scan; **scan line** = one of the horizontal lines of phosphor (or phosphor dots) on the inside of a CRT or monitor; the monitor's picture beam sweeps along each scan line to create the image on the screen; **scan rate** = number of times every second that the image on a CRT is redrawn; **raster scan** = one sweep of the picture beam horizontally across the front of the CRT screen **2** *verb* to examine and produce data from the shape *or* state of an object *or* drawing *or* file *or* list of items; *the facsimile machine scans the picture and converts this to digital form before transmission; the machine scans at up to 300 dpi resolution*

◊ **ScanDisk** utility supplied with MS-DOS (which is also part of Windows 95) that will check the hard disk for any problems and will try and correct problems that it finds

scanner *noun* **(a)** device which scans; *a scanner reads the bar-code on the product label using a laser beam and photodiode* **(b)** (usual term for) a device which uses photo-electric cells to convert an image *or* drawing *or* photograph *or* document into graphical data which can be manipulated by a computer; a scanner is connected and controlled by a computer which can then display or process the image data; **flat-bed scanner** = device with a flat sheet of glass on which the image *or* photograph *or* document is placed; the scan head moves below the glass and converts the image into data which can be manipulated by a computer; **hand-held scanner** = device that is held in your hand and contains a row of photo-electric cells which, when moved over an image, convert it into data which can be manipulated by a computer; **image scanner** = input device that converts documents *or* drawings *or* photographs into digitized machine-readable form; **optical scanner** = equipment which converts an image into electrical signals which can be stored in and displayed on a computer; **scanner memory** = memory area allocated to store images which have been scanned

COMMENT: a scanner can be a device using photoelectric cells as in an image digitizer, or a device that samples data from a process. Flat-bed scanners are more accurate than hand-held scanners.

Ricoh's Fax 300L Computer Link is connected to a PC via a RS232C serial interface, and enables users to send faxes from within Dos and Windows applications without printing a hard copy: It can also act as a scanner for graphics, and a printer for documents.

Computing

scanning *noun* action of examining and producing data from the shape of an object *or* drawing; **scanning error** = error introduced while scanning an image; **scanning line** = path traced on a CRT screen by the picture beam; **scanning rate** = time taken to scan one line of a CRT image; **scanning**

resolution = ability of a scanner to distinguish between small points (usual resolution is 300 dpi); **scanning software** = dedicated program that controls a scanner and allows certain operations (rotate *or* edit *or* store, etc.) to be performed on a scanned image; **scanning speed** = how fast a line *or* image is scanned; *throughput is 1.3 inches per second scanning speed; its scanning speed is 9.9 seconds for an 8.5 inch by 11 inch document;* **auto-baud scanning** *or* **auto-baud sensing** = (of a modem) circuit that can automatically sense and select the correct baud rate for a line

COMMENT: a modem with auto-baud scanning can automatically sense which baud rate to operate on and switches automatically to that baud rate

scanning time per page ranged from about 30 seconds to three minutes

PC Business World

scatter load *verb* to load sequential data into various (non-continuous) locations in memory

◊ **scatter read** *verb* to access and read sequential data stored in various (non-continuous) locations

scavenging *noun* searching through and access database material without permission

schedule *noun* order in which tasks are to be done *or* order in which CPU time will be allocated to processes in a multi-user system

◊ **Schedule+**™ (Microsoft Windows 95) software program that provides personal information management features, including a diary

◊ **scheduled circuits** *noun* telephone lines for data communications only

◊ **scheduler** *noun* **(a)** program which organizes use of a CPU *or* of peripherals which are shared by several users **(b)** utility software that helps users organise their meetings, appointments or use of a resources (such as a boardroom)

◊ **scheduling** *noun* method of working which allows several users to share the use of a CPU; **job scheduling** = arranging the order in which jobs are to be processed

schema *noun* graphical description of a process *or* database structure

schematic *adjective & noun* (diagram) showing system components and how they are connected

scissoring *noun* (i) defining an area of an image and then cutting out this part of the image so it can then be pasted into another image; (ii) defining an area of an image and deleting any information that is outside this area

scope *noun* range of values that a variable can contain

SCR = SEQUENCE CONTROL REGISTER

scramble *verb* to code speech *or* data which is transmitted in such a way that it cannot be understood unless it is decoded

◊ **scrambler** *noun* device that codes a data stream into a pseudorandom form before transmission to eliminate any series of ones or zeros *or* alternate ones and zeros that would cause synchronization problems at the receiver

scrapbook *noun* utility (on an Apple Macintosh) that stores frequently used graphic images; *we store our logo in the scrapbook*

scratch 1 *noun* (a) area of memory *or* file used for temporary storage of data (b) mark on the surface of a disk; *this scratch makes the disk unreadable* **2** *verb* to delete *or* move an area of memory to provide room for other data

◊ **scratch file** *or* **work file** *noun* work area which is being used for current work; **scratch tape** = magnetic tape used for a scratch file

◊ **scratchpad** *noun* workspace *or* area of high speed memory used for temporary storage of data currently in use; **scratchpad memory** = cache memory used to buffer data being transferred between a fast processor and a slow I/O device (such as a disk drive)

```
Mathcad is described as an
easy-to-use "handy scratch pad
for quick number crunching",
which is positioned as an
alternative to popular
spreadsheets.
```
Computing

screen 1 *noun* **(a)** display device capable of showing a quantity of information, such as a CRT *or* VDU; *see also* READOUT; **on-screen** = information displayed on a screen; **screen angle** = angle at which a screen is set before the photograph is taken; **screen attribute** = (in some operating systems, including DOS) attribute bits which define how each character will be displayed on screen; they set background and foreground colour and bold, italic or underline; **screen border** = margin around text displayed on a screen; **screen buffer** = temporary storage area for characters *or* graphics before they are displayed screen burn =; **problem caused if a stationary image is displayed for too long on a monitor, burning the phosphor** screen capture = to store the image currently displayed on screen in a file; **screen dump** = outputting the text *or* graphics displayed on a screen to a printer; **screen editor** *or* **text editor** = software which allows the user to edit text on-screen, with one complete screen of information being displayed at a time; **screen flicker** = (on a display) image that moves slightly or whose brightness alternates due to a low image refresh rate *or* signal corruption; **screen font** = (in a GUI) typeface and size designed to be used to display text on screen rather than be printed out; *the screen font is displayed at 72dpi on a monitor, rather than printed at 300dpi on this laser printer;* **screen format** = way in which a screen is laid out; **screen grab** = (i) digitizing a single frame from a display *or* television; (ii) capturing what is displayed on a monitor and storing it as a graphics file; **screen memory** = in a memory-mapped screen, the area of memory representing the whole screen, usually with one byte representing one *or* a number of pixels; *the dtp package offers on-screen font display;* **screen saver** = software which, after a pre-determined period of user inactivity, replaces the existing image on screen and displays moving objects to protect against screen burn; **text screen** = area of a computer screen set up to display text; **touch screen** = computer display which allows the user to control the cursor position by touching the screen **(b)** something which protects; **magnetic screen** = metal screen to prevent stray magnetic fields affecting electronic components; *without the metal screen over the power supply unit, the computer just produced garbage* **2** *verb* **(a)** to protect something with a screen; *the PSU is screened against interference* **(b)** to select

◊ **screenful** *noun* complete frame of information displayed on a screen

---

the screen memory is, in fact
a total of 4K in size, the first
2K hold the character codes, of
which   1K   is   displayed.
Scrolling brings the remaining
area into view

Computing Today

---

script *noun* set of instructions which carry out a function, normally used with a macro language or batch language; *I log in automatically using this script with my communications software;* **scripting language** = simple programming language (normally proprietary to an application) that allows a user to automate the application's functions; *this communications software has a scripting language that lets me dial and log in automatically*

◊ **ScriptX™** authoring tool and utilities that allow a developer to write multimedia applications that can be played (unchanged) on a range of different platforms

scroll *verb* to move displayed text vertically up *or* down the screen, one line *or* pixel at a time; **roll scroll** = displayed text that moves up *or* down the screen one line at a time; **scroll arrows** = (in a GUI) arrows that when clicked, move the contents of the window up or down or sideways; **scroll bar** = (in a GUI) bar displayed along the side of a window with a marker which indicates how far you have scrolled; *the marker is in the middle of the scroll bar so I know I am in the middle of the document;* **Scroll Lock key** = key (on an IBM PC keyboard) that changes how the cursor control keys operate; their function is dependent on the application; **scroll mode** = terminal mode which transmits every key press and displays what is received; **smooth scroll** = text which is moved up a screen pixel by pixel rather than line by line, which gives a smoother movement

scrub *verb* to wipe information off a disk *or* remove data from store; *scrub all files with the .BAK extension*

SCSI = SMALL COMPUTER SYSTEM INTERFACE standard high-speed parallel interface used to connect computers to peripheral devices (such as disk drives and scanners); **Fast-SCSI** = development that allows data to be transferred at a higher rate than with the original SCSI specification; **SCSI-2** = newer standard that provides a wider data bus and transfers data faster than the original SCSI specification that supports 16-bit data transfers and can control 15 devices; **Ultra SCSI** = extension to the SCSI hard disk interface that supports either 8-bit data transfers at a rate of 20Mbits/second or 16-bit data transfers at a rate of 40Mbits/second; this standard can support 15 devices; **Ultra-2 SCSI** = extension to the SCSI hard disk interface that supports either 8-bit data transfers at a rate of 40Mbits/second or 16-bit data transfers at a rate of 80Mbits/second; this standard can support 15 devices; **Wide-SCSI** = development that provides a wider data bus than the original SCSI specification, so can transfer more data at a time

---

the   system   uses   SCSI   for
connecting to the host and ESDI
for   interconnecting   among
drives   within   a   multidrive
system

Byte

SD = SINGLE DENSITY (DISK)

SDLC = SYNCHRONOUS DATA LINK CONTROL data transmission protocol most often used in IBM's Systems Network Architecture (SNA) and defines how synchronous data is transmitted

SDR = STORE DATA REGISTER register in a CPU which holds data before it is processed *or* moved to memory location

SDRAM = SYNCHRONIZED DYNMANIC RAM enhanced memory component that is replacing traditional DRAM; the memory access cycle is synchronized with the main processor clock, eliminating wait time between memory operations

seal *verb* to close something tightly so that it cannot be opened; *the hard disk is in a sealed case*

seamless integration *noun* the process of including a new device or software into a system without any problems; *it took a lot of careful planning, but we succeeded in a seamless integration of the new application*

search 1 *noun* process of looking for and identifying a character *or* word *or* section of data in a document *or* file; **search key** = (i) word *or* phrase that is to be found in a text; (ii) field and other data used to select various records in a database; **search engine** = (on the internet) software that carries out a search of a database when a user asks it to find information; **search memory** = method of data retrieval that uses part of the data rather than an address to locate the data; **chaining search** = searching a file of elements arranged as a chained list; **linear search** = search method which compares each item in a list with the search key until the correct entry is found (starting with the first item and working sequentially towards the end); **retrospective search** = search of documents on a certain subject since a certain date; **sequential search** = search where each item in a list (starting at the beginning) is checked until the required one is found **2** *verb* to look for an item of data

a linear search of 1,000 items takes 500 comparisons to find the target, and 1,000 to report that it isn't present. A binary search of the same set of items takes roughly ten divisions

either to find or not to find the target
Personal Computer World

◊ **search and replace** *noun* feature on word-processors which allows the user to find certain words *or* phrases, then replace them with another word *or* phrase; **global search and replace** = word-processor search and replace function covering a complete file *or* document

◊ **searching storage** *noun* method of data retrieval that uses part of the data rather than an address to locate the data

second *adjective* (thing) which comes after the first; *we have two computers, the second one being used if the first is being repaired;* **second generation computers** = computer which used transistors instead of valves; **second-level addressing** = instruction that contains an address at which the operand is stored; **second sourcing** = granting a licence to another manufacturer to produce an electronic item *or* component when production capacity is not great enough to meet demand; **second user** *or* **second hand** = (old equipment) which has already been used and is being sold again

secondary *adjective* second in importance *or* less important than the first; **secondary channel** = second channel containing control information transmitted at the same time as data; **secondary service provider** = organisation that provide internet access for a particular region of a country; **secondary station** = temporary status of a station receiving data; **secondary storage** = any data storage medium (such as magnetic tape *or* floppy disk) that is not the main, high-speed computer storage (RAM)

COMMENT: this type of storage is usually of a higher capacity, lower cost and slower access time than main memory

section *noun* part of a main program which can be executed in its own right, without the rest of the main program being required

sector 1 *noun* smallest area on a magnetic disk which can be addressed by a computer;

the disk is divided into concentric tracks, and each track is divided into sectors which, typically, can store 512 bytes of data; **bad sector** = sector which has been identified as faulty and cannot be used to reliably store data (bad sectors are stored in a sector map); **(disk) sector formatting** = dividing a disk into a series of addressable sectors (a table of their addresses is also formed, allowing each sector to be accessed); **sector interleave** = ratio of sectors skipped between access operations on a hard disk; in a hard disk with an interleave of 3, the first sector is read, then three sectors are skipped and the next sector is read; this is used to allow hard disks with slow access time to store more data on the disk.; **sector map** = table which contains the addresses of unusable sectors on a hard disk **2** *verb* to divide a disk into a series of sectors; **sectoring hole** = hole in the edge of a disk to indicate where the first sector is located; **hard-sectored** = disk with sector start locations described by holes *or* other physical marks on the disk, which are set when the disk is manufactured; **soft-sectored** = disk where sectors are described by an address and start code data written onto it when the disk is formatted; *see also* FORMAT

> COMMENT: a disk is divided into many tracks, each of which is then divided into a number of sectors which can hold a certain number of bits

secure electronic transactions

(SET) standards created by a group of banks and internet companies that allow users to buy goods over the internet without risk of hackers; *see also* SSL

secure encryption payment protocol (SEPP)
system developed to provide a secure link between a user's browser and a vendor's Web site to allow the user to pay for goods over the internet; *see also* PGP, S-HTTP, SSL, STT

secure hypertext transfer protocol (S-HTTP)
extension of the HTTP protocol that allows an encrypted and authenticated session between a user's web browser and a secure web server

secure/MIME *or* **S/MIME** method of sending encrypted mail messages and file attachments, the encryption is public-key so it also provides authentication of the identity of the sender; *see also* MIME

secure sockets layer encrypted transmission protocol designed by Netscape that provides secure communications between a browser and a web server over the internet; *see also* PGP, SEPP, SET, STT

secure system *noun* system that cannot be accessed without authorization

secure transaction technology (STT) system developed by Microsoft to provide a secure link between a user's browser and a vendor's Web site to allow the user to pay for goods over the internet; *see also* PGP, SEPP, SET, S-HTTP, SSL

secured *adjective* (file) which is protected against accidental writing *or* deletion *or* against unauthorized access

security *noun* being protected *or* being secret; *the system has been designed to assure the security of the stored data;* **security backup** = copy of a disk *or* tape *or* file kept in a safe place in case the working copy is lost *or* damaged; **security check** = identification of authorized users (by a password) before granting access

seed *noun* starting value used when generating random or pseudorandom numbers

seek *verb* to try to find; **seek area** = section of memory to be searched for a particular item of data *or* a word; **seek time** = time taken by a read/write head to find the right track on a disk; *the new hard disk drive has a seek time of just 35mS*

segment 1 *noun* section of a main program which can be executed in its own right, without the rest of the main program being required; **segmented address space** = memory address space divided into areas called segments; to address a particular location, the segment and offset values must be specified; **LAN segment** = (i) (in a bus network) an electrically continuous piece of cable; (ii) part of a network separated from the rest by a bridge **2** *verb* to divide a long program into shorter sections which can then be called up when required; *see also* OVERLAY

---

you can also write in smaller program segments. This simplifies debugging and testing

Personal Computer World

---

select *verb* to find and retrieve specific information from a database; **chip select (CS)** = single line on a chip that will enable it to function when a signal is present (often ICs do not function even when power is applied, until a CS signal is provided)

◊ **selectable** *adjective* which can be selected; **jumper-selectable** = circuit *or* device whose options can be selected by positioning various wire connections; **selectable attributes** = the function *or* attributes of a device which can be chosen by the user; **user-selectable** = which can be chosen or selected by the user; **this modem has user-selectable baud rates** = the receive and transmit baud rates of the modem can be chosen by the user, and are not preset

◊ **selection** *noun* action *or* process of selecting; *selection of information from a large database may take some time;* **selection handle** = small square displayed on a frame around a selected area that allows the user to change the shape of the area; **selection tool** = (in a paint or drawing program) icon in a toolbar that allows a user to select an area of an image which can then be cut, copied or processed in some way

◊ **selective** *adjective* which chooses certain items; **selective dump** = display *or* printout of a selected area of memory; **selective sort** = sorting a section of data items into order

◊ **selector** *noun* mechanical device which allows a user to choose an option *or* function

self- *prefix* referring to oneself; **self-adapting system** = system which is able to adapt itself to various tasks; **self-checking system** = system which carries out diagnostic tests on itself usually at switch on;

self-checking code = character coding system which is able to detect an error *or* bad character but not correct it; **self-correcting codes** = character coding system which is able to detect and correct an error *or* bad character; **self-diagnostic** = computer that runs a series of diagnostic programs (usually when it is switched on) to ensure that it is all working correctly; often memory, peripherals and disk drives are tested; **self-documenting program** = computer program providing the user with operating instructions as it runs; **self extracting archive** = compressed file that includes the program to de-compress the contents; **self-learning** = (expert system) that adds each new piece of information or rule to its database, improving its knowledge, expertise and performance as it is used; **self-refreshing RAM** = dynamic RAM chip with built-in circuitry to generate refresh signals, allowing data to be retained when the power is off, using battery back-up; **self-relocating program** = program that can be loaded into any part of memory (that will modify its addresses depending on the program origin address); **self-resetting** *or* **self-restoring loop** = loop that returns any locations *or* registers accessed during its execution to the state they were in

semantics *noun* (i) part of language which deals with the meaning of words, parts of words or combinations of words; (ii) (in computing) meanings of words or symbols used in programs; **semantic error** = error due to use of an incorrect symbol within a program instruction

semaphore *noun* coordination of two jobs and appropriate handshaking to prevent lock-outs *or* other problems when both require a peripheral *or* function

semi- *prefix* meaning half *or* partly

◊ **semi-processed data** *noun* raw data which has had some processing carried out, such as sorting, recording, error detection, etc.

semicolon *noun* printed sign (;) which marks the end of a program line *or* statement in some languages (such as C and Pascal)

semicompiled *adjective* (object code) program converted from a source code program, but not containing the code for functions from libraries, etc., that were used in the source code

semiconductor *noun* material with conductive properties between those of a conductor (such as a metal) and an insulator; **semiconductor device** = electronic component constructed on a small piece of semiconductor (the components on the device are constructed using patterns of insulator *or* conductor *or* semiconductor material whose properties can be changed by doping); **semiconductor memory** = storage using capacitors (dynamic memory) *or* latches and bistables (static memory) constructed as a semiconductor device to store bits of data

> COMMENT: semiconductor material (such as silicon) is used as a base for manufacturing integrated circuits and other solid-state components, usually by depositing various types of doping substances on or into its surface

sender *noun* person who sends a message

◊ **send-only device** *noun* device such as a terminal which cannot receive data, but only transmit it

◊ **Send To command** *noun* menu command, available from the File menu of new Windows 95 applications, that allows a user to send the file or data currently open in the application to another application

sense *verb* to examine the state of a device *or* electronic component; *the condition of the switch was sensed by the program; this device senses the holes punched in a paper tape;* **auto-baud sensing;** *see* SCANNING; **sense recovery time** = time that a RAM takes to switch from read to write mode; **sense switch** = switch on a computer front panel whose state can by examined by the computer

◊ **sensitive** *adjective* which can sense even small changes; *the computer is sensitive even to very slight changes in current*

◊ **sensitivity** *noun* (a) being sensitive to something; *the scanner's sensitivity to small objects* (b) minimum power of a received

signal that is necessary for a receiver to distinguish the signal

◊ **sensor** *noun* electronic device which produces an output dependent upon the condition *or* physical state of a process; *see also* TRANSDUCER; *the sensor's output varies with temperature; the process is monitored by a bank of sensors;* **image sensor** = photoelectric device which produces a signal related to the amount of light falling on it

sentinel *noun* (i) marker *or* pointer to a special section of data; (ii) a flag which reports the status of a register after a mathematical *or* logical operation

separate 1 *adjective* not together; **separate channel signalling** = using independent communications channel *or* bands in a multichannel system to send the control data and messages **2** *verb* to divide; **separated graphics** = displayed characters that do not take up the whole of a character matrix, resulting in spaces between them

◊ **separation** *noun* act of separating

◊ **separator** *noun* symbol used to distinguish parts of an instruction line in a program, such as command and argument; *see also* DELIMITER

SEPP = SECURE ENCRYPTION PAYMENT PROTOCOL system developed to provide a secure link between a user's browser and a vendor's Web site to allow the user to pay for goods over the internet; *see also* PGP, S-HTTP, SSL, STT

septet *noun* word made up of seven bits

sequence *noun* number of items *or* data arranged as a logical, ordered list; *the sequence of names is arranged alphabetically; the program instructions are arranged in sequence according to line numbers;* **binary sequence** = series of binary digits; **control sequence** = (series of) codes containing a control character and various arguments, used to carry out a process *or* change mode in a device; **sequence check** = check to ensure that sorted data is in the correct order; **sequence control register (SCR)** *or* **sequence counter** *or* **sequence**

register *or* **instruction address register** = CPU register which contains the address of the next instruction to be processed; **the logon sequence** = order in which user number, password and other authorization codes are to be entered when attempting to access a system

sequencer *noun* section within a bit-slice microprocessor which contains the next microprogram address

sequential *adjective* arranged in an ordered manner; **sequential batch processing** = completing one job in a batch before the next can be started; **sequential computer** = type of computer, for which each instruction must be completed before the next is started, and so cannot handle parallel processing; **sequential file** *or* **serial file** = stored file whose records are accessed sequentially; **sequential logic** = logical circuit whose output depends on the logic state of the previous inputs; *if the input sequence to the sequential logic circuit is 1101 the output will always be zero (0)* compare COMBINATIONAL CIRCUIT; **sequential mode** = mode where each instruction in a program is stored in consecutive locations; **sequential operation** = operations executed one after the other; **sequential packet exchange** (SPX) = network transport protocol developed by Novell and used to carry IPX network traffic; **sequential processing** = data *or* instructions processed sequentially, in the same order as they are accessed; *see also* INDEXED; **sequential search** = search where each item in a list (starting at the beginning) is checked until the required one is found

sequential access *noun* method of retrieving data from a storage device by starting at the beginning of the medium (such as tape) and reading each record until the required data is found; **queued indexed sequential access method** (QISAM) = indexed sequential file that is read item by item into a buffer; **queued sequential access method** (QSAM) = queue of blocks waiting to be processed, retrieved using a sequential access method; **sequential access storage** = storage medium in which the data is accessed sequentially

sequentially *adverb* (done) one after the other, in sequence

> COMMENT: a tape storage system uses sequential access, since the tape has to be played through until the section required is found. The access time of sequential access storage is dependent on the position in the file of the data, compared with random access which has the same access time for any piece of data in a list

serial *adjective* (data *or* instructions) ordered sequentially (one after the other) and not in parallel; **serial access** = one item of the data accessed by reading through all the data in a list until the correct one is found (as on a tape); **serial-access memory** (SAM) = storage where a particular data item can only be accessed by reading all the previous items in the list (as opposed to random access); **serial adder** = addition circuit which acts on one digit at a time from a larger number; **serial computer** = computer system which has a single ALU and carries out instructions one at a time; *see also* SEQUENTIAL COMPUTER; **serial data transmission** *or* **communications** = transmission of the separate bits that make up data words, one at a time down a single line; **serial file** = stored file whose records are accessed sequentially; **serial input/output** (SIO); *see* SERIAL TRANSMISSION; **serial input/parallel output** (SIPO) *or* **serial to parallel converter** = device which can accept serial data and transmit parallel data; **serial input/serial output** (SISO) =; *see* SERIAL TRANSMISSION; **serial interface** *or* **port** = circuit used to convert parallel data in a computer to and from a serial form, and which allows serial data to be transmitted and received from other equipment (the most common form is the RS232C interface); *parallel connections are usually less trouble to set up and use than serial interfaces, but are usually limited to 20 feet in length;* **serial line internet protocol** (SLIP) = method of sending TCP/IP network traffic over a serial line, such as a telephone modem connection (normally used to connect a user's computer to the internet via a modem link); **serial memory** = memory in which data is stored sequentially, only allowing sequential access; **serial mouse** = mouse which connects to the serial port of a PC and transfers positional data via the serial port; **serial operation** = working of a device on data in a sequential manner; **serial port** = connector and circuit used to convert parallel data in a computer to and from a serial form in which each bit is transmitted one at a time over a single wire; **serial printer** = printer which prints characters one at a time; **serial processing** = data *or* instructions processed sequentially, in the same order as they are retrieved; **serial storage** = storage which only allows sequential access; **serial to parallel converter** = electronic device which converts data from a serial form to a parallel form; **serial transmission** *or* **serial input/output** = data transmitted one bit at a time (this is the normal method of transmission over long distances, since although slower it uses fewer lines and so is cheaper than parallel transmission); **word serial** = data words transmitted one after the other, along a parallel bus

◊ **serially** *adverb* one after the other *or* in a series; *their transmission rate is 64,000 bits per second through a parallel connection or 19,200 serially*

◊ **series** *noun* group of related items ordered sequentially; **series circuit** = circuit in which the components are connected serially

> COMMENT: in a series circuit the same current flows through each component; in a parallel circuit the current flow is dependent upon the component impedance

server *noun* dedicated computer which provides a function to a network; **file server** = computer connected to a network which runs a network operating system software to manage user accounts, file sharing and printer sharing; **LAN server** = dedicated computer and backing storage facility used by terminals and operators of a LAN; **LAN Server** = network operating system for the

PC developed by IBM; **print server** = computer in a network which is dedicated to managing print queues and printers; **server-based application** = application program, stored on a server's hard disk, which can be accessed (and executed) by several users at one time; **server message block (SMB)** = system (developed by Microsoft) which allows a user to access another computer's files and peripherals over a network as if they were local resources; **service side includes (SSI)** = special extensions to a web server that allow the web page, scripts and programs to access special features, such as a count of visitors to a site

> COMMENT: in a network the hard disk machine is called the 'server' and the floppy disk units the 'satellites'. In a star network each satellite is linked individually to a central server

> Sequent Computer Systems' Platform division will focus on hardware and software manufacture, procurement and marketing, with the Enterprise division concentrating on services and server implementation.
>
> *Computing*

service *verb* to check *or* repair *or* maintain a system; *the disk drives were serviced yesterday and are working well;* **service bit** = transmitted bit used for control rather than data; **service bureau** = company which provides a specialist service, such as outputting DTP files to a typesetter, converting files or creating slides from graphics files; **service contract** = agreement that an engineer will service equipment if it goes wrong; **service program** = useful program used for routine activities such as file searching, copying, sorting, debugging, etc.

◊ **services** *noun* (i) set of functions provided by a device; (ii) (in an OSI network model) set of functions provided by one OSI layer for use by a higher layer

session *noun* (i) period of work; (ii) time during which a program *or* process is running or active; **session layer** = fifth layer in the

ISO/OSI standard model which makes the connection/disconnection between transmitter and receiver

set 1 *noun* number of related data items; **character set** = all the characters which can be displayed *or* printed; **set theory** = mathematics related to numerical sets **2** *verb* **(a)** (i) to make one variable equal to a value; (ii) to define a parameter value; *we set the right-hand margin at 80 characters;* **set breakpoints** = to define the position of breakpoints within a program being debugged; **tab settings** = preset points along a line, where the printing head *or* cursor will stop for each tabulation command **(b)** to give a bit the value of 1

SET = SECURE ELECTRONIC TRANSACTIONS standards created by a group of banks and internet companies that allow users to buy goods over the internet without risk of hackers; *see also* SSL

set up *verb* to configure *or* initialize *or* define *or* start an application *or* system; *the new computer worked well as soon as the engineer had set it up;* **setup option** = the choices available when setting up a system; **setup program** = utility program that helps a user configure their computer *or* new software application; **setup time** = period of time between a signal to start an operation and the start

sexadecimal *see* HEXADECIMAL

sex changer *noun* device for changing a female connection to a male or vice versa

sextet *noun* byte made up of six bits

sf signalling = SINGLE FREQUENCY SIGNALLING

SGML = STANDARD GENERALIZED MARKUP LANGUAGE hardware-independent standard which defines how documents should be marked up to indicate bolds, italics, margins and so on

shadowmask *noun* sheet with holes placed just behind the front of a colour monitor screen to separate the three-colour picture beams

◊ **shadow memory** *or* **page** *noun* duplicate memory locations accessed by a special code; **shadow page table** = conversion table which lists real memory locations with their equivalent shadow memory locations; *see also* VIRTUAL

◊ **shadow RAM** *noun* method of improving the performance of a PC by copying the contents of a (slow) ROM chip to a faster RAM chip when the computer is first switched on

◊ **shadow ROM** *noun* read-only shadow memory

shannon *noun* measure of the information content of a transmission

◊ **Shannon's Law** *noun* law defining the maximum information carrying capacity of a transmission line

COMMENT: Shannon's Law is defined as B lg(1 + S/N) where B = Bandwidth, lg is logarithm to the base two and S/N is Signal to Noise ratio

share *verb* to own *or* use something together with someone else; *the facility is shared by several independent companies;* **share-level access** = method used to set up network security to protect local resources; **share level security** = network operating system which assigns passwords to resources rather than setting up user accounts to limit access; **shared access** = use of a computer *or* peripheral by more than one person *or* system; *see also* TIME-SHARING SYSTEM, MULTI-USER; **shared bus** = one bus used (usually) for address and data transfer between the CPU and a peripheral; **shared directory** = directory (on a file server or workstation) which can be accessed by several users connected to a network; **shared file** = stored file which can be accessed by more than one user *or* system; **shared folder** = folder of files stored on a computer's local hard disk drive that can be used (or shared) by other users on the network; **shared logic system** = one computer and backing storage device used by a number of people in a network for an application; **shared logic text processor** = word-processing available to a number of users of a shared logic system;

shared memory = memory accessed by more than one CPU; **shared network directory** = directory (on a file server or workstation) which can be accessed by several users connected to a network; **shared resources system** = system where one peripheral *or* backing storage device *or* other resource is used by a number of users

◊ **shareware** *noun* software which is available free to try, but if kept the user is expected to pay a fee to the writer (often confused with public domain software which is completely free)

Bulletin board users know the dangers of 'flaming' (receiving hostile comments following a naive or ridiculous assertion) and of being seen 'troughing' (grabbing every bit of shareware on the network).

Computing

---

sheet *noun* large piece of paper; **(single) sheet feed** = paper feed system which puts single sheets of paper into a printer, one at a time; **sheet feed attachment** = device which can be attached to a printer to allow single sheets of paper to be fed in automatically

shell *noun* software which operates between the user and the operating system, often to try and make the operating system more friendly or easier to use; *MS-DOS's COMMAND.COM is a basic shell that interprets commands typed in at the prompt; the Macintosh Finder is a sophisticated shell with a GUI front-end*

shell out *verb* (when running an application) to exit to the operating system, whilst the original application is still in memory; the user then returns to the application; *I shelled out from the word-processor to check which files were on the floppy, then went back to the program*

shell sort *noun* algorithm for sorting data items, in which items can be moved more than one position per sort action

shield 1 *noun* metal screen connected to earth, used to prevent harmful voltages *or*

interference reaching sensitive electronic equipment **2** *verb* to protect a signal *or* device from external interference *or* harmful voltages; **shielded cable** = cable made up of a conductive core surrounded by an insulator, then a conductive layer to protect the transmitted signal against interference; **shielded twisted pair (STP) cable** = cable consisting of two insulated copper wires twisted around each other (to reduce induction and so interference), the pair of wires are then wrapped in an insulated shielding layer to further reduce interference; **unshielded twisted pair (UTP) cable** = cable made of two insulated copper wires twisted around each other (to reduce induction and so interference), unlike STP cable the pair of wires are not wrapped in any other layer; *see also* ETHERNET, 10BASE-T, TWISTED PAIR

shift *verb* **(a)** to move a bit *or* word of data left or right by a certain amount (usually one bit); **arithmetic shift** = word *or* data moved one bit to the right *or* left inside a register, losing the bit shifted off the end; **cyclic shift** = rotation of bits in a word with the previous last bit inserted in the first bit position; **logical shift** = data movement to the left *or* right in a word, the bits falling outside the word boundary are discarded, the free positions are filled with zeros; **shift instruction** = computer command to shift the contents of a register to the left or right; **shift left** = left arithmetic shift of data in a word (the number is doubled for each left shift); *0110 left shifted once is 1100;* **shift register** = temporary storage into which data can be shifted; **shift right** = right arithmetic shift of data in a word (the number is halved for each right shift) **(b)** to change from one character set to another, allowing other characters (such as capitals) to be used; **shift character** = transmitted character code which indicates that the following code is to be shifted; **shift code** = method of increasing total possible bit combinations by using a number of bits to indicate if the following code is to be shifted

Shift key *noun* (key on a keyboard) which switches secondary functions for keys, such as another character set, by changing the output to upper case

Shockwave™ system developed by Macromedia that allows Web browsers to display complex multimedia effects

short *adjective* not long; **short card =** add-on expansion board which is shorter than a standard size; **shortcut =** feature of Windows 95 that allows a user to define an icon that links to another file or application; **short haul modem =** modem used to transmit data over short distances (often within a building), usually without using a carrier

◊ **shorten** *verb* to make shorter; *we had to shorten the file to be able to save it on one floppy*

shout *verb* (term of abuse) typing a message or electronic mail in capital letters

S-HTTP = SECURE HYPERTEXT TRANSFER PROTOCOL system developed to provide a secure link between a user's browser and a vendor's Web site to allow the user to pay for goods over the internet; *see also* PGP, SEPP, SET, SSL, STT

shut down *verb* to switch off and stop the functions of a machine *or* system

◊ **ShutDown** (in Windows 95) command that will close down Windows and, if the user has a compatible PC, will switch off the computer

◊ **shut-off mechanism** *noun* device which stops a process in case of fault

> COMMENT: most hard disks have an automatic shut-off mechanism to pull the head back from the read position when the power is turned off

sideways ROM *noun* software which allows selection of a particular memory bank *or* ROM device

SIG = SPECIAL INTEREST GROUP group of people (within a larger club) who are interested in a particular aspect of software or hardware; *our local computer club has a SIG for comms and networking*

sign 1 *noun* polarity of a number *or* signal (whether it is positive *or* negative); **sign bit** *or* **sign indicator** = single bit which indicates if a binary number is positive *or* negative (usually 0 = positive, 1 = negative); **sign digit** = one digit which indicates if a number is positive *or* negative; **sign and magnitude** *or* **signed magnitude** = number representation in which the most significant bit indicates the sign of the number, the rest of the bits its value; **sign and modulus** = way of representing numbers, where one bit shows if the number is positive *or* negative (usually 0 = positive, 1 = negative); **sign position** = digit *or* bit position which contains the sign bit *or* digit **2** *verb* **(a)** to identify oneself to a computer using a personalized signature; **to sign off** = to logoff a system; **to sign on** = to logon to a system **(b)**; **signed field** = storage field which can contain a number and a sign bit

signal 1 *noun* (i) generated analog *or* digital waveform used to carry information; (ii) short message used to carry control codes; *the signal received from the computer contained the answer;* **interrupt signal** = voltage pulse from a peripheral sent to the CPU requesting attention; **signal conditioning** = converting *or* translating a signal into a form that is accepted by a device; **signal conversion** = processing, changing or modulating a signal; **signal distance** = number of bit positions with different contents in two data words; *see also* HAMMING; **signal element** = smallest basic unit used when transmitting digital data; *the signal element in this system is a short voltage pulse, indicating a binary one; the signal elements for the radio transmission system are 10mS of 40KHz and 10mS of 60KHz for binary 0 and 1 respectively;* **signal processing** = processing of signals to extract the information contained; *the system is used by students doing research on signal processing techniques; the message was recovered by carrier signal processing;* **signal to noise ratio** (S/N) = difference between the power of the transmitted signal and the noise on the line **2** *verb* to send a message to a computer; *signal to the network that we are busy*

◊ **signalling** *noun* (i) method used by a transmitter to warn a receiver that a message is to be sent; (ii) communication to the transmitter about the state of the receiver; **in band signalling** = use of a normal voice grade channel for data transmission

signature *noun* special authentication code, such as a password, which a user gives prior to access to a system *or* prior to the execution of a task (to prove identity)

signify *verb* to mean; *a carriage return code signifies the end of an input line*

◊ **significance** *noun* special meaning

◊ **significant** *adjective* which has a special meaning; **significant digit codes** *or* **faceted codes** = codes which indicate various details of an item, by assigning each one a value

silicon *noun* element with semiconductor properties, used in crystal form as a base for IC manufacture; **silicon chip** = small piece of silicon in and on the surface of which a complete circuit *or* logic function has been produced (by depositing other substances *or* by doping); **silicon disk** *or* **RAM disk** = section of RAM made to look and behave like a high speed disk drive; **silicon foundry** = machine used to create crystals of silicon, then slice them into silicon wafers; **Silicon Valley** = area in California where many US semiconductor device manufacturers are based; **silicon wafer** = thin slice of a pure silicon crystal, usually around 4 inches in diameter on which integrated circuits are produced (these are then cut out of the wafer to produce individual chips)

COMMENT: silicon is used in the electronics industry as a base material for integrated circuits. It is grown as a long crystal which is then sliced into wafers before being etched or treated, producing several hundred chips per wafer. Other materials, such as germanium or gallium arsenide, are also used as a base for ICs

SIMD = SINGLE INSTRUCTION STREAM MULTIPLE DATA STREAM architecture of a parallel computer that has a number of ALUs and data buses with one control unit

SIMM = SINGLE IN-LINE MEMORY MODULE small, compact circuit board with an edge connector along one edge that carries densely-packed memory chips; *you can expand the main memory of your PC by plugging in two more SIMMs*

simple *adjective* not complicated, not difficult; **simple device** = multimedia device that does not require a data file for playback, such as a CD drive used to play audio CDs; **simple to use** = (machine *or* software) easy to use and operate

simple mail transfer protocol

(SMTP) standard protocol which allows electronic mail messages to be transferred from one system to another; normally used as the method of transferring mail from one internet server to another or to send mail from your computer to a server *compare with* POP3

simple network management

protocol (SNMP) network management system which defines how status data is sent from monitored nodes back to a control station; SNMP is able to work with virtually any type of network hardware and software

simplex *noun* data transmission in only one direction (NOTE: opposite is **duplex)**

simplify *verb* to make something simpler; *function keys simplify program operation*

simulate *verb* to copy the behaviour of a system *or* device with another; *this software simulates the action of an aircraft*

◊ **simulator** *noun* device which simulates another system; **flight simulator** = computer program which allows a user to pilot a plane, showing a realistic control panel and moving scenes (either as training programme *or* computer game)

◊ **simulation** *noun* operation where a computer is made to imitate a real life situation *or* a machine, and shows how something works *or* will work in the future; *simulation techniques have reached a high degree of sophistication*

simultaneity *noun* in which the CPU and the I/O sections of a computer can handle different data *or* tasks at the same time

simultaneous *adjective* which takes place at the same time as something else; **simultaneous processing** = two or more processes executed at the same time; **simultaneous transmission** = transmission of data *or* control codes in two directions at the same time (NOTE: same as **duplex**)

◊ **simultaneously** *adverb* at the same time

> COMMENT: true simultaneous processing requires two processors, but can be imitated by switching rapidly between two tasks with a single processor

single *adjective* only one; **single address code** *or* **instruction** = machine code instruction which contains one operator and one address; **single address message** = message with a single destination; **single attachment station (SAS)** = (in an FDDI network) station with only one port through which to attach to the network; SAS stations are connected to the FDDI ring through a concentrator; **single board computer (SBC)** = micro *or* mini computer whose components are all contained on a single printed circuit board; **single density disk (SD)** = standard magnetic disk and drive able to store data; **single frequency signalling** *or* **sf signalling** = use of various frequency signals to represent different control codes; **single function software** = applications program used for one kind of task only; **single instruction stream multiple data stream (SIMD)** = architecture of a parallel computer which has a number of ALUs and data buses with one control unit; **single in-line memory module (SIMM)** = small, compact circuit board with an edge connector along one edge that carries densely-packed memory chips; **single in-line package (SIP)** = electronic component which has all its leads on one side of its package; **single instruction stream single data stream (SISD)** = architecture of a serial computer, which has one ALU and data bus, with one control unit; **single key response** = software which requires only one

key to be pressed (no CR required) to select an option; **single length precision** = number stored in one word *compare* DOUBLE, MULTIPLE LENGTH; **single length working** = using numbers that can be stored within a single word; **single line display** = small screen which displays a single line of characters at a time; **single mode** *or* **monomode fibre** *or* **fiber** = optic fibre that has a very narrow diameter (or 10 microns or less) and is designed to transmit a single light signal over a long distance; this type of fibre has a bandwidth of 5Gbits/second and is normally used for long distance telephone networks; **single operand instruction;** *see* SINGLE ADDRESS INSTRUCTION; **single operation** = communications system which allows data to travel in only one direction at a time (controlled by codes S/O = send only, R/O = receive only, S/R = send or receive); *see also* SIMPLEX; **single pass operation** = software which produces the required result *or* carries out a task after one run; **single precision** = number stored in one word; **single sheet feed** = device attached to a printer to allow single sheets of paper to be used instead of continuous stationery; **single-sided disk (SSD)** = floppy disk that can only store data on one side, because of the way it is manufactured *or* formatted; **single speed** = speed at which a CD-ROM is spun by a drive - normally 230rpm; *see also* DOUBLE-SPEED DRIVE, QUAD-SPEED DRIVE; **single step** = executing a program one instruction at a time; **single-strike ribbon** = printer ribbon which can only be used once *compare* MULTI-STRIKE; **single-system image** = operational view of multiple networks, distributed databases or multiple computer systems as if they were one system; **single-user system** = computer system which can only be used by a single user at a time (as opposed to a multi-user system)

sink *noun* receiving end of a communications line; **sink tree** = description in a routing table of all the paths in a network to a destination (NOTE: the opposite of **sink** is **source**)

SIO = SERIAL INPUT/OUTPUT

SIP = SINGLE IN-LINE PACKAGE

SIPO = SERIAL INPUT/PARALLEL OUTPUT

SISD = SINGLE INSTRUCTION STREAM SINGLE DATA STREAM

SISO = SERIAL INPUT/SERIAL OUTPUT

site *noun* place where something is based; **site licence** = licence between a software publisher and a user which allows any number of users in that site to use the software; *we have negotiated a good deal for the site licence for our 1200 employees in our HQ;* **web site** = collection of web pages that are linked and related and can be accessed by a user with a web browser; for example, the Peter Collin Publishing web site has different web pages for each dictionary, a web page for new titles and an online dictionary, it can be accessed from the home page at the URL 'http://www.pcp.co.uk'

◊ **site poll** *verb* to poll all the terminals *or* devices in a particular location *or* area; *see also* POLLING

sixteen-bit *adjective* (microcomputer system *or* CPU) which handles data in sixteen bit words, providing much faster operation than older eight-bit systems

size 1 *noun* physical dimensions of an image *or* object *or* page; **screen size** = (i) number of characters a computer display can show horizontally and vertically; (ii) size of a monitor screen based on international paper sizes **2** *verb* to calculate the resources available, and those required to carry out a particular job

skeletal code *noun* program which is not complete, with the basic structure coded

skew 1 *noun* the amount by which something which is not correctly aligned **2** *verb* to align something incorrectly; *this page is badly skewed*

skip *verb* to ignore an instruction in a sequence of instructions; *the printer skipped the next three lines of text;* **skip capability** =

feature of certain word-processors to allow the user to jump backwards *or* forwards by a quantity of text in a document; **skip instruction** = null computer command which directs the CPU to the next instruction; **high-speed skip** = rapid movement of paper in a printer, ignoring the normal line advance

slashed zero *noun* a printed *or* written sign (Ø)

> COMMENT: the zero appears on the screen with a line across it to distinguish a zero from the letter Ø

slave *noun* remote secondary computer *or* terminal controlled by a central computer; **bus slave** = data sink which receives data from a bus master; **slave cache** *or* **store** = section of high-speed memory which stores data that the CPU can access quickly; **slave processor** = dedicated processor controlled by a master processor; **slave terminal** = terminal controlled by a main computer *or* terminal; **slave tube** = second CRT display connected to another so that it shows exactly the same information

sleep *noun* state of a system that is waiting for a signal (log-on) before doing anything; *see also* WAKE-UP

sleeve *noun* paper *or* plastic cover for a magnetic disk

slew *noun* rapid movement of paper in a printer, ignoring the normal line advance

slice *noun* section *or* piece of something; **bit-slice architecture** = construction of a large word size CPU by joining a number of smaller word size blocks; *the bit-slice design uses four four-bit word processors to make a sixteen-bit processor;* **time slice** = period of time allocated for a user *or* program *or* job within a multitasking system; amount of time allowed for a single task in a time-sharing system *or* in multiprogramming

slide *verb* to move smoothly across a surface; *the disk cover slides on and off easily*

SLIP = SERIAL LINE INTERNET PROTOCOL method of sending TCP/IP network traffic over a serial line, such as a telephone modem connection (normally used to connect a user's computer to the internet via a modem link)

slot 1 *noun* **(a)** long thin hole; *the system disk should be inserted into the left-hand slot on the front of the computer;* **expansion slot** = connector inside a computer into which an expansion card can be plugged; *there are two free slots in the micro, you only need one for the add-on board* **(b)**; **message slot** = number of bits that can hold a message which circulates round a ring network **2** *verb* to insert an object into a hole; *the disk slots into one of the floppy drive apertures*

SLSI = SUPER LARGE SCALE INTEGRATION

small *adjective* not large

◊ **small computer systems interface (SCSI)** *noun* standard high-speed parallel interface used to connect computers to peripheral devices (such as disk drives and scanners)

◊ **small scale integration (SSI)** *noun* integrated circuit with 1 to 10 components

Smalltalk object-oriented programming language developed by Xerox

smart *adjective* intelligent; **smart card** = plastic card with a memory and microprocessor embedded in it, so that it can be used for direct money transfer *or* for identification of the user; *see also* PID; **smart terminal** *or* **intelligent terminal** = computer terminal which can process information; **smart wiring hub** = network hub *or* concentrator which can transmit status information back to a managing station and allows management software to configure each port remotely; *using this management software, I can shut down Tom's port on the remote smart wiring hub*

SMB = SERVER MESSAGE BLOCK system (developed by Microsoft) which allows a user to access another computer's files and peripherals over a network as if they were local resources

smiley *noun* face created with text characters, used to provide the real meaning to an email message; for example, :-) means laughter or a joke, and :-(means sad

smog *noun;* **electronic smog** = excessive stray electromagnetic fields and static electricity generated by large numbers of electronic equipment (this can damage equipment and a person's health)

smoke test *noun (informal)* casual test which indicates that the machine must be working if no smoke appears when it is switched on

SMT = SURFACE-MOUNT TECHNOLOGY method of manufacturing circuit boards in which the electronic components are bonded directly onto the surface of the board rather than being inserted into holes and soldered into place; *surface-mount technology is faster and more space-efficient than soldering*

SMTP = SIMPLE MAIL TRANSFER PROTOCOL standard protocol which allows electronic mail messages to be transferred from one system to another; normally used as the method of transferring mail from one internet server to another or to send mail from your computer to a server; *compare with* POP3

SNA = SYSTEMS NETWORK ARCHITECTURE design methods developed by IBM which define how communications in a network should occur and allow different hardware to communicate

snail mail *noun* slang term used to refer to the normal (slow) postal delivery rather than (near instant) electronic mail delivery

snapshot *noun* (i) recording of all the states of a computer at a particular instant; (ii) storing in main memory the contents of a screen full of information at an instant; **snapshot dump** = printout of all the registers and a section of memory at a particular instant, used when debugging a program

snd (SouND) filename extension used to indicate a file that contains digitized sound data

SNMP = SIMPLE NETWORK MANAGEMENT PROTOCOL

SNOBOL = STRING ORIENTATED SYMBOLIC LANGUAGE high-level programming language which uses string processing methods

snow *noun* interference displayed as flickering white flecks on a monitor

soak *verb* to run a program *or* device continuously for a period of time to make sure it functions correctly; *the device was soak-tested prior to delivery*

socket *noun* device with a set of holes, into which a plug fits; **female socket** = hole into which a pin *or* plug can be inserted to make an electrical connection

---

the mouse and keyboard sockets are the same, and could lead to the kind of confusion that arose with the early PCs when the keyboard could be connected to the tape socket

PC User

---

soft *adjective* **(a)** (material) which loses its magnetic effects when removed from a magnetic field **(b)** (data) which is not permanently stored in hardware (soft usually refers to data stored on magnetic medium); **soft copy** = text listed on screen (as opposed to hard copy on paper); **soft error** = random error caused by software or data errors (this type of error is very difficult to trace and identify since it only appears under certain conditions) *compare* HARD ERROR; **soft-fail** = (system) which is still partly operational even after a part of the system has failed; **soft font** = fonts *or* typefaces stored on a disk, which can be downloaded *or* sent to a printer and stored in temporary memory *or* RAM; **soft hyphen** = hyphen which is inserted when a word is split at the end of a line, but is not present when the word is written normally; **soft keys** = keys which can be changed by means of a program; **soft keyboard** = keyboard where the functions of

the keys can be changed by programs; **soft-reset** = instruction which terminates any program execution and returns the user to the monitor program *or* BIOS *compare* HARD RESET; **soft-sectored disk** = disk where the sectors are described by an address and start code data written onto it when the disk is formatted; **soft zone** = text area to the left of the right margin in a word-processed document, where if a word does not fit completely, a hyphen is automatically inserted

software *noun* any program *or* group of programs which instructs the hardware on how it should perform, including operating systems, word processors and applications programs; **applications software** = programs which are used by the user to perform a certain task; **bundled software** = software which is included in the price of the system; **common software** = useful routines that can be used by any program; **network software** = software which is used to establish the link between a users' program and a network; **pirate software** = illegal copy of a software package; **system software** = programs which direct the basic functions, input-output control, etc., of a computer; **unbundled software** = software which is not included in the price of a system; **user-friendly software** = program which is easy for a non-expert to use and interact with; **software compatible** = (computer) which will load and run programs written for another computer; **software development** = processes required to produce working programs from an initial idea; **software documentation** = information, notes and diagrams describing the function, use and operation of a piece of software; **software engineer** = person who can write working software to fit an application; **software engineering** = field of study covering all software-related subjects; **software house** = company which develops and sells computer programs; **software interrupt** = high priority program generated signal, requesting the use of the central processor; **software library** = number of specially written routines, stored in a library file which can be inserted into a program, saving time and effort; **software licence** =

agreement between a user and a software house, giving details of the rights of the user to use *or* copy the software; **software life cycle** = period of time when a piece of software exists, from its initial design to the moment when it becomes out of date; **software maintenance** = carrying out updates and modifications to a software package to make sure the program is up to date Vapourware; **software-only video playback** = ability to display full-motion video standard on any multimedia computer, that does not need special hardware; **software package** = complete set of programs (and the manual) which allow a certain task to be performed; **software piracy** = illegal copying of software for sale; **software quality assurance (SQA)** = making sure that software will perform as intended; **software reliability** = ability of a piece of software to perform the task required correctly; **software specification** = detailed information about a piece of software's abilities, functions and methods; **software system** = all the programs required for one or more tasks; **software tool** = program used in the development of other programs (NOTE: no plural for **software**; for the plural say **pieces of software**)

solid *adjective;* **solid colour** = colour that can be displayed on a screen or printed on a colour printer without dithering; **solid error** = error that is always present when certain equipment is used; **solid font printer** = printer which uses a whole character shape to print in one movement, such as a daisy wheel printer; **solid modelling** = function in a graphics program that creates three-dimensional solid-looking objects by shading

◊ **solid-state** *adjective* referring to semiconductor devices; **solid-state device** = electronic device which operates by using the effects of electrical *or* magnetic signals in a solid semiconductor material; **solid-state memory device** = solid-state memory storage device (usually in the form of RAM or ROM chips)

solution *noun* answer to a problem

solve *verb* to find the answer to a problem

son file *noun* latest working version of a file *compare* FATHER FILE, GRANDFATHER FILE

sophisticated *adjective* technically advanced; *a sophisticated desktop publishing program*

◊ **sophistication** *noun* being technically advanced; *the sophistication of the new package is remarkable*

sort *verb* to put data into order, according to a system, on the instructions of the user; *to sort addresses into alphabetical order; to sort orders according to account numbers;* **bubble sort** = sorting method which repeatedly exchanges various pairs of data items until they are in order; **shell sort** = algorithm for sorting data items, in which items can be moved more than position per sort action; **sort/merge** = program which allows new files to be sorted and then merged in correct order into existing files; **tree selection sort** = rapid form of selection where the information from the first sort pass is used in the second pass to speed up selection

◊ **sortkey** *or* **sort field** *noun* field in a stored file which is used to sort the file; *the orders were sorted according to dates by assigning the date field as the sortkey*

sound *noun* noise; **sound bandwidth** = range of frequencies that a human ear can register, normally from 20Hz to 20KHz; **sound capture** = conversion of an analog sound into a digital form that can be used by a computer; *see also* ANALOG TO DIGITAL CONVERSION; **sound card** = expansion card which produces analog sound signals under the control of a computer; *this software lets you create almost any sound - but you can only hear them if you have a sound card fitted;* **sound hood** = cover which cuts down the noise from a noisy printer; **sound file** = file stored on disk that contains sound data

◊ **Sound Blaster**™ type of sound card for PC compatibles developed by Creative Labs that allows sounds to be recorded to disk (using a microphone) and played back

◊ **Sound Recorder** utility included with Microsoft Windows that allows a user to play back digitized sound files or record sound onto disk and carry out very basic editing

source *noun* **(a)** point where a transmitted signal enters a network (NOTE: opposite is **sink**) **(b)** original *or* initial point; **source address filtering** = feature of some bridges which detects a particular address in the received packet and either rejects or forwards the data; **source code** = set of codes written by the programmer which cannot be directly executed by the computer, but has to be translated into an object code program by a compiler *or* interpreter; **source deck** *or* **pack** = set of punched cards which contain the source code for a program; **source document** = form *or* document from which data is extracted prior to entering it into a database; **source editor** = software which allows the user to alter, delete or add instructions in a program source file; **source file** = program written in source language, which is then converted to machine code by a compiler; **source listing** = (i) listing of a text in its original form; (ii) listing of a source program; **source machine** = computer which can compile source code *compare* OBJECT MACHINE; **source object** = (in Windows) within a drag and drop operation the source object is the object that is first clicked on and then dragged; **source program** = program, prior to translation, written in a programming language by a programmer; **source routing** = method (originally developed by IBM for its Token Ring networks) of moving data between two networks which examines the data within the token and passes the data to the correct station; **source transparent routing (SRT)** = standard developed by IBM and the IEEE; it allows IBM networks and non-IBM Token Ring networks to be bridged and so exchange data

source language *noun* (i) language in which a program is originally written in; (ii) language of a program prior to translation (NOTE: opposite is **object** *or* **target language**)

SP = STACK POINTER

space 1 *noun* **(a)** gap between characters or lines; **space character** = character code which prints a space; **space bar** = long bar at the bottom of a keyboard, which inserts a space into the text when pressed **2** *verb* to spread out text; *the line of characters was evenly spaced out across the page*

spacer *noun;* **intelligent spacer** = facility on a word-processing system used to prevent words from being hyphenated *or* separated at the wrong point

spacing *noun* putting spaces between characters or lines of printed text; *the spacing on some lines is very uneven*

spam *noun slang* (i) article that has been posted to more than one newsgroup, so is likely to contain commercial messages; (ii) unwanted and unrequested email sent to lots of people at the same time, normally to advertise a produce; **anti-spam** = feature of some email programs that will automatically delete any unwanted spam messages that are received

span *noun* set of allowed values between a maximum and minimum

spanning tree *noun* method of creating a network topology that does not contain any loops and provides redundancy in case of a network fault or problem

SPARC = SCALAR PROCESSOR ARCHITECTURE RISC processor designed by Sun Microsystems which is used in its range of workstations

spark printer *noun* thermal printer which produces characters on thermal paper by electric sparks

sparse array *noun* data matrix structure containing mainly zero *or* null entries

spatial measurement *noun* method of allowing a computer to determine the position of a pointer within three dimensions (often using a sensitive glove)

spec *(informal)* = SPECIFICATION; **high-spec** = high specification

special *adjective* which is different *or* not usual; **special character** = character which is not a normal one in a certain font (such as a certain accent *or* a symbol); **special purpose** = system designed for a specific *or* limited range of applications; **special sort** = extra printing character not in the standard font range

special interest group (SIG) *noun*

group (within a larger club) which is interested in a particular aspect of software or hardware; *our local computer club has a SIG for comms and networking*

specialist *noun* expert in a certain field of study; *you need a specialist programmer to help devise a new word-processing program*

specialize *verb* to study and be an expert in a subject; *he specializes in the design of CAD systems*

specific address *noun* storage address which directly, without any modification, accesses a location *or* device

specific code *noun* binary code which directly operates the central processing unit, using only absolute addresses and values; **specific coding** = program code which has been written so that it only uses absolute addresses and values

specificity *noun* ratio of non-relevant entries not retrieved to the total number of non-relevant entries contained in a file, database or library

specify *verb* to state clearly what is needed

specification *noun* detailed information about what is to be supplied *or* about a job to be done; **to work to standard specifications** = to work to specifications which are accepted anywhere in the same industry; **the work is not up to specification** *or* **does not meet the customer's specifications** = the product was not manufactured in the way which was detailed in the specifications; **high specification** *or* **high spec** = high degree of accuracy *or* large number of features; *high spec cabling needs to be very carefully handled;* **program specification** = detailed information about a program's abilities, features and methods

speech *noun* speaking *or* making words with the voice; **speech chip** = integrated circuit which generates sounds (usually phonemes) which when played together sound like human speech; **speech recognition** = analysing spoken words in such a way that a computer can recognize spoken words and commands; **speech synthesis** = production of spoken words by a speech synthesizer; **speech synthesizer** = device which takes data from a computer and outputs it as spoken words

> speech conveys information, and the primary task of computer speech processing is the transmission and reception of that information
> *Personal Computer World*

speed *noun* time taken for a movement divided by the distance travelled; **speed of loop** = method of benchmarking a computer by measuring the number of loops executed in a certain time; **playback speed** = rate at which tape travels past a playback head

spellcheck *verb* to check the spelling in a text by comparing it with a dictionary held in the computer

◊ **spellchecker** *or* **spelling checker** *noun* dictionary of correctly spelled words, held in a computer, and used to check the spelling of a text; *the program will be upgraded with a word-processor and a spelling checker*

spherization *noun* special effect provided by a computer graphics program that converts an image into a sphere, or 'wraps' the image over a spherical shape

spike *noun* very short duration voltage pulse

spillage *noun* situation when too much data is being processed and cannot be contained in a buffer

spin *verb* to turn round fast; *the disk was spun by the drive; the disk drive motor spins at a constant velocity*

spindle *noun* object which grips and spins a disk in the centre hole

spindling *noun* turning a disk by hand

splash screen *noun* initial screen that is displayed for a few seconds when a program is started; *the splash screen normally displays the product logo and gives basic copyright information*

splice *verb* to join two lengths of magnetic tape, forming a continuous length; **splicing tape** = non-magnetic tape which is applied to the back of the two ends of tape to be spliced

split screen *noun* software which can divide the display into two or more independent areas, to display two text files or a graph and a text file; *we use split screen mode to show the text being worked on and another text from memory for comparison*

spool 1 *noun* reel on which a tape *or* printer ribbon is wound **2** *verb* to transfer data from a disk to a tape

◊ **spooler** *or* **spooling device**   *noun* device which holds a tape and which receives information from a disk for storage

◊ **spooling** *noun* transferring data to a disk from which it can be printed at the normal speed of the printer, leaving the computer available to do something else

sporadic fault *noun* error which occurs occasionally

spreadsheet *noun* (i) program which allows calculations to be carried out on several columns of numbers; (ii) printout of calculations on wide computer stationary

sprite *noun* object which moves round the screen in computer graphics

sprocket *or* **sprocket wheel**   *noun* wheel with teeth round it which fit into holes in continuous stationery *or* punched tape

◊ **sprocket feed** *noun* paper feed, where the printer pulls the paper by turning sprocket wheels which fit into a series of holes along each edge of the sheet; *see also* TRACTOR FEED

◊ **sprocket holes** *noun* series of small holes on each edge of continuous stationery, which allow the sheet to be pulled through the printer

square wave *noun* pulse that rises vertically, levels off, then drops vertically; the ideal shape for a digital signal

SPX 1 = SEQUENCED PACKET EXCHANGE network transport protocol developed by Novell and used to carry IPX network traffic **2** = SIMPLEX data transmission in only one direction (NOTE: opposite is **duplex)**

SQA = SOFTWARE QUALITY ASSURANCE

SQL = STRUCTURED QUERY LANGUAGE simple, commonly used standard, database programming language that is only used to create queries to retrieve data from the database

SRAM *see* STATIC RAM

SRT = SOURCE TRANSPARENT ROUTING

SSD = SINGLE-SIDED DISK

SSI = SMALL SCALE INTEGRATION

SSL = SECURE SOCKETS LAYER protocol designed by Netscape that provides secure communications over the internet; *see also* PGP, SEPP, SET, STT

ST connector *noun* connector used to terminate optical fibres

ST506 standard *noun* (old) disk interface standard used in early IBM PCs, developed by Seagate; *the ST506 standard has now been replaced by IDE and SCSI*

stable *adjective* not moving *or* not changing; **stable state** = the state of a system when no external signals are applied

◊ **stability** *noun* being stable; **image stability** = ability of a display screen to provide a flicker-free picture

stack *noun* temporary storage for data, registers *or* tasks where items are added and retrieved from the same end of the list; *see also* LIFO; **stack address** = location pointed to by the stack pointer; **stack base** = address of the origin *or* base of a stack; **stack job**

processor = storing a number of jobs to be processed in a stack and automatically executing one after the other; **stack overflow** = error message that is sometimes displayed when there is not enough free memory on a computer for a program's needs; **stack pointer (SP)** = address register containing the location of the most recently stored item of data *or* the location of the next item of data to be retrieved; **stackware** = application developed using the Apple Macintosh HyperCard system; **push-down stack** *or* **push-down list** = method of storing data, where the last item stored is always at the same location, the rest of the list being pushed down by one address; **virtual memory stack** = temporary store for pages in a virtual memory system

stage *noun* one of several points in a process; *the text is ready for the printing stage; we are in the first stage of running in the new computer system*

◊ **staged** *adjective* carried out in stages, one after the other; **staged change-over** = change between an old and a new system in a series of stages

stand-alone *or* standalone *adjective & noun* (device *or* system) which can operate without the need of any other devices; *the workstations have been networked together rather than used as stand-alone systems;* **stand-alone system** = system which can operate independently; **stand-alone terminal** = computer terminal with a processor and memory which can be directly connected to a modem, without being a member of a network *or* cluster

standard *adjective* normal *or* usual; **standard colours** = range of colours that are available on a particular system and can be shared by all applications; **standard document** *or* **standard form** *or* **standard paragraph** *or* **standard text** = normal printed document *or* form *or* paragraph which is used many times (with different names and addresses often inserted - as in a form letter); **standard function** = special feature included as normal in a computer system; **Standard Generalized Markup Language;** *see* SGML; **standard interface** = interface

between two or more systems which conforms to pre-defined standards; **standard letter** = letter which is sent without any change to the main text, but which is personalized by inserting the names and addresses of different people; **standard memory** = first 1Mb of memory in a PC; *see also* EXPANDED MEMORY, UPPER MEMORY; **standard mode** = (in an IBM PC) mode of operation of Microsoft Windows which uses extended memory but does not allow multitasking of DOS applications; **standard subroutine** = routine which carries out an often used function, such as keyboard input *or* screen display

◊ **standardize** *verb* to make a series of things conform to a standard; *to standardize control of transmission links*

◊ **standard** *noun* normal quality *or* normal conditions which are used to judge other things; **up to standard** = of an acceptable quality; *this batch of disks is not up to standard;* **standards converter** = device to convert received signals conforming to one standard into a different standard; **modem standards** = rules defining transmitting frequencies, etc., which allow different modems to communicate; **production standards** = quality of production

COMMENT: modem standards are set by the CCITT in the UK, the Commonwealth and most of Europe, while the USA and part of South America use modem standards set by Bell

standby *adjective & noun* (device *or* program) which is ready for use in case of failure; **standby equipment** = secondary system identical to the main system, to be used if the main system breaks down; **cold standby** = backup system which will allow the equipment to continue running but with the loss of any volatile data; **hot standby** = backup equipment which is kept operational at all times in case of system failure

before fault-tolerant systems, users had to rely on the cold standby, that is switching on a second machine when the first developed a fault; the alternative was the hot

standby, where a second
computer was kept running
continuously

Computer News

star network topology *noun* network
of several machines where each node is
linked individually to a central hub *compare*
BUS NETWORK, RING NETWORK

◊ **star program** *noun* perfect program
which runs (first time) without any errors or
bugs

start *adjective* beginning *or* first part; **cold
start** = switching on a computer *or* to run a
program from its original start point; **start bit**
or **element** = transmitted bit used (in
asynchronous communications) to indicate
the start of a character (NOTE: opposite is **stop
bit**); **warm start** = restarting a program
which has stopped, without losing any data;
start of header = transmitted code indicating
the start of header (address *or* destination)
information for a following message; **start of
text (SOT** *or* **STX)** = transmitted code
indicating the end of control *or* address
information and the start of the message

◊ **Start button** *noun* button that is
normally in the bottom left-hand corner of a
Windows 95 Desktop screen and provides a
convenient route to the programs and files on
the computer

◊ **startup disk** *noun* floppy disk which
holds the operating system and system
configuration files which can, in case of hard
disk failure, be used to boot the computer

◊ **Startup folder** *noun* special folder on a
hard disk that contains programs that will be
run automatically when the user next starts
Windows

◊ **startup screen** *noun* text or graphics
displayed when an application or multimedia
book is run

state *noun* the way something is; **active
state** = state in which an action can *or* does
occur; **steady state** = circuit *or* device *or*
program state in which no action is occurring
but can accept an input

statement *noun* (i) expression used to
convey an instruction *or* define a process; (ii)
instruction in a source language which is

translated into several machine code
instructions; **conditional statement** =
program instruction which will redirect
program control according to the outcome of
an event; **control statement** = (i) program
instruction which directs a program (to
another branch, etc.); (ii) program instruction
which directs a CPU to provide controlling
actions *or* controls the actions of the CPU;
directive statement = program instruction
used to control the language translator,
compiler, etc.; **input statement** = computer
programming command which waits for data
entry from a port *or* keyboard;
multi-statement line = line from a computer
program which contains more than one
instruction *or* statement; **narrative statement**
= statement which sets variables and
allocates storage; **statement number** =
number assigned (in a sequential way) to a
series of instruction statements; *see also*
LINE NUMBER

state-of-the-art *adjective* very modern *or*
technically as advanced as possible

the main PCB is decidedly
non-state-of-the-art

Personal Computer World

static *adjective* (i) (data) which does not
change with time; (ii) (system) which is not
dynamic; **static dump** = printout of the state
of a system when it has finished a process;
static electricity = electrical charge that can
build up in a person or electronic component;
static memory = non-volatile memory that
does not require refreshing; **static RAM
(SRAM)** = RAM which retains data for as
long as the power supply is on, and where the
data does not have to be refreshed *compare*
DYNAMIC RAM; **static subroutine** =
subroutine which uses no variables apart
from the operand addresses

COMMENT: static RAM uses bistable
devices such as flip-flops to store data;
these take up more space on a chip than
the capacitive storage method of
dynamic RAM but do not require
refreshing

station *noun* point in a network *or*
communications system which contains

devices to control the input and output of messages, allowing it to be used as a sink *or* source; **secondary station** = temporary status of the station that is receiving data; **station management (SMT)** = software and hardware within the FDDI specification which provides control information; **workstation** = desk with computer, keyboard, monitor, printers, etc., where a person works

stationery *noun* office supplies for writing, especially paper, envelopes, labels, etc.; **computer stationery** = paper specially made for use in a computer printer; **continuous stationery** = printer stationery which takes the form of a single long sheet; **preprinted stationery** = computer stationery (such as invoices) which is preprinted with the company heading and form layout onto which the details will be printed by the computer

statistics *noun* (study of) facts in the form of figures

◊ **statistical** *adjective* based on statistics

status *noun* importance *or* position; **status bar** = line at the top or bottom of a screen which gives information about the task currently being worked on (position of cursor, number of lines, filename, time, etc.); **status bit** = single bit in a word used to provide information about the state *or* result of an operation; **status line** = line at the top *or* bottom of a screen which gives information about the task currently being worked on (number of lines, number of columns, filename, time, etc.); **status poll** = signal from a computer requesting information on the current status of a terminal; **status register** = register containing information on the status of a peripheral device; **program status word (PSW)** = word which contains a number of status bits, such as carry flag, zero flag, overflow bit, etc.

steady state *noun* circuit *or* device *or* program state in which no action is occurring but can accept an input

stencil *noun;* **flowchart stencil** *or* **template** = plastic sheet with template

symbols cut out, to allow flowcharts to be quickly and clearly drawn

step 1 *noun* a single unit; **single step** = executing a computer program one instruction at a time, used for debugging **2** *verb* to move forward *or* backwards by one unit; *we stepped forward through the file one record at a time*

◊ **step frame** *verb* to capture a video sequence one frame at a time, used when the computer is not powerful or fast enough to capture real-time full-motion video

◊ **stepper motor** *or* **stepping motor** *noun* motor which turns in small steps as instructed by a computer (used in printers, disk drives and robots)

◊ **step through** *noun* function of a debugger that allows a developer to execute a program one instruction at a time to see where the fault lies

stereo *or* **stereophonic** sound recorded onto two separate channels from two separate microphone elements and played back through a pair of headphones or two speakers

stochastic model *noun* mathematical representation of a system which includes the effects of random actions

stock control program *noun* software designed to help manage stock in a business

stop 1 *verb* to cease doing something; **stop and wait protocol** = communications protocol in which the transmitter waits for a signal from the receiver that the message was correctly received before transmitting further data; **stop bit** *or* **stop element** = transmitted bit used in asynchronous communications to indicate the end of a character; **stop code** = instruction which temporarily stops a process to allow the user to enter data; **stop instruction** = computer programming instruction which stops program execution; **stop list** = list of words which are not to be used *or* are not significant for a file *or* library search; **stop time** = time taken for a spinning disk to come to a stop after it is no longer powered **2** *noun* not doing any action; **tab stop** = preset point along a line, where the printing head *or* cursor will stop for each tabulation command

storage *noun* memory *or* part of the computer system in which data *or* programs are kept for further use; **archive storage** = storage of data for a long period of time; **auxiliary storage** = any data storage medium (such as magnetic tape *or* disk) that is not the main, high speed memory; **dynamic storage** *or* **memory** = memory that requires its contents to be updated regularly; **external storage** = storage device which is located outside the main computer system but which can be accessed by the CPU; **information storage** = storing data in a form which allows it to be processed at a later date; **instruction storage** = section of memory used to store instructions; **intermediate storage** = temporary area of memory for items which are currently being processed; **mass storage system** = data storage which can hold more than one million million bits of data; **nonerasable storage** = storage medium which cannot be erased and re-used; **primary storage** = (i) small fast-access internal memory of a system which contains the program currently being executed; (ii) main internal memory of a system; **secondary storage** = any data storage medium (such as magnetic tape *or* floppy disk) which is not the main, high-speed computer storage; **static storage** = non-volatile memory which does not require refreshing; **temporary storage** = storage which is not permanent; **volatile storage** = memory *or* storage medium which loses data stored when the power supply is switched off; **storage allocation** = how memory is allocated for different uses, such as programs, variables, data, etc.; **storage capacity** = amount of space available for storage of data; **storage density** = number of bits which can be recorded per unit area of storage medium; **storage device** = any device which can store data and then allow it to retrieved when required; **storage disk** = disk used to store data; **storage dump** = printout of all the contents of an area of storage space; **storage media** = the various materials which are able to store data; **storage tube** = special CRT used for computer graphics; it retains an image on screen without the need for refresh actions; *see also* REFRESH

◊ **store 1** *noun* memory *or* part of the computer system in which data *or* programs are kept for further use; **store address register (SAR)** = register in a CPU which contains the address of the next location to be accessed; **store data register (SDR)** = register in a CPU which holds data before it is processed *or* moved to a memory location; **store location** *or* **cell** = unit in a computer system which can store information **2** *verb* to save data, which can then be used again as necessary; *storing a page of high resolution graphics can require 3Mb;* **store and forward** = electronic mail communications system which stores a number of messages before retransmitting them; **stored program** = computer program which is stored in memory (if it is stored in dynamic RAM it will be lost when the machine is switched off, if stored on disk or tape (backing store) it will be permanently retained); **stored program signalling** = system of storing communications control signals on computer in the form of a program

COMMENT: storage devices include hard and floppy disk, RAM, punched paper tape and magnetic tape

story board *noun* series of pictures or drawings that show how a video or animation progresses

STP *see* = SHIELDED TWISTED PAIR

straight-line coding *noun* program written to avoid the use of loops and branches, providing a faster execution time

stray *adjective* lost *or* wandering; (something) which has avoided being stopped; *the metal screen protects the CPU against stray electromagnetic effects from the PSU*

stream *noun* long flow of serial data; **job stream** = number of tasks arranged in order waiting to be processed in a batch system

◊ **streamer** *noun;* **tape streamer** *or* **streaming tape drive** = (device containing a)

continuous loop of tape, used as backing storage

> the product has 16Mb of memory, 45Mb of Winchester disk storage and 95Mb streaming tape storage
>
> *Minicomputer News*

string *noun* any series of consecutive alphanumeric characters *or* words that are manipulated and treated as a single unit by the computer; **alphanumeric** *or* **character string** = storage allocated for a series of alphanumeric characters; **numeric string** = string which contains only numbers; **null** *or* **blank string** = string which contains nothing; **string area** = section of memory in which strings of alphanumeric characters are stored; **string concatenation** = linking a series of strings together; **string function** = program operation which can act on strings; **string length** = the number of characters in a string; **string name** = identification label assigned to a string; **string orientated symbolic language (SNOBOL)** = high-level programming language that uses string processing methods; **string variable** = variable used in a computer language that can contain alphanumeric characters as well as numbers

◊ **stringy floppy** *or* **tape streamer** *noun* continuous loop of tape, used for backing storage

strip 1 *noun* long thin piece of material; **strip window** = display which shows a single line of text; **magnetic strip** = layer of magnetic material on the surface of a plastic card, used for recording data 2 *verb* to remove the control data from a received message, leaving only the relevant information

strobe 1 *verb* to send a pulse (usually on the selection line) of an electronic circuit 2 *noun* pulse of an electric circuit; **address strobe** = signal indicating that a valid address is on the address bus; **data strobe** = signal indicating that valid data is on the data bus

stroke *noun* (i) width (in pixels) of a pen or brush used to draw on-screen; (ii) thickness of a printed character

structure 1 *noun* way in which something is organized *or* formed; **network structure** = data structure which allows each node to be connected to any of the others 2 *verb* to organize *or* to arrange in a certain way; *you first structure a document to meet your requirements and then fill in the blanks;* **structured cabling** = (organisation which is cabled) using UTP cable feeding into hubs designed in such a way that it is easy to trace and repair cable faults and also to add new stations or more cable; **structured design** = a number of interconnected modules which are intended to solve problems; **structured programming** = well-ordered and logical technique of assembling programs; **structured query language (SQL)** = simple, commonly used, standard database programming language which is only used to create queries to retrieve data from the database; **structured wiring** = planned installation of all the cables that will be required in an office or building for computer networks and telephone

STT = SECURE TRANSACTION TECHNOLOGY system developed to provide a secure link between a user's browser and a vendor's Web site to allow the user to pay for goods over the internet; *see also* PGP, SEPP, SET, S-HTTP, SSL

STX = START OF TEXT

stub *noun* short program routine which contains comments to describe the executable code that will, eventually, be inserted into the routine

stuck beacon *noun* (error condition in which) a station continuously transmits beacon frames

style *noun* typeface, font, point size, colour, spacing and margins of text in a formatted document

◊ **style sheet** *noun* template which can be preformatted to generate automatically the style *or* layout of a document such as a manual, a book, a newsletter, etc.

stylus *noun* pen-like device which is used in computer graphics systems to dictate cursor position on the screen; *use the stylus to draw on the graphics tablet;* **stylus printer** = printer that prints using a pen, normally by drawing tiny dots on the paper to form characters and graphics; *compare* INK-JET PRINTER

sub- *prefix* meaning less (important) than *or* lower than; **subaddress** = peripheral identification code, used to access one peripheral (this is then followed by address data to access a location within the peripheral's memory); **subclass** = number of data items related to one item in a master class

subdirectory *noun* directory of disk *or* tape contents contained within the main directory

> if you delete a file and then delete the subdirectory where it was located, you cannot restore the file because the directory does not exist
> *Personal Computer World*

sub-domain *noun* second level of addressing on the internet that normally refers to a department name within a larger organisation

◊ **submenu** *noun* secondary menu displayed as a choice from a menu

◊ **subprogram** *noun* (i) subroutine in a program; (ii) program called up by a main program

subroutine *noun* section of a program which performs a required function and can be called upon at any time from inside the main program; **closed** *or* **linked subroutine** = number of computer instructions in a program which can be called at any time, with control being returned on completion to the next instruction after the call; **open subroutine** = code for a subroutine which is copied into memory whenever a call instruction is found; **static subroutine** = subroutine which uses no variables apart from the operand addresses; **two-level subroutine** = subroutine containing another subroutine; **subroutine call** = computer programming instruction which directs control to a subroutine

> COMMENT: a subroutine is executed by a call instruction which directs the processor to its address; when finished it returns to the instruction after the call instruction in the main program

subscribe *verb* to add your name to a mailing list or listserv list so that you will receive any messages for the group

◊ **subscriber** *noun* (i) person who has a telephone; (ii) person who pays for access to a service such as a BBS

subscript *noun* small character which is printed below the line of other characters; *see also* SUPERSCRIPT (NOTE: used in chemical formulae: CO_2)

◊ **subscripted variable** *noun* element in an array, which is identified by a subscript

◊ **subset** *noun* small set of data items which forms part of a another larger set

◊ **subsegment** *noun* small section of a segment

substitute *verb* to put something in the place of something else (NOTE: you substitute one thing **for** another)

◊ **substitute character** *noun* character which is displayed if a received character is not recognized

◊ **substitution** *noun* replacing something by something else; **substitution error** = error made by a scanner which mistakes one character *or* letter for another; **substitution table** = list of characters *or* codes which are to be inserted instead of received codes

substrate *noun* base material on which an integrated circuit is constructed; *see also* INTEGRATED CIRCUIT

subsystem *noun* one smaller part of a large system

subtraction *noun* taking one number away from another

◊ **subtrahend** *noun* in a subtraction operation, the number to be subtracted from the minuend

sub-woofer *noun* large loudspeaker that can reproduce very low frequency sounds (normally with frequencies between 20 to

100Hz) that is used with normal loudspeakers to enhance the overall sound quality

successive *adjective* which follow one after the other; *each successive operation adds further characters to the string*

suffix notation *noun* mathematical operations written in a logical way, so that the symbol appears after the numbers to be acted upon; *see also* POSTFIX NOTATION

suitcase *noun* (in the Apple Macintosh environment) icon which contains a screen font and allows fonts to be easily installed onto the system

suite of programs *noun* (i) group of programs which run one after the other; (ii) number of programs used for a particular task; *the word-processing system uses a suite of three programs, editor, spelling checker and printing controller*

sum *noun* total of a number of items added together

◊ **summation check** *noun* error detection check performed by adding together the characters received and comparing with the required total

Sun Microsystems™ company that developed the Java programming system used to extend Web pages

super- *prefix* meaning very good *or* very powerful; **supercomputer** = very powerful mainframe computer used for high speed mathematical tasks; **super VGA (SVGA)** = enhancement to the standard VGA graphics display system which allows resolutions of up to 800x600pixels with 16million colours

◊ **super large scale integration (SLSI)** *noun* integrated circuit with more than 100,000 components

superimpose *verb* to place something on top of something else

superior number *noun* superscript figure

superscript *noun* small character printed higher than the normal line of characters;

compare SUBSCRIPT (NOTE: used often in mathematics: 10^5 say: **ten to the power five**)

supersede *verb* to take the place of something which is older *or* less useful; *the new program supersedes the earlier one, and is much faster*

supervise *verb* to watch carefully to see if work is well done; *the manufacture of circuit boards is very carefully supervised*

◊ **supervision** *noun* being supervised

◊ **supervisor** *noun* (i) person who makes sure that equipment is always working correctly; (ii) section of a computer operating system that regulates the use of peripherals and the operations undertaken by the CPU

◊ **supervisory** *adjective* as a supervisor; **supervisory program** *or* **executive program** = master program in a computer system that controls the execution of other programs; **supervisory sequence** = combination of control codes that perform a controlling function in a data communications network; **supervisory signal** = (i) signal that indicates if a circuit is busy; (ii) signal which provides an indication of the state of a device

supply 1 *noun* providing goods *or* products *or* services; *the electricity supply has failed; they signed a contract for the supply of computer stationery* **2** *verb* to provide something which is needed (for which someone will pay); *the computer was supplied by a recognized dealer; they have signed a contract to supply on-line information*

◊ **supplier** *noun* company which supplies; *a supplier of computer parts; a supplier of disk drives or a disk drive supplier; Japanese suppliers have set up warehouses in the country*

support *verb* to give help to *or* to help to run; *the main computer supports six workstations;* **support chip** = dedicated IC which works with a CPU, and carries out an additional function *or* a standard function very rapidly, so speeding up the processing time; *the maths support chip can be plugged in here*

suppress *verb* to remove; *the filter is used to suppress the noise due to static interference*

◊ **suppression** *noun* act of suppressing

◊ **suppressor** *noun* device which suppresses interference

surf *verb* to explore a web site looking at the web pages in no particular order, but simply moving between pages using the links

surface-mount technology (SMT)

noun method of manufacturing circuit boards in which the electronic components are bonded directly onto the surface of the board rather than being inserted into holes and soldered into place; *surface-mount technology is faster and more space-efficient than soldering*

surge *noun* sudden increase in electrical power in a system, due to a fault *or* noise *or* component failure; **surge protector** = electronic device which cuts off the power supply to sensitive equipment if it detects a power surge that could cause damage

COMMENT: power surges can burn out circuits before you have time to pull the plug; a surge protector between your computer and the wall outlet will help prevent damage

suspend *verb* command that is used when running Windows 95 on a battery-powered laptop computer to shut down almost all of the electronic components of the laptop

SVGA = SUPER VGA enhancement to the standard VGA graphics display system which allows resolutions of up to 800x600pixels with 16million colours

swap 1 *noun* = SWAPPING **2** *verb* to stop using one program, put it into store temporarily, run another program, and when that is finished, return to the first one; **swap file** = file stored on the hard disk used as a temporary storage area for data held in RAM, to provide virtual memory

◊ **swapping** *or* **swap** *noun* (in a virtual memory system) activity in which program data is moved from main memory to disk,

whilst another program is loaded or run; *see also* VIRTUAL MEMORY

swim *noun* computer graphics which move slightly due to a faulty display unit

switch 1 *noun* (a) (in some command-line operating systems) an additional character entered on the same line as the program command and which affects how the program runs; *add the switch '/W' to the DOS command DIR and the directory listing will be displayed across the screen* (b) point in a computer program where control can be passed to one of a number of choices (c) mechanical *or* solid state device that can electrically connect *or* isolate two or more lines **2** *verb* (a) to connect *or* disconnect two lines by activating a switch; **to switch on** = to start to provide power to a system by using a switch to connect the power supply lines to the circuit; **to switch off** = to disconnect the power supply to a device (b); **to switch over** = to start using an alternative device when the primary one becomes faulty

◊ **switched network backup** *noun* user's choice of a secondary route through a network if the first is busy

◊ **switching** *noun* constant update of connections between changing sinks and sources in a network; **switching centre** = point in a communications network where messages can be switched to and from the various lines and circuits that end there; **switching circuit** = electronic circuit that can direct messages from one line *or* circuit to another in a switching centre; **line switching** = communication line and circuit established on demand and held until no longer required

SX type of processor chip derived from the basic 80386 or 80486 processor that is slightly cheaper to manufacture and buy but is slower because of design changes that include an internal 32-bit data bus with an external 16-bit data bus

symbol *noun* sign *or* picture which represents something; *this language uses the symbol ? to represent the print command;* **logic symbol** = graphical symbol used to represent a type of logic function in a diagram; **symbol table** *or* **library** = list of labels *or* names in a compiler *or* assembler, which relate to their addresses in the machine code program

Symbol font *noun* TrueType font that is included with Windows and includes all sorts of symbols and Greek characters; *see also* TrueType

symbolic *adjective* which acts as a symbol *or* which uses a symbol name *or* label; **symbolic address** = address represented by a symbol *or* name; **symbolic code** *or* **instruction** = instruction that is in mnemonic form rather than a binary number; **symbolic debugging** = debugger that allows symbolic representation of variables *or* locations; **symbolic language** = (i) any computer language where locations are represented by names; (ii) any language used to write source code; **symbolic logic** = study of reasoning and thought (formal logic); **symbolic name** = name used as a label for a variable *or* location; **symbolic programming** = writing a program in a source language

symmetrical compression *noun* compression system that requires the same processing power and time scale to compress and decompress an image

symmetric difference *noun* logical function whose output is true if either (of 2) inputs is true, and false if both inputs are the same

sync *noun* *(informal)* = SYNCHRONIZATION; **sync bit** = transmitted bit used to synchronize devices; **sync character** = transmitted character used to synchronize devices; **sync pulses** = transmitted pulses used to make sure that the receiver is synchronized with the transmitter; **in sync** = synchronized; **the two devices are out of sync** = the two devices are not properly synchronized

◊ **synchronization** *noun* action of synchronizing two or more devices; **synchronization pulses** = transmitted pulses used to make sure that the receiver is synchronized with the transmitter

◊ **synchronize** *verb* to make sure that two or more devices *or* processes are coordinated

in time or action; **synchronized dynamic RAM (SDRAM)** = enhanced memory component that is replacing traditional DRAM; the memory access cycle is synchronized with the main processor clock, eliminating wait time between memory operations

◊ **synchronizer** *noun* device that will perform a function when it receives a signal from another device

◊ **synchronous** *adjective* which runs in sync with something else (such as a main clock); **synchronous cache** = high-speed secondary cache system used in many computers that use the Pentium processor chip; **synchronous computer** = computer in which each action can only take place when a timing pulse arrives; **synchronous data link control (SDLC)** = data transmission protocol most often used in IBM's Systems Network Architecture (SNA) and defines how synchronous data is transmitted; **synchronous data network** = communications network in which all the actions throughout the network are controlled by a single timing signal; **synchronous DRAM** = new high-speed memory technology in which the memory components work from the same clock signal as the main processor, so are synchronized; **synchronous idle character** = character transmitted by a DTE to ensure correct synchronization when no other character is being transmitted; **synchronous mode** = system mode in which operations and events are synchronized with a clock signal; **synchronous network** = network in which all the links are synchronized with a single timing signal; **synchronous system** = system in which all devices are synchronized to a main clock signal; **synchronous transmission** = transmission of data from one device to another, where both devices are controlled by the same clock, and the transmitted data is synchronized with the clock signal

syntactic error *noun* programming error in which the program statement does not follow the syntax of the language

syntax *noun* grammatical rules which apply to a programming language; **syntax**

analysis = stage in compilation where statements are checked to see if they obey the rules of syntax; **syntax error** = programming error in which the program statement does not follow the syntax of the language

synthesis *noun* producing something artificially (from a number of smaller elements)

synthesize *verb* to produce something artificially (from a number of smaller elements)

synthesizer *noun* device which generates something (signals *or* sound *or* speech); **speech synthesizer** = device which generates sounds which are similar to the human voice

---

despite the fact that speech can now be synthesized with very acceptable quality, all it conveys is linguistic information

Personal Computer World

---

synthetic address *noun* location used by a program produced by instructions within the program; **synthetic language** = programming language in which the source program is written

sysgen = SYSTEM GENERATION

sysop *noun* person who maintains a bulletin board system *or* network

system *noun* any group of hardware *or* software *or* peripherals, etc., which work together; **adaptive system** = system which is able to alter its responses and processes according to inputs *or* situations; **computer system** = central processor with storage and associated peripherals which make up a working computer; **expert system** = software which applies the knowledge, advice and rules defined by experts in a particular field to a user's data to help solve a problem; **information system** = computer system which provides information according to a user's requests; **interactive system** = system which provides an immediate response to the user's commands *or* programs *or* data; **operating system (op sys)** = basic software that controls the running of the hardware and

the management of data files, without the user having to operate it; **secure system** = system which cannot be accessed without authorization; **system backup** = copy of all the data stored on a computer, server or network; **system board;** *see* MOTHERBOARD; **system check** = running diagnostic routines to ensure that there are no problems; **system clock** = electronic component that generates a regular signal that is used to synchronize all the components in the computer; **system colours** = palette of 20 colours that are used by Windows for colouring window elements such as borders, captions, buttons; **system console** = main terminal or control centre for a computer which includes status lights and control switches; **system control panel** = main computer system control switches and status indicators; **system crash** = situation where the operating system stops working and has to be restarted; **system design** = identifying and investigating possible solutions to a problem, and deciding upon the most appropriate system to solve the problem; **system diagnostics** = tests, features and messages that help find hardware *or* software faults; **system disk** = disk which holds the system software; **system firmware** = basic operating system functions and routines in a ROM device; **system flowchart** = diagram which shows each step of the computer procedures needed in a system; **system folder** = (in the Apple Macintosh environment) folder that contains the program files for the operating system and Finder; **system generation** *or* **sysgen** = process of producing an optimum operating system for a particular task; **system library** = stored files that hold the various parts of a computer's operating system; **system life cycle** = time when a system exists, between its initial design and its becoming out of date; **system log** = record of computer processor operations; **system prompt** = prompt which indicates the operating system is ready and waiting for the user to enter a system command; **system security** = measures, such as password, priority protection, authorization codes, etc., designed to stop browsers and hackers; **system software** = software which makes applications run on hardware; **system specifications** = details of hardware and software required to perform certain tasks; **system support** = group of people who maintain and operate a system; **system unit** = main terminal or control centre for a computer which includes status lights and control switches; **system variable** = variable that contains data generated by the system software that can be used by applications

System 7™   version of the operating system for the Apple Macintosh personal computer that introduces multitasking, virtual memory and peer-to-peer file sharing

System 8™ new version of the Apple Macintosh operating system that improves reliability and multitasking functions

System Monitor Windows 95 utility that allows a user to view how the resources on their PC are performing and, if they have shared the device, who else on the network is using the resources

systems analysis *noun* (i) analysing a process *or* system to see if it could be more efficiently carried out by a computer; (ii) examining an existing system with the aim of

improving *or* replacing it; **systems analyst** = person who undertakes system analysis; **systems integration** = combining different products from different manufacturers to create a system; **systems program** = program which controls the way in which a computer system works; **systems programmer** = person who writes system software

Systems Application Architecture (SAA) *noun* standard developed by IBM which defines the look and feel of an application regardless of the hardware platform; SAA defines which keystrokes carry out standard functions (such as F1 to display help), the application's display and how the application interacts with the operating system

Systems Network Architecture (SNA) *noun* design methods developed by IBM which define how communications in a network should occur and allow different hardware to communicate

the core of an expert system is its database of rules

Personal Computer World

Tt

T = TERA- prefix meaning 10^{12}; one million million

T carrier *noun* US standard for digital data transmission lines, such as T1, T1C, and corresponding signal standards DS1, DS1C

T connector *noun* coaxial connector, shaped like the letter 'T', which connects two thin coaxial cables using BNC plugs and provides a third connection for another cable or network interface card

T junction *noun* connection at right angles with a main signal *or* power carrying cable

T1 committee *noun* ANSI committee which sets digital communications standards for the US, particularly ISDN services

T1 link *noun* (in the US) high speed, long distance data transmission link (not related to the T1 committee) that can carry data at 1.544Mbits per second

◊ **T2 link** *noun* (in the US) high speed, long distance data transmission link equivalent to four T1 lines that can carry data at 6.3Mbits per second

◊ **T3 link** *noun* (in the US) high speed, long distance data transmission link equivalent to 28 T1 lines that can carry data at 44.736Mbits per second

TAB = TABULATE

tab *verb* to tabulate *or* to arrange text in columns with the cursor automatically running from one column to the next in keyboarding; *the list was neatly lined up by tabbing to column 10 at the start of each new line;* **tab character** = ASCII character 09hex which is used to align text at a preset tab stop; **tab key** = key on a keyboard, normally positioned on the far left, beside the 'Q' key, with two arrows pointing opposite horizontal directions, used to insert a tab character into text and so align the text at a preset tab stop; **tab memory** = ability of a editing program (usually a word-processor) to store details about various tab settings; **tab rack** *or* **ruler line** = graduated scale, displayed on the screen, showing the position of tabulation columns; *the tab rack shows you the left and right margins;* **tab settings** *or* **tab stops** = preset points along a line, where the printing head *or* cursor will stop for each tabulation command

◊ **tabbing** *noun* movement of the cursor in a word-processing program from one tab stop to the next; *tabbing can be done from inside the program;* **tabbing order** = order in which the focus moves from one button or field to the next as the user presses the tab key; **decimal tabbing** = adjusting a column of numbers so that the decimal points are aligned vertically

table *noun* (a) list of data in columns and rows on a printed page *or* on the screen; **decision table** = list of all possible events *or* states that could happen and the actions taken (sometimes used instead of a flowchart); **lookup table** = collection of stored results which can be accessed very rapidly; *this is the value of the key pressed, use a lookup table to find its ASCII value;* **reference program table** = list produced by a compiler *or* system of the location, size and type of the variables, routines and macros within a program; **symbol table** = list of all the symbols which are accepted by a language *or* compiler and their object code translation; **table lookup** = using one known value to select one entry in a table, providing a secondary value; **table of contents** = (i) (in a

CD) data at the start of the disc that describes how many tracks are on the CD, their position and length; (ii) (in a multimedia title) page with a list of the headings of all the other main pages in the title and links so that a user can move to them **(b)** (in a relational database) structure which shows how records and data items are linked by relations between the rows and columns of the table

tablet *noun;* **graphics tablet** = graphics pad *or* flat device which allows a user to input graphical information into a computer by drawing on its surface; *it is much easier to draw accurately with a tablet than with a mouse*

tabulate *verb* to arrange text in columns, with the cursor moving to each new column automatically as the text is keyboarded

◊ **tabular** *adjective;* **in tabular form** = arranged in a table

◊ **tabulating** *noun* processing punched cards, such as a sorting operation

◊ **tabulation** *noun* (i) arrangement of a table of figures; (ii) moving a printing head *or* cursor a preset distance along a line; **tabulation markers** = symbols displayed to indicate the position of tabulation stops; **tabulation stops** = preset points along a line at which a printing head *or* cursor will stop for each tabulation command

◊ **tabulator** *noun* part of a typewriter *or* word-processor which automatically sets words *or* figures into columns

tactile *adjective* using the sense of touch; **tactile keyboard** = keyboard that provides some indication that a key has been pressed, such as a beep

tag *noun* **(a)** one section of a computer instruction **(b)** identifying characters attached to a file *or* item (of data); *each file has a three letter tag for rapid identification*

◊ **tag image file format (TIFF)** *noun* standard file format used to store graphic images

tail *noun* **(a)** data recognized as the end of a list of data **(b)** control code used to signal the end of a message

takedown *verb* to remove paper *or* disks *or* tape from a peripheral after one job and prepare it for the next; **takedown time** = amount of time required to takedown a peripheral ready for another job

take-up reel *noun* reel onto which magnetic tape is collected; *put the full reel on this spindle, and feed the tape into the take-up reel on the other spindle*

Taligent™ *'noun* operating system developed by IBM and Apple that can be used on both PC and Macintosh platforms

talk *verb* to speak *or* to communicate

a variety of technologies exist which allow computers to talk to one another

Which PC?

tandem *noun;* **tandem processors** = two processors connected so that if one fails, the second takes over; **working in tandem** = situation where two devices are working together

tape *noun* long thin flat piece of material; **cassette tape** = tape stored on two small reels protected by a solid casing; *cassette tape is mainly used with home computers;* **(magnetic) tape** = narrow length of thin plastic coated with a magnetic material used to store signals magnetically; **master tape** = magnetic tape which contains all the vital operating system routines, loaded by the initial program loader once when the computer is switched on *or* hard reset; **(paper) tape** *or* **punched tape** = strip of paper on which information can be recorded in the form of punched holes; **streaming tape drive** = device containing a continuous loop of tape, used as backing store; **tape archive;** *see* TAR; **tape backup** = using (usually magnetic) tape as a medium for storing back-ups from faster main *or* secondary storage (such as RAM *or* hard disk); **tape cable** *or* **ribbon cable** = number of insulated conductors arranged next to each other forming a flat cable; **tape cartridge** = cassette box containing magnetic tape (on a reel); **tape cassette** = small box containing a reel of magnetic tape and a pickup reel; **tape**

code = coding system used for punched data representation on paper tape; **tape deck** = device which plays back and records data onto magnetic tape; **tape drive** = mechanism which controls magnetic tape movement over the tape heads; *our new product has a 96Mb streaming tape drive;* **tape format** = way in which blocks of data, control codes and location data is stored on tape; **tape guide** = method by which the tape is correctly positioned over the tape head; *the tape is out of alignment because one of the tape guides has broken;* **tape head** = transducer which can read and write signals onto the surface of magnetic tape; **tape header** = identification information at the beginning of a tape; **tape label** = tape header and trailer containing information about the contents of a tape; **tape library** = (i) secure area for the storage of computer data tapes; (ii) series of computer tapes kept in store for reference; **tape loadpoint** = position on a magnetic tape at which reading should commence to load a file; **tape punch** = machine that punches holes into paper tape; **tape reader** = machine which reads punched holes in paper tape *or* signals on magnetic tape; **tape streamer** = continuous loop of tape used for backing storage; **tape to card converter** = device which reads data from magnetic tape and stores it on punched cards; **tape transmitter** = device which reads data from paper tape and transmits it to another point; **tape trailer** = identification information at the beginning of a tape; **tape transport** = method (in a magnetic tape recorder) by which the tape is moved smoothly from reel to reel over the magnetic heads

COMMENT: cassettes or reels of tape are easy to use and cheaper than disks, the cassette casing usually conforms to a standard size. They are less adaptable and only provide sequential access, usually being used for master copies or making back-ups

TAPI = TELEPHONY APPLICATION PROGRAMMING INTERFACE

tar = TAPE ARCHIVE file compression system used on a computer running the Unix operating system

Targa *noun* (i) graphics file format (which uses the .TGA extension on a PC) developed by Truevision to store raster graphic images in 16-, 24- and 32-bit colour; (ii) high-resolution colour graphics adapter made by Truevision

target *noun* goal which you aim to achieve; **target computer** = computer on which software is to be run (but not necessarily written on, for example using a cross-assembler); **target disk** = disk onto which a file is to be copied; **target language** = language into which a language will be translated from its source language; *the target language for this PASCAL program is machine code;* **target level** = interpretative processing mode for program execution; **target** *or* **run phase** = period of time during which the target program is run; **target program** = object program *or* computer program in object code form, produced by a compiler; **target window** = window in which text or graphics will be displayed

the target board is connected to the machine through the in-circuit emulator cable
Electronics & Wireless World

tariff *noun* charge incurred by a user of a communications *or* computer system; *there is a set tariff for logging on, then a rate for every minute of computer time used*

task *noun* job which is to be carried out by a computer; **task management** = system software which controls the use and allocation of resources to programs; **task queue** = temporary storage of jobs waiting to be processed; **task swapping** *or* **switching** = exchanging one program in memory for another which is temporarily stored on disk; task switching is not the same as multitasking which can execute several programs at once; *see also* MULTITASKING

◊ **taskbar** *noun* bar that is normally displayed along the bottom of the screen in Windows 95 and displays the Start button and a list of other programs or windows that are currently active

TAT = TURNAROUND TIME

TCP = TRANSMISSION CONTROL PROTOCOL standard data transmission protocol that provides full duplex transmission, the protocol bundles data into packets and checks for errors

◊ **TCP/IP** = TRANSMISSION CONTROL PROTOCOL/INTERFACE PROGRAM data transfer protocol used in networks and communications systems (often used in Unix-based networks); this protocol is used for all communications over the inter

TDM = TIME DIVISION MULTIPLEXING method of combining several signals into one high-speed transmission carrier; each input signal is sampled in turn and the result transmitted, the receiver re-constructs the signals

TDR = TIME DOMAIN REFLECTOMETRY test that identifies where cable faults lie by sending a signal down the cable and measuring how long it takes for the reflection to come back

TDS = TRANSACTION-DRIVEN SYSTEM computer system that will normally run batch processing tasks until interrupted by a new transaction, at which point it allocates resources to the new transaction

technical *adjective* referring to a particular machine *or* process; *the document gives all the technical details on the new computer;* **technical support** = (person who provides) technical advice to a user to explain how to use software *or* hardware or explain why it might not work

◊ **technician** *noun* person who is specialized in industrial work; *the computer technicians installed the new system*

◊ **technique** *noun* skilled way of doing a job; *the company has developed a new technique for processing customers' disks; he has a special technique for answering complaints from users of the software*

technology *noun* applying scientific knowledge to industrial processes; **information technology (IT)** = technology involved in acquiring, storing, processing,

and distributing information by electronic means (including radio, TV, telephone and computers); **new technology** = electronic instruments which have recently been developed; **the introduction of new technology** = putting new electronic equipment into a business *or* industry

◊ **technological** *adjective* referring to technology; **the technological revolution** = changing of industrial methods by introducing new technology

tele- *prefix* meaning long distance

◊ **telecommunications** *noun* technology of passing and receiving messages over a distance (as in radio, telephone, telegram, satellite broadcast, etc.)

◊ **telecommuting** *noun* practice of working on a computer in one place (normally from home) that is linked by modem to the company's central office allowing messages and data to be transferred

◊ **teleconferencing** *noun* to link video, audio and computer signals from different locations so that distant people can talk and see each other, as if in a conference room

◊ **teleinformatic services** *noun* any data only service, such as telex, facsimile, which uses telecommunications

telematics *noun* interaction of all data processing and communications devices (computers, networks, etc.)

telephone *noun* machine used for speaking to someone *or* communicating with another computer (using modems) over a long distance; **telephone (data carrier)** = using a modem to send binary data as sound signals over a telephone line

telephony *adjective & noun* series of standards that define the way in which computers can work with a telephone system to provide voice-mail, telephone answering, and fax services; **telephony application programming interface (TAPI)** = system developed by Microsoft and Intel that allows a PC to control a telephone; **telephony services application programming interface (TSAPI)** = system developed by Novell and AT&T that allows a PC to control a PBX telephone exchange (compare with TAPI that controls a single telephone)

teleprinter *noun* device that is capable of sending and receiving data from a distant point by means of a telegraphic circuit, and printing out the message on a printer; *you can drive a teleprinter from this modified serial port;* **teleprinter interface** = terminal interface *or* hardware and software combination required to control the functions of a terminal; **teleprinter roll** = roll of paper onto which messages are printed

teleprocessing (TP) *noun* processing of data at a distance (as on a central computer from outside terminals)

telesoftware (TSW) *noun* software which is received from a viewdata *or* teletext service; *the telesoftware was downloaded yesterday*

teletext *noun* method of transmitting text and information with a normal television signal, usually as a serial bit stream which can be displayed using a special decoder

teletype (TTY) *noun* term used for teleprinter equipment

◊ **teletypewriter** *noun* keyboard and printer attached to a computer system which can input data either direct *or* by making punched paper tape

television (TV) *noun* device which can receive (modulated) video signals from a computer *or* broadcast signals with an aerial and display images on a CRT screen with sound; **television monitor** = device able to display signals from a computer without sound, but not broadcast signals (this is usually because there is no demodulator device which is needed for broadcast signals); **television receiver/monitor** = device able to act as a TV receiver *or* monitor; **television scan** = horizontal movement of the picture beam over the screen, producing one line of an image; **television tube** = CRT with electronic devices which provide the line by line horizontal and vertical scanning movement of the picture beam; *see also* CRT, RGB

telnet *noun* TCP/IP protocol that allows a user to connect to and control via the internet a remote computer as if they were there and type in commands as if they were sitting in front of the computer

template *noun* (i) plastic *or* metal sheet with cut-out symbols to help the drawing of flowcharts and circuit diagrams; (ii) (in text processing) standard text (such as a standard letter *or* invoice) into which specific details (company address *or* prices *or* quantities) can be added; **template command** = command which allows functions *or* other commands to be easily set; *a template paragraph command enables the user to specify the number of spaces each paragraph should be indented; see also* STANDARD, FORM LETTER

tempo *noun* (i) (in MIDI or music) the speed at which the notes are played, measured in beats per minute; *a typical MIDI tempo is 120bpm;* (ii) (in a multimedia title) the speed at which frames are displayed

temporary storage *noun* storage which is not permanent; **temporary register** = register used for temporary storage for the results of an ALU operation; **temporary swap file** = file on a hard disk which is used by software to store data temporarily or for software that implements virtual memory, such as Microsoft's Windows

◊ **temporarily** *adverb* for a certain time *or* not permanently

ten's complement *noun* formed by adding one to the nine's complement of a decimal number

10Base2 IEEE Ethernet standard specification for running Ethernet over thin coaxial cable

◊ **10Base5** IEEE Ethernet standard specification for running Ethernet over thick coaxial cable

◊ **10BaseFX** version of the IEEE Ethernet standard that allows data to be transferred at 10Mbps over a fibre optic cable

◊ **10BaseT** IEEE Ethernet standard specification for running Ethernet over unshielded twisted pair cable

tera- (T) *prefix* prefix meaning 10^{12}; one million million

◊ **terabyte** *noun* one thousand gigabytes or one million megabytes of data

terminal 1 *noun* **(a)** device usually made up of a display unit and a keyboard which allows entry and display of information when on-line to a central computer system (computer terminals can be intelligent, smart or dumb according to the inbuilt processing capabilities); **addressable terminal** = terminal which will only accept data if it has the correct address and identification data in the message header; *all the messages go to all the terminals since none are addressable terminals;* **applications terminal** = terminal (such as at a sales desk) which is specifically configured to carry out certain tasks; **dumb terminal** = peripheral which can only receive and transmit data, and is not capable of processing data; **central terminal** = terminal which controls communications between a central *or* host computer and remote terminals; **intelligent terminal** *or* **smart terminal** = computer terminal which contains a CPU and memory, allowing basic data processing to be carried out, usually with the facility to allow the user to program it independently of the host computer; *the new intelligent terminal has a built-in text editor;* **master terminal** = one terminal in a network which has priority over any other, used by the system manager to set-up the system *or* carry out privileged commands; *the system manager uses the master terminal to restart the system;* **remote terminal** = computer terminal connected to a distant computer system; **slave terminal** = terminal controlled by a main computer *or* terminal; **terminal area** = part of a printed circuit board at which edge connectors can be connected; **terminal character set** = range of characters available for a particular type of terminal, these might include graphics *or* customized characters; **terminal controller** = hardware device *or* IC which controls a terminal including data communications and display; **terminal emulation** = ability of a terminal to emulate the functions of another type of terminal so that display codes can be correctly decoded and displayed and

keystrokes correctly coded and transmitted; **terminal identity** = unique code transmitted by a viewdata terminal to provide identification and authorization of a user; **terminal interface** = hardware and software combination required to control the functions of a terminal from a computer; *the network controller has 16 terminal interfaces (slang);* **terminal junky (T.J)** = person (a hacker) who is obsessed by computers; *my son has turned into a real terminal junky;* **terminal keyboard** = standard QWERTY *or* special keyboard allowing input at a terminal; **terminal session** = period of time when a terminal is on-line or in use **(b)** an electrical connection point; **terminal strip** = row of electrical connectors that allow pairs of wires to be electrically connected using a screw-down metal plate **(c)** point in a network where a message can be transmitted *or* received; *see also* SOURCE, SINK **2** *adjective* fatal *or* which cannot be repaired; *the computer has a terminal fault*

```
The London Borough of Hackney
has standardised on terminal
emulator      software      from
Omniplex to allow its networked
desktop users to select Unix or
DOS applications from a single
menu.
```
Computing

---

terminate *verb* to end

◊ **terminate and stay resident (TSR) program** *noun* program which loads itself into main memory and carries out a function when activated; *when you hit Ctrl-F5, you will activate the TSR program and it will display your day's diary*

◊ **termination** *noun* ending *or* stopping; **abnormal termination** = unexpected stoppage of a program which is being run, caused by a fault *or* power failure

◊ **terminator** *noun* **(a)** (i) (in a LAN) resistor that fits onto the each end of a coaxial cable in a bus network to create an electrical circuit; (ii) (in a SCSI installation) resistor that fits onto the last SCSI device in the daisy-chain, creating an electrical circuit **(b)** item in a list of data, which indicates the end of a list

ternary *adjective* (number system) with three possible states

tessellate *verb* to reduce a complex shape into a collection of simple shapes, often triangles

test 1 *noun* action carried out on a device *or* program to establish whether it is working correctly, and if not, which component *or* instruction is not working; **test bed** = (software) environment used to test programs; **test data** = data with known results prepared to allow a new program to be tested; **test equipment** = special equipment which tests hardware *or* software; *the engineer has special test equipment for this model;* **test numeric** = check to ensure that numerical information is numerical; **test run** = program run with test data to ensure that the software is working correctly; *a test run will soon show up any errors* **2** *verb* to carry out an examination of a device *or* program to see if it is working correctly; **saturation testing** = testing a communications network by transmitting large quantities of data and messages over it

texel *noun* collection of pixels that are treated as a single unit when applying a texture map over an object

text *noun* alphanumeric characters that convey information; **ragged text** = unjustified text, text with a ragged right margin; **start-of-text (SOT** *or* **STX)** = transmitted code indicating the end of control and address information and the start of the message; **text compression** = reducing the space required by a section of text, using one code to represent more than one character, and removing spaces and punctuation marks, etc.; **text-editing facilities** = word-processing system which allows the user to add, delete, move, insert and correct sections of text; **text-editing function** = option in a program which provides text-editing facilities; *the program includes a built-in text-editing function;* **text editor** = piece of software which provides the user with text-editing facilities; *the text editor will only read files smaller than 64Kbytes long;* **text file** = stored file on a computer

containing text rather than digits *or* data; **text formatter** = program which arranges a text file according to preset rules, such as line width and page size; *people use the text formatter as a basic desk-top publishing program;* **text management** = facilities which allow text to be written, stored, retrieved, edited and printed; **text manipulation** = facilities which allow text editing, changing, inserting and deleting; **text mode** = operating mode of a computer or display screen that will only display pre-defined characters and will not allow graphic images to be displayed; *MS-DOS normally operates in a text mode;* **text processing** = word-processing *or* using a computer to keyboard, edit and output text, in the forms of letters, labels, etc.; **text register** = temporary computer storage register for text characters only; **text retrieval** = information retrieval system which allows the user to examine complete documents rather than just a reference to one; **text screen** = area of computer screen which has been set up to display text; **text-to-speech converter** = electronic device which uses a speech synthesizer to produce the spoken equivalent of a piece of text that has been entered

texture mapping *noun* (i) special computer graphics effect using algorithms to produce an image that looks like the surface of something (such as marble, brick, stone or water); (ii) to cover one image with another to give the first a texture

TFT screen = THIN FILM TRANSISTOR SCREEN method of creating a high-quality LCD display often used in laptop computers

thermal *adjective* referring to heat; **thermal inkjet printer** = computer printer which produces characters by sending a stream of tiny drops, (created by heating the ink) of electrically charged ink onto the paper (the movement of the ink drops is controlled by an electric field; this is a non-impact printer with few moving parts); **thermal paper** = special paper whose coating turns black when heated, allowing characters to be printed by using a matrix of small heating elements; **thermal printer** = type of printer where the character is formed on thermal paper with a printhead containing a matrix of small heating elements

> COMMENT: this type of printer is very quiet in operation since the printing head does not strike the paper

◊ **thermal transfer** *or* **thermal wax** *or* **thermal wax transfer printer** *noun* method of printing where the colours are produced by melting coloured wax onto the paper; *thermal wax transfer technology still provides the best colour representation on paper for PC output*

thesaurus *noun* file which contains synonyms that are displayed as alternatives to a misspelt word during a spell-check

thick *adjective* with a large distance between two surfaces; **thick film** = miniature electronic circuit design in which miniature components are mounted on an insulating base, then connected as required

> COMMENT: this provides a package which is larger but cheaper for short runs than chips

◊ **thick-Ethernet** *noun* network implemented using thick coaxial cable and transceivers to connect branch cables; can stretch long distances; *see also* ETHERNET; THIN-ETHERNET

thimble printer *noun* computer printer using a printing head similar to a daisy wheel but shaped like a thimble

thin *adjective* with only a small distance between two surfaces; **thin film** = method of constructing integrated circuits by depositing in a vacuum very thin patterns of various materials onto a substrate to form the required interconnected components; *see also* CHIP, SUBSTRATE; **thin film memory** = high-speed access RAM device using a matrix of magnetic cells and a matrix of read/write heads to access them; **thin film transistor screen;** *see* TFT screen; **thin window** = single line display window

◊ **thin-Ethernet** *noun* (the most popular type of Ethernet) network implemented using

thin coaxial cable and BNC connectors; it is limited to distances of around 1000m

third *adjective* coming after second; **third generation computers** = range of computers where integrated circuits were used instead of transistors; **third party** = company which supplies items *or* services for a system sold by one party (the seller) to another (the buyer)

> COMMENT: a third party might supply computer maintenance or might write programs, etc.

they expect third party developers to enhance the operating systems by adding their own libraries

PC Business World

thirty-two bit system *noun* microcomputer system *or* CPU that handles data in thirty-two bit words

thrashing *noun* (i) excessive disk activity; (ii) configuration *or* program fault in a virtual memory system, that results in a CPU wasting time moving pages of data between main memory and disk or backing store

thread *noun* program which consists of many independent smaller sections or beads; **threaded file** = file in which an entry will contain data and an address to the next entry that has the same data content (allowing rapid retrieval of all identical records); **threaded language** = programming language which allows many small sections of code to be written then used by a main program; **threaded tree** = structure in which each node contains a pointer to other nodes

WigWam makes it easier for a user to follow a thread in a bulletin-board conference topic by ordering responses using a hierarchical indent simlar to that found in outline processor.

Computing

three-address instruction *noun* instruction which contains the addresses of two operands and the location where the result is to be stored

◊ **three-dimensional** *or* **3D**   *adjective* (image) which has three dimensions (width, breadth and depth), and therefore gives the impression of being solid

◊ **three input adder** *see* FULL ADDER

three-pin plug *noun* standard plug with three connections, to connect an electric device to the mains electricity supply

> COMMENT: the three pins are for the live, neutral and earth connections

three state logic *noun* logic gate *or* IC which has three possible output states (rather than the usual two): logic high, logic low and high impedance

threshold *noun* preset level which causes an action if a signal exceeds or drops below it

throughput *noun* rate of production by a machine *or* system, measured as total useful information processed in a set period of time; *for this machine throughput is 1.3 inches per second (ips) scanning speed;* **rated throughput** = maximum throughput of a device which will still meet original specifications

thumbnail *noun* miniature graphical representation of an image; used as a quick and convenient method of viewing the contents of graphics or DTP files before they are retrieved

TIFF = TAG IMAGE FILE FORMAT standard file format used to store graphic images

tile *verb* (in a GUI) to arrange a group of windows so that they are displayed side by side without overlapping

tilt and swivel *adjective* (monitor) which is mounted on a pivot so that it can be moved to point in the most convenient direction for the operator

time 1 *noun* period expressed in hours, minutes, seconds, etc.; **addition time** = time an adder takes to carry out an addition operation; **cycle time** = time between start and stop of an operation, especially between addressing a memory location and receiving the data; **queuing time** = period of time messages have to wait before they are processed *or* transmitted; **real time** = actions *or* processing time that is of the same order of magnitude as the problem to be solved (i.e. the processing time is within the same time as the problem to be solved, so that the result can influence the source of the data); **response time** = (i) time which passes between the user starting an action (by pressing a key) and the result appearing on the screen; (ii) speed with which a system responds to a stimulus; **stop time** = time taken for a spinning disk to come to rest after it is no longer powered; **time base** = (i) signal used as a basis for timing purposes; (ii) regular sawtooth signal used in an oscilloscope to sweep the beam across the screen; **time division multiplexing (TDM)** = method of combining several signals into one high-speed transmission carrier; each input signal is sampled in turn and the result transmitted, the receiver re-constructs the signals; **time domain reflectometry (TDR)** = test which identifies where cable faults lie by sending a signal down the cable and measuring how long it takes for the reflection to come back; **time slice** = amount of time allowed for a single task in a time-sharing system *or* in multiprogramming; period of time allocated for a user *or* program *or* job within a multitasking system **2** *verb* to measure the time taken by an operation; **microprocessor timing** = correct selection of system clock frequency to allow for slower peripherals, etc.; **network timing** = signals which correctly synchronize the transmission of data; **timed backup** = backup which occurs automatically after a period of time, or at a particular time each day; **timing loop** = computer program loop which is repeated a number of times to produce a certain time delay; **timing master** = clock signal which synchronizes all the components in a system

◊ **timeout** *noun* (i) logoff procedure carried out if no data is entered on an on-line terminal; (ii) period of time reserved for an operation

◊ **time out** *verb* (of an event or option) to become no longer valid after a period of time; *if you do not answer this question within* *one minute, the program times out and moves onto the next question*

◊ **timer** *noun* device which records the time taken for an operation to be completed

◊ **time-sharing** *noun* computer system which allows several independent users to use it *or* be on-line at the same time

> COMMENT: in time-sharing, each user appears to be using the computer all the time, when in fact each is using the CPU for a short time slice only; the CPU processing one user for a short time then moving on to the next

tiny model *noun* memory model of the Intel 80x86 processor family that allows a combined total of 64Kb for data and code

title *noun* identification name given to a file *or* program *or* disk; **title bar** = horizontal bar at the top of a window which displays the title of the window or application; **title of disk** = identification of a disk, referring to its contents

toggle *verb* to switch between two states; **toggle switch** = electrical switch which has only two positions

```
the symbols can be toggled on
or off the display
```
Micro Decision

token *noun* (a) internal code which replaces a reserved word *or* program statement in a high-level language (b) (in a local area network) control packet which is passed between workstations to control access to the network

◊ **token bus network** *noun* IEEE 802.4 standard for a local area network formed with a bus-topology cable; workstations transfer data by passing a token

◊ **token passing** *noun* method of controlling access to a local area network by using a token packet: a workstation cannot transmit data until it receives the token

◊ **token ring network** *noun* IEEE 802.5 standard that uses a token passed from one workstation to the next in a ring network, a workstation can only transmit data if it captures the token (Token Ring networks, although logically a ring, are often physically

wired in a star topology); *Token Ring networks are very democratic and retain performance against increasing load*

toner *noun* finely powdered ink (usually black) that is used in laser printers; the toner is transferred onto the paper by electrical charge, then fixed permanently to the paper by heating; *if you get toner on your hands, you can only wash it off with cold water;* **toner cartridge** = plastic container which holds powdered toner for use in a laser printer

toolbar *noun* window that contains a range of icons that access tools

◊ **Toolbook** *noun* multimedia authoring tool developed by Asymetrix, which uses the OpenScript script language to control objects and actions

◊ **toolbox** *noun* (a) box containing instruments needed to repair *or* maintain *or* install equipment (b) set of predefined routines *or* functions that are used when writing a program

◊ **Toolbox** *noun* (in an Apple Macintosh) set of utility programs stored in ROM to provide graphic functions

◊ **toolkit** *noun* series of functions which help a programmer write *or* debug programs

◊ **tools** *noun* set of utility programs (backup, format, etc.) in a computer system

◊ **ToolTips** feature of applications that work under Windows that display a line of descriptive text under an icon when the user moves the pointer over the icon

top *noun* part which is the highest point of something; **top down programming** *or* **structured programming** = method of writing programs where a complete system is divided into simple blocks *or* tasks, each block unit is written and tested before proceeding with the next one; **top of stack** = the newest data item added to a stack

topology *noun* way in which the various elements in a network are interconnected; **bus topology** = network topology in which all devices are connected to a single cable which has terminators at each end; *Ethernet is a network that uses the bus topology; token ring uses a ring topology;* **network**

topology = layout of machines in a network (such as a star network *or* a ring network *or* a bus network) which will determine what cabling and interfaces are needed and what possibilities the network can offer; **star topology** = network topology in which all devices are connected by individual cable to a single central hub; *if one workstation cable snaps in a star topology, the rest continue, unlike a bus topology*

total *noun* **hash total** = total of a number of hashed entries, used for error detection

touch *verb* to make contact with something with the fingers; **touch pad** = flat device which can sense where on its surface and when it is touched, used to control a cursor position *or* switch a device on or off; **touch screen** = computer display which has a grid of infrared transmitters and receivers, positioned on either side of the screen used to control a cursor position (when a user wants to make a selection *or* move the cursor, he points to the screen, breaking two of the beams, which gives the position of his finger)

TP   =   TELEPROCESSING, TRANSACTION PROCESSING

TPI = TRACKS PER INCH

trace *noun* method of verifying that a program is functioning correctly, in which the current status and contents of the registers and variables used are displayed after each instruction step; **trace program** = diagnostic program which executes a program that is being debugged, one instruction at a time, displaying the states and registers; **trace trap** = selective breakpoint where a tracing program stops, allowing registers to be examined

◊ **tracing** *noun* function of a graphics program that takes a bitmap image and processes it to find the edges of the shapes and so convert these into a vector line image that can be more easily manipulated

track 1 *noun* one of a series of thin concentric rings on a magnetic disk *or* thin lines on a tape, which the read/write head accesses and along which the data is stored in separate sectors; **address track** = track on a magnetic disk containing the address of files, etc., stored on the other tracks; **track address** = location of a particular track on a magnetic disk; **tracks per inch (TPI)** = number of concentric data tracks on a disk surface per inch **2** *verb* to follow a path *or* track correctly; *the read head is not tracking the recorded track correctly*

> COMMENT: the first track on a tape is along the edge and the tape may have up to nine different tracks on it, while a disk has many concentric tracks around the central hub; the track and sector addresses are set-up during formatting

trackball *noun* device used to move a cursor on-screen, which is controlled by turning a ball contained in a case

tractor feed *noun* method of feeding paper into a printer, where sprocket wheels on the printer connect with the sprocket holes on either edge of the paper to pull the paper through

```
the printer is fairly standard
with both tractor and cut sheet
feed system
```
Which PC?

traffic *noun* term covering all the messages and other signals processed by a system *or* carried by a communications link; *our Ethernet network begins to slow down if the traffic reaches 60 per cent of the bandwidth;* **traffic analysis** = study of the times, types and quantities of messages and signals being processed by a system; **traffic density** = number of messages and data transmitted over a network *or* system in a period of time; **traffic intensity** = ratio of messages entering a queue against those leaving the queue within a certain time; **incoming traffic** = data and messages received

trail *noun* line followed by something; **audit trail** = recording details of the use made of a system by noting transactions carried out (used for checking on illegal use *or* malfunction)

◊ **trailer** *noun* final byte of a file containing control *or* file characteristics; **trailer record**

= last record in a file containing control *or* file characteristics

transaction *noun* one single action which affects a database (a sale, a change of address, a new customer, etc.); **transaction-driven system (TDS)** = computer system that will normally run batch processing tasks until interrupted by a new transaction, at which point it allocates resources to the transaction; **transaction file** *or* **change file** *or* **detail file** *or* **movement file** = file containing recent changes *or* transactions to records which is then used to update a master file; **transaction processing (TP)** = interactive processing in which a user enters commands and data on a terminal which is linked to a central computer, with results being displayed on-screen; **transaction record** *or* **change record** = record containing new data which is to be used to update a master record

---

At present, users implementing client-server strategies are focusing on decision support systems before implementing online transaction processing and other mission-critical applications.

Computing

---

transceiver *noun* transmitter and receiver *or* device which can both transmit and receive signals (such as a terminal *or* modem)

transcribe *verb* to copy data from one backing storage unit *or* medium to another

transfer 1 *verb* **(a)** to change command or control; *all processing activities have been transferred to the mainframe;* **transfer command** = instruction that directs processor control from one part of a program to another; *see also* JUMP, CALL; **transfer control** = when a branch *or* jump instruction within a program is executed, control is transferred to another point in the program **(b)** to copy a section of memory to another location; **transfer rate** = speed at which data is transferred from backing store to main memory *or* from one device to another; *with a good telephone line, this pair of modems can achieve a transfer rate of 14.4Kbps;*

transfer time = time taken to transfer data between devices *or* locations **2** *noun* changing command or control; **conditional transfer** = programming instruction which provides a jump to a section of a program if a certain condition is met; **radial transfer** = data transfer between two peripherals *or* programs that are on different layers of a structured system (such as an OSI/ISO system); **transfer check** = check that a data transfer is correct according to a set of rules

transform *verb* to change something from one state to another

◊ **transformation** *noun* action of changing

◊ **transformational rules** *noun* set of rules applied to data which is to be transformed into coded form

transient 1 *adjective* state *or* signal which is present for a short period of time; **transient area** = section of memory for user programs and data; **transient error** = temporary error which occurs for a short period of time **2** *noun* something which is present for a short period; **transient suppressor** = device which suppresses voltage transients; **power transient** = very short duration voltage pulse *or* spike; **voltage transient** = sudden surge in voltage

transistor *noun* electronic semiconductor device which can control the current flow in a circuit (there are two main types of transistors: bipolar and unipolar); **bipolar** *or* **junction transistor (BJT)** = transistor constructed of three layers of alternating types of doped semiconductor (p-n-p or n-p-n), each layer has a terminal labelled emitter, base and collector, usually the base controls the current flow between emitter and collector; **field effect transistor (FET)** = electronic device that can act as a variable current flow control (an external signal varies the resistance of the device and current flow by changing the width of a conducting channel by means of a field; it has three terminals: source, gate and drain); **transistor-transistor logic (TTL)** = most common family of logic gates and high-speed transistor circuit design, in which the bipolar transistors are directly connected (usually collector to base) to provide the logic function; **unipolar transistor** = FIELD EFFECT TRANSISTOR

transition *noun* change from one state to another; **transition point** = point in a program *or* system where a transition occurs

translate *verb* to convert data from one form into another

◊ **translation tables** *or* **conversion tables** *noun* lookup tables *or* collection of stored results that can be accessed very rapidly by a process without the need to calculate each result when needed

◊ **translator (program)** *noun* program which translates a high level language program into another language (usually machine code); *see also* INTERPRETER, COMPILER

transmission control protocol/interface program *see* TCP/IP

transmit *verb* to send information from one device to another, using any medium, such as radio, cable, wire link, etc.

◊ **transmission** *noun* sending of signals from one device to another; **neutral transmission** = (transmission) in which a voltage pulse and zero volts represent the binary digits 1 and 0; **parallel transmission** = number of data lines carrying all the bits of a data word simultaneously; **serial transmission** = data transmission one bit at a time (this is the normal method of transmission over longer distances, since although slower, it uses fewer lines and so is cheaper than parallel); **synchronous transmission** = transmission of data from one device to another, where both devices are controlled by the same clock, and the transmitted data is synchronized with the clock signal; **transmission channel** = physical connection between two points which allows data to be transmitted (such as a link between a CPU and a peripheral); **transmission control protocol;** *see* TCP, TCP/IP; **transmission errors** = errors due to noise on the line; **transmission media** = means by which data can be transmitted, such

as radio, light, etc.; **transmission rate** = measure of the amount of data transmitted in a certain time; *their average transmission is 64,000 bits per second (bps) through a parallel connection or 19,200 bps through a serial connection*

◊ **transmission control protocol/interface program (TCP/IP)** *noun* data transfer protocol used in networks and communications systems (often used in Unix-based networks)

◊ **transmissive disk** *noun* optical data storage disk in which the reading laser beam shines through the disk to a detector below

◊ **transmitter (TX)** *noun* device which will take an input signal, process it (modulate *or* convert to sound, etc.) then transmit it by some medium (radio, light, etc.)

transparency *noun* (in graphics) amount one image shows of another image beneath it

◊ **transparent** *noun* computer program which is not obvious to the user *or* which cannot be seen by the user when it is running; **transparent interrupts** = mode in which, if an interrupt occurs, all program and machine states are saved; the interrupt is serviced and then the system is restored to its previous states; **transparent paging** = software which allows the user to access any memory location in a paged memory system as if it were not paged

transphasor *noun* optical transistor, which is constructed from a crystal which is able to switch a main beam of light according to a smaller input signal

COMMENT: this is used in the latest research for an optical computer which could run at very high speeds, i.e., at the speed of light

transport *verb* to carry from one place to another; **transport layer** = fourth layer in the ISO/OSI network model that provides a reliable connection and checks and controls the quality of the connection; *see also* LAYER

◊ **transportable** *adjective* which can be carried; *a transportable computer is not as small as a portable or a laptop*

WSL has potential as the repository's 'meta transport layer for program objects', claims Healey, but it would need to be significantly extended. 'It only handles a 10th of the translation problem,' says Healey.

Computing

transputer *noun* single large very powerful chip containing a 32-bit microprocessor running at around 10 MIPS, that can be connected together to form a parallel processing system (running OCCAM)

TAOS kernels are now available from TKS for the Intel 486 and Pentium, the Apple/Olivetti ARM, the Inmos T800/T9000 transputer and the Mips R3000 series.

Computing

trap *noun* device, software or hardware that will catch something, such as a variable, fault or value; **trace trap** = selective breakpoint where a tracing program stops, allowing registers to be examined; **trap handler** = software that accepts interrupt signals and acts on them (such as running a special routine *or* sending data to a peripheral)

◊ **trapdoor** *noun* way of getting into a system to change data *or* browse *or* hack

trashcan *noun* (in a GUI) icon which looks like a dustbin or trash can; it deletes any file that is dragged onto it

tree *noun;* **tree (structure)** = data structure system where each item of data is linked to several others by branches (as opposed to a line system where each item leads on to the next); **tree and branch network system** = system of networking where data is transmitted along a single output line, from which other lines branch out, forming a tree structure that feeds individual stations; **tree of folders** = view of all the folders stored on your disk arranged to show folders and sub-folders; **tree selection sort** = rapid form of selection where the information from the first sort pass is used in the second pass to

speed up selection; **binary tree** = data system where each item of data *or* node has only two branches

trellis coding *noun* method of modulating a signal that uses both amplitude and phase modulation to give a greater throughput and lower error rates for data transmission speeds of over 9600bits per second

triad *noun* (i) three elements *or* characters *or* bits; (ii) triangular shaped grouping of the red, green and blue colour phosphor spots at each pixel location on the screen of a colour RGB monitor

Trojan Horse *noun* program inserted into a system by a hacker; it will perform a harmless function while copying information held in a classified file into a file with a low priority, which the hacker can then access without the authorized user knowing

troubleshoot *verb* (i) to debug computer software; (ii) to locate and repair faults in hardware

◊ **troubleshooter** *noun* person who troubleshoots hardware *or* software

TRUE *noun* logical condition (representing binary one) *compare* FALSE

TrueType™ outline font technology introduced by Apple and Microsoft as a means of printing exactly what is displayed on screen

truncate *verb* (a) to cut short (b) to give an approximate value to a number by reducing it to a certain number of digits

◊ **truncation** *noun* removal of digits from a number so that it is a certain length; *3.5678 truncated to 3.56;* **truncation error** = error caused when a number is truncated

trunk *noun* bus *or* communication link consisting of wires *or* leads, which connect different parts of a hardware system

truth table *noun* method of defining a logic function as the output state for all possible inputs; **truth value** = two values (true *or* false, T *or* F, 1 *or* 0) used in Boolean algebra

TSAPI = TELEPHONY SERVICES APPLICATION PROGRAMMING INTERFACE

Tseng Labs manufacturer of chipsets used in graphics adapters

TSR = TERMINATE AND STAY RESIDENT (PROGRAM)

TSW = TELESOFTWARE

TTL = TRANSISTOR-TRANSISTOR LOGIC most common family of logic gates and high-speed transistor circuit design in which the bipolar transistors are directly connected (usually collector to base); **TTL compatible** = MOS or other electronic circuits *or* components that can directly connect to and drive TTL circuits; **TTL logic** = use of TTL design and components to implement logic circuits and gates; **TTL monitor** = design of monitor which can only accept digital signals, so can only display monochrome images or a limited range of colours

TTY = TELETYPE

tune *verb* to set a system at its optimum point by careful adjustment; **to fine tune** = to adjust by small amounts the parameters of hardware *or* software to improve performance

tunnelling *noun* method of enclosing a packet of data from one type of network within another packet so that it can be sent over a different, incompatible, network

Turing machine *noun* mathematical model of a device which could read and write data to a controllable tape storage while altering its internal states

◊ **Turing test** *noun* test to decide if a computer is 'intelligent'

turn off *verb* to switch off *or* to disconnect the power supply to a machine; *turn off the power before unplugging the monitor*

◊ **turn on** *verb* to switch on *or* to connect the power supply to a machine

◊ **turnaround document** *noun* document which is printed out from a computer, sent to a user and returned by the user with new notes *or* information written on it, which can be read by a document reader

◊ **turnaround time (TAT)** *noun* **(a)** length of time it takes to switch data flow direction in a half duplex system **(b)** *US* time taken to activate a program and produce the result which the user has asked for

◊ **turnkey system** *noun* complete system which is designed to a customer's needs and is ready to use (to operate it, the user only has to switch it on or turn a key)

turtle *noun* device whose movements and position are controllable; it is used to draw graphics (with instructions in the computer language LOGO); it is either a device which works on a flat surface (floor turtle) or one which draws on a VDU screen (screen turtle), and is often used as a teaching aid; **turtle graphics** = graphic images created using a turtle and a series of commands; *the charts were prepared using turtle graphics*

TWAIN application programming interface standard developed by Hewlett-Packard, Logitech, Eastman Kodak, Aldus, and Caere that allows software to control image hardware

tweak *verb* to make small adjustments to a program *or* hardware to improve performance

tweening *noun* (in computer graphics) calculating the intermediate images that lead from a starting image to a different finished image; *using tweening, we can show how a frog turns into a princess in five steps*

twisted-pair cable *noun* cable which consists of two insulated copper wires twisted around each other (to reduce induction and so interference); **shielded twisted pair (STP) cable** = cable which consists of two insulated copper wires twisted around each other (to reduce induction and so interference), the pair of wires are then wrapped in an insulated shielding layer to further reduce interference; **unshielded twisted pair (UTP) cable** = cable which consists of two insulated copper wires twisted around each other (to reduce induction and so interference), unlike STP cable the pair of wires are not wrapped in any other layer; *see also* ETHERNET, 10BASET, UTP

COMMENT: The EIA specifies five levels of cable for different purposes. The *Category 1* standard defines an older-style unshielded twisted-pair cable that is formed by loosely twisting two insulated wires together to reduce noise and interference; this type of cable is not suitable for data transmission. The *Category 2* (part of the EIA/TIA 568 specification) standard defines a type of unshielded twisted-pair cable that can be used to transmit data at rates up to 4MHz. The *Category 3* (part of the EIA/TIA 568 specification) standard defines a type of unshielded twisted-pair cable that can be used to transmit data at rates up to 10MHz; this type of cable is the minimum standard of cable required for a 10BaseT network (NOTE: the standard suggests that the cable should have three twists per foot of cable). The *Category 4* (part of the EIA/TIA 568 specification) standard defines a type of unshielded twisted-pair cable that is the minimum standard of cable required for data transmission rates up to 16Mbit/second on a Token Ring network. The *Category 5* (part of the EIA/TIA 568 specification) standard defines a type of cable that can carry data transmitted at up to 100MHz and is suitable for FDDI over copper wire, 100BaseT or other high-speed networks

two-address instruction *noun* instruction format containing the location of two operands, the result being stored in one of the operand locations; **two-plus-one instruction** = instruction containing the locations of two operands and an address for the result

◊ **two-dimensional** *adjective* which has two dimensions (that is, flat, with no depth); **two-dimensional array** = array which locates items both vertically and horizontally

◊ **two input adder** ; *see* HALF ADDER

◊ **two-level subroutine** *noun* subroutine containing another subroutine

◊ **two-part** *noun* paper (for computers *or* typewriters) with a top sheet for the original and a second sheet for a copy; *two-part invoices; two-part stationery*

◊ **two-pass assembler** *noun* assembler which converts an assembly language program into machine code in two passes; the first pass stores symbolic addresses, the second converts them to absolute addresses

◊ **two-phase commit** *noun* (in a database) function that ensures that each step of a transaction is correct and valid before committing the changes to the database; *see also* COMMIT, TRANSACTION

two's complement *noun* formed by adding one to the one's complement of a binary number, often used to represent negative binary numbers

TX = TRANSMITTER

type 1 *noun* definition of the processes *or* sorts of data which a variable in a computer can contain (this can be numbers, text only, etc.); **variable data type** = variable that can contain any sort of data, such as numerical, text, etc.; **string type** = variable that can contain alphanumeric characters only **2** *verb* to enter information via a keyboard; *I typed in the command again, but it still didn't work*

◊ **Type cable** *noun* specification for cables defined by IBM; **Type 1** = four wires arranged as two pairs of solid wires surrounded by a braided shield to reduce interference; **Type 2** = twelve wires arranged as six pairs of wires, used for voice transmission; **Type 3** = two wires, twisted pair used for telephone wire; **Type 5** = 100-140micron diameter fibre optic cable; **Type 6** = four separate wires arranged as two pairs; each wire is made up of strands of fine wire; **Type 8** = four separate wires arranged as two pairs, shielded cable with no twists

typeface *noun* set of characters in a particular design and particular weight; *most of this book is set in the Times typeface;*

typesetter = machine which produces very high-quality text output using a laser to create an image on photosensitive paper (normally at a resolution of 1275 or 2450dpi); **type size** = size of a font, measured in points; **type style** = weight and angle of a font, such as bold or italic

Uu

UA = USER AGENT (in an X.400 email system) software that ensures a mail message has the correct header information and then delivers it to the message transfer agent which send the message to its destination

UART = UNIVERSAL ASYNCHRONOUS RECEIVER/TRANSMITTER chip which converts asynchronous serial bit streams to a parallel form *or* parallel data to a serial bit stream; **UART controller** = circuit that uses a UART to convert (serial) data from a terminal into a parallel form, then transmits it over a network; *see also* USART

UBC = UNIVERSAL BLOCK CHANNEL

UDP = USER DATAGRAM PROTOCOL protocol that is part of TCP/IP that is often used in network management and SNMP applications

UHF = ULTRA HIGH FREQUENCY range of frequencies normally used to transmit television signals

ULA = UNCOMMITTED LOGIC ARRAY chip containing a number of unconnected logic circuits and gates which can then be connected by a customer to provide a required function

-law *noun* method of encoding digital sound samples so that an eight bit word can store a 14-bit sound sample

Ultimedia™ multimedia concept developed by IBM that combines sound, video, images, and text, and defines the hardware required to run it

ultra- *prefix* meaning very large *or* further than; **ultra high frequency (UHF)** = range of frequencies normally used to transmit television signals

ultraviolet (UV) light *noun* electromagnetic radiation with wavelength just greater than the visible spectrum, from 200 to 4000 angstrom; **ultraviolet erasable PROM** = EPROM whose contents are erased by exposing to UV light

unallowable digit *noun* illegal combination of bits in a word, according to predefined rules

unauthorized *adjective* which has not been authorized; *the use of a password is to prevent unauthorized access to the data*

unary operation *noun* computing operation on only one operand, such as the logical NOT operation

unattended operation *noun* system which can operate without the need for a person to supervise

unbundled software *noun* software which is not included in the price of the equipment

unclocked *adjective* electronic circuit *or* flip-flop which changes state as soon as an input changes, not with a clock signal

uncommitted logic array (ULA) *noun* chip containing a number of unconnected logic circuits and gates which can then be connected by a customer to provide a required function; **uncommitted storage list** = table of the areas of memory in a system that are free *or* have not been allocated

unconditional *adjective* which does not depend on any condition being met; **unconditional branch** *or* **jump** *or* **transfer =** instruction which transfers control from one point in the program to another, without depending on any condition being met (NOTE: opposite is **conditional**)

undelete *verb* to restore deleted information *or* a deleted file; *don't worry, this function will undelete your cuts to the letter*

underflow *noun* result of a numerical operation that is too small to be represented with the given accuracy of a computer

underline *or* **underscore 1** *noun* line drawn *or* printed under a piece of text **2** *verb* to print *or* write a line under a piece of text; **underlining** = word-processing command which underlines text

undertake *verb* to agree to do something; *he has undertaken to reprogram the whole system*

undetected *adjective* which has not been detected; *the programming error remained undetected for some time*

undo *verb* (option in a program) to reverse the previous action, normally an editing command; *you've just deleted the paragraph, but you can undo it from the option in the Edit menu*

unedited *adjective* which has not been edited

unformatted *adjective* (i) text file which contains no formatting commands, margins or typographical commands; (ii) (disk) which has not been formatted; *it is impossible to copy to an unformatted disk; the cartridge drive provides 12.7Mbyte of unformatted storage;* **unformatted capacity** = capacity of a magnetic disk before it has been formatted; **unformatted disk** = magnetic disk which has not been formatted (disks must be formatted before use)

uni- *prefix* meaning one *or* single

◊ **uniform resource locator (URL)** *noun* (internet) system used to standardize the way in which WWW addresses are written; *the URL of the Peter Collin Publishing home page is 'http://www.pcp.co.uk'*

◊ **union** *noun* logical function which produces a true output if any input is true

◊ **unipolar** *adjective* **(a)** (transistor) which can act as a variable current flow control (an external signal varies the resistance of the device); *see also* FET, TRANSISTOR **(b)** (transmission system) in which a positive voltage pulse and zero volts represents the binary bits 1 and 0; **unipolar signal** = signal that uses only positive voltage levels *compare* POLAR

uninterruptable power supply (UPS) *noun* power supply which can continue to provide a regulated supply to equipment even after a mains power failure (using a battery)

unique *adjective* which is different from everything else; *each separate memory byte has its own unique address;* **unique identifier** = set of characters used to distinguish between different resources in a multimedia book

unit *noun* **(a)** smallest element; **unit buffer** = buffer which is one character long (NOTE: usually used to mean that there are no buffering facilities); **unit record** = single record of information **(b)** single machine (possibly with many different parts); **arithmetic and logic unit (ALU)** = section of the CPU which performs all the mathematical and logical functions; **central processing unit (CPU)** = group of circuits which perform the basic functions of a computer, made up of three main parts: the control unit, the arithmetic and logic unit and the input/output unit; **control unit** = section of the CPU which selects and executes instructions; **desk top unit** = computer *or* machine which will fit onto a desk; **input/output unit** *or* **device** = peripheral (such as a terminal in a workstation) which can be used both for inputting and outputting data to a processor

universal *adjective* which applies everywhere *or* which can be used everywhere *or* used for a number of tasks; **universal asynchronous receiver/transmitter (UART)** = chip which converts an asynchronous serial bit stream to a parallel form *or* parallel data to a serial bit stream; **universal block channel (UBC)** = communications channel allowing high speed transfer of blocks of data to and from high speed peripherals; **universal device** = (i) UART; (ii) USRT; (iii) USART; **universal product code (UPC)** = standard printed bar coding system used to identify products in a shop (using a bar code reader *or* at a EPOS); *see also* EAN; **universal programming** = writing a program which is not specific to one machine, so that it can run on several machines; **universal resource locator (URL)** = (internet) system used to standardize the way in which WWW addresses are written; made up of three parts: the first is the protocol (such as HTTP or FTP), then the domain name of the service and finally the directory or file name - 'http://www.pcp.co.uk/index.html'; *the URL of the Peter Collin Publishing home page is 'http://www.pcp.co.uk';* **universal set** = complete set of elements which conform to a set of rules; *the universal set of prime numbers less than ten and greater than two is 3,5,7;* **universal synchronous asynchronous receiver-transmitter (USART)** = chip that can be instructed by a CPU to communicate with asynchronous or synchronous bit streams *or* parallel data lines; **universal synchronous receiver/transmitter (USRT)** = single integrated circuit which can carry out all the serial to parallel and interfacing operations required between a computer and transmission line

UNIX *noun* popular multiuser, multitasking operating system developed by AT&T Bell Laboratories to run on almost any computer, from a PC, to minicomputers and large mainframes; **UNIX-to-UNIX copy (UUCP)** = software utilities that help make it easier for a user to copy data from one computer (running UNIX) via a serial link to another computer (running UNIX)

Hampshire fire brigade is investing £2 million in a command and control system based on the new SeriesFT fault-tolerant Unix machine from Motorola.

Computing

unjustified *adjective* (text) which has not been justified; **unjustified tape** *or* **idiot tape** = tape containing unformatted text, which cannot be printed until formatting data (such as justification, line width and page size) has been added by a computer

unlock *verb* action to allow other users to write to a file *or* access a system

unmoderated list *noun* mailing list that sends any material submitted to the listserv on to all the subscribers without a person reading or checking the content

unmodified instruction *noun* program instruction which is directly processed without modification to obtain the operation to be performed

unmodulated *adjective* (signal) which has not been modulated; *see also* BASE BAND

unmount *verb* (i) to remove a disk from a disk drive; (ii) (instruction) to inform the operating system that a disk drive is no longer in active use

unpack *verb* to remove packed data from storage and expand it to its former state; *this routine unpacks the archived file*

unplug *verb* to take a plug out of a socket; *do not move the system without unplugging it; simply unplug the old drive and plug-in a new one*

unpopulated *adjective* printed circuit board which does not yet contain any components *or* whose sockets are empty; *you can buy an unpopulated RAM card and fit your own RAM chips*

unprotected *adjective* (data) which can be modified and is not protected by a security measure; **unprotected field** = section of a computer display that a user can modify

unrecoverable error *noun* computer hardware *or* software error which causes a program to crash

unshielded twisted-pair (UTP) cable

cable *noun* cable consisting of two insulated copper wires twisted around each other (to reduce induction and so interference), unlike STP cable the pair of wires are not wrapped in any other layer; *see* CATEGORY CABLE, UTP

> COMMENT: UTP is normally used for telephone cabling, but is also the cabling used in the IEEE 802.3 (10BaseT) standard that defines Ethernet running over UTP at rates of up to 10Mbits per second.

unsigned *adjective* (number system) which does not represent negative numbers

unsorted *adjective* (data) which has not been sorted; *it took four times as long to search the unsorted file*

unwanted *adjective* which is not needed; *use the global delete command to remove large areas of unwanted text*

up *adverb* (*of computer or program*) working *or* running; *they must have found the fault - the computer is finally up and running*

◊ **up time** *or* **uptime** *noun* time during which a device is operational and error free (NOTE: opposite is **down**)

UPC = UNIVERSAL PRODUCT CODE

update 1 *noun* (i) master file which has been made up-to-date by adding new material; (ii) printed information which is an up-to-date revision of earlier information; (iii) new version of a system which is sent to users of the existing system; **update file** *or* **transaction file** = file containing recent changes *or* transactions to records which is used to update the master file **2** *verb* to change *or* add to specific data in a master file so as to make the information up-to-date; *he has the original and updated documents on disks*

> it means that any item of data stored in the system need be updated only once
> *Which PC?*

up/down counter *noun* electronic counter which can increment *or* decrement a counter with each input pulse

upgrade *verb* to make (a system) more powerful *or* more up-to-date by adding new equipment; *they can upgrade the printer; the single processor with 2Mbytes of memory can be upgraded to 4Mbytes; all three models have an on-site upgrade facility*

> the cost of upgrading a PC to support CAD clearly depends on the peripheral devices added
> *PC Business World*

upkeep *noun* keeping data up-to-date; keeping devices in working order; *the upkeep of the files means reviewing them every six months*

uplink *noun* transmission link from an earth station to a satellite

upload *verb* (i) to transfer data files *or* programs from a small computer to a main CPU; (ii) to transfer a file from one computer to a BBS or host computer; *the user can upload PC data to update mainframe applications; the image can be manipulated before uploading to the host computer* (NOTE: the opposite is **download**)

◊ **uploading** *noun* action of transferring files to a main CPU

upper memory *noun* (in an IBM PC) 384Kb of memory located between the 640Kb and 1Mb limits

UPS = UNINTERRUPTABLE POWER SUPPLY power supply which can continue to provide a regulated supply to equipment even after a mains power failure (using a battery)

> Magnum Power Systems has launched a new UPS for PCs. The BI-UPS prevents loss of data due to power dips or

'brown-outs' - voltage drops because of circuit overload.

Computing

upper case *noun* capital letters and other symbols on a typewriter *or* keyboard, which are accessed by pressing the shift key

upper memory *noun* (in an IBM PC) 384Kb of memory located between the 640Kb and 1Mb limits; upper memory is after the 640Kb conventional memory but before the high memory areas above the 1Mb range

uptime *noun* time when a computer is functioning correctly (as opposed to downtime)

upwards compatible *or US* **upward compatible** *adjective* (hardware *or* software) designed to be compatible either with earlier models *or* with future models which have not yet been invented

URL = UNIFORM RESOURCE LOCATOR (internet) system used to standardize the way in which WWW addresses are written; made up of three parts: the first is the protocol (such as HTTP or FTP), then the domain name of the service and finally the directory or file name - 'http://www.pcp.co.uk/index.html'; *the URL of the Peter Collin Publishing home page is 'http://www.pcp.co.uk'*

usable *adjective* which can be used *or* which is available for use; *the PC has 512K of usable memory*

◊ **usability** *noun* the ease with which hardware *or* software can be used; *we have studied usability tests and found that a GUI is easier for new users than a command line*

USART = UNIVERSAL SYNCHRONOUS ASYNCHRONOUS RECEIVER-TRANSMITTER chip which can be instructed by a CPU to communicate with asynchronous *or* synchronous bit streams or parallel data lines

USASCII = USA STANDARD CODE FOR INFORMATION INTERCHANGE; *see* ASCII

use 1 *noun* (a) way in which something can be used; *the printer has been in use for the last two hours; the use of the that file is restricted;* to make use of something = to use something (b) value; being useful; *what use is an extra disk drive? it's no use, I cannot find the error;* in use = already in operation; *sorry, the printer is already in use* **2** *verb* (a) to operate something; *if you use the computer for processing the labels, it will be much quicker; the computer is used too often by the sales staff* (b) to consume heat, light, etc.; *it's using too much electricity*

◊ **used** *adjective* which is not new; *special offer on used terminals; our latest system is hardly used*

Usenet *noun* section of the internet that provides forums (called newsgroups) in which any user can add a message or comment on any other message; *see also* NEWSGROUP

user *noun* (i) person who uses a computer *or* machine *or* software; (ii) especially, a keyboard operator; **user account** = (in a network *or* multiuser system) record which identifies a user, contains his password and holds his rights to use resources; *I have a new user account on this LAN but I cannot remember my password;* user area = part of the memory which is available for the user, and does not contain the operating system; **user agent (UA)** = (in an X.400 email system) software that ensures a mail message has the correct header information and then delivers it to the message transfer agent which send the message to its destination; **user datagram protocol (UDP)** = protocol that is part of TCP/IP that is often used in network management and SNMP applications; **user-definable** = feature *or* section of a program that a user can customize as required; *the style sheet contains 125 user-definable symbols;* **user-defined characters** = characters which are created by the user and added to the standard character set; **user documentation** = documentation provided with a program which helps the user run it; *using the package was easy with the excellent user* *documentation;* **user group** = association *or* club of users of a particular system *or* computer; *I found how to solve the problem by asking people at the user group meeting;* **user guide** = manual describing how to use a software package *or* system; **user ID** = unique identification code which allows a computer to recognize a user; *if you forget your user ID, you will not be able to logon;* **user interface** = hardware *or* software designed to make it easier for a user to communicate with the machine; *see also* COMMAND LINE, GUI; **user level** = (in authoring software) one of two modes that allows a user to run and interact with a multimedia application, but not modify it in any way; **user name** = (in a network *or* multiuser system) name by which a user is known to the system and which opens the correct user account; **user-operated language** = high-level programming language which allows certain problems *or* procedures to be easily expressed; **user port** = socket which allows peripherals to be connected to a computer; **user's program** = computer software written by a user rather than a manufacturer; **user-selectable** = which can be chosen *or* selected by the user; *the video resolution of 640 by 300, 240 or 200 pixels is user-selectable*

> the user's guides are designed for people who have never seen a computer, but some sections have been spoiled by careless checking
>
> *PC User*

◊ **user-friendly** *adjective* (language *or* system *or* program) which is easy to use and interact with; *it's such a user-friendly machine; compared with the previous version this one is very user-friendly*

> ModelMaker saves researchers a great deal of time and effort, and provides a highly user-friendly environment using menus and 'buttons', instant output, and instant access to a wide variety of mathematical techniques built into the system.
>
> *Computing*

> the first popular microcomputer to have a user-friendly interface built into its operating system
>
> *Micro Decision*

USRT = UNIVERSAL SYNCHRONOUS RECEIVER/TRANSMITTER

utility (program) *noun* useful program which is concerned with such routine activities as file searching, copying files, file directories, sorting and debugging and various mathematical functions; *a lost file cannot be found without a file-recovery utility; on the disk is a utility for backing up a hard disk*

UTP cable = UNSHIELDED TWISTED-PAIR CABLE

UUCP = UNIX-TO-UNIX COPY

Uuencoding *noun* method of converting documents and files to a pseudo-text format that allows them to be transmitted as an electronic mail message

> COMMENT: this gets around the internet's inability to transfer messages that are not text. Now been largely replaced by MIME

UV light = ULTRAVIOLET LIGHT

Vv

V = VOLTAGE

V20, V30 processor made by NEC, which are compatible with the Intel 8088 and 8086

V & V = VERIFICATION & VALIDATION

V format *noun* data organization, in which variable length records are stored with a header which contains their length

V series *noun* CCITT standards for data transmission using a modem

COMMENT: **V.21** = 300 bits/second transmit and receive, full duplex; **V.22** = 1200 bits/second transmit and receive, half duplex; **V.22 BIS** = 1200 bits/second transmit and receive, full duplex; **V.23** = 75 bits/second transmit, 1200 bits/second receive, half duplex; **V.24** = interchange circuits between a DTE and a DCE; **V.25 BIS** = automatic calling and answering equipment on a PSTN; **V.26** = 2400 bits/second transmission over leased lines; **V.26 BIS** = 2400 bits/second transmit, 1200 bits/second receive, half duplex for use on a PSTN; **V.26 TER** = 2400 bits/second transmit, 1200 bits/second receive, full duplex for use on a PSTN; **V.27** = 4800 bits/second modem for use on a leased line; **V.27 BIS** = 4800 bits/second transmit, 2400 bits/second receive for use on a leased line; **V.27 TER** = 4800 bits/second transmit, 2400 bits/second receive for use on a PSTN; **V.29** = 9600 bits/second modem for use on a PSTN or leased line; **V.32** = data transmission rate is 9600 bits/second; **V.32bis** = data transmission rate is 14,400 bits/second; **V.32terbo** = pseudo-standard developed by AT&T, among others, that supports transmission at 19200 bits/second; **V.42** = error control and correction protocol; **V.42 BIS** = data compression used with V.42 error control

vaccine *noun* software utility used to check a system to see if any viruses are present, and remove any that are found

valid *adjective* correct, according to a set of rules; **valid memory address** = signal on control bus indicating that an address is available on the address bus

◊ **validate** *verb* to check that an input *or* data is correct according to a set of rules

◊ **validation** *noun* check performed to validate data; *see also* VERIFICATION

◊ **validity** *noun* correctness of an instruction *or* password; **validity check** = check that data *or* results are realistic

value *noun* what something is worth (either in money *or* as a quantity); **absolute value** = value of a number regardless of its sign; *the absolute value of -62.34 is 62.34;* **initial value** = starting point (usually zero) set when initializing variables at the beginning of a program

◊ **value-added** *adjective* (something) with extra benefit for a user; **value-added network (VAN)** = commercial network which offers information services, such as stock prices, weather, email or advice as well as basic file transfer; **value-added reseller (VAR)** = company that buys hardware *or* software and adds another feature, customizes or offers an extra service to attract customers

VAN = VALUE-ADDED NETWORK

vanishing point perspective *noun* graphics displayed in two-dimensions that have the appearance of depth as all lines converge at a vanishing point and objects appear smaller as they are further from the user

vapourware *noun* (*informal*) products which exist in name only

Rivals dismissed the initiative as IBM vapourware, designed to protect its installed base of machines running under widely differing operating systems.

Computing

VAR = VALUE-ADDED RESELLER

variable 1 *adjective* which is able to change; **variable data** = data which can be modified, and is not write-protected; **variable length record** = record which can be of any length; **variable word length computer** = computer in which the number of bits which make up a word is variable, and varies according to the type of data **2** *noun* (computer program identifier for a) register *or* storage location which can contain any number *or* characters and which may vary during the program run; **global variable** = number that can be accessed by any routine *or* structure in a program; **local variable** = number which can only be accessed by certain routines in a certain section of a computer program

◊ **vary** *verb* to change; *the clarity of the signal can vary with the power supply*

VB = VISUAL BASIC programming tool, developed by Microsoft, that allows users to create Windows applications very easily

◊ **VBA** = VISUAL BASIC FOR APPLICATIONS complex macro language developed by Microsoft from its Visual Basic programming tool

◊ **VBScript** set of programming commands that can be included within a normal Web page (that is written using HTML commands) *compare with* JAVASCRIPT

VDT *or* **VDU** = VISUAL DISPLAY TERMINAL, VISUAL DISPLAY UNIT terminal with a screen and a keyboard, on which text *or* graphics can be viewed and information entered

it normally consists of a keyboard to input information and either a printing terminal

or a VDU screen to display messages and results

Practical Computing

---

a VDU is a device used with a computer that displays information in the form of characters and drawings on a screen

Electronics & Power

---

vector *noun* **(a)** address which directs a computer to a new memory location **(b)** coordinate that consists of a magnitude and direction; **vector font** = shape of characters within a font that are drawn using curves and lines (vector graphics) allowing the characters to be scaled to almost any size without changing the quality *compare* BIT-MAPPED FONT; **vector graphics** *or* **vector image** *or* **vector scan** = computer drawing system which uses line length and direction from an origin to plot lines; **vector processor** = coprocessor that operates on one row or column of an array at a time

◊ **vectored interrupt** *noun* interrupt signal which directs the processor to a routine at a particular address

the great advantage of the vector-scan display is that it requires little memory to store a picture

Electronics & Power

Veitch diagram *noun* graphical representation of a truth table

velocity *noun* speed; *the disk drive motor spins at a constant velocity*

vendor *noun* person who manufactures *or* sells or supplies hardware *or* software products; **vendor independent** = hardware *or* software that will work with hardware and software manufactured by other vendors *opposite* is PROPRIETARY; **vendor-independent messaging** =; *see* VIM

Venn diagram *noun* graphical representation of the relationships between the states in a system *or* circuit

verify *verb* to check that data recorded *or* entered is correct

◊ **verification** *noun* checking that data has been keyboarded correctly *or* that data transferred from one medium to another has been transferred correctly; **verification and validation (V & V)** = testing a system to check that it is functioning correctly and that it is suitable for the tasks intended; **keystroke verification** = check made on each key pressed to make sure it is valid for a particular application

◊ **verifier** *noun* special device for verifying input data

Veronica tool that works with Gopher to help a user find information or files on the WWW

version *noun* copy *or* program *or* statement which is slightly different from others; *the latest version of the software includes an improved graphics routine;* **version control** = utility software that allows several programmers to work on a source file and monitors the changes that have been made by each programmer; **version number** = number of the version of a product

vertex *noun* point in space defined by the three coordinates x, y, and z

vertical *adjective* at right angles to the horizontal; **vertical application** = application software that has been designed for a specific use, rather than for general use; *your new software to manage a florist's is a good vertical application;* **vertical blanking interval;** *see* RASTER; **vertical format unit (VFU)** = part of the control system of a printer which governs the vertical format of the document to be printed (such as vertical spacing, page length); **vertical justification** = adjustment of the spacing between lines of text to fit a section of text into a page; **vertical parity check** = error detection test in which the bits of a word are added and compared with a correct total; **vertical redundancy check (VRC)** = (odd) parity check on each character of a block received, to detect any errors; **vertical scrolling** = displayed text which moves up or down the computer screen one line at a time; **vertical**

sync signal = (in a video signal) signal which indicates the end of the last trace at the bottom of the display; **vertical tab** = number of lines that should be skipped before printing starts again

◊ **vertically** *adverb* from top to bottom *or* going up and down at right angles to the horizontal; *the page has been justified vertically*

very large scale integration (VLSI) *noun* integrated circuit with 10,000 to 100,000 components

VESA = VIDEO ELECTRONICS STANDARDS ASSOCIATION; **VESA local bus** *or* **VL-bus** = (in an IBM PC) standard defined by VESA which allows up to three special expansion slots that provide direct, bus-master control of the central processor and allow very high speed data transfers between main memory and the expansion card without using the processor; *for a high-performance PC, choose one with a VESA bus*

VFU = VERTICAL FORMAT UNIT

VFW *see* VIDEO FOR WINDOWS

VGA VIDEO GRAPHICS ARRAY (in an IBM PC) standard of video adapter developed by IBM that can support a display with a resolution up to 640x480 pixels in up to 256 colours, superseded by SVGA; **VGA feature connector** = 26-pin edge connector or port (normally at the top edge) of a VGA display adapter that allows another device to access its palette information and clock signals; **super VGA (SVGA)** = enhancement to the standard VGA graphics display system that allows resolutions of up to 800x600pixels with 16 million colours

VHD = VERY HIGH DENSITY capacitance type video disk able to store very large quantities of data

via *preposition* going through something *or* using something to get to a destination; *the signals have reached us via satellite; you can download the data to the CPU via a modem*

VidCap utility program used in the Microsoft Video for Windows system to capture a video sequence

video *noun* text *or* images *or* graphics viewed on television *or* a monitor; **video adapter** *or* **board** *or* **controller** = add-in board which converts data into electrical signals to drive a monitor and display text and graphics; **video buffer** = memory in a video adapter that is used to store the bit-map of the image being displayed; **video capture board** = board that plugs into an expansion socket inside a PC and lets a user capture a TV picture and store it in memory so that it can then be processed by a computer; **video-CD** = CD-ROM that stores digital video data conforming to the Philips White Book standard and uses MPEG compression for the full-motion video data; **video codec** = electronic device to convert a video signal to or from a digital form; **video conferencing** = linking video, audio and computer signals from different locations so that distant people can talk and see each other, as if in a conference room; **video digitiser** = high speed digital sampling circuit which stores a TV picture in memory so that it can then be processed by a computer; **videodisc** = optical disc used to store television pictures and sound; **video display** = device which can display text *or* graphical information, such as a CRT; **video editing** = method of editing a video sequence in which the video is digitized and stored in a computer; **video editor** = computer that controls two videotape recorders to allow an operator to play back sequences from one and record these on the second machine; **Video Electronics Standards Association;** *see* VESA; **video game** = game played on a computer, with action shown on a video display; **video graphics array (VGA)** = (in an IBM PC) standard of video adapter developed by IBM that can support a display with a resolution up to 640x480 pixels in up to 256 colours, superseded by SVGA; **video graphics card** *or* **overlay card** = expansion card that fits into an expansion slot inside a PC and that allows a computer to display both generated text and graphics and moving video images from an external camera or

VCR; **video interface chip** = chip which controls a video display allowing information stored in a computer (text, graphics) to be displayed; **video lookup table** = collection of pre-calculated values of the different colours that are stored in memory and can be examined very quickly to produce an answer without the need to recalculate; **video memory** *or* **video RAM (VRAM)** = high speed random access memory used to store computer-generated *or* digitized images; **video monitor** = device able to display, without sound, signals from a computer; **video scanner** = device which allows images of objects *or* pictures to be entered into a computer; *new video scanners are designed to scan three-dimensional objects;* **video server** = dedicated computer on a network used to store video sequences *(informal);* **video signal** = signal which provides line picture information and synchronization pulses; **video terminal** = keyboard with a monitor; *see also* VESA

Video for Windows (VFW) set of software drivers and utilities for Microsoft Windows 3.1, developed by Microsoft, that allows AVI-format video files to be played back in a window

◊ **videotext** *or* **videotex** *noun* system for transmitting text and displaying it on a screen

COMMENT: this covers information transmitted either by TV signals (teletext) or by signals sent down telephone lines (viewdata)

Vision Dynamics has upgraded its video capture and display boards for PCs. Elvis II will now display TV pictures on a VGA screen at a resolution of 1,024 x 768 square pixels and 2 million colours to provide enhanced picture quality from PAL, NTSC and S-VHS sources.
Computing

view *verb* to look at something, especially something displayed on a screen; *the user has to pay a charge for viewing pages on a bulletin board*

◊ **viewdata** *noun* interactive system for transmitting text *or* graphics from a database to a user's terminal by telephone lines, providing facilities for information retrieval, transactions, education, games and recreation

> COMMENT: the user calls up the page of information required, using the telephone and a modem, as opposed to teletext, where the pages of information are repeated one after the other automatically

◊ **viewer** *noun* utility that allows a user to see what is contained in an image or formatted document file, without having to start the program that created it

◊ **Viewer**™ multimedia authoring tool for Microsoft Windows and Sony DataDiscman platforms, developed by Microsoft, which uses RTF formatted files with embedded commands

VIM = VENDOR-INDEPENDENT MESSAGING set of standards developed by IBM, Borland, Novell and Apple, that provides a way of sending electronic mail messages between applications *compare* MAPI

virgin *adjective* (tape) that has not been recorded on before

virtual *adjective* (feature *or* device) which does not actually exist but which is simulated by a computer and can be used by a user as if it did exist; **virtual address** = an address referring to virtual storage; **virtual circuit** = link established between a source and sink (in a packet-switching network) for the duration of the call; **virtual desktop** *or* **screen** = area that is bigger than the physical limits of the monitor, and which can contain text, images, windows, etc.; **virtual disk** = section of RAM used with a short controlling program as if it were a fast disk storage system; **virtual image** = complete image stored in memory rather than the part of it that is displayed; **virtual machine** = simulated machine and its operations; **virtual memory** *or* **virtual storage (VS)** = large imaginary main memory made available by loading smaller pages from a backing store into the available main memory only as and when

they are required; **virtual reality** = simulation of a real-life scene or environment by computer; *this new virtual reality software can create a three-dimensional room that you can navigate around;* **virtual reality modeling language;** *see* VRML; **virtual terminal** = ideal terminal specifications used as a model by a real terminal

> Autodesk suggests that anyone wishing to build Virtual Reality applications with the Cyberspace Developer's Kit should have solid knowledge of programming in C++ along with general knowledge of computer graphics.
>
> *Computing*

virus *noun* program which adds itself to an executable file and copies (or spreads) itself to other executable files each time an infected file is run; a virus can corrupt data, display a message or do nothing; *if your PC is infected with a virus, your data is at risk;* **anti-virus software** = software which removes a virus from a file; **virus checker** = software that is used to try and detect and remove unwanted virus programs from the hard disk of a computer; **virus detector** = utility software which checks executable files to see if they contain (have been infected) with a known virus

> COMMENT: viruses are spread by downloading unchecked files from a bulletin board system or via unregulated networks or by inserting an unchecked floppy disk into your PC - always use a virus detector.

visible *adjective* which can be seen

visual *adjective* which can be seen *or* which is used by sight; **visual programming** = method of programming a computer by dragging icons into a flowchart that describes the program's actions rather than writing a series of instructions

◊ **Visual Basic**™ (VB) programming tool, developed by Microsoft, that allows users to create Windows applications very easily

◊ **Visual Basic for Applications** (VBA) complex macro language developed by Microsoft from its Visual Basic programming tool

◊ **Visual Basic Script** *see* VBSCRIPT

◊ **Visual C** development product by Microsoft that allows Windows applications to be created by drawing the user interface and attaching C code

visual display terminal (VDT) *or* **visual display unit (VDU)** *noun* terminal with a screen and a keyboard, on which text *or* graphics can be viewed and information entered

visualization *noun* conversion of numbers or data into a graphical format that can be more easily understood

Vivo™ data storage format used to deliver video over the internet

VL-bus *or* **VL local bus** *noun* standard defined by VESA which allows up to three special expansion slots that provide direct, bus-master control of the central processor and allow very high speed data transfers between main memory and the expansion card without using the processor; *for a high-performance PC, choose one with a VL-bus*

VLSI = VERY LARGE SCALE INTEGRATION system with between 10,000 and 100,000 components on a single IC

voice *noun* sound of human speech; **voice answer back** = computerized response service using a synthesized voice to answer enquiries; **voice data entry** *or* **input** = input of information into a computer using a speech recognition system and the user's voice; **voice mail** = computer linked to a telephone exchange that answers a person's telephone when they are not there and allows messages to be recorded (in digital form); *I checked my voice mail to see if anyone had left me a message;* **voice output** = production of sounds which sound like human speech, made as a result of voice synthesis; **voice recognition** = ability of a computer to recognize certain words in a human voice and provide a suitable response; **voice response** = VOICE OUTPUT; **voice synthesis** = reproduction of sounds similar to those of the human voice; **voice synthesizer** = device which generates sounds which are similar to the human voice

---

the technology of voice output is reasonably difficult, but the technology of voice recognition is much more complex

Personal Computer World

---

volatile memory *or* **volatile store** *or* **volatile dynamic storage** *noun* memory *or* storage medium which loses data stored in it when the power supply is switched off (NOTE: opposite is **non-volatile memory**)

◊ **volatility** *noun* number of records that are added *or* deleted from a computer system compared to the total number in store

volt *noun* SI unit of electrical potential, defined as voltage across a one ohm resistance when one amp is flowing

◊ **voltage** *noun* electromotive force expressed in volts; **voltage regulator** = device which provides a steady output voltage even if the input supply varies; **voltage transient** = spike of voltage which is caused by a time delay in two devices switching *or* by noise on the line

---

COMMENT: electricity supply can have peaks and troughs of current, depending on the users in the area. Fluctuations in voltage can affect computers; a voltage regulator will provide a steady supply of electricity

---

volume *noun* (a) disk *or* tape *or* storage device; **volume label** *or* **name** = name assigned to identify a particular disk *or* tape (b) total space occupied by data in a storage system

VR *see* VIRTUAL REALITY

VRAM = VIDEO RANDOM ACCESS MEMORY high speed random access memory used to store computer-generated *or* digitized images

VRC = VERTICAL REDUNDANCY CHECK (odd) parity check on each character of a block received, to detect any errors

VRML = VIRTUAL REALITY MODELING LANGUAGE system that allows developers to create three-dimensional worlds within a Web page

VS = VIRTUAL STORAGE

VT-terminal emulation *noun* standard set of codes developed by Digital Equipment Corporation to control how text and graphics are displayed on its range of terminals; **VT-52** = popular standard of a terminal that defines the codes used to display text and graphics

Vxtreme format used to deliver streaming video sequences over the internet

Ww

wafer *noun* thin round slice of a large single crystal of silicon onto which hundreds of individual integrated circuits are constructed, before being cut into individual chips

◊ **wafer scale integration** *noun* one large chip, the size of a wafer, made up of smaller integrated circuits connected together (these are still in the research stage)

Rockwell International has signed a letter of intent to buy Western Digital's silicon wafer fabrication facility in Irvine, California for a proposed price of $115 million (£77 million).

Computing

WAIS = WIDE AREA INFORMATION SERVER system that allows a user to search for information stored on the internet

wait condition *or* **state** *noun* (i) state where a processor is not active, but waiting for input from peripherals; (ii) null instruction which is used to slow down a processor so that slower memory *or* a peripheral can keep up

◊ **wait loop** *noun* processor that repeats one loop of program until some action occurs

◊ **wait time** *noun* time delay between the moment when an instruction is given and the execution of the instruction *or* return of a result (such as the delay between a request for data and the data being transferred from memory)

◊ **waiting list** *see* QUEUE

◊ **waiting state** *noun* computer state, in which a program requires an input *or* signal before continuing execution

wake up *verb* to switch on *or* start *or* initiate; **wake-up code** = code entered at a remote terminal to indicate to the central computer that someone is trying to log-on at that location

walk through *verb* to examine each step of a piece of software

wallpaper *noun* (in a GUI) image or pattern used as a background in a window

WAN = WIDE AREA NETWORK *opposite is* LAN

wand *noun* bar code reader *or* optical device which is held in the hand to read bar codes on products in a store

warm boot *noun* system restart which normally reloads the operating system but does not reset or check the hardware *compare* HARD RESET

◊ **warm standby** *noun* secondary backup device which can be switched into action a short time after the main system fails *compare* COLD STANDBY, HOT STANDBY

◊ **warm start** *noun* restarting a programme which has stopped, but without losing any data *compare* COLD START

◊ **warm up** *verb* to allow a machine to stand idle for a time after switching on, to reach the optimum operating conditions

warm-up time measures how long each printer takes to get ready to begin printing

Byte

warn *verb* to say that something dangerous is about to happen; to say that there is a possible danger; *he warned the keyboarders that the system might become overloaded* (NOTE: you warn someone **of** something, or **that** something may happen)

warning *noun* notice of possible danger; *to issue a warning; warning notices were put up around the high powered laser;* **warning light** = (small light) which lights up to show that something dangerous may happen; *when the warning light on the front panel comes on, switch off the system*

wash PROM *verb* to erase the data from a PROM

waste instruction *noun* instruction that does not carry out any action (except increasing the program counter to the location of next instruction)

Watt *noun* SI unit of measurement of electrical power, defined as power produced when one amp of current flows through a load that has one volt of voltage across it

wave *noun* signal motion which rises and falls periodically as it travels through a medium

◊ **WAVE** *or* **WAV file** standard method of storing an analog signal in digital form under Microsoft Windows (files have the .WAV extension)

◊ **waveform** *noun* shape of a wave; **waveform digitization** = conversion and storing a waveform in numerical form using an A/D converter

◊ **wavelength division multiplexing (WDM)** method of increasing the data capacity of an optic fibre by transmitting several light signals at different wavelengths along the same fibre

◊ **wavetable** *noun* memory in a sound card that contains a recording of a real musical instrument that is played back

WDM = WAVELENGTH DIVISION MULTIPLEXING

WebBot™ feature used in Microsoft internet web server software that automatically provides a particular function in a Web page and avoids the need for programming

Web browser software program that is used to display and navigate through WWW pages stored on the internet in HTML format

COMMENT: a browser program asks the internet server (called the HTTP server) to send it a page of information; this page is stored in the HTML layout language that is decoded by the browser and displayed on screen. The browser displays text formatting, images and any hotspots and will jump to another page if the user clicks on a hotspot hyperlink

Web crawler *noun* software that moves over every new Web page on the internet and produces an index based on the content of the Web pages

Web page *noun* single file stored on a Web server that contains formatted text, graphics and hypertext links to other pages on the internet or within a web site

Web server *noun* computer that stores the collection of Web pages that make up a Web site

Web site *noun* collection of web pages that are linked and related and can be accessed by a user with a web browser; for example, the Peter Collin Publishing web site has different web pages for each dictionary, a web page for new titles and an online dictionary, it can be accessed from the home page at the URL 'http://www.pcp.co.uk'; *see also* BROWSER, HYPERLINK, URL, WEB PAGE

weighted bit *noun* each bit having a different value depending on its position in a word

weighting *noun* sorting of users, programs or data by their importance or priority

well-behaved *adjective* (program) which does not make any non-standard system calls, using only the standard BIOS input/output calls rather than directly addressing peripherals *or* memory

COMMENT: if well-behaved, the software should work on all machines using the same operating system

wetware *noun* US (*informal*) the human brain, intelligence which writes software to be used with hardware

What-You-See-Is-All-You-Get
(WYSIAYG) *noun* program where the output on screen cannot be printed out in any other form (that is, it cannot contain hidden print *or* formatting commands)

What-You-See-Is-What-You-Get
(WYSIWYG) *noun* program where the output on the screen is exactly the same as the output on printout, including graphics and special fonts

while-loop *noun* conditional program instructions that carries out a loop while a condition is true

white *adjective & noun* the colour of snow; **white pages** = database of users and their email address stored on the internet to help other users find an email address; **white writer** = laser printer which directs its laser beam on the points that are not printed (NOTE: the opposite is **black writer)**

> COMMENT: with a white writer, the black areas are printed evenly but edges and borders are not so sharp

◊ **White Book** *noun* formal video-CD standard published by Philips and JVC that defines how digital video can be stored on a CD-ROM

wide area information server *see* WAIS

wide area network (WAN) *noun* network where the various terminals are far apart and linked by radio, satellite and cable *compare* LAN

> COMMENT: WANs use modems, radio and other long distance transmission methods; LANs use cables or optical fibre links

wideband *noun* (in local area networks or communications) transmission method that combines several channels of data onto a carrier signal and can carry the data over long distances *compare* BASEBAND

width *noun* size of something from side to side; **page width** *or* **line width** = number of characters across a page *or* line

wild card character *noun* symbol used when searching for files *or* data which represents all files; *a wild card can be used to find all files names beginning DIC*

> COMMENT: in DOS, UNIX and PC operating systems, the wild card character '?' will match any single character in this position; the wild card character '*' means match any number of any characters

WIMP = WINDOW, ICON, MOUSE, POINTERS program display which uses graphics *or* icons to control the software and make it easier to use; system commands do not have to be typed in; *see also* ENVIRONMENT, GUI *compare* COMMAND LINE INTERFACE

> COMMENT: WIMPs normally use a combination of windows, icons and a mouse to control the operating system. In many GUIs, such as Microsoft Windows, Apple Macintosh System 7 and DR-GEM, you can control all the functions of the operating system just using the mouse. Icons represent programs and files; instead of entering the file name, you select it by moving a pointer with a mouse

Winchester disk *or* **drive** *noun* compact high-capacity hard disk which is usually built into a computer system and cannot be removed; **removable Winchester** = small hard disk in a sealed unit, which can be detached from a computer when full *or* when not required

window 1 *noun* (i) reserved section of screen used to display special information, that can be selected and looked at at any time and which overwrites information already on the screen; (ii) part of a document currently displayed on a screen; (iii) area of memory *or* access to a storage device; *several remote stations are connected to the network and each has its own window onto the hard disk; the operating system will allow other programs to be displayed on-screen at the same time in different windows;* **active window** = area of the display screen where the operator is currently working; **command**

window = area of the screen that always displays the range of commands available; *the command window is a single line at the bottom of the screen;* **edit window** = area of the screen in which the user can display and edit text *or* graphics; **text window** = window in a graphics system, where the text is held in a small space on the screen before being allocated to a final area; **window, icon, mouse, pointer (WIMP)** = program display which uses graphics *or* icons to control the software and make it easier to use; system commands do not have to be typed in **2** *verb* to set up a section of screen by defining the coordinates of its corners, that allows information to be temporarily displayed, overwriting previous information but without altering information in the workspace

when an output window overlaps another, the interpreter does not save the contents of the obscured window
Personal Computer World

you can connect more satellites to the network, each having its own window onto the hard disk
PC Plus

windowing *noun* (i) action of setting up a window to show information on the screen; (ii) displaying *or* accessing information via a window; *the network system uses the latest windowing techniques*

For instance, if you define a screen window using PowerBuilder, you can build a whole family of windows, which automatically inherit the characteristics of the first.
Computing

windowing facilities make use of virtual screens as well as physical screens
Byte

the network system uses the latest windowing techniques
Desktop Publishing

the functions are integrated via a windowing system with

pull-down menus used to select different operations
Byte

Windows™ multitasking graphical user interface for the IBM PC developed by Microsoft Corp. that is designed to be easy to use; Windows uses icons to represent files and devices and can be controlled using a mouse, unlike MS-DOS which requires commands to be typed in

◊ **Windows 3.1** first of the new generation of Windows which provided features including OLE and drag and drop

◊ **Windows 3.11** *see* WINDOWS FOR WORKGROUPS

◊ **Windows 3.1x** refers to any version of Windows after version 3, including 3.1 and 3.11

◊ **Windows 95** version of Microsoft's Windows that provides support for long filenames, an interface that is easier to use and better support for networks and the internet

◊ **Windows 98** enhanced version of Microsoft's Windows 95 that provides more communications and internet features and is easier to use and configure

◊ **Windows API** set of standard functions and commands, defined by Microsoft, that allow a programmer to control the Windows operating system from a programming language

◊ **Windows CE** software operating system developed by Microsoft and designed to run on small PDA or palmtop computers that use either a pen input or a keyboard instead of a mouse

◊ **Windows Explorer** software utility included with Windows 95 that lets a user view the folders and files on their hard disk, floppy disk, CD-ROM and any shared network drives; **Windows for Workgroups** = version of Windows that includes basic peer-to-peer file-sharing functions and email, fax and scheduler utilities

◊ **Windows GDI** set of standard functions, defined by Microsoft, that allow a programmer to draw images in windows within the Windows operating system; **Windows NT** = high-performance GUI derived from Windows that does not use DOS as an operating system and features 32-bit code; **Windows SDK** = set of software tools, including definitions of the Windows API, that make it easier for a programmer to write applications that will work under the Windows operating system

Winsock *noun* utility software that is required to control the modem when connecting to the internet under MS-DOS or Windows 3 and allows the computer to communicate using the TCP/IP protocol

wipe *verb* to clean data from a disk; *by reformatting you will wipe the disk clean*

wire 1 *noun* (a) thin metal conductor; **wire printer** = dot-matrix printer; **wire wrap** = simple method of electrically connecting component terminals together using thin insulated wire wrapped around each terminal, which is then soldered into place, usually used for prototype systems 2 *verb* to install wiring; **wired** *or* **hardwired program computer** = computer with a program built into the hardware which cannot be changed; *see also* HARDWIRED

◊ **wire frame model** *noun* (in graphics and CAD) objects displayed using lines and arcs rather than filled areas or having the appearance of being solid

◊ **wireless network** *or* **LAN** *noun* network that does not use cable to transmit the data between computers, but instead uses radio or infrared signals to transmit signals; *see also* IRDA

◊ **wiring** *noun* series of wires; *the wiring in the system had to be replaced;* **wiring closet** = box in which the cabling for a network or part of network is terminated and interconnected; **wiring frame** = metal structure used to support incoming cables and provide connectors to allow cables to be interconnected

WISC = WRITABLE INSTRUCTION SET COMPUTER CPU design that allows a programmer to add extra machine code instructions using microcode, to customize the instruction set

wizard *noun* software utility that helps you create something

word *noun* (a) separate item of language, which is used with others to form speech *or* writing which can be understood; **words per minute (wpm** *or* **WPM)** = method of measuring the speed of a printer; **word break** = division of a word at the end of a line, where part of the word is left on one line with a hyphen, and the rest of the word is taken over to begin the next line; **word count** = number of words in a file *or* text; **word wrap** *or* **wraparound** = system in word processing where the operator does not have to indicate the line endings, but can keyboard continuously, leaving the program to insert word breaks and to continue the text on the next line (b) separate item of data on a computer, formed of a group of bits, stored in a single location in a memory; **word length** = length of a computer word, counted as the number of bits; **word mark** = symbol indicating the start of a word in a variable word length machine; **word serial** = data words transmitted along a parallel bus one after the other; **word time** = time taken to transfer a word from one memory area *or* device to another; **word wrap** *or* **wraparound** = system in an editing or word processing application in which the operator does not have to indicate the line endings, but can keyboard continuously, leaving the program to insert word breaks and to continue the text on the next line

◊ **Word™** popular word-processing application developed by Microsoft Corp. to run on a wide range of hardware platforms and operating systems

◊ **Word for Windows™** popular word-processing application developed by Microsoft Corp. to run under the Microsoft Windows operating system

◊ **WordPad™** software utility included with Windows 95 that provides the basic functions of Microsoft Word 6

◊ **WordPerfect™** popular word-processing application developed by WordPerfect Corp. to run on a wide range of hardware platforms and operating systems

◊ **word-process** *verb* to edit, store and manipulate text using a computer; *it is quite easy to read word-processed files*

◊ **wordprocessing** *or* **word-processing (WP)** *noun* using a computer to keyboard, edit, and output text, in the form of letters, labels, address lists, etc.; *load the word-processing program before you start keyboarding;* **word-processing bureau =** office which specializes in word-processing for other companies

word-processor *noun* **(a)** small computer *or* typewriter with a computer in it, used for word-processing text and documents **(b)** word-processing package *or* program for a computer which allows the editing and manipulation and output of text, such as letters, labels, address lists, etc.

WordStar™ popular word-processing application originally developed by MicroPro International for CP/M and IBM PC computers

work 1 *noun;* **work area =** memory space which is being used by an operator; **work disk =** disk on which current work is stored; **work file** *or* **scratch file** temporary work area which is being used for current work

◊ **workflow** *noun* software designed to improve the flow of electronic documents around an office network, from user to user

◊ **workgroup** *noun* small group of users who are working on a project *or* connected with a local area network; **workgroup enabled =** feature added to standard software package to give it more appeal to a group of networked users; *this word-processor is workgroup enabled which adds an email gateway from the standard menus;* **workgroup software =** application designed to be used by many users in a group to improve productivity - such as a diary or scheduler **2** *verb* to function; *the computer system has never worked properly since it was installed*

◊ **working** *adjective* (something) which is operating correctly; **working store** *or* **scratch pad =** area of high-speed memory used for temporary storage of data in current use

◊ **workload** *noun* amount of work which a person *or* computer has to do; *he has difficulty in dealing with his heavy workload*

◊ **workspace** *noun* space on memory, which is available for use *or* is being used currently by an operator

◊ **worksheet** *noun* (in a spreadsheet program) a two-dimensional matrix of rows and columns that contains cells which can, themselves, contain equations

◊ **workstation** *noun* place where a computer user works, with a terminal, VDU, printer, modem, etc.; *the system includes five workstations linked together in a ring network; the archive storage has a total capacity of 1200 Mb between seven workstations*

```
an      image      processing
workstation must provide three
basic facilities: the means to
digitize,    display    and
manipulate the image data
```
Byte

world *noun* three-dimensional scene that is displayed on a web site and allows a user to move around the scene exploring the objects visible; *see also* VRML

World Wide Web *see* WWW

WORM = WRITE ONCE READ MANY times memory

WP = WORD-PROCESSING

WPM *or* **wpm =** WORDS PER MINUTE

wraparound *or* **word wrap** *noun* system in word-processing where the operator does not have to indicate the line endings, but can keyboard continuously, leaving the program to insert word breaks and to continue the text on the next line; **horizontal wraparound =** movement of a cursor on a computer display from the end of one line to the beginning of the next

writable instruction set computer (WISC) *noun* CPU design that allows a programmer to add extra machine code instructions using microcode, to customize the instruction set

write *verb* **(a)** to put words *or* figures on to paper; *she wrote a letter of complaint to the manager; the telephone number is written at the bottom of the notepaper* **(b)** to put text *or* data onto a disk *or* tape; *access time is the time taken to read from or write to a location in memory;* **write** *or* **write-back** *or* **write-behind cache** = temporary storage used to hold data intended for a storage device until the device is ready; *write-back cacheing improves performance, but can be dangerous; see also* CACHE, READ CACHE; **write error** = error reported when trying to save data onto a magnetic storage medium; **write head** = transducer that can write data onto a magnetic medium; **write once, read many times memory (WORM)** = optical disk storage system that allows one writing action but many reading actions in its life; **writing pad** = special device which allows a computer to read in handwritten characters which have been written onto a special pad; *see* OCR; **write time** = time between requesting data transfer to a storage location and it being written (NOTE: you write data **to** a file)

◊ **write black printer** *noun* printer where toner sticks to the points hit by the laser beam when the image drum is scanned *compare* WHITE WRITER

COMMENT: a write black printer produces sharp edges and graphics, but large areas of black are muddy

◊ **write-permit ring** *noun* ring on a reel of magnetic tape which allows the tape to be overwritten *or* erased

◊ **write protect** *verb* to make it impossible to write to a floppy disk *or* tape by moving a special write-protect tab; **write-protect tab** = tab on a floppy disk which if moved, prevents any writing to *or* erasing from the disk

writer *see* BLACK WRITER, WHITE WRITER

writing *noun* something which has been written

WWW = WORLD WIDE WEB collection of the millions of Web sites and Web pages that together form the part of the internet that is most often seen by users; *see also* BROWSER, CERN, HTML, HTTP, INTERNET, WEB PAGE

COMMENT: to view a WWW page, a user needs a browser and an internet connection (or a link to an intranet); the browser asks for the WWW page using HTTP commands and receives a page coded in the HTML language

WYSIAYG = WHAT YOU SEE IS ALL YOU GET

WYSIWYG = WHAT YOU SEE IS WHAT YOU GET

Xx Yy Zz

X = EXTENSION

X *see* X-WINDOW SYSTEM

X.25 CCITT standard that defines the connection between a terminal and a packet-switching network

X.400 CCITT standard that defines an electronic mail transfer method; *see also* MESSAGE TRANSFER AGENT, USER AGENT

X.500 CCITT standard that defines a method of global naming that allows every individual user to have a unique identity and allows any user to address an electronic mail message to any other user; *see also* DIRECTORY SERVICES

X-axis *noun* horizontal axis of a graph

X-coordinate *noun* horizontal axis position coordinate

X direction *noun* movement horizontally

X distance *noun* distance along an X-axis from an origin

xerographic printer *noun* printer (such as a photocopier) where charged ink is attracted to areas of a charged picture

Xerox PARC Xerox development centre that has developed a wide range of important products including the mouse and GUI

Xerox Network System (XNS) *noun* network protocol developed by Xerox that has provided the basis for the Novell IPX network protocols; *see also* IPX, NETBEUI

XGA EXTENDED GRAPHICS ARRAY standard for colour video graphics adapter for PCs, developed by IBM, which has a resolution of 1,024x768 pixels with 256 colours on an interlaced display

XMODEM standard file transfer and error-detecting protocol used in asynchronous (modem) data transmissions; **XMODEM 1K** = version of XMODEM that transfers 1024-byte blocks of data; **XMODEM CRC** = enhanced version of XMODEM that includes error checking

XMS = EXTENDED MEMORY SPECIFICATION rules that define how a program should access extended memory fitted in a PC

XNS = XEROX NETWORK SYSTEM network protocol developed by Xerox that has provided the basis for the Novell IPX network protocols; *see also* IPX, NETBEUI

XON/XOFF asynchronous transmission protocol in which each end can regulate the data flow by transmitting special codes

X/OPEN group of vendors that are responsible for promoting open systems

x punch *noun* card punch for column 11, often used to represent a negative number

X-series *noun* recommendations for data communications over public data networks

XT version of the original IBM PC, developed by IBM, that used an 8088 processor and included a hard disk; **XT keyboard** = keyboard used with the IBM PC which had ten function keys running in two columns along the left-hand side of the keyboard

X-Window System or X-Windows

graphical interface normally used on Unix workstation computers; made up of a set of API commands and display handling routines, that provides a hardware-independent programming interface for applications; originally developed for UNIX workstations, it can also run on a PC or minicomputer terminals; the Open Software Foundation has a version of X-Window called Motif, Sun and Hewlett Packard have a version called OpenLook

---

X is the underlying technology which allows Unix applications to run under a multi-user, multitasking GUI. It has been adopted as the standard for the Common Open Software Environment, proposed recently by top Unix vendors including Digital, IBM and Sun.

Computing

X-Y *noun* coordinates for drawing a graph, where X is the horizontal and Y the vertical value; **X-Y plotter** = device for drawing lines on paper between given coordinates

Y-axis *noun* vertical axis of a graph

◊ **Y-coordinate** *noun* vertical axis position coordinate

◊ **Y-direction** *noun* vertical movement

◊ **Y-distance** *noun* distance along an Y-axis from an origin

Yellow Book *noun* formal specification for CD-ROM published by Philips, includes data storage formats and has an extension to cover the CD-ROM XA standard

YMCK = YELLOW, MAGENTA, CYAN, BLACK colour definition based on these four colours used in DTP software when creating separate colour film to use for printing

YMODEM variation of the XMODEM file transfer protocol that uses 1024-byte blocks and can send multiple files

yoke *noun;* **deflection yoke** = magnetic coils around a TV tube used to control the position of the picture beam

y punch *noun* card punch for column 12 (often used to indicate a positive number)

Z = IMPEDANCE

Z80 8-bit processor developed by Zilog, used in many early popular computers

zap *verb* to wipe off all data currently in the workspace; *he pressed CONTROL Z and zapped all the text*

z-axis *noun* axis for depth in a three-dimensional graph *or* plot

◊ **z buffer** *noun* area of memory used to store the z-axis information for a graphics object displayed on screen

zero 1 *noun* (i) the digit 0; (ii) equivalent of logical off or false state; *the code for international calls is zero one zero (010);* **jump on zero** = conditional jump executed if a flag *or* register is zero; **zero compression** *or* **zero suppression** = shortening of a file by the removal of unnecessary zeros; **zero flag** = indicator that the contents of a register *or* result is zero; *the jump on zero instruction tests the zero flag;* **zero-level address** *or* **immediate address** = instruction in which the address is the operand **2** *verb* to erase *or* clear a file; **to zero a device** = to erase the contents of a programmable device; **to zero fill** = to fill a section of memory with zero values

◊ **zero insertion force (ZIF) socket** *noun* chip socket that has movable connection terminals, allowing the chip to be inserted without using any force, then a small lever is turned to grip the legs of the chip

◊ **zero slot LAN** *noun* local area network that does not use internal expansion adapters, instead it uses the serial port (or sometimes an external pocket network adapters connected to the printer port)

◊ **zero wait state** *noun* state of a device (normally processor *or* memory chips) that is fast enough to run at the same speed as the other components in a computer, so does not have to be artificially slowed down by inserting wait states

ZIF *see* ZERO INSERTION FORCE SOCKET

ZIP filename extension given to files that contain compressed data, normally generated by the PKZIP shareware utility program

ZMODEM enhanced version of the XMODEM file transfer protocol that includes error detection and the ability to re-start a transfer where it left off if the connection is cut

zone *noun* region *or* part of a screen defined for specialized printing; **hot zone** = text area to the left of the right margin in a word-processed document, if a word does not fit completely into the line, a hyphen is automatically inserted

zoom *verb* to enlarge an area of text (to make it easier to work on)

◊ **zooming** *noun* enlarging an area of text *or* graphics; *variable zooming from 25% to 400% of actual size*

there are many options to allow you to zoom into an area for precision work

Electronics & Wireless World

any window can be zoomed to full-screen size by pressing the F-5 function key

Byte

SUPPLEMENT

SINGLE BUS COMPUTER

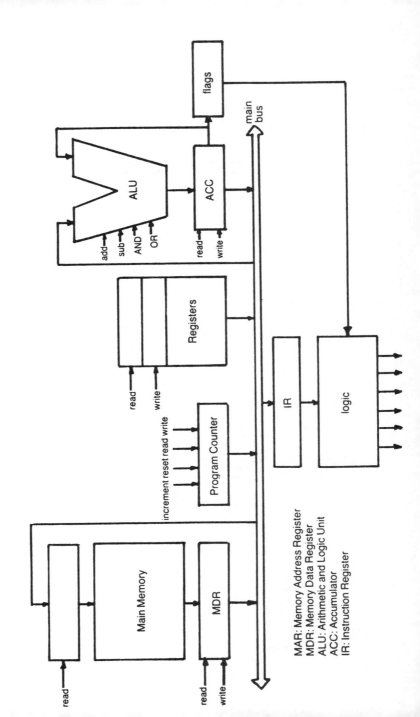

MAR: Memory Address Register
MDR: Memory Data Register
ALU: Arithmetic and Logic Unit
ACC: Accumulator
IR: Instruction Register

MULTI-USER COMPUTER SYSTEM

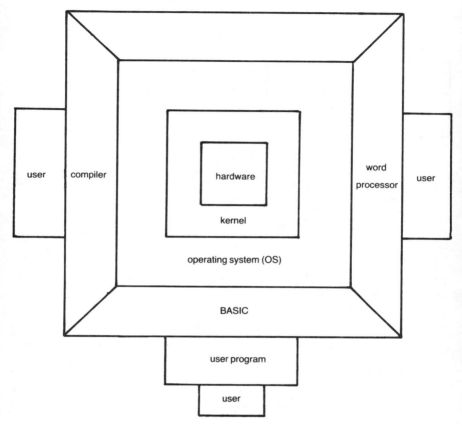

Architecture of a multi-user computer system

hardware:
the base of the system, including the CPU and
memory
kernel:
routines used by every hardware operation
(access restricted to privileged users)
operating system:
system software used by all users (access
restricted to privileged users)
applications:
a user can select applications such as a compiler
or word-processing software

HANDSHAKING

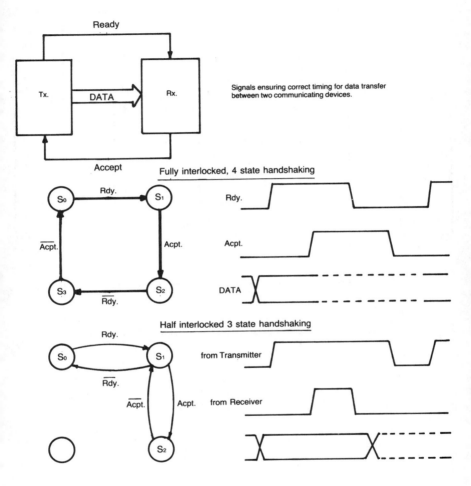

Signals ensuring correct timing for data transfer between two communicating devices.

Fully interlocked, 4 state handshaking

Half interlocked 3 state handshaking

RS232 SIGNALS

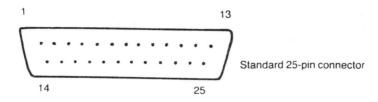

1   13

Standard 25-pin connector

14   25

Pin	Description	Name
1	frame ground	FG
2	transmit data to equipment	TxD
3	receive data from equipment	RxD
4	request to send	RTS
5	clear to send	CTS
6	data set ready	DSR
7	signal ground	SG
8	data carrier detect	DCD
9	positive DC test voltage	+V
10	negative DC test voltage	−V
11	equalizer mode	QM
12	secondary DCD	(S)DCD
13	secondary clear to send	(S)CTS
14	secondary transmit data	(S)TxD
15	transmitter clock	TxC
16	secondary receive data	(S)RD
17	receiver clock	RxC
18	not used	
19	secondary RTS	(S)RTS
20	data terminal ready	DTR
21	signal quality detect	SQ
22	ring indicator	RI
23	data rate selector	
24	external transmitter clock	(TC)
25	not used	

PROGRAMMING LANGUAGES

The following demonstrates the differernces in programming languages for a similar function: an input, n, is requested from the user (defining the number of entries in the list) then a loop repeats n times, asking for an entry and comparing it with the current biggest number entered. The biggest entry is then printed out.

ALGOL

```
begin
  integer n, i, x, big;

  q := 0;
  read(n);
  for i := 1 step 1 until n do begin
        read(x);
        if x > q then
              q := x;
        end;
        print (q);
  end
```

BASIC

```
5   BIG=0
10  INPUT"How many numbers ";N
20  FOR I=1 TO N
30  INPUT X
40  IF X>BIG THEN BIG=X
50  NEXT I
60  PRINT BIG
70  END
```

C

```c
main()
{
 int n, i, x, big;
 big=0;
 scanf("%d", &n);
 (for (i=0; i<n; i++)
 {
       scanf("%d", &x);
       if (x>big)
               big=x;
 }
 printf("%d", big);
}
```

FORTRAN

```fortran
      INTEGER BIG
      BIG=0
      READ,N
      DO 2 I=1,N
      READ,C
2     IF (X.GT.BIG)BIG=X
      PRINT,BIG
      STOP
      END
```

PASCAL

```pascal
program bignum(input, output);
var n,i,x,big : integer;
begin
       big := 0;
       read(n);
       for i:=1 to n do;
       begin
              read(x);
              if x>big then big:=x
       end;
       write(big)
end
```

ASCII IN DECIMAL, HEXADECIMAL

dec.	HEX	CHAR	dec.	HEX	CHAR	dec.	HEX	CHAR	dec.	HEX	CHAR
0	00	NUL	32	20	SP	64	40	@	96	60	
1	01	SOH	33	21	!	65	41	A	97	61	a
2	02	STX	34	22	"	66	42	B	98	62	b
3	03	ETX	35	23	#	67	43	C	99	63	c
4	04	EOT	36	24	$	68	44	D	100	64	d
5	05	ENQ	37	25	%	69	45	E	101	65	e
6	06	ACK	38	26	&	70	46	F	102	66	f
7	07	BEL	39	27	'	71	47	G	103	67	g
8	08	BS	40	28	(	72	48	H	104	68	h
9	09	HT	41	29	)	73	49	I	105	69	i
10	0A	LF	42	2A	*	74	4A	J	106	6A	j
11	0B	VT	43	2B	+	75	4B	K	107	6B	k
12	0C	FF	44	2C	,	76	4C	L	108	6C	l
13	0D	CR	45	2D	-	77	4D	M	109	6D	m
14	0E	SO	46	2E	.	78	4E	N	110	6E	n
15	0F	SI	47	2F	/	79	4F	O	111	6F	o
16	10	DLE	48	30	0	80	50	P	112	70	p
17	11	DC1	49	31	1	81	51	Q	113	71	q
18	12	DC2	50	32	2	82	52	R	114	72	r
19	13	DC3	51	33	3	83	53	S	115	73	s
20	14	DC4	52	34	4	84	54	T	116	74	t
21	15	NAK	53	35	5	85	55	U	117	75	u
22	16	SYN	54	36	3	86	56	V	118	76	v
23	17	ETB	55	37	7	87	57	W	119	77	w
24	18	CAN	56	38	8	88	58	X	120	78	x
25	19	EM	57	39	9	89	59	Y	121	79	y
26	1A	SUB	58	3A	:	90	5A	Z	122	7A	z
27	1B	ESC	59	3B	;	91	5B	[	123	7B	{
28	1C	FS	60	3C	<	92	5C	\	124	7C	|
29	1D	GS	61	3D	=	93	5D	]	125	7D	}
30	1E	RS	62	3E	>	94	5E	↑	126	7E	~
31	1F	US	63	3F	?	95	5F	_	127	7F	DEL

THE ASCII SYMBOLS

NUL	Null	DLE	Data Link Escape
SOH	Start of Heading	DC	Device Control
STX	Start of Text	NAK	Negative Acknowledge
ETX	End of Text	SYN	Synchronous Idle
EOT	End of Transmission	ETB	End of Transmission Block
ENQ	Enquiry	CAN	Cancel
ACK	Acknowledge	EM	End of Medium
BEL	Bell	SUB	Substitute
BS	Backspace	ESC	Escape
HT	Horizontal Tabulation	FS	File Separator
LF	Line Feed	GS	Group Separator
VT	Vertical Tabulation	RS	Record Separator
FF	Form Feed	US	Unit Separator
CR	Carriage Return	SP	Space (Blank)
SO	Shift Out	DEL	Delete
SI	Shift In		

EBCDIC code

bits 0, 1, 2, 3

bits 4,5,6,7 ↓ \ 0,1,2,3 →	0	1	2	3	4	5	6	7	8	9	10	11	12	13	14	15
0	NUL	DLE			SP	&	—									0
1	SOH	DC_1					/		a	j			A	J		1
2	STX	DC_2		SYN					b	k	s		B	K	S	2
3	ETX	DC_3							c	l	t		C	L	T	3
4									d	m	u		D	M	U	4
5	HT	NL	LF						e	n	v		E	N	V	5
6	LC	BS	ETB						f	o	w		F	O	W	6
7	DEL		ESC	EOT					g	p	x		G	P	X	7
8									h	q	y		H	Q	Y	8
9									i	r	z		I	R	Z	9
10	RPT				¢	!		:								
11	VT				.	$	,	#								
12	FF	IFS		DC_4	<	★	%	@								
13	CR	IGS	ENQ	NAK	(	)	_	'								
14		IRS	ACK		+	;	>	=								
15			BEL			¬	?	'								

For further details, please tick the titles of interest and return this form to:
Peter Collin Publishing, 1 Cambridge Road, Teddington, TW11 8DT, UK
fax: +44 181 943 1673   tel: +44 181 943 3386   email: info@pcp.co.uk
For full details, visit our web site: http://www.pcp.co.uk

Title	ISBN	Send Details
English Dictionaries		
Accounting	0-948549-27-0	❏
Agriculture, 2nd ed	0-948549-78-5	❏
American Business	0-948549-11-4	❏
Automobile Engineering	0-948549-66-1	❏
Banking & Finance	0-948549-12-2	❏
Business, 2nd ed	0-948549-51-3	❏
Computing, 3rd ed	1-901659-04-6	❏
Ecology & Environment, 3ed	0-948549-74-2	❏
Government & Politics, 2ed	0-948549-89-0	❏
Hotel, Tourism, Catering Mg	0-948549-40-8	❏
Human Resource & Personnel, 2ed	0-948549-79-3	❏
Information Technology, 2nd ed	0-948549-88-2	❏
Law, 2nd ed	0-948549-33-5	❏
Library & Information Management	0-948549-68-8	❏
Marketing, 2nd ed	0-948549-73-4	❏
Medicine, 2nd ed	0-948549-36-X	❏
Printing & Publishing, 2nd ed	0-948549-99-8	❏
Science & Technology	0-948549-67-X	❏
Vocabulary Workbooks		
Banking & Finance	0-948549-96-3	❏
Business	0-948549-72-6	❏
Computing	0-948549-58-0	❏
Colloquial English	0-948549-97-1	❏
Hotels, Tourism, Catering	0-948549-75-0	❏
Law	0-948549-62-9	❏
Medicine	0-948549-59-9	❏
Professional/General		
Astronomy	0-948549-43-2	❏
Economics	0-948549-91-2	❏
Multimedia, 2nd ed	1-901659-01-1	❏
PC & the Internet	0-948549-93-9	❏
Bradford Crossword Solver	1-901659-03-8	❏
Bilingual Dictionaries		
French-English/English-French Dictionaries		❏
German-English/English-German Dictionaries		❏
Spanish-English/English-Spanish Dictionaries		❏
Swedish-English/English-Swedish Dictionaries		❏

Name: ....

Address: ....

....

....Postcode:............................